Global Hollywood 2

**Toby Miller, Nitin Govil, John McMurria,
Richard Maxwell and Ting Wang**

 Publishing

First published in 2005 by the
British Film Institute
21 Stephen Street, London W1T 1LN

The British Film Institute promotes greater understanding of,
and access to, film and moving image culture in the UK.

Cover design: ketchup
Back cover illustration: 'D-Day' © Andy Singer, 1998

Set in Minion by Fakenham Photosetting Limited, Fakenham, Norfolk
Printed in Great Britain by Cromwell Press, Trowbridge, Wiltshire

British Library Cataloguing-in-Publication Data
A catalogue record for this book is available from the British Library
ISBN 1–84457–039–8 pbk
ISBN 1–84457–049–5 hbk

Contents

Acknowledgments

The authors wish to thank the following for their assistance during this project: Manuel Alvarado, Jonathan Buchsbaum, the US Bureau of Labor Statistics, Edward Buscombe, the Center for Ideas and Society at the University of California Riverside, Joe Chang, Sophia Contento (who was at the BFI for the second edition), David Craig, the US Department of Commerce, Glen Creeber, Sean Delaney, Taryn Drongowski, Greg Elmer, Michael Everett, Mike Gasher, Faye Ginsburg, James Hay, John Hill, Aparna John, Joe Karaganis, Noel King, Chuck Kleinhans, Orntima Kularb, Geoffrey Lawrence, Marie Leger, Andrew Lockett (at the BFI for the first edition), Anna McCarthy, Denise McKenna, Luke Maxwell, Steve Mellano, Albert Moran, Julia Nevarez, Ana Maria Ochoa, Colleen Petruzzi, Dana Polan, Luis Reygadas, Naomi Schiller, Marita Sturken, Michael Tapper, Janet Wasko, Mike Wayne, Marion Wilson, Deborah Wuliger, Cynthia Young, George Yúdice and all the workers involved in producing this book, as well as the first one. Thanks to the conference audiences and the journals and writers that reviewed or otherwise engaged with the first edition. You confirmed many of our thoughts and offered others. The spirit of Jack Valenti inspired us every step of the way.

Note on *Global Hollywood 2*

We finished the first edition of this book in the northern spring of 2001, and the BFI approached us about updating it in 2002. Much had already happened that affected Hollywood, notably the recession and September 11, while other changes have emerged since, such as shifts in the exchange rate, transformations in US foreign policy and significant developments in trade agreements, consumer technology and ownership regimes.

As well as being joined by a new co-author, Ting Wang, we have substantially revised each chapter and added major new sections on India and China. While the key methodological, theoretical and political tendencies of *Global Hollywood* continue to animate us, *Global Hollywood 2* both brings the story up to date and offers new case studies to illuminate our analysis. We have also redisposed and retheorised much of the existing material. This is the director's cut, with expanded features.

Note on Authorship

Global Hollywod 2 has been a collaborative writing project, with research, ideas and words proliferating between us. Primary responsibility for writing specific chapters was as follows: Introduction and Chapter One (Miller); Chapter Two (Miller, Wang and Govil); Chapter Three (McMurria); Chapter Four (Govil), Chapter Five (Maxwell, Miller, Govil and Wang); and Conclusion (Miller, Govil, McMurria and Maxwell).

Introduction

(handwritten annotations: "2 — colonized?" above the first quote)

[T]he Americans have colonized our subconscious.

(Wim Wenders, 1991: 98)

It is a fact, blessedly confirmed, that the American movie is affectionately received by audiences of all races, cultures and creeds on all continents; amid turmoil and stress as well as hope and promise. This isn't happenstance. It is the confluence of creative reach, story telling skill, decision making by top studio executives and the interlocking exertions of distribution and marketing artisans.

(Jack Valenti, 1998a)

Hollywood is a place you can't geographically define. We don't really know where it is.

(John Ford on BBC Television, 1964; quoted in Bordwell *et al.*, 1988: xiii)

We are all experts at understanding Hollywood movies. We have to be, given their presence on most cinema and television screens. Each year, more movie tickets are sold than there are people on the planet ('Global Cinema', 2002). Those audiences are mostly watching fiction conceived, made and owned by Hollywood. It symbolises an invitation to replication and domination, an invitation both desired and disavowed – one that many of us resist or are troubled by, but that draws a sixth of the world's population to telecasts of its annual commercial, the Academy Awards.

What is it about *le défi américain* that makes it hegemonic, yet troubles people so? In his fateful address to Congress on 20 September 2001, George Bush Minor quoted the words of a woman who, as she emerged from the rubble of the World Trade Center, asked '*why do they hate us?*' Although Motion Picture Association of America (MPAA)[1] maven Valenti maintained in the wake of the disaster that '[g]oing to the movies is the American remedy for anxieties of daily life' (quoted in European Audiovisual Laboratory, 2002: 4), many answered the question with reference to Hollywood. Novelist Don DeLillo (2001) suggested the problem lay in 'the power of American culture to penetrate every wall, home, life and mind'. The European Audiovisual Laboratory (2002) warned that, regardless of its cultural messages, Hollywood was involved because of the part it played in an international economy that excluded and dominated most of the world's population. Standard & Poors' 2002 survey of the industry referred to an 'expanding global empire'. And the ever-oleaginous Newt Gingrich, former Speaker of the House of Representatives, suggested that Hollywood, not US foreign policy, had landed the country in turmoil. He insisted on a new public diplomacy that would 'put the world in touch with real Americans, not celluloid Americans' (Gingrich and Schweizer, 2003).

It may well be that blaming popular culture is a means of deceiving the US public about the reality of its governments' foreign policies, distracting attention away from militarism, authoritarianism and exploitation and towards genres, stars and fantasies. A 2001 *International Herald Tribune* poll of opinion leaders found that 58 per cent of them outside the US attributed the loathing it attracts to its policies, while only 18 per cent inside the US thought so (Sardar and Davies, 2002: 9–10).

The influence of the US around the world 'is simultaneously embraced and rejected by world publics'. Opinion polling post-9/11 2001 reveals rejection of US ideology both in states where the US is otherwise well regarded (by 50 per cent of Britons and 54 per cent of Canadians) as well as where it is disliked (in Pakistan by 81 per cent of people and Argentina by 73 per cent). Conversely, 80 per cent of US citizens favour the global dissemination of their culture (Pew

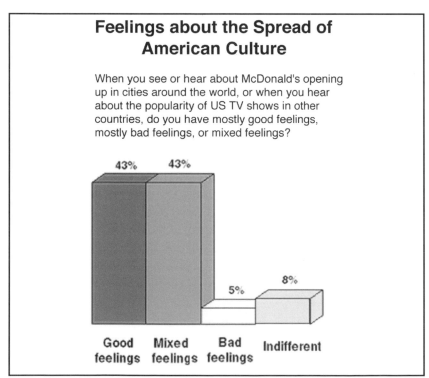

SOURCE: Program on International Policy Attitudes, 2002

Research Center for the People & the Press, 2002) but with certain reservations.

These issues surpass the arenas of cinema and television. They address our very frameworks of culture and politics – and our experience of US state terrorism and commercial domination. Meanwhile, some are questioning the extent to which Hollywood remains a national icon. The 1990 Academy Awards took as their theme the international significance of the cinema at a key moment in the decline of European state socialism and the promise of total US military hegemony, plus new ideological markets provided by deregulation and technology. In celebration of these opportunities, the Oscars were presented from Britain, Australia, the future Russia, Argentina and Japan (Acland, 2003: 8). Ten years later, at the 2000 Academy Awards, three of the five candidates for Best Picture were set outside the US. And something else global happened that went almost unnoticed: Ernst and Young released its annual *Guide to International Film Production*, which outlined tax incentives available to Hollywood companies that spent over US$10 billion a year in overseas location shooting ('Global Investing', 2001). Covering forty countries, the report explained 'corporate, personal and indirect tax issues; the pitfalls of filming and marketing abroad; locations of foreign public and private financing sources and a list of resources to help with local film production' ('Guide', 2000). The next year, none of the nominees for Best Picture were filmed in Hollywood, and three were made outside the US (Wicker, 2003: 471). Despite this internationalism, Hollywood symbolises the extraordinary contradictions of one particular nation. Is something afoot here? We think so. We shall show the link between these events as the book unfolds. For now, let us say that each Awards ceremony gave Hollywood good reason to celebrate globalism.

The quotations that open this Introduction disclose multiple sides to the screen industries' attitudes to Hollywood's power and the immensity of US popular culture (valued at US$31 billion in 2000) ('Saving Hollywood', 2001). Whereas the pan-European auteur Wenders provides a pithy evocation of despair in the face of US cultural domination, Valenti offers a Panglossian account of talent rising to the top. If Wenders represents a supposedly superior aesthetic that would like to anoint Western European civilisation to world cultural leadership, Valenti stands for a human spectre haunting world film and television, the personification of hearty, gum-chewing US populism. Both quips contain grains of truth, albeit running the way of each man's 'wood'. But the elitism of Wenders and the celebrationism of Valenti are as unsatisfying politically as they are analytically. We hope to read against the grain of each.

We are conventionally told today that two models govern the economics of cinema. The first is *laissez-faire*, represented by Bollywood, Hong Kong and, *primus inter pares*, Hollywood. The second is *dirigisme*, represented by Western Europe and most of the global South. Let's look at the binary oppositions that supposedly sustain this distinction.

LAISSEZ-FAIRE FILM INDUSTRY	*DIRIGISTE* FILM INDUSTRY
No state investment in training, production, distribution or exhibition	Major state subvention of training and production, minimal or no support for distribution and exhibition
No governmental censorship or some governmental censorship	Governmental censorship
Copyright protection	Copyright protection
Monopoly restrictions	Monopoly restrictions
Export orientation	Import substitution
Market model	Mixed-economy model
Ideology of pleasure before nation	Ideology of nation before pleasure
Governmental anxiety over the impact of film sex and violence on the population	Governmental anxiety over the impact of imported film on the population

In the left column we have a set of ideal-types generated from neoclassical economics. Their equivalents on the right derive from cultural policy. While they have some items in common, such as the role of the state in policing property, their fundamental missions seem incompatible. In fact, we shall observe how these ideal-types overlap throughout *Global Hollywood 2*, then revisit the binary map to redraw it in our Conclusion.

We seek to explain the national and international success of Hollywood without being beholden to the above grid. In this sense *Global Hollywood 2* differs from most contemporary studies of the phenomenon, which veer between uncritical celebration (Olson, 1999; Demers, 1999), neoclassical economic conservatism (Hoskins *et al.*, 1997) and empiricist archivism (Thompson, 1985; Jarvie, 1998). Such approaches tend to agree that Hollywood's international success results from the 'narrative transparency' of its continuity storytelling, necessitated by the vast and internally differentiated US public of immigrants from diverse cultures. Neoconservative proselytisers for pluralism often confound logic with their simultaneous claims that the US' migrant history and contemporaneity make art that is universally appealing because its polysemy is available to 'indigenous readings', even as they tell us that Hollywood narratives address uniquely universal themes, that other nations' cinemas are less popular because they receive state support, *and* that the US itself excludes other nations' films because it is entirely Anglo-insular (Olson, 1999). By turning itself into a particular narrative form and visual style, we are told, Hollywood aestheticised its localness out of existence. In responding to market pleasures it lost its national qualities and became a benignly universal product, amenable to all audiences and now available to all producers. As per entertainment consultant Michael Wolf's claim that '*the human imagination*' best explains US dominance (1999: 296), or journalist-historian Neal Gabler's (2003) rather alarming assertion that Hollywood has a unique purchase on a 'primal aesthetic of excitement and individualism', this mixture allegedly makes for a universal alchemy of entertainment that attracts foreign consumers. It just so happens that Hollywood unlocked the 'golden mean for images', which can be reused by all and sundry in a Panglossian world (Olson, 2000). And internally, the success of Hollywood is due to the operation of a market in information where the consumer is sovereign and taste emerges through the divinity of supply and demand. Ownership patterns do not matter, because the industry is 'wildly volatile', animated entirely by 'the unpredictable choice of the audience' (De Vany, 2004: 1, 140). The industry itself likes such accounts of the all-powerful viewer determining what it produces. So, *Life* magazine's triumphant cover story on conglomerates taking over the studios in 1970 trumpeted the 'fact' that

> Involved youth, raised in a crisis society and educated by saturation communication, had become 75% of the moviegoing public. They wanted relevant movies reflecting reality as *they* saw it, and they got them: a rash of 'small films' like *Easy Rider* [Dennis Hopper, 1969], made on location for peanuts.
>
> ('The Day', 1970: 39)

How sweet.

Conversely, we are working in a Marxist tradition (Larner, 2002; Guback, 1969, 1974, 1984, 1985 and 1987; Rhines, 1996; Hozic, 2001; Wasko, 1994 and 2003; Trumpbour, 2002). It emphasises corporate and state domination, with the US government instigating and facilitating capital accumulation generally and screen trade in particular. We regard films as commodities whose value is derived from the labour that makes them. Because Hollywood's cultural products travel through time, space and population, their material properties and practices of circulation must be addressed in a way that blends disciplinary perspectives, rather than obeying restricted orders of discourse, be they dustily academic or utopically brassy.

Unlike economic neoconservatives, we do not assume the primacy of markets in allocating preferences. Unlike market researchers, we do not accept Hollywood's version of itself as a narrator of universal stories. Unlike textual reductionists, we do not assume that it is adequate to interpret a film's internal qualities or its supposed 'positioning' of mythic spectators. And unlike the psy-complexes (psychology, psychoanalysis, psychotherapy and psychiatry), we do not seek to divine what is going on inside audiences' heads. Instead, we address global Hollywood both theoretically and empirically, deploying a mixture of methods from screen studies (the left-liberal humanities bent to what are variously termed film, cinema and media studies) and communications (the radical end to social-science approaches), via an admixture of critical political economy and cultural studies. Our aim is to challenge both *laissez-faire* celebrations and *étatiste* denunciations of Hollywood, aware always that the economy and culture are duelling twins whose relations are clumsily theorised whenever one term is privileged over the other (DiMaggio, 1994: 27).

Socio-economic analysis is a natural ally of representational analysis in seeking to explain global Hollywood. But a certain tendency on both sides has maintained that they are mutually exclusive, on the grounds that one approach is concerned with structures of the economy, and the other with structures of meaning. This need not be the case. Historically, the best critical political economy and the best cultural studies have worked through the imbrication of power and signification at all points on the cultural continuum. Graham Murdock puts the task well:

> Critical political economy is at its strongest in explaining who gets to speak to whom and what forms these symbolic encounters take in the major spaces of public culture. But cultural studies, at its best, has much of value to say about ... how discourse and imagery are organised in complex and shifting patterns of meaning and how these meanings are reproduced, negotiated, and struggled over in the flow and flux of everyday life.
>
> (Murdock, 1995: 94)

Ideally, blending the two approaches would heal the 'sterile fissure' (Michael Wayne, 2003: 84) between fact and interpretation and between the social sciences and the humanities, under the sign of a principled approach to cultural democracy. To that end, Lawrence Grossberg recommends 'politicizing theory and theorizing politics' to combine abstraction and grounded analysis. This requires a focus on the contradictions of organisational structures, their articulations with everyday living and textuality, and their intrication with the polity and economy, refusing any bifurcation that opposes the study of production and consumption, or fails to address axes of social stratification (Grossberg, 1997: 4–5, 9–10). That focus has animated our work here. It seems the best way to understand the conundrum of our third foundational epigraph, Ford's provocation about Hollywood's 'nowhereness' – that there is no 'there there'. As Robert Park put it sixty years ago, Hollywood is 'visible but remote' even to Angelinos (1943: 732), while at the same time appearing 'so much like any other American town, only more so', in Budd Schulberg's (1950) memorable phrase. For their part, conservatives of today claim that 'Hollywood has become an aesthetic and is no longer a place in California', because there are now multiple sites of screen power across the world (Olson, 2000). Picking up from Ralph L. Beals' suggestion in the 1950s that whereas he once thought it was 'something special' but came to see that it was 'just another bank – or university' (1951: 550), we have a less fanciful answer. Hollywood's 'real' location lies in its division of labour.

Global Hollywood 2 commences with a statistical account of exported US film and TV to establish the dimensions of the phenomenon. Then we evaluate screen studies' attempts to address and challenge this situation, from both a humanities and social-scientific perspective, and the legacy of those approaches for debate over audiences in particular. Chapter 1 analyses the industry's history of globalisation and the dilemmas it poses as an ideological sign and a perceived threat to national cultures, as detailed in the discourse of cultural imperialism and its alternatives, such as conventional ideas from the industry itself and neoclassical economics. Chapter 2 foregrounds the competing concept of a New International Division of Cultural Labour (NICL)[2] to explain 'runaway film production', the journalistic, governmental and industry shorthand for Hollywood productions undertaken overseas:

> **rún·a·way pro·dúc·tion** *n* 1: those US productions which are developed and are intended for initial release, exhibition, or broadcast in the US and that appear to be made in the US, but are actually filmed in another country.
> **2**: that hissing sound you hear as $10 billion drains out of the US economy every year.
>
> (Film and Television Action Commitee, 2002)

While we explain the NICL in greatest detail in Chapter 2, it is the governing theory that underpins *Global Hollywood 2*, as part of an emerging paradigm across music, cultural policy, sport and film (Ochoa, 2003; Yúdice, 2003; Miller *et al.*, 2001; Gasher, 2002; Acland, 2003). After these initial ground-clearing chapters, the book turns to the nitty-gritty of how Hollywood texts live and die, their existence as commodity chains (Wallerstein, 2000), with Chapters 3, 4 and 5 addressing co-production, copyright and marketing. We seek to answer three questions:

- Is Hollywood global – and in what sense?
- What are the implications of that dominance?
- Where is Hollywood?

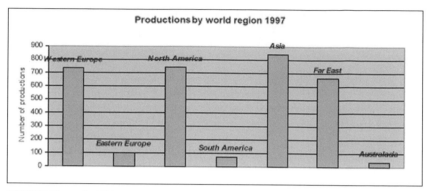

SOURCE: Hancock, 1999

	Feature Films Produced 1996	Of which are co-productions 1996	Feature Films Produced 1997	Of which are co-productions 1997	Feature Films Produced 1998	Of which are co-productions 1998
	GLOBAL FILM PRODUCTION AND CO-PRODUCTION LEVELS Feature films produced and co-produced in the major territories, 1996–98					
Australia	24	0	34	2	38	1
Brazil	41	0	30	0	40	0
Canada	53	16	60	28	64	32
China	224	21	88	12	80	6
France	133	60	163	77	182	81
Germany	64	22	61	14	119	30
Hong Kong	116	15	94	16	91	20
India	649	–	697	–	693	–
Italy	99	22	87	16	92	13
Japan	278	3	278	3	249	8
Spain	91	25	80	25	65	18
UK	111	52	108	40	87	–
USA	715	43	676	13	661	9
Rest of World	739	146	853	107	672	32
World Total	3,225	425	3,309	353	3,133	250

SOURCE: www.netribution.co.uk

The Statistical Backdrop[3]

Variety colorfully used the headline 'Earth to H'wood: You Win' for an article estimating that US films earned 90 percent of the global box office.

(Frederick Wasser, 2001: 193)

US companies own between 40 and 90 per cent of the movies shown in most parts of the world. This is not to deny the importance of other screen cultures: non-US based people of colour are the majority global film-makers, with much more diverse ideological projects and patterns of distribution than Hollywood. For example, the various language groups in India produce about a thousand films a year and employ two and a half million people across the industry. Arthur Anderson predicted in 2000 that Indian cinema would earn US$3.4 billion in overseas sales by 2005 ('Anderson Report', 2000) – but given that firm's probity, we must wait to find out! For even with its vast production, strong export trade and extraordinary film-making tradition, China's total overseas sales of films between 1996 and 2000 amounted to just US$13.86 million ('Chinese Film Industry', 2001).

Los Angeles–New York culture and commerce dominate screen entertainment around the globe, either directly or as an implied other, and the dramatic success of US film since the First World War has been a model for its export of music, television, advertising, the Internet and sport. Shifts towards a neoliberal, multinational investment climate over the past decade have reinforced global Hollywood's strategic power over the NICL through the privatisation of media ownership, a unified Western European market, openings in the former Soviet bloc, and the spread of satellite TV, the Web and the VCR, combined with deregulation of national broadcasting in Europe and Latin America (Rockwell, 1994: H1; Shohat and Stam, 1994: 27; Wasko, 1994: 233; Wasser, 2001: 193). In 1996,

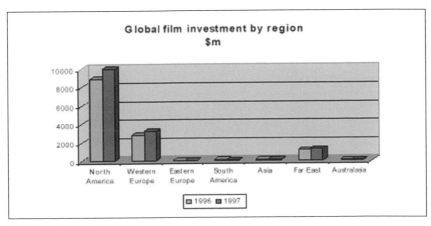

SOURCE: Hancock, 1998

cultural-industry sales (of film, music, television, software, journals and books) became the US' largest exports, ahead of aerospace, defence, cars and farming. Between 1977 and 1996, US copyright industries – as it likes to call them, over-writing the term 'culture' and ensuring comprehensive governmentalisation and commodification – grew three times as quickly as the overall economy. Between 1980 and 1998, annual world trade in texts from the cultural industries increased from US$95.3 billion to US$387.9 billion (UNESCO, 2002). The recession of 2001 was the first year since 1983 that trade in services (TIS), i.e. entertainment, finance, health and other unproductive, non-manufacturing, non-subsistence industries, declined (World Trade Organization, 2003: 3).

The world market is crucial to the US. In 1998, the major US film studios increased their foreign rentals by one-fifth on 1997; the overseas box office of US$6.821 billion virtually equalled the domestic figure of US$6.877 billion. The most popular thirty-nine films across the world in 1998 came from the US, and as that happened, the condition of other major film-making countries was declining: the percentage of the box office taken by indigenous films was down to 10 per cent in Germany, 12 per cent in Britain, 26 per cent in France, 12 per cent in Spain, 2 per cent in Canada, 4 per cent in Australia and 5 per cent in Brazil – all dramatic decreases, to record low levels in some cases. These figures were certainly driven in part by the phenomenal impact of *Titanic* (James Cameron, 1997), which made US$1 billion outside the US, but they represented a significant change from the earlier part of the decade, when European audi-ences for domestic films had increased (*Screen Digest*, August 1997: 177, 183; Dawtrey *et al.*, 2000). In Eastern Europe, the story was equally dramatic. Whereas the USSR had released 215 films in 1990, this had fallen to just 82 by 1995, half the number of US imports (Rantanen, 2002: 86).

Hollywood's proportion of the world market is double what it was in 1990, and the European film industry is one-ninth of its size in 1945. Hollywood's overseas receipts were US$6.6 billion in 1999 and US$6.4 billion in 2000 (the reduction was due to foreign-exchange depreciation rather than any drop in admissions [Groves, 2001b]). In 2000, most 'star-driven event films' from Hol-lywood obtained more revenue overseas than domestically, with eighteen movies accumulating over US$100 million internationally, figures not attained by even one film from any other national cinema (Groves, 2000b). For 2001 and 2002, all the top twenty films in the world were from the US, if one allows for co-production conceits that describe, for example, *Scooby-Doo* (Raja Gosnell, 2002) as Australian, *Bridget Jones's Diary* (Sharon Maguire, 2001) as British and the *Lord of the Rings* trilogy (Peter Jackson, 2001–03) as a New Zealand film. Between 1996 and 2002, of the most remunerative twenty films released in Europe, each one was from the US, with the exception of *Notting Hill* (Roger Michell, 1999) and some co-productions that used British studios, such as the Bond franchise (European Audiovisual Observatory, 2003: 9, 25; Calder, 2003).

In 2002, Hollywood box office overall increased by 13.2 per cent, the biggest

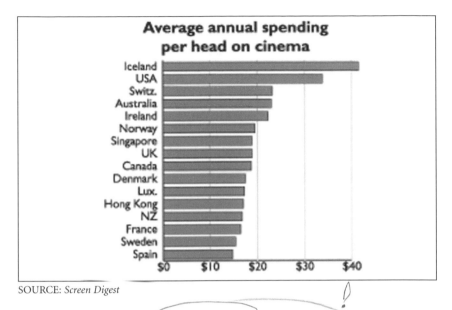

Average annual spending per head on cinema

SOURCE: *Screen Digest*

growth in two decades (European Audiovisual Observatory, 2003: 4). International revenue was US$9.64 billion, up 20 per cent from 2001 (European Audiovisual Observatory, 2003: 11). The figures become very arresting when we consider the most successful films. For example, *Lord of the Rings: The Two Towers* earned US$341 million domestically (i.e. in the US) out of a worldwide figure of US$921 million, and at the beginning of 2004, *Lord of the Rings: The Return of the King* had made US$292 million at home and US$677 million abroad (Muñoz, 2004).

PriceWaterhouseCoopers estimates that US companies make almost US$11 billion by exporting film and that Hollywood will receive close to US$14 billion in export revenue in 2004 (Winslow, 2001). In 2003, Hollywood accounted for the preponderance of revenue in all major markets.

SITE	US MARKET SHARE (%)
Britain	82
France	52
Italy	65
Spain	70
Netherlands	68
Australia	92
Russia	75

SOURCE: Adapted from Guider *et al.*, 2004

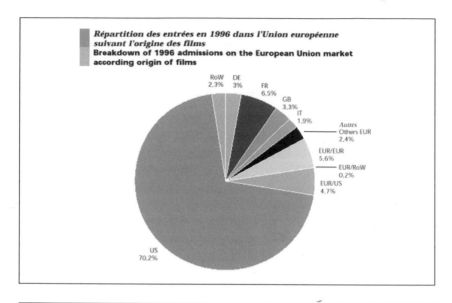

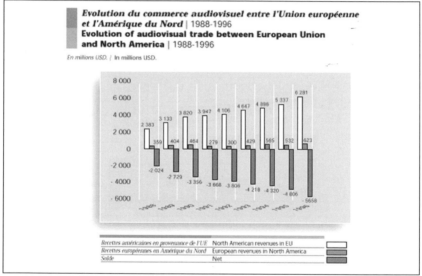

SOURCE: European Audiovisual Observatory, 1998

To give an idea of how new this trend is, the corollary numbers for the 1970s saw Hollywood's market share at 33.7 per cent in Italy, 35.2 per cent in France and 35 per cent in Spain (Cook, 2000: 21). Despite a few aberrant moments, such as 1946 and 1965, when foreign revenue accounted for over 50 per cent of Hollywood's sales as domestic moviegoing plummeted, in 1980 the US film industry relied on exports for one-third of its annual income – the same proportion as 1950.

The past decade has seen a truly foundational change (Augros, 2000: 157; Schatz, 1997: 297). And there is minimal reciprocity, as these US figures for

GLOBAL FILM MARKET IN 1949	
SITE	US MARKET SHARE (%)
Europe	56
South America	64
Mexico and Central America	75
Africa	62
Pacific	75
Middle East	52
Far East	47

SOURCE: Adapted from Schatz, 1997: 303

importing sound recordings on 35mm motion pictures, positive release prints and other 35mm features indicate.

SOUND RECORDINGS ON 35MM	October 2003		2003, through October	
	Quantity	Value	Quantity	Value
WORLD TOTAL	13,488	14	5,323,854	1,272
Australia	0	0	1,000	3
Canada	0	0	4,974,282	1,043
Dominican Republic	0	0	7,429	3
Germany	0	0	11,714	6
France	0	0	4,746	17
India	0	0	822	8
Italy	0	0	209,960	21
Japan	0	0	3,944	2
Korea, South	0	0	2,515	3
New Zealand	0	0	1	3
Romania	0	0	76,071	139
Spain	2,637	10	11,597	12
Thailand	0	0	8,570	6
United Kingdom	10,851	4	11,203	7

POSITIVE RELEASE PRINTS				
	October 2003		2003, through October	
	Quantity	Value	Quantity	Value
WORLD TOTAL	**65,087,463**	**19,263**	**587,450,504**	**172,966**
Austria	2,600	4	2,600	4
Brazil	0	0	3,309	23
Canada	65,023,990	19,221	561,175,003	163,515
Croatia	0	0	31,800	18
Czech Republic	0	0	2,500	3
Germany	0	0	58,698	17
France	0	0	225,956	72
India	28,201	17	405,857	315
Italy	3,588	5	25,054,026	8,684
Japan	2,591	4	40,668	45
Korea, South	0	0	5,970	19
Netherlands	0	0	8,000	2
Poland	0	0	23,828	3
Spain	626	4	139,229	57
Switzerland	0	0	6,283	103
United Kingdom	25,867	10	264,477	84
Yugoslavia	0	0	2,300	4

OTHER FEATURES				
	October 2003		2003, through October	
	Quantity	Value	Quantity	Value
WORLD TOTAL	**12,024,038**	**4,743**	**63,999,271**	**31,927**
Argentina	0	0	74,494	26
Australia	0	0	597,083	107
Austria	0	0	3	5
Brazil	0	0	167	10
Bulgaria	0	0	133,454	166
Canada	11,742,247	4,611	56,432,485	28,134
Czech Republic	0	0	57,143	8
Dominican Rep.	0	0	2,788	5
Germany	0	0	20,797	29
France	0	0	209,022	184
Hong Kong	0	0	13,497	29
India	430	14	32,546	234
Italy	10,519	3	1,321,799	408
Japan	6,171	33	89,688	108
Korea, South	0	0	9,189	23
Mexico	0	0	299,219	104
New Zealand	0	0	742,915	1,144
Panama	0	0	48	20
Romania	0	0	53,223	117
Russia	0	0	19,887	14
South Africa	0	0	115,239	12
Spain	0	0	680,050	263
Switzerland	0	0	25,006	45
Thailand	3,083	3	72,023	44
United Kingdom	261,588	80	2,997,506	689

35MM OR MORE				
	October 2003		2003, through October	
	Quantity	Value	Quantity	Value
WORLD TOTAL	967,503	822	18,338,016	7,180
Argentina	0	0	7,110	10
Australia	0	0	266,677	13
Austria	0	0	209	2
Belgium	245	4	245	4
Brazil	0	0	8,900	19
Bulgaria	732	144	15,736	157
Canada	876,324	641	13,661,381	5,539
Czech Republic	4,200	2	12,104	8
Germany	0	0	50,850	22
France	78,382	29	115,734	84
Hong Kong	0	0	22,073	10
India	0	0	23,950	55
Ireland	0	0	4,000	2
Italy	0	0	3,496,363	772
Japan	0	0	4,247	12
Kenya	0	0	694	7
Korea, South	0	0	5,406	36
Netherlands	0	0	27,737	2
Spain	0	0	196,243	20
Sweden	0	0	4,201	18
Switzerland	0	0	1,100	30
United Kingdom	7,620	3	413,056	358

SOURCE: Foreign Trade Division, US Census Bureau. Presented by Office of Trade and Economic Analysis (OTEA), International Trade Administration, US Department of Commerce.

These huge disparities in textual trade show up on the screen, where the large and wealthy domestic US audience for television and video versions of movies is crucial to enabling high budgets for theatrical releases, even though very few films are profitable in cinemas (Waterman and Jayakar, 2000). In 1999, domestic consumers spent US$40.7 billion on filmed entertainment across these sectors, up 5 per cent on 1998 (Veronis Suhler, 2000). Over the decade, average individual annual expenditure on audiovisual popular culture in the US rose from US$365 to US$641 (Pew Internet & American Life Project, 2003). The US box office for 2002 was US$9.5 billion, up 13 per cent on 2001 despite the massive uptake of DVD and pay-per-view technology at the same time, and twice the 1987 amount (Motion Picture Association of America Worldwide Market Research, 2003: 3–4).

The impact of a large domestic audience with high disposable income is clear when we compare the budgets of Hollywood films to those of other First World nations. Differences in the amounts of money behind and on the screen become apparent.

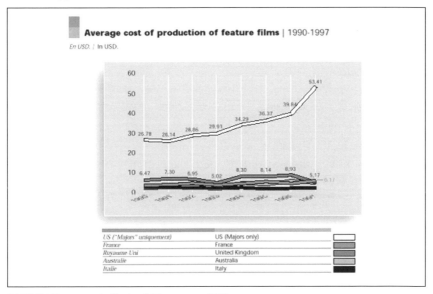

SOURCE: European Audiovisual Observatory, 1998

The trend towards US dominance is indubitable. For example, in 1985, 41 per cent of film tickets bought in Western Europe were for Hollywood fare. In 1995, the proportion was 75 per cent. And 70 per cent of films on European television come from the US. Measured in box-office receipts, Europe is Hollywood's most valuable territory. Overall revenue there in 1997 was half the US figure, but twice that of Asia and four times larger than Latin America. In 1999, 65 per cent of US film and tape rental exports were to Western Europe, 17.4 per cent to Asia and the Pacific, 13 per cent to Latin America and 2.3 per cent to the Middle East and Africa (Scott, 2002: 970). The majors collected over 60 per cent of their box-office revenues from outside the US in the top five European markets, and Hollywood's share of the market in 1996 ranged from 45–55 per cent in France, Italy and Spain, to 70–80 per cent in Germany and the UK. Hollywood's proportion of total video revenues mirrored theatrical box office – between 60 and 80 per cent across Europe (*Screen Digest*, September 1999: 232; *Screen Digest*, November 1999: 296; *Screen Digest*, January 2000: 30; De Bens and de Smaele, 2001). In 1997, the balance of film trade between the US and Europe favoured the former by a third (UNESCO, 2000a). In 2000, a re-release of *The Exorcist* (William Friedkin, 1973) took more money in Italy than the most successful local title (Dawtrey *et al.*, 2000)! Here is the situation in Italy throughout the 1990s:

Market share(%)	1990	1991	1992	1993	1994	1995	1996	1997	1998
National Italian films	21%	26.8%	24.4%	17.3%	23.7%	21.1%	24.8%	32.9%	24.7%
US Films	70%	58.6%	59.4%	70%	61.4%	63.2%	59.7%	46.7%	63.8%
Films from the row	9%	14.6%	16.2%	12.7%	14.9%	15.7%	15.5%	20.4%	11.5%

SOURCE: Bodo, 2000

In 2001, Hollywood's European market share was 66 per cent, down from 73 per cent in 2000 and the lowest since 1997. But the trend was distinct: in 2000, Europe had a US$8.2 billion deficit in cultural trade with the US, an increase of a billion dollars on 1999. And the exchange of audiovisual programmes between 1992 and 2000 followed a distinctly lopsided shape, with the deficit growing from US$4.1 billion to US$9 billion (European Audiovisual Observatory, 2002: 5, 24, 12). In 2002, Hollywood's European market share was restored to its prior level, at 71 per cent (European Audiovisual Observatory, 2003: 20).

International Hollywood receipts in theatres attained record levels in 2002 at US$9.64 billion, 20 per cent up on the previous year. Fifty per cent came from Europe/Middle East/Africa, followed by the Asia-Pacific with 40 per cent and Latin America with 10 per cent (Motion Picture Association of America Worldwide Market Research, 2003). Beyond Europe, the percentage of imports from Hollywood has shown astonishing growth: US films accounted for 57.4 per cent of screenings in Barbados in 1970 and 97.8 per cent in 1991; 39.7 per cent in Canada in 1970 and 63.9 per cent in 1990; 59.2 per cent in Costa Rica in 1985 and 95.9 per cent in 1995; 8.9 per cent in Cuba in 1970 and 40.9 per cent in 1993. Africa is the largest proportional importer of Hollywood films, which account for 70 per cent of exhibition in Anglophone nations and 40 per cent in Francophone countries. It is easier today to find

PERCENTAGE MARKET SHARE FOR US FILMS ON THE EUROPEAN UNION
MARKET (1996–2001)

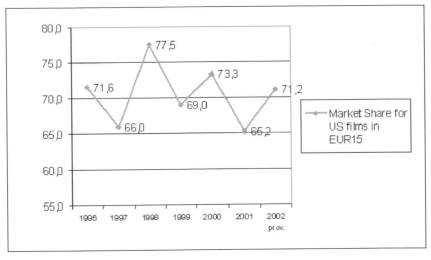

SOURCE: *Lumiere*, 2003

ESTIMATES OF THE TRADE OF AUDIOVISUAL PROGRAMMES BETWEEN
EUROPEAN UNION AND NORTH AMERICA (1988–2000) – US$ MILLIONS

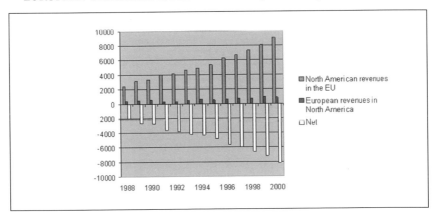

SOURCE: 'The Imbalance', 2002

an African film screened in Europe or the US than on home territory. Following the hyperinflation of the 1970s and 1980s, which decimated film
production in Mexico and Argentina, the percentage of Hollywood films
exhibited in Latin America has increased dramatically (thanks also to the
labours of MPA-America Latina) ('Home Alone', 1997; Woods, 2000;
UNESCO, 2000a; Hayes, 2001; UNESCO, 2000b; Primo, 1999: 190; Amin,
1997: 322–24, 326; Armes, 1987: 49; Mattelart, 1979: 194; Diawara, 1992: 106;
Ukadike, 1994: 63; Himpele, 1996: 52; O'Regan, 1992: 304).

Since the mid-1980s, Japan has been a critical source of Hollywood's revenue, providing 10–20 per cent of worldwide grosses on blockbuster releases
(Cook, 2000: 21; Hayes, 2001), while 96 per cent of the Taiwanese box office
and 78 per cent of the Thai go to Hollywood (Klein, 2003). Great potential
growth lies in this region, as China and India account for over two-thirds of
film screens around the world (Guider, 2000b). Hollywood is optimistic about
the market potential of China's 65,000 film theatres, and India's 12,000, despite
severe restrictions on imports since their revolution (PRC, 1949) and independence (India, 1947), respectively (European Audiovisual Observatory, 2003:
44). While total US revenues from the PRC are low, because only twenty films
can be imported each year, many expect that a large percentage of its 1.3 billion people, who are used to a steady stream of pirated media product, will
become 'conventional' consumers. In January 2001, half of Shanghai's theatrical takings came from five of its 130 venues, and 80 per cent of their screenings
came from Hollywood (Groves, 2001a; 'Chinese Film Producers', 2001). In 1999
in India, of the 154 films released in Hindi, the dominant language of entertainment, 16 were dubbed US titles (Ganti, 2002: 298 n. 7). The benchmark for
a successful Hollywood release there has ballooned almost 1,000 per cent over
the past ten years, from US$100,000 to US$1 million. By 2015, Asia could be
responsible for 60 per cent of Hollywood box-office revenue (Major, 1997)
(Chapter 5 contains a more detailed examination of these two countries). Consider this depiction of Hollywood's market share of imported features in 1999:

Site	Total Imports	US Imports
Algeria	26	21
Azerbaijan	47	42
Bolivia	118	102
Bulgaria	149	118
Canada	383	204
Colombia	222	126
Croatia	67	57
Cyprus	118	107
Czech Republic	135	84
Denmark	176	95
Estonia	79	57
Germany	347	134
Iceland	191	158

Site	Total Imports	US Imports
India	203	–
Ireland	161	111
Kenya	389	–
Latvia	118	86
Lebanon	557	455
Libyan Arab Jamahiriya	39	21
Lithuania	109	73
Macao	345	–
Macedonia	26	23
Mauritius	232	–
Mexico	306	203
New Zealand	191	133
Nicaragua	140	140
Norway	232	123
Pakistan	61	38
Panama	143	134
Poland	140	93
Portugal	166	118
Republic of Korea	297	200
Republic of Moldova	110	48
Romania	105	72
Russia	127	63
Slovakia	130	81
Slovenia	96	67
Spain	397	216
Sweden	210	108
Tunisia	88	60
Ukraine	105	76
Zimbabwe	36	26

SOURCE: Adapted from UNESCO Office of Statistics, 2000b

Of course, theatrical exhibition accounts for barely a quarter of Hollywood's global revenues (29 per cent in 1999). Video provides 25 per cent and television 46 per cent ('Global Media Breakdown', 2001). In 1995, 89 per cent of films screened on Brazil's cable channels were US imports, which occupied 61 per cent of time dedicated to cinema on Mexican TV, while in Egypt, the last twenty years have seen Hollywood prevail over Arab national cinemas both theatrically and in video rental (Duke, 2000; Nain, 1996: 168, 170; Sánchez-Ruiz, 2001: 100). Following the opening up of cable and satellite in the Middle East during the 1990s, there was a scramble both to 'secure access to Western content' and 'Arabise existing Western shows', with an influx of US film channels, along with a special Arab-dedicated Disney channel of dubbed 'family' fare. By 1999, Disney was selling US$100 million a month in the Middle East (Sakr, 2001: 93–94), and in 2002, Showtime offered ten new channels through Nilesat. From its earliest days in the 1960s, Malaysian television relied on US films for content. The trend has never let up and dominates prime time. The same is true in Sri Lanka and the Philippines, where local films are rarely seen on television (Mahendra, 1996: 223; Kenny and Pernia, 1998: 84, 99). Eurodata TV's 1999 analysis of films on television found that fourteen Hollywood pictures drew the highest audiences in twenty-seven nations across all continents. And television drama in 2000 accounted for almost 50 per cent of worldwide television exchange ('1999: Une Année', 2000). In 1974, the Soviet Union imported 5 per cent of its programming, and in 1984, 8 per cent; but Russia imported 60 per cent of its TV in 1997, much of it from the US (Rantanen, 2002: 86).

Television drama more generally shows the same trend. In 1983, the US was estimated to have 60 per cent of global TV sales. By 1999, the US figure had grown to 68 per cent, thanks to 85 per cent of exported children's programming and 81 per cent of TV movies. The only sizeable trade the other way was Britain's paltry export figure of US$85 million; the following year its share of world television exchange stood at 9 per cent, France's and Australia's at 3 per cent. The British went from a small TV trade surplus in 1989 to a deficit of £272 million in 1997 and £403 million in 2000 – the result of fashions in public policy, as the proliferation of channels following deregulation created new opportunities for English-language text from Hollywood's archive. Meanwhile, British TV exports dropped by 10 per cent in 1999 and 11 per cent in 2000, victims of the tendency to buy British formats rather than programmes, thereby minimising price and maximising local signification. Cool Britannia, anyone? In 1998, Europe bought US$2 billion of US programming. The one failure was the decline of US soap opera in the face of indigenous productions that mimic it, and the loss of a domestic audience in prime time. But even the Latin American internal market in *telenovelas* meant that only 6 per cent of imported television was pan-continental in 1996 – 86 per cent came from the US. US imports could be priced to best local costs very easily (Augros, 2000: 228; Freedman, 2003a: 29–30, 32, 36; Foreman *et al.*, 1999; *Screen Digest*, September 1999:

232; *Screen Digest*, November 1999: 296; *Screen Digest*, January 2000: 30; Durie *et al.*, 2000: 87; Olson, 1999: 1; 'A World View', 1997; European Audiovisual Observatory, 1998; O'Donnell, 1999: 213; Sinclair, 1999: 156; Tuohy, 2003). Here are comparative data over four decades:

PERCENTAGES OF US PROGRAMMING				
SITE	1962	1972	1982	1992
Japan	7	9	4	5
South Korea	24	19	10	9
Hong Kong	69	28	9	2
Taiwan	36	21	9	20
India	N/A	3	0	0
France	0	3	6	22
Spain	13	24	11	31
Sweden	8	2	4	34
Israel	N/A	13	15	15
Lebanon	24	41	34	29
Dominican Rep.	14	22	36	N/A
Colombia	18	10	23	N/A
Chile	4	38	28	22
Brazil	31	44	37	20
Mexico	38	26	35	24
Anglo-Canada	49	50	53	51
Franco-Canada	35	38	38	39
Trinidad	29	50	59	69
Jamaica	30	46	55	65
Barbados	31	31	52	N/A

SOURCE: Adapted from Straubhaar, 2001:148

These figures reflect changing local arrangements, such as increases in local TV production (most nations), the departure of colonial rulers (Hong Kong) and the proliferation of channels following deregulation (Germany, Britain, Italy, France, Spain and Belgium had fourteen TV stations in 1980, one of which was private, and thirty-six in 1990, of which nineteen were private) (Augros, 2000: 229).

To give a sense of how differential pricing can aid entry into these markets, we shall briefly consider the key world television market, MIPCOM, in 2002. Sales were made on a sliding scale, with features the most expensive, followed by TV movies, drama series, situation comedies, documentaries and children's programmes. The fees paid reflect, of course, wealth, gullibility and domestic competition rather than audience desire.

SITES, GENRES AND US$ PRICES FOR US TEXTS IN TELEVISION MARKET, 2002 (DRAMA PER HOUR, OTHERS PER HALF-HOUR)

GENRE SITE	FEATURE	TV MOVIE	DRAMA	COMEDY	DOCU	CHILD
Australia	1,000,000	30,000	10,000	5,000	4,000	3,000
Brazil	60,000	16,000	9,000	2,500	3,000	2,250
Canada	125,000	100,000	50,000	35,000	5,000	25,000
Czech Rep.	30,000	3,500	3,000	800	800	500
France	2,000,000	90,000	55,000	25,000	12,000	10,000
Germany	5,000,000	200,000	75,000	20,000	18,000	14,000
Italy	1,000,000	100,000	30,000	10,000	7,000	7,000
Japan	1,400,000	30,000	23,000	7,000	16,000	5,000
Mexico	40,000	15,000	8,000	6,000	2,000	2,000
Nordic	200,000	18,000	7,000	4,500	3,500	2,500
Spain	1,000,000	50,000	20,000	6,000	5,000	3,000
Britain	2,000,000	35,000	50,000	25,000	20,000	22,500

SOURCE: Adapted from 'Global Programming', 2002

TV mixed in without explanation

ORIGIN OF IMPORTED FICTION PROGRAMMES (FILM + TV FICTION) TRANSMITTED BY 101 EUROPEAN UNION NETWORKS IN 2000

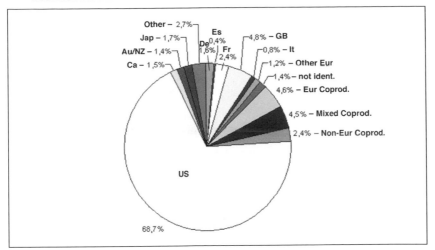

SOURCE: 'The Imbalance', 2002

ORIGIN OF IMPORTED FICTION BROADCAST BY TV CHANNELS IN WESTERN EUROPE (1994–2001) BY BROADCAST HOURS

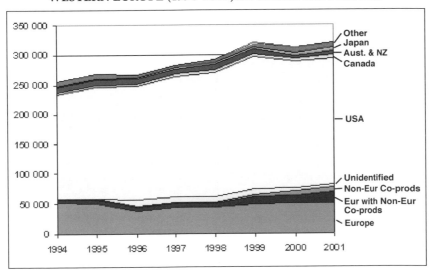

SOURCE: 'American Fiction', 2003

Even when the volume of US television exports decreases, revenue frequently increases. In 2000, receipts from US programming in Europe grew by 15.9 per cent, although the number of programmes sold diminished from 223,000 hours to 214,000, and the audiovisual imbalance of trade stood at US$8.2 billion, up 14 per cent on 1999. In 2001, volume diminished again, by 1 per cent. Co-productions account for the change in imported hours: many are undertaken with the US but count as European. The few competitors for the European market have fallen away recently, notably New Zealand and Australian soap operas, which were briefly successful during the mid-1990s. The volume of US exports to Western Europe may be unstable, but their value is not. And these figures are principally derived from the major public and private networks. Dedicated genre channels, which anecdotally rely massively on US imports, are mostly excluded from official statistics. Although prime time

REVENUES OF US COMPANIES IN THE EUROPEAN UNION MARKET
(BROADCASTERS NOT INCLUDED – IN $US MILLIONS)

MPA – Theatrical rental		AFMA – TV sales	
1995	1001	1995	407
1996	1155	1996	443
1997	1188	1997	473
1998	1405	1998	576
1999	1270	1999	831
2000	1240	2000	784
AFMA – Theatrical sales		**MPA – Video rental**	
1995	177	1995	1930
1996	237	1996	2026
1997	306	1997	2030
1998	329	1998	2034
1999	451	1999	2124
2000	510	2000	2570
MPA – TV rental		**AFMA – Video sales**	
1995	1655	1995	162
1996	2202	1996	198
1997	2407	1997	242
1998	2611	1998	358
1999	2950	1999	416
2000	3600	2000	328
		TOTAL	
		1995	5331
		1996	6262
		1997	6645
		1998	7313
		1999	8042
		2000	9031

SOURCE: Adapted from 'The Imbalance', 2002

n/ clear, where only

GEOGRAPHICAL ORIGINS OF TELEVISION FICTION PROGRAMMED BY MAJOR NETWORKS (SAMPLE WEEK 12–18 MARCH 2000) ⟵

		Domestic	US	European	Other
	Whole day	47%	43%	0%	10%
	Prime Time only	51%	49%	0%	0%
	Whole day	36%	57%	5%	2%
	Prime Time only	56%	44%	0%	0%
	Whole day	25%	56%	15%	5%
	Prime Time only	75%	25%	0%	0%
	Whole day	19%	64%	4%	13%
	Prime Time only	43%	51%	6%	0%
	Whole day	20%	56%	7%	17%
	Prime Time only	51%	37%	12%	0%

SOURCE: 'TV Fiction', 2001

VOLUME OF US-ORIGINATED FICTIONAL TV AND FILMS IMPORTED AND BROADCAST ON TELEVISION CHANNELS IN THE FIVE PRINCIPAL EUROPEAN MARKETS IN 2001 AS PERCENTAGE OF THE TOTAL VOLUME OF FICTIONAL TV AND FILM IMPORTED AND BROADCAST

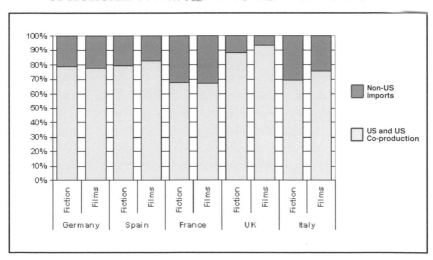

SOURCE: 'American Fiction', 2003

is usually occupied by local television, a vast amount of potential investment
in the European industry goes into buying Hollywood programmes. And
between 1999 and 2000, video rights showed startling growth for Hollywood,
up 21 per cent on 1999, while theatrical receipts grew just 1.7 per cent, as European distributors gained control of some key US features ('The Imbalance',
2002; 'TV Fiction', 2001; 'American Fiction', 2003).

Yet, while its mounting dominance is there for all to see, US governments
and businesses object when other countries assert rights to national self-determination on-screen via barriers to imports. Washington has the world on
notice that it will use the notorious provisions of the 1974 Trade Act against
any cultural protectionism it dislikes. Hong Kong, for instance, is often accused
of what the US likes to call screen 'piracy',[4] and the European Union (EU) is a
particular target because of its wealth and continued insistence on public support for non-US screen alternatives. So, what have independent critics offered
by way of engagement with this behemoth?

A Problem of Knowledge

[T]he feature film market is continually reconstituted through the
introduction of new, short-lived products. As a result, basic questions of
identity arise on an ongoing basis. In this respect, the feature film market
resembles the market for assistant professorships.

(Ezra W. Zuckerman and Tai-Young Kim, 2003: 31)

As noted above, later chapters examine the climate that generated and sustains
global Hollywood, and the policy actions that animate it. The remainder of this
Introduction questions whether the contemporary state of screen studies
equips us to address such issues through its blend of textual analysis, the psy-
complexes and bourgeois business history. Has screen studies contributed
significantly to public debate? Here are some test cases:

- In the domain of film financing, major court cases have pitted the studios
  against insurance companies that invested in foolhardy risk assessments of
  Hollywood across the 1990s. These cases involved billions of dollars, and
  were precipitating forces in the collapse of Australia's largest private insurer,
  HIH ('Customer Comments', 2003). Screen studies has had nothing to offer
  the discussion.
- In 2002, the Tisch School of the Arts at New York University, where several
  of us have worked, received a formal note from the MPAA advising that
  copyrighted films were being illegally distributed from a computer registered with a particular School maven. Did administrators turn to the
  Department of Cinema Studies for advice on the legal, political, educational, textual, audience, technological or privacy implications of the
  downloading and its surveillance by the Association?

- If one peruses the American Academy of Pediatrics' *Media Matters* programme (2001), notably its advocacy of a letter-writing campaign about
  cinema and support for the egregious 'TV-Turnoff Week' (see also Mittell,
  2000), there is no engagement with screen studies, and with good reason –
  we don't engage with dominant discourse.

Yet there is a long history of linking intellectuals to the screen in public culture.

- In the silent era, ethical critic Vachel Lindsay referred to 'the moving picture man as a local social force ... the mere formula of [whose] activities'
  keeps the public well-tempered (Lindsay, 1970: 243). Films were connected to gambling and horse racing in various forms of social criticism and
  were plundered as raw material by the emergent discipline of psychology,
  where obsessions with eyesight and the cinema gave professors something
  to do. At the same time, social reformers looked to film as a potential
  forum for moral uplift. If the screen could drive the young to madness, it
  might also provoke social responsibility (Austin, 1989: 33–35). Film
  bureaucrat Will Hays regarded the industry as riveting 'the girders of
  society' (Hays, 1927: 29).
- In the 1930s, social research into the impact of cinema on American youth
  via the Payne Fund Studies (Blumer, 1933; Blumer and Hauser, 1933) inaugurated mass social-science panic about young people at the cinema, driven
  by academic, religious and familial iconophobia in the face of large groups
  of people engaged by popular culture and seemingly beyond the control of
  the state and the ruling class.
- After the Second World War, the anthropology of Hortense Powdermaker
  (1950: 12–15) and the sociology of J. P. Mayer (1946: 24) revealed anxieties
  about Hollywood's intrication of education and entertainment and the need
  for counter-knowledge among the population.
- In 1957, Pope Pius XII issued *Miranda Prorsus: Encyclical Letter on
  Motion Pictures, Radio and Television*, stating that 'Catholic Film critics
  can have much influence; they ought to set the moral issue of the plots
  in its proper light, defending those judgments which will act as a safeguard against falling into so-called "relative morality", or the overthrow
  of that right order in which the lesser issues yield place to the more
  important'.

Such a history of social engagement, however problematic, might have produced public intellectuals who made major policy and critical contributions to
transforming Hollywood. But in the hegemonic world of US–UK screen
studies, this has not happened – even though Powdermaker anticipated Ford
in realising that 'Hollywood itself is not an exact geographical area' (1950: 18)
and showed a way forward to the kind of analysis we favour.

We are sometimes told today that, to quote one recent film-theory anthology, there has been 'a general movement in approaches to film from a preoccupation with authorship (broadly defined), through a concentration upon the text and textuality, to an investigation of audiences' (Hollows and Jancovich, 1995: 8); or, to paraphrase the fifth edition of a widely used anthology, a progression from a pursuit of knowledge about film form, to realism, followed by language, and, finally, cultural politics (Braudy and Cohen, 1999: xv–xvi). Such accounts approximate the history of some humanities-based academic work, but disengage it from popular cinema criticism, social-science technique, and cultural policy as applied to the screen via formal analysis of films, identification of directors with movies, studies of the audience through psychology and psychoanalysis, workplace analysis of the industry, and governmental programmes of research and support. All of these have been around, quite doggedly, for almost a century (Worth, 1981: 39), but their remarkable continuity of concerns about audiences is secreted in favour of a heroic, Whiggish narrative of teleological, textualist development that animates the *doxa* of the humanities screen academy.

This is not to gainsay important screen-studies achievements. Questions of pleasure and suppression, for example, have become central more recently, as analysts have sought to account for and resist narrative stereotypes and exclusions – to explain, in Richard Dyer's words, 'why socialists and feminists liked things they thought they ought not to' (1992: 4), and why some voices and images have been excluded or systematically distorted. This difficulty over pleasure, presence and absence accounts for film theory being highly critical of prevailing representations, but never reifying itself into the Puritanism alleged by critics of political correctness. The extraordinary diversity of latter-day film anthologies makes the point clear. Contemporary feminist film collections certainly focus on issues of representation and production of common concern to many women, but they also attend, routinely, to differences of race, history, class, sexuality and nation, alongside and as part of theoretical difference (Carson *et al.*, 1994), while black film volumes divide between spectatorial and aesthetic dimensions (Diawara, 1993), and queer ones identify links between social oppression and film and video practice (Gever *et al.*, 1993; Holmlund and Fuchs, 1997). The implicit and explicit masculinism, Eurocentrism and universalism of earlier theory have been questioned by social movements and Third and Fourth World discourses that highlight exclusions and generate new methods (Shohat and Stam, 1994; Carson and Friedman, 1995).

Crucial elements are left out, though, from today's dominant discourse of screen studies – the major journals, book series, conferences and graduate programmes. Our anecdotes about finance, copyright and anti-television campaigns point to the irrelevance of screen studies to *both* popular *and* policy-driven discussion of films, flowing from a lack of engagement with the sense-making practices of criticism and research conducted outside the textu-

alist and historical side to the humanities. For example, humanities work on
stardom seldom addresses the excellent research on that topic in the social sciences.[5] Adding this material to the textual, theoreticist and biographical
preferences of humanities critics could offer knowledge of the impact of stars
on box office, via regression analysis, and of work practices, via labour studies.
This neglect is symptomatic – screen studies frequently fails to engage political
and social history and social theory on the human subject, the nation, cultural
policy, the law and the economy. It is especially odd to find that there is precious little concern for working conditions in what is avowedly a progressive
discipline (Tashiro, 2002: 27).

   This can be explained partly by rent-seeking academic professionalism,
where latter-day lines divide communication, cultural and screen studies from
each other. The theorisation of production and spectatorship relations between
film and television, for instance, continues to be dogged by the separation of
mass communication's interest in economics, technology and policy from film
theory's preoccupation with aesthetics and cultural address. Of course, much
social-science work on the media is leaden-footed positivism that counts and
counts while interpreting not a whit, and is driven by a controversial media-
effects epistemology. On the economics front, a similarly disabling distinction
has been drawn between value and labour. This distinction has precluded a
political-economic approach. At one high-profile 2003 US academic event on
the economics of Hollywood, every single paper from business and economics
faculties focused exclusively on one topic – how firms could increase their revenues. What a stunning indictment of social irresponsibility in academia,
worse by far than the largely irrelevant world of film theory. This leads us
to consider one field where academic work on the screen, picking up on
Payne Fund and Papal anxieties, has made a major, but deeply problematic,
contribution.

Actually Existing Policy Influence – Audiences

   Violence is harder to catalog than sensuality. There either is copulation or
   there isn't. There is writhing or there isn't. But it's hard to measure gradations
   of violence. John Wayne hitting the beaches at Iwo Jima and mowing down
   2,000 people – how do you equate that with a fellow being fellated? It's pretty
   difficult.

                                           (Jack Valenti quoted in Svetkey, 1994: 32)
   Yes, Jack.
       (Peter Sellers in *Dr Strangelove, or How I Learned to Stop Worrying and Love the
                                               Bomb*, Stanley Kubrick, 1964)

Perhaps the most striking example of successful applied academic work on the
screen comes from communication studies and the psy-complexes. They
fix on the audience and how to understand it, which inevitably connects them

to practical applications. Production executives invoke the audience to measure success and claim knowledge of what people want. Regulators do the same in order to administer, and lobby groups to change content. Hence the link to panics about education, violence and apathy, supposedly engendered by the screen and routinely investigated by the state, psychology, Marxism, neoconservatism, religion, liberal feminism and others. By contrast, our starting point is the provocation that the audience is artificial, a creature of the industry, the state and academia, which proceed to act upon their creation.

Many discussions of the audience are signs of domestic anxiety about the US: commercial laments for bountiful profits that regret the turn towards cable and the Internet away from broadcast television, or sociological laments for civic culture that correlate heavy film viewing with increased violence and declining membership of parent-teacher associations. Communitarian philosophy and sociology rail against rampant individualism, secular selfishness and the absence of civic responsibility. An allegedly active public is contrasted with a putatively inactive screen audience:

> we are not happy when we are watching television, even though most of us spend many hours a week doing so, because we feel we are 'on hold' rather than really living during that time. We are happiest when we are successfully meeting challenges at work, in our private lives, and in our communities.
>
> (Bellah et al., 1992: 49)

For seventy years, social science has worked from an effects model of film and TV. Effects models assume the screen *does* things *to* people, with the citizen understood as an audience member that can be a 'dope', abjuring interpersonal responsibility. This model, dominant in the US and exported around the world, is typically applied without consideration of place. We call it the *domestic* effects model, or DEM. It is universalist and psychological. The DEM offers analysis and critique of such crucial citizenship questions as education and civic order. It views the screen as a machine that can either pervert or direct the citizen-consumer. Entering young minds osmotically, it can enable or imperil learning and drive the citizen to violence through aggressive and misogynistic images and narratives. The DEM is found in a variety of sites, including laboratories, clinics, prisons, schools, newspapers, psychology journals, television network and film studio research and publicity departments, everyday talk, programme-classification regulations, conference papers, parliamentary debates and state-of-our-youth or state-of-our-civil-society moral panics (see Buckingham, 1997; Hartley, 1996). The DEM is embodied in the nationwide US media theatrics that ensued after the Columbine high-school shootings, which questioned the role of violent images (not firearms or straight white religious masculinity) in creating violent citizens. This led Bill Clinton to charge the Federal Trade Commission with the task of producing a study of the culture industries that target children with violent texts. Over a period of several months, the Commission undertook this charge, *inter alia*, by spying on teenagers across the country as they entered movie theatres, in what it described as an 'undercover shopper survey' (Federal Trade Commission, 2000: 20, Appendix F – for more on social science as surveillance, see Chapter 5). The DEM is also evident in panics about the impact of television advertisements on the environment, health or politics.

A recent content analysis published by the American Medical Association (AMA) concerns feature-length animation films made in the US between 1937 and 1997, and the way in which they associate legal but damaging recreational drugs with heroic characters (Goldstein *et al.*, 1999). The study received major public attention via AMA endorsement, a press conference, numerous media stories and formal replies from Disney. Similar interest surrounded the 2001 release of findings that despite the film industry and 'big' tobacco companies agreeing to a voluntary ban on product placement in 1989, the incidence of stars smoking cigarettes in Hollywood films since that time has increased elevenfold, mostly to get around bans on television commercials, while its use in youth-oriented films has doubled since the 1998 Master Settlement Agreement between the tobacco companies and forty-six US states. In addition to placing their products on-screen, the industry also provides stars with free cigarettes and cigars, and encourages them to smoke in public and during photographic and interview sessions as a quid pro quo (Laurance, 2001; Mekemson and Glantz, 2002; Ng and Dakake, 2002). The American Lung Association funded a key public-relations campaign on the topic to coincide with the 2002 Academy Awards, seeking to embarrass the MPAA into including warnings in its film ratings about tobacco use, alongside alcohol advisories (American Lung Association, website). And a major campaign and set of studies have been undertaken by the Massachusetts Public Interest Research Group (toughontobacco.org) and the University of California, San Francisco Medical School (smokefreemovies.ucsf.edu) that offer the following information:

> **Fact**: Today's movies are the smokiest since 1950. And unlike the old Hollywood, today they're promoting actual brands on-screen.
> **Fact**: The tobacco industry has a history of behind-the-scenes payoffs in Hollywood – with everyone involved publicly denying it.
> **Fact**: More powerful than traditional advertising, movies recruit over half of all adolescent smokers, upwards of 1,000 new smokers every day, eventually killing 50% more of them than illegal drugs, gun violence, suicide, drink driving and AIDS *combined*.
> **Fact**: Hollywood leaders could stop on-screen tobacco promotion in a heartbeat. But in public, few even admit there's a problem.
> **Is Hollywood corrupt? Or stupid?**

You decide. Then act.

This award-winning website opens secret industry files, names names and gives you all the facts you need to protect yourself, your family and your community against this solidly documented, deadly assault on a rising generation worldwide.

Smoke Free Movies' voluntary, commonsense solutions are endorsed by the World Health Organization (WHO), American Medical Association, American Academy of Pediatrics, American Legacy Foundation ('truth'), LA Department of Health Services, and other medical and public health leaders worldwide.

This is a truly global policy issue, again unaddressed and unaffected by screen studies.

Today, industries, governments and critics often work with shared empirical data, but to very different ends. When we read that the average US resident spent 9.3 hours of each day in 1999 using the various entertainment media, that this is projected to rise to 10.4 hours per day in 2004 (Veronis Suhler, 2000), and that theatrical revenues have risen by nearly 60 per cent since 1990 (Valenti, 2001c), these are not simple numbers. They are indices and auguries of opportunity, triviality, docility, violence and bigotry, depending on one's reading position.

There is a reason for all this censorious DEM activity: the cultural audience is not so much a specifiable group *within* the social order as the principal site *of* that order, a virtual screen control that mirrors direct policing of the streets. Audiences participate in the most global (but local), communal (yet individual) and time-consuming practice of making meaning in world history. The concept and the occasion of being an audience are textual links between society and person, for viewing involves solitary interpretation as well as collective behaviour.

Various different groups may construct the audience as consumers, students, felons, voters and idiots. Such approaches fix on what Harold Garfinkel in 1967 called the 'cultural dope', a mythic figure 'who produces the stable features of the society by acting in compliance with pre-established and legitimate alternatives of action that the common culture provides'. The 'common sense rationalities . . . of here and now situations' that people use are obscured by this condescending categorisation (Garfinkel, 1992: 68).

One hundred and fifty years ago, it was taken as read that audiences were active, given their unruly and overtly engaged conduct at cultural events. But the spread of public education in the West in the nineteenth century, allied to the emergence of literary criticism and psychology, shifted critical rhetoric about audiences (Butsch, 2000: 3) towards Garfinkel's 'dope'. Ever since the advent of the mass media, much energy has been devoted to evaluating the active versus passive sides to media audiences. This is because popular-culture texts are 'symbols for time' (Hartley, 1987: 133). The alleged misuse of time has become integral to the desire to police everyday life.

Sometimes the criticisms are about particular genres (e.g. action-adventure cinema is mindless and talk shows trivialise current affairs, whereas character-driven drama builds moral fibre in the audience and 'real' journalism informs the electorate). This is often a gendered critique, as Michèle Mattelart explains:

> in the everyday time of domestic life ... the fundamental discrimination of sex roles is expressed. ... The hierachy of values finds expression through the positive value attached to masculine time (defined by action, change and history) and the negative value attached to feminine time which, for all its potential richness, is implicitly discriminated against in our society, interiorized and lived through as the time of banal everyday life, repetition and monotony.
>
> (Mattelart, 1986: 65)

There is also a class and race dimension to these concerns, as illustrated by the 'third-person effect', in which middle-class Europeans often exhibit more concern about the impact of US popular culture on others than on themselves, just as censors can allegedly safely imbibe materials that they deem harmful to others (Willnat *et al.*, 2002).

When the audience is invoked as a category by the industry or its critics and regulators, it immediately becomes such a 'dope', which links the DEM to the global effects model, or GEM, which is central to debates about global Hollywood. The GEM, primarily utilised in non-US discourse, is specific and political rather than universalist and psychological. Whereas the DEM focuses on the cognition and emotion of individual human subjects via replicable experimentation, the GEM looks to the knowledge of custom and patriotic feeling exhibited by collective human subjects, the grout of national culture. In place of psychology, it is concerned with politics. The screen does not make you a well or an ill-educated person, a wild or a self-controlled one. Rather, it makes you a knowledgeable and loyal national subject, or a duped viewer who lacks an appreciation of local custom and history. Cultural belonging, not psychic wholeness, is the touchstone of the global effects model. Instead of measuring responses electronically or behaviourally, as its domestic counterpart does, the GEM looks to the national origin of screen texts and the themes and styles they embody, paying particular attention to the putatively nation-building genres of drama, news, sport and current affairs. GEM adherents hold that local citizens should control local broadcast networks, because they alone can be relied upon to be loyal reporters in the event of war, while in the case of fiction, only locally sensitised producers make narratives that are true to tradition and custom. This model is found in the discourses of cultural imperialism, everyday talk, broadcast and telecommunications policy, international organisations, newspapers, heritage, cultural diplomacy, post-industrial service-sector planning and national cinemas. The enumeration of national authenticity in screen texts

GEM — global effects model

through fractional ownership has been a common practice in countries concerned to protect their national cultural economies from foreign imports. The GEM favours 'creativity, not consumerism', as UNESCO's 'Screens Without Frontiers' initiative puts it (Tricot, 2000).

The GEM's concentration on national culture is as problematic as the DEM's focus on individual conduct. It:

- denies the potentially liberatory and pleasurable nature of different takes on the popular
- forgets the internal differentiation of viewing publics
- valorises frequently oppressive and/or unrepresentative local bourgeoisies in the name of national culture's maintenance and development; and
- ignores the demographic realities of its 'own' terrain.

The marketing impulses of the DEM can sometimes run counter to the marketing impulses of the GEM. Consider the history of *Crocodile Dundee* (Peter Faiman, 1986), one of the most popular imported films in US history. Paramount, the US distributor, worked with a particular view of its audience when it cut five minutes from the original Australian version by removing scenic segments and altering the sound mix to foreground dialogue, thereby increasing the film's pace and concentrating even further on the creation of a heterosexual couple (Crofts, 1998: 129, 137, 141). Conversely, the Australian government's promotion of the film had been based on showcasing this ultimately excluded scenery to potential tourists. Clearly, different conceptions of the audience produce radically divergent versions of a film. This involves a marked disdain for ordinary people, as this Paramount executive's account of marketing overseas suggests:

> [M]ost of our films are dubbed because they have mass appeal; we tend to focus on action, however something we have discovered lately is that the subject is crucial. Indian audiences are becoming intelligent enough to decipher the difference between a good subject, and a bad one.
>
> (quoted in Kumar, 2002)

Much non-Hollywood-oriented cinema is charged by the state with turning audience dopes into a public of thinkers beyond the home – civic-minded participants in a political and social system as well as an economy of purchasing. National cinemas in Europe, Asia, the Pacific, Latin America and Africa are expected to win viewers and train them in a way that complements the profit-driven sector. Entertainment is secondary to providing what the commercial market does not 'naturally' deliver. The GEM encourages audiences not just to watch and consume, but to act differently, to be 'better' people than their 'dope' status as Hollywood viewers. The GEM links national cinema to the historic mission of public broadcasting, and such links are frequently institutional as well as discursive.

The DEM and the GEM have supporters on both the left and the right, and across the social sciences and the humanities. In opposition to these *données*, an active-audience tradition picks up on Garfinkel's cultural-dope insight. Rather than issuing jeremiads, it claims that audiences are so clever and able that they outwit the institutions of the state, capitalism and criticism that seek to control and measure them and their interpretations. In one sense, this position has a venerable tradition, through literary-theory Nazis like Hans Robert Jauss (1982) and his aesthetics of reception to Marxists such as Jean-Paul Sartre (1990) and his philosophy of the mutual intrication of writer and reader in making meaning (Mattelart and Mattelart, 1998: 119–20, 123). In screen culture, the idea really spread with the medievalist Umberto Eco's mid-1960s development of a notion of encoding–decoding, open texts and aberrant readings, developed as part of a consultancy for Italian television (1972). This was picked up by sociologists Frank Parkin (1971) and Stuart Hall (1980), on the left, and on the right by uses-and-gratifications functionalist Elihu Katz (1990).

Counter-critique attacks criticisms of the screen for failing to allot the people's machine its due as a populist apparatus that subverts patriarchy, capitalism and other forms of oppression (or diminishes the tension of social divisions, depending on your politics). The screen is held to be subversive (or a release), because, almost regardless of content, its output is decoded by audiences in keeping with their own social situation (Seiter, 1999). The active audience is said to be weak at the level of cultural production, but strong as an interpretative community. Consider the special skills of cultish fans. They construct parasocial, imagined connections to celebrities or actants, who fulfil the functions of friendship or serve as spaces for projecting and evaluating schemas that make sense of human interaction. In addition to adoring texts, cult audiences domesticate characters, removing them from the overall story and quoting their escapades and proclivities as part of a fan's world that is opened up to others through quizzes and rankings. References to favourite scenes, the behaviour of actants or the qualities of stars catalyse memories. Sequences and tendencies are disarticulated from screen time, reshaped and redisposed to contrast with one's own social circumstances (Leets *et al.*, 1995: 102–04; Harrington and Bielby, 1995: 102–04, 110; Eco, 1987: 198). In addition, the despised genres listed earlier are recuperated: Hong Kong action becomes carnivalesque, and talk shows address hitherto suppressed topics of public debate.

This active-audience position may be the most visible aspect of cultural studies. In 1999, Virginia Postrel wrote an op-ed piece for the right-wing US financial newspaper the *Wall Street Journal* welcoming such research, describing it as 'deeply threatening to traditional leftist views of commerce', because active media consumption seemed so close to the sovereign consumer beloved of the right. Postrel suggests that 'cultural-studies mavens are betraying the

leftist cause, lending support to the corporate enemy and even training graduate students who wind up doing market research' (Postrel, 1999). And Todd
Gitlin argues that some sectors of cultural studies are indeed in synch with neoclassical economics and the right: 'What the group wants, buys, demands is *ipso
facto* the voice of the people. Supply has meshed with demand' (1997: 32). As
Herbert I. Schiller puts it, the direct opposition that is frequently drawn
between political economy (production matters) and active-audience theory
(interpretation matters) assumes that the fragmentation of audience niches
and responses nullifies the concentration and reach of economic power in mass
culture – that pluralism ensures diversity (1989: 147–48, 153). But is this credible? Perhaps a 'shared interest in [a TV] show is an end in itself and seldom
leads to some action beyond that interest, some larger political purpose'
(Butsch, 2000: 291).

And yet, leading bourgeois economist Jagdish Bhagwati (2002) is convinced
that cultural studies and the media are parties to global grassroots activism
against globalisation. This suggests there is hope. After all, many of those
actions have been taken against neoliberalism. So we need to move towards
an alternative cultural studies, closer to Bhagwati's fears than the *Journal*'s
celebrations.

Meaghan Morris glosses, enacts and criticises the dilemma of this position
in her account of *The Lucille Ball Show*, as seen on 1950s Australian television.
This isolated image of women evading patriarchal control had dramatic effects
on the Morris household – mother and daughter revelled in the show, while
father absented himself. But the programme was also a sign of political economy and diplomacy: it represented the resiting of Australian geopolitical
culture away from Britain and towards the US. The screen is certainly amenable
to notions of localism, resistance and feminism, working via the 'subversive
pleasure of the female spectators' to produce an active engagement with both
the text and the family. But this can become a critic's alibi for social speculation.
Our suspicions should be aroused when academic theory cites 'the people' as
demotic supports for its own preoccupations, because when 'the people'
become one more text to be read and interpreted, they stand for the critic's own
practice of reading. Far from being sources of information, they have been
transmogrified into delegates that endow the critic's *own* account with a populist ring (Morris, 1990: 15–16, 21–23). Aberrant decoding by fans becomes a
means of making the output of the culture industries isomorphic with a professor's anti-capitalist, anti-patriarchal, anti-racist politics.

In reaction to models of the cultural dope and the active audience, Alec
McHoul and Tom O'Regan (1992) criticise the idea that 'local instances' of
people 'embracing' or 'refusing' the dominant interpretations preferred by global producers 'guarantee any general statement about textual meaning'. Instead,
they propose a 'discursive analysis of particular actor networks, technologies of
textual exchange, circuits of communicational and textual effectivity, traditions

of exegesis, commentary and critical practice'. In other words, the specific 'uptake' of a text by a community should be our focus; but not because this reveals something essential to the properties of screen texts or their likely uptake anywhere else or at any other time. We can only discern a 'general out-line' of 'interests', applied to specific cases 'upon a piecemeal and local inspection' (McHoul and O'Regan, 1992: 5–6, 8–9). The screen is an instrument of instruction and response that varies with place, time, genre and audience (O'Shea, 1989: 376–77). As Justin Lewis says, 'viewing is a cultural practice, and like all cultural practices, it involves not only "doing it" but "ways of doing it" ' (1991: 49). The crucial link between theories of the text and spectatorship – one that abjures the extremes of the dope and its opposite – may come from a spec-ification of occasionality, that moment when a spectator moves from being 'the hypothetical point of address of filmic discourse' to membership in 'a plural, social audience'; for that moment can produce surprises (Hansen, 1994: 2).

For those of us schooled in pub-talk or Leavisite talk, whether about sport, art, politics, literature, friends or television, there is nothing necessarily new or socially subversive about evaluations by fans – or the idiocies forwarded to explain them by studios, psychologists, censors or cultural critics. None of which is to say that, on the other side, the anti-populists are correct in their infantalisation of audiences. The DEM suffers from all the disadvantages of ideal-typical psychological reasoning. Each massively costly laboratory test of media effects, based on, as the refrain goes, 'a large university in the mid-West', is countered by a similar experiment, with conflicting results. As politicians, grant-givers and jeremiad-wielding pundits call for more and more research to prove that the screen makes you stupid, violent, unpatriotic and apathetic – or the opposite – academics line up at the trough to indulge their contempt for popular culture and ordinary life and their rent-seeking urge for public money. As Pierre Bourdieu suggests in criticising the GEM, 'paternalistic-pedagogical television' is 'no less opposed to a truly democratic use of the means of mass circulation than populist spontaneism and demagogic capitulation to popular tastes' (1998: 48).

Guided by that insight, there are examples of screen-studies interventions into policy discussions of this type, such as Stuart Cunningham's 1980s sub-missions on film and television violence for public inquiries in Australia, which carefully adumbrated conventional approaches while adding theorisa-tion of the state, capital and social movements to the normal science of effects research (1992: 137–67). The humanities side to screen studies in the US caught up with this kind of work fifteen years later, when a group of scholars supported video-game industrialists in a law case against a commercial ordi-nance that required manufacturers to advise parents that their products were risky for young people ('Brief *Amici Curiae*', 2003). Such actions stood out in a field that had eschewed engagement with the public interest in favour of a narcissistic parthenogenesis (but for a sobering critique of this brief, see Kline,

2003). In each case, the analysts were dealing with the bottom line in these debates, of citizenship versus consumption.

The Citsumer

The customer knows precisely what is attractive and valuable. . . . It is the local citizenry casting their own votes, not the American film industry.

(Jack Valenti, 1993: 147, 149)

Combining good pictures with good citizenship

(Studio slogan, quoted in Powdermaker, 1950: 108)

Our movies and TV programs are hospitably received by citizens around the world.

(Jack Valenti, quoted in Gershon, 1997: 47)

As opposed to his earlier difficulty with militarism and oral sex, here Valenti is finding it hard to distinguish between citizens and consumers. This section of our book is designed to help him sort out this complex difference. It leads us to the heart of the *laissez-faire* bifurcation between Hollywood and its others, between audiences as citizens and consumers. We do not provide a comprehensive account of 'citizen' and 'consumer', but we do spell out certain rationalities that mobilise these terms in transnational cultural battles, challenging assertions made in their name while recognising their necessity.

There is a complicated relationship between the citizen and its logocentric double, the consumer. The citizen is a wizened figure from the ancient past. The consumer, by contrast, is naïve, essentially a creature of the nineteenth century. Each shadows the other, the *national* subject versus (or is it *as*?) the *rational* subject. We all know how popular the consumer is with neoclassical economists and policy wonks: the market is said to operate in response to this ratiocinative agent, who, endowed with perfect knowledge, negotiates between alternative suppliers and his or her own demands, such that an appropriate price is paid for desired commodities. The consumer has become the sexless, ageless, unprincipled, magical agent of social value in a multitude of discourses and institutions since that time. Unmarked in this rationality by national origins, consumers are runaways from national culture, animated by individual preferences.

What of the other side to our couplet, the citizen, currently invoked in Europe against US demands for a free market? The citizen has also undergone a major revival in the last decade. Social theorists and policy-makers have nominated it as a magical agent of historical change. More easily identified than class, and more easily mobilised as a justification for state action, citizenship has become a site of hope for a left that has lost its actually existing alternative to international capital. We now address the utility of this move in the context of film and television.

Once we add some history, spatiality and politics to the DEM/GEM, they become more complicated, not least as consumption and citizenship have a dynamic relationship to right and left discourse. Citizen-consumers are said to be both constructed and corrupted through popular culture. On one side of the debate, the exercise of choice through purchase is supposed to guarantee the democratic workings of a market-driven society, because the culture industries are simply providing what the consuming public desires. But for today's progressives, choice may also effect social change – for example, Denny's restaurant chain is boycotted by some leftists in the US because of its racist hiring practices. Many such activists also use the Working Assets long-distance telephone service because it donates a portion of its proceeds to left-wing causes. At certain moments, those on the left who resist authoritarian politics may embrace ideologies of liberal individualism and free choice, whereas at other times they may foreground questions of labour rather than consumption in a struggle for collective justice. Nation-building moments exhibit a similar slippage between citizen and consumer, depending on the historical moment and geographical location. For example, state-based modernisation projects in Latin America between the 1930s and the 1960s utilised the mass media – song in Brazil, radio in Argentina and cinema in Mexico – to turn the masses, newly migrated to the cities, into citizens (Martín-Barbero, 1993). Conversely, the 1990s brought a wave of deregulation in the mass media, because of neoliberalism and reactions against the clientelism and *dirigisme* of earlier decades. In lieu of citizen-building, the new logic of the culture industries is the construction of consumers. Néstor García-Canclini notes that this shift in emphasis from citizen to consumer is sometimes linked to the change in Latin America's dependency from Europe to the US: 'We Latin Americans presumably learned to be citizens through our relationship to Europe; our relationship to the United States will, however, reduce us to consumers' (2001: 1). And in the name of the consumer, ideas of the national popular are eschewed – consumer choice becomes an alibi for structural adjustment policies imposed by international lending institutions that call for privatisation of the media. So what is the way forward?

Getting it Right

I was engulfed in a nice fireball, actually.

(Australian movie fan, Brian Concannon, burned while performing a stunt he copied from the American film *Jackass: The Movie* [Jeff Tremaine, 2002], quoted in 'Fiery End', 2003)

Perhaps the most significant innovation that we need – and it inspires this volume – comes from critical political economy and cultural studies. These areas have witnessed a radical historicisation of context, such that the analysis of textual properties and spectatorial processes must now be supplemented by an account of *occasionality* that details the conditions under which a text is made, circulated, received, interpreted and criticised. The life of any popular or praised film is a passage across space and time, a life remade again and again by institutions, discourses and practices of distribution and reception. To understand texts, we must consider all the shifts and shocks that characterise their existence as cultural commodities, their ongoing renewal as the temporary 'property' of varied, productive workers and publics and the abiding 'property' of businesspeople.

This push for a radical contextualisation of interpretation is aided by a surprising turn – the reprise of the early history of film as part of a vaudeville bill. The moving image is again part of a multi-form network of entertainment, via CD-ROMs, computer games, the Web, DVDs and multiplexes. The brief moment when cinema could be viewed as a fairly unitary phenomenon in terms of exhibition (say, 1920 to 1950) set up the *conceptual* prospect of its textual fetishisation in academia, something that became *technologically feasible* with video-cassette recorders – just when that technology's popularity compromised the very discourse of stable aestheticisation! Now that viewing environments, audiences, technologies and genres are so multiple, the cinema is restored to a mixed-medium mode. No wonder some argue that 'a film today is merely a billboard stretched out in time, designed to showcase tomorrow's classics in the video stores and television reruns' (Elsaesser, 2001: 11), that cinema is the aesthetic 'engine driving the interlinked global entertainment markets' (Prince, 2000: 141). The US Federal Government's official classification of screen production (Department of Commerce, 2001: 14, 16 n. 12) includes features, made-for-television films, television series, commercials and music videos – and so should screen studies' 'official classification'.

In short, if it is to make an impact on the power and status of global Hollywood, screen studies needs an overhaul. The current orthodoxy is:

- use of certain limited, seemingly arbitrarily selected, theories of subject-formation
- solitary or classroom textual analysis of 'films' that is actually conducted on a television screen, an analysis that magically stands for other audiences, subjectivities, cultures and occasions of viewing
- neglect of cultural bureaucrats and industry workers in favour of attention to individuals, collectives or (by magical proxy) social movements, because artists are privileged over governments and unions, and scholarly critics decree themselves able to divine meaning for whole classes of the population, prizing spectacularity over the mundane; and
- use of the DEM and/or GEM models.

These are interesting things to do, but they are insufficient as political-economic-textual-anthropological accounts, and their politics are all too frequently limited to the academy or to servicing reactionary epistemologies and policies.

Instead, we should acknowledge the policy, distributional, promotional and exhibitionary protocols of the screen at each site as much as their textual ones. Enough talk of 'economic reductionism' without also problematising 'textual reductionism'. Enough valorisation of close reading and armchair or behavioural accounts of human interiority without ethical and political regard for the conditions of global cultural labour and the significance of workers, texts and subjectivities within social movements and demographic cohorts. Enough denial of the role of government. Enough teaching classes on animation, for instance, without reference to effects work, content analysis and the international political economy that sees an episode of *The Simpsons* decrying globalisation when the programme has itself been made by non-union animators in South-East Asia. These issues – cultural labour, industry frameworks, audience experiences and cultural policy – should be integral.

Fortunately, while the disciplinary division of labour in screen studies is encouraged by orthodox rent-seeking, it is imperilled by three factors:

1 The excellent work done on, for instance, race and the media by the likes of Thomas Nakayama (1994 and 1997; Nakayama and Krizek, 1995; Nakayama and Martin, 1999; Martin and Nakayama, 2000) and Oscar Gandy (1992a, 1992b and 1998; Gandy and Matabane, 1989), and the ethnographic and political-economic studies of Faye Ginsburg *et al.* (2002; see also Himpele, 1996, and Jacob, 1998). But are they referenced by the hegemons and acolytes of screen studies?

2 Many college jobs in film now come not from the usual suspect – a literature department in search of a partial make-over – but from communication and media studies.

3 From the other end, globalisation has pushed neoclassical economics and rational-choice political science towards some acknowledgment of the need to allow actually existing social politics and financial transactions to exist and interpenetrate, given that the 'business of government is everywhere increasingly organised along the lines of the government of business' (Higgott, 1999: 29–30; see also Ollman, 2000) – though we question how far this can go, given that the seductive 'line of least mathematical resistance' is so wedded to formal modelling (Krugman, 2000: 49).

Institutions do not have to be arid areas of study, and the links to everyday life are real. The remarkable international actions of young people against globalisation at the dawn of the twenty-first century show that they can be energised around such topics, notably the world division of labour – so let screen studies 'get' real, too. It already does better than literary studies: who today in such classes, on either side of the power point, can explain the material histories of books through ownership, control and labour? At least screen studies does look at such issues. But screen studies engaged in disciplinary gatekeeping too early on life, as if following Papal instructions would give it disciplinary strength. Now is the time to open up. At the same time, there are risks, as we saw with how audiences are made up by social science.

Dan Schiller (1996: 194) proposes a way beyond the graceless antinomies of production-centred analysis versus DEM-GEM or active-audience screen studies. Screen production need not be thought of in opposition to consumption, with one practice 'productive' and the other not, or one side trumping the other. Instead, the work of screen employees is one moment of labouring activity, and the work of screen audiences is another. Rather than embarking on *either* active interpretation *or* passive reception, audience members' labour includes self-understanding – but that labour cannot and should not be conceptualised in isolation from their day jobs, the work of others in bringing television to them or, as we discuss in Chapter 5, how such labour can be exploited through the surveillance networks of market research (see also Maxwell, 2001).

We need to view the screen through twin theoretical prisms. On the one hand, it can be understood as the newest component of sovereignty, a twentieth-century cultural addition to ideas of patrimony and rights that sits alongside such traditional topics as territory, language, history and schooling. On the other hand, the screen is a cluster of culture industries (Porter, 2000: 254). It is subject to exactly the rent-seeking practices and exclusionary representational protocols that characterise liaisons between state and capital. We must ask:

- Is screen studies serving phantasmatic projections of humanities critics' narcissism, or does it actively engage cultural policies and social-movement politics?
- Is Hollywood really giving the people of the world what they want, or does it operate via monopoly-capitalist business practice?
- Is non-Hollywood, state-supported screen culture expanding the vision and availability of the good life to include the ability of a people to control its representation on-screen?
- Is that 'alternative' culture merely a free ride for fractions of a *comprador*, cosmopolitan or social-movement bourgeoisie?
- To what extent do national cinemas engage their rhetorical publics, and do those audiences spend more time watching imports than their 'own' films?
- Is there a way out of the DEM-GEM and active-audience discourses?
- What place does labour have in giving culture value?
- How can screen studies intervene in the public sphere?

The political audit we make of an audiovisual space should consider its openness, both on and off camera, to the demographics of those inhabiting it. No cinema that claims resistance to Hollywood in the name of national or social-movement specificity is worthy of endorsement if it does not actually attend to sexual and racial minorities and women, along with class politics.

What would it take for screen studies to matter more? We have three proposals: (a) influencing public media discourse on the screen; (b) engaging public policy and not-for-profit and commercial practice; and (c) avoiding the reproduction of 'screen studies' in favour of work that studies the screen, regardless of its intellectual provenance. When it comes to key questions of texts and audiences – what gets produced and circulated and how it is read – policy analysis, political economy, ethnography, movement activism and the use of the social-science archive are crucial. The idea is to embark on an analysis of hysterisis, whereby overlapping causes and sites can be understood. That necessitates both macro and micro scales and a focus on: (i) the global, where capitalism is ordered; (ii) the national, where ideology is produced; and (iii) the local, where work is done (adapted from Herod, 2001: 39–41). We hope, therefore, that this book contributes not only to the debate about global Hollywood but also to how screen studies goes about its business.

For us, that means engaging the labour process of making meaning, the material relations that describe a screen text's life through script development, pre-production, production, post-production, marketing, distribution, exhibition and reception (see Chapter 2). Film remains at the apex semiotically, but not financially.

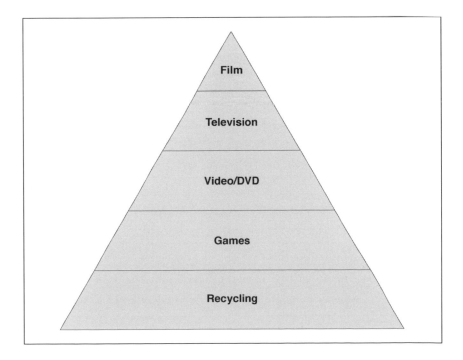

Film is the site of origin for these other forms and has the most venerable status, so it is positioned at the top of the pyramid. Video and television are the most popular and games generate the most revenue, so they come next and broaden out the diagram. As the newest manifestation, recycling is at the bottom, but it has potentially the greatest economic effect, through recycling film stock from old movies as polyester, or metals retrieved from old computers and televisions (Mallory, 2003). Pre-teen Chinese girls pick away without protection of any kind at discarded First-World televisions and computers in order to find precious metals, then dump the remains in landfills. The metals are sold to recyclers, who do not use landfills or labour in the First World because of environmental and industrial legislation against the damage caused to soil, water and workers by the dozens of poisonous chemicals and gases in these dangerous machines (Basel Action Network and Silicon Valley Toxics Coalition, 2002). The reality of much screen production is exorbitant water consumption for computer technology, and an 'hourglass' economy, with increased inequality because of low-level, non-unionised positions (Shiva, 2002; Waters, 2003). Making semi-conductors requires the use of hazardous chemicals, including some known carcinogens, and the waste from discarded electronics is one of the biggest sources of heavy metals and toxic pollutants in US trash piles. Whereas the main focus of this book is on the upper reaches of the pyramid, we wish to signal our recognition of what happens at its base, and the potentially vast economic impact of this dangerous and costly side to the industry.

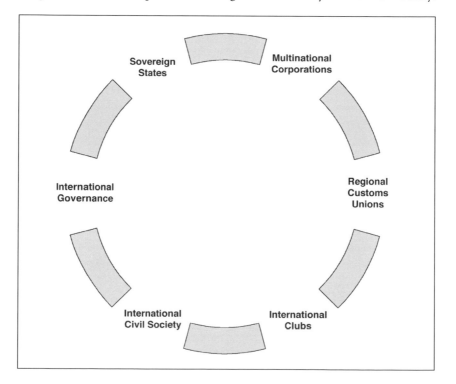

Within this pyramid lies the dynamising force of work, part of the centrifugal and centripetal forces that may simultaneously and contradictorily favour growth at both the core and the periphery. This is the place where we find 'the realities of the power struggle all along the assembly line of creation' (Powdermaker, 1967: 217).

In turn, international organisations are key actors in our analysis.

Picking up on these multi-sited realities, we commend the approaches to global production offered in Zsuzsa Gille and Séan Ó Riain's (2002) suggestive methodological *parti pris*. They investigate not a mythic, placeless site of ideal consumer–producer exchange, but rather the relationship between space and society, via networks, flows, groups and sites across and between nations, localities, firms, civil society, states and global concerns. This is in keeping with some of the earliest work on globalisation, which emphasised the relocation of jobs from Third World to the First. That research has latterly been enriched by ethnographic approaches that incorporate the experience of these workers – their co-optations and resistances, and the gendered and racialised elements of capitalism's extended reach. This brings agency into what had seemed a deterministic paradigm, while walking a fine line alongside the putative voluntarism of bourgeois individualism. Such approaches have encouraged both our project and others seeking to get to grips with the global division of cultural work (Miller *et al.*, 2001; Connell and Wood, 2002; Freeman, 2000; Baldoz *et al.*, 2001; Burawoy *et al.*, 2000); or as it is politely described by corporate leeches and their lackeys, 'business process outsourcing' (Srinivas, 2003).

Membership of these institutions may overlap and even converge as the dividing lines between public and private are redrawn, new institutions are created and old ones discarded or devalued in order to manage the global economy. They are not all of equal power at all times and in all venues. But they do represent a mix of global, regional, national and sub-national institutions that can link and decouple promiscuously (Scott, 1998c: 10). In media terms, the relevant agencies encompass copyright, labour, the environment, technology, travel, censorship, subsidy, macro-economic policy and conglomeration (see Raboy, 2002). Such topics form the core of our book, and we think they should be at the heart of any screen-studies curriculum (see Blair *et al.*, 2001).

We have inspirations and fellow-travellers in this project, notably the example of Powdermaker. Half a century ago, she wrote what remains the key ethnography of Hollywood. This is how she looked back on the experience:

> As I left Hollywood after a year and drove past marking the boundaries of Los Angeles, I burst into song, as is my habit when feeling joy. But even that reaction did not make me realize how deeply I hated the place. When leaving other field sites, I have usually been both glad and sorry – glad to depart because I have been tired and fed-up; sorry to leave my friends and life in the field. Except for the Hollywood situation, I have never been joyous on leaving, nor have I hated a society I studied. Although it might be difficult, there is no

reason why an anthropologist could not study a society he hated, so long as he was aware of his feelings at the time, and was able to cope with them. But my rage was bottled up, and never fully conscious.

I happen to be a person of strong feelings, and it might have been predicted from the previous conditioning of my personality that I would feel rage in Hollywood. The plunge into the labor movement had been a rebellion from authority in the family and against the subjugation of unorganized workers by employers. Nor was it irrelevant that World War II, in which we fought a totalitarian concept of man, had just ended before I went to Hollywood, or that I had always been (and still am) concerned with the moral problem of freedom. I had, also, always been hostile to a way of life in which the accumulation of wealth was the primary motive. My identifications had long been with scientists and artists, and I have never seen any real ideological or temperamental incompatibility between them.

(Powdermaker, 1967: 225)

This is a shocking but inspirational epigraph.

Of course, in producing *Global Hollywood 2*, we have entered the strange world of the sequel, a cliché of Hollywood franchising that is on the increase (twenty such titles in 2002 and twenty-seven in 2003). The word derives from the Middle-Ages French *séquelle* and the Middle-English *sequele*. It was a term of derision in those times, referring to blind followers of a leader (European Audiovisual Observatory, 2003: 4). To the extent that we form a band of followers, our exemplars are those, like Powdermaker, who strive for alternatives to Yanqui[6] domination and wholesale commodification at the expense of the marginal and the oppressed. Such company seems worth keeping.

Notes

1   The MPAA is comprised of the major studios in Hollywood. The working definition of 'independent' in the US film industry covers all films made by producers who are not MPAA members and are mostly represented by the American Film Marketing Association (AFMA). Although the two entities are responsible for the release of about the same number of films (more than 200 each annually), MPAA members outspend AFMA members eleven to one (Department of Commerce, 2001: 14).

2   We chose to use the acronym NICL rather than NIDCL to offer a homonym for 'nickel', the US five-cent coin.

3   Figures for cinema attendance and receipts are extremely difficult to calculate with confidence. France, Germany, Sweden, Spain and Italy mandate the declaration of receipts by theatre owners. Some European countries, such as Portugal, Greece, Iceland, Luxembourg, Russia and Hungary, and most in the Third World, have no data collection. Others see data promulgated by professional associations (the Netherlands), distributors (Slovakia,

Switzerland and the Czech Republic), magazines and private companies (the US, Ireland, the UK, Belgium, France, Spain, Germany and Italy) or governmental statisticians (Finland and Denmark). Major research entities use the AMADEUS database (*Lumiere*, n. d.; also see Lange, 2003).

4   Odd, is it not, that this concept is never put into dialectical play with the development dictum of the free exchange of ideas and open communication?

5   In addition to the papers we cite elsewhere, see Simonet, 1980; Rosen, 1981; Adler, 1985; Chung and Cox, 1994; Wallace *et al.*, 1993; Albert, 1998; Peters, 1974; Peters and Cantor, 1982; Levy, 1989; Baker and Faulkner, 1991; De Vany and Walls, 1996, 1997 and 1999; Lauzen and Dozier, 1999; Clark, 1995; Marvasti, 2000; Nelson *et al.*, 2001; Sedgwick, 2002; Zuckerman *et al.*, 2003; Pokorny and Sedgwick, 2001; Ravid, 1999; Sedgwick and Pokorny, 1998; Weinstein, 1998; Jones and DeFillippi, 1996; Eliashberg and Shugan, 1997; Faulkner and Anderson, 1987; and Sochay, 1994. Ask your film professor what to make of this work.

6   The word 'American' or 'America' is frequently used to describe the United States of America, its people and culture. This is both offensive and misleading, as dozens of other countries are part of the Americas, including the other components of North America (Mexico and Canada). In our usage we therefore move between Hollywood, the US and Yanqui as descriptors. In Latin America, people from the US are often referred to as 'Norte Americanos' or 'Gringos', and the country is given its own adjectival form, 'estadunidense'. Use of the term 'Yanqui' is in keeping with Chicano/a usage within the US.

1

Globalisation + Hollywood History + Cultural Imperialism + the GATT and Friends = *Laissez-Faire* Hollywood or State Business?

If I could control the medium of the American motion picture, I would need nothing else to convert the entire world to Communism.

(Joseph Stalin, quoted in Trumpbour, 2002: 2)

Exposure of the multi billion-dollar gravy train enjoyed by media executives would be a shock to stockholders and the public. All would see that the inflated production costs are not due solely to a few highly paid actors. Raking money off the top, bouncing revenues and expenses between TV stations, cable channels, ancillary markets and numerous overseas machinations would be open to question. Enough slack exists to allow for creative bookkeeping practices that would baffle even Arthur Anderson's successors. *Hollywood Creative Bookkeeping* is a picture they hope will never be made or shown.

(Haskell Wexler, 2002)

What happens when Hollywood and Bombay meet, Siva only knows.

('Movies Abroad', 1959)

We inhabit a moment popularly understood, in Eric Hobsbawm's words, as 'the global triumph of the United States and its way of life' (1998: 1). From a very different perspective, Henry Kissinger (1999) goes so far as to say that 'globalisation is really another name for the dominant role of the United States'. His consulting firm, Kissinger Associates, advises that this era must see the US 'win the battle of the world's information flows, dominating the airwaves as Great Britain once ruled the seas', not least because 'Americans should not deny the fact that of all the nations in the history of the world, theirs is the most just, the most tolerant, the most willing to constantly reassess and improve itself, and the best model for the future' (Rothkopf, 1997: 38, 47).

For all the misery within the US (in 2000, even as 74 per cent of college students expected to become millionaires, 44 million people had no medical coverage), it has international influence beyond the reach of other regimes, with the military and popular culture a key. And the speed with which its culture can spread around the world is accelerating. Whereas radio reached 50 million homes after forty years, it took television just thirteen years, and the Internet attained that figure in four years (International Labour Office, 2000a). In addition, the thirteen largest Internet companies in the world in 2003 were based in the US (Rice-Oxley, 2004). With ever-increasing homogeneity of ownership and control, and rapidly developing economies of scale, the capacity to dominate the exchange of ideas is strengthened. The NICL is central to that mission, as we demonstrate in chapters to come.

The source of Hollywood's power extends far beyond the history of cinema, to the cultural-communications complex that has been an integral component of capitalist exchange since the end of the nineteenth century. In the second half of the twentieth century, Third World activists, artists, writers and critical political economists nominated that complex as cultural imperialism. By the late twentieth century, it became fashionable to think of this power in terms of globalisation, a maddeningly euphemistic term laden with desire, fantasy, fear – and intellectual imprecision (Jacka, 1992: 5, 2; Jameson, 2000). 'Hollywood' appears in nearly all descriptions of globalisation's effects – left, right and third ways – as a floating signifier, a kind of cultural smoke rising from a US-led struggle to convert the world to capitalism.

Cultural diffusion has always been international, but the velocity and profundity of its processes seem to be on the increase (Mann, 1993: 119). There is an indissoluble link that ties and even mixes the 'ideology of corporate globalization' with the 'ideology of worldwide communication' through five decades of European and US government and corporate funding for intellectuals who have assiduously cultivated the mythology of communications technologies as signs of freedom, even as these innovations enabled 'a world ruled by the logic of social and economic segregation' (Mattelart, 2002: 591–92, 596–99). Tony Blair's vision of politics positions the media at the centre of global economic success: 'Free trade has proved itself a motor for economic development, political co-operation and cultural exchange. The development of modern global media will intensify this process' (quoted in Freedman, 2003a: 27).

For this reason, theories of globalisation put space and speed at the centre of both analytic and business concerns. Capital moves at high velocity, alighting on areas and countries in a promiscuous way, and the manner in which materials and people are exchanged simultaneously across the globe is profoundly asymmetrical (Sankowski, 1992: 6; Rockwell, 1994: H1; Frow, 1992: 14–15). Put another way, the military domination of empire suffered by First Peoples is now experienced – in milder form – as corporate domination by former colonisers and colonised alike – the 'Americanisation' that Charles Baudelaire referred to as a 'vast cage, a great accounting establishment' (quoted in Grantham, 1998: 60). For Hollywood both animates and is animated by globalisation. And what distinguishes Hollywood from other industries in the present stage of capitalist expansion, but also makes the organisation of film and television crucial signs of the future, is the industry's command of the New International Division of Cultural Labour. We prepare the way here for a description in subsequent chapters of how Hollywood reproduces and regulates the NICL through its control over cultural labour markets, international co-production, intellectual property, marketing, distribution and exhibition. The goal is to expand existing theories of global Hollywood's power, and modify current thinking about cultural policies that both enable and resist it. We start with an account of globalisation, proceeding from there to examine Hollywood's global history, resistance to it via cultural-imperialism critique and contemporary debates over screen trade, culminating in an evaluation of the claim that Hollywood exemplifies private enterprise.

Globalisation

[T]he US enters the 21st century in a position of unrivalled dominance that surpasses anything it experienced in the 20th. . . . America's free-market ideology is now the world's ideology; and the nation's Internet and biotechnology businesses are pioneering the technologies of tomorrow.

(Alan Murray, 1999)

Early capitalism predated the existence of states, and cultures were usually organised by other points of affinity, such as religion or language. Networks of information and trade connected the Pacific, the Mediterranean, Asia and Africa through the fifteenth century, but the slavery, militarism and technology of imperialism wiped out these routes. Intra-continental communications came to rely on Europe as a conduit, and new ideologies followed, such as racial supremacy and the conversion mission of Christianity (Hamelink, 1990: 223–24). Eurocentric networks circulated the assumptions of social evolutionists, not only in their narcissism, but in their search for a unanimity that would

Big Bad World by P. J. Polyp
SOURCE: *New Internationalist* 337, 2001

bind humanity in singular directions and forms of development. This discourse enabled its owners to observe themselves in an earlier stage of maturation, by investigating life in the southern hemisphere, and to police and co-ordinate what they found there, in keeping with a drive towards uniformity and opti-mality of human definition, achievement and organisation (Axtmann, 1993: 64–65).

The coordinates for compressing space and time under contemporary glob-alisation derive from three key imperial events: the Treaty of Tordesillas in 1494 and the Washington and Berlin Conferences of 1884. The Tordesillas Treaty acknowledged the emergence of empire, as the Pope mediated rivalries between Portugal and Spain through a bifurcation of the world – the first recorded con-ceptualisation of the globe as a site of conquest and exploitation. The Washington Conference standardised Greenwich as the axis of time and car-tography, while the imperial division of Africa was outlined at the Conference of Berlin in the same year. These developments effectively marked out the world as a site of interconnected government and commerce (Schaeffer, 1997: 2, 7, 10–11), with Western Europe and the US as its domineering epicentre.

Capitalism's uneven and unequal development has paralleled the violent cartographies of Tordesillas, Washington and Berlin. The mercantilist accumu-lation and imperialism of 1500 to 1800 were followed by the classical era of capital and its Industrial Revolution, founded on the use of natural resources for manufacturing copper, steel and fuel. Northern industrial development and agrarian change were partnered by European emigration to the Americas (to deal with population overflow) and the division of Africa and Asia (to obtain raw materials and enslaved labour) (Amin, 1997: 1, x; Reich, 1999; Chase-Dunn, 2002). These transformations had their utopic corollaries and contradictions via religious, imperial, economic and revolutionary ideologies that promised truth and beauty (Mattelart, 2002: 594–95).

Cinema technology and narrative emerged around the same time, at the turn of the twentieth century, when the US invented and appropriated a vast array of culturally significant machines – the airplane, the typewriter, electric light and the telephone. These devices made the nation the very image of a mech-anical dream or nightmare, depending on where you stood (Grantham, 2000: 13). There were also transformations in colonial politics: the US seized the Philippines and Cuba, the European powers ran Africa, and Native American resistance was crushed. While First Peoples' rights were being trampled under foot, commercial cultural export and sovereign authority were synchronising (with an array of genocidal stories enacted on-screen). A key economic shift also occurred between 1870 and 1914: average annual global output and exchange increased by more than 3 per cent – an unprecedented figure (Hirst, 1997: 411). Not surprisingly, Bahá'u'lláh coined the phrase 'New World Order' in 1873 (quoted in Calkins and Vézina, 1996: 311).[1] In response to these gov-ernmental and business developments, European and US socialists, syndicalists and anarchists formed large international associations of working people (Herod, 1997: 167).

Up to the Second World War, international trade focused on national capitals, controlled by sovereign-states. In the First World, the period from 1945 to 1973 represented an 'interregnum between the age of competing imperial powers and the coming of the global economy' (Teeple, 1995: 57), based on US military and diplomatic hegemony, articulated to the expansionary needs of its corporations. As other economies grew, so did interdependence between nations, and between companies within nations. After 1950, world trade was dominated by the triad of Europe, Japan and the US, 'each with their immense hinterland of satellite states' (Jameson, 1996: 2). Between 1950 and 1973, total trade increased by almost 10 per cent annually, and output by more than 5 per cent, most of it between the triad (Hirst, 1997: 411). Whereas modern manufacturing techniques had been restricted in the nineteenth century to Europe and the north-eastern US, they came to proliferate across the world, as applied intellect and science deterritorialised (Hindley, 1999; Reich, 1999). Politically, the Cold War constructed a polarised world of two totalising ideologies that struggled for control, just as empires had done over the previous century. This totality, which obscured other differences, encouraged the view that the future would see the triumph of one pole (Bauman, 1998: 58). Hence today's mavens of *laissez-faire* celebrating the supposed demise of the state – the sense that the US' anti-Soviet security policy of 'Containment' has been displaced by 'Entertainment', that 'MTV has gone where the CIA could never penetrate' (Gardels, 1998: 2).

The back-story to this division of the world is complex, and it need not have gone the way that it did. Starting in 1945, two historic promises were made by established and emergent governments: to secure both the economic welfare of citizens and their political sovereignty. At the end of the Second World War, the promise of economic welfare in the First World seemed locally workable, via state-based management of supply and demand and the creation of industries to substitute imports with domestically produced items. The promise of political sovereignty in the Third World required concerted international action to convince the colonial powers (principally Britain, the Netherlands, Belgium, France and Portugal) that the peoples whom they had enslaved should be given the right of self-determination via nationalism. The latter became a powerful ideology of political mobilisation as a supposed precursor to liberation. When this second promise was made good, the resulting post-colonial governments undertook to deliver the first promise. Most followed import-substitution industrialisation (ISI), frequently via state enterprises or on the coat-tails of multinational corporations (MNCs) that established local presences. MNCs had first appeared in the mid-sixteenth century, when the first ever joint-stock company financed an English expedition to Moscow. They were effectively granted shareholder-immunity from direct responsibility for their failures with

Britain's 1855 Limited Liability Act, which restricted investors' responsibilities to the value of their shares. By the 1880s, the US was dominated by such entities, which quickly looked to overseas profits, in keeping with their origins (Ferguson and Henderson, 2003). Following decolonisation in the middle of the twentieth century, MNCs were well placed to expand their involvement in the global South.

Despite the bright promise of self-determination that had accompanied their successful movements of national liberation, post-colonial Third World states suffered dependent underdevelopment and were mostly unable to grow economically. Their formal *political* post-coloniality rarely became *economic*, apart from some Asian states that pursued Export-Oriented Industrialisation (EOI) and service-based expansion. The ISI of the 1950s and 1960s was progressively problematised and dismantled from the 1970s to today, a tendency that grew in velocity and scope with the erosion of state socialism.

With the crises of the 1970s, even those developed Western states that had a bourgeoisie with sufficient capital formation to permit a welfare system found that stagflation had undermined their capacity to hedge employment against inflation. We know the consequences: 'the space of economic management of capital accumulation [no longer] coincided with that of its political and social dimensions' (Amin, 1997: xi). Today, governments are supposed to deliver the two promises to voters via ongoing formal sovereignty and controlled financial markets, but neoclassical orthodoxy and business priorities call for free international capital markets. This amounts to what the *Economist* calls an '[i]mpossible trinity' ('Global Finance', 1999: 4 Survey Global Finance).

The corollary of open markets is that national governments cannot guarantee the economic well-being of their citizens. The loan-granting power of the World Bank and the International Monetary Fund (IMF) has forced a shift away from the local provision of basic needs. The original task of the Fund was to sustain demand at the same time as it allowed employment to remain stable. Suffering nations could turn to it instead of deflating their economies or erecting trade barriers against their neighbours, and the interests of international finance were subordinated to those of the popular classes. Today, markets are held to be perfect if they operate without such interventions. The IMF does not have enough money of its own to function, so it frequently relies on private banks. The result has often maximised profit, rather than alleviating misery, such that the late-1990s multimillion intervention in East Asia was in part a bail-out of US financial institutions that had made bad investments. And IMF loans to the Third World are in dollars, often through US banks, which require a quid pro quo for what should be a truly disinterested venue of international public policy (Hutton, 2002; Stiglitz, 2002). So globalisation does not offer an end to centre–periphery inequalities, competition between states or macro-decision-making by corporations; it just reduces the capacity of the state system to control such transactions, and relegates responsibility for the protection and well-being

of the cultural workforce to multinational corporate entities and financial institutions (McMichael, 1996: 27–29; Marshall, 1996; Connelly, 1996: 12–13;
Wallerstein, 1989: 10–11). At the same time, the claim that globalisation has seen
an equivalent undermining of the welfare state in the First World has been challenged (Navarro et al., 2004). One rule for the South, another for the North.

Globalisation stands for a sense from across time, space and nation that those
very categories are in peril. (Our sense of the temporal is questioned – think of
the panic generated by computers dealing with the difference between 1900 and
2000.) Space, too, is problematised, as jobs are undertaken by people on the
basis of price and docility rather than locale. And nations are threatened by corporate control, as unelected, far-distant elites displace or instruct locally
'accountable' politicians. In each category, the cultural corollary is clear. Time
is manipulated in concert with the interests of global capital, space is torn asun-
der, and traditional social bonds are compromised by ownership based on
profit rather than township. At the political, economic and class level, this can
lead to 'social and economic fatalism and chronic insecurity'. Democracies
seem unable to deal with economic forces (Held et al., 1999: 1).

In the global economic system that has evolved since the mid-1970s, Northern class fractions support a transnational capital that has displaced
non-capitalist systems elsewhere (Robinson, 1996: 14–15). Regulatory and
other mechanisms have been set in place to liberalise world trade, contain
socialism, promote legislation favourable to capitalist expansion and aggregate
world markets (for harmonisation of copyright, see Chapter 4). World markets,
including the EU and other trade groupings, have been crucial for the promotion of free trade in the 1980s and beyond (though trade since then has not
exceeded that of the post-war quarter-century [Hirst, 1997: 412]). The growth
of corporate power is so strong that corporations can demand the removal of
national barriers to trade, such that the spread of foreign capital and currency
markets has meant that economic decisions are taken outside the context of the
sovereign-state, in ways that favour the market. And by 1994, half of the one
hundred biggest economies in the world 'belonged' not to nation-states, but to
MNCs (Donnelly, 1996: 239). The Fortune 500's revenue represented over 44
per cent of world Gross Domestic Product (GDP). Four hundred of the group
accounted for two-thirds of fixed assets and 70 per cent of trade, while there
were over a quarter of a million international subsidiaries of major firms
(Robinson, 1996: 20; Scott, 1998c: 36). But the US, Western Europe and Japan
are really the only key sites of MNC activity, housing more than two-thirds of
MNC sales and assets. Direct foreign investment elsewhere is limited (Hirst,
1997: 418; Kozul-Wright and Rowthorn, 1998). Perhaps one in twenty MNCs
actually function globally (Gibson-Graham, 1996–97: 7–8). Multinationals
look around for marginal utility and then retreat to what is known and con-
trollable – so the explosion of foreign investment in the three years from 1994
saw an increase of 40 per cent in MNC money flowing into the US, while invest-

ment the other way was primarily in Britain, the Netherlands, Canada, France and Australia ('Trade Barriers', 1997).

Viewing the market as a deterritorialising movement does not imply a borderless world, but it does mean a transformation of the state. Through structural adjustment and liberalisation, states adopt policies to manage global, rather than national, economic relations. These policies facilitate global circuits of money and commodities at the expense of social stability and environmental security within the sovereign-state. At a fundamental level, they do violence to open debate over national and global cultural policies and promote malevolence and condescension towards any cultural policy that does not facilitate the NICL.

Today's prevailing neoliberal 'Washington Consensus' has vanquished the key politico-economic questions of the last half-century (there is less need for 'Conferences' now, with the World Trade Organization [WTO] and the Global Business Dialogue). After the shocks of 2001, the US government issued a chilling directive to the world via its *National Security Strategy*, which criticised 'the enemies of civilisation' while promoting the 'single sustainable model for national success: freedom, democracy, and free enterprise' (The White House, 2002). Dominant since the late 1970s, the 'Consensus' (surely by now better named 'Washington Control') favours open trade, comparative advantage, deregulation of financial markets and low inflation, correlating open markets with media exchange (Yang and Shanahan, 2003). It has, of course, presided over slower worldwide growth and greater worldwide inequality than any time since the Depression. Job security and real wages are down and working hours are up. By the year 2000, Yanquis were working close to an average of 2,000 hours annually, the only developed country beside Sweden in which obligatory work hours increased (average annual hours fell from 1,809 to 1,656 in France, from 2,121 to 1,889 in Japan, and from 1,512 to 1,399 in Norway) (International Labour Office, 1999: 166). Between 1973 and 1998, working hours per capita declined by 12 per cent in Europe, but increased by the same extent in the US (Gindin and Panitch, 2002). At the same time, the richest 20 per cent of the world's people earned seventy-four times the amount of the world's poorest in 1997, up from sixty times in 1990 and thirty times in 1960 (UNDP, 1999: 3). The following year, according to World Bank estimates, 56 per cent of the global population made less than US$2 a day. Poverty is their norm (Sutcliffe, 2003: 3). But despite the manifold catastrophes of the 'Consensus' across the late 1990s (Mexico, South-East Asia, Russia and Brazil), it is still hailed as exemplary policy. Repeated failures are deemed aberrations by apologists, who confidently await 'the long run', when equilibrium will be attained (Palley, 1999: 49; Levinson, 1999: 21; Galbraith, 1999: 13; Stiglitz, 2002). The 'Consensus' is animated by neoliberalism's mantra of individual freedom, the marketplace and minimal government involvement in economic matters. This provides the intellectual alibi for a comparatively unimpeded flow of capital across national boundaries, and the rejection of labour, capital and the state managing the economy together.

In sum, global exchange has been with us for a long time. But since the 1970s, financial and managerial decisions made in one part of the world have taken very rapid effect elsewhere. New international currency markets sprang up at that time following the decline of a fixed exchange rate, matching regulated systems with piratical financial institutions that crossed borders. Speculation brought greater rewards than production, as the trade in securities and debts outstripped profits from selling cars or building houses. The world circulation of money created the conditions for imposing international creditworthiness tests on all countries. At a policy level, this put an end to ISI and the very legitimacy of national economies. These concepts were supplanted by EOI and the idea of an international economy. With productive investment less profitable than financial investment, and companies rationalising production, the worlds of marketing, labour and administration were reconceived on an international scale, with services, notably entertainment, a crucial category.

The US has become an extraordinary trader – to the value of US$3.4 trillion in 2000, a 15 per cent increase in exports from the previous year. Annual expansion in trade between 1970 and 2000 averaged 11.4 per cent, compared to 7.8 per cent yearly growth in GDP. Services are central to this figure. The US has long been adept at innovation in the services sector. Even as the economy was undergoing its dramatic agricultural and manufacturing growth, the services area, too, was expanding. Although, of course, services were not theorised as such at the time, changes had been evident for some time prior to the Depression and the GATT. The counting house became the modern office as new technologies, educational investments and systems of labour hierarchy emerged from the 1870s, helping the US to overtake Britain as the key centre of world productivity in a general shift from personalised, customised, low-volume production to anonymous, standardised, high-volume manufacture. These transformations began in communications and transport, before widening to finance and cultural distribution (Broadberry and Ghosal, 2002).

The US today has 86 million private-sector jobs in services. They created one dollar in seven of total world production and exported US$295 billion in 2000, producing a US$80 billion surplus in service-industry balance of payments (Office of the US Trade Representative, 2001a: 1, 10, 15). Well over half of US job growth between 1988 and 2000 was in this sector (Goodman and Steadman, 2002). Media industry merchant bank Veronis Suhler (2000) says that communications was the fastest-growing component of the US economy in the five years to 1999 and will continue to be so throughout 2004. Within the service sector the screen industries are unusual, in that they serve both audiences and other industries, from films and television drama to training videos and commercials. The split is roughly equal. Jobs in this sector increased by 74 per cent over the 1990s (Goodman and Steadman, 2002: 13–14).

US Services Exports						
Exports:	1997	1998	1999	2000*	99–00*	90–00*
	Billions of Dollars				*Percent Change*	
Total (BOP basis)	**257.2**	**262.7**	**271.9**	**295.0**	**8.5**	**99.5**
Travel	73.4	71.3	74.9	84.8	13.3	97.2
Passenger Fares	20.9	20.1	19.8	21.3	7.9	39.5
Other Transportation	27.0	25.6	27.0	29.9	10.7	36.0
Royalties and Licensing Fees	33.6	36.2	36.5	37.7	3.3	120.3
Other Private Services	84.5	90.9	96.5	106.0	9.8	163.0
Transfers under US Military Sales Contracts	16.8	17.6	16.3	14.5	−11.5	49.1
US Government Miscellaneous Services	1.0	0.9.	0.9	0.8	−4.2	21.1

*Annualised based on January–November 2000 data.
SOURCE: Office of the US Trade Representative, 2001a

The US has become a very significant exporter of services such as popular culture to other prongs of the triad. In 1999, private-sector sales of services to Western Europe amounted to US$85 billion, and US$30 billion to Japan (Office of the US Trade Representative, 2001c). Of course, other players in the triad are also important. In 1990, Japan, Germany, Britain and the US accounted for 55.4 per cent of the world's exports of culture, while 47 per cent of total imports were made to France, Germany, Britain and the US. By 1998, China had become the third largest exporter. The US, Japan, China, Britain and Germany were now responsible for 53 per cent of cultural exports and 57 per cent of such imports (UNESCO, 2002). In December 2002, the US ran a trade deficit in goods of US$48.4 billion, relying on services for a surplus of US$4.1 billion. Annual service exports amounted to US$290.4 billion that year (Department of Commerce, 2003: 1, 3). Again, the screen industries provide both a key surplus through net exports that is also significant as a proportion of overall output (Goodman and Steadman, 2002: 14).

In the next section, we examine the micro-screen corollaries to these macro-historical developments. In general, however, one can say that public investment has been directed towards sectors supposedly endowed with comparative advantage. In the domain of the screen, this means that 'if your cultural workers aren't already making movies profitably, don't start or you will be punished'.

Hollywood History

[T]ransformations of the American film industry ... can all be traced to ... the way in which manufacturers and merchants have transposed their own conflict over economic space onto the regulation of moral space.

(Aida Hozic, 2001: 33)

Why do we allow our people to become inebriated with such bald-faced Americanism? This twinkle-eyed, white-toothed wonder, Deanna Durbin, stirs up crazed emotions among the public. And what are they getting out of it? It only reinforces their long-time worship of the *keto* [racial epithet for white people]. This, plus the eight hundred thousand yen in precious national reserves handed over to the Americans, makes the film a double menace to the nation.

(Representative Noguchi Kazumi, 1937, quoted in High, 2003: 78)

In keeping with the conflictual story that flows from a historical perspective on capitalism, the balance of textual trade was not always as it is today: France sold a dozen films a week to the US early in the twentieth century, and in 1914, most movies and much moviemaking technology in North America were imported, while Italy and France dominated exhibition in Latin America. On the other hand, the US film production company Vitagraph was producing two negatives for every reel by 1907, one for European and one for domestic use, and China was receiving US films from 1897. By 1909, Yanqui companies could rely on the local market to recoup costs, and were tailoring export prices to meet other markets. Director Alice Guy-Blanché moved from France to the US in 1910 and made many films with her own production company, for example. But that international control over the business, and associated openness to women directors and producers, was a victim of two processes (Cherneff, 1991: 435). The drive towards what Richard Abel (1999) calls the 'Americanisation' of the domestic market was aided by the legal codification of film as intellectual property and mysterious confiscations of French equipment by US customs (Grantham, 2000: 44). Since that time, the US film industry has prospered internationally because it has understood that intellectual-property protection is part of the infrastructure that binds otherwise competing companies together, and because it has had a willing servant in the state. The creation of the studio system also ended women's access to decision-making authority for decades (Cherneff, 1991: 435–36).

Legal battles in the US during the early 1900s over motion-picture camera patents, held in monopoly by The Edison Company alongside Biograph's patented device, threatened distribution of overseas film in the US unless foreign companies ceded to the newly formed Motion Picture Patents Company (MPPC). Until it succumbed to US anti-trust legislation and action by the Federal Trade Commission in the early teens, the MPPC cartel licensed filmmaking technology to producers, and projectors to exhibitors. A few foreign producers were allowed to license from the company. On the surface, it seemed that the cartel was designed to deter upstarts in film technology (it signed an exclusive agreement with Eastman Kodak to sell raw stock to bona fide licensees only). In reality, the MPPC sought to stem the tide of foreign film imports that dominated American screens in the first decade of the 1900s (Bowser, 1990: 21–36; Ye, 2003: 10–11; Jones, 2001). Its success has continued unabated: by the 1990s, the US supplied over 80 per cent of the world's film stock (Olson, 1999: 60).

This marks a convergence of warring fractions of the film bourgeoisie, between those interested in technology and those concerned with content, a distinction going back to their respective origins in manufacturing and retail (Jones, 2001). The mythology of rag-trading immigrants turned moguls hides the reality of a rapidly managerialising, professionalising class in the 1920s and 1930s that ran much of Hollywood not from the remnants of the lower East Side, but from alumni associations of the Ivy Leagues who engaged in intra-class conflict over the primacy of mercantile and manufacturing capital. This was California's blend of a 'feudal manor' and a 'modern urban environment' (Cooper, 2003: 23; Hozic, 2001: 54, 56; Kennedy, 1927).

Between 1915 and 1916, US exports rose from 36 million feet of film to 159 million feet, while imports fell from 16 million feet before the First World War to 7 million by the mid-1920s. As the feature film took off during those years, Hollywood began to sell to Asia and Latin America, almost wiping out Brazilian production, for example, by purchasing local distributors. The State Department set up a motion-picture section in 1916. In 1918, Congress passed the Webb-Pomerene Act, which permitted overseas trusts that were illegal domestically. This enabled an international distribution cartel for the next forty years. Export prices and terms of trade were centrally determined by the Motion Picture Export Association of America (MPEAA), which also worked to ensure blind bidding and block booking. From 1919, overseas receipts were factored into Hollywood budgets. In the 1920s, Hollywood's leading export sites were Britain, Australia, Argentina and Brazil, and the Federal Government institutionalised commercial attachés in its embassies. In return, supposedly non-interventionist Republican administrations of the day routinely drew on US finance, film and industry to achieve political objectives (Balio, 1993: 32–33; Grantham, 2000: 53; de Grazia, 1989: 57; Bjork, 2000; O'Regan, 1992: 313; Kent, 1927: 206, 208; Cochrane, 1927: 255).

Silent film titles from Hollywood were available in thirty-six languages in the 1920s, with export departments' translators creating electrotypes of publicity material to go across the world, where they were further customised. US English was itself localised to conform with other *anglo-parlante* dialects. By the 1930s, foreign sales provided between one-third and one-half of film industry returns. The *Harvard Business Review* estimated that Hollywood was responsible for up to 80 per cent of all films screened around the world and took in US$200 million of total global receipts of US$275 million. Many of the first sound films made in Spanish were shot in Hollywood and exported to Spain and Latin America. From 1927 to 1939, Hollywood sold 4,000 movies to China. In 1933, the local industry produced 89 features and 421 were imported, of which 309 were from Hollywood. In 1936, 328 of the 367 films imported there came from the US. Hollywood films occupied 78.9 per cent of screening space in Mexico City across the 1930s. When sound was standardised, non-English speakers were courted by the musical. Studios set up shop in key countries and created foreign-language versions of domestic successes, subtitles or voiceover narration (Handel, 1950: 220) similar to the service available to unsighted listeners of films on digital cable today. The industry also achieved horizontal integration by linking the sale of radios and records to the musical film – US music was often a precursor to US film. In 1939, the Department of Commerce estimated that Hollywood supplied 65 per cent of films exhibited worldwide (Harley, 1940: 21). By the early 1950s, two-thirds of global cinema revenue went to the US, with 135 million foreigners watching (Litman, 1998: 91; Ulff-Moller, 1999: 182–83; Strauss, 1930: 307; Ye, 2003: 14; Hu, 2003: 20; Hoskins *et al.*, 1997: 46–47; King, 1990: 10, 22; Trumpbour, 2002: 115; Triana-Toribio, 2003: 28–29; Shohat and Stam, 1994: 28; Armes, 1987: 48; Tunstall, 1981: 175, 91; Berg, 1992: 13; Greenwald, 1952: 39).

The two world wars complicate any notion of narrative transparency, managerial sophistication or global consumer preferences explaining American dominance. The 1914–18 and 1939–45 conflicts left national production across Europe either shut down or slowed, as conscription led to death, deskilling and the end of any competition with Hollywood for the US audience (Ramsaye, 1947: 7).

Of course, some of the success resulted from textual appeal, but even that was mediated via state relations. In 1920s and 1930s Italy, for example, Hollywood projected a fabulous modernity that even fascinated Mussolini. Beauty, youth and wealth merged under the sign of fun. Local marketing played up the extraordinary pleasures of this world, and its difference from traditional Italian life. At the same time, the local industry was held back by the growth of US-owned distribution, new government taxes and a reliance on importing Hollywood technology (Hay, 1987: 66–71). Part of this was due to Hollywood's cultivation of fascists, as then-MPAA head Will Hays revealed:

> A producer was going to make 'The Eternal City.' I called the Italian
> Ambassador, Signor Caetani, on the telephone, and told him we wanted to
> make this correctly from Italy's standpoint. He came to New York the next day.

Signor Caetani is a most distinguished man, the richest man in Italy, a graduate of Columbia University who examined mines in this country, then went back and marched beside Mussolini in a black shirt in Rome. He collaborated with us ... We made a picture thoroughly sympathetic and pleasing to Italy.

(Hays, 1927: 53)

The nature of such 'collaborations' with 'distinguished' fascists changed in 1945. The compulsory dismantling of state filmmaking institutions among the Axis powers complemented Hollywood profit plans with anti-fascist and anti-communist political agendas that ensured the defeated regimes would hold off on protectionist film legislation and take up lost years of Hollywood inventory (Greenwald, 1952). At the same time, a declining British economy drove Hollywood to expand its other sources of foreign revenue (Schatz, 1997: 300, 302; Lev, 2003: 147). A plenitude of unseen US inventory waited to be unleashed (Italy was sent over 2,000 features in the four years from 1945), while the developing US shipping industry improved transport infrastructure.

With profits endangered at home by anti-monopoly laws and the arrival of television, the world market grew in importance for Hollywood during the 1950s. Vertical integration through ownership of production, distribution and exhibition may have been outlawed domestically, but not on a global scale. Peter Lev (2003: 148) offers an interesting study of *Strangers on a Train* (Alfred Hitchcock, 1951). It cost US$1,568,246, and after three years had earned US$1,691,213 in the US and US$86,541 in Canada. Overseas, the key source of revenue was Britain (US$365,000) but it brought in over US$20,000 from ten other countries across four continents. These receipts made the film safely profitable. Fifty years later, the situation was more varied and complex still for anyone seeking to track the life of the commodity sign. Estimates of how *Pearl Harbor* (Michael Way, 2001) would eventually make a profit illustrate the complex dependence of domestic and international sales across formats. Its US$475 million budget was to be returned over eight to ten years like this:

- 22 per cent from US theatres
- 22 per cent from international theatres
- 22 per cent from US video and DVD sales
- 14 per cent from international video and DVD sales
- 12 per cent from domestic television
- 8 per cent from international television.

('The Monster', 2001)

Britain and Latin America were Hollywood's most lucrative importers until the 1970s. In both cases, economic downturn and the failure to invest in new theatres diminished attendance at that time. As a result, Hollywood turned to

new forms of internal commercial exploitation (as in the 1970s 'discovery' of
the African-American audience and the emergence of blaxploitation) until
recapitalisation and the studios' acquisition by conglomerates. The new
owners could spread risk across different business activities, from mineral
extraction to real estate. They were happy to turn studios into shopping malls.
Externally, US government and industry set up new cartels to market films
everywhere, with special agencies created for anglophone and francophone
Africa. Hollywood's American Motion Picture Export Company of Africa, for
example, dominated cinema sales to former British colonies from the 1960s,
when the continent screened about 350 films a year, perhaps half of them
from the US (Armes, 1987: 49; Mattelart, 1979: 194–208; Diawara, 1992: 106;
Balio, 1998a: 61; Hozic, 2001: 104; Ukadike, 1994: 63; Sama, 1996: 150).

The link between military might and Hollywood was clarified in 1947 when
an MPAA maven referred to the peoples freed in Europe by the Allies as showing 'pathetic zeal' in their attendance at US movies, a pathos matched only by
their welcome of 'our advancing armies' (Mayer, 1947: 31). With such tactless-
ness afoot, a reaction was inevitable. No wonder that *A Foreign Affair* (Billy
Wilder, 1948) depicted a member of the US Congress referring to post-war
relief efforts in Europe in the following way: 'If you give them food, it's democracy. If you leave the labels on, it's imperialism.' The complaints were soon to
grow louder, and they were directly linked to the idea that the screen brought
political and economic as well as textual messages.

Cultural Imperialism

America is not just interested in exporting its films. It is interested in
exporting its way of life.

(Gilles Jacob, Cannes Film Festival director, quoted in 'Culture Wars', 1998)

[W]hen Saddam Hussein chose Frank Sinatra's globally recognized 'My Way'
as the theme song for his 54th birthday party, it wasn't as a result of American
Imperialist pressure.

(Michael Eisner, quoted in Costa-Gavras *et al.*, 1995: 10)

In 1820, the noted essayist Sydney Smith asked: 'In the four quarters of the
globe, who reads an American book? or goes to an American play? or looks at
an American picture or statue?' (1844: 141). Not surprisingly, the US soon
became an early-modern exponent of anti-cultural imperialist, pro-nation-
building sentiment. Herman Melville opposed the US literary establishment's
devotion to all things English, questioning the compatibility of this Eurocen-
trically cringing import culture with efforts to 'carry Republicanism into
literature' (Newcomb, 1996: 94). At the same time, a discourse in opposition to
the Western cultural domination that so troubled nativist Yanquis was also
developing among Islamic leaders (Mowlana, 2000: 107–08). But a century

later, *Time* magazine referred to Hollywood as 'the new maharajahs' in 1959 India ('Movies Abroad', 1959). And today, Rupert Murdoch confidently predicts that three companies will soon dominate the world's media – Comcast, Fox and Time Warner (Schulze and Elliott, 2004). What happened to make the US culturally hegemonic?

In the mid-nineteenth century, when the first international copyright treaties were being negotiated on the European continent, the US refused to protect foreign literary works – a belligerent stance that it would denounce today as piratical. As a net importer of books seeking to develop a national literary patrimony of its own – an 'American Literature' – Washington was not interested in extending protection to foreign works that might hinder its own printers, publishers or authors from making a profit. This mix of indebtedness and *ressentiment* characterises the relation of import to export cultures, where taste and domination versus market choice and cultural control are graceless antinomies. It also characterises the dependent relationship of development, a lesson that the US learned quickly and used to do unto others as had been done to it. Gramscian to the core, US business and government recognised that commercial empires must make modernity both mundane and extraordinary via control and consent, as per a history that stretched from Dutch art to British fiction (Hozic, 2001: 32). The memo to self read: practise ISI, preach EOI.

As early as 1912, Hollywood exporters were also aware that where their films travelled, demand was created for other US goods. Commerce Secretary Herbert Hoover praised the industry in the 1920s for putting forward 'intellectual ideas and national ideals', for its trade earnings 'and as a powerful influence on behalf of American goods' (Hays, 1931: 15; Hoover quoted in Bjork, 2000, and Grantham, 2000: 53). Joseph P. Kennedy, one of the eastern-establishment moguls, acknowledged that 'films were serving as silent salesmen for other products of American industry' (1927: 6). Hays, who worked closely with Hoover to ensure that the studios operated as an overseas distribution cartel to deal with recalcitrant foreign powers, asserted that 'Hollywood has become a tremendous influence upon the peoples of all the world'. In 1927, he informed the bright young things of Harvard's Business School that 'I could spend all of my allotted time telling you how the motion picture is selling goods abroad for every American manufacturer ... "Trade follows the film"' (37–38); and he went on to advise the J. Walter Thompson advertising agency in 1930 that 'every foot of American film sells $1.00 worth of manufactured products some place in the world'. Hays twinned this with the claim that Hollywood was crucial to '[w]orld peace' (quoted in Trumpbour, 2002: 17).

By the late 1930s, stories of heroic merchandising links between cinema and sales were legion, such as the ones that told of a new Javanese market for US sewing machines that followed screenings of factory conditions, Hollywood-style; and a Brazilian taste for bungalows that mimicked Angelino high life. Producer Walter Wanger even expressed delight at a strike by Paris stenographers in protest over the gap between their conditions and those of office workers in US films, the impact of what he called '120,000 American Ambassadors' (a reference to the number of prints exported each year). By the 1950s, the industry confidently claimed that 'business follows the film as well as the flag' (Greenwald, 1952: 39). The association between cinema and democratisation was not without the odd *non-alignment*, however. When Indonesia's President Sukarno visited Hollywood in 1956, he embraced moviemakers as fellow revolutionaries, thanking them for their inspiration to anti-colonial struggles. Sukarno declared that Hollywood-style conspicuous consumption of goods such as cars and refrigerators helped to 'build up the sense of deprivation on man's birthright' that fuelled the formation of consumer markets in newly decolonised nations (quoted in Pryor, 1956).

US mass production and marketing transformed values. On the one hand, they required intense productive discipline; on the other, they promised transcendence through intense commodity consumption. Such links are encapsulated in two famous scenes involving Clark Gable. In the 1930s, a deputation of Argentinian businessmen protested to the US embassy about *It Happened One Night* (Frank Capra, 1934) because Gable was seen removing his shirt, revealing no singlet below. This supposedly created an undershirt inventory surplus in their warehouses – overnight! A quarter of a century later, *It Started in Naples* (Melville Shavelson, 1960) found Gable showing a local boy how to eat a hamburger, which produced public controversy about compromising Mediterranean cuisine. Thirty years on, the task of tying commodities to films was completed by another kind of envoy, as Disney coordinated the release of *Pocahontas* (Mike Gabriel and Erik Goldberg, 1995) with McDonald's new 'McChief Burger' – early fruit from their ten-year agreement for cross-promotion in 109 countries (Grantham, 1998: 62; Wanger, 1939: 50, 45; King, 1990: 32; Sardar, 1998: 26; McChesney, 1999: 108).

The politics of Hollywood images have drawn critical reactions from many sources. Although anxieties about screen stereotypes are often identified with a contemporary liberal sensibility, they have in fact been a long-standing concern, both for domestic conservatives frightened by sex, and other nations objecting to stereotypes.

In 1921, the Great Wall Motion Picture Studio was founded in New York by Chinese expatriates angered by US industry and government neglect of their complaints about representations of Chinese characters. The studio produced films for export home as well the US market (Hu, 2003: 51–52). In 1922, Mexico placed embargoes on film imports because of the repugnant 'greaser' genre. It was supported by other Latin American countries, Canada, France and Spain (De Los Reyes, 1996: 29–31). Powdermaker's ethnography records one production decision to change the subjectivity of some streetfighters from Mexican to gypsy/Romany/traveller/*gitano* because the latter 'had no country or organization to register a protest' (1950: 64). Similar problems recurred throughout the 1930s. French soldiers rioted against their portrayal in *Hot for Paris* (Raoul Walsh, 1929) (Trumpbour, 2002: 28, 31, 40). And official complaints from Germany, England, France, Italy and Spain over cultural slurs were made during the same decade (Vasey, 1992: 618, 620–21, 624, 627, 631).

This period saw countries across Western Europe enacting quota provisions to protect national film culture, based on a German model (Strauss, 1930: 310–11), fearing Hollywood's 'serious menace to their trade' (Kennedy, 1927: 5). The change in imported films between 1925 and 1928 is illustrative of the shift occasioned by such policies.

PERCENTAGE OF US FILMS OF TEXTS SCREENED		
SITE	1925	1928
BRITAIN	95	81
GERMANY	60	47
AUSTRALASIA	95	86
SCANDINAVIA	85	65
ARGENTINA	90	90
CANADA	95	95
FRANCE	70	63
JAPAN	30	22
BRAZIL	95	85
AUSTRIA, HUNGARY, CZECHOSLOVAKIA	70	59
ITALY	65	70
SPAIN AND PORTUGAL	90	85
MEXICO	90	95

SOURCE: Adapted from Strauss, 1930: 309, 311

Further reductions occurred with the Great Depression and the rise of fascism, so Hollywood focused on exporting to Latin America and Australia (Greenwald, 1952: 44).

The industry's 1927 list of 'Don'ts and Be Carefuls' instructed producers to 'avoid picturizing in an unfavorable light another country's religion, history, institutions, prominent people, and citizenry'. Foreigners were hired to vet productions and the government also offered advice. Hays noted that 'We cooperate with the governments of all nations, that our pictures may correctly portray the habits and customs of every country to the citizens of every other country and thus bring better understanding between the peoples of the world' (1927: 50).

Hays' successor, Eric Johnston, euphemised the need for a careful cultural politics as a means to 'break down barriers of misunderstanding among nations as readily as it has broken down lesser barriers within this country' (1947: 98). The assiduous political correctness that had courted Italian blackshirts was ongoing. The British insisted on the unrepresentability of Christ, so he was absent from *The Last Days of Pompeii* (Ernest B. Schoedsack, 1935), and United Artists renamed *His Majesty, the American* (Joseph Henabery, 1919) as *Born to the Blood* for its British release (Walsh, 1997: 8), while Samuel Goldwyn complained that 'the only villain we dare show today [1936] is a white American' (quoted in Harley, 1940: 23), and Siegfried Kracauer (1949: 56) argued that the industry was perennially afraid of placing overseas revenues in jeopardy through misrepresentation. Only Hollywood's audience surveillance was able to persuade the British government that Yanquis liked the image of the British in *Mrs Miniver* (William Wyler, 1942) (Bakker, 2003: 114).

On the other hand, in the 1930s, the Japanese were threatened with narrative stereotyping as criminals if they denied access to Hollywood films. Censors there had for some time been rejecting anti-war films, and a new Film Law became a key article of fascist ideology. It was administered to give preference to Italian and German films from what became the Axis powers (High, 2003: 77). Franco's Spain enthusiastically embraced the pro-capitalist side to Hollywood while abjuring its pro-worker, anti-fascist and libertarian films. *The Grapes of Wrath* (John Ford, 1940), *The Great Dictator* (Charles Chaplin, 1940), *How Green Was My Valley* (John Ford, 1941), *To Be or Not to Be* (Ernst Lubitsch, 1942) and *Some Like it Hot* (Billy Wilder, 1959) were too dangerous to be seen there until after Franco's death in 1975, while Orson Welles' International Brigade past was excised from *The Lady from Shanghai* (1948) (Wanger, 1950: 445; Bosch and del Rincón, 2000: 108–09, 111). The MPAA also advised against any negative representation of the fascist Spanish state even after the war (Powdermaker, 1950: 65).

In 1926, the British Cabinet Office issued a paper to participants at the Imperial Economic Conference warning that 'so very large a proportion of the films shown throughout the Empire ... present modes of life and forms of conduct which are not typically British'. By the following year, the *Daily Express* newspaper worried that the exposure of British youth to US entertainment was making them 'temporary American citizens' (quoted in de Grazia, 1989: 53). Pius XI's 1936 *Encyclical Letter of Pope Pius XI on the Motion Picture Vigilanti Cura* to US bishops offered the following Olympian remark:

> We were deeply anguished to note with each passing day the lamentable
> progress – *magni passus extra viam* – of the motion picture art and industry in
> the portrayal of sin and vice. ....

> There is no need to point out the fact that millions of people go to the motion pictures every day; that motion picture theatres are being opened in ever increasing number in civilized and semi-civilized countries; that the motion picture has become the most popular form of diversion which is offered for the leisure hours not only of the rich but of all classes of society.

This critique is a fascinating amalgam of the DEM and the GEM. It became a core element in the dialectic between sexualisation and conservatism that has characterised US cultural production – not merely part of local Puritanism, but a contradictory calculus that is crucially connected to selling sex on world markets.

Throughout the 1920s and early 1930s, British authorities in India criticised Hollywood films as potential sources of nationalist unruliness, forms of contagion that might infect the precarious management of the native body politic. Though these critiques were couched in the sort of primordialism that characterised early colonial contact – that the nefarious 'perversity' of Hollywood film upset the traditional sexual and social foundations of 'native culture' – the forked and ambivalent nature of colonial administration recognised the possible problems posed by films that undermined whiteness (via caricature or hyperbole) through melodrama and comedy. Alert to possible cracks in the representational armature of white mastery, the British House of Commons held long debates on possible correctives, such as the production of 'quality' British features. But with Britain entrenched as Hollywood's largest export market in the pre-war years, and unwilling to support production in India, British film industrialists felt stymied in seeking large-scale production of films as cultural buttresses for the maintenance of colonial power (see Jaikumar, 1999).

In 1926, the *Times of India* editorialised that 'no language is too strong to condemn the films with which America is plaguing India' (quoted in Segrave, 1997: 56–57). Making matters worse, the publication of the Indian Cinematograph Committee findings in 1928, commissioned partially to combat the tide of Hollywood imports with new censorship restrictions, refused to give British films preferential treatment and advocated the support of Indian film production through protectionist measures such as the abolition of duty fees on raw stock and financial incentives to filmmakers and producers. Not surprisingly, colonial authorities ignored the findings of the Indian committee majority. And though the 1929 crash muted Hollywood enthusiasm for Indian market penetration, the Production Code Administration (PCA) welcomed the relative exoneration of US film and used the report to criticise British film protectionism. The British Board of Film Classification of the 1930s insisted that Hollywood films released in imperial possessions follow the rule that 'white men may not be shown in a state of degradation amidst native surroundings' (quoted in Barker, 1993: 11). At the same time, the British government in India banned foreign films 'likely to encourage revolutionary tendencies': for example, *Viva Villa* (Jack Conway, Howard Hawks and William A. Wellman, 1934), *Declaration of Independence* (Crane Wilbur, 1938) and *Give Me Liberty* (B. Reeves Eason, 1936) (Bagai, *c*.1938; Abbas, 1940: 192).

As independence became more and more of a political reality, import tensions were evident. The Vice-President of the Indian Chamber of Commerce, citing the physical resemblance of the thugee high priest in *Gunga Din* (George Stevens, 1939) to Gandhi, called for the Indian National Congress to boycott US films alongside a 'national protest under the signature of our Indian leaders in public life and business, national organizations and Chambers of Commerce' and a message advising Will Hays of these 'malicious and slanderous attacks' ('Boycott', *c*.1938). Also in the late 1930s, in addition to *Gunga Din, Clive of India* (Richard Boleslawski, 1935), *The Lives of a Bengal Lancer* (Henry Hathaway, 1935), the German *Der Tiger von Eschnapur* (Richard Eichberg, 1938) and Zoltan Korda's *The Drum* (1938) were cited as anti-Indian propaganda, with the editor of the *Bombay Chronicle* calling Korda's film a 'glorification of British Imperialism'; such protests resulted in the editor of *Filmindia* calling on the prime ministers of provincial governments to 'uphold national prestige' through boycotts ('Ban Those', n. d.). In addition, Hollywood continued to be influenced in its depictions of Indian history by Katherine Mayo's 1927 excoriation of Hindu superstition and Indian sexual perversity, *Mother India* (Rotter, 2000: 3).

A US Department of Commerce report that summed up motion-picture business in a number of countries noted that of the sixteen US films reviewed by Bombay censors in August 1947, three were banned and four heavily edited. The government of Madras authorised its censors to delete drinking scenes to facilitate the introduction of prohibition into the province; films like *The Best Years of Our Lives* (William Wyler, 1946) underwent severe censorship; drinking scenes, for example, must seek to 'ridicule drink, to hold it in abhorrence, to show it as poisonous, to paint the drinking habit as ungentlemanly, unhealthy or anti-social or condemn it in various ways' ('Censors', 1947; 'India Bans', 1948). At a screening of *Call Me Madam* (Walter Lang, 1953), members of the New Delhi US colony were heard remarking in response to a character's speech that 'you cannot buy everything with gold': 'Just like our own Nehru's attitude towards America' (Katz, 1954). As an exemplar of cascading Cold War ire, in late 1954, the *Hollywood Reporter* ran a front-page headline 'India Censors on Rampage', complaining about the cutting of 'Diamonds Are a Girl's Best Friend' from *Gentlemen Prefer Blondes* (Howard Hawks, 1953) and the drinking song from *Student Prince* (Richard Thorpe and Curtis Bernhardt, 1954) because it contained the word 'drink' and depicted Heidelberg students drinking beer, along with the outright banning of *Dial M for Murder* (Alfred Hitchcock, 1954), *The Moon is Blue* (Otto Preminger, 1953), *Fort Algiers* (Lesley Selander, 1953), *Cease Fire!* (Owen Crump, 1953), *Arrowhead* (Charles Marquis Warren, 1953), *The Wild One* (László Benedek, 1953), *Phantom of the*

Rue Morgue (Roy Del Ruth, 1954), *Man in the Attic* (Hugo Fregonese, 1953), *I, the Jury* (Harry Essex, 1953), *Flame and the Flesh* (Richard Brooks, 1954) and *French Line* (Lloyd Bacon, 1954) ('India Censors', 1954).

A new edict issued by the Indian government in 1954 mandated that only 'neutral' films would be permitted for exhibition, having just banned Paramount's feature about the Korean War, *Cease Fire!*, on the grounds that 'to allow this film to be shown would bring pressure for permission to exhibit films containing communist propaganda'. In addition, and somewhat cryptically, the Information Ministry claimed that since the Korean War was over, the film had 'no meaning' ('India to Permit', *c.*1954). Non-alignment also held sway over censorship decisions – according to Bombay censors, Soviet films were notoriously propagandistic – and if a film tended 'to mould the susceptibilities of foreign nations or to disparage the heads of foreign states', it was subject to rejection. The Central Board of Censors also decided that 'films on African subjects which fail to depict people of Africa in proper perspective, will not in the future be licensed for exhibition in India'. *The African Queen* (John Huston, 1951), *West of Zanzibar* (Harry Watt, 1954), *The Snows of Kilimanjaro* (Henry King, 1952), *Below the Sahara* (Armand Denis, 1953), *Mogambo* (John Ford, 1953), *Tanganyika* (André De Toth, 1954), *African Adventure* (Robert Ruark, 1954) and *Untamed* (Henry King, 1955) were all prohibited ('India Ban', 1955; Rosenthal, 1955; 'India's Ban', 1956).The DEM met the GEM.

'Progressive' films continued to be relatively popular in India. One commentator noted that

[the] most successful film ever shown in Bombay is [*The*] *Life of Emile Zola* [William Dieterle, 1937] which ran for six weeks continuously. Thousands who saw it did not know a word of English. They had read the synopsis in some vernacular paper and vaguely knew that Zola was a fighter for freedom and justice. The Indian cinema audiences are demonstrative and every time Zola or Dreyfus appeared in later sequences they cheer. Somehow they saw in them the symbols of humanity's fight against oppression and tyranny. Some other foreign films which have been notable successes here are *Modern Times* [Charles Chaplin, 1936], [*The Story of*] *Louis Pasteur* [William Dieterle, 1935], the French version of *Les Misérables* [Raymond Bernard, 1934], *Blockade* [William Dieterle, 1938] and *Dead End* [William Wyler, 1937]. Recently the Progressive Film Society has shown documentary films about China and Spain to appreciative audiences all over India, and there is now a demand for more such progressive pictures.

(Abbas, 1940: 193–4)

With the advent of sound technology and tightening censorship by fascist European governments threatening to shrink US film exports, Hollywood became more sensitive to the needs of its largest export market and placated

both its critics in the US Motion Picture Research Council and British industrial representatives by encouraging the production of 'Empire' films that
celebrated colonial conquest. This genre was capped by the release of *Gunga
Din*, whose allusions to Gandhian nationalism had a clear pedagogic imperative. Belgium's 1945 decision to ban Hollywood film in Congo came from
concerns that it could incite anti-colonial agitation. The US itself wisely elec-
ted not to screen *Gone with the Wind* (Victor Fleming, 1939) in Germany after
the war, in the light of its horrendous racism (Trumpbour, 2002: 101) and held
back *Tobacco Road* (John Ford, 1941) and *The Grapes of Wrath* from foreign
release lest they be 'used as propaganda against the United States' in their focus
on 'the American dispossessed', which would 'offer considerable embarrassment to our State Department' (Rosten, 1947: 119). Meanwhile, the tendency
of US culture to assume full responsibility for victory in 'just' wars and ignore
complicity in other wars led to derision and anger. After both world wars, complaints came from Australia, France, Britain and Canada when Hollywood
fictionalised those epic conflicts as exclusively US triumphs (Trumpbour, 2002:
172, 184–85). After all, what are 25 million dead Soviets next to the glamour of
the 'Greatest Generation'?

The history of intersections with foreign governments is a complex one in
Asia and the Arab world as well. In China, the high point of Maoism and the
Cultural Revolution saw Hollywood excluded after an early period of exchange
that broke down with the Korean War, and was not resumed until the late 1970s
(Ye, 2003: 15–16). The liberalisation of film imports in the 1970s was curtailed
when Hollywood turned to anti-China themes (Ye, 2003: 18) in *Kundun* (Martin Scorsese, 1997 – shot in Morocco, Canada and Idaho), *Red Corner* (Jon
Avnet, 1997 – partially shot undercover in Beijing and including footage of exe-
cutions that was supposedly smuggled out) and *Seven Years in Tibet*
(Jean-Jacques Annaud, 1997 – shot in Argentina, Austria, Chile, Britain, Canada
and, secretly, Tibet). Star of the latter film, Brad Pitt, was banned from entry to
the PRC. Complaints came not just from the state; these texts were regarded by
critics as 'laughable gimmicks . . . elaborately cooked up for the sake of "demo-
nizing" China' ('A Renewed', 2003: 50). And for decades, Thailand has banned
Hollywood's clumsy representations of its monarchy ('Thailand', 1999). Even
at the height of the Iranian Revolution, many Hollywood films were still
released, despite the opposition they incurred (Naficy, 2002). Disney's lucrative
1990s deals in the Middle East were jeopardised by a bizarre exhibit at its Epcot
theme park in Orlando that naturalised Jerusalem as Israel's capital (Sakr, 2001:
94), while the company carefully recalibrated its Latin American stereotypes in
order to assist the sale of TV networks there (Mike Wayne, 2003: 74).

In short, the power of Hollywood has long triggered responses from both left
and right. European progressives have admired the US for its secular modernity, egalitarianism and change, even as they have deplored its racism,
monopoly capitalism and class exploitation and their corollaries on camera,

while the right has been disturbed by the *mestizo* qualities of African-American and Jewish contributions to the popular (Wagnleitner and May, 2000: 5–6). Since the Second World War, widespread reaction against the discourses of modernisation has foregrounded the US capitalist media as crucial components in the formation of commodities, mass culture and economic and political organisation in the Third World. Examples include the export of Hollywood screen products and infrastructure as well as US dominance of international communications technology (Nigeria, for example, was first tied to US television through the supply of equipment, which was then articulated to the sale of programmes, genres and formats [Owens-Ibie, 2000: 133]). Critics claim that the rhetoric of development through commercialism was responsible for decelerating economic growth and disenfranchising local culture, with emergent ruling classes in dependent nations exercising local power only at the cost of relying on foreign capital and ideology.

As noted earlier, the US had reached international political-economic domination by the end of the Second World War. The ensuing export of modernisation ignored the way in which the very life of the modern had been defined in colonial and international experience, both by differentiating the metropole from the periphery and importing ideas, fashions and people back to the core. In the 1950s, modernity was designated as a complex imbrication of industrial, economic, social, cultural and political development, towards which all peoples of the world were progressively headed. The founders and husbands of this discourse were First World political scientists and economists, mostly associated with US universities, research institutes, foundations and corporations, or with international organisations. Among the premises of this modernity were nationalist fellow feeling and individual/state sovereignty as habits of thought. The daily prayer called for a 'modern individual' who would not fall into the temptation of Marxism-Leninism. Development necessitated displacement of 'the particularistic norms' of tradition by 'more universalistic' blends of the modern to help create 'achievement-oriented' society (Pye, 1965: 19). The successful importation of media technologies and forms of communication from the US were touted as critical components in this replicant figure, as elite sectors of society were trained to be exemplars and leaders for a wider populace said to be mired in backward, folkloric forms of thought and lacking the trust in national organisations required for modernisation.

The theory of cultural imperialism comprehensively challenged this implausibly solipsistic model. Apart from the latter's unreconstructed narcissism, its precepts disavowed the existing international division of labour and the success of imperial and commercial powers in annexing states and/or their labour forces. Although diffusionist theorists and others came up with neomodernisation models that were more locally sensitive to conflicts over wealth, influence and status, they did not measure up to critical theories of dependent development, underdevelopment, unequal exchange, world-systems history, centre–

periphery relations and cultural and media imperialism. These radical critiques of capitalist modernisation shared the view that the transfer of technology, politics and economics had become unattainable, because the emergence of MNCs united business and government to regulate cheap labour markets, produce new consumers and guarantee pliant regimes (Reeves, 1993: 24–25, 30).

The DEM and GEM were somewhat allied in this first era, as questions of sexual conduct were closely tied to fears of a loss of tradition. Consider the Indian writer Baburo Patel's 1951 article, 'Rape of Our Heritage' (Patel, 1951). It is worth quoting at some length:

> Hollywood undertook this cultural insemination of 400 million people with their most powerful weapon in the world – the movies. Pictures after pictures were sent to India during the two wars – pictures that taught us to dance rhumbas and sambas; pictures that taught us to coo and woo; pictures that taught us to kill and steal; pictures that taught us to utter 'Hi' and 'Gee'; pictures that taught us deviltry and divorce and pictures that took us to jinks and drinks ...
>
> Hollywood stripped our women of the beautiful cholis and saris and wrapped them in shirts and slacks. Hollywood dropped our women into swimming pools with more skin than cloth on them. Hollywood turned our seashores into bedrooms of illicit romance. Hollywood tore shirts from our men's backs and covered them with multi-colored blouses. Hollywood robbed our men of their character and gave them guns to rob others. Hollywood ruined our homes and built clubs and dance halls on their ruins. Hollywood debauched the sanctity of our married life and glorified the illicit thrills of free love. Hollywood destroyed the philosophic fibre of the East and turned us into a frenzied mob of neurotics.
>
> Hollywood has vitiated our food, water, air, arts, music, culture, costumes, philosophy, life and human relations. Whatever Hollywood touched was contaminated. A thousand American sins became as many Indian fashions. That is how Hollywood taught us the 'American Way of Life' through entertainment. For a few good pictures like '[The Life of] Emile Zola', '[The Story of] Louis Pasteur', 'Juarez' [William Dieterle, 1939], etc., we have been shown thousands of rotten ones.

This kind of sustained critique assisted in the development of a cultural-imperialism thesis during the 1960s. It argued that the US, as the world's leading screen exporter, was transferring its dominant value system to others, with a corresponding diminution in the vitality and standing of local languages and traditions that had nurtured national identity.

The theory attributed US cultural hegemony to control of news agencies, advertising, market research, public opinion, screen trade, technology, propaganda, telecommunications and security (Primo, 1999: 183). US involvement

in South-East Asian wars during the 1960s led to critiques of its military interventions against struggles of national liberation and in turn targeted links
between the military-industrial complex and the media, pointing to the ways
that communications and cultural MNCs bolstered US foreign policy and military strategy and enabled the more general expansion of multinationals, which
were seen as substantial power brokers in their own right.

From this complex background, major studies deriving from cultural-
imperialism critique have looked at US control of world media, the role of
international press agencies, television programme flow, village versus corporate values, the export of US screen products and distribution systems, and
Yanqui dominance of international communications technology and infrastructure. Another major area of work has deconstructed the rhetoric of
development via commercialism, particularly in advertising, which was found
to discourage the allocation of resources to industrialisation (Reeves, 1993:
30–35; Roach, 1997: 47; Mowlana, 1993).

During the 1960s and 1970s, cultural-imperialism discourse found a voice in
the Non-Aligned Movement and the United Nations Educational, Scientific
and Cultural Organization (UNESCO) (an irony this, as the US had fought
strenuously after the Second World War for the organisation to emphasise the
impact of the mass media and information flows [Sewell, 1974: 142–43]). In
the 1970s, UNESCO was run by the Frenchman Jean Maheu and the Senegalese
Amadou Mahtar M'Bow, who set up the MacBride Commission to investigate
cultural and communication issues in North–South flows and power. At the
same time, Third World countries lobbied for a New International Information
Order or New World Information and Communication Order (NWICO), mir-
roring calls for a New International Economic Order and a revised
North–South dialogue. The MacBride Commission reported in 1980 on the
need for equal distribution of the electronic spectrum, reduced postal rates for
international texts, protection against satellites crossing borders and an emphasis on the media as tools of development and democracy rather than commerce.
There continue to be annual roundtables on the Commission's legacy, but the
insistence by the US on the free-flow paradigm was a successful riposte to
NWICO strategies and claims (Mattelart and Mattelart, 1998: 94–97; Roach,
1997: 48; Mowlana, 1993: 61).

UNESCO has ceased to be the critical site for NWICO debate. The US and
the UK withdrew from the organisation in 1985 on the grounds that it was ille-
gitimately politicised, supposedly evidenced by its denunciation of Zionist
racism and support for state intervention against private-press hegemony. The
past decade has seen UNESCrats distancing themselves from NWICO in the
hope of attracting their critics back to the fold. The UN has also downplayed
its prior commitment to a New Order (Gerbner, 1994: 112–13; Gerbner et al.,
1994: xi–xii). The US rejoined in 2003 in time to make noises about the organisation's plans for a convention on cultural diversity that might sequester

culture from neoliberal trade arrangements (Fraser, 2003) – the wrong kind of globalisation, presumably because it might be arrived at democratically! Negotiations saw the US arguing officially that texts are not culture, which it defined as the less commodifiable and governable spheres of religion and language (Ford, 2003).

Not surprisingly, calls for a NWICO have become less influential in both the political and intellectual registers since that time. The NWICO position was vulnerable from all sides for its inadequate theorisation of capitalism, the post-colonial condition, internal and international class relations, the role of the state, the mediating power of indigenous culture and its own complex *frottage* – a pluralism that insisted on the relativistic equivalence of all cultures and defied chauvinism, but rubbed up against a distinctively powerful equation of national identities with cultural forms (Schlesinger, 1991: 145).

In a telling accommodation, the UN began to sponsor large international conferences in the late 1990s, such as the World Television Forum, to promote partnerships between commercial media managers, entrepreneurs and investors from the US and Europe and their poorer counterparts from Africa, Asia and Latin America. And while UNESCO is a supporter of the 'Screens Without Frontiers' (2000) initiative, which aims to facilitate a 'readjustment movement of North–South information exchanges' within the rubric of quality and public service, i.e. to encourage First World broadcasters to give away non-commodity-oriented programmes, even this project was endorsed, provided it was not funded from the UNESCO budget (Tricot, 2000). By 2003, there was talk of a NWICO *redux* – this time under US hegemony, with UNESCO and culture displaced as sites and priorities by the WTO and commerce (Pauwels and Loisen, 2003: 292).

There were also conceptual limitations to cultural imperialism:

> Cultural imperialism is a perspective that has largely been identified with
> leftist analysts ... and is therefore often dismissed ... [because it allegedly]
> blots out any capacity of the world's citizens to resist or appropriate in their
> own fashion the messages of global advertising or US television, and
> additionally presumes that worries about cultural survival are uniquely
> provoked by the policies of the major powers, and not equally by nation-states
> against ethnic minorities within their own frontier.
>
> (Downing, 1996: 223)

As per the GEM and the DEM, anxieties about local confrontations with the NICL are frequently expressed under the guise of a concern for spurious effects on national or regional cultures or identities that may themselves be repressive or phantasmatic. Opponents of cultural-imperialism critique argue that such worries, and the cultural protectionism they inspire, derive from a Puritanism that denies the liberatory aspects of much US entertainment for stifling class structures (Federico Fellini famously equated 'America, democracy ... Fred Astaire' [quoted in Hay, 1987: 64]). Critics of the cultural-imperialism thesis note that its analyses of transplanted culture take a very totalising view that is insufficiently alive to specificities of region, nation, audience and so on (O'Regan, 1992: 75). They argue that customisation is critical, as evidenced in the capacity to fuse imported strands of popular culture with indigenous ones (e.g. Nigerian juju and Afro-Beat), to rediscover and remodel a heritage via intersections with imported musical genres. Mattel's Barbie doll has been successfully exported to 140 countries with company customisation, but there are also local, unauthorised adaptations that trope Barbie while undermining its MNC exclusivity (MacDougall, 2003). This is said to indicate the power of audience preferences against US dominance.

Similarly, when national cinemas refuse to take a critical distance from Hollywood cinema as some damned other, seeking instead to imitate it – notably the 1980s *Si Boy* cycle in Indonesia, with its youth culture of fast cars and English-speaking servants – they are fusing imported strands of popular culture with indigenous cultural labour. This embrace of imported Hollywood texts might indeed rework cultural identity, as in Irish cinema, or act as a buffer against cultural imports that are too close for comfort, as when Pakistanis prefer the difference of North America to the similarity of India. In the case of a text such as *Moulin Rouge!* (Baz Luhrmann, 2001), the oddity of Ewan McGregor bursting into song is cradled in a familiarity with Bollywood as much as Hollywood intertexts, while Bollywood itself has drawn on Hollywood storylines and star images for decades, as have the Chinese, Japanese and Brazilians (Sen, 1994: 64, 73, 129–30; Rockett et al., 1988: 147; O'Regan, 1992: 343; Byrne, 2002; Pendakur, 2003: 108; Ganti, 2002; Mishra, 2002: 126; Ye, 2003; Hu, 2003; High, 2003: 79; Shaw, 2003).

The central claim of cultural-imperialist critique, that there has been a transfer of taste without a transfer of technology between the global North and South, sometimes looks hard to sustain. Consider India. In a September 1932 letter to the President of the American Academy of Motion Picture Arts and Sciences, the Chairman of the Technical Committee of the newly formed Motion Picture Society of India proposed increasing the country's international film profile by encouraging a 'more scientific interest in the entire technique of motion pictures, both silent and talkie'. After describing the archival, organisational, scientific and experimental aims of the new Bombay-based Society, the writer asked for Hollywood's help in providing surplus organisational literature that was now 'intrinsically of little value' to the presumably fully developed American Academy. In return for help in modelling the institutionalisation of the Indian film industry, the writer offered Hollywood increased publicity (Kantebet, 1932). Universal opened the first Hollywood studio offices there in 1916. The waning presence of a British imperial cinema (see Jaikumar, 1999) cleared the way for further collaborations in the early 1930s, as domestic film producers took advantage of the country's linguistic heterogeneity by spurring investment in new sound technologies for regional film industries. Indicative of these early efforts, Ardeshir M. Irani, the Bombay producer credited with making the first Hindi-language sound film (*Alam Ara*, 1931), purchased substandard equipment from the US and brought over a Hollywood sound technician, Wilford Deming, to work on the film.

The mediation of Hollywood's output by indigenous cultures has been particularly important in qualifying the cultural-imperialism thesis as per active audiences. Michel Foucault's story (1989: 193) of a white psychologist's visit to Africa is instructive in its detail of differing aesthetic systems: when the academic asks local viewers to recount a narrative he has screened, they focus on 'the passage of light and shadows through the trees' in preference to his interest in character and plot. In their study of the reception of the television soap opera *Dallas* in Israel, Japan and the US, conservative functionalists Tamar Liebes and Katz (1990: 3–4, v) establish three prerequisites for the successful communication of US ideology: the text contains information designed to assist the US overseas, it is decoded as it was encrypted, and it enters the receiving culture as a norm. They 'found only very few innocent minds' across the different cultural groups that discussed the programme; instead, a variety of interpretative frames led to a multiplicity of readings, because accommodation always already involves transformation by a local culture, and an increasing awareness of the heterogeneous and conflictual nature of US culture itself (Schou, 1992: 143–45). Screen studies tells us of men identifying with women in melodramas, women identifying with male action heroes, Native Americans identifying with Western pioneers – in short, the theatre as a site of carnival as much as machinery, where viewers transcend the dross of their ordinary social and psychological lives (Stam, 1989: 224). Jacqueline Bobo's analysis of black women viewers of *The Color Purple* (Steven Spielberg, 1985) shows how watching the film and discussing it drew them back to Alice Walker's novel and invoked their historical experience in ways quite unparalleled in dominant culture – a far cry from the dismissal of the film by critics. These women 'sifted through the incongruent parts of the film and reacted favorably to elements with which they could identify' (Bobo, 1995: 3). Similarly, gay Asian-Caribbean-Canadian videomaker Richard Fung (1991) talks about searching for Asian genitals in the much-demonised genre of pornography, an account that is unavailable in conventional denunciations of porn and its impact on minorities. And when JoEllen Shively (1992) returned as a researcher to the reservation where she had grown up, she found that her fellow Native Americans had continued their practice of reading the Western genre in an actantial rather than political way, cheering for the 'cowboys' over the 'Indians' because of narrative position, not race.

Should this be regarded as false consciousness, or the capacity to interpret films through their particular story worlds as well as via the horizon of personal life? Neither answer will do. The worldwide divergence of filmgoers' labours of interpretation and judgment is not reducible to a choice between false consciousness or polysemy. Historicised specificity is a valuable antidote to any purely textual or symptomatic reading – it alerts us to encounters of divergent tastes, even as the NICL regulates distinctions in the fusion of imported strands of popular culture with indigenous cultural labour.

Clearly, these are cases of a strategic making-do, not of being overwhelmed. The cycles of interdependency locate a form of authority in Hollywood, but the respect is provisional, offered as a gesture to knowledge and technical exchange. The national becomes an improvisational stabiliser of difference that allows commercial image industries to respond to shifting climates of commodity exchange.

A television survey by the *Economist* in 1994 remarks that cultural politics is always so localised in its first and last instances that the 'electronic bonds' of exported drama are 'threadbare' (Heilemann, 1994: Survey 4). And it is certainly true that part of the talent of the cultural commodity is that it pursues a lengthy career and can be retrained to suit new circumstances. As Liberace once put it: 'If I play Tchaikovsky I play his melodies and skip his spiritual struggles. . . . I have to know just how many notes my audience will stand for' (quoted in Hall and Whannell, 1965: 70). Because culture covers aesthetic discrimination as much as monetary exchange, it is simultaneously the key to international textual trade and one of its limiting factors. Ethics, affect, custom and other forms of knowledge both enable and restrict the processes of commodification (Frow, 1992: 18–20). For example, Tokyo Disneyland is owned by the Oriental Land Company, a Japanese firm. It is a successful replica of Anaheim's often de-provincialising, sometimes enchanting dross, but has been modified to suit local culture (Raz, 2003). Disney television in Australia consisted of rebroadcast US programmes in the 1960s; by the 1990s, they went through a superficial localisation, via young Australian presenters (Nightingale, 2001: 73). And General Motors, which own Australia's General Motors Holden, translates its 'hot dogs, baseball, apple pie, and Chevrolet' jingle into 'meat pies, football, kangaroos, and Holden cars' for the Australian market.

Sony, Warners and Disney all produce thousands of hours of television texts in foreign markets each year, designed for local audiences. Similar stories apply to material produced by the Spanish-owned Endemol in the Netherlands, Action Time, Granada and All American Fremantle. In Italy, *The Nanny* was dubbed to make Fran Drescher's character Sicilian rather than Jewish, thereby connoting someone adjacent but marginal to the dominant culture (Bielby and Harrington, 2002: 220). Granada, for instance, has customised the British soap opera *Coronation Street* for China (*Joy Luck Street*) and Hollywood finally won over a key segment of the Indian market with a localised *Who Wants to be a*

Millionaire?. *Joy Luck Street* is shown on cable for free, with the advertising revenue going to Granada. This means that small cable networks can fill airtime and global companies can move easily and cheaply into markets (Landler, 2001; Fry, 2001).

While criticisms have been made of MTV Asia, for example, because of the preponderance of Western material, a logic of intercultural communication suggests that Saudi and Taiwanese audiences could be alienated by the 'foreignness' of either culture on-screen, but feel familiar with the 'internationalism' of Yanqui product. And in any event, when Rupert Murdoch bought the parent Star TV, he insisted that market forces would make indigenous programming critical to success in China, Indonesia and India (Reeves, 1993: 36, 62; Fitzpatrick, 1993: 22; Heilemann, 1994: Survey 12). MTV gradually became regional rather than local or Yanqui in its global programming, as did other cross-national networks such as news channels (Chalaby, 2003: 465).

These instances can be read as an indication of the paradigmatic nature of the national in an era of global companies, or as the requirement to reference the local in a form that is obliged to do something with cultural-economic meeting-grounds. In the end, the sale is local, and its interpretation too, in the opinion of ambitious MNCs and active-audience critics alike.

An additional problem with the NWICO version of cultural imperialism is that it risks cloaking the interests of emergent bourgeoisies seeking to advance their own market power under the sign of national cultural self-determination. Such a framework disavows the NICL, neglecting questions of labour in favour of questions of textuality via a cultural nationalism. It encourages cultural-imperialism theorists to champion hierarchical and narrow accounts of culture as discrete and super-legitimate phenomena that, they soon discovered, mostly served as a warrant for an asphyxiating parochialism created and policed by cultural bureaucrats (Mattelart and Mattelart, 1992: 175–77; Roach, 1997: 49). We may lose sight of the NICL if, as per NWICO, we identify economic effects of globalisation with cultural ones (Golding and Harris, 1997: 5). Then we only perceive the oppositions discerned by the neoliberal business columnist 'Lexington' (1999) – 'Pokémania v. Globophobia' – or Mario Vargas Llosa: 'preferences and intimate motivations' against a 'delirium of persecution' (2000).

Concerns about cultural imperialism were not restricted to the Third World. At Mondiacult 1982, the Mexico City world conference on cultural production, the French Minister for Culture Jack Lang made the following remark:

> We hope that this conference will be an occasion for peoples, through their governments, to call for genuine cultural resistance, a real crusade against this domination, against – let us call a spade a spade – this financial and intellectual imperialism.
>
> (**Quoted** in Mattelart *et al.*, 1988: 19–20)

While the leftist connotations of this rhetoric are not universally welcome, its moral fervour resonates widely and profoundly, such that all Western European countries now echo it, and the Association of South-East Asian Nations (ASEAN) issued a statement in the 1990s calling for 'a united response to the phenomenon of cultural globalization in order to protect and advance cherished Asian values and traditions which are being threatened by the proliferation of Western media content' (quoted in Chadha and Kavoori, 2000: 417). These states are caught between the desire to police representations and languages along racial and religious lines and financial commitments to internationalism (Hamilton, 1992: 82–85, 90; Fitzpatrick, 1993: 22). The fact that Germany's huge post-production company Das Werk launches a subsidiary in Spain and calls it '42nd Street' is signal testimony to this ambiguity/ambivalence and the continuing force of the US as an index of capitalist entertainment, whatever its origin (Hopewell, 2001). *Bruce Almighty* (Tom Shadyac, 2003), beloved by young Yanqui Christians, was banned in Egypt because 'it harms the Almighty by daring to have him incarnated by an actor', according to censor Madkour Thabet (Eygpt also banned *The Matrix Reloaded* (Andy and Larry Wachowski, 2003) as sacrilegious). Marketers were, however, able to position *Bruce Almighty* in Jordan, despite official protests, after comic allusions to Moses parting the Red Sea were cut ('Egyptian Censors', 2003). It is no wonder young Indonesian and Egyptian artists called for a ban on the screening of US and British material during the 2003 imperialist invasion of the Middle East, while Chinese film critics worried about 'a powerful cultural offensive' from Hollywood that was 'a sort of plundering' of Chinese youth ('Indonesian', 2003; 'A Renewed', 2003: 48–49). In Greece, the Union of Greek filmmakers organised a boycott of Hollywood, including the DVD release of *My Big Fat Greek Wedding* (Joel Zwick, 2002) (Nathan, 2003: 16). In attending to these concerns, and the alarming rise in eating disorders among Greek women following the deregulation of TV and the advent of more and more US popular-culture body fetishes (Davenport, 2002), we must both acknowledge nationalist and feminist concerns, and investigate the economic correlatives of this textual effect and other formations of bodies in the cultural labour market. Once more, the GEM and the DEM meet.

In this light, self-satisfied Yanqui arguments against cultural imperialism become disingenuous, inane – and revealing: 'Authoritarians left and right, religious fundamentalists and cultural conservatives – whether in China, India, Pakistan, Bangladesh or France – look warily at American film imports as conveyors of value disease' (Plate, 2002). The very basis for this statement, that the message matters and that it signifies something broader about the US, gives the lie to the claim that the industry is only interested in business questions, while the array of villains lined up against Hollywood is so diffuse and improbable in any other context as to suggest that something else is in fact going on.

Instead, we need to link the unequal trade in culture to the labour that makes it happen, from production through distribution to reception. We shall see how labour is central to the real story in Chapter 2.

Ironically, there are now many critics in the US who fear that it has lost its own culture, because the Ford motor company's credo ('To be a multinational group, it is necessary to be national everywhere') spread to Hollywood cinema in the 1970s, and texts were tailored to foreign consumption (Mattelart, 1979: 218). The desire for sales overseas also depresses budgets for African-American situation comedies, because they are perceived to have limited appeal elsewhere, and TV drama requires three seasons to qualify for effective syndication, while initial network licensing fees do not cover costs. This forces ethnically specific formats to lose themselves in middle-class whiteness in order to secure major international distribution, since multiple domestic seasons are rarely obtained (Havens, 2002). Just as oppositional voices in the US characterise the flight of capital as a reaction to unfair trading that sees state subsidies precluding open competition on the basis of efficiency and effectiveness, there are equivalent culturalist anxieties, whereby any incursion on this cherished nativist territory is quickly countered. In 1974, the Australian singer Olivia Newton-John won Country Female Artist of the Year from the US Country Music Association. This immediately led to the formation at Tammy Wynette's home of the Academy of Country Entertainers in protest at 'cultural carpetbagging' (Peterson, 1978). Today, the American Film Institute is concerned about the loss of cultural heritage to internationalism. Laments that British costume history crowds out the space for indigenous 'quality' television also claim that there was more Australian high-end drama on US television in the 1980s than locally produced material (Quester, 1990: 57). Political economists argue that a newly transnational Hollywood no longer addresses its nominal audience (Wasser, 1995: 433), and that the opening of screen markets to freer trade will adversely affect the localism of US cinema still further (Keil, 2001). Soap-opera producers seek to avoid storylines or customs that will be illegible to other audiences (Bielby and Harrington, 2002: 222).

The *Economist* magazine advises that 'many of America's neoconservatives (and some liberals) see [US cultural domination] as a perilous solvent acting on the United States itself', because of ethnically specific local marketing and media and a cinema that no longer showcases 'core' Northern European values and subjectivities. The Film and Television Action Committee (FTAC), a Hollywood coalition opposed to runaway production, with endorsement from unions representing actors, directors, teamsters and others, protests that 'the American motion picture and television industry is a part of our national cultural heritage, not to be surrendered to another nation' – almost a case of cultural-imperialist concerns ('Culture Wars', 1998; Film and Television Action Committee, 1999)! Even the US government now speaks in these terms:

Some industry insiders consider the significant increase of American television and film production moving offshore to be more than an economic issue. They point out that, throughout the twentieth century, democratic and free market ideals were the cornerstone of American films successfully produced, exhibited, and distributed throughout the world. In addition to serving as one of our most lucrative exports, the entertainment industry provided the world's population with a clear understanding of a democratic society. America exported stories defining a system of government that could withstand open criticism and still grow stronger (*Mr Smith Goes to Washington* [Frank Capra, 1939], *Gentleman's Agreement* [Elia Kazan, 1947]); stories demonstrating that talent and hard work could surpass birth into a social class as determinants of wealth or fame (*Rocky* [John G. Avildsen, 1976]); stories about one person's ability to make a difference (*Norma Rae* [Martin Ritt, 1979]), and to overcome persecution and prejudice (*To Kill a Mockingbird* [Robert Mulligan, 1962]); stories exploring the impact of American slavery and prejudice and the struggle to transform society into one of equal rights for all (*Roots*). Many of these American films and television programs have helped promote freedom and democratic values, the same values that encouraged throngs of people throughout the world to rise up and challenge repressive governments, contributing to the end of the Cold War, the destruction of the Berlin Wall, and the events in Tiananmen Square before the crackdown. Many foreign incentive programs were initially created to encourage production that reflected the local language and characteristics of that population. However, these incentives, particularly when paired with quotas, often require that the major creators and artists be citizens or hold passports of the country providing the funding, limiting the opportunity for Americans to participate in the production. In addition, these incentive programs bring with them a requirement to consider the creative opinions of the local partner, whether a broadcaster or a governmental entity. Some American storytellers have questioned whether their messages will have to change in order to meet the financial incentives created by foreign interests.

(Department of Commerce, 2001: 6, adapted from an essay by Meryl Marshall, Chairman of the Board and Chief Executive Officer of the Academy of Television Arts and Sciences)

This is rather a bad-faith argument, given the effective abandonment of a national public-interest address in the deregulatory fervour that has characterised US media since the 1980s, with TV now 'a medium of formats' as per radio amid the decline of 'a single dominant popular culture' (Hirsch, 2000: 357). But it has great currency. On all sides, cultural imperialism and nationalism are foundational, generative discourses, however much one might wish it otherwise.

Against the currently fashionable idea that globalisation eradicates difference in a dialectic of cultural homogeneity/integration versus heterogeneity/

fragmentation, Mike Featherstone (1990: 1–2) argues that we must question who is served by globalisation – the *cui bono* question. Here we return the emphasis to Hollywood's power over the geographical coordinates of the NICL. As Herbert I. Schiller expressed it, 'the media-cultural component in a developed, corporate economy supports the economic objectives of the decisive industrial-financial sectors (i.e. the creation and extension of the consumer society)' (1976). This insight should counter such charmingly hyperbolic rhetoric as Masao Miyoshi's assertion that the 'formation of a highly complex web across national borders of industrial production and distribution (transnationalization) largely invalidates disputes over surpluses and deficits in trade' (1993: 745). In bitter response to this imagined *pax munda*, the cultural workers of the world might chortle, 'Yeah, right'.

In one sense, there are now four distinct varieties of cultural-imperialism discourse. First, Africa, the Middle East and Latin America continue the long-standing debate about local democratic participation and control. Second, the major economic powers of Western Europe argue about the need to build pan-Europeanism in contrast to the homogenising forces of Americanisation. Third, the former state-socialist polities of Eastern and Central Europe seek to develop independent civil societies with privatised media (Mowlana, 1993: 66–67). And finally, there is the nativist fear that the US has lost its own national address in the surge to overseas markets. There can be no better illustration of the durability of cultural-imperialist analysis and its stimulus to cultural policy. To be more useful, it needs to work through the NICL as well. That means looking into the various international organisations that establish the terrain for cultural exchange.

The GATT and Friends

If the European Commission governments truly care about their citizens' cultural preferences, they would permit them the freedom to see and hear works of their choosing; if they are really concerned about a nation's cultural heritage, they would encourage the distribution of programming reflecting that heritage.

(Jack Golodner, President of the Department for Professional Employees, American Federation of Labor-Council of Industrial Organizations, 1994)

Given the choice between Arnie killing lots of bad people, and a bunch of menopausal women going naked and talking about buns, I know which I'd prefer.

(Peter Briffa, 2003)

Whether your source is an old-school US union official or a populist pundit from the London *Times*, you will probably have encountered strong views about public policy and cinema. Much of that discussion has been had over the past decade in the context of the General Agreement on Tariffs and Trade (GATT). From its emergence in the late 1940s as one of several new international financial and trading protocols, the GATT embodied in contractual terms the First World's rules of economic prosperity: non-discrimination; codified regulations policed outside the terrain of individual sovereign-states; and multilateralism. They were in opposition to the main struts of cultural policy:

- subsidies
- domestic-content guarantees
- market-access restrictions
- licensing restrictions
- taxes on foreign investment
- copyright protection
- import tariffs; and
- regional co-productions and customs unions.

Born under the logic of growth evangelism, whereby standardised industrial methods, vast scales of production and an endless expansion of markets would engineer economic recovery and development for the Western European detritus of the Second World War and preclude any turn to Marxism-Leninism, the GATT helped to restructure capitalism. The General Agreement was a paradoxically bureaucratic voice of neoclassical economics, rejecting parochial national interests and state intervention in favour of free trade. Officials worked like Puritans ordered by intellectual manifest destiny to disrupt trading blocs and restrict distortions to the putatively natural rhythms of supply and demand as determined by consumer sovereignty and comparative advantage.

After the Second World War, the US immediately sought coverage of cinema under the GATT, and later television. The 1948 Beirut Agreement eliminated duty and licensing costs for educational audiovisual imports, but not for texts designated as cultural or popular (Marvasti, 2000: 108 n. 3). Film quotas were permitted because the Europeans maintained, against the US, that screen texts were services, not commodities. In any event, as we have seen, US exports increased rapidly. In the 1950s, when Britain was the only country with anything like the proportion of television households that the US had, it quickly became a staple customer for US programming. This established a trend of deficit financing for US material based on overseas sales that obliged it to continue to press for 'open' markets (Tunstall and Machin, 1999: 26; McDonald, 1999).

Although it briefly had a TV programmes panel in 1961, the GATT was slow to recognise TIS. This was in part because the frequently object-free exchanges that characterise the 'human' side to the sector (restaurants, for example) were not especially amenable to conceptualisation and enumeration. But as the Western powers saw capital fly from manufacturing, they sought to become net exporters of services. The US argued against public subsidies for television and film during the Agreement's Tokyo Round of negotiations between 1973 and 1979, to no great effect. But the Punta del Este Declaration of 1986, which began the seven-year-long Uruguay Round of the GATT, put TIS at the centre of GATT negotiations for the first time, because of pressure from the US in the service of lobbyists for American Express, Citibank, IBM and Hollywood (Loeb, 2000: 308; Sjolander, 1992–93: 54 n. 5; Footer and Graber, 2000: 118; Grey, 1990: 6–9). The stakes were high: by the late 1990s, TIS accounted for 60 per cent of GDP in the industrialised market economies (IMECS) and more than a quarter of world trade. In 1999, total world TIS was valued at US$1,350 billion, with the US responsible for 33.8 per cent. Of course, this is part of a discursive change as well, for 'the cultural term "work" has been supplanted by the market notions of "service" and "product" ' (Mattelart, 2002: 604).

After the US failed to have cultural industries incorporated in the 1988 Free Trade Agreement with Canada, its diplomats and trade officials tried to thwart EU plans for import quotas on audiovisual texts. EU law enshrines freedom of expression through media access – the Union's alibi for putting quotas on US screen texts, along with the continuing claim that the screen is not a good but a service. The EU's 'Television Without [intra-Western European] Frontiers' directive (adopted in 1989 and amended in 1997) drew particular ire for an annual limit on texts imported by member nations of 49 per cent of broadcast time (World Trade Organization, 2000; Theiler, 1999: 558; McDonald, 1999). But US attempts to have the GATT's Uruguay Round derail such policies were almost universally opposed in the name of cultural sovereignty, with significant participation from Canada, Japan, Australia, Europe and the Third World. This position equated the culture industries with environmental protection or the armed forces, as spheres that exist beyond neoclassicism: their social impact could not be reduced to price. In 1993, thousands of European artists, intellectuals and producers signed a petition in major newspapers calling for culture to be exempted from the GATT's no-holds barred commodification (Van Elteren, 1996a: 47), in what became known as the 'Cola and Zola' debate (Kakabadse, 1995). The 1993 coalition opposed the idea that the GATT ensure open access to screen markets, on the grounds that culture is inalienable (non-commodifiable).

To US critics, however, cultural rights merely concealed the protection of inefficient industries and outmoded *dirigisme* (Kessler, 1995; Van Elteren, 1996b; Venturelli, 1998: 61). The US argued from a *laissez-faire* position, maintaining that the revelation of consumer preferences should be the deciding factor as to who has comparative advantage in television and film production – whether Los Angeles or Sydney is the logical production site for audiovisual texts. 'Washwood' claimed there was no room for the public sector in screen production, because it crowded out private investment, which was necessarily more in tune with popular taste. Both the active face of public subvention (national cinemas and broadcasters) and the negative face of public proscrip-

tion (import barriers to encourage local production) were derided for obstruct-
ing market forces. This smokescreen obscured the constitutive nature of the
NICL in deciding the Los Angeles versus Sydney question, which we explore in
greater detail in Chapter 2. As always, Washwood's moralism on this question
is contingent – it's fine for Israel to exclude certain items and practices from
free trade with the US based on cultural specificity (Loeb, 2000: 305). But that
conditionality is itself never taken as a precedent for cases involving states that
are not fellow rogues of the international system.

François Mitterand's memorable argument of the mid-1990s stressed that
cultural struggle over the GATT was not 'the culture of Europe' versus 'the New
World'. Rather, it was about the preservation of 'the universality of culture'
(quoted in Strode, 2000: 67). Over forty countries exempted audiovisual sectors
from their eventual endorsement of the Agreement – including the US (World
Trade Organization, 1998)!

These struggles have not prevented Hollywood from peddling its wares internationally. As noted in our Introduction, half of Hollywood's revenue comes
from overseas. The US supplies three-quarters of the West European market, up
from half a decade ago. The consolidation of 'wealthy' Europe into one sales site
has been a huge boon to Hollywood, along with the deregulation of television.
Over the first eight years of 'Television Without Frontiers', net audiovisual trade
between the EU and the US saw Europe's annual culture industries deficit rise
from US$2 billion to US$5.6 billion. The screen-trade imbalance grew from
US$4.8 billion to US$5.65 billion between 1995 and 1996 ('After GATT', 1994:
16; 'Culture Wars', 1998; Van Elteren, 1996b; European Audiovisual Observatory, 1998; Hill, 1994b: 2, 7 n. 4; 'Déjà Vu', 1994: 3). Meanwhile, the studios
fretted that their 55 per cent proportion of these other nations' box-office takes
had been cut by foreign-exchange controls and assorted barriers to 42–43 per
cent ('You're Not', 1995)!

In 1995, the WTO replaced the GATT and bought the services of its GAT-
Tocrats. The WTO has a legal personality, a secretariat and biennial ministerial
conferences. This new machinery makes it easier for MNCs to dominate trade
via the diplomatic services of their home governments' representatives.
Environmental concerns and other matters of public interest no longer have the
entrée that the GATT gave to non-governmental, not-for-profit organisations.
Multinationals now find it easier to be regarded as local firms in their host
countries, and Third World agricultural production has been further opened
up to foreign ownership (Lang and Hines, 1993: 48–50; Dobson, 1993: 573–76).

Despite its high-theory commitment to pure/perfect competition, political pressures mean the GATT had at least nodded in the direction of
archaeological, artistic and historic exemptions to free-trade totalisations
(Chartrand, 1992: 137). Commodities and knowledges previously excluded
from the GATT, such as artworks and international export controls, are
included in the WTO's remit, with extra-economic questions of national

sovereignty eluding the written word of trade negotiation, but thoroughly suffusing its implementation and consequences (Zolberg, 1995). The WTO's operating protocols stress transparency, most-favoured nation precepts, national treatment (identical policies on imported and local commodities), tariffs in preference to other protective measures and formal methods of settling disputes. The organisation's initial focus on the service industries highlighted the lucrative telecommunications market, but its oleaginous hand is turning to culture. When Canada and France tried to remove cultural issues from the WTO and place them within the purview of UNESCO, they met with little support (Department of Commerce, 2001: 82).

In 1997, the WTO made its first major movement into the culture industries, in cases concerning Turkish limitations on foreign films and taxation of US film revenue (WT/DS43 – subsequently settled privately with the Turks agreeing to harmonise taxes on local and imported texts) and the Canadian version of *Sports Illustrated* magazine. The organisation ruled that Canada could not impose tariffs on the magazine for enticing advertisers away from local periodicals. This case is regarded as the beginning of the WTO's cultural push (World Trade Organization, 2001: 71; Valentine, 1997; Herold, 2003; Magder, 1998). The new US move is to cluster cultural issues under the catch-all rubric of intellectual property, which saw it bring WTO cases against Greece for allowing the rebroadcast of US television programmes without regard to copyright. This prodded the Greek government to legislate on television copyright and then close down television stations that broke the law. Washington also opposed Croatian and Latvian membership of the organisation because of those states' desire to follow EU policies on screen imports (Venturelli, 1998: 62, 66; World Trade Organization, 2001: 51; 'Administration Settles', 2001; Freedman, 2003b: 287).[2]

Anything on television is now governed by the General Agreement on Trade in Services (GATS). It is the WTO's protocol on TIS from the Uruguay Round that emerged from lobbying by Yanqui banks and insurance companies via their Coalition of Service Industries, which, of course, excluded labour from the 400 apparatchiks it sent scurrying around the Uruguay Round's closing moments (Wesselius, 2002). Now an Entertainment Industry Coalition for Free Trade has been set up to do similar work (Boliek, 2003).

Although the GATS stipulates that there must be easy market access and no differential treatment of national and foreign suppliers of services, it gives room to exempt certain services from these principles. This margin for manoeuvre is utilised, for example, by the EU in setting quotas for films (Hoskins *et al.*, 1997: 5–7). European states objected to incorporating the audiovisual field within discussions. They constructed a most-favoured nation (MFN) system of 'cultural exceptions' for this sector, plus libraries, museums and archives. Publishing was not included. Of the fifty states involved in the GATS talks, only fourteen included culture on their list for liberalisation, and it was agreed to maintain the film exemption from the old GATT (UNESCO, 2002). The WTO convened GATS 2000, a round of negotiations lasting until the end of 2002 that further addressed the liberalisation of goods and services 'to entrench privatization and deregulation worldwide' (Gould, 2001) and rein in democratic controls over corporations across a broad swathe of business activity (Sinclair, 2000; see also Office of the US Trade Representative, 2001c). GATS and GATS 2000 have been ineffective in liberalising film and television, because civil society groups from all over the world have responded critically (Wesselius, 2002: 3) and many governments have been loath to permit Yanqui domination. Only the Central African Republic and the US have signed on to all the Agreements' categories (Freedman, 2003b).

One major issue is the future of virtual goods. Clearly, the digitisation of text will soon make use of the term 'good' over 'service' rather outdated anyway, as objects will not cross borders. For now, theatrical films are deemed to be goods by the WTO, and other screen texts are services. Meanwhile, the quota provision endures, but it is unclear whether other forms of local support or foreign exclusion are exempted by the WTO's rules, and some argue that cultural exemptions would not hold water legally (Herold, 2003; Pauwels and Loisen, 2003; Sauvé and Steinfatt, 2000: 324). As audiovisual services are absorbed into concepts such as electronic commerce, information and entertainment, the distinction between goods and services begins to blur. The EU fears that the US will muscle its way into film and television through insisting on free-market access to new communication services, using 'the Internet as a Trojan Horse to undermine the Community's "Television Without Frontiers" directive' (Wheeler, 2000: 258).

The US has been like a child with a toy in the WTO, proud that it has filed more complaints than any other country and has prevailed so often (Barshefsky, 1998). And just in case it should fail to destroy cultural policies through international trading institutions, it has lodged the EU on its internal Special 301 'Priority Watch List' for sanctions (USIA, 1997). Again, there is a sense of a child, this time keeping a list of most-hated peers and real or imagined 'meanness'. In 2000, Washington sent an official paper to the WTO's Council for Trade in Services on 'Audiovisual and Related Services' that it hoped would give the organisation a framework to assist 'the continued growth of this sector by ensuring an open and predictable environment' that would allegedly enable greater diversity of artistic output. Clearly, this was the key to the US' *laissez-faire* politics. But there was now recognition of a countervailing legitimacy, that this environment must pay heed to 'the preservation and promotion of cultural values and identity', just as nations retain control over local prudential rules for their domestic financial systems (United States Government, 2000). It remains to be seen whether this is one more invocation of national concerns on behalf of a bourgeoisie, as per the cynical use of culturalism by other countries' media producers in favour of state support for national cinemas and broadcasters.

The GATS has become known as 'an agreement to disagree', with the cultural industries exempted *de facto* if not *de jure* and the new Doha Round of talks expected to turn into a terrain of struggle, once more pitting the US against the rest of the world over the issue of culture, with the former wielding trade rules and the latter UNESCO's *Universal Declaration on Cultural Diversity*. While one side preaches continuity with its liberal intent, the other proclaims continuity with the GATT's cultural exemptions (Herold, 2003). Each party trades off concessions in other areas via a diplomacy that is rarely unveiled in anything approximating to democratic openness (Pauwels and Loisen, 2003: 292).

Does this make for a transformation of the world system, away from state-centrism? In addition to setting public servants to work on its behalf at the WTO, the international ruling class also holds its own parties. The Global Business Dialogue on Electronic Commerce, which held its first meeting in 1999, works with parallel imperatives to the WTO. Cees Hamelink (2001: 15) describes this meeting of '500 top executives from media and IT industries (among them CEOs from Time Warner, Bertelsmann, Nokia, AOL, and Japanese NTT)', in which the cultural MNC leadership 'discussed policy topics such as taxation, data protection, intellectual property rights, tariffs, information security and authentication. ... Basically global business leaders told governments what to do in the governance of CyberSpace.' Of the hundred government representatives present, none received more than observer treatment. This MNC leadership set up 'a 29-member steering committee with representatives from the private sector only' to shape strategies and policy initiatives. Among the main industry-led policies are lifting Internet taxes, eliminating export restrictions on encryption software as well as 'third party arbitration in e-commerce disputes', and relaxing EU privacy laws, which the Global Business Dialogue rejects as a barrier to global trading.

Certain critics argue that the promiscuous nature of capital has been over-stated, that the sovereign-state, far from being a series of 'glorified local authorities' (Hirst, 1997: 409), is in fact crucial to the regulation of MNCs, with regional blocs strengthening, rather than weakening, the ability of the state to govern – that the GATT and its friends rely on, work through and in part serve the world of states. And people around the world continue to look to the latter for both economic sanction and return (Smith, 1996: 580). While the 'relationship between capitalism and territoriality' has shifted (Robinson, 1996: 18), it remains governed by inter-state bodies, albeit dominated by the G8 (Hirst, 1997: 413; McMichael, 2000a: 177). Capital markets, for example, operate internationally but with national supervision and regulation; all conceivable plans for dealing with their transnational reach still necessitate formal governance ('Global Finance', 1999). A supposedly exemplary open-market specimen, the North American Free Trade Agreement/Tratado de Libre Comercio Norteamericano (NAFTA) needs a mere one thousand pages of governmental rules to 'work' (Palley, 1999: 50), while the last GATT amounted to twenty-thousand pages of protocols, weighing 850 kilograms! As far as investment is concerned, in a global age, governments continue to matter. So does the sum of the tendencies we have outlined support the claim that global Hollywood is the acme of neoliberalism (Feigenbaum, 2002)?

Laissez-Faire Hollywood?

> The core of globalization is to achieve economic hegemony of a few rich states, the United States of America in particular, as well as the hegemony of Western consumer culture, threatening the peoples' cultures, methods of living and spiritual values.
>
> (Tariq Aziz, then Prime Minister of Iraq, quoted in Landers, 2000)

Conventional economics explains Hollywood's historical success in terms of 'a flexible managerial culture and an open and innovative financial system' (Acheson and Maule, 1994: 271–73) that have adapted to changing economic and social conditions. On this account, which we briefly adumbrated in the Introduction, in the silent era, films were made for the big domestic market that could also be sold in other English-speaking countries. Because English was a very international First World language by contrast with those of other wealthy linguistic groups, the coming of sound aided the process, while the diverse ethnic mix of the US population encouraged a universal mode of storytelling. As Terry Ramsaye put it over half a century ago, '[t]he American motion picture born to serve a vast polyglottic patronage was born international in its own home market' (1947: 8). The argument goes that these strengths have been built on since, under the guiding principle of free-enterprise competitiveness, to produce a product that is popular with audiences (Wildman and Siwek, 1993; Dupagne and Waterman, 1998; Noam, 1993). Global corporate media firms are seen as solutions to the market's low productivity and inefficiency – an effective means of delivering consumers what they want, while opening up cultures to change in ways that encourage liberal democracy through new ideas (Demers, 1999: 5). Hollywood's own account of itself intersects with these neoclassical economics *nostra* in claiming that comparative advantage determines the location of globally successful cinema. Hollywood 'wins' because it is set in a melting-pot society and obeys *laissez-faire* protocols (Pollock in Peres and Pollack, 1998).

Conversely, this section questions whether Hollywood is truly a free market based purely on consumer demand, and whether the industry realises the stated aims of public policy based on the tenets of neoclassical economics. We use three tests of worth, outlined below, based on the promises and premises of that discourse. Then we focus in particular on the grand claim of both *laissez-faire* and Hollywood – that private enterprise is central to success and the state is either a barrier or irrelevant.

1   Freedom of entry to new starters?

Neoclassical economics says that the degree of real competitiveness in an industry can be gauged by the openness of its markets to new entrants. But because of their links to broadcasting, several studios have at different moments received substantial protection. So Washington blocked a takeover attempt by the Banque de Paris et de Pays-Bas for Columbia in 1966 (Ulich and Simmons, 2001: 362). The global injection of money from video sales in the 1980s gave independent financing some new heft because of additional outlets, and foreign companies such as Carolco, De Laurentiis and Cannon briefly entered Hollywood, utilising funds from pre-sales to produce ten pictures a year, but their lack of plant and library left them undercapitalised and vulnerable when the stock market collapsed in 1987 (Wasser, 2001: 125). While it is certainly true that some of the major Hollywood studios have had new owners over the past fifteen years – for example, Australia's Channel Seven and News Corporation, Canada's Seagrams, France's Canal Plus/Vivendi and Japan's Matsushita and Sony, plus a new domestic venture in DreamWorks that gained key support from Korea's Cheil Jedang Corporation – control of studio output remains in California and New York. What matters spatially is not the company's headquarters, or the location of its major shareholders, but the site of its actual product development and management. Given that US entertainment antitrust has been a joke since the 1980s, and television is closely tied to film following the deregulation of domestic cross-ownership rules, continued governmental limits of 25 per cent foreign ownership of US radio and television stations minimise external participation, even as they encourage domestic oligopoly (Stokes, 1999). With large conglomerates owning studios and networks, and Wall Street demanding routine success by industries that are used to routine failure, there is an increasing tendency for films to be made with this foreign investment (Groves and D'Alessandro, 2001). Control of these funds remains firmly in US hands, just as it did during unsuccessful purchases of studios by others over the previous decade.

2   A relationship between the cost of production and consumption?

Unlike most forms of manufacturing, the production of film drama is dominated by a small number of large companies with limited, individually differentiated outputs. After the televisualisation and suburbanisation of the 1940s, the B-movie was no longer a cheap commodity, and the studios focused on seeking hits rather than staples; thus, the economics of cinema shifted from seeking returns on all texts to a few – a precursor to most popular-cultural industries, which are characterised by a high volume of expensive production but an increasingly narrow band of successes (Robins, 1993: 107, 115). Most investments are complete failures, a financial burden that can only be borne by the big firms. The absolute significance of story over cost for audiences – who are accustomed to paying the same amount for all releases – goes against neoclassical economics' standard assumptions about the role of price in balancing supply and demand. Because of textual meaning's centrality to film, again unlike manufactured goods, screen texts have very short product lives and only minimal opportunities for the reuse of already extant 'parts'. Instead, films are transformed from services to products and then to services again as they move between theatrical, video, televisual and Internet forms of life (Litman, 1998: 25, 1). Costs are not reflected in ticket prices or cable fees. They are amortised through a huge array of venues, so reusable is each full copy of each text. Unlike a car or painting, it grows in value with use (Venturelli, n. d.: 7–8). Although the means of production are standardised, economies of scale are rare when each project is costly and unlikely to succeed. Prices at major theatres are based on the class composition of audiences as determined by rental space and national income, as these 2004 figures indicate:

UNITED STATES	INTERNATIONAL
Layton US$7.25	Buenos Aires US$2.25
Allentown US$7.50	Marshall Islands US$5.00
Nashville US$8.00	Dubai US$8.20
Austin US$8.00	Paris US$10.80
Milwaukee US$8.50	Sydney US$11.25
New York US$10.25	Tokyo US$16.80
Los Angeles US$11.75	London US$19.00

SOURCE: Adapted from Mackey, 2004

Whereas the average cost of feature films in France, the UK, Australia and Italy barely rose between 1990 and 1997 (it remained well below US$10 million), the average cost of features in the US went from US$26 million in 1990 to US$39 million in 1996 and US$53 million in 1997. In 1999, Hollywood spent US$8.7 billion, a total far in excess of all other national cinemas combined (European Audiovisual Observatory, 1998; 'Film Production and Distribution', 2000). Overall average film costs have doubled in less than a decade (Waters, 1999), increasing by 6.5 per cent between 1999 and 2000, to US$54.8 million (Valenti, 2001c). In 2002 the average feature cost US$89.4 million, of which US$58.8 million went on production and US$30.6 million on marketing. This figure was up 10.2 per cent on 2001 (Motion Picture Association of America Worldwide Market Research, 2003: 17). In no case does this alter ticket prices, domestically or abroad. And in television there is a clear correlation between GDP, public-sector broadcasting and the purchase of US television in both Asia

2001 US Economic Review			Theatrical Costs	
MPAA Average **Negative Costs** **($ millions)** (includes production costs, studio overhead and capitalized interest)	Year	Cost Per Feature	Yearly Change	2001 Versus
	2001*	47.7	-13.0%	--
	2000*	54.8	6.5%	-13.0%
	1999	51.5	-2.3%	-7.3%
	1998	52.7	-1.4%	-9.5%
	1997	53.4	34.1%	-10.7%
	1996	39.8	9.5%	19.7%
	1995	36.4	6.1%	31.1%
	1994	34.3	14.6%	39.0%
	1993	29.9	3.6%	59.4%
	1992	28.9	10.4%	65.2%
	1991	26.1	-2.4%	82.4%
	1990	26.8	14.2%	78.0%
	1989	23.5	29.9%	103.3%
	1988	18.1	-9.9%	164.0%
	1987	20.1	14.9%	137.8%
	1986	17.5	4.0%	173.1%
	1985	16.8	16.4%	184.1%
	1984	14.4	21.3%	230.8%
*Due to changes in financial reporting regulations, abandoned project costs are no longer included in studio overhead, and as such, are no longer a part total Negative Costs	1983	11.9	0.3%	301.1%
	1982	11.8	4.5%	302.3%
	1981	11.3	20.8%	320.6%
Source: MPAA	1980	9.4	--	408.1%
MPAA Worldwide Market Research				**-14-**

and Europe – the richer the nation and the stronger its public media, the less need it has for Hollywood material (Dupagne and Waterman, 1998). This indicates that economic power exploits poor countries, not that prices are determined by consumer desire.

3   Textual diversity?

Open markets supposedly make for diverse products, permitting extensive freedom of choice for customers. Do we have this on US screens? In the 1960s, imports accounted for 10 per cent of the US film market. In 1986, that figure was 7 per cent. Today, it is 0.75 per cent if one excludes co-productions, which are rarely significant apart from UK films that look, sound and are marketed as Hollywood products ('The Imbalance', 2002). Foreign films are essentially excluded from the US as never before, and large-scale studies show that people all over the world have experienced more and more imported music, cinema and TV – with one exception (Pew Research Center for the People & the Press, 2003: 72–73)! Neoclassical reactionaries attribute this to US audiences, who are seen as 'unusually insular and intolerant of foreign programming or films, because historically they are exposed to very little' (Hoskins et al., 1997: 45). The industry magazine Variety.com refers to 'uptight, subtitle-averse America', while the leftist weekly The Nation speaks of 'no-subtitles America' (Bloom, 2002; Rich, 2001). As a country with a thriving Spanish-language cultural market, and in which non-English languages are used extensively every day, this account of the US is flawed – and also ironic, given that the early Hollywood moguls attributed their start to 'the foreign born, who could not speak or understand our tongue, who had no theatre where he could hear his own tongue' (Fox, 1927: 302). Most Hollywood films are now released domestically in Spanish on VHS and, very recently, DVD. In the TV market, Paramount makes Spanish-language videos of its Nickelodeon children's series, and Buena Vista Home Entertainment promotes Disney texts in Spanish-language versions (Bennett, 2001; Villa, 2002). Disney sold its first Spanish-language interactive video games in 2001 ('Disney Games', 2001). Ground Zero Entertainment has a Latino film division whose express purpose is to make and release movies direct to video (Netherby, 2001). Yet foreign-film distributors face the problem of what to emphasise in trailers – usually the only publicity they can afford apart from small notices in newspapers. Miramax trailers, for example, tend to hide the fact when its movies are not in English, even in art-house circuits (Henné, 2001: 142), while Fox TV in Los Angeles refuses to air commercials for movies in Spanish (Puente, 2001). Barriers to the distribution of foreign films in the US also include the cost of subtitling and dubbing (Sánchez-Ruiz, 2001: 107).

Minimal screen diversity is due to the corporatisation of cinema exhibition, in combination with increases in promotional and real-estate costs for independent distributors and exhibitors and higher demands from the original producers, who have had to put more and more money 'on the screen' to compete with the Hollywood 'look'. This has reached the point where the costs of subtitling and dubbing have become insupportable – the average Hollywood film had US$21 million budgeted for advertising in 1999, an unthinkable figure for European rights-holders (Stanbery, 2001). In television, the proliferation of channels in the US over the past ten years has required companies to change their drama offerings significantly. Action adventure, the most expensive television genre, occupied 20 per cent of prime time on the networks in 1990; four years later, the figure was around 1 per cent (Balio, 1998b: 65; Schwab, 1994; Martin, 1995). Reality television, fixed upon by cultural critics who either mourn it as representative of a decline in journalistic standards or celebrate it as the sign of a newly feminised public sphere, should actually be understood as a cost-cutting measure and an instance of niche marketing. This has not led to significant variety or quality. The US has a 'culture blockade', extending from tariffs on imported CDs, through bans on foreign owners of broadcast licences, and on to film-distribution collusion (Ledbetter, 2002). This deregulated media world has delivered the most protectionist culture in world history.

State Business

Neoclassical reactionaries claim that state subsidies in other countries undertaken in the name of cultural sovereignty impede the free market and disadvantage other nations because, allegedly *ipso facto*, such intervention stifles innovation, thereby aiding US dominance (Marvasti, 2000). For his part, Valenti claims it is a 'delusion' that governments know how best to build a thriving cinema industry (quoted in 'Clarity', 1999). These *laissez-faire* shibboleths and Hollywood fictions woefully misread the constitutive nature of US governmental assistance to Hollywood. The local film industry has been aided through decades of tax-credit schemes, State and Commerce Department representation, the Informational Media Guaranty Program's currency assistance (Izod, 1988: 61–63, 82, 118; Guback, 1987: 92–93; Schatz, 1988: 160; Muscio, 2000: 117–19; Powdermaker, 1950: 6; Harley, 1940: 3; Elsaesser, 1989: 10–11) and oligopolistic domestic buying and overseas selling practices that keep the primary market essentially closed to imports on the grounds of popular taste (without much good evidence for doing so). We could start with the 30 per cent tax on box office for imported films during the inter-war period and go on from there (Greenwald, 1952: 46).

The US Department of Commerce continues to produce materials on media globalisation for Congress that run lines about both economic development and ideological influence, problematising claims that Hollywood is pure free enterprise and that the US government is uninterested in blending trade with cultural change. The US has a vast array of state, regional and city film commissions coordinated by Film US, hidden subsidies to the film industry (via reduced local taxes, free provision of police services and the blocking of public thoroughfares), Small Business Administration financing through loans and support of independents, along with State and Commerce Department briefings and plenipotentiary representation. This is typical of the overall economy, which routinely starts and maintains industries with major public investment, then seeks to destroy foreign competition by arguing that it should follow *laissez-faire* rules. The alibi for subsidising digital, aerospace and other sectors is, for example, the 'rhetorical shield of "defence policy" ' (Wade, 2003).

Having originated in the late 1940s, by 2000, the number of publicly funded US film and television commissions stood at 205 (Wasko, 2003: 38; Stevens, 2000: 797–804), although some have been defunded with the budgetary crises of the Bush Minor era (Center for Entertainment Industry Data and Research, 2002). In 2002 there were fifty-six municipal film offices across California alone (M. Jones, 2002: 41). Their work represents a major subsidy. For example, the New York City Office of Film, Theatre and Broadcasting (2000) offers exemption from sales tax on all production consumables, rentals and purchases. The Minnesota Film Board (2000) has a 'Minnesota Film Jobs Fund' that gives a 5 per cent rebate on wages, not to mention paying producers' first-class airfares and providing free accommodation for them and tax-free accommodation for their workers, as well as tax-avoidance schemes. The California Film Commission (2000) reimburses public personnel costs, along with permit and equipment fees. Hotel and sales tax rebates are almost universal across the country, and such services even extend in some cases to constructing studio sites, as in North Carolina (Rettig, 1998; Ross and Walker, 2000). The Californian State Government offers a 'Film California First Program' that covers everything from free services through to a major wage tax credit, and was about to introduce a new tax credit in 2004, until this was overturned at the appropriations stage due to the state's deficit (Hozic, 1999; Directors Guild of America, 2000; 'Americans', 2001; Wicker, 2003: 493; Pietrolungo and Tinkham, 2002–03). Cincinnati promises 'Harlem in the 1950s, Manhattan and Queens in the 1940s, Chicago in the late 1910s, and the present-day New Jersey' (quoted in Hozic, 2001: 88).

Consider state film commissions' array of tax incentives as the new century arrived:

US TAX INCENTIVES FOR FILM

STATE	TAX INCENTIVES
Alabama	Sales tax exemption for hotel accommodations after 30 days. Some local option tax exemptions exist on hotel rooms after 60 days.
Alaska	No state sales tax. No state individual income tax.
Arizona	A 50 per cent sales (transaction privilege) and use tax rebate on the purchase or lease of tangible personal property if producers spend over $1 million in Arizona filming movies for theaters, television, video, industrial or education films or commercial advertising. A second threshold of expenditures of $250,000 applies to television commercial or advertising in commercials aired in two minutes or less. No withholding tax from wages of nonresidents engaged in any phase of motion picture production. A 1996 law provided for an exemption of retail sales tax on the purchase of machinery and equipment used primarily at sound stages constructed between 1 July 1996 and 1 January 2002. No state tax on lodging after 30 days.
Arkansas	Full gross receipts and use tax refund on the purchase of property and services including in connection with production costs. To qualify, a production company must spend at least $500,000 within six months or $1 million within 12 months in connection with the production.
California	No sales or use tax on production or post-production services on a motion picture or TV film. No sales and use tax on

services generally. Such industry-specific services include writing, acting, directing, casting and storyboarding. Five per cent sales tax exemption on the purchase or lease of post-production equipment by qualified persons.

No sales and use tax on 45 per cent of the charges for sets, including labour to design, construct and strike, and no sales tax on the full charge for the rental of personal property.

No state hotel tax on occupancy; however, cities or countries that impose a local tax have a tax exemption for occupancies in excess of 30 days.

Colorado	No sales and use tax on film company services if, in fact, the company is providing a service and not tangible personal property.
Connecticut	Sales and use tax exemption for the purchase, lease, use, storage or other consumption of motion picture, video production or sound recording equipment for use in the state for production activities that become an ingredient of any motion picture, audio tape or recording produced for commercial entertainment. No hotel occupancy tax for hotel stays in excess of 30 days.
Delaware	No state sales tax.
Florida	Sales and use tax refund for the purchase or lease of motion picture, video or other equipment (depreciable equipment with a useful life of at least three years) if used exclusively as an integral part of production activities in preparation of motion pictures, tapes, TV or productions produced for commercial use or sale. If equipment and personnel used belong to the producer of a qualified motion picture, there is no tax on fabrication labour. Repair of motion picture equipment if used exclusively by the producer as an integral part of production activities. No state individual income tax.
Hawaii	Income tax credit up to 4 per cent, which is deductible from net income tax liability of the costs incurred in the state in the production of motion picture and television films; and up to 6 per cent for costs incurred in the state for actual expenditures for transient accommodations. Must spend at

least $2 million in Hawaii for motion pictures or at least $750,000 to produce a television episode, pilot, or movie of the week. If the tax credit exceeds the income tax liability, the excess will be refunded to the taxpayer.

Idaho	No hotel occupancy tax on hotel stays of 30 days or longer.
Illinois	Sales and use tax exemption for products of photo-processing produced for use in motion pictures for public commercial exhibition. The 14.9 per cent hotel tax is reimbursed for stays in excess of 30 days.
Kansas	Sales tax refund for certain film, television, commercial or video production expenditures. Must spend at least $200,000 per project in Kansas. Expires 30 June 2000.
Kentucky	Sales and use tax refund for purchases made by a motion picture production company in connection with filming in Kentucky if the company films or produces one or more motion pictures in the state during any 12-month period.
Louisiana	State sales and use tax refund on purchases made in connection with filming or production if purchases exceed $1 million or more in a 12-month period. After 30 consecutive days, the 14.9 per cent hotel tax is reimbursed and no further taxes are charged.
Maine	Hotel occupancy taxes are rebated after 28 consecutive days.
Maryland	No state sales tax for hotel stays in excess of 30 days.
Mississippi	A 1998 attorney general opinion declared film production a manufacturing process. This would provide a sales and use tax cap of 1.5 per cent on the purchase of machinery, equipment and tangible personal property used in the production of motion pictures, television programs, commercials and documentaries. This opinion requires clarification by the State Revenue Department.

Minnesota	Provides for an annual appropriation of $500,000 per year for payments to producers for a portion of services and wages paid for in-state production jobs up to a maximum of $100,000 per film. No sales tax on hotel stays of 30 days or more.
Missouri	Provides an income tax credit up to 25 per cent of expenditures in the state to a maximum of $250,000 in tax credits per project. Productions must spend a minimum of $300,000 in the state. No sales tax on hotel stays after 31 days.
Montana	No sales tax. No property tax on out-of-state equipment used exclusively in motion picture or commercial production. No accommodation tax for hotel says in excess of 30 days.
Nebraska	No hotel occupancy tax for stays in excess of 30 days.
Nevada	No corporate or individual income tax. Low hotel room tax.
New Hampshire	No state sales tax. Individual income tax on interest and dividends only.
New Jersey	Sales tax exemption for all film and video related machinery and equipment as well as services of installing or repairing equipment used directly in production and post-production of motion pictures, television or commercials.
New Mexico	State sales tax exemption on all production costs including set construction, wardrobe, facility and equipment rental, all production and post-production services. After 30 days, the 4 per cent ledgers tax is waived for hotel guests.
New York	Comprehensive state and New York City sales and use tax exemption for machinery, equipment and services used in production and post-production activities in the production of feature-length films, television programs, music videos and commercials. Film, television and commercial production are considered a manufacturing process.

North Carolina Reduced sales and use tax (1 per cent rate) on the purchase and rentals for motion picture production films of cameras, films, set construction materials; as well as chemicals and equipment used to develop and edit film that is used to produce release prints. Full exemption for the purchase of film that becomes a component part of release prints sold or leased. Chemicals used to develop prints for sale or lease are also exempt. A 1997 law included a sales tax exemption for audiovisual master tapes made or used in production.

Ohio No state sales tax on hotel stays in excess of 30 days.

Oklahoma Sales tax exemption on sales of tangible, personal property, or services to a motion picture or television production company to be used or consumed in connection with an 'eligible production'. An eligible production is defined as all television productions (not including commercials), television pilot or ongoing series televised on a network or a feature-length motion picture intended for theatrical release. State sales tax rebate on hotels after 30 days.

Oregon No state sales tax.

Pennsylvania A 1997 law granted a 6 per cent sales and use tax for the purchase or rental of any tangible personal property in Pennsylvania used directly in the production of a feature-length commercial motion picture distributed to a national audience. The exemption covers props, sets, supplies, tools, production and post-production services including processing, editing, etc.

South Carolina Sales and use tax exemption for all suppliers, technical equipment, machinery and electricity sold to motion picture companies for use in the filming or producing of motion pictures. For tax years after 1998, corporate and personal income tax credits for investments in South Carolina production projects or facilities.

South Dakota No state individual income tax.

Tennessee Sales and use tax refund for out-of-state motion picture companies for use in filming or producing motion pictures. For tax years after 1998, corporate and personal income tax credits for investments in Tennessee production projects or facilities.

Texas	Comprehensive sales and use tax exemption for purchased or rented equipment or services used in the production of a motion picture or video recording for ultimate sale, license or broadcast (including cable broadcast). No sales tax on hotel rooms for stays in excess of 30 days.
Utah	Transient occupancy tax rebate after 30 days.
Vermont	Credit for non-resident income tax for commercial film production if Vermont income tax exceeds income tax rate in state of residence. No tax on hotel stays in excess of 30 days.
Virginia	Sales and use tax exemption for production services or fabrication in connection with the production of any portion of exempt audio/visual work, feature or made-for-television films, programs, documentaries, commercials, etc. Tangible personal property including scripts, artwork, supplies, equipment and accessories are also exempt.
Washington	Sales and use tax exemption for the purchase or rental of production equipment and services used in motion picture or video production or post-production. No sales and use tax on vehicles used in production. No tax on hotel stays in excess of 30 days. No state individual income tax.
Wyoming	No tax on hotel stays in excess of 30 days. No state corporate or individual income tax.

SOURCE: Boryskavich and Bowler, 2002

A stunning example of this is Miami, the centre of runaway production *into* the US from Latin America. Miami has become the third-largest audiovisual production hub in the US after Los Angeles and New York, and perhaps the largest *for* Latin America. This was achieved not by chance or convenience of location, but through very deliberate policy. The Miami Beach Enterprise Zone offers incentives to businesses expanding or relocating there that include property tax credits, tax credits on wages paid to Enterprise Zone residents and sales tax refunds. The Façade Renovation Grant programme provides matching grants to qualifying businesses for the rehabilitation of storefronts and the correction of interior code violations. As a consequence of this promotional activity, the Miami entertainment industries generated about US$2 billion in 1997, more than any entertainment capital in Latin America, and boasted a workforce of 10,000 employees (García, 1998; Martín, 1998). By 2000, volume had increased to US$2.5 billion. Other Miami counties are also renewing their initiatives to woo the entertainment industries. To diminish the difficulties that producers and film companies encounter with the complicated bureaucracy of the numerous municipalities in the area, which have their own regulations, Miami-Dade's Film Commission led an initiative to draw more film and TV business to South Florida (Miller and Yúdice, 2002: 80).

Federally, Congress considered legislation in 1991 to limit foreign owner-ship of the culture industries to 50 per cent, a xenophobia that retreated along with the Japanese economy, but returned with Canadian runaways. The House of Representatives continues to contemplate a bill from 2000 that would provide subvention to low-budget films and new production-wage tax invest-ments incentives or research-and-development tax credits regularly come before Congress (Steinbock, 1995: 21; Blankstein, 2001; Goldman, 2000; 'Con-gress', 2001), and there is now a Congressional Entertainment Industry Taskforce dedicated to retaining cultural industry jobs in the US (Boryskavich and Bowler, 2002: 35).

Internationally, negotiations on so-called video piracy have seen PRC offend-ers face beheading, even as the US claims to be watching Chinese human rights as part of its most-favoured nation treatment. Protests by Indonesian filmmak-ers against Hollywood that are supported by their government have led to threats of retaliation from Washington via a vast array of industrial sanctions. The delegation to Hanoi in the mid-1990s of congressmen who had fought in Vietnam ushered in film scouts, multiplex salespeople and Hollywood films on TV. And the US pressured South Korea to drop its screen quotas as part of the 1998–99 negotiations on a Bilateral Investment Treaty ('Commerce Secretary', 2001; Robinson, 2000: 51; Devine, 1999: xvii; Kim, 2000: 362). Copyright limi-tations prevent the free flow of information, and foreign funds have often been raised through overseas tax shelters (Acheson and Maule, 1991; Guback, 1984, 1985 and 1987). For example, nearly 20 per cent of the US$15 billion expended on Hollywood production in 2000 was German, based on tax subsidies and lax listing rules on its high-technology Neuer Markt – in 2001 the figure amounted to US$2 billion (Zwick, 2000; Kirschbaum, 2001; European Audiovisual Obser-vatory, 2003: 5; Crayford, 2002). In 2004, while US cable-TV companies might politely receive callers from US film commissions seeking their business, they were planning production in Canada, based on funds derived from annual rebate incentives for 'the dentists of Hamburg'. Once more, we find public fund-ing at the heart of this putatively private endeavour. The domestic Export-Import Bank Film Production Guarantee Program of 2001 (Wheeler, 2000: 490–91) is only the latest incarnation of the state off-screen.

No wonder, then, that *Canadian Business* magazine – archly, and with a deeply endearing hypocrisy – refers to 'Hollywood's welfare bums' (Chidley, 2000). Even *Time*'s European business correspondent (Ledbetter, 2002) acknowledges the world-historical extent of cultural protectionism in the US, which applies across the entertainment spectrum – what William I. Greenwald half a century ago memorably named 'the virtual embargo' (1952: 48; see also Slotin, 2002; Miller *et al.*, 2003). The FTAC and other leftist groups doubt the efficacy of additional, local corporate welfare as a counter to foreign corporate welfare, since the media giants that utilised such subsidies are international in their operation. Activists favour rooting out all such policies (Cooper, 2000a) – almost a link to the neoclassical ideal – in the name of saving Hollywood from 'rustbelt' status thanks to NAFTA (Bacon, 1999; see also Talcin, n. d.). For their employers, competition is an end rather than a means, as in other forms of capitalism.

As for propaganda, in the embarrassingly macho language of US political science, the media represent 'soft power' to match the 'hard power' of the military and the economy (Nye, 2002–03). The state has a long history of direct participation in production (Hearon, 1938) and control, starting with the screening of Hollywood films on ships bringing migrants to the US, through to sending 'films to leper colonies in the Canal Zone and in the Philippines' (Hays, 1927: 50). During the First World War, films from the Central Powers were banned across the US. Immediately afterwards, the Department of the Interior recruited the industry to its policy of the 'Americanisation' of immigrants (Walsh, 1997: 10) and Paramount-Famous-Lasky executive Sidney R. Kent proudly referred to films as 'silent propaganda' (1927: 208). In 1927, the fan magazine *Film Fun* printed an unsigned article by an immigrant who had grown up in Paraguay:

> Hizzoner, Uncle Sam, tells us it takes five years for a furriner to become Americanized. Hizzoner is looking up the wrong street; any furriner who goes to the movies in Europe can become an American in almost no time ...
>
> When I got to America they told us we would have to go to Ellis Island the next day. I wanted to get into the swim right away ...
>
> They turned me loose. I knew just what to do. The movies I had seen had taught me all about America. I bought a gun the second day, a horse the third, and the Woolworth building the fourth; the man who sold it to me was such a nice fellow, I'd like to meet him again some day.
>
> So you see, it really doesn't take long to become Yankeeized when one has seen the cinema.
>
> ('A Yank', 1927)

In the 1920s and 1930s, Hollywood lobbyists regarded the US Departments of State and Commerce as its 'message boys'. The State Department undertook market research and shared business intelligence. The Commerce Department pressured other countries to permit cinema free access and favourable terms of trade.

In the 1940s, the US opened an Office of the Coordinator of Inter-American Affairs (OCIAA). Its most visible programme was the Motion Picture Division, headed by John Hay Whitney, former co-producer of *Gone with the Wind* and future secret agent and front man for the CIA's news service, Forum World Features (Stonor Saunders, 1999: 311–12). He brought in public-relations specialists and noted filmmakers like Luis Buñuel to analyse the propaganda value of German and Japanese films, and, in particular, their construction of ethnic stereotypes. He sought to formulate a programme for revising Hollywood movies, which were obstacles to gaining solidarity from Latin Americans for the US war efforts, and was responsible for getting Hollywood to distribute *Simón Bolívar* (Miguel Contreras Torres, 1942) and produce *Saludos Amigos* (Norman Ferguson and Wilfred Jackson, 1943) and *The Three Caballeros* (Norman Ferguson, 1944). Some production costs were borne by the OCIAA in exchange for the distribution of free prints to the US embassies and consulates in Latin America. Whitney even accompanied Walt Disney and the star of his film, Donald Duck, who made a guest appearance in Rio de Janeiro (Kahn, 1981: 145), and the Office ordered the reshooting of a film because it showed Mexican children shoeless in the street (Powdermaker, 1950: 71). The successful integration of Brazilian comic-book and cartoon characters into Disney products at this time paved the way for its post-war success in opening up the Brazilian market to extensive Disney merchandise (Reis, 2001: 89–90).

During the invasion of Europe in 1944 and 1945, the military prohibited the screening of Axis films, closed down their industry and insisted on the release of US movies. The quid pro quo for the Marshall Plan was the abolition of customs restrictions, among which were limits on film imports (Trumpbour, 2002: 63, 3–4, 62, 98; Pauwels and Loisen, 2003: 293). In the case of Japan, the occupation immediately changed the face of cinema. When theatres reopened for the first time after the US had dropped its atomic bombs, all films and posters with war themes had been removed. Previously censored Hollywood texts were on screens. The occupying troops immediately established the Information Dissemination Section (soon to become the Civilian Information and Education Section) in its Psychological Warfare Branch, to imbue the local population with guilt and 'teach American values' through movies (High, 2003: 503–04).

Meanwhile, with the Cold War under way, the CIA's Psychological Warfare Workshop employed future Watergate criminal E. Howard Hunt, who clandestinely funded the rights purchase and production of *Animal Farm* (Joy Batchelor and John Halas, 1954) and *1984* (Michael Anderson, 1956) (Cohen, 2003). On a more routine basis, the United States Information Service, located all over the world as part of Cold War expansion, maintained a lending library of films as a key part of its public diplomacy (Lazarsfeld, 1950: xi).

The MPEAA referred to itself as 'the little State Department' in the 1940s, so isomorphic were its methods and ideology with US policy and politics. This was also the era when the industry's self-regulating Production Code appended to its bizarre litany of sexual anxieties two items requested by the 'other' State Department: selling the American way of life around the world and, as we have seen, avoiding negative representations of 'a foreign country with which we have cordial relations' (Powdermaker, 1950: 36).

Wanger (1950) trumpeted the meshing of what he called 'Donald Duck and Diplomacy' as 'a Marshall Plan for ideas ... a veritable celluloid Athens' (444) that meant the state needed Hollywood 'more than ... the H bomb' (446) – this from the man who had hailed Mussolini as 'a marvelous man' in 1936 (quoted in Trumpbour, 2002: 37). Clearly not a premature anti-fascist. MPAA/MPEAA head Johnston, fresh from his prior post as Secretary of Commerce, sought to dispatch 'messengers from a free country'. Harry Truman agreed, referring to movies as 'ambassadors of goodwill' during his presidency (quoted in Johnston, 1950; also see Hozic, 2001: 77). And when the advent of the NICL threatened Hollywood jobs as production moved offshore, union official H. O'Neil Shanks spoke in these terms to Congress' 1961 House Education and Labor Subcommittee on the Impact of Imports and Exports on American Employment:

> Apart from the fact that thousands of job opportunities for motion picture technicians, musicians, and players are being 'exported' to other countries at the expense of American citizens residing in the State of California, the State of New York, and in other States because of runaway production this unfortunate trend ... threatens to destroy a valuable national asset in the field of world-wide mass communications, which is vital to our national interest and security. If Hollywood is thus permitted to become 'obsolete as a production center' and the United States voluntarily surrenders its position of world leadership in the field of theatrical motion pictures, the chance to present a more favorable American image on the movie screens of non-Communist countries in reply to the cold war attacks of our Soviet adversaries will be lost forever.
>
> (Quoted in Ulich and Simmons, 2001: 359–60)

The Legislative Research Service prepared a report for the House Committee on Foreign Affairs' Subcommittee on International Organizations and Movements in 1964 with a title that made the point bluntly: *The U.S. Ideological Effort: Government Agencies and Programs*. The report explained that 'the US ideological effort has become more important than ever', because 'The Communist movement is working actively to bring ... underdeveloped lands under Communist control' (1964: 1). It included John F. Kennedy's instruction to the US Information Agency that it use film and television, *inter alia*, to propagandise (9), and noted that at that date, the government paid for 226 film centres in 106 countries with 7,541 projectors (19). This is *laissez-faire*? Four decades later, union officials soberly intoned that 'Although the Cold War is no longer a reason to protect cultural identity, today U.S.-produced pictures are still a conduit through which our values, such as democracy and freedom, are promoted' (Ulich and Simmons, 2001: 365).

Today's hybrid of SiliWood blends Northern Californian technology, Hollywood methods and military funding. The interactivity underpinning this hybrid has evolved through the articulation since the mid-1980s of Southern and Northern California semi-conductor and computer manufacture and systems and software development (a massively military-inflected and supported industry until after the Cold War) to Hollywood screen content. Disused aircraft-production hangars were symbolically converted into entertainment sites. After the additional stimulus of the dot-com boom, the 2001–03 recession hit these sectors very hard, especially when added to the force of international employment practices, despite Hollywood's supposed counter-cyclical resilience (Aksoy and Robins, 1992; Scott, 1998a and b: 31; Porter, 1998; Bureau of Labor Statistics, 2000a: 205; Vogel, 1998: 33; International Labour Office, 2000a; Sedgwick, 2002; Raco, 1999; Waters, 1999; Goodman, 2001). But the links are ongoing. Stephen Spielberg is a recipient of the Defense Department's Medal for Distinguished Public Service, Silicon Graphics feverishly designs material for use by the empire in both its military and cultural aspects, and virtual-reality research veers between soldierly and audience applications, much of it subsidised by the Federal Technology Reinvestment Project and Advanced Technology Program. This has further submerged killing machines from public scrutiny, even as they surface superficially, doubling as Hollywood props (Directors Guild of America, 2000; Hozic, 2001: 140–41, 148–51). This link was clearly evident in the way the film industry sprang into militaristic action in concert with Pentagon preferences after 9/11 and even became a consultant on possible attacks (Grover, 2001; McClintock, 2002; Gorman, 2002; Calvo and Welkos, 2002; 'Americans', 2001). The University of Southern California's Institute for Creative Technologies uses military money and Hollywood directors to test out homicidal technologies and narrative scenarios. And with NASA struggling to renovate its image, who better to invite to a lunch than Hollywood producers, so they would produce new scripts featuring the Agency as a benign, dynamic entity ('Hollywood Reaches', 2002)? Why not form a 'White House-Hollywood Committee' while you're at it, to ensure coordination between the nations we bomb and the messages we export (Chambers, 2002)? Valenti (2003a) has even argued before Congress that this is a key initiative against terrorism, since copying funds transnational extra-political violence.

Lastly, with the Republican Party owned by minerals and manufacturing and mistrustful of film's putative liberalism, the service industries have their bidding done by purchasing Democrat lobbyists. In return for campaign funds, the Democratic Party obeys the will of the studios via protectionist legislation such as the Consumer Broadband and Digital Television Promotion Act and various anti-counterfeiting amendments to attack file-sharing and the use of multiple platforms for watching films (Koerner, 2003). Caught between conflicting pressures of expansion, stability and political legitimacy (Streeter, 1996: 264), Hollywood studios have poured donations into the campaign coffers of politicians who support copyright extensions, ratification of the World Intellectual Property Organization Treaty and anti-piracy technologies.

CINEMA, TELEVISION AND MUSIC INDUSTRY CONTRIBUTIONS TO US POLITICAL PARTIES

YEAR	TOTAL	INDIVI-DUALS	PACS	SOFT MONEY	DEM	REPUB
2002	$39,910,667	$7,923,442	$4,327,202	$27,660,023	78%	22%
2000	$37,936,084	$15,228,134	$3,976,294	$18,731,656	64%	36%
1998	$16,430,185	$6,921,670	$3,398,946	$6,109,569	62%	38%
1996	$19,597,100	$7,778,591	$3,195,514	$8,622,995	62%	37%
1994	$9,744,657	$4,804,969	$2,604,878	$2,334,810	71%	29%
1992	$13,722,121	$7,880,176	$2,809,985	$3,031,960	74%	26%
1990	$5,755,469	$3,381,999	$2,373,470	N/A	74%	26%

SOURCE: Adapted from www.opensecrets.org

For all its rhetoric of pure competition, therefore, the US government has devoted massive resources to generate and sustain 'private-sector' film in the interests of ideology and money, and the industry has responded in commercial and ideological kind. All in all, this represents a wide array of subsidies and regulations that virtually no one in screen studies or media-reform movements seems to debate or even notice.

Conclusion

Let there be no misunderstanding, the United States will continue to advance the values that define this nation – openness, opportunity, democracy and compassion. Trade reinforces these values, serving as an engine of growth and a source of hope for workers and families in the United States and the world.
(Robert Zoellick, US Trade Representative, Doha WTO Round, 14 November 2001,
quoted in Given, 2003: 11)

In summary, the neoclassical vision of Hollywood asserts that the supposedly neutral mechanism of market competition exchanges materials at costs that ensure the most efficient people are producing, and their customers are content. While this model may occasionally describe life in some fruit and vegetable markets today, as a historical account, it is of no value. The US, France, Germany, Japan, Korea, China – each story of successful industrialisation follows the same path: state subsidy, import taxation, high regulation, welfare protection. *Then* there was liberalisation, the results of which remain as yet unclear (Mann, 2003: 69). The rhythms of supply and demand, operating unfettered by states, religions, unions, superstition and fashion, have never existed as such. Or rather, they have existed as enormously potent prescriptive signs in the rhetoric of international financial organisations, bureaucrats and journalists, at least since economists achieved their hegemony via the Keynesian end to the Great Depression, and then worked to maintain it, despite 1970s stagflation, via their mass conversion from demand- to supply-side doctrines.

This chapter has explained global Hollywood's presence and power both via an engagement with previously underused theoretical and empirical material in screen studies, and through an encounter with orthodox claims. While the industry's commanding position is entangled with the fortunes and projects of US-led capitalist expansion, such domination is uneven – fraught with resistance, failure and competition. Other states' notions of cultural sovereignty underpin concerns vis-à-vis the US, but so too does support for monopoly capital (Burgelman and Pauwels, 1992). That the EU must to some degree shape its cultural labour markets and deliver its cultural workforce to the NICL ensures that its culture industries must continue to struggle with Hollywood for control of the NICL. This is most obvious in the area of international co-production, as Chapter 3 will show. Meanwhile, the old notions of state cultural sovereignty that were so crucial to Europe's political traditions are being attenuated by the twin forces of '*bruxellois* centralisation' from outside and separatist ethnicities from within (Berman, 1992: 1515).

More broadly, we have reached a point where it is said that 'the state remains a pre-eminent political actor on the global stage', but 'the aggregation of states ... is no longer in control of the global policy process'. In their place is a fundamentally non-normative system, run by banks, corporations and finance traders (Falk, 1997: 124–25, 129–30). Core and periphery are blurred, the spatial mobility of capital is enhanced, the strategic strength of labour is undermined and the power of the state is circumscribed by the ability of capital to move across borders. A fundamental shift in bargaining and power relations between capital and labour has been facilitated by transportation and information technologies and trends towards casualisation, though it continues to display the traces of specific national modes of integration into the NICL. We shall see more of this in Chapter 2 (Ross and Trachte, 1990: 63; Thompson and Smith, 1999: 197; Broad, 1995a).

Of course, the demise of the sovereign-state and the emergence of international sovereignty have been routinely – and mistakenly – predicted over the past century. More and more states appear, even as the discourse announcing their departure becomes increasingly insistent (Miller, 1981: 16–18). But as we have seen, the internationalism of new communications technologies and patterns of ownership and control, and increases in the variety and extent of global diasporas, *extend* the significance of the state as a regulatory and stimulatory entity. The corollary has been a developing need for each state to create a national subjectivity from disparate identities. Internationalisation is perhaps nowhere better exemplified than in the work done by states to build the concept of belonging among their polyethnic populations, and the labour performed by those populations to seek new forms of state representation. Clearly, the screen industries are crucial actors in this sphere, not only because of issues of collective identity, as per the GEM, but in the material realm of engendering and reproducing the NICL. The major corporations active in Hollywood follow Time Warner's specification for globalisation: horizontal expansion to enter new markets worldwide, vertical expansion to work with independent producers, and partnership with foreign investors to spread risks and increase capitalisation (Balio, 1998a: 58).

Consider for a moment the cosmic arrogance – or perhaps the sense of a peer dialogue – in Valenti's 2003 letter to Vicente Fox, the President of Mexico, after the government had announced a levy of 1 peso on each film ticket in order to support local production. The tone is truly Olympian: '[T]he adoption of such a measure without previously consulting [the MPA] could force us to cancel our backing for the Mexican film industry ... this also would cause difficulties to our mutual relations' (quoted in de la Fuente and Goodridge, 2003).

The effects of screen trade are not merely registered in cultural identities, but on the very bodies and dispositions of cultural workers. As Dana Polan suggests, 'globalism's mode is embodied, and its embodiment occurs locally' (1996: 258). Global Hollywood is an institution of global capitalism that seeks to render bodies that are intelligible and responsive to the New International Division of Cultural Labour.

Notes

1   It took over a century for George Bush Senior to pick up on the idea. That family always was on the slow side.
2   Ironically, the first case of this nature (WT/DS160/1) went against the US. The WTO found that US copyright law violated global trade rules by permitting large businesses to play recorded versions of music by foreign artists without paying royalties (Newman and Phillips, 2000; World Trade Organization, 2001: 20).

Chapter Two

The New International Division of Cultural Labour

'Bring Hollywood Back to the USA.'
> (Film and Television Action Committee [FTAC] banner, 2000)

Hollywood's not in Hollywood.
> (William Faulkner, quoted in Augros, 2000: 9)

Christopher B. MacCabe, an actor who coaches more than 300 dialect students, works between Toronto and Montreal, training people for auditions. He advises his students to chew gum in the front of their mouths to help perfect their New York accent. Frequent phrases that he tackles are 'fegettabowit,' 'how yuh doin'?' and 'tamarra' for tomorrow.
> (Joanne Latimer, 2003)

Chapter 1 demonstrated that Hollywood's success has been a coordinated, if sometimes conflictual and chaotic, attempt by capital and the state to establish and maintain a position of market and ideological dominance, in ways that find US governments every bit as crucial as audiences and firms. Now we turn to labour, searching for 'the economic geography of capitalism through the eyes of labor' (Herod, 2001:18). Émile Durkheim noted a century ago that conventional economists see the division of labour as a 'higher law of human societies and the condition for progress' (1984: 1), and Hollywood has certainly embraced that analysis in practice if not theory. Picking up from industrial practice and Marxist theory in place of industrial rhetoric and neoclassical theory, this chapter looks to labour as the source of international screen value.

Following an introduction to the idea of the NICL, we address the issues of:

- ownership and control
- merchandise
- animation
- copyright; and
- in much greater detail, runaway production.

We focus in particular on the division of labour, as derived from its classical origins:

> One man draws out the wire, another straightens it, a third cuts it, a fourth points it, a fifth grinds it at the top for receiving the head; to make the head requires three distinct operations; to put it on is a peculiar business, to whiten the pins is another; it is even a trade by itself to put them into the paper ...
> The division of labour ... occasions, in every art, a proportionable increase of the productive powers of labour.
>
> (Smith, 1970: 110)

Today, the expression 'division of labour' is used to describe: sectoral differences in an economy; the occupations and skills of a labour force and the organisation of tasks within a firm. Neoclassical economists suggest that it functions like this:

- wages increase with age, at a diminishing rate
- unemployment and earnings are related to skills
- already highly trained people benefit from ongoing training
- the market determines the division of labour; and
- human-capital investments are less predictably valuable than more material investments.

(Becker, 1983: 16)

Most labour-economics theory is based on neoclassical assumptions as applied to the US, with little regard either for empirical evidence from elsewhere or theories based on labour as a source of value, rather than a limit on it. Marxism offers a different story from these supply-and-demand magicians. For one thing, it conducts research, by talking to people, going to places, uncovering the past and adding and subtracting actually existing numbers. This is what it finds.

Objects and services obtain their surplus value as commodities through the exploitation of the value derived from the labour that makes them. Once these commodities enter circulation with a price, they attain exchange value. The power gained by capitalism, through ever-widening exchange, includes both surplus value, realised as profit, and authority over the conditions and possibilities of labour. The division of labour is the mechanism for this linkage of productivity, exploitation and social control. As its subdivisions multiply and spread geographically, it acquires a talent for hiding the cooperation of labour that constitutes it (Marx, 1906: 49, 83). But the process is visible to those administering it: some distance from Marxism, Adam Smith himself saw that the market must be extended internationally in order to sustain this division of labour (Scott, 1998c: 15), and the International Monetary Fund (2000) positions the division of labour at the centre of globalisation, in keeping with Smith's desire for a worldwide factory and mercantile republic (Mattelart, 2002: 595).

The development of surplus production and the division of labour correspond to four distinct phases of trading history. In the fourteenth and fifteenth centuries, a mercantile system arose from calculations, appropriations and exchanges of climate, geography, flora and fauna. Exchanges of goods turned into exchanges of labour. As food commodities made their way around the globe, so did people, often as slaves. When machinery was developed, work split into an industrial mode. Across the sixteenth, seventeenth and eighteenth centuries, cities grew into manufacturing sites, populations urbanised and wages displaced farming as the basis of subsistence (Lang and Hines, 1993: 15). This is the moment of Smith's famous example of pin-making quoted above. In the twentieth century, assembly-line control, with its quid pro quo of sufficient wages to buy the products being assembled, became a Fordist paradigm. The labour force was divided between blue-collar workers undertaking tasks on the line, and white-collar workers observing and timing them (Scott, 1998c: 18).

When developed countries moved onto the global stage, new forms of labour were institutionalised in empire. In the eighteenth and nineteenth centuries, manufacturing went on at the centre, with food and raw materials imported from the periphery. Differences of opinion emerged about the significance of the balance of trade to a country's well-being. Mercantilists thought it should be controlled, but free traders wanted market forces to rule, in accordance with factor endowments and an international division of labour. Keynesian responses to the Depression made protectionism a more legitimate position in economic theory, until stagflation emerged from the transnational phase that commenced after the war. By the mid-1980s, the volume of offshore production by multinationals exceeded the amount of trade between states for the first time. Today, life-cycle models of international products suggest that they are first made and consumed in the centre, in a major industrial economy, then exported to the periphery, and finally produced and consumed 'out there', once technology is standardised and savings can be made on the labour front. Goods and services owned and vended by the periphery rarely make their way into the centre as imports. The global capitalist economy depends on the integration of production processes; even when geographically dispersed, they remain governed by states and parastatal institutions in the service of capital accumulation (Strange, 1995b: 293; Keynes, 1957: 333–34; Cohen, 1991: 129, 133–39; Evans, 1979: 27–28; Wallerstein, 1989). How does this work in the new, TIS-driven era?

In the film industry, labour can take manifold forms, from special effects, sound recording, editing, film processing, music and dialogue coaching, to acting, directing, filming, scouting locations, building sets, catering, government relations, set publicity, watching and interpreting. Here are some models of the process, beginning with production.

Since the demise of the Hollywood studio system of production that more or less applied between about 1920 and 1970, but was eroding by the late 1950s,

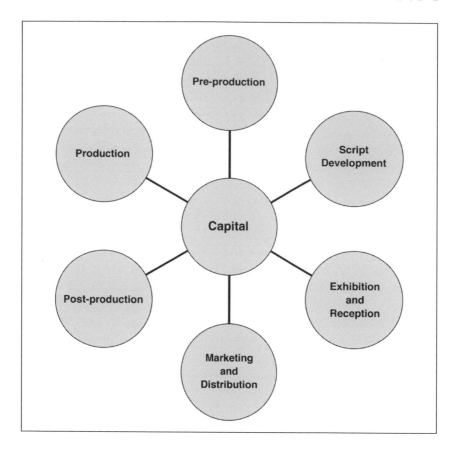

the industry has been a pioneer in the loose model of employment beloved of contemporary management, in that jobs are constantly ending and starting (Jones, 1996). This is characterised by a shift from 'company employees' to 'freelance, franchised or casualised labour' (McRobbie, 2002: 98). Hollywood provides the exemplar of 'flexible specialisation' in its economic commitment to 'permanent innovation' and its political commitment to control its environment (Piore and Sabel, 1984: 17). The key difference is that Hollywood has horizontal unionisation to protect workers from the caprice and exploitation of capital, rather than an enterprise-based system. Within this context, workers and bosses strike complex, transitory arrangements on a project basis via temporary organisations, with small numbers of diverse hands involved at each stage other than production, when sizeable crews function both together and semi-autonomously. Places and networks matter in terms of textual cues, policy incentives, educational support, financing and skills, and time matters because of cost and marketing (DeFillippi and Arthur, 1998; Scott, 1996; Amman, 2002). Work may be subject to the local, national, regional and international fetishisation of each component, matching the way that the labour undertaken is itself largely fetishised away from the final text. Conventional organisational charts are inadequate to the task, especially if one seeks to elude the conventions of hierarchy through capital while recognising the eternal presence of managerial surveillance. Business leeches want *flexibility* in the numbers they employ, the technology they use, the place where they produce and the amount that they pay. They want *inflexibility* in terms of ownership and control (Eisenmann and Bower, 2000). This description is not so far removed from Schulberg's account of half a century ago: 'Old World values, American big business methods, individual standards of integrity and assembly line art' (1950). We can represent the core of the labour process like this:

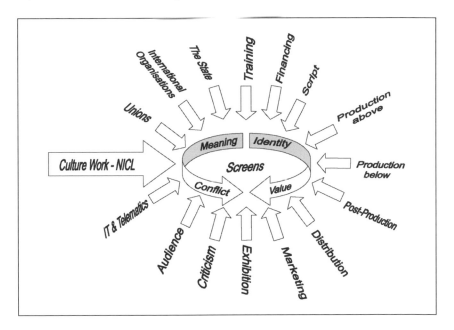

All aspects of Hollywood work have thus been transformed by both new technologies and new work relations. For example, the advent of digital technology has diminished the prior necessity for editors to keep a vast array of information under control as they ploughed through analogic changes. Nonlinear editing permits randomness as workers gain skills in the latest machines – and lose them in the latest narratives (Pierson, 2002: 143). And there are key distinctions between primary and secondary labour markets. In the primary market, employment may be relatively regular and workers receive benefits and pensions. In the secondary market, peripheral employees are caught in perennial uncertainty and lack anything beyond contingent wages (Barnatt and Starkey, 1994: 252). For some, this is a story of loss, for others it is about transition, and in cheerleading versions, a celebration of autonomy (McRobbie, 2002: 102).

In 2002 there were 3,500 film and television companies in Southern California (M. Jones, 2002: 11). Perhaps 0.1 per cent of these firms hire over a thousand people, while about 75 per cent have no more than four employees (Los Angeles County Economic Development Corporation, 2001: 4). This makes the industry appear dispersed and open. But perhaps Hollywood is in a period of *'decentralized accumulation'* (Michael Wayne, 2003: 84), in which the power and logic of domination by a small number of vast entities is achieved via a huge and globalising network of subcontracted firms and individuals, in turn mediated through unions, employer associations, education and the state (Scott, 2002). The accuracy of this account may vary with the genre under discussion – for example, soap operas and sport might be covered by teams that are kept together for entire seasons in order to minimise the transaction costs incurred in starting ventures anew (Saundry, 1998: 155). In addition, as we noted above, Hollywood has shifted its signification, such that it is now effectively one part of a diversified system for recycling texts in different salesrooms and one (flagship) component of conglomerate activity.

Services are much-touted in contemporary mixed-economy capitalist societies as a route to economic development. In the words of populist UK analyst John Howkins, 'people who own ideas have become more powerful than people who work machines and, in many cases, more powerful than people who own machines' (quoted in Tepper, 2002). Howkins' opinion is shared by many in the British government and its seemingly endless cadre of *faux* and fallen leftist academic apparatchiks, along with advocates of 'free labour' (i.e. non-union work) in the US who maintain that collectivities such as class, race and gender will wither because of transformations associated with new information technology that will grant 'creatives' a new individuation (May, 2002: 319). They divine that in today's TIS-driven US economy, there is an almost holy distinction between 'humdrum' and 'artistic' workers (Caves, 2000). This delightful bifurcation is sometimes called 'generic labour' versus 'self-reprogrammable labour' (Flew, 2003: 70). Essentially, it is reinstating a Fordist distinction between blue and white collar.

No surprise, then, that the UK Film Council (2003) endorses three aspects in its charter: 'creativity', 'enterprise' and 'imagination'. Putting aside the chintzy humanism of 'creative-society' mantras and their oleaginous elision of industrial realities, such positions also offend because of New Labour's blathering ignorance that the model of 'entrepreneurial corporatism' was developed by US electronics firms between the 1920s and 1960s as a means of fostering obedient innovation among workers under cover of pseudo-independence (Lécuyer, 2003).

Conventional analysts explain the division of labour in the 'new' economy with reference to:

- flexibility (for which read contingent labour);
- human capital (which means skill); and
- social capital (signifying class, race and gender).

Harnessing the skills of the population is meant to replace lost agricultural and manufacturing jobs with creative-sector employment. Creativity is also seen as a social-policy answer to the dislocation caused by deindustrialisation. In other words, we'll address the poverty and collective distress caused by our closure of the coal mines by setting up museums that detail what life was like in those mines; or, we'll establish a slavery tourism trail that will provide jobs for poor whites and blacks by attracting affluent blacks to visit their heritage. In the US, the National Governors' Association argues that 'innovative commercial businesses, non-profit institutions and independent artists all have become necessary ingredients in a successful region's "habitat"' (quoted in Tepper, 2002), while the Conference of Mayors adopted a resolution in 2001 opposing runaway production, emphasising the importance of the culture industries.

ADOPTED RESOLUTIONS: ARTS, CULTURE AND RECREATION
RUNAWAY FILM PRODUCTION

WHEREAS, the production of filmed entertainment is a cornerstone of America's economy; and

WHEREAS, globalization and the emergence of new technologies has changed the nature of how motion pictures are made, sending ripples through the workforce and displacing thousands of working men and women; and

WHEREAS, nations like Canada have targeted the motion picture industry and its jobs by enticing producers with tax incentives, funded with tax dollars from Canada's federal and provincial governments; and

WHEREAS, foreign give-backs have penalized America's below-the-line workforce by creating a financial variable that precludes them from competing for these jobs, since their counterparts in Canada or Australia are working with subsidized wages, and

WHEREAS, furthering complicating matters for American motion picture industry workers is the emergence of computer-generated imaging (CGI) and related digital technologies, which not only creates the need for newly-trained workers skilled in these areas but also may likely render some industry workers obsolete; and

WHEREAS, municipalities across the country rely on the entertainment industry as an economic development tool, particularly those cities that serve as production centers, employing thousands from the crews behind the camera to those working in the prop houses or equipment rental companies; and

WHEREAS, a January 2001 study by the US Department of Commerce on the impact of runaway production on US workers and small business further underscored that a compelling case can be made that runaway production threatens to disrupt important segments of a vital American industry and the thousands small businesses and below the line workers who depend on it; and

WHEREAS, it is vital that policy makers at every level of government act to preserve the well-being of this industry, and ensure the men and women who comprise its workforce have the tools and ability to ensure its continued growth and contributions to our local economies; and

WHEREAS, a National Entertainment Alliance of organizations and guilds representing the film and TV industries have long studied the runaway film production problem and its devastating effects on US jobs; and

WHEREAS, the National Entertainment Alliance has agreed that the most effective approach for producers is one that levels the playing field;

NOW, THEREFORE, BE IT RESOLVED that the US Conference of Mayors recognizes the importance of the entertainment industry and its workforce to the health and prosperity of America's cities; and,

BE IT FURTHER RESOLVED that the US Conference of Mayors urges the US. Congress to recognize the need for action at the federal level and adopt legislation that promotes domestic film production in the form of a Federal income tax credit and other options that would provide similar financial relief to filmmakers that produce motion picture projects in the United States.

Projected Cost: Unknown

This recognition was exemplified in the state of California's decision in the mid-1980s to increase the number of hours that child labour could be required on-set, 'to induce producers to stay in California' (quoted in Tashiro, 2002: 35). That is the ugly side to the Janus face that UNESCO (2002) identifies in its account of the cultural industries as sites where knowledge and labour combine to generate both wealth and popular memory: a 'twofold nature – both cultural and economic'.

Ranging across the cultural sector, figurational sociology and 'Creative-Industries' economics account for the global and national division of cultural labour in sport (Maguire, 1999) and cinema (Blair, 2003) as benign instances of workers' capacities to control their destiny even under neoliberalism – and indeed, services such as Mandy.com are predicated on a visa-laden globetrotter who will eagerly relocate in search of work wherever and whenever. Key tasks of integration are seemingly more managerial, but are frequently under-taken by neoartisans. Such analyses note that these tasks may be performed under flexible, post-Fordist circumstances, but in geographical clusters.

Groups like the British trade-union movement have offered translations of the 'creative economy' diatribe that construct the film industry as the harbin-ger of newly empowered and free workers, revealing them instead to be in the vanguard of newly exploited and casualiscd labour (Blair and Rainnie, 1998). In the US, activists such as Ed Asner have campaigned fervently on this point. Consider his commentary on Court TV's *Taking a Stand* of May 2001, which ties runaways to other trade policies designed to disempower workers:

> Our only hope is to prove that the companies making film in Canada are merely extensions or vertical companies of companies existing in the states who have ongoing contracts with the SAG [the Screen Actors Guild], and that they must thereby abide by those contracts whether filming in France or Canada.
>
> (www.courttv.com/talk/chat_transcripts/2001/0504asner.html)

Hollywood distinguishes between 'above-the-line' and 'below-the-line' costs. The former lies within the key sector of budgets and includes supposedly 'proactive' workers, such as writers, producers, stars and directors, while the lat-ter term covers 'reactive' workers, or proletarians such as make-up artists, carpenters, costumiers, set designers and electricians (NZ Institute of Econ-omic Research, 2002: 16, 55). Above-the-line workers' salaries are set in concert with high-level agents, distributors and financiers. With this mercantile power at work, the variable in limiting budgets takes place below the line, where union power can be eluded by shooting elsewhere, *ceteris paribus* (Hozic, 2001: 115). The first segment sees leading talent transplanted back to the core, while the second is more likely to provide contingent runaway employment under the NICL. Hollywood's NICL operates through a blend of comprehensive studio facilities and fetishised roles in the labour process that rely on the disaggrega-tion of production across space (Goldsmith and O'Regan, 2003: 9).

Any analysis of global Hollywood must take account of the politics, exploita-tion and stratification of labour. In a 2001 report, the US Department of Commerce noted the following:

> Since there are no distinct, physical locations for making movies, it is difficult to quantif[y] all the skills, equipment, technology, or even number of workers that contribute to the production of a film or television show. Films and television productions tend to be short-term projects lasting only a few months. Often there are different combinations of crews and workers involved in different projects. Because of these factors, motion picture and television production is less visible than a stationary manufacturing facility, such as an

automobile plant. Moreover, in 'floating factories' film workers tend to be relatively fragmented, belonging to literally dozens of professional associations and unions, and lacking a unified national identity akin to workers in the steel or auto industry.

Correspondingly, when production is lost, it neither generates the same tangible, visual image of unemployed workers standing outside the fence of a shuttered physical factory, nor does it elicit a cohesive nationwide industry response. However, the economic impact and job loss are no less real or important to local communities.

(Department of Commerce, 2001: 12)

The conservative British newspaper the *Financial Times* called this 'a whine of a report', noting that Hollywood has 'self-righteous unions' ('Why Hollywood', 2001). Surely, the hysteria of that response indicates that the Department had highlighted a profound historical truth!

Any adequate analysis of the division of labour must account for how practices and labourers are concentrated in one place and disciplined by their access to local labour markets, while establishing increasingly globalised 'means for co-ordination and control under the despotic authority of the capitalist'. This distant power reacts to competition's 'progressive concentration of activity (until, presumably, all economies of scale are exhausted)' by 'tightening authority structures and control mechanisms within the workplace'. This leads our interrogation of the NICL towards a confrontation with processes in global Hollywood that go hand in hand with globalisation of the 'hierarchical organisation and forms of specialisation which stratify the working class and create a social layer of administrators and overseers who rule – in the name of capital – over the day-to-day operations in the workplace' (Harvey, 1999: 31).

In seeking a more politicised understanding of work in global Hollywood – how an international division of labour links productivity, exploitation and social control – we deploy the concept of the NICL to account for:

- differentiation of cultural labour
- globalisation of labour processes
- the means by which Hollywood coordinates and defends its authority over cultural labour markets; and
- the role national governments play in collusion with MNCs.

The NICL is adapted from the idea of a New International Division of Labour (NIDL): developing markets for labour and sales, and the shift from the spatial *sen*sitivities of electrics to the spatial *in*sensitivities of electronics, pushed businesses beyond treating Third World countries as suppliers of raw materials, to look on them as shadow-setters of the price of work, competing among themselves and with the First World for employment. As production was split across continents, the prior division of the globe into a small number of IMECs and a majority of underdeveloped countries was compromised. Folker Fröbel and his collaborators (1980) christened this trend the NIDL. Whereas the old IDL kept labour costs down through the formal and informal slavery of colonialism (the trade in people and indentureship) and importation of cheap raw materials with value added in the metropole, this eventually produced successful action by the working class at the centre to redistribute income away from the bourgeoisie. The response from capital was to export production to the Third World, focusing especially on young women workers. As INTEL puts it, 'We hire girls because they have less energy, are more disciplined and are easier to control'. The upshot has been that any decision by a multinational firm to invest in a particular national formation carries the seeds of insecurity, because companies move on when tax incentives or other factors of production beckon – or at least threaten to do so, thereby generating anxiety and obedience in the proletariat (Allan, 1988: 325–26; Browett and Leaver, 1989: 38; Welch and Luostarinen, 1988; Fröbel et al., 1980: 2–8, 13–15, 45–48; Mies, 1998: 112–13; INTEL quoted in Mies, 1998: 117). At the same time, these poor dears are faced with the issue of how to control a displaced workforce, euphemistically described as 'new challenges for strategic management' (Robins, 1993: 103).

The implication of the NICL is that rather than technology's putatively inherent freedoms generating a revolution in social relations that empowers citizens, consumers and workers, as per cybertarianism's touching but ultimately pitiable 'New-Economy' mythology, we should regard the 'information society' as one more moment of transformation to secure capital's continuing domination of labour (May, 2002; Schiller, 1981 and 1984).

A quarter of all MNCs have their headquarters in the US, where union-busting is a central strut of management. When operating overseas, they adopt highly centralised systems of labour control, run from home (Edwards and Ferner, 2002). Because of their mobility and links to the US government, these MNCs operate similarly wherever they are located, disciplining both labour and the state such that the former is advised on 'appropriate' forms of life by the AFL-CIO (American Federation of Labor and Congress of Industrial Organizations), in keeping with the latter's strong opposition to Marxism-Leninism over many decades (Herod, 1997: 172, 175), and the latter is reluctant to impose new taxes, constraints or pro-worker policies in the face of possible declining investment (not to mention settling for spectator status in the Global Business Dialogue). The labour forces of the 'uncompetitive' countries of the Arab world and Africa are bracketed by MNCs as a reserve army of low-cost potential workers who can be imported to the North as required (Amin, 1997: ix), while throughout the world, 'household and informal sector activities ... sustain global reproduction' (Peterson, 1996: 10). Third World peoples experience 'comparative advantage' as exploitation, working long hours for meagre pay on commodities that expose their countries to the flights of fancy and instability of global markets in a form of 'primitive Taylorism' (Robles, 1994: 1–2, 136–37). The state undermines the union movement on behalf of capital through policies designed to 'free' labour from employment laws. In the process, the Keynesian welfare system, which helped to redistribute funds to the working class, is being dismantled. Ralph Nader refers to this as 'a slow motion *coup d'état*', in which the historic gains of representative discussion and social welfare made by working people and subaltern groups are displaced by corporate power (1999: 7).

Although most of the literature on migration focuses on the poor, international skill exchange has accelerated in the past twenty years, with the departure of professionals often representing a ghastly loss – Ghana saw 60 per cent of its doctors leave in the early 1980s, and the African continent loses 20,000 professionals annually (Stalker, 2000: 107). NICL recruitment via the Web has already instantiated racist and sexist cultural stereotypes (Tyner, 1998). Hollywood has managed to export and even refine domestic disciplinary systems, effectively disempowering and deskilling the workers they hire offshore by monopoly practices, thereby undermining the indigenous bourgeoisies' capacity for capital formation (Prasad, 1998). Cultural production has mostly relocated within English-language IMECs, as factors of production, including state assistance, lure business. This is happening at the level of popular textual production, marketing and information – data-processing everything from airline bookings and customer warranties to the literary canon and pornographic novels – as well as high-culture, limited-edition work. The UN Development Programme estimates the value of offshore information and chip-insertion services at US$30–40 billion annually, and growing at twice the rate of the world economy. The claim that workers in the South benefit from the relocation of jobs there has not been sustained empirically. Competition for this market frequently leads to grotesque working conditions endured by contingent, 'disposable' labour: the Asian Monitor Resource Center reported in 1999 that Mattel toys were being assembled by workers in China who were required to be on the job ten to sixteen hours a day, seven days a week. The feminisation of labour in Asia for Northern service industries refutes any assertion that participating in the formal labour market is necessarily empowering under capitalist development (Greider, 2000: 152–53; Dicken, 1998: 398; 'Technology-Labor', 1999; Burawoy et al., 2000: 175–202; Gills, 2002).

The NICL became a topic of major debate in 2002 when projections emerged to the effect that 3.3 million white-collar US positions, including 500,000 in information technology, would go offshore by 2015, a tendency that is said already to have created a 'global labour arbitrage' and 'jobless recoveries' in the North. Washington responded in 2002 by reducing the number of visas to South Asian software engineers from 195,000 to 65,000, a dramatic trend given the industry's talismanic role in US leadership of a 'New Economy'. Start-ups were being advised to get their loans in US financial markets, and make their hires in Indian intellectual ones (Lakha, 1999; Gaither, 2003; Monbiot, 2003; 'Relocating', 2003). This is some distance from the supposedly newly free worker who has been emancipated from collectivity, dross and employer power through the autonomy granted by information technology (May, 2002: 319).

Today, India is presented to the US as a threat to jobs through the NICL because of its labour-force's technical and linguistic skill vis-à-vis wages. With the PRC mandating the study of English at all levels of education, the Philippines producing hundreds of thousands of *anglo-parlante* graduates annually, and Malaysia also well placed, that may soon change (Srinivas, 2003; 'Relocating', 2003).

The NICL is designed to cover a variety of workers within the culture industries, whatever their part in the commodity chain. So, it includes janitors, accountants, drivers and tourism commissioners as well as scriptwriters, best boys and radio announcers (Throsby, 2001: 256). Cinema is now rather like the telephone-based systems of banking, marketing and ticketing (Bain and Taylor, 2002) in its twenty-four-hour 'follow-the-sun' use of regional hubs that service various nations and industrial sectors, be they in otherwise less-developed or highly developed nations (Larner, 2002; Audirac, 2003). Advances in communications technology permit electronic off-line editing, synchronised special effects and musical scores across the world through digital networks (International Labour Office, 2000b), thereby problematising the very need for location shooting. The universal Integrated Services Digital Network permits the instantaneous transfer of digital video (Pierson, 2002: 160), and labour is fetishised through its disarticulation from texts in terms of both work and place, while employees are further disempowered through flexible hiring arrangements that are organised on a project-by-project basis – contingent labour as a way of life. In the hope of protecting themselves from this exploitation, workers may aspire to informal connections, links that see the same group rehired for additional projects. Risk and uncertainty are constitutive (Blair, 2003), and even highly skilled labour is at its best artisanal (Kerr and Flynn, 2003). Organising workers as a class becomes extremely difficult under such circumstances; but as alienation increases, and neoliberalism's promises turn to dross, there are signs of worker activism (Bain and Taylor, 2002). At the same time, the shibboleth that innovation is positively correlated with the flexibility to hire and fire and do away with permanent employment is being discredited, and the contribution of unions in delivering stability with newness is being recognised (Scott, 1996: 316; Michie and Sheehan, 2003; see also Baron *et al.*, 2001). With this in mind, we can investigate the array of NICL forms inside screen production.

Ownership and Control
US financial institutions have bought foreign theatres and distribution

companies, thus sharing risk and profit with local businesses (see Chapter 5). This is in keeping with the close historic relationship between the film industry and finance capital: as Yanqui banks looked overseas for sources of profit through the 1960s, so they endorsed and assisted efforts by Hollywood to spread risk and investment as widely as possible. By the end of the 1980s, overseas firms were crucial suppliers of funds invested in US film or loans against distribution rights in their countries of origin. Joint production arrangements are now well established between US enterprises and French, British, Swedish, Australian and Italian companies, with connections to television, theme parks, cable, satellite, video and the Internet (Lent, 1998: 243; Wasser, 1995: 424, 431; Monitor, 1999; Buck, 1992: 119, 123; Briller, 1990: 75–78; Wasko, 1994: 33; Miège, 1989: 46; Wasko, 1982: 206–07; Marvasti, 1994; Kessler, 1995; 'The Poly-Gram Test', 1998; Wasko, 1998: 180–81; Puttnam with Watson, 1998: 202-05). Hollywood producers and networks are also purchasing satellite and broadcast space across Europe, with Time Warner, Disney-ABC, Viacom, NBC and others jostling their way into the centre of the vast and growing Western European industry as a site of production and a dumping-ground for old material. As we saw in Chapter 1, the new stations throughout Europe invest in local programming with cost savings from scheduling US filler (Stevenson, 1994: 6). A huge increase in the number of channels and systems of supply and payment is also producing an unprecedented concentration of television ownership and significant horizontal licensing and joint ventures that mirror domestic retailing systems (Schwab, 1994: 14; Roddick, 1994: 30).

Disney ensures that it profits from unsuccessful films through merchandising (46 per cent of annual revenue is from such sales). Much of that manufacturing is undertaken in Third World countries by subcontractors who exploit low-paid women workers. *The Hunchback of Notre Dame* (Gary Trousdale and Kirk Wise, 1996) performed poorly at the box office but sensationally in toy stores, with products made in Taiwan, Hong Kong, Mexico, Brazil, El Salvador, Thailand, Malaysia, St Lucia, Colombia, the Philippines, Honduras, the Dominican Republic, India, Bangladesh, Sri Lanka, China, Haiti, the US, Japan, Denmark and Canada. Disney's labour abuses in China (sixteen-hour days, seven-day weeks, US$0.135–0.36 an hour), uncovered by the Hong Kong Christian Industrial Committee (2001) and others, show how exploitation puts the company into super-profit through 660 Disney retail outlets worldwide that sell the products manufactured by exploited workers. Even Eisner can make a profit when Haitian workers are sewing *101 Dalmatians* (Stephen Herrek, 1996) T-shirts for 12 cents an hour. Animation is especially appealing as a source of profit from licensing activities, because it offers a direct route to children through the original text (McCann, 1998; Madigan, 1999a and 1999b; 'Culture Wars', 1998; Tracy, 1999; McChesney, 1999: 94; Gills, 2002: 108; 'Animation', 2001; 'Disney Labor', 1999). We return to merchandising in Chapter 5.

Animation

Japanese animators were drawing US cartoons from the early 1960s, and it has long been common to transport 'key drawings' by US animators to Asia, where cheap labour is employed to create the frames in-between (Eberts and Norcliffe, 1998: 124). The possibilities of real-time creative collaboration between inter-national sites – over the Internet and dedicated satellite links – has invigorated the global animation and special-effects industry, which is forecast to grow from US$25 billion in 2001 to over US$70 billion in 2005 ('Global Animation', 2001). So, an animation firm may work on medical imaging, film post-production or websites (Eberts and Norcliffe, 1998: 126). As the labour of cultural production departmentalises into units working on multiple tasks in multiple locations, technologies of connectivity have also become integral to managerial oversight. And workers may be physically dispersed and articulated to large concerns versus small companies. Comic-book firms such as Dark Horse employ writers and artists living in the US, Britain, Australia, Canada, Spain, Japan, Taiwan, Uruguay, the Philippines, Mexico, Croatia, New Zealand and France, clustering within those countries in particular cities (Norcliffe and Rendace, 2003). The 2002 Asian Media Festival brought together 1,500 ani-mation producers and distributors from Asia, Europe and the US to discuss regional integration and the global animation trade. Three positions emerged that cut across the classic alignment of cultural heritage and national sover-eignty. Most festival participants agreed that growth in international animation offered regional industries the opportunity to showcase local cultural forms and expertise. However, some worried that growth in Asian animation would lead inexorably to greater exploitation by the US media, which were already looking to consolidate offshore labour pools as Wall Street forced Hollywood to the bottom-line of quarterly-earnings reports. In addition, the accounting allure of increasingly popular package or 'turnkey' productions – where pro-ject costs and implementation are fixed in advance – worked best by demonstrating the cost benefits of cheap labour. Finally, the major players in Asian animation noted that aesthetic difference and outsourced revenue encouraged the building of more local studios with greater technological exper-tise. The same position was advocated by the general animation manager for India's UTV Toons in 2001, who noted that 'a mature domestic market will go a long way in projecting India as a talent hub' (quoted in De and Glancy, 2001).

Copyright

The NICL also holds implications for copyright (see Chapter 4). As part of the framework for the NICL, issues of the territory of a text's first publication, its producer's domicile and the location of its owner's corporate headquarters are often crucial in international intellectual property disputes, as when the estates of John Huston and Ben Maddows claimed that, as director and co-screenwriter respectively of *The Asphalt Jungle* (1950), their moral rights had been infringed when a French television station scheduled the broadcast of a colourised version in 1988. Under US law, the heirs would have had little legal recourse, since the Turner Entertainment Company owned the copyright in the film, having bought it from MGM-Loews in 1986 (which had contracted Huston and Maddows as 'workers for hire'). Turner could do whatever it wanted with the film, including colourising it. After an injunction to prevent broadcast on French television, the lower court deemed that, under civil law moral rights, colourisation had not been authorised by those with a perpetual moral right to the film (namely Huston and Maddows). An appeals court reversed the decision by invoking authorial domicile, finding that US law held jurisdiction, but the highest French civil court confirmed the original decision, on the grounds that only natural persons (not corporate entities) could qualify for the authorship associated with copyright by French law. Jane Ginsberg and Pierre Sirinelli (1991) suggest that the Huston ruling will not necessarily result in a flurry of offshore copyright-infringement claims from US-based artists suing corporate copyright owners in moral-rights friendly countries. Instead, corporate owners might simply strengthen the contractual language in 'work-for-hire' agreements, fleshing out the transfer of rights. Strengthening such language would, in the case of *The Asphalt Jungle*, align US 'work-for-hire' agreements with France's recognition of a written transfer of exploitation rights. Recognition of the subtleties of international legislative difference might inoculate 'owners' from international infringement claims. While the moral legitimacy of a national cultural custodianship underlies claims by the directors' descendants that colourisation is a 'conspiracy to degrade our national character', and the American Film Institute's assertion that 'colorization will destroy our national film history' (Grainge, 1999: 627), the internationalisation of film copyright is harmonising the values that form the basis of domestic cultural policies, in keeping with the need for universal rules to facilitate the NICL. This pliability of the image will continue to transform labour. The coming generation of screen workers are synthespians or vactors – virtual actors. Labour is fetishised as never before when the facial images of dead stars are reanimated onto images of somatotypically similar living actors. The law suggests at this early stage that copyright holders will have greater artistic and financial control over the results than the estates of the deceased, and that residuals will not be payable to the living, since it is not exactly 'their performance' that we see onscreen (International Labour Office, 2000b).

Runaway Production

Nowadays, once a film is shot, it is transferred to videotape format, digitalized, transmitted over the internet, and an editor sitting at any location in the world can use powerful computers and sophisticated software programs to perform his tasks. The editor can then get feedback almost immediately from directors, actors, and others, no matter where they happen to be, and re-edit the 'film' to produce the final product. Long distances and geographical borders are simply not as important as they once were. This phenomenon holds true for many other specialists involved in film production, particularly those involved in the post-production phase.

(Department of Commerce, 2001: 4)

Production is the most important site of all for Hollywood's use of the NICL. Labour-market slackness, increased profits and developments in global transportation and communications technology have diminished the need for co-location of these factors, depressing labour costs and deskilling workers. This has been especially true of cinema and television in the period since 1980, when the compound annual rate of increase of screen production costs has well outstripped inflation. Newness is endemic to capitalism's propensity for continual disruption of production, a restless expansion-contraction-dispersion dynamic that sees companies move in concert with the revised social conditions they have helped to generate. This ultimately leads to raised worker expectations and hence a need for businesses to move on in order to avoid meeting those expectations. So rather than a national scale to economic growth, our model is based on three international foundations:

- first, a world centre (Hollywood);
- second, intermediate zones nearby of secondary importance (Western Europe, North America and Australia); and
- third, outlying regions of labour subordinate to the centre (the rest of the world) (Mattelart and Mattelart, 1998: 92).

How did this globalisation of the labour process come about? The standard argument about Hollywood's industrial history is as follows: the earliest film-makers modelled their organisation on theatres, but their financial backers, from vaudeville and the nickelodeons, wanted mass-production systems that could provide routines for getting films to the emergent immigrant audience. This encouraged standardisation via continuity scripts. Thus a quasi-artisanal, quasi-industrial system obtained in New York from the early 1900s until the wholesale shift to California in the 1920s (ironically, undertaken in part to elude the powerful eastern union movement, given the west's stature as an anti-union state, along with the fires and coal prices afflicting New York studios). Los Angeles was originally known as a 'citadel of the open shop' where wages were 25–50 per cent lower than New York. But following New Deal legislation, notably the Wagner Act, and the post-sound arrival of leftist actors and writers from Broadway, the Californian film industry unionised rapidly, culminating in pitched battles with the police after the war. The anti-labour work done by moral codification and Marxist-baiting, along with block-booking and the threat of relocation, have characterised struggles ever since, as workers have sought to obtain profit-sharing with each new market and technology (Storper, 1994: 200–01; Hozic, 2001: 56, 70–72, 75, 78–79; Milkman, 2000; Ross, 1947: 58).

From the 1920s to the 1940s, vertically integrated industrialisation took the form of a studio system that in some ways made and distributed films like car manufacturers made and distributed jalopies, through rationalised techniques of mass production, albeit with ancillary specialist industries, as per the classic norms of partitioned resources, with the latter responsible for innovation and the former for standardisation (Mezias and Mezias, 2000: 307, 320). One important caveat on the notion that Hollywood was a true Fordist production comes at the point of work. Films were made en masse, but the deskilling that manufacturing machinery forced on workers in allied sectors did not apply to the same extent in cinema, because many studio employees understood and participated at several points in the labour process, and their labour was not clearly substitutable as on a line. Many skilled workers surplus to immediate requirements were hired, much raw material was thrown away and there was social interaction across class barriers because of face-to-face interaction (Powdermaker, 1950: 169). The *Hollywood Reporter* of 1947 differentiated the industry from others: '[m]otion pictures are not an assembly-line mass-production enterprise like automobiles or prefabricated houses', because Hollywood relied on its instincts about public tastes rather than on technological innovation or financial wizardry (quoted in Powdermaker, 1950: 92).

In any event, during the 1940s the system was undermined by governmental trust-busting, televisualisation and suburbanisation: the state called on Hollywood to divest ownership of theatres, even as the spread of television and housing away from city centres diminished box-office receipts. The number of films released in 1956 was 28 per cent less than in 1946. In addition, blockbusters emerged as the route to large profits, and an ever-smaller proportion of films made money theatrically. The studios were said by some to have entered a post-Fordist phase of flexible specialisation at that point, through product differentiation and vertical disintegration that relied on:

- high-end genres, not B-movies, newsreels and short subjects;
- subcontracted independent producers, pre- and post-production companies and global locations, rather than comprehensive in-house services; and
- technological innovations designed to transform filmgoing from an everyday diurnal norm to a spectacular leisure event.

From the 1950s, the studios increasingly looked to independent producers for more differentiated films that reduced labour costs through the use of project contracts. Unions were now 'hiring halls'. Meanwhile, the made-for-television movie became a source of staple funding from the mid-1960s. The studios confronted unused lots and used-up libraries that TV no longer wanted, and when independents cut costs, these huge institutions increasingly began to appear like relics (Storper, 1994: 205–09). A property-based industry, where beds, bars and stars were 'owned' as assets, gave way to a knowledge-based environment, where skills and networks were key (Miller and Shamsie, 1996).

Short on profits but long on assets, in the 1970s the studios were purchased by financial and industrial conglomerates, a trend that has intensified since. These institutions show minimal interest in lifelong employment. They are focused on profit and practices across their concerns. Internationalisation and synergy are keywords, and subcontracting spreads risk across the workforce. Today, there are literally hundreds of multimedia production houses in Southern California, and most film and distribution businesses there employ fewer than ten workers. They add up to an interconnecting critical mass, a cluster of technology, labour and capital that operates through contracts with and investments from the studios, rather than ownership by them (Scott, 1996 and 1998a). The system works because of four factors:

1 flexible delivery of services by specialised companies
2 intense interaction between small units that are part of a dynamic global industrial sector
3 highly diverse and skilful labour; and
4 functioning institutional infrastructure.

When external shocks or internal reforms have threatened or shaken the industry, the unions have been crucial sources of stability, maintaining and developing compensation systems to ensure that minimum pay, individual negotiation and industry-wide residuals can all be encompassed – a highly innovative package that blends collectivity with individuality (Paul and Kleingartner, 1994). Today, major Hollywood screen unions include the American Federation of Television and Radio Artists (AFTRA), the Directors Guild of America (DGA), the International Alliance of Theatrical and Stage Employees (IATSE), the International Brotherhood of Teamsters, the Producers Guild of America (PGA), SAG and the Writers Guild of America (WGA). For all their differences and problems, between horizontal and vertical organisation and different material interests, their success through the dismal days of the 1980s and since stands as a beacon for labour across the country, proving that high levels of unionisation are compatible with innovation and expansion. IATSE has grown over the so-called post-union era to well over 100,000 members, while the DGA and the WGA have 12,000 each – all dramatic upsurges by contrast with the 1980s (Amman, 2002), even though employment can be as chaotic as pay (Wasko, 2003: 18–19). And many are immigrants.

The US film industry has always imported cultural producers, such as the German Expressionists. (Alfred Hitchcock used to reprimand Yanqui-hating Britons with '[t]here are no Americans. America is full of foreigners' [quoted in Truffaut with Scott, 1967: 54].) In the mid-1920s, a survey revealed that the leaders among camera operators, actors and directors included the following national origins:

SITE	NUMBER
Britain	60
Canada	26
Germany	23
Soviet Union	16
France	12
Sweden	11
Austria	10
Italy	7
Hungary	6
Japan	4
Mexico	3
Denmark	3
India	1
Argentina	1
China	1
Romania	1
Brazil	1
Poland	1
Czechoslovakia	1
Serbia	1
Switzerland	1
Turkey	1
Ireland	1

SOURCE: Adapted from Hays, 1927: 51

The conventional argument runs that three waves of immigration formed colonies in Hollywood, as Europeans fled poverty, fascism and state socialism (Langman, 2000). But as usual, Yanqui reasoning that sites the US at the centre of the rest of the world's dreams is as inaccurate as it is self-serving. Much of this personnel recruitment was a deliberate strategy to counter competitive industries in other countries. As one executive put it in the 1920s:

[W]e are trying to lessen sales resistance in those countries that want to build up their own industries. We are trying to do that by internationalizing this art, by drawing on the old countries for the best talent that they possess in the way of artists, directors, and technicians and bringing these people over to our country, by drawing on their literary talents, taking their choicest stories and producing them in our own way.

(Kent, 1927: 225–26)

This was a deliberate cultural policy, designed to ensure that Hollywood 'continued to fortify its world position by the acquisition of the outstanding talent of production abroad as rapidly as it appeared' (Ramsaye, 1947: 8). During his tenure as Valenti's pre-war predecessor, Hays referred to this as 'drawing into the American art industry the talent of other nations in order to make it more truly universal' (quoted in Higson and Maltby, 1999: 5). Nor was this benign in terms of the opportunities they received once they got there. One of the twenty Indian actors working in the US film industry in the early 1940s maintained that Hollywood frequently cast Chinese and Japanese actors in Indian roles (quoted in 'Ignored', 1941). And Antonio Gramsci referred to the 30,000 Italian women who, after hearing that *Ben-Hur* (Fred Niblo and Alfred Raboch, 1925) was to be shot there, sent photographs of themselves in bathing suits to Hollywood, as would-be 'luxury mammals' (1978: 306). The long-term trend in Hollywood is for the US to attract or otherwise exploit talent originally developed by national cinemas to compete with it. But while the industry has always been international, in the sense of hiring workers from different countries, its sense of what counts as its own face is severely restricted.

Our critique argues that Hollywood's hegemony is built upon and sustained by the internal suppression of worker rights, the exploitation of a global division of labour and the impact of colonialism on language – so Hollywood might fancy the not-too-threatening difference of a Pakeha New Zealand director who works in the US (Roger Donaldson) or a Scottish actor/British national

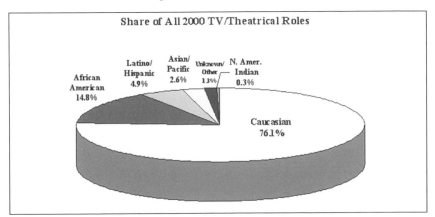

SOURCE: Screen Actors Guild, 2001

resident in Spain who works in the US and avoids British tax by a special deal that he limit his time spent there (Sean Connery) to the ready credentials of a USC alum (Hoskins *et al.*, 1997: 40–43; Tunstall and Machin, 1999: 18). When the European Audiovisual Observatory argues that casting Hollywood stars in partly European-funded and -set films enables the latter's 'reconquest of market share' (2003: 5), this reads like a fanciful gloss.

Attempts by the French film industry in the 1980s to bring in Hollywood investment may ultimately lead to US studio takeovers (Hayward, 1993: 385). Director Peter Weir's post-production for *The Truman Show* (1998) or *Witness* (1985) might take place in Australia, satisfying off-screen indices of localism in order to obtain state financing, but does that make for a real alternative to the US? What does it mean that Michael Apted, director of James Bond and the *7 Up* series, can speak with optimism of a 'European-izing of Hollywood', when Gaumont points out that 'a co-production with the Americans . . . usually turns out to be just another U.S. film shot on location' (see Chapter 3), and Guillermo del Toro turns the success of his Mexican film *Cronos* (1995) into a big-budget Hollywood career with *Mimic* (1997) ('Top', 1994; Apted quoted in Dawtrey, 1994: 75; Gaumont quoted in Kessler, 1995: n. 143; López, 2000: 434)?

In any event, cultural workers from other nations are subject to the Immigration and Naturalization and Judicial Naturalization Acts under the jurisdiction of the state, with union input. By the mid-1980s they formed the largest single group of temporary foreign workers admitted for special projects, though the overall numbers of 'alien cultural workers' and their classifications are not publicly available (Cherbo, 2001). Since the attacks of 2001, scrutiny of these applications has increased massively, as cultural workers from across the Third World find themselves targeted for additional surveillance via digital fingerprinting, photographing and interview, and visa-appeal processes are cancelled (Hostetter, 2004). Opera singers from Europe are increasingly deciding not to enter the US because of the way they are treated at the border, and there have been headlines across the globe about the experiences of Iranian filmmakers passing through (Verini, 2004). Again, it would be laughable to regard this as a free market in labour. The US is extremely protectionist. Politics, labour power and elite tastes are applied across such issues as Cuban artists, union arguments and operatic glamour. That charming word 'alien' occurs again and again in the legislation and the literature.

NICL exchanges were mostly one-way during the classical Hollywood era, although as early as 1938, when MGM was establishing a studio in Britain, unions in Los Angeles were expressing concern about job losses overseas, and in 1941, the Federal Government encouraged Disney to go offshore, in part to undermine striking workers. The decade from 1946 saw increased overseas production. Location shooting became a means of differentiating stories, once colour and widescreen formats became fashionable and portable recording technology was available. Studios purchased facilities around the world to utilise cheap, docile labour, and stars and directors were encouraged by the new post-war US tax system to set up production companies overseas, avoiding the cost of renting studio space in Los Angeles and paying pension and welfare-fund contributions. By investing in local industry, Hollywood avoided foreign-exchange drawback rules that prevented the expatriation of profits, simultaneously benefiting from host-state subvention of 'local' films (Townson, 1999: 9; Leff, 2000; Kehr, 1999; Smoodin, 1993: 147).

In 1949, there were 19 runaway productions. Twenty years on, the figure was 183, mostly in Europe. In 1957, the American Federation of Labor's peak industry body, the Film Council, issued a report revealing that in the eight years since 1949, of the 314 films produced by United Artists, MGM, Columbia and Fox, 159 (50.6 per cent) had utilised the NICL, mostly in Britain, Mexico, Germany, Italy and France. In 1960, a six-month strike sought royalties and fees from overseas revenue, while the MPAA rejected the concept of the runaway, arguing that TV work had substituted for the old-style studios and that overseas projects were better understood as 'supplemental international production', to quote Johnston's fine euphemism (these texts were also called 'American-interest' films). In 1960, Charlton Heston, one of the delightful people that SAG from time to time elects as its head prior to Presidency of either the country or the National Rifle Association, blamed fellow-workers for the runaways, asserting that the shift was due to the Screen Extras Guild calling for decent pay. Offshore production that year extended to 40 per cent of all features. Between 1950 and 1973, just 60 per cent of Hollywood films in production began their lives in the US, and foreign direct investment by the US in offshore production increased by a factor of five between 1977 and 1993. In 1984, 151 of Hollywood's 318 major features were runaways (Johnston quoted in Hozic, 2001: 96; Lev, 2003: 150, 149; Monaco, 2001: 11–12, 14; Ulich and Simmons, 2001: 358–59; Christopherson and Storper, 1986; Marvasti, 2000; Hozic, 2001: 79, 85, 93–94).

In addition to a danger to local labour, this also represented the decision by mercantile capital to loosen manufacturing-style organisation and industry in a return to the pre-Hollywood era. Producers had become subordinated to financiers and distributors. A 'company town' had become 'a global factory'. Concerns of time had become secondary to concerns of space. Both were subject to the rule of mercantile rather than manufacturing capital (Hozic, 2001: 93, 102–03).

Many of these texts were cheap and nasty compared to those shot at home. The aura of second-rate production is thematised in particularly stark form in a 1966 episode of the television programme *I Spy*, starring Robert Culp and Bill Cosby. 'The Trouble with Temple', itself shot offshore in the interests of a cosmopolitan look, is set in Spain, during the production of a downmarket

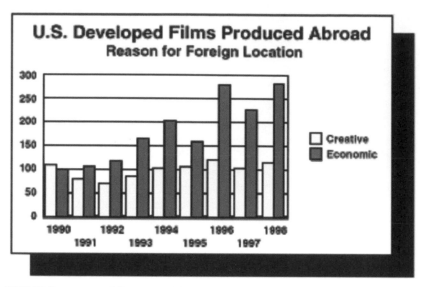

U.S. Developed Films Produced Abroad
Reason for Foreign Location

SOURCE: Department of Commerce, 2001: 26

Hollywood film. The movie features a producer-star derided by his female counterpart as an 'All-American boy with time snapping at his heels', who later turns out to be a traitor in 'real' life. As we shall see, this sense of runaway producers as disloyal has significant resonance today, when the opposition of creativity and economics continues to characterise reasons for shooting abroad.

It is estimated that 270,000 jobs in the US are directly involved in screen production. Many are in the below-the-line sectors, which are easily filled on the site of runaways by the NICL (Department of Commerce, 2001: 5, 10). As at January 2003, the US' Standard Industrial Classification identifies 150,000 such jobs in Southern California, divided between film and video (97,400), sound (7,800) and radio, TV and cable (44,400). But those figures exclude both ancillary work, such as entertainment catering, and the hyper-contingent labour of contractors who work freelance. The difficulty of gathering accurate data is exemplified in separate estimates from 1996 that calculated the Hollywood workforce as anywhere between 127,000 and 480,000 (Jim Bates, 2003). For the entirety of the US film industry, the Bureau of Labor Statistics estimates that nationwide in 2002 there were 259,000 people employed in production and services, 142,000 in theatres, 164,000 in retail rental and 18,000 in ancillary sectors, out of a total of 583,000, compared to 401,000 in 1992 (Motion Picture Association of America Worldwide Market Research, 2003: 27). While the runaway trend is still a relatively small threat to Hollywood workers when compared to plant closures and jobs moved overseas in sectors like textiles and apparel (Bronfenbrenner, 2000: 25), US entertainment unions fear that if the NICL expands, there will be further disemployment in

Average Direct Labour Hourly Cost by Country, 2001

Country	2001 Direct Hourly Rate (US$)
Germany	11.80
England	9.90
USA	9.60
Japan	9.05
Ireland	8.50
Spain	6.40
Mexico	3.25
Hungary	2.80
Singapore	2.60
Taiwan	2.05
Malaysia	1.30
India	1.25
Philippines	1.25
Thailand	1.20
Indonesia	0.90
China	0.85

SOURCE: Electronic Trend Publications

construction, hotels, catering, driving, carpentry and electrical trades. Across the 1990s, Southern California had lost 145,000 jobs as the aerospace sector was demilitarised (perhaps temporarily). Could something similar happen to Hollywood? In 2001, 12 per cent of the workforce, or 17,000 people, were disemployed as digitisation merged with risk aversion and recession (Parkes, 2002). In 2003, 7,500 more jobs were lost (Los Angeles County Economic Development Corporation, 2004: 59). Many losses were in advertising (to the recession), mini-series and made-for-television films (to Canada). The latter is a key sector in terms of regular production work for cable networks and training grounds for new workers. The NICL is also a source of concern for Hollywood workers. The US Federal Government first investigated runaway production in the 1960s, when a number of members of Congress proposed

labels that would identify films made in the US. In 1979, US animators went
on strike against runaways, achieving a contract clause that Los Angeles-based
unionists should be given first option on work. But producers blithely ignored
it, regardless of stiff fines (Lent, 1998: 240). With the advent of producers'
demands for special effects and the spread of the necessary technology and
skill across the world, job loss to fetishised segments of the labour process has
become a major issue, if less glamorous than fully-fledged offshore filmmaking. The proportion of feature budgets allocated to post-production has grown
from 13 per cent in 2000 to 25 per cent in 2002 (UK Film Council, 2003).

When we consider the past, present and projected future of California, and
Los Angeles in particular, the amount of wealth created might give pause before
lamenting the movement of jobs offshore.

But these figures cloak both technical and felt exploitation. This is no labour
aristocracy. Average 1999 earnings for actors in the film industry were
US$26,000, although the hourly wage of US$20.57 compares favourably with
private industry's overall average of US$13.44. Adding in all directors and pro-

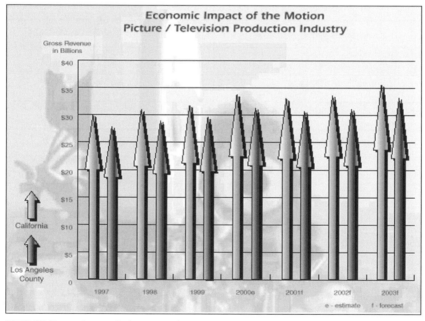

SOURCE: Entertainment Industry Development Corporation, 2001

ducers as well produced a mean 1998 salary of just US$27,400. Eighty per cent
of unionised actors in the US who make television commercials earn less than
US$5,000 per year in residuals, and a struggle over that issue in 2000 saw them
link with central labour councils in unprecedented ways that overcame
professional–proletarian divisions. Further up the pay scale, the strike over tele-

vision commercials drew donations to a fund from Britney Spears and 'N Sync (but found Tiger Woods filming Buick advertisements in Canada and Elizabeth Hurley also breaking the picket – although Hurley claimed she was unaware of the protest). The high level of offshore flight to make commercials suggested itself to many observers as a long-term union-busting strategy. SAG puts runaway production 'at the very top of our legislative and organizational agenda' (Gray and Seeber, 1996a: 34; Gray and Seeber, 1996b: 4, 7; Christopherson, 1996: 87, 105–06; Lauzen and Dozier, 1999; Wasko, 1998: 179, 184 n. 4, 185–86; Vogel, 1998: 75; Toto, 2000; Screen Actors Guild, 2000; Mallet, 2001; Bureau of Labor Statistics 2000b: 256; Cooper, 2000b; Association of Internet Professionals, 2000; Barrett, 2000; Department of Commerce, 2001: 17; Weller, 1999; Johnson, 2000; SAG quoted in Cooper, 2000a). In 2001, contracts for writers and actors were up for renewal, leading to what became known as a '*de facto*' strike, in that it never happened; however, so much production had been scheduled to avoid the period when industrial action was anticipated that there was a major slump in production and employment in 2002 (Los Angeles County Economic Development Corporation, 2004: 59).

For all the Clinton administration's boasts that information technology was responsible for a third of US job growth between 1995 and 2000, there has been no credible analysis of job losses in the sector over that period, or the loss of 'good' jobs that have been casualised and proletarianised into freelance employment (Anderson, 2001). The International Labour Office (2000b) suggests that 125,100 jobs were lost to runaway production between 1990 and 1998, mostly by below-the-line workers, and it is common for multimedia firms to supplement a small group of full-time employees with part-timers and freelancers on an ad hoc basis (Scott, 1998a: 150–51).

Runaway television and film production from the US amounted to US$500 million in 1990 and US$2.8 billion in 1998. By the end of the 1990s, the NICL was allegedly costing Los Angeles US$7.5 billion annually in multiplier effects, plus 20,000 jobs, with a further US$12.5 billion purportedly lost to the national economy through production and its multiplier effects gone from elsewhere in the country (Wicker, 2003: 461–62).

Hollywood's proportion of productions shot overseas in the last decade accelerated from 7 to 27 per cent, according to a study undertaken by the Monitor Group in 2000 for the DGA and SAG. Eighty-one per cent went to Canada out of a total of 232 in 1998 compared to 63 in 1990, and 10 per cent to Britain and Australia. This latest runaway trend depends on countries that have the right skills, language, familiarity, business links and foreign-exchange rates. It is a form of 'peripheral Taylorism', in that highly developed efficiencies are available from a skilled working class in places that nevertheless continue to import what is made on 'their' territory, but which is never under their control (Robles, 1994: 137, 151). The vagaries of foreign exchange are crucial. The Canadian, Australian and British currencies declined by between 15 and 23 per cent against the US dollar across the 1990s, with the Australian and Canadian dollars undervalued against it by as much as 35 and 15 per cent respectively in 2002 (Ulich and Simmons, 2001: 365; Center for Entertainment Industry Data and Research, 2002).

For both commercial and cultural reasons, governments see positive as well as negative implications in the NICL. Aware that 30 per cent of runaway budgets is spent on location, they seek ways to utilise the new internationalism to create or tend their own screen industries and tourism (Seguin, 2003). It is estimated that 250 jurisdictions vie for runaways (Gasher, 2002: 97), and between 1990 and 1998, thirty-one national film commissions were set up across the globe, many to attract foreign capital (Guttridge, 1996). For two decades, there has been an Association of Film Commissioners International, which publishes *Location Magazine* and convenes annual Location Expos in Los Angeles (Hozic, 2001: 87). These agencies' ambitions appear limitless: Fiji's Audio Visual Commission has a website that announces its intention 'to make Fiji the world's best country to produce and distribute audiovisual products' via 'the world's best tax incentives'. Toronto is abjectly promoted as 'any-city USA', while Israel promises 'a unique opportunity to cast actors and extras from its population representing ethnic types of Europeans, Africans or Asians of all ages and backgrounds' (quoted in Hozic, 2001: 88). They could find no Sephardim or Arabs? Meanwhile, Dollywood Studios recently opened in the United Arab Emirates. It was set up to permit workers from across the world to work on projects without restrictions, a 'neutral production house' whose avowed identity was post-national as a means of making Dubai 'the hub of [the] film industry' (Ahmed, 2003). Dollywood was the principal rival to the Egyptian Media Production City, established in the late 1990s as part of a Media Free Zone, by which was meant a zone free of taxes rather than the media, free of socialism (guarantees of no nationalisation) and free of censorship (for texts not shown in Egypt). For many years a hub of regional film, Cairo was being recast as a global centre of TV and commercial production as well. In late 2003, 'Hollywood of the East' was set to begin shooting Sylvester Stallone's co-produced television series *International Investigators Incorporated* (Kandil, 2000; Forrester, 2001; 'Sony-Led', 1997; Kamel, 2000; Helmi, 2003).

Proponents regard the NICL as a sign of successful post-Fordist flexible accumulation, whereby unions work with business and government to operate competitively in a tripartite heaven (Murphy, 1997; Shatilla, 1996). In other areas, the pharmaceutical sector looks to the film industry's labour exploitation and avoidance of risk as a model for its own pernicious development (Franco, 2002; Surowiecki, 2004). Other nations' screen industries, which are mostly built on policy responses to external cultural domination, may now, ironically, be enabling that domination, because they governmentalise and commodify locations as industrial settings of sites and services (Menon, 2001; Mokhiber and Weissman, 1999; Gailey, 2001). This de-localisation permits reterritorialisation in the lens of the foreigner, making Canada, for example, not 'Hollywood North' so much as 'Mexico North' (Gasher, 1995). So the *Lord of the Rings* cycle was made courtesy of a tax loss to the host government of NZ$217 million, which nevertheless wasted no time promulgating 'growth' figures to the effect that the local industry had grown sixteen-fold (NZ Institute of Economic Research, 2002). No wonder Billy Crystal made such fun of them on Oscar night in 2004.

Based on the key locations identified below, we shall now consider some case studies that address the role of the state in facilitating the leading players in the NICL, concentrating on Canada, Australia, Italy, the PRC, the Czech Republic, South Africa, India, Britain, Mexico and South-East Asia. The key question for us is whether, in the terminology of neoclassical economics, these nations are developing ongoing cultural capacity and impact, such as technical infrastructure and their own library, or just transitory supply responses to investment, like one-off enterprises that cater to foreign filmmakers (NZ Institute of Econ-

ESTIMATED BUDGETS OF HOLLYWOOD FILMS IN US$ MILLIONS AND SITES OF EXPENDITURE

SITE	1998	1999	2000	2001
Worldwide	**5,557.0**	**5,029.0**	**5,450.0**	**5,599.0**
US/Canada	4,357.0	3,966.0	4,387.0	4,291.0
%	78.4	78.9	80.5	76.6
Asia	47.0	105.0	131.0	117.0
%	0.8	2.1	2.4	2.1
Australasia	111.0	115.0	299.0	67.0
%	2.0	2.3	5.5	1.2
Eastern Europe	30.0	85.0	70.0	208.0
%	0.5	1.7	1.3	3.7
Mexico	269.0	85.0	3.0	65.0
%	4.8	1.7	0.1	1.2
Britain	486.0	450.0	245.0	414.0
%	8.7	8.9	4.5	7.4
RoW	49.0	132.0	39.0	0.0
%	0.9	2.6	0.7	0.0

SOURCE: Adapted from Center for Entertainment Industry Data and Research, 2002

omic Research, 2002: 2). The choice is between setting up one's own, dynamic bourgeoisie, or remaining locked in a dependent underdevelopment that is vulnerable to disinvestment.

Canada

Regarded as 'domestic' for the purposes of US theatrical box-office statistics, Canada has provided the raw material for hundreds of Hollywood stories (500 between 1910 and 1957), mostly shot in Los Angeles (Magder and Burston, 2001: 208). Perhaps they were the original runaways. Buttressed by First World money, physical proximity, English-language expertise, geo-historical variety, malleable unions, an infrastructure established through public broadcasting and filmmaking, major tax breaks, federal and provincial state subsidies and a frequently weak currency, Canada has become the centre of NICL struggles. Most runaways head there, where they are euphemistically referred to as 'service productions' (Canadian Film and Television Production Association/ Association des Producteurs de Films et de Télévision du Québec, 2003).

British Columbia hired Ivan Stauffer as its Los Angeles representative in 1971 to promote the province's 'unparalleled scenery' to the industry, but, of course, not 'to take away any production that could be done in Hollywood' – though he disingenuously stressed 'production costs are considerably less here' (quoted in Gasher, 2002: 70). By 1982, British Columbia was dubbed 'Hollywood North', with film commissioner Dianne Neufeld guaranteeing that it could double as 'Nowheresville, USA'. *First Blood* (Ted Kotcheff, 1982) branded it as a major destination (Gasher, 2002: 77, 81). But there were struggles before Canada could establish itself as the NICL's first production option. A 'Welcome to Hollywood North' symposium planned for Los Angeles in 1988 was cancelled, due to what one trade magazine termed 'lack of interest' (quoted in Acland, 2003: 163). But it was noted that US$200,000 paid for ten days of filming in Toronto, while Manhattan cost US$1.5 million (Augros, 2000: 135).

All this took place before the full impact of restructuring the Californian economy in the wake of Reagan's destructive deregulation and the Cold War's conclusion. In the contemporary moment, there is a clear link between the deregulatory policies adopted by successive US governments and the rush to Canada. Because major conglomerates have been permitted cross-media ownership in a way that would have horrified pro-competition reformers of the mid-twentieth century, they have been able to reuse texts across media and hence cut costs. To compete with this strategy, those premium cable channels that have limited other venues for reruns save money by shooting movies and series in Canada, cutting costs by as much as US$400,000 an hour (Wicker, 2003: 465). While Canada has moralised at every turn about the inalienability of culture in international fora, forming coalitions of cultural policy against US commodification, it has also mounted bad-faith arguments, since domestic policy has worked for massive media concentration, assisting accumulation by a small number of multinationals that otherwise would be hampered by the size of the domestic market (McDowell, 2001: 126). Enticements to runaway productions are part of this neomercantilist strategy.

Vancouver and Toronto are the busiest locations for North American screen production after Los Angeles and New York, due to exchange rates and tax rebates on labour costs. Whereas the minimum weekly salary of a US assistant director is US$3,285 for studio work and US$4,595 on location, the Canadian equivalent is US$2,927. Tax rebates and credits offset as much as 25 per cent of costs in Canada (Wicker, 2003: 469). Disney even announced its intention to set up an animation studio in Toronto in 1995 (Eberts and Norcliffe, 1998: 129).

Toronto has doubled as New York City in over one hundred films. When it played the role of Chicago in *Blues Brothers 2000* (John Landis, 1998), officials had the nerve to telephone the Chicago Film Commission for pointers, while producers boast their readiness to import trees in refrigeration trucks when there is a need to impersonate California. In television, *Due South*'s use of Toronto as Chicago was estimated to have saved 40 per cent in costs. The number of made-for-television movies lost to the NICL rose from 30 in 1990 to 139 in 1998, a 363 per cent increase. The US share of movies-of-the-week dropped from 62 per cent in 1994–95 to 41 per cent in 1999–2000, and 45 per cent of the genre was shot in Canada in 1998–99. Opponents are more concerned about this sector than the occasional high-profile features that are made there. Between 1998 and 2001, the number of US features shot in Canada increased from 23 to 39 (Wicker, 2003: 470–71). Of the 1,075 US-funded fiction films and programmes screened on US television in 1998, 27 per cent were filmed abroad, twice the proportion in 1990 (Coe, 2000; 'Culture Wars', 1998; Masur and Shea, 1999; Weller, 1999 and 2000; Entertainment Industry Development Corporation, 2001; Gasher, 1995; Grumiau, 2000; Connell, 2000; Center for Entertainment Industry Data and Research, 2002).

In 1999, Canada boasted 696 weeks of television film production, California just 152 (Department of Commerce, 2001: 31). The first six months of 2000 saw an increase in the value of film production in Toronto of 15.2 per cent on the corresponding period the previous year, to US$352.8 million (Brown, 2000). That year, runaways increased in value by 37 per cent on the year before (Wicker, 2003: 466). In 2001–02, Canada received C$1.76 billion in runaway funding from Hollywood, 51 per cent in Vancouver, 33 per cent to Montreal, and 10 per cent for Toronto (Seguin, 2003). There have been major declines in production since 1995 in several US sites (North Carolina down 36 per cent, Illinois down 20 per cent, Texas down 31 per cent and Washington down 37 per cent). But the two key Canadian locations' 1998 production slates, of just under US$1.5 billion, are well behind California's total of US$28 billion, which incorporated almost 70 per cent of US film production that year and 60 per cent of national screen employment. Expenditure on screen production in Los Angeles County was US$29.4 billion in 1999, and an estimated US$31.2 billion in

2000, with five times the number of shooting days of Toronto. In the twelve years to 1999, the number of culture-industry jobs in California rose by 137 per cent. And Canadian officials point out that while they represent 10 per cent of the world audience for US texts, only 3 per cent of film production takes place there (Kempster, 2001; Bates, 2000; Madigan, 2000; Monitor, 1999).

Canadian unions upped the ante in 1999 by agreeing to a 13–16 per cent pay cut plus a reduction in vacation and retirement pay and health and welfare benefits (Ryan, 1999; Brinsley, 1999; Madigan, 1999c; Swift, 1999; Brown, 2000; Department of Commerce, 2001: 19; Lowry, 2000; Center for Entertainment Industry Data and Research, 2002; Vlessing and Kiefer, 2003). Canadians argued that they were 'stealing peanuts from an elephant' (quoted in Wicker, 2003: 470). No wonder Norman Jewison preferred them to California crews, on the grounds that '[t]hey are still running, they don't walk' (quoted in Hozic, 2001: 116).

But the picture is becoming unstable in Canada. The advent of reality TV reduced US costs, as fewer workers were required for shorter periods, and most came from cable, an under-unionised sector of the industry. The short-term implications for movies-of-the-week, a Canadian staple, were dire (Jim Bates, 2003; Seguin, 2003; Rendon, 2004). At the same moment, the Canadian Federal Government rescinded its tax shelter for runaways. Toronto NICL employment was decimated in 2003 due to the outbreak of Severe Airborne Respiratory Syndrome, with the C$200 million runaway commercial industry halved. Then the Canadian dollar strengthened, ramifying the impact. The government's lone response was to increase wage tax credits for foreign productions from 11 per cent to 16 per cent (Whyte, 2003). Meanwhile, local critics were asking about the cultural value of this public support, when, for the first time, Toronto had seen more foreign than local production in 2000, with reduced money going to Canadian films, and a third of the Canadian industry's worth coming from off-shore. In Ontario, foreign productions accounted for 57 per cent of output in 2001 (Wicker, 2003: 488). Federal subsidies had increased for foreign investors, and decreased for domestic production (Vlessing and Kiefer, 2003). A cultural-

FEATURES SHOT IN THE US AND CANADA

	US				CAN			
	1998	1999	2000	2001	1998	1999	2000	2001
NUMBER	127	123	108	119	23	18	37	39
%	85	87	74	75	15	13	26	25
US$ BN	3.93	3.55	3.37	3.24	0.43	0.41	1.02	1.05
%	90	90	77	76	10	10	23	24

SOURCE: Adapted from Center for Entertainment Industry Data and Research, 2002

nationalist logic was under threat from a cultural-industries logic, a victory for EOI over ISI. Meanwhile, the Mounties, no longer key to Hollywood's iconography, reversed the relationship, signing a merchandising arrangement to be promoted by Disney (Wasko, 2001: 23).

Australia

Similar questions could be asked in Australia. *Kangaroo* (Lewis Milestone, 1952) and *The Return of Captain Invincible* (Philippe Mora, 1983) provide chronological and conceptual limit-cases of US screen investment in other film industries. *Kangaroo* was the first of several Hollywood features shot in Australia during the 1950s. 20th Century-Fox dispatched a crew and most of the cast, because its Australian-based capital reserves had been frozen to prevent foreign exchange leaving the country. Shooting took place in Zanuckville, obsequiously named to honour the studio head. A formulaic Western, the film failed, but then the need to use money lying idle was probably the sole reason for its production. Three decades later, *Captain Invincible* represented another outcome of the state's encouragement of foreign filmmaking. Taxation incentives designed to make Australian cinema more attentive to the private sector saw the local Treasury subsidising Hollywood to make a film set almost 'nowhere'. The text concerns a lapsed US superhero, played by Alan Arkin, who migrates to Australia and falls into dipsomania following McCarthyite persecution, reviving his powers and sobriety to thwart a villainous Christopher Lee. Recut by its producers following difficulties obtaining US distribution, the text was disavowed by its director and denied certification by the Australian government on the grounds that it was insufficiently local by comparison with its original script. A court challenge against this ruling succeeded, but the tax haven designed to boost commercial production was politically and culturally compromised from that point (Miller, 1998a). Nevertheless, the policy paradox of a cultural inalienability that can be governmentalised even as it is commodified and globalised remains central to film support (Australian Film Commission, 2002a).

When Dino De Laurentiis was choosing between Sydney and Queensland's Gold Coast as locations for a joint-venture studio with the Australian company Village Roadshow in 1987, one factor in the latter's favour was the A$7.5 million low-interest loan patched together by the then Queensland Film Corporation, which attracted A$55 million via a local share-issue (another was lax labour laws that enabled easy exploitation of children). De Laurentiis' company collapsed after the stock-market crash that year, and the space seemed destined to fail. Touted as a new Disneyland site or a multifunction polis, neither plan succeeded. But in 1988, a 150-day strike by the WGA over creative- and residual-rights payments led to a chronic shortfall in new programmes. Village Roadshow responded by refinancing its investment with Warner Bros. and seeking foreign business. The first major series shot on the Gold Coast was the

television show *Mission: Impossible* in 1988. The Queensland Film Development Office immediately advertised the state to prospective producers like this:
'the production company of a recent American primetime television series
found a diverse range of "international locations", from London to the Greek
Islands in Queensland'. Village Roadshow-Warner Bros. announced a studio
expansion in 1989 courtesy of a construction subsidy that became part of the
studios' promotional material. Well might the Queensland Tourist and Travel
Corporation refer to itself as the 'last frontier', replete with 'smiling locals'.
(Runaway workers from Hollywood call it 'the Mississippi of Australia'.) For
Stanley O'Toole, managing director of what later became the studio, Queensland was 'LA without the smog'. The studio came to be part-owned by Warner
Bros. and named Warner Roadshow. The Pacific Film and Television Commission, formed to promote the state to international and Australian
filmmakers, offers a revolving fund for low-interest loans secured against guarantees and presales, rebates on payroll tax and subsidised crewing costs (Miller,
1998a). In its fifteen years of operation, the studio has drawn NICL investment
from CBS, Viacom, ABC, Fox TV, Disney TV, Disney Channel, Fox and Warner
Bros., aided by Australian government tax credits on labour of up to 10 per cent
in its first decade (Hanrahan, 2000; Monitor, 1999). In 2003, Warners reduced
its commitment. Village Roadshow took over and, along with Greater Union,
assumed responsibility for their multiplexes. Roadshow was in major financial
difficulty by this point, with declining profits from production and its theme
park (Kay, 2003; Given, 2003: 51; 'Warner Bros. Exits', 2003; Frew, 2004). On
the animation front, Walt Disney Television Australia bought the successful
Hanna-Barbera company in 1989 and turned it into a site for making cartoon
series derived from films and direct-to-video texts that are conceived in the US
(Nightingale, 2001: 76–77). For its part, Fox built Sydney studios in 1998, again
with public assistance, and has hosted *Mission: Impossible 2* (John Woo, 2000),
Star Wars: Episode 3 (George Lucas, 2003) and *The Matrix Reloaded* (Goldsmith
and O'Regan, 2003: 90). In 2004, new studios opened in Melbourne, again with
massive public subvention ('Docklands', 2004).

Total runaway production to Australia increased an average of 26 per cent
across the 1990s. In 1990–91 one foreign feature was shot in Australia; in
2001–02 the number was seven, while runway and co-produced television
increased from six projects to eleven and local employment trebled (Given,
2003: 52–53). By 2001, the local audiovisual sector was worth A$1.8 billion, of
which A$325 million came from offshore (Gailey, 2001). That year, the balance
of domestic and runaway feature production changed. Just 8 per cent of local
movies had budgets of more than A$6 million, whereas the corollary number
for overseas investments was close to 50 per cent (European Audiovisual Observatory, 2002: 19). Half of all screen expenditure in Australia across 2001 and
2002 was foreign (European Audiovisual Observatory, 2003: 19). From 2002,
the Federal Government gave an offset of 12.5 per cent to foreign production

after pressure from US studios (Wicker, 2003: 480–81; Groves, 2002a) and sought to organise post-production companies to meet the desire for fragmented production across countries (Goldsmith and O'Regan, 2002: 3). It also established a body named Ausfilm, resident in Los Angeles, which is charged with promoting the NICL (Department of Commerce, 2001: 50), but the government was holding out against pressure to open the offset up to television ('Hollywood Downunder', 2004). There are now business opportunities for Australian managers who reside in Los Angeles and promote Australian crew and talent to US producers of TV commercials looking to save by shooting offshore (Huck and Gurvich, 2003).

The shooting of high-profile movies like *Mission: Impossible 2* and *The Matrix* (Andy and Larry Wachowski, 1999) in Australia saw savings on LA prices of up to 30 per cent – not to mention the fact that US$100 million of their budgets was German and US$12 million came from Australian tax incentives (Waxman, 1999; Zwick, 2000; Ulich and Simmons, 2001: 361). At 2002 prices for actors, for example, the appeal was clear even before subsidies and exchange rates.

Rich McCallum, co-producer of the *Star Wars* sequels in production in Australia, prefers it to Hollywood, which 'represents everything repugnant ... it's so unionized'. He and his colleague George Lucas like Australia so much that 'I made the commitment to two films', a sign that '[t]his isn't rape and pillage'

CONTRACT ITEM	AUSTRALIA	HOLLYWOOD
Daily pay	A$400–30	A$635
Royalties	Zero before profit	Guaranteed
Daily shift	10 hours	12 hours
Pension contribution	8 per cent	13.5 per cent

SOURCE: Coslovich and Zion, 2002

(McCallum quoted in Fitzgerald, 2000). Warner Bros.' President of Production Lorenzo di Bonaventura put it somewhat less brashly but with equal condescension: 'They are very embracing' (quoted in Ulich and Simmons, 2001: 361). Such neediness has seen Hollywood producers refer to Queenslanders as 'Mexicans with mobiles', which has become a sore point with the local Screen Directors' Guild (quoted in 'Australia', 1998; Fitzgerald, 2000). Runaway moguls also adore the lack of worker solidarity through demarcation. As Columbia Pictures executive Scott Siegler put it: 'You don't hear anyone saying "I don't pull cables, I only move cameras"' (quoted in Hozic, 2001: 116). Of course, not all jurisdictions are keen to be exploited. The producers of the television series *Baywatch*, then screened in 144 countries, decided to move to Australia in the late 1990s (prior to its relocation, this time diegetically as well as physically, to

Egypt). Australian beaches are public property, and residents of Avalon in Sydney protested when their local politicians offered to sign the space over. But Queensland's Gold Coast was ready to help out ('Baywatch', 1999; 'Egypt's Censorship', 2003).

Like Canada, the film-making skills available in Australia derive from long-standing cultural policies parlayed into capital accumulation. Consider the Grundy Organisation. It produced Australian television drama and game shows from the 1950s that were bought on licence from the US. Then the company expanded to sell such texts across the world, operating with a strategy called 'parochial internationalism' that meant leaving Australia rather than exporting in isolation from relevant industrial, taste and regulatory frameworks. Following patterns established in the advertising industry, it bought production houses around the world, making programmes in local languages based on formats imported from Australia that had originally drawn on US models. From a base in Bermuda, the organisation produced about fifty hours of television a week in seventy countries across Europe, Oceania, Asia and North America, until its sale in 1995 to Pearson for US$280 million. This exemplified the NICL offshore – a company utilising experience in the Australian commercial reproduction industry to manufacture US palimpsests in countries relatively new to profit-centred television. The benefits to Australia, where a regulatory framework had generated this expertise by requiring the networks to support such productions as part of cultural protection, are unclear. As Greg Dyke, the Pearson executive responsible for the Grundy purchase and later the head of the BBC, proudly put it, the typical Grundy programme *Man O Man* 'has no redeeming social values' (Cunningham and Jacka, 1996: 81–87; Moran, 1998: 41–71; Short, 1996; Stevenson, 1994: 1; Tunstall and Machin, 1999: 30; Dyke quoted in Short, 1996).

Australian state apparatchiks see the NICL providing impressive signs of foreign investment, acting both to stimulate and validate local actors in the industry. But at whose cost? For screen-industry unions, globalisation is double-edged: employment from runaways is available, but so is 'cultural oblivion' (Gailey, 2001). The Australian situation resembles the classic relation of dependency for comprador bourgeoisies, whose power is finally undermined by cultural policy. And that link is always conditional. The Australian Federal Government's 2002 offset did not apply to TV series, the staple for large studio spaces, and this saw a drop-off of more than 50 per cent in US TV shot there, as well as doubts about new studios planned in Sydney. A combination of risk aversion after 9/11 and changing exchange rates was doing its work. For all the claims made by the government that other factors attracted runaways, the exchange rate was crucial (Australian Film Commission, 2002b; Phillips, 2003). Having dropped 33 per cent between 1997 and 2002, by the end of 2003, the Australian dollar had strengthened against its US equivalent, from 50 to 70 cents. The result was predictable: the Mexicans with mobiles were in crisis

(Bodey, 2003; Australian Film Commission, 2002b; Quinlivan, 2003; Mitchell, 2003). Meanwhile, in new bilateral trade talks, Washington was seeking the removal of local-content TV rules, which gave 30 per cent of screen time to local drama, but seemed satisfied with its 94 per cent domination of the local box office (Day, 2003). The eventual Free Trade Agreement was trumpeted from the Australian side as 'Protecting Australian Voices' (2004) and from the US as 'important and unprecedented provisions to improve market access for U.S. films and television' ('US and Australia', 2004). Critics viewed it as a triumph for the US overall (Beams, 2004), while Australian arts ministers agitated over what the deal really meant for the media ('SA Premier', 2004).

But there was something positive. *The Matrix* series was providing rich material (off-offshore) for *The Meatrix*, a short flash animation that features a youthful pig waging the battle for survival on a factory farm. The text offers links to alternatives to unsustainable anti-animal brutality. Would that Australian energies were headed in this direction instead of masquerading as the US of the future.

Italy

Italy has a long history of runaway production – in the 1920s, several Hollywood studios had post-production facilities there (Nowell-Smith *et al.*, 1996: 2). But Mussolini's gradual adoption of anti-US cultural politics restricted business for many years. As part of post-war reconstruction, the government enacted a Cinema Law in 1949 that guaranteed screening time to locally made films (as had been the case from the 1920s until Allied occupation), but otherwise did little by way of cultural protection. Although this aspect of the legislation was observed more in the breach than the observance, the law also required that revenue from Hollywood releases remain in Italy, which encouraged US expenditure on plant and production. The majors invested in the state-owned studio Cinecittà and began co-productions, with skilled crews and fresh locations an additional means of sweetening what was effectively mandated investment. In the early 1950s, following the making of *Quo Vadis?* (Mervyn LeRoy, 1951), the studios were attracted by blocked accounts and docile labour. Stars moved to Italy, independent producers sought new settings and US workers denied employment at home because of their leftism were welcomed. Jules Dassin, John Berry, Michael Wilson, Cy Endfield, Bernard Vorhaus, Joseph Losey and Ben Barzman all worked in Italy, along with Welles, Huston and Robert Rossen, in what became known as 'Hollywood on the Tiber'. In all, twenty-seven Hollywood films were produced in Italy between 1950 and 1965, and by 1960, most of Italy's 114 features had some US investment or participation (Nowell-Smith *et al.*, 1996: 5, 140; Seguin, 2003; Muscio, 2000: 120–21; Bono, 1995; Monaco, 2001: 14).

It was said that *Roman Holiday* (William Wyler, 1953) jump-started US tourism to Italy, and other well-known films with extravagant on- and off-camera narratives included *Beat the Devil* (John Huston, 1954), *Alexander the Great* (Robert Rossen, 1956), *Ben-Hur* (William Wyler, 1959), *Lawrence of Arabia* (David Lean, 1962) and *55 Days at Peking* (Nicholas Ray, 1962). Italy became a luxury site of excess, as immortalised in Fellini's *La dolce vita* (1960), culminating with *Cleopatra* (Joseph L. Mankiewicz, 1963), which ran so far over budget during four years of production that it became legendary, not least thanks to Italian Communist Party boycotts against the film's depiction of slaves. Its financial difficulties (ninety-six hours of footage costing US$60–90 million) and rising labour costs saw the end of 'Hollywood on the Tiber'. Redemption came in the late 1960s with the 'Spaghetti Western', which used Italy and Spain as stand-ins for Mexico and California, and featured US television stars such as Clint Eastwood. They provided a way back into the world market until producers were perturbed by the Red Brigades, then seduced elsewhere by post-state socialist privatisation, while Italy's deregulation of television produced a tabloid effect that cut into film production, employment and skills (Weil, 1998; Hozic, 2001: 98, 100; Bodo, 2000).

In the 1990s, Cinecittà was mostly a site for television production, along with some features, such as *The English Patient* (Anthony Minghella, 1996), *Daylight* (Rob Cohen, 1996), *Titus* (Julie Taymor, 1999), *The Talented Mr Ripley* (Anthony Minghella, 1999) and *U-571* (Jonathan Mostow, 2000) (Vivarelli, 2003), plus a new twist on runaways: Hollywood idols who eschew US television commercials as signs of failure, but appear on Italian television promoting products for huge sums, with sturdy guarantees that they not be broadcast at home. Brad Pitt (jewellery), Kevin Costner (footwear), Harrison Ford (cars), Marlon Brando, Leonardo DiCaprio and Woody Allen (telecommunications), Richard Gere (sweetmeats) and Sharon Stone and George Clooney (alcohol) all made appearances in 2000 (Lyman, 2000), adding huge advertising costs to the price of Italian consumables, and sending the money offshore.

Following restructuring in 1997, when it was partially privatised, Cinecittà built new sound stages, developed digital imaging and became a theme park. Television commercials stars were not alone in the new century. The government established an Italian Film Commission in Los Angeles (Goldsmith and O'Regan, 2003: 104). Miramax looked for cheap local texts to form the new genre Miramaxizzazione (Coletti, 2000), Martin Scorsese shot *Gangs of New York* (2002), Lucas filmed parts of the second *Star Wars* prequel and Mel Gibson's creepy-Christian *The Passion of the Christ* (2003) was produced at the studio, thus eluding Hollywood union wages and capitalising on the convention that screen workers should work between fifty and fifty-seven hours a week before overtime, with their pay set in relation to budgets rather than skills and relativities (Horst, 2002; Hancock, 1999; Seguin, 2003). And as an answer to Lucas' two-year-old taunt to Scorsese, 'why didn't you just use a computer?'

(quoted in Harford, 2003), Cinecittà opened a new digital facility in 2001. Meanwhile, systems of state subvention were revised to discourage art cinema and attract private investment (Rooney, 2002).

The PRC

For racial, linguistic and political reasons, China has not been a key locus of Hollywood runaway productions, but there are signs that the situation is changing, as is the case in so many other offshore industries. The first Shanghai movie studio was founded by a Yanqui in 1909, and in 1926, the American-Oriental Picture Company was formed. It planned to make films in China for sale there and in the US, utilising cheap labour, exotic scenery and a history of drama. But the Second Civil War and the War against Fascism shut down production from 1927, and Hollywood came to look on the country as an export location only (Ye, 2003: 13) (for which see Chapter 5).

The 1949 Revolution was met with intense hostility from the US that lasted over two decades and precluded political-economic relationships. On China's side, the bad experiences with the Soviet Union and doubts about neocolonialism turned it away from technological exchange and towards a mostly ISI form of planning, albeit with some foreign, but non-Yanqui, participation. Fears built up that nearby imperialist wars would develop into a project of invasion. Once the US finally recognised that governmental and economic relations with China were not so terrifying, and the fortress mentality of Beijing leaders changed with the passing of the Cultural Revolution, there was a quick turn towards EOI and the encouragement of private investment. The Gang-of-Four catch-cry 'Better Socialist Weeds than Capitalist Rice' was replaced with Deng Xiaoping's slogan, 'It Doesn't Matter Whether the Cats are Black or White, as Long as They Catch Mice' (Sklair, 2002: 244, 246, quotations at 251).

The first major Hollywood studio production shot in the PRC was Spielberg's 1987 film *Empire of the Sun* for Warner Bros., a Second World War epic set in Shanghai (Welkos, 1999). Facilitated by the China Film Co-Production Corporation (CFCC), the official entity coordinating and supervising foreign production in China, the Shanghai Film Studio provided both above- and below-the-line crew, ranging from the art director to prop men as well as production facilities. Parts of Shanghai in 1987 resembled its appearance during the 1940s, which diminished the cost of re-creating the past and offered authenticity. But skilled and inexpensive labour was also a key attraction, and thousands of Chinese extras were used for the invasion and battle scenes. At the same time, it may be significant that *Empire of the Sun* took in 75 per cent of its box office outside the US (Augros, 2000: 158–59). The film was able to enter China only as an import, labelled an 'assist-production' to differentiate it from a co-production. This remained the format for a very small number of Holly-

productions in China through the late 1990s. In 1991 and 1992, shot two relatively small films in China with the assistance of the Beijing Film Studio: *The Amazing Panda Adventure* (Christopher _, and *M. Butterfly* (David Cronenberg, 1993). In the case of the former, pandas from a local circus were used, and location shooting took place in Sichuan, where panda preserves fitted both storyline and scenery. A large part of the latter film was shot on location, because the Beijing Opera was crucial to a plot set in 1960s China.

At this time, Sony Pictures TriStar became the first studio to appreciate the market potential of Chinese-language films, not only in Asia but throughout the world. It launched a Hong Kong-based production unit in 1998 as part of the studio's long-term localisation strategy to produce and acquire local Chinese films for global distribution, yet with an eye particularly on Chinese and culturally proximate audiences (Welkos, 1999).

Through Mandarin-language projects like the US$15 million *Crouching Tiger, Hidden Dragon* (Ang Lee, 2000), co-invested and co-produced with China's Huayi Brothers and Taiye Film Investment Co., as well as United China Vision of UK, Sony Pictures TriStar enjoyed access to the otherwise-restricted Chinese film market. In 2002, Miramax filmed key scenes from John Dahl's US$40 million Second World War epic *The Great Raid* in Shanghai. This provided the second location for the film after Australia, which was disguised as 1940s colonial Philippines (the latter having been passed over for fear of terrorism) (A. Jones, 2002). The science-fiction TV series *Flatland*, starring Dennis Hopper, was also shot in Shanghai in 2002, aimed at both East and West television markets (Cummins, 2003).

Quentin Tarantino's *Kill Bill* (2003) marked the first occasion that China was disguised as another place, in this case, Japan. Cheap labour and a relatively weak exchange rate were the biggest draw, representing a half or a third of US costs. Moreover, the control exerted by the government over daily life makes the filmmakers feel secure, an added attraction compared to other Third World Asian locations. With most of its production crew and cast recruited from China, and Beijing Film Studio sound stages providing the set for much of its two-month shooting in the country, *Kill Bill* benefited from significant cost savings. A publicist explained the decision to replace skilled Japanese swordsmen with Chinese extras once their characters had died: 'They're dead on the floor, so we don't need to pay so much' (quoted in Chang, 2002a: B1). This gave the production team flexibility in their filming schedule and allowed them to shoot the action sequences via stunts rather than the machine-facilitated or computer-simulated segments that are typical of Hollywood productions. This added authenticity as well as an exotic, Far Eastern flavour (Brogan, 2002). The absence of unions in China meant that the crew often worked fourteen-hour days, six days a week. By contrast, SAG rules stipulate a twelve-hour break for actors between two successive shootings (Chang, 2002b).

Post-production has generally been done in Thailand or Australia, with special effects completed in Hong Kong and the US, but now some computer work is being undertaken on-site (Brown, 2003). Immediately after gaining its independence from Britain, Hong Kong had set up a Film Services Office to attract digital post-production ('Hong Kong', 2002). Though still falling short of the digital post-production infrastructure of some well-established film-making centres, China has witnessed a significant leap forward in the skills and experience of film professionals in recent years. In 2003, for the first time, high-technology post-production work on Hollywood productions was completed in China (Brown, 2003). Coupled with the country's low labour costs and appeal as a potential highly lucrative market, the PRC looks set to become a key NICL site. Unlike other places where this has occurred, the size of the Chinese audience, and the latter's unfamiliarity with Hollywood, means that this latest location for labour exploitation may at least generate some culturally specific films, rather than becoming yet one more site of commercial despoliation. On the other hand, the disciplining voice of US capital will always be ready to speak: 'Yesterday they had 900 school kids wandering around in the back-ground. We were promised that they would curtail activities. They will be hearing from us about that' (Marty Katz, producer of *The Great Raid*, quoted in A. Jones, 2002).

The Czech Republic

Under state socialism, Czechoslovakia had stunning success as a film centre, pro-ducing many classics at its famous Barrandov Studios, and attracting occasional foreign productions, such as *Amadeus* (Milos Forman, 1983) (Farnam, 2002). In some ways, it represents the 'Washington Consensus' at work on-set, since the Czech Republic was the first post-Soviet state to embark on mass privatisation, which was pushed through against popular objections by claims that it merely restored private property to its rightful owners (Earle and Gehlbach, 2003). Of course, the Czech Republic is often cited as an instance of privatisation without mass unemployment. But that story hides major declines in labour-force par-ticipation (Gitter and Scheuer, 1998) and political opposition. The decision by the government to sell 75 per cent of the studios was opposed by the local film-makers' union, who pointed out its illegality – the process was begun in 1991, two years before the passage of a law ending the state monopoly on filmmaking. In 1994, directors who called for retention of a national cultural policy were told 'Don't even think about it' by Prime Minister Vaclav Klaus, under whom domes-tic films dropped to 2 per cent of the studio's output. Such world-renowned artists as Jiri Menzel and Vera Chytilova were excluded from filmmaking altogether (Hames, 2000). The detritus of state socialism, public investment in plant and skill, left Prague a capitalist screen centre, not a cultural one.

One of privatisation's architects, Michael Millea, joyously recounts a visit to Prague with the US Agency for International Development (USAID), where he found that 'the former Czechoslovakia was carpetbagger heaven' (1997: 489), with five hundred skilled below-the-liners, eleven sound stages and on-site laboratories waiting to serve. Millea may have been referring to Hollywood filmmakers, but of course he was the carpetbagger wonk in this story. The plan to privatise was predicated by USAID on data about US studios that correlated favourable exchange rates and comparatively low budgets with decisions to shoot offshore. Based on the Agency's projections, the successful tender proposed translating Barrandov's output from nationally framed texts to US ones, extending even to converting studio space into shopping centres and hotels for visiting crews. The competitor, a plan drawn up by filmmakers that favoured domestic production, was rejected by USAID. Millea concludes his memoir with the triumphant observation that the shooting of the first *Mission Impossible* (Brian De Palma, 1996) film in Prague indicated how 'capitalism has taken firm root in the Czech Republic' (1997: 504).

The 'firm root' immediately fired 85 per cent of Barrandov's employees, despite the fact that labour was 40 per cent cheaper than in Los Angeles – in 2001, for example, union painters were paid less than US$3 an hour, while extras 'commanded' US$15 a day, as opposed to Hollywood's US$100 ('Hollywood on the Vltava', 2001; 'Hollywood Cashes', n. d.; Hejma, 2000; Holley, 2000). A studio manager boasted in 2000 of 'one artist working on set-building for the last two months who's been earning about as much in a week as his British counterparts earn in a day and he just happens to be a famous Czech sculptor', while a non-union workforce meant that injuries to locals did not require compensation (quoted in l'Anson-Sparks, 2000) – hence their doing the stunts for *Titanic* that DiCaprio cared to avoid (Farnam, 2002). The eventual buyer of Barrandov, Moravia Steel, did not invest in plant (relying instead on stages built when the Nazis were in occupation), and so cultural forces within the nation have called for a re-nationalisation (MacMillan, 2003a; Farnam, 2002).

Stillking Films and Milk and Honey Films, two international film-production service companies with ties to US and British clients, facilitated an influx of commercials in the mid-1990s, followed by television-movies, mini-series and feature films. Six of the seven majors shot there in 1999–2000. Productions include the mini-series *The Scarlet Pimpernel* (a BBC and A&E co-production), *Dune* (Sci-Fi Channel), *Mists of Avalon* (TNT) and *The Candy Bomber* (HBO), along with several features: *Messenger: The Story of Joan of Arc* (Luc Besson, 1999), *Dungeons and Dragons* (Courtney Solomon, 2000), *The Bourne Identity* (Doug Liman, 2001), *Blade II: Bloodlust* (Guillermo del Toro, 2001), *Hart's War* (Gregory Hoblit, 2002), *Bad Company* (Joel Schumacher, 2002), *XXX* (Rob

Cohen, 2002) and *Shanghai Knights* (David Dubkin, 2003), complete with a Big-Ben simulacrum (Meils, 1998, 2000a, 2000b and 2000c; Klein, 2003; Connolly, 2002). Del Toro returned in 2003 to film *Hellboy*, and DreamWorks arrived that year for the first time (MacMillan, 2003b and 2003c). *Blade II* spent US$15 million of its US$70 million budget in Prague, where local films were in production for less than US$1 million (Farnam, 2002). Well over sixty Hollywood films have now been made there.

Meanwhile, every conceivable disused relic of state socialism has been refitted for film, from hangars to sports grounds (Connolly, 2002). The industry claims that the NICL has had a fourfold multiplier effect on the national economy, because Yanqui filmmakers spend US$200 million each year while in town (MacMillan, 2002). The local government bids Hollywood a supine welcome, via such paradoxical cultural policies as permitting producers to set off fireworks in the downtown area in the middle of the night, but diverting air traffic for several hours in the interests of 'quiet on the set' (Krosnar *et al.*, 2001). The NICL facilitates the free movement of screen capital into cheap production locations, contains labour mobility and undermines labour internationalism – all brokered on the exploitation of skills and facilities developed under state socialism.

Since the entry of the Republic into the EU in 2004, US filmmakers have looked to move on in order to elude the worker protections and other restrictions that would follow expectations of that system (Krosnar *et al.*, 2001). The city council responded by reducing location fees by 75 per cent (MacMillan, 2002), and companies rushed to create new post-production facilities that would permit fibre-optic links to LA and London (Meils, 2002–03). It may be significant that Romania, which offers foreigners major film subsidies, docile workers and space owned by American Central European Media Enterprises, was selected to re-create the US Civil War in *Cold Mountain* (Anthony Minghella, 2003) (Seguin, 2003; Farnam, 2002; Dragomir, 2003) – unless you can believe the director's remarks made on ABC's *20/20* that he could find no part of the southern US that 'had not been touched by the twentieth and twenty-first century'. Perhaps Prague will retain one comparative advantage as it runs its skilled workers into the ground in a paradigm case of 'de-development', of socialism gutted by neoliberalism (Meurs and Ranasinghe, 2003): the city's Archbishop now offers filmmakers use of his palace exterior for just US$1,000 (Connolly, 2002). But word is out that Wesley Snipes and his colleagues were drawn to make *Blade II* not by the city's baroque and Gothic monuments, but its empty warehouses (Sorrosa A., 2001).

South Africa

Although sub-Saharan Africa was the setting for some runaway productions that used 'authentic locations' in the 1950s, such as *King Solomon's Mines*

18-DAY MOVIE BUDGET	EXCLUDING CONTINGENCY & BOND	24-DAY MOVIE BUDGET
USA		**South Africa**
100,000	Rights	100,000
275,000	Producer	275,000
175,000	Director	100,000
900,000	Cast	750,000
1,450,000	**TOTAL ABOVE THE LINE**	**1,225,000**
162,667	Production Costs	70,000
196,000	Art, Set & Dress	110,000
53,333	Set Operation	30,000
50,000	Special Effects	30,000
150,000	Props & Picture Veh.	120,000
96,000	Wardrobe	40,000
40,000	Make-up & Hair	10,000
80,000	Electrical	70,000
70,000	Camera Department	70,000
26,667	Sound Department	14,000
206,000	Transport Unit	90,000
175,000	Location	125,000
86,667	Film & Processing	86,667
1,392,334	**TOTAL PRODUCTION**	**865,667**
232,000	Editing	120,000
55,000	Music	55,000
65,000	Post-Sound	50,000
50,000	Post-Laboratory	50,000
402,000	**TOTAL POST PRODUCTION**	**275,000**
65,000	Insurances	35,000
120,000	General Expenses	85,000
185,000	Total Miscellaneous	120,000
$3,429,334	**TOTAL**	**$2,485,667**

(Compton Bennett and Andrew Marton, 1950), *The African Queen, The Snows of Kilimanjaro, Mogambo* and *The Roots of Heaven* (John Huston, 1958) (Lev, 2003: 150–51), the continent has only become a key site fairly recently. South Africa is the only sizeable country in Africa with the appropriate infrastructure to attract the NICL. Following the overthrow of apartheid, its first major Hollywood runaway was *The Ghost and the Darkness* (Stephen Hopkins, 1996) (DeWayne, 2002: 67). Costs are 30–40 per cent below the US and Europe and 20 per cent less than in Australia. This encouraged entry to the NICL, along with the Los Angeles Consulate-General of South Africa's guarantee that 'Union activity in the industry is low key' (www.link2southafrica.com). The trend began with commercials: 182 were shot in South Africa in the year to March 1997, up 40 per cent on the previous year, with major governmental subvention. By 2002, the number was 1,000, generating US$187 million in investment (Grumaiu, 1998; Department of Commerce, 1997; 'Africa's Hollywood', 1997; Guider, 2001; 'Telenovela de Caracol', 2001; Moore, 2002).

At 2002 prices, film workers making US$550 a day in LA or US$290 in Vancouver received US$165 in the Cape. ScreenAfrica (screenafrica.com) advertises the following comparison, in association with Film Afrika and Sasani Limited. The figures on page 154 compare the eighteen days it takes to film a made-for-TV movie in the US with a twenty-four-day shoot in South Africa.

Cape Town doubles for Toronto in Canadian beer commercials, and its residents rent out their homes to film crews for a week, which pays for three months' mortgage, while happy young householders in Johannesburg and Durban are now in line for the same benefit, and white pensioners find themselves in demand as extras (Nevin, 2002). The exploitative nature of the NICL is nowhere better evidenced than in a continent desperately in need of investment, where a country of segregated wealth is the sole site of appeal to Hollywood. Watching the output and the government's promotional materials, 'it is easy to forget that South Africa is a predominantly black nation' (Moore, 2002). The Cape Town Film Office, the KwaZulu-Natal Department of Economic Development and Tourism and the Gauteng Film Office all look to attract music videos, commercials, game shows and mini-series from the North, offering as incentives a weak Rand, experienced workers – and perhaps a safari, for that post-shooting experience that exoticises what is otherwise disguised as familiar terrain.

With the NICL in full swing, the Apollo Awards, the nation's principal film festival, did not select a Best Feature Film in 2002 (Nevin, 2002). At that very moment, Gauteng Film Office bureaucrat Themba Sikebo avowed that she was trying to 'co-opt local film-makers into formalising the industry by taking an aggressive stand and marketing the province to the international market . . . The Johannesburg CBD [central business district] could easily be the backdrop for a European city' (quoted in Nevin, 2002). Again, there can be no better indication of how dependent development limits cultural expression.

India

Despite India's image of cultural independence from the US, the Biograph Company and other firms shot newsreels there from 1911. Universal established the first Hollywood studio in India in 1916, and producer-director Ezra Mir served a five-year apprenticeship at Universal Studios in the US, learning about editing techniques and screenwriting before returning to India (Mahmood, 1980). But for decades, India stood largely on the sidelines of the NICL, primarily because of perceived inadequacies in the technical infrastructure of the domestic film industry. As the distributor J. P. Jhalani noted in 1947 on a trip to the US with producer/director Mehboob Khan, 'if a reciprocal agreement could be made with some large American company to help us build up our studios and equip them with the best American facilities, it would be of material benefit to both our countries' (quoted in Fox, 1947).

Post-independence India followed a different path to assimilation into the global economy from the PRC, but it was equally complex. Committed to a multicultural blend of religions under the sign of secular nationalism, and to economic development through ISI, capitalism was mostly welcomed, but with a view to the germination of local industry, local bourgeoisies and public-service enterprise, sometimes via nationalisation. Low growth rates up to 1980 led to a rethinking of the equation of development and secular nationalism and to a movement into world capitalism via deregulation by the 1990s that was tied domestically to an emergent Hindu nationalism – for all that it was as much the outcome of IMF evangelism (Rajagopal, 2001: 35–42). This is the backdrop both to the development of the Indian screen and its new prospects as a NICL site.

In 1965, it was understood that between the major Indian film-production centres of Bombay, Calcutta and Madras, only five to seven studios could handle the demands of foreign producers. Hollywood studios interested in Indian co-production edited Indian footage in the US and added post-production effects in London. Herbert Coleman, who arrived in India in early 1967 to direct the television series *Maya* for MGM and NBC, noted that, despite the absence of 'script supervisors, special effects men and ... western-oriented makeup men and hairdressers', India was an attractive place for US media companies because of blocked funds and low production costs (Coleman, 1975). Co-production agreements, such as the low-budget location shooting production deal struck between Mark Druck and Bombay/Calcutta studios, were drawn up in the mid-1970s. With the US guaranteeing global distribution, story and cast approval lay with the Indian co-producers. Druck stressed that the Indian 'company will provide personnel and services to cover below-the-line elements', while the films will 'be American in story, treatment, completion and music'. The Rank Organisation also expressed interest in using blocked funds for the production of British films in Asia and buying Indian films for distribution in the West, in return for wider distribution of British film in India (Pelegrine, 1976; 'Rank', 1976). Blocked funds became available, subject to script and story approval by the government (*Nine Hours to Rama* [Mark Robson, 1963] was banned). Blocked funds were used to film parts of Spielberg's *Close Encounters of the Third Kind* (1977) outside Bombay. With the industry dubbing sound in post-production, stars booked years in advance and laboratories backed up for weeks – making daily rushes an impossibility – Western co-productions needed to be flexible (Weatherall, 1978). In 1975, India's total investment in studios and laboratories was around US$65 million, with a workforce of about 25,000 people. Yet Hollywood took note of the fact that out of nearly sixty studios and laboratories, only a few run by state governments provided facilities for outside producers on a for-hire basis ('60 Studios', 1975).

The release of *Gandhi* (Richard Attenborough, 1982) sparked interest in Indian location shooting. Two British television serials – *Jewel in the Crown* and *The Far Pavilions* – utilised India, as did David Lean's *A Passage to India* (1984). A Lean festival was held at the Chanakya theatre in Delhi in 1985, with proceeds going to the Prime Minister's Relief Fund. But the weighty bureaucratic system – including the required script, income tax, customs and foreign-equipment clearances from a number of different agencies – turned away producers as well, notably Spielberg, who shot *Raiders of the Lost Ark* (1981) in Sri Lanka instead (Sethi, 1984).

Despite the success of India's film industries, some domestically and others internationally (notably Bollywood, plus auteur art cinema), the early 1990s liberalisation of the economy via a shift from ISI to EOI and its large numbers of highly trained engineers and programmers has latterly seen a turn towards Hollywood that is more precise and targeted than other NICL standard-bearers. At the 2002 Cannes Film Festival, the Minister of Information and Broadcasting noted that 'there is more to Indian creative talent than snake charmers and monkeys', and 'we have a new generation of directors who understand that the outside world is watching. This in turn is reflected in what appears on screen' (quoted in Frater, 2002). The cultural momentum of deregulation peaked in 2002 when foreign companies were permitted to invest in local media (Callahan, 2004).

In 2003, an Indian media and technology seminar featured talks on India's potential as a 'major back-end operations hub for animation and special effects, with rushes of mega-budget films shot in the US and the UK being outsourced to India for processing and editing' ('Hollywood May', 2003). While the Western European and Japanese film industries had considered India as a NICL site in recent years, the commercial digital-graphics sector was especially interested in providing editing and other post-production work (including digital animation and computer-generated images, compositing, colour correction and digital sound) for big-budget, effects-intensive Hollywood features. Graphics studios in Bombay and Madras, and information-technology laboratories in Bangalore and Hyderabad, had already undertaken post-production work for *Independence Day* (Roland Emmerich, 1996), *Men in Black* (Barry Sonenberg,

1997), *Titanic, Gladiator* (Ridley Scott, 2000), *Nutty Professor II: The Klumps* (Peter Segal, 2000) *Swordfish* (Dominic Sena, 2001) and *Spider-Man* (Sam Raimi, 2002). As digital post-production technologies integrated into larger commercial film industries worldwide, and special effects shifted from being markers of science-fiction film (see McQuire, 1999), Indian special-effects studios jostled for position in the globalisation of contracted film labour.

According to the National Association of Software and Service Companies (Nasscom), outsourced work provided by Indian companies like Crest Communications, FX Factory, United Television, Toonz Animation India, Maya Entertainment, Ramoji Rao, Western Outdoor and Pentamedia Graphics will account for US$1.5 billion in animation revenue by 2005. Many of these digital media companies had consolidated their position within the domestic Indian market by riding the wave of computer-led graphics in the 1990s, designing commercials for Indian cable-television channels and marketing portfolios for the fashion industry. For Indian graphics companies with significant stakes in digital animation, however, international outsourcing extends beyond TV and fashion. Indian multimedia firms are becoming internationally recognised sites for 'video and TV programs, commercial advertising, corporate presentations and films, gaming consoles, interactive CD and DVD presentations ... architectural walkthroughs [and] forensic analyses' (De, 2002).

Hollywood studios and multinational firms like Sony, Apple, Kodak and Silicon Graphics are increasingly drawn to the comparatively low costs of Indian multimedia. Silicon Graphics, for example, whose Maya animation and special-effects software suite is used extensively by Hollywood majors, has continued its Indian expansion, even as the company pulls back from other locations because of economic downturns (particularly in the US). Compudyne Winfosystems gained a US presence when it acquired the US media company Digital Arts Media and has done work for a number of Hollywood spectaculars. It claims that Indian 'artistic traditions in this country are so ancient, so we draw on that' (quoted in Sharma, 2003).

But Hollywood draws on them as well. Undercutting the redemptive alignment of cultural heritage with international outsourcing, Pentamedia completed the three-dimensional animation for *The King and I* (Richard Rich, 1999) and *Sinbad: Beyond the Veil of Mists* (Evan Ricks, 2000). A key NICL player, Pentamedia occupies 10,000 square feet of Hollywood, connected to its Madras digital-imaging studio by a dedicated satellite Internet link. The Hollywood office focuses on pre- and post-production, acts as Pentamedia's 'cultural antenna and interface with the US film industry' and specifies up to 60 per cent of the total production work done in India (Seneviratne, 2002; Guha, 1999). Commenting upon the company's opportunities in Hollywood, its chair fears that 'our people still draw an "Indian" face rather than an "American" face when they work on films for US markets. We will have to adjust' (quoted in Merchant, 2001).

The Confederation of Indian Industry designated 2002–03 the 'Year of Multimedia', in recognition of NICL success. The Indian graphics, animation and digital-media industry is currently valued at about US$600 million dollars (expected to grow to between US$5 and 15 billion by 2008), while post-production is estimated to be worth over US$100 million. Currently, about US$300 million is outsourced to India and other South-East Asian markets by Hollywood studios, only a small part of the US$8 billion software NICL. Still, animation outsourcing in India is valued at US$100 million and growing by 200 per cent per year (Sharma, 2003; Nagaraj, 1999; Seno and Mitton, 2001; De, 2002; Subramaniam, 2003). This growth is directly related to cost savings for the international media producer. Animation costs about US$70–100 per hour in India, a third of the US rate. Senior animators earn US$100,000 a year in the US, US$50,000 in South Korea and about US$12,000 in India. A recent Nasscom study shows that the average cost of production for half an hour of animated television in the US or Canada is US$250,000–$400,000 versus US$60,000 in India (Seno and Mitton, 2001). However, the Indian chapter of the International Animated Film Society (ASIFA) notes that although there are over 250 animation and new media companies in the country, India is 'generally seen by the international animation community as an emerging animation resource . . . one with serious quality and delivery issues that must be overcome' ('Welcome Note', 2002). As a consequence, animation outsourcing to India continues to feature predominantly two-dimensional animation and labour-intensive clean-up tasks for three-dimensional work.

In 2002, another newly formed Indian trade organisation, the Animation Producers Association of India, was charged with capturing a greater share of the NICL. In addition, the Indian chapter of ASIFA joined the Federation of Indian Chambers of Commerce and Industry (FICCI), which had been formed in 1927 to consolidate the gains made by counter-colonial agitation to open industry to greater Indian management and participation. FICCI commissioned a report from the now-defunct Arthur Anderson, who did the work for free in the hope of special consideration, as Indian media companies looked to Yanqui tax and auditing firms when a new corporate accountability movement began (interestingly enough, another US firm that provides auditing support for the Indian film industry, Ernst and Young, issues an annual guide to international production, and recently began sending tax returns to its Indian office for processing). The 2000 FICCI report laid out global opportunities for Indian media, noting the increased export potential of cinema beyond diasporic audiences in Britain, the Gulf and the US. The Indian government had granted 'industry status' to the domestic film trade in 1998, which opened it up to tax, investment, insurance and other financial considerations previously reserved for manufacturing and other service sectors. Breathlessly extolling the virtues of foreign exchange, tax revenue and international media partnerships that bolstered skilled job creation, the report maintains that

'Indian as well as American analysts estimate that' the country's share of the NICL can 'be given a big boost in view of India's strong technical human capital foundation and growing reputation' (Federation of Indian Chambers of Commerce and Industry, 2000: 28). A number of companies, from Disney to News Corp, disclosed plans to build film studios in India. Fox announced a US$100 million partnership with a major Indian steel magnate to open a film and TV production centre in Bombay in 2000, after Murdoch was assured speedy clearance from the chief minister of the state.

With the reconceptualisation of Indian labour as a post-production service hub, the continuing development of the graphics business has become a primary concern for technocrats and policy advocates alike. Alarmed that there were an estimated 15,000 people in digital content and only about 1,000 animators in 2000, one advocacy group suggested that India would need 300,000 professionals in the fields of animation and digital content by 2008 (De and Glancy, 2001). Not surprisingly, calls for the construction of new training facilities have increased. Such facilities encourage local industries to invest in digital media training, while opening up opportunities for foreign investment and the formation of trade associations to represent the industry internationally. Indian students interested in the special-effects industry are bombarded with press accounts of the nation's proud place in transnational work. Successful stories of knowledge exchange and migration – widely circulated on the Web (see Chakravartty, 2001) – certify the attractiveness of transnational labour to young Indian students. For example, on the heels of glittering accounts of wealthy expatriate Indians in the US software industry, particularly Yogesh Gupta at Computer Associates, the graphics training industry was buoyed by the success of three Indian animators who were part of the team that won an Oscar for *Shrek* (Andrew Adamson, Vicky Jenson and Scott Marshall, 2001) (they subsequently left India for graduate work in the US).

Britain

Runaways really began in Britain. When the government introduced legislation in 1927 via a Quota Act that mandated cinemas show a minimum number of local films, US studios responded by investing in what became known colloquially as 'quota quickies', paying small British companies to make dross that the studios' distribution arms would release. The poor quality of these texts ensured that there was no effective competition for imports, thus beginning a long history during which UK film policy was used by Hollywood to further its interests (Blair and Rainnie, 1998). Post-Second World War runaways began thanks to Britain's 1948 Anglo-American Film Agreement, which required the majors to leave US$40 million a year of their receipts in blocked accounts (Nowell-Smith *et al.*, 1996: 139). Even after its abandonment, later state incentives continued to encourage runaways via the Eady Levy, which reinvested a proportion of theatrical revenue into British production, again 'inviting' Hollywood to use the money to make films in Britain – 105 between 1950 and 1957 (Lev, 2003: 153). By 1956, a third of British films involved the US, and the figure soared to two-thirds across the next decade, many produced at MGM's studio there (Monaco, 2001: 14). Between 1949 and 1961, Britain accounted for over a third of US runaways (Hozic, 2001: 95–96). The Levy also became a way of utilising Hollywood's reserve army of domestic labour, as superannuated actors and technicians were dispatched to Britain to make the 'quickies' (Greenwald, 1952: 42). Later on, films like *Superman II* (Richard Lester, 1980) and *Flash Gordon* (Mike Hodges, 1980) cashed in on similar measures designed to encourage local production, but much post-production went on elsewhere (Hill, 1999: 36 n. 18, 43).

In order to keep British studios going while avoiding such misuse, regulations were promulgated in the mid-1990s that meant films entirely made in Britain counted as British, regardless of theme, setting or stars. This meant that *Judge Dredd* (Danny Cannon, 1995) with Stallone was 'British', but *The English Patient*, whose post-production work was mainly done abroad, did not qualify. Until 1998, 92 per cent of a film had to be created in Britain. At the end of that year, the government reduced this requirement to 75 per cent to attract Hollywood (Woolf, 1998).

The government's decision to float the pound and free the Bank of England from democratic consultation contributed to a situation in 1998 where a strengthening currency raised costs for overseas investors and encouraged locals to spend their money elsewhere, with severe implications for offshore film funds. But a 100 per cent tax write-off is now available for film and television production, provided that most crew members are EU citizens and half the equipment is owned by British firms. Failure to qualify under these terms may still mean eligibility for a lease-back scheme, whereby a local company buys the film rights then leases them back to the producer. There is also a production-equity tax break (Department of Commerce, 2001: 72; 'Soft Money', 2002) and public investment in infrastructure. Between 1997 and 2002, the Hertsmere Borough Council spent £10 million renovating Elstree Film Studios (Goldsmith and O'Regan, 2002: 4).

On the labour front, the long-term strategy of successive governments since 1979 has been to break up unions within the media in order to become a Euro-Hollywood by default: the skills generated in a regulated domain of the screen – TV – would be retained without the 'inefficiency' of the so-called 'X-factor' – labour. In short, 'flexibility' has supplanted wage stability, with non-union negotiations conducted at a highly individual level, and texts oriented towards export. Associated deregulation has produced a proliferation of networks and the inevitable search for cheap overseas content. As a consequence, the UK now has a negative balance of screen trade for the first time in its history (Cornford and Robins, 1998: 207–09; Hancock, 1999; Ursell, 2000). Contracts for production workers frequently exclude provisions for overtime, travel, public holidays, sickness benefits and mutual-fund contributions, and require Dickensian work hours (Blair and Rainnie, 1998).

The UK Film Council International (until 2003, the British Film Commission) markets production expertise and locations by providing overseas producers with a free service articulating talent, sites and subsidies, and runs a national network of urban and regional film commissions. The government also opened a British Film Office in Los Angeles to normalise traffic with Hollywood by offering liaison services to the industry and promoting British locations and crews. Its priority is 'to attract more overseas film-makers' (Hiscock, 1998; British Film Commission, n. d.). The London Film Commission promotes the capital to overseas filmmakers, arranges police permits and negotiates with local residents and businesses. Its defining moment was the first *Mission: Impossible* film, when the Commissioner proudly said of that film's Hollywood producers: 'They came up with all these demands and I just went on insisting that, as long as they gave us notice, we could schedule it' (Jury, 1996). Lest we forget. After all, the trailer for the movie could not be differentiated from Macintosh's 'Mission: Impossible. The Web Adventure' television commercial until their respective punch lines: either 'Expect the Impossible May 22 1996' or 'Your mission, should you choose to accept it, begins at http://www.mission.apple.com'. Commodification undertaken in the name of local culture saw seven Hollywood movies account for 54 per cent of expenditure on feature-film production in Britain in 1997.

Five years later, Alan Parker, Film Council maven and Hollywood director, declared that the industry would 'die slowly like a frog in a saucepan' without more state aid to draw in Hollywood, because 'the brutal age of global capitalism' would not countenance local British cinema ('Bond', 2003; Parker, 2002). How dramatically different this is from Keynes' address to the nation when he inaugurated the Arts Council in 1945: 'Let every part of Merry England be merry in its own way. Death to Hollywood' (quoted in Mayer, 1946: 40)! Localism had become a problem, not a virtue. According to David Bruce:

> Location shooting by overseas companies in 1995 ... [was] at a record level
> and Scotland would be appearing on screen in its own right, or doubling for
> somewhere else, all over the world. (Someone said that had there been a 1996
> Oscar for 'best supporting country' Scotland would have won.)
>
> (1996: 4)

Some of this lust for attention becomes quite heinous, as when the Liverpool Film Commission advertises itself internationally as 'a lookalike for ... Nazi Germany, and cities of the Eastern bloc' (Afilm.com, 1998).

The looming threat of strikes by actors and writers in Hollywood in 2001 meant that British studios and post-production facilities were heavily booked as offshore union-busting sites. Utilisation of post-production and special effects as well as studios and film production increased by over 30 per cent in 2000, thanks to US investment (Richard, 2000; Gibbons, 2000; Department of Commerce, 2001: 49; 'Film Production Soars', 2001).

As part of a contest with other nations to attract HBO's *Band of Brothers* project in 2001, Tony Blair, who had depicted his government as the vanguard of a new, 'creative', 'cool' Britain, intervened to repeal lease-back laws (Wicker, 2003: 480). As with all such dependent relationships, the investment is highly contingent. The number of films produced by Hollywood in Britain fell from thirteen to three in 2001, before recovering to six in 2002, with investment dropping from £418.9 million to £200 million, before rising to £267.8 million for films and £133.8 million for co-productions. The recovery was due to investment in large productions, notably *Die Another Day* (Lee Tamahori, 2002) and *Lara Croft Tomb Raider: The Cradle of Life* (Jan de Bont, 2003). Again, the problem of a reliance on the kindness of strangers appearing with extravagant feature requirements marked a major structural weakness in the industry that left it vulnerable to shifts in the political economy (European Audiovisual Observatory, 2003: 37; 'New Film Council', 2003). The reaction was to devise new work conditions that would necessitate seventy-two-hour weeks, no guaranteed overtime pay, basic wages and smaller crews (Minns, 2002). Meanwhile, 2002 saw an end to FilmFour, Channel Four's innovative financing system.

However, film investments in Britain doubled in 2003 on the previous year, stemming in large part from growth in co-productions, which comprised 102 of the 177 'British' films made in 2003 (Jury, 2004). But in response to what one commentator described as 'carpetbagging foreign producers raiding Treasury coffers', the Department of Media, Culture and Sport raised the minimum investment in co-productions for Canadian participants to 40 per cent from 20 per cent. Of the fifty British-Canadian co-productions made in the three previous years, only three would qualify under the new revenue requirements. The most prolific co-producer of such films, Spice Factory, warned that lower-budget films would migrate to less parsimonious nations such as Belgium. Other financiers argued that the new standards would only create safer subject matter (Adler, 2003d). Clearly, the policy field in Britain had been split between supporting producers or distributors, even as it remained committed to attracting runaways (Canadian Film and Television Production Association/Association des Producteurs de Films et de Télévision du Québec, 2003).

Mexico

The US has been a crucial participant in Mexican filmmaking for sixty years. The '*Época de Oro*' of the 1940s and 1950s was built on the Second World War infrastructure provided by the US to encourage anti-fascist, pro-US propaganda (Robinson, 2000). Most notably, Mexico City's Churubusco Studios were built by RKO, Emilio Azcarraga (founder of Televisa) and Harry Wright in the 1940s as a place where RKO could invest in the local industry and reap the benefits of the continental *hispano-hablante* market (Tegel, 2001b). In the 1960s and 1970s, auteurs such as John Huston and Sam Peckinpah filmed in Mexico for the scenery, and Richard Burton, Elizabeth Taylor and their attendant paparazzi turned Puerto Vallarta into a tourist destination (Tegel, 2001a). Durango was the site for over a hundred Westerns and genre films in the same decades, because it had non-unionised workers, and in the 1980s, *Dune* (David Lynch, 1984), *Under the Volcano* (John Huston, 1984), *Predator* (John McTiernan, 1987), *Licence to Kill* (John Glen, 1989) and *Total Recall* (Paul Verhoeven, 1990) were shot there, but runaway productions shifted as other locations vied for studio attention and complaints grew about bureaucracy, extortion and skill levels (Berg, 1992: 215; 'Hollywood Heads South', 2000; Bensinger, 2002: B4).

Mexico again became a key site for offshore production following the success of *Titanic*, the refurbishment of Churubusco and the establishment of a National Film Commission in 1995 with satellites across the country's thirty-one states, offering everything from trips in governors' helicopters to many other, less exotic, services (Bensinger, 2002: B1; Tegel, 2001b and 2002). Restoring Mexico to the Hollywood map gained James Cameron the Order of the Aztec Eagle from a grateful government, which offers docile labour, minimal bureaucracy, a weak peso, many US-trained technicians and liaison services. The National Film Commission's website states that almost 3,000 foreign productions were shot there between 1995 and 2002, from airline commercials to *The Mask of Zorro* (Martin Campbell, 1998) and *Romeo and Juliet* (Baz Luhrmann, 1996), which saved 35 per cent on Italian prices. Plans have been announced for a new runaway studio in San Miguel de Allende, a favoured retirement spot for Yanquis that also has a new golf course in development. There will be six sound stages, putting it beyond anything else in the country, and without the urban life of Mexico City to disturb anxious Anglos ('San Miguelwood', 2004).

Local workers on *Titanic* in Rosarito, a maquiladora sixty miles south of the border that became Fox Baja Studios and then the theme park Foxploration, reported horrific levels of exploitation and mistreatment, as the state forced out a leftist union in favour of management stooges. Mexico's new film 'union' even maintains an office in Los Angeles to reassure anxious industry mavens of its cooperativeness and to remain up to date on US pay rates – in order to undercut them (Sutter, 1998a and b; Swift, 1999; Bacon, 1999, 2000a and b). In the words of Film Commissioner Sergio Molina, extolling the virtues of local workers permitting the importation of LA expertise: 'The local unions have made themselves very flexible in the past few years. It's all negotiable now' (quoted in Bensinger, 2002: B4). Tony Mark, the producer of HBO's *Starring Pancho Villa as Himself* (2003) put it this way: 'They are prepared to bend over backwards for us. How could you not be impressed by that?' (quoted in Tegel, 2002). How indeed?

Pearl Harbor, Kung Pow: Enter the Fist (Steve Oederkerk, 2002) and *Master and Commander: The Far Side of the World* (Peter Weir, 2003) are among the runaways to Fox Baja (Goldsmith and O'Regan, 2003: 106). In 1999, a union carpenter in Hollywood earned US$275 for eight hours. A union carpenter in Mexico earned US$216 for fifty-five hours. 'Mexico is becoming a "maquiladora" for movies of the week' (Riley, 1999), in the same way that it is a low-cost cross-border site for automobile assembly. It even offers non-*mestizaje* Mennonite extras, to compensate for the fact that otherwise, 'the people look different' (Riley, 1999). When Durango stood in for Texas in TNT's *King of Texas* (2002), it was actually a nice reversal of Yanqui imperialism's violent annexations, and Arizona and Sonora now coordinate efforts to attract film investment (Bensinger, 2002: B4). Little wonder that despite his florid anti-runaway rhetoric as a candidate for the governorship of California, Arnold Schwarzenegger shot several films in Mexico, including *Collateral Damage* (Andrew Davis, 2002). Good deals inevitably attracted the rodents of Disney, who began their first Mexican film in 2003 via a joint venture with Admira from Spain, while Warner Bros. mounted productions with Coyoacan Films, and Televisa's Videocine and Columbia TriStar co-produced films for Mexico itself (de la Fuente and Goodridge, 2003).

The Mexican (Gore Verbinski, 2001) was partly shot in Real de Catorce, the first location in San Luis Potosí used by Hollywood. Much was made of the fact that the production invested US$10,000 on new water pipes and to tap a spring in an abandoned mine – doubtless so that its stars Brad Pitt and Julia Roberts would have the best *agua* each morning – and that the local grocer's sales increased 20 per cent during filming. Meanwhile, construction workers were paid US$12 a day to match Pitt and Roberts' US$40 million salaries (Pfister, 2000). Two years later, *Master and Commander*'s producers obtained an IATSE contract that dissident members saw as an outrage. It mandated the exposure of US workers in Mexico to occupational and safety risks without danger money, and stipulated special conditions below US standards ('Masters Command', 2002; 'IATSE', 2002).

Not surprisingly, Rupert Murdoch (1998) cites approvingly the number of European workers invisibly employed in the making of *Titanic*: 'this cross-border cultural co-operation is not the result of regulation, but market forces. It's the freedom to move capital, technology and talent around the world that adds value, invigorates ailing markets, creates new ones.' How ironic that the workers submerged at the end of the credits (or not listed at all) should 'owe' their livelihoods to a boat sunk by invisible ice and business hubris, and that the continuing livelihood of people in Popotla has been endangered by *Titanic* – since the production, the local catch of fish has declined by one-third because of Fox's chlorination project (Pfister, 2000). It was also revealed that the overall cost of the film could have provided safe drinking water to 600,000 people for a year (Elsaesser, 2001: 17). Meanwhile, National Public Radio reported that Rupert's very own Fox company was asking the Mexican government to offer financial incentives for runaways (broadcast of 24 March 2000), and the

privatisation of the film industry during the 1990s had decimated local production (Riley, 1999). The majority of post-production was completed over the
border in San Diego (Goldsmith and O'Regan, 2003: 106), and by the mid-
1990s, Mexico City had lost its monopoly on dubbing English-language
television into Spanish to Los Angeles and Miami – the latter, of course, an anti-
union, 'right-to-work' jurisdiction, as well as a cosmopolitan cultural *entrepôt*
driven by the subsidies we mentioned in Chapter 1 (Sinclair, 1999: 165; Augros,
2000: 135; Mato, 2003). Nevertheless, US-based Spanish-language television
networks frequently produce voiceovers for commercials in Mexico via high-
quality phone lines, to utilise non-union labour (Porter, 2000).

The present conjuncture is a screen testimony to NAFTA, which has seen the
average number of offshore productions in Mexico per year increase from seven
to seventeen as the shipment of film stock and special-effects equipment is facilitated, especially for low-budget productions (LaFranchi, 1999; Riley, 1999),
while local production spiralled downwards, from 747 films in the decade prior
to the Treaty, to 212 in the decade since (Ugalde, 2004). The NICL's cold contingency was wreaking its usual havoc.

East Asia

In addition to these national formations, regions are also becoming part of the
Hollywood atlas, advertising cost-cutting measures and favourable exchange
rates as they strive to displace the Anglo white-settler colonies and Britain as
NICL locations. The adoption across the 1990s of an Asia-Pacific Information
Infrastructure policy features references to diverse content that promise cultural distinctiveness, but it is largely an attempt to restrict textual flow (via
copyright) and enable labour flow (via deregulation) (Sum, 2003). The outcome thus far has opened the sector to foreign capital. In 2004, Vietnam, South
Korea, Malaysia, Japan, Russia, Indonesia and China (not all from this region,
of course, but all parts of Asia) formed the Asian Film Commissions Network
to engage in joint marketing (Paquet, 2004). They had much to build on that
had already been done to join the NICL.

Animation, for example, is frequently undertaken in South-East Asia by
employees on much lower pay than US workers (who still do well, because
deregulation created so many dedicated-genre US television networks). There
are 239 major producers spread across 39 countries, with 90 per cent of the
world's television cartoons made in Asia, from *The Simpsons* to *Ninja Turtles*.
Manila's studios produce half an hour for US$120–160,000, whereas the US
cost is US$300,000. The equipment can now be bought for the price of a car.
Even the US Public Broadcasting Service sends cartooning offshore. It is sometimes claimed that high-technology changes to the craft have repatriated work
to Southern California, but South-East Asian nations are constantly upgrading
their equipment and downgrading labour as the storing of images, scanning,
modelling, lip-synching and so on becomes much easier. The prediction is that

2004 will bring the region a third of all computer-animation revenues (Vogel, 1998: 72; 'Asia's Toonville', 1997; Lent, 1998; 'Animation', 2001; Freeman, 2000: 2, 9; Scott, 1998a: 147; Jagannathan, 2002; Holson, 2003a).

In the feature sector, Columbia Asia is shooting texts for the regional market (Kay, 2002). RSVP Film Studios advertises the Philippines as 'a non-union town where labor is delightfully inexpensive' and 'filming 16 hour days is not uncommon' (Woods, 1999b; Monitor, 1999; Pendakur, 1998: 229; Brown, 2000; RSVP, n. d.), although producers have to deal with the fact that 'Filipinos like to eat regularly ... None of this six hours work and then you have lunch at midnight' (DeWayne, 2002: 75). But despite that cultural 'oddity', labour has proven very malleable, with actors' salaries massively depressed. Productions often relocate there as a means of securing good distribution of US film through partnerships with comprador media elites (DeWayne, 2002: 228). The Philippines is now a hub for labour-intensive two-dimensional animation, and in addition to partnerships with Yanqui companies like Hanna-Barbera and Walt Disney Productions, Filipino studios are providing outsourcing services to Canadian, European, Japanese, Korean and Australian media producers. Local production has halved in a decade of 'openness' (Prelypchan, 2003).

Thai environmental and pro-democracy activists publicised the arrogant despoliation they witnessed when Fox was making *The Beach* (Danny Boyle, 2000) in Maya Bay, part of Phi Phi Islands National Park. Natural scenery was bulldozed in late 1998 because it did not fit the fantasy of a tropical idyll, sand dunes were relocated, flora rearranged and a 'new' strip of coconut palms planted. The producers paid off the government with a donation to the Royal Forestry Department and a campaign with the Tourism Authority of Thailand to twin the film as a promotion for the country. Meanwhile, following the next monsoon, the damaged sand dunes of the region collapsed, as the land's natural defences against erosion had been destroyed by Hollywood bulldozers. All the while, director Boyle claimed the film was 'raising environmental consciousness' among a local population that was allegedly 'behind' US levels of 'awareness' – typical Hollywood arrogance, and especially idiotic when there was no US legislation capable of handling the environmental scandal, which was dealt with in overseas litigation where proper laws and precedents existed, via the local Environment Act (Justice for Maya Bay International Alliance, 2000; Ghosh, 2003; Flanigan, 2002: 84). Thailand formed a Film Commission in 2003 – not to prevent despoliation, but to encourage the NICL, along with changes in taxes levied on foreign actors and corporate income-tax 'holidays' ('Bangkok', 2002: 14–15). It also announced its intention to become Asia's 'film-making hub' via joint ventures ('Thailand Wants', 2004).

At 2002 rates in US dollars, here is one example of a budget calculated for production in the US versus Thailand that covers labour, equipment hire and fees. It helps to explain why low-budget US features are increasingly relocating there (DeWayne, 2002: 99):

ITEM	THAILAND	US
Crew	22,490	55,450
Lighting	3,062	7,533
Grip	1,450	1,662
Camera	2,399	4,107
Sound	220	250
Expenses	1,550	2,650
Transport	3,860	6,963
Picture Vehicles	1,085	4,975
Aeroplane	2,010	6,500
Catering	858	2,675
Location Fee	2,350	9,750
Casting	650	0
Talent	1,430	9,400
State	133	0
Mise en scène	3,450	4,000
Costume	665	2,050
Make-up	175	150
Accommodation	826	4,808
Insurance	N/A	2,500
TOTAL	**US$48,663**	**US$125,423**

SOURCE: Adapted from DeWayne, 2002: 174

Much of *Tomb Raider* (Simon West, 2001) was shot at Angkor Wat, Cambodian sandstone temple ruins dating from the ninth century. After
Paramount brought in minesweepers to check the location set for leftover
Khmer Rouge *matériel*, Cambodian conservation authorities charged the
company US$10,000 a day to film. Interestingly enough, popular accounts of
the process emphasise not tourist or conservation dollars, assistance from the
army or the pittance received by local labour, but opportunities for the decimated local film industry to witness Hollywood at work. After UNESCO
protested Cambodia's support of a film about tomb-raiding at the very
moment that Khmer antiquities were being looted from temples, Hollywood's

newly anointed ambassador, Angelina Jolie, insisted that 'Lara is not a looter … and she'd probably shoot you for saying so' (Rosenberg, 2001; Seno, 2001; Jolie quoted in East, 2000).

Four other Hollywood films went into production there soon afterwards. The producers sought new and cheap terrain (they pay just US$10,000 a day to film in a wonder of the world, with the money going to a petroleum company that inherited the preservation department's duties as part of privatisation; and the filmmakers had roads built for them by the military). The government sought to promote filmmaking in concert with Thailand (under the slogan 'two countries, one film locale' and 'Destination Thailand') and a boost to tourism that showed the country as safe in its post-Khmer Rouge incarnation. Critics feared destruction of ancient treasures by visitors and the association of the ruins with the hyper violence of *Tomb Raider* (the state allowed foreigners to bear arms – normally against the law – in order to ensure that Jolie felt safe) (Seno and Reap, 2001; Rosenberg, 2001; 'Movie Shoot', 2000; 'Tough Girl', 2000).

Meanwhile, Korean activists, actors and directors were shaving their heads, protesting in the streets, organising a Coalition for Diversity in Moving Images and going on hunger strikes against their government's deal with the US to cut screen quotas, likening the decision to the experience of the Japanese empire, and calling for a cultural exception in bilateral talks. After Valenti's servants in the US government had required Seoul to minimise quotas on domestic film exhibition in return for other industrial arrangements, he promised training for Korean filmmakers in order to enter the NICL, which meant that the reduction in local-film quota from 40 per cent to 20 per cent would allegedly not matter (Kim, 2000: 363–65; Paquet, 2002; Park, 2003)! Therefore, at the same time as greater access is obtained for releasing films, a new cheap labour force is constructed to produce them. More than that, consider this tale of *anglo-parlante* remake producer Roy Lee's negotiations there:

> Lee began hawking his Asian remake possibilities. 'I forgot to bring you this review of "Saving My Hubby," ' he said. 'Terrible title, but it's a Korean movie about a woman kicking ass in the 'hood, supposedly modeled on some Greek mythology thing about a woman entering somewhere and doing something. Maybe we could do that as a remake, setting it up with Queen Latifah.'
>
> (Quoted in Friend, 2003: 42)

Following the success of the US remake of *Ringu* (Hideo Nakata, 1998), *In the Mood for Love* (Wong Kar-Wai, 2000) and *Crouching Tiger, Hidden Dragon*, 'big studios have been scouring Asia for the next hit'. Vertigo Entertainment alone has marketed remake rights to the majors for about twenty films from Japan, South Korea, Hong Kong and elsewhere (Mazurkewich, 2003; Mi-hui, 2003). In 2002 and 2003, the studios purchased the rights to remake eight

Korean movies, for US$300,000–1 million (Park, 2003; Frater, 2003). As industry executive Ken Kamins puts it, 'The fact that it's foreign in origin does not necessarily mean it's a foreign concept' (quoted in Lyons, 2002).

Meanwhile, the Korean government's successful redisposal of its state-aided EOI manufacturing policies to culture reached its apogee with successful pan-Asian marketing of the 'Korean wave', signalling a capacity to exploit US popular-cultural techniques for regional audiences (Yong-Shik, 2002). No wonder Ang Lee refers to Asia as *Sense and Sensibility* with martial arts' in describing *Crouching Tiger* (quoted in Campbell, 2003), and *Variety* can – taste-lessly but aptly – begin a major story with 'Americans are gearing up for another invasion of Vietnam'. No longer frightened by state socialism, and alarmed that the country's usual double in Hollywood films, the Philippines, has been demonised as Islamic, Hollywood was keen to shoot there (Bing, 2002: 9).

Hollywood's characteristic exploitation of uneven development in national regulatory policies has, however, suffered from one of the great unintended consequences of US-led globalisation initiatives: the growth of regional affil-iations and trading blocs. A significant feature of the 1996 Asia-Pacific Economic Cooperation Forum was the use of NAFTA's language to justify a wall against US media imports. This has brought together some unlikely part-ners. Along with co-hosting the 2002 World Cup men's football finals, Japan and Korea started working together on new film initiatives. Buoyed by the relaxation of a fifty-year-old Korean ban on Japanese cultural products, some producers foresee a regional Japan-Korea-China media bloc, a single market facilitated by South-East Asian storylines that speak better to local popu-lations than Hollywood does (Alford and Herskovitz, 2001), and facilitated by the long-standing visibility of Korean, Japanese and Chinese actors across satellite television in the region. Co-productions are on the rise, such as the first Thai-Hong Kong film (*Jan Dara*) in 2001. The same year, several pan-Asian films were in production in Hong Kong (Beals, 2001). On the domestic front, South Korea has been prominent in recent efforts to reinforce screen quotas and cultural exemptions for audiovisual products, recalling the French call for similar exemptions during GATT negotiations in the 1990s. And recently, five major US distributors in Seoul were found guilty by the Korean Fair Trade Commission of anti-competitive practices, including collusion and cartel formation, a charge to which the officials of the MPA quickly admitted to avoid further punitive actions (Mann, 1997). The US Office of the Trade Representative subsequently placed Korea on a 'watch list', because people were buying US movies outside the market price and arrangement ('US Elevates', 2004).

Conclusion

Those patriotic corporations never lost a beat after 911. Given the choice they flew the American flag on their SUVs while visas, passports and currency conversion calculators in Gucci cases were loaded on corporate jets bound for anywhere cheaper, anywhere greed dictated.

(Haskell Wexler, 2002)

Clearly, the NICL is uneven. It relies on cultural consanguinity, favourable rates of exchange, supine governments, minimal worker internationalism and high levels of skill equivalency – but it is real. In the words of *Canadian Business* magazine, 'a mobile elite happily exploits whichever country charges the least' (Seguin, 2003).

Of course, in responding to disinvestment, many US workers embark on a neonativist critique that can appear lacking in generosity regarding their brothers and sisters elsewhere in the world, a Yanqui cultural nationalism that is chauvinistic and narrow-minded. But looked at from three other perspectives, their reaction becomes quite reasonable. First, their livelihoods are being threatened by the decisions of high-priests of *laissez-faire* capitalism, who in fact use every public resource imaginable to increase their own net worth without giving any thought to the lives that prop them up. Second, the loss of local US culture in this most 'American' of art forms is at least as legitimate an argument as those made in support of national cinemas. Third, they are dealing with a group of studios that continues to exert massive control over their destinies, for all the rhetoric of networks, projects and post-Fordist freedoms-that-are-really-fiefdoms.

Everyone knows that the impact of the NICL on workers in a nation without a competent healthcare system (i.e. the US) is potentially catastrophic, as producers who are signatories to SAG contracts under its 'Rule One' arrangements contribute 13.8 per cent of each employee's wages to the union's Pension and Health Fund. By 2001, millions of retirement and healthcare dollars had been lost because of runaways, which employed approximately 1,500 SAG members a year but did not yield such contributions. In 2002, SAG enforced its 'Global Rule One', prohibiting members from working without a SAG contract offshore, thereby ensuring pension contributions, occupational safety rules and pay rates. This brought the union into line with the decades-old practice regarding directors and writers (Roth, 2002). There was opposition from workers elsewhere and from domestic employers (Pietrolungo and Tinkham, 2002–03; Wicker, 2003: 484–85; 'Producers Warn', 2002). Meanwhile, labour-law 'experts' were ready to offer legal justifications and protection for scab workers (see, for example, Levin and Li, 2001).

The hypocrisy of global Hollywood's masters reached its apogee in 2003 when Fox released a trailer that criticised 'piracy'. It sought the empathy and sympathy of viewers with below-the-liners, whose jobs were supposedly in jeopardy (Muñoz, 2003) from a phenomenon that is all about super-profit. The absence of an equivalent argument against runaway production reveals the cynicism of such a tactic.

We can already see that the grid from our Introduction (see p. 4), with its binary opposition between free-enterprise and public cinema, is fatally flawed. In the next two chapters, we investigate the NICL through specific practices – co-production and copyright – that exemplify the complexities of transnational culture businesses and their use of public funding and law that are supposedly dedicated to preserving and developing national heritage and creativity.

Chapter Three
Co-producing Hollywood

We have created a product that by, say, putting the name of Warner Brothers on it is a stamp of credibility. But that could be an Arnon Milchan film, directed by Paul Verhoeven, starring Gérard Depardieu and Anthony Hopkins, and shot in France and Italy, and made with foreign money.
(John Ptak, Creative Artists Agency of Hollywood, quoted in Weinraub, 1993)

On 16 April 2002, employees of France's revered pay-TV network Canal Plus seized control of the station to protest the sacking of chief executive Pierre Lescure. The protesters interrupted scheduled programming to allow Lescure the opportunity to vent against his former boss, Jean-Maire Messier, whom Lescure described as consumed by a 'pathological egotism'. Messier, who prefers to be called J6M (Jean-Marie Messier 'moi-même, maître du monde' – myself, master of the world), found time on a competing station to explain that his decision was based on Lescure's failure to reverse the network's five years of losses and a shrinking subscriber base. The controversy came during the height of the French presidential campaign, with candidates supporting Lescure and the pay-TV network, French cinema's leading source of financing. Even incumbent President Jacques Chirac backed Lescure, whose satirical puppet show, *Les Guignols*, characterised the French leader as a caped 'superliar'. Green Party candidate Noel Mamere claimed Messier linked the 'future of Canal Plus to the CAC40 [the French stock-market index]' (quoted in Campbell and Rush, 2002). All this referenced Messier's infamous statement made a few months earlier that the 'French cultural exception is dead', which implied that he saw the French system of government subsidies and quotas in support of audiovisual culture as no longer relevant within an increasingly global and neoliberal economy. In the previous two years, Messier had transformed a water-utility company into a global media conglomerate by acquiring Canal Plus, a major Hollywood studio, the world's largest music group, several US cable networks and financial interests in mobile phone and Internet companies. The value of Canal Plus and the French film industry's future within the giant Vivendi Universal became symbolically clear when Messier relocated to a US$17.5 million apartment in New York City, and referred to France as 'a small, exotic country' (quoted in Sabbagh, 2002).

Because the US has long dominated film and television exports around the world, globalisation in the audiovisual industries has mostly registered as Americanisation. But if the presidential candidates and the French press protested against the impending Americanisation of French culture, North American Vivendi Universal board members first campaigned for Messier's removal (Snoddy, 2002). Motivated less by concerns about a US invasion of French culture, the Canadian directors worried that Messier had failed to understand the culture of Hollywood. As an adviser to the French government on privatisation projects in the 1980s, his commitment to deregulation had followed a growing neoliberal consensus among business and government leaders that favoured lifting trade barriers and selling state-run industries. But the neoclassical economic theories that represent markets as neutral, equalising forces that optimise supply-and-demand chains among nations do not account for the widespread support for cultural provision in the Canal Plus protests or for the continuing support for exempting cultural sectors within world trade fora. Indeed, audiovisual culture became the spoiler in Vivendi Universal's quest to build a transatlantic conglomeration – in 2003, Vivendi agreed to sell its US entertainment assets, save for Universal Music, to NBC (Tagliabue, 2003), itself a subsidiary of the major arms manufacturer General Electric.

But if the cultural exception is not dead, its future is unclear within a rapidly changing audiovisual environment where national public broadcasting services struggle to exist alongside hundreds of commercial cable/satellite pay-TV commercial channels, and where the neoliberal policies of the European Commission (EC) favour transnational media conglomerates. According to the Informa Media Group, in 2002, the governments of the EU spent €1.8 billion to subsidise the film sector, 74 per cent of which supported production, 15 per

BREAKDOWN OF 2002 ADMISSIONS IN THE EUROPEAN UNION ACCORDING TO THE ORIGIN OF FILMS

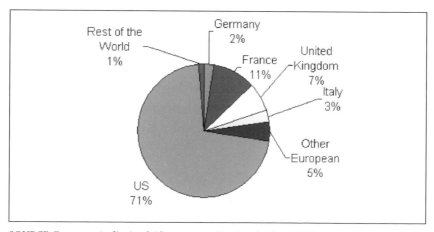

SOURCE: European Audiovisual Observatory – Lumiere database, 2003

cent training and 11 per cent distribution. France, indeed, leads this cultural exception with €552 million, followed by Britain (€261 million), Spain (€245 million), Italy (€210 million), Germany (€186 million), Ireland (€71 million) and the Netherlands (€49 million). However, the EC has considered further limits to film subsidies, in part through distinguishing between 'commercial' and 'cultural' films, in an effort to reduce so-called unfair competition. The fifteen film councils of the EU states oppose this (Adler, 2003b). Despite these subsidies, which take the form of tax breaks and direct grants, and on average make up 42 per cent of European film budgets, Hollywood accounted for 71 per cent of EU box-office admissions in 2002.

This chapter considers the collaborative efforts of EU nations to create a pan-European industry to challenge Hollywood's continuing domination. Concurrent with these struggles between advocates of economic liberalisation and proponents of national film subsidisation are co-production policies that attempt to foster a pan-European film culture by subsidising collaboration among national filmmakers and film industries. We begin with a sketch of world co-production activity, then focus on government policy and industry transformation in the EU, the most active co-production region, and Hollywood's most valuable intermediate zone in the NICL. Distinguishing between treaty co-productions that receive direct public support, and equity co-productions principally financed by multinational capital, we first consider the efficacy of funding procedures for treaty co-production and other government provisions in meeting the challenges of combating Hollywood's proliferation, then ask how a NICL-oriented approach might re-conceive policy objectives currently based on supporting individual artists and cultural affiliation via economic trading blocs. In turning to equity co-production, we trace the rise of pan-European pay-TV conglomerates, and consider their role in fostering, rather than challenging, the Hollywood NICL. Canal Plus is our case study, which is of particular interest, as it invests French money in Hollywood independents and London lottery franchises. The final section considers how renewed neoliberal discourse about a digital 'revolution' has threatened to dismantle the cultural exception. Under the rubric of 'convergence', telecommunications policies in the US and Europe have begun to dismantle regulatory barriers that once separated the telephone, cable and broadcast industries. The rules that have prevented these telecommunications industries from entering each other's business are said to jeopardise the economic and cultural promises of the new 'information era'. Yet Vivendi's failed strategy of merging programming networks and a Hollywood studio with telephone and Internet investments at the height of the dot-com bubble proved that convergence has been promising in theory, but not practice. Our conclusion addresses the challenges European media policy faces, given the vast imbalances between European investments in Hollywood and treaty provisions crafted to impede its continued growth.

Economies of Scale: Cultures of Cash

> I would argue that ... the entertainment industry of this country is not so
> much Americanizing the world as planetizing entertainment.
>
> (Michael Eisner in Costa-Gavras *et al.*, 1995: 9)

On 9 October 1992, three days prior to the so-called Christopher Columbus
quincentenary, Paramount Pictures released *1492: Conquest of Paradise* in more
than 3,000 theatres across thirty countries. French actor Gérard Depardieu
played the Italian-born Spanish explorer, under the direction of ex-British television commercials guru Ridley Scott. Co-produced by the venerable French
film studio Gaumont on the eve of its own centenary, *1492* was the first in a
series of Gaumont English-language features intended to reach both the valuable US market and a worldwide audience, through Hollywood's global
distribution cartel. Shot in Spain and Costa Rica, the production hired 170
Indians from Costa Rica (at US$35 per day) and six Waunana Indians from
Colombia who had acted in *The Mission* (Roland Joffé, 1986). If Costa Rica provided both the First Peoples and the cheap labour to keep the budget under
US$40 million, it was perhaps also chosen at the request of the executive pro-
ducer's husband, the head of the newly born Costa Rica Film Commission. An
official British-French-Spanish co-production, *1492* qualified for public funding under co-production treaties between the three countries that had been
struck to protect national cultural expression and support national culture
industries. While the Spanish cultural heritage of this story is clear, the tri-
national status of the film aligns it more closely with industry and labour
imperatives than cultural protection: a British director and post-production
work, a French actor and production company, and Spanish/ex-Spanish possession locations and crews. The film failed in the US, but topped the European
box office (except for Italy, where it did particularly poorly in Genoa, Columbus' birthplace) (Williams, 1994; Berkman, 1992; Jäckel, 1996; Groves, 1992).
It was one of a stream of films celebrating masculinity and national conquest
that came, ironically, from highly fractured labour processes across the 1990s,
utilising forms of work that were far from the staple of permanent male
employment under Fordism (Radner, 2001). The film did not mark a boom for
its host, however. Because Costa Rica bans explosions by filmmakers, Brazil is
a preferred alternative (DeWayne, 2002: 4).

If the *year* 1492 reminds us of the colonial legacies that have structured globalisation's long history via the pursuit of gold, commodities and labour (Broad,
1995b), the *film 1492* exemplifies the legacies of 'America's' twentieth-century
economic ascendance, including a cultural legacy that finds sovereign-states
around the world vying for expressive space and cultural industrialisation in
the face of Hollywood's continued proliferation. Just as the birth of sovereign-
states in the colonised world occurred through struggles for independence from

colonial domination, the co-production protocols that brought *1492* to the screen are among more than 135 bilateral and multilateral treaties between over 85 countries outside the US. Designed to combat Hollywood's domination of screen culture, they frequently enable the very NICL that ratifies it (Taylor, 1998: 134). In the light of the dominance of reactionary explanations for how Hollywood functions, how else could we comprehend its success – utilising data such as the *1492* story, and recalling its 1492 intertext of imperialism?

International co-production policies simultaneously inscribe and destabilise national descriptors of cultural value. As a practice of international cultural collaboration, co-productions call into question national measures of cultural identity, but reinscribe them in treaty language that struggles to specify national cultural preservation. Co-production marks a site of transformation in cultural scale, from the local and national to the regional and global. As Erik Swyngedouw argues, 'scale becomes the arena and moment, both discursively and materially, where sociospatial power relations are contested and compromises are negotiated and regulated'. The sections below on treaty and equity co-production address various points of transformation across such scales of cultural production. Because 'theoretical and political priority . . . never resides in a particular geographical scale, but rather in the process through which particular scales become (re)constituted' (Swyngedouw, 1997: 140–41), we seek to identify the institutions, from culture ministries to corporate conglomerates, that reconstitute the scale-politics of audiovisual co-production.

Treaty and equity co-productions intersect scales of political modernity (the super- and supra-national), vertical industrial scales (production, distribution and exhibition) and horizontal industrial scales (conglomeration and synergy). Neoclassical economists sever the relations between these scales when they argue that audiovisual products follow unique economic laws that pertain to 'joint-consumption' goods, those with high initial costs and low reproduction expenses. As we saw in Chapter 1, these laws are said to explain 'the high volume of [audiovisual] trade', because production costs are 'largely unaffected by the number of viewers', with the US enjoying an economic advantage in film and television trade, given the wealth of the English-language market, and a competitive advantage born in a vigorous domestic free market, where 'sophisticated and demanding' film and television buyers cater to a 'polyglot' US audience, resulting in the 'new universal art form' that is Hollywood. This is the exceptional-birthplace equation: migrant democracies + free markets = textual universalism. Yet 'melting-pot' viewers are also 'unusually insular and intolerant of foreign programming or films'. Even as these micro-economists recognise Hollywood's cartel control over world film distribution, their methodological focus on segmented economic units and assumptions about audience sophistication (or not) lead to these glaring contradictions in ascribing Hollywood's success. The stilted concept of 'cultural discount' attempts to quantify the imperceptibility of imported programming, to codify rigid national cultural indices by predominantly measuring cultural value in vulgar national economic chunks (Hoskins *et al.*, 1997: 12–36, 44–45, 51–67, 40). We prefer what John Frow describes as a 'regimes of value' approach, which considers the institutional contexts that produce sets of criteria, the degree to which these criteria are open to a diversity of participants and the effectivity of policy decisions made on the basis of these criteria. This blend of political-economic concerns for structure with a cultural-studies approach to institutional hierarchies of value better accounts for the complexities of co-production contexts. As debates over government-subsidised co-production often hinge on questions of artistic value versus commercial marketability, this approach helps to 'rethink the relation between canonical (or "high") and non-canonical (or "popular") culture, as practices of value rather than as collections of texts with a necessary coherence' (Frow, 1995: 144–51).

For example, the dominant regime of value that has animated *dirigiste* EU media policy is the conceit of a common pan-European cultural heritage: to fortify a regional economic trading block – as we shall see, this conceit is largely derived from a high-cultural, white colonial Christianity. Meanwhile, the popular is assigned to *laissez-faire* market forces, which have seen European industry up its investments in Hollywood as the gold standard for pleasure. In traversing the rise in international co-production, we ask how pan-Europeanism excludes or enables diversity, and how values of art and commerce negotiate pan-European popular pleasures.

World Co-productions

A great shaggy beast prowling the movie forest, a fiscal Godzilla slouching toward our future.

(Jack Valenti on the costs of releasing a Hollywood film, quoted in Fuson, 1998)

Co-production results often surprise: *JFK* (Oliver Stone, 1991) was funded by a Hollywood studio, a French cable network, a German production house and a Dutch financier, while *The Full Monty* (Peter Cattaneo, 1997), supposedly the *ur*-British film of its generation, is of course owned by Fox. Although co-production statistics are unevenly reported, according to the industry trade magazine *Screen Digest* (see table below), at least 35 per cent of all feature films in Europe in 1998 were co-productions. Hong Kong is the most active co-producer in Asia, with 22 per cent co-productions that year, followed by China with 7 per cent (down from 19 per cent in 1996), and just 8 of 249 for Japan. France, Spain and Germany are the co-production centres in Europe, as many smaller film markets seek to tap into larger industries.

SITES	FEATURES		CO-PRODUCTIONS			
	1998	1991	1998	%	1991	%
United States	661	583	9	1%	n/a	
EUROPE						
France	183	156	81	44%	83	53%
Italy	92	129	13	14%	18	14%
UK	87	46	24	28%	22	48%
Spain	65	64	18	28%	18	28%
Germany	50	72	11	22%	19	26%
Poland	25	25	2	8%	9	36%
Sweden	20	27	7	35%	17	63%
Romania	12	19	8	67%	4	21%
LATIN AMERICA						
Mexico	23	32	n/a		1	3%
Argentina	23	21	6	26%	6	29%
Chile	4	n/a	2	50%	n/a	
ASIA						
Japan	249	230	8	3%	n/a	
Hong Kong	92	211	20	22%	4	2%
China	82	100	6	7%	n/a	
Australia	38	27	1	3%	4	15%

SOURCE: Adapted from *Screen Digest*, May 1997: 105–06; June 1999: 130–31; June 2000: 182–83

Although co-productions can fluctuate widely from year to year, between 1994 and 1998, French co-productions averaged 49 per cent of total production, Spanish 28 per cent and German 29 per cent. Britain co-produces with the US and Canada more than with the rest of Europe, and co-production accounted for between 37 and 47 per cent of its total over the 1990s. Argentina co-produced six of twenty-three features in 1998, four with Spain and one each with Mexico and Mali (*Screen Digest*, May 1997: 105; *Screen Digest*, June 1999: 129–35; *Screen Digest*, June 2000: 182–83).

Television Business International compiled a database of over 2,000 co-productions, from 1978 to 1995 (see table below). Most were concentrated in drama and documentary television, while 21 per cent were feature films. Again, the vast majority of television co-production activity took place in Europe. The most frequent co-producers were Britain and France, which together comprised 32 per cent of all co-productions. Documentary co-productions in the US are found on public broadcasting and reality-based thematic channels like the Discovery Channel. Drama co-productions are principally high-profile made-for-television movies and mini-series that air on the major broadcast and cable networks, and action-adventure series in syndication and on cable networks such as USA and Sci-Fi. Canada (7 per cent) and Australia (4 per cent) are the most frequent co-producers outside Europe and the US, often with each other and Britain. Many of these English-language co-productions seek higher production values that will open up the US market (Brown, 1995: 2.1.1–2.1.3).

TELEVISION BUSINESS INTERNATIONAL: DATABASE OF TV/FILM CO-PRODUCTIONS 1978–1995

SITE	%	GENRE	%
Britain	16	Drama (all)	41
France	16	Documentary	24
US	14	Feature films	21
Germany	10	Drama: mini-series	8
Canada	7	Drama: TV movies	7
Italy	6	Animation	7
Spain	4	Drama: series	6
Australia	4	Children's (exc. animation)	3
Japan	3	Comedy	1
Switzerland	2		
Belgium	2		

SOURCE: Brown, 1995

While the volume of US fiction programming imported by Western European broadcast television channels fell slightly between 1997 and 2001, an increase in the volume of US co-productions has more than made up for this decline.

IMPORTED US, EUROPEAN AND OTHER FICTIONAL PROGRAMMING BROADCAST ON TV CHANNELS IN WESTERN EUROPE AS A PERCENTAGE OF TOTAL IMPORTED FICTIONAL PROGRAMMING (1997–2001)

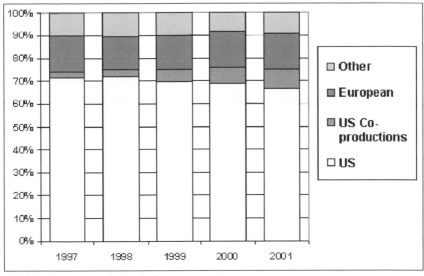

SOURCE: European Audiovisual Observatory, 2002

Also, of all imported programming on Western European broadcast channels in 2001, 13 per cent were co-productions, up from 6 per cent in 1997.

VOLUME OF NON-EUROPEAN/NON-US FICTION PROGRAMMING AND OF INTERNATIONAL CO-PRODUCTIONS IMPORTED AND BROADCAST BY WESTERN EUROPEAN TELEVISION CHANNELS (1994–2001) IN HOURS BROADCAST

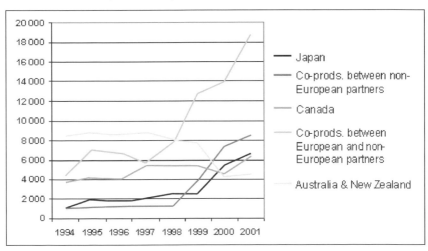

SOURCE: ETS/European Audiovisual Observatory, 2003

These figures are mostly for 'official' co-productions, meaning that each participant's national government recognised the work as a product of national culture, and accordingly granted subsidies and tax breaks in the name of protecting national culture or fortifying national industry. But the figures also include non-treaty co-productions, where international partners find economic and cultural benefits in sharing resources, despite not meeting the criteria for treaty provisions. In these cases, partners usually hold equity, which means they take a percentage ownership in a project or production company, rather than buying territory rights for initial distribution. Equity partners have a voice in the projects that are developed, but the level of input into creative decisions can vary considerably. If the audiovisual industries often use the terms co-financing and co-production interchangeably, the conceptual distinction usually hinges on whether there is a shared creative component in the planning or execution (Light, 1994: 79–80). It is difficult to plot the market share of co-productions, because, as we saw in the Introduction, nationally gathered statistics tend to claim such texts as their own (*Goldeneye* [Martin Campbell, 1995] is said to be British, for example). As a percentage of total EU box-office admissions, EU co-productions had a slim 5.6 per cent market share in 1996, and less than 3 per cent in 1997.

This contrasts with the growing presence of US–European co-productions, in which the box-office successes of *The English Patient, Tomorrow Never Dies* (Roger Spottiswoode, 1997) and *Evita* (Alan Parker, 1996) contributed to a 5 per cent share of the European market in 1996, and a 6 per cent share in 1997 (Lange, 1998). Also, US film studios have escalated their involvement in non-English-language co-productions. For example, 20th Century-Fox International participated in films such as *Y tu mama también* (2001) by Mexican director Alfonso Cuarón and the Italian co-production *Io No* (Simona Izzo and Riccardo Tognazzi, 2003), and distributed *Lisbela and the Prisoner* (Guel Arreas, 2003) in Brazil and *Hero* (Yimou Zhang, 2002) in East Asia. In 2003, Fox created a European local-language co-production unit run by Theresa Moneo, who previously acquired films for Miramax and others, including *Central Station* (Walter Salles, 1998), *Strawberry and Chocolate* (Tomás Gutiérrez Alea and Juan Carlos Tabío, 1993), *The Others* (Alejandro Amenábar, 2001) and *Life is Beautiful* (Roberto Benigni, 1997), as well as executive-producing *Dirty Pretty Things* (Stephen Frears, 2003) and *Malèna* (Giuseppe Tornatore, 2000) (Brodesser, 2003). Columbia TriStar and Warner Bros. completed their first Spanish productions in 2003. This brought the US-studio share of the Spanish market to 75 per cent, up from 70 per cent in 2002 (Hopewell, 2003), and Warners' revenues from non-English-language films in 2003 tripled the previous year's total (Guider *et al.*, 2004). Since 2001, Hollywood co-productions with the PRC have also accelerated.

PRC (by Ting Wang)

In an effort to win over the Chinese audience, in 2001, Columbia Pictures Film Production Asia co-produced a black comedy entitled *Big Shot's Funeral* by director Xiaogang Feng with the Huayi Brothers, the Taihe Film Investment Co. and Beijing Film Studio. Shot in China with a budget of US$3.5 million, starring Donald Sutherland from the US and Chinese stars Ge You from the mainland and Rosamund Kwan from Hong Kong, the film broke commercial box-office records in mainland China by grossing over US$4 million in less than one month (Mazurkewich, 2002); yet its comic depiction of modern China was unfamiliar to Western audiences, and the director's obscurity in the West prevented it from taking off overseas. For its next project, Columbia Pictures Film Production Asia tried to strike a chord with both Chinese and Western audiences with *Warriors of Heaven and Earth*, directed by He Ping, a Chinese fifth-generation auteur well recognised at home. The film was jointly produced with the Huayi Brothers, the Taihe Film Investment Co. and Xi'an Film Studio at a budget of around US$10 million, well over the average for a Chinese film. A mix of epic, kung fu, suspense and romance that resembled a Chinese Western, the film was made by a crew composed mostly of local film professionals, including digital artists. Backed by a strong mixed cast, including veteran Chinese star Wen Jiang and Japanese screen idol Kiichi Nakai, and Hollywood-style massive publicity, including a grand national premiere within the Forbidden City and China's first official website promoting a single movie, the film did well from its 2003 opening, garnering US$724,000 in the first two weeks in Beijing and nearly US$250,000 within a few days of opening in Shanghai, outshining *Matrix II* and *Finding Nemo* (Andrew Stanton and Lee Unkrich, 2003), and maintaining a strong momentum in other cities as well (Huayi Brothers and Taihe Investment Company Website, 2003). Whether Columbia Pictures Film Production Asia has finally found the right formula for its financing of Chinese domestic blockbusters still remains to be seen, pending the film's release under the label of Columbia TriStar in the US and other territories yet to come, and its candidacy for best foreign-language film at the 2004 Academy Awards.

Sony Pictures Tristar is not alone in its co-production venture in China, though it has been the most committed. Universal Studio made its foray into this area in 1999 with the Beijing Film Studio's *Pavilion of Women* (Ho Yim, 2001). A period romantic drama set in 1930s China, based on Pearl S. Buck's 1946 novel and starring Willem Dafoe and Luo Yan (a US-educated Chinese actress, also producer and co-scriptwriter), it was shot entirely in China in English, and targeted the hard-sought-after billion-plus Chinese audiences as well as the global market. Again, low cost and market access were the major calculation. In a rare move, a high-level ten-strong delegation from the studio attended the film's premiere in major Chinese cities (Groves, 2001c). Warner Bros. recently co-produced ten 90-minute made-for-TV films with a Chinese film company affiliated to the China Film Group and Salon Films of Hong Kong. Entitled *Swordsmen of the Passes*, they are set in China's Qing dynasty. Shot in high-definition digital video with Salon's advanced equipment on location in the Chinese mainland at a relatively low cost, and set to be distributed both in China and overseas, the films were successful in 2003; and a plan is under way to reproduce two of them as features (Hong Kong Trade Development Council, 2003). To the Chinese film industry, foreign productions in China can enhance domestic production by introducing the world's advanced filmmaking technology and management expertise, boost the image of local films and film artists in the NICL and stimulate the domestic film market. More recently, there has been increasing liberalisation of foreign film (co)production, including easier project green-lighting with simplified application and approval procedures, more flexible crew and cast composition and arrangement, and the elimination of the requirement that stories be set in China.

Treaty Co-productions and Hollywood

Critics of protectionism question the reality of ... European culture, asking whether Spain actually has more in common culturally with Sweden than with Argentina ... noting that a great deal of England's cultural content, including its language, is more like that in the United States than in Greece.

(Baker, 2000: 1373)

Co-production treaties between two or more national governments create rules for collaborative projects to qualify for subsidies and fulfil quota restrictions. As legacies of nation-state formations under modernity, treaties measure cultural specificity by way of national borders, a demarcation that necessitates folding intra-national cultural diversity under an exclusionary sign of unity, failing to gauge supra-national cultural affiliations across borders. So, although national audiovisual industries have used co-production to stall Hollywood dominance by pooling resources to create audiovisual products with greater international appeal, co-production treaties also inscribe boundaries that distinguish a product of national cultural expression from one that is not. Such treaties institutionalise normative and static conceptions of national culture in the very process of international collaboration.

Multilateral treaties seek to harmonise international treaty provisions along the axes of economic trading blocs or regional language markets. The Conferencia de Autoridades de Ibero-América covers Latin America, while the Pacific Rim Consortium for Public Broadcasting (PACRIM) facilitates transpacific co-productions (Taylor, 1995). In the European context, the Council of Europe (COE) set out to harmonise co-production rules and make access to funds easier for producers by creating the pan-European co-production fund Eurimages in 1989, and convened a European Convention on Cinematographic Co-production in 1992 to establish common criteria for eligibility. These pan-

European cultural initiatives have their roots in desires for a common market, beginning with the formation of the COE in 1949, and the European Community, founded by the Treaty of Rome in 1957. While the Community sought economic unity for Europe, the COE was equally concerned with the cultural mission of 'safeguarding and realising the ideals and principles which are their common heritage'. The cinema was considered an important medium for giving expression to 'European identity'. And when the 1992 Maastricht Treaty folded the Community into the EU, culture was addressed in article 128: 'The Community shall contribute to the flowering of the cultures of the Member States, while respecting their national and regional diversity and at the same time bringing their common cultural heritage to the fore.' The audiovisual policies of the COE and the EU have set out to meet the economic imperatives of unification through cultural imperatives, to foster 'unity in diversity' (Hainsworth, 1994: 13–15, 29).

Eurimages' stated goal is to 'promote the European film industry'. It supports distribution and exhibition, but allocates most money to co-production. Designed to augment existing bilateral treaties between members, Eurimages initially only funded co-productions with three or more participating countries, but in 1997 began accepting bilateral co-productions. Eurimages is run by a board of management with one representative from each member. To determine that each project meets a sufficient level of 'European Character', the board follows a point system established in the European Convention on Cinematographic Co-production, which weighs the value of individual cultural labourers according to their production assignments. Projects must have a director who lives in Europe. The director, scriptwriter and leading actor all receive three points on a nineteen-point scale. Two points are awarded for supporting-actor roles, and one point each for craft labourers such as the camera operator, sound recorder, editor, art director and studio, shooting and post-production locations. A total of fifteen points is required for a screen text to qualify as 'European' (Council of Europe, 2000a: 6–8; Council of Europe, 1992).

This scheme sets out, then, to regulate the NICL along two axes, of work and culture, through the labour residency of a few above-the-line culture workers. Board members also bring their own cultural preferences and those of their representative nations to bear when making decisions. But the fund's policies privilege bureaucratic elite decision-making based on authorial measures of cultural value. That is, the locus of cultural expression is found in the transcendental and creative potential of 'artists', as per the Western concept of subjectivity that valorises individuals as producers of cultural value through personal expression (Crofts, 1998: 310–13). This cultural measure has had a long history in Europe, from the influential French critics/filmmakers of the 1950s affiliated with *Cahiers du cinéma*, who established the cultural worth of motion pictures via the expressive signature of the director or auteur, to the internationally recognised art-house cinema of North Asian and Western and Eastern European filmmakers. As Tom Ryall has noted,

> it is an irony that the critical acceptance of Hollywood cinema was initially achieved through its extensive mapping, by the critics of *Cahiers du cinéma*, in terms of authorial oeuvres rather than in terms of the genres that, along with the stars, have defined its image for the moviegoing public.

> (1998: 327)

Often privileging personal vision over plot, formal experimentation over generic forms, and nuanced character studies rather than causal narratives, art-house and auteur cinema have secured only limited distribution and funds for marketing, and have rarely been popular in Europe (Nowell-Smith, 1998: 6).

The majority of total financing on projects must come from Eurimages members, with no more than 30 per cent from outside Europe, and no partner can exceed 80 per cent participation. In 2003, the fund had twenty-eight member-states in Western, Central and Eastern Europe, with Croatia the latest to join. France provides half the budget and has been a co-producer of half the projects funded so far. Britain did not sign on until 1993, and left the fund in 1995. The co-production budget decreased from €22 million in 1994 to €20 million in 1999, and remained frozen at that level through 2003. Since 1988, the fund has assisted nearly a thousand films, including support for such internationally known directors as Lars Von Trier (*Europa*, 1991), Chantal Akerman (*Nuit et jour*, 1991), Krzysztof Kieslowski (*Bleu*, 1993), Emir Kusturica (*Underground*, 1996), Theo Angelopoulous (*Eternity and a Day*, 1998) and Peter Greenaway (*Eight and a Half Women*, 2000). Although all funding is repayable from net box-office receipts, no more than a million euro has been returned to Eurimages in any given year. The programme to faciliate pan-European distribution has largely failed, as less than half the sponsored films have been seen outside their countries of origin (Jäckel, 1999: 187–88; Taylor, 1998: 137; *Screen Digest*, July 1999; Council of Europe, 2000a: 9–18; Adler, 2003a).

In part to address these failings, Eurimages implemented reforms in 2000 that split funding between two schemes. The first awards money on the basis of 'circulation potential' and the second on the basis of 'artistic value'. The first scheme assesses the commercial viability of a project based on 'pre-sales and sales estimates, the number and quality of distribution commitments, the percentage of market financing confirmed and the experience of the producers and the director' (Council of Europe, 2000b: 12). The second scheme funds lower-budget 'arthouse films with strong artistic potential, and films that are more innovative in their form and subject' (Council of Europe, 2000a: 9). Decisions regarding the potential for wider audience engagement are not based on content criteria, but are the opinions of marketplace gatekeepers. This suggests that if these elite committees are more qualified and intent on gauging artistic potential, they have no criteria for gauging popular appeal outside existing market mechanisms.

The fund was criticised in 2003 for 'having an interfering secretariat and for the lack of transparency when backing projects'. The president resigned in 2002 in protest over the executive secretary bypassing the board in choosing projects. A report commissioned by the Centre National de la Cinématographie in France found Eurimages overly bureaucratic and underfunded, with little determining role for launching co-productions, and France considered dropping out. A new president in 2003 set up a working party to reconsider combining the artistic and commercial systems, and talked of raising matching bank financing and introducing 'business sponsors' for films, but added that decisions would continue to be based on artistic criteria (Adler, 2003a).

Despite these bureaucratic and elite biases, Eurimages has greatly expanded the range and diversity of projects from European countries that had been minority participants in EU commercial filmmaking. For example, in 2003 the fund sponsored *Vodka Lemon*, a French, Swiss, Armenian and Italian co-production directed by the Kurdish filmmaker Hiner Saleem, with Armenian, Russian and Kurdish dialogue (Stratton, 2003). In December 2003, the fund awarded €650,000 to a Hungarian film adaptation of Imre Kertesz's Nobel Prize-winning novel *Fateless* (Lajos Koltai) and €180,000 to a Turkish–Cypriot–Hungarian co-production ('Eurimages', 2003). One way to bridge the gap between high artistic films with little popular appeal from smaller EU countries and commercial markets which favour Britain, France and Germany is to expand co-production policies beyond those that privilege auteur directors to include cultural workers who serve both art and commerce – those who labour 'below-the-line'. This vast majority of screen proletarians receive a maximum of two points for their indirect association with production and/or post-production location. Anchored in the physical plant of production infrastructures, they are held hostage to the fiscal vicissitudes of national currency markets and runaway production, whereas well-compensated above-the-line talent is guaranteed a free ride to the production location *du jour*. Screen policy needs to address this fundamental imbalance between labour and capital mobility in the NICL, and protect and fortify screen labour in the east, west, north and south of the expanded EU. As European screen production is subject to the vagaries of currency markets (as we saw with Britain in Chapter 2), tax incentives (see the Dutch scheme below) and cheapest production facilities (as in the case of Prague in Chapter 2), international labour standards should be a fundamental aspect of pan-European screen policy.

The COE's Eurimages has worked in tandem with the more economically minded EU, which initiated two principal audiovisual policies to create a unified European market. First, as we have seen, the 'Television Without Frontiers' (TWF) directive sought to form a single European television market by liberalising broadcast trade between members and setting content quotas for European television. The directive has been criticised for fostering the expansion of commercial channels faster than the European revenue base and production infrastructure could fill them. This led to an influx of cheap imported programmes from the US, unimpeded by the weak language of the quota provision (Collins, 1999: 200–02). Of course, the policy provisions are not without frontiers, but these parameters have shifted from the national to the continental. After years of trying to bring together public-television systems to create a deliberately European drama series, producers continue to encounter difficulties with notions of discrete national dramaturgies and fears of creating the ultimate blandness of 'un Euro-pudding', which works so hard to include multiple linguistic, audience and production norms that it loses form. A classic example is the resounding failure of the Joseph Conrad Nostromo adaptation, funded by three European public broadcasters (the BBC, Italy's RAI and Spain's TVE), and with British and Italian stars. These stuttering attempts at compiling a European television text have given birth to a policy initiative with the best acrónym ever: BABEL (Broadcasting Across the Barriers of European Languages) (Ungureit, 1991: 16; McDonald, 1999: 2004; Field, 2000: 100; Theiler, 1999: 570). Sony Entertainment published a report in mid-1994 that argued against quotas as inimical to the very producers they were designed to assist, with many commercial television networks failing to observe national production quotas (Stern, 1994a; Zecchinelli, 1994; Stern, 1994b: 1).

Second, the Measures for the Encouragement of the Development of the Industry of Audiovisual Production programme (MEDIA) has funded the distribution and exhibition of European motion pictures and strengthened the Community's audiovisual technological capacity. Initiated in 1990, MEDIA was designed to 'encourage market liberalization whilst avoiding cultural uniformity', but has been underfunded, and created conflict between France, which supported it, and Britain, which did not. In 1995, MEDIA II allocated €265 million over five years, a 55 per cent increase over MEDIA I, but still just 0.5 per cent of the total European audiovisual sector. MEDIA II had three priorities: 'vocational training, development of projects and businesses, transnational distribution of films and audiovisual programmes'. As of 1998, forty projects were completed or under way, including Elizabeth (Shekahar Kapur, 1998) and The Million Dollar Hotel (Wim Wenders, 2000). The latter fused the unlikely combination of an art-house director and the ex-Australian resident, Hollywood star, creepy Christian and co-producer Mel Gibson, who called the film 'as boring as a dog's ass' (quoted in Mackenzie, 2000). One hundred and ten films labelled 'difficult works' were awarded €2.3 million for distribution outside their country of origin, including Breaking the Waves (Lars Von Trier, 1996), Carne Tremula (Pedro Almodóvar, 1997) and Secrets and Lies (Mike Leigh, 1996). The programme includes an automatic system for reinvestment that channels loan repayments back into the industry. In two years, the programme helped European films find 75 million filmgoers outside their national territory. Through these admissions, it reinvested €19 million into the programme (Hainsworth, 1994: 19; 'Commission', 1999: 2, 8–10). European co-productions peaked in 1995 at 50.2 per cent and dropped to 36 per cent in 1998 (*Screen Digest*, May 1997: 105; *Screen Digest*, June 1999).

With the extremely limited resources of Eurimages and MEDIA, local film provision has been swimming against a tide of European-financed Hollywood films, as we shall see. And just as the total 1999 domestic take of national productions in the five largest European markets struggled to survive, so cinemas rooted in national cultural contexts have struggled to circulate across borders. Reasons for this include limited pan-European distribution, small marketing budgets and limited audience appeal. For example, German and Spanish films took no more than 0.3 per cent of the national box office in the five core European markets outside their own, and French films comprised no more than 1.5 per cent of box office in any country. British films fare better in other European countries, ranging from 4 to 6 per cent of the box office. Italian films comprised 4 per cent of the Spanish market, but no more than 1.2 per cent elsewhere. However, European co-productions do much better in perspective markets, achieving near parity with domestic market shares in France, Germany and Spain. Accordingly, European co-productions hold a certain promise for regional economic sustainability in Europe, perhaps as the place where trans-border identifications and pan-European popular cultural expressions can take place outside what otherwise appears to be a fragmented European film industry (*Screen Digest*, June 2000: 189). In 2002, MEDIA II's successor MEDIA Plus awarded eighteen European sales agents, including Britain's FilmFour, France's Pathé International and Italy's Adriana Chiesa Enterprises, €700,000 to promote pan-European distribution of European films. However, as *Gosford Park* (Robert Altman, 2001) and *The Others* received assistance, it is less clear from their above-the-line labour whether this assisted pan-European or pan-Atlantic cultural expression ('International Film', 2002).

However successful the MEDIA programmes have been in circulating films throughout the EU, their scale of provision is dwarfed by competing national tax incentives, such as a 1999 Dutch scheme of write-offs and depreciation that injected an estimated US$150 million into the local industry. It is telling that one of the first projects to receive assistance was *Hollywood Sign* (Sönke Wortmann, 2000), starring Rod Steiger and Burt Reynolds. As MEDIA Plus got under way, the Dutch government lobbied to decrease the budget because of its newfound source of film financing (Edmunds, 2000a and b). From an industry standpoint, the MEDIA programmes, with proportionally small budgets, are largely ineffective at combating the audiovisual trade deficit ('Commission', 1999: 1). Even this marginal level of support for European film is threatened in negotiations for MEDIA Plus' successor, as the EC has become increasingly hostile to cultural provisions in its efforts to liberalise the EU. As one trade journal reported, 'some commissioners see film and television as a thorn in the side of the European project', that TV 'takes a consistently Eurosceptic approach' (Adler, 2003c). An important issue for the future of the MEDIA programmes will be how new members such as Estonia, Latvia and Poland benefit from the programme. The COE's Audiovisual Eureka organisation held a conference in Macedonia in 2002 to assist new members in the south-east to harmonise tax breaks and co-production rules, but Estonia and Latvia have struggled just to make the initial €250,000 contribution required of members (Adler, 2002). Also, Western European priorities have meant the loss of funding for Eastern European filmmaking, forcing aspiring filmmakers to migrate to the West (Iordanova, 2002).

Astérix vs. Hollywood

> If Europeans were producing better movies instead of intellectual bull ...
> people would flock to see them.
>
> (Jean-Paul Vignon, Hollywood Association of French Actors, quoted in 'Hollywood
> Defends Itself', 1998)

On 3 February 1999, a different kind of blockbuster opened in a record 764 theatres across Europe. *Astérix et Obélix vs. Caesar* (Claude Zidi) was shot in French for US$45 million. It ultimately grossed over US$111 million in world-wide box-office receipts, less than US$1 million of which came from the US market (Rawsthorn, 1997; Frater, 2000; D'Alessandro, 2000). A French (51 per cent), German (33 per cent) and Italian (16 per cent) co-production that qual-ified for Eurimages funding, *Astérix* is based on popular French comic-book characters who defend Gaul against invading Romans in 50 BC (Elley, 1999). The comic book has sold over 280 million copies since 1959 and been trans-lated into 88 languages, but has had only limited release in the US since 1994 (Riding, 1999; 'Jacques Chirac', 2003). The successful Disneyesque Parc Astérix was built outside Paris in 1989, and an Astérix video game went into produc-tion in 2000 (Cox, 2000). A second film, *Astérix et Obélix: Mission Cléopatre* (Alain Chabat, 2002) cost more but made less at the domestic and foreign box office (Kasilag, 2003). In the first film, Astérix, Obélix and a group of misfits prevent Caesar from reaching the English Channel/La Manche through the aid of a magic Druid potion that turns them into superior warriors. In the second instalment, they help Cléopatre and the Egyptians resist Caesar, with added spoofs of *Star Wars* (George Lucas, 1977) and *Crouching Tiger, Hidden Dragon*.

Do these marauding cartoon figures represent the promise of an econom-ically self-generating pan-European expressive screen culture to combat Hollywood's domination? The French newspaper *Le Monde* seemed to think so when it hailed *Astérix* as 'the image of resistance to American cinemato-graphic imperialism' (quoted in Riding, 1999: 2). With over sixty actors, 1,500 extras and expensive special effects, *Astérix* borrows Hollywood's own tactics, creating spectacular action-adventure formulae for international markets. But does this mean *Astérix* represents a future European cinema that mimics Hollywood at the expense of a diverse alternative cinema of smaller budgets and local expressivity? John Hill has suggested that strategies to build a big-budget pan-European cinema are neither economically feasible nor culturally desirable. Pan-European policies based on notions of a common heritage or European identity are suspect, given their heritage of 'whiteness, colonialism, Christianity, and High Culture'. As the countries of Europe, unlike the US, share no popular sensibilities or traditions except those emanating from Hollywood itself, Hill and others have advocated that rather than sponsor big-budget international filmmaking in Europe, 'the mobilization of transnational resources in support of national and regional cinemas rooted in specific cultures' will further a 'genuinely European cinema' (Hill *et al.*, 1994: 1–7; Hill, 1994a: 59–68).

Given these important concerns, it is worth considering *Astérix* as an example, though an exceptional one, of a big-budget genre film based on non-US, pan-European popular-cultural currents. Unlike the auteur and textual traditions cited above, which measure diversity by way of knowing artists and readers, genre criticism has located cultural meaning within broader social contexts, where cultural forms and textuality intersect with culture industries and lived publics. Genre is a cultural referencing system that provides pleasures for filmgoers as well as pre-sold forms for risk-averse industries. Generic cultural forms are products of modernity, where technologies of mass production and distribution privilege formal standardisation. These industrial imperatives regulate cultural production within historical contexts that engage with widespread public recognition and consent. In this sense, genres both shape and are shaped by cultural specificities at particular moments and across various geographical scales. Verisimilitude and variation are equally important to genre, as viewers find pleasure in recognising stylistic and thematic protocols, even as they experience novelty and difference (Neale, 1995) – a blend of familiarity and surprise. Hollywood genres such as the Western, musical, horror, romantic comedy or action film are said to be variants of the broader genre of the Hollywood narrative film, which is composed of core characteristics such as quickly paced linear storylines, goal-oriented central protagonists and stars, with bigger-budget films deploying increasing use of special effects and spectacular action sequences (Ryall, 1998: 332).

Astérix is a product of three generic coding systems: the Astérix comic strip, the popular Greco-Roman era muscle-man epics of post-war Europe and the Hollywood narrative film. It is hard to overestimate the popularity of the comic strip in France. A decade after René Goscinny and Albert Urderzo created the characters in 1959, a national survey revealed that two-thirds of the French population had read one of the comic books. In 1965, France's first space satellite was named after the cartoon marauders. In reviewing a republished collection of the classic *Astérix* comic strips released in 2003, one commentator embraced the authors' use of parody and mixture of the high- and lowbrow:

> There is high art (pastiches of work by Breughel, Géricault, Rembrandt, Doré, Rodin) and there is film (Fellini's *Satyricon* satirised, Sean Connery appearing as agent Dubbelosix, Laurel and Hardy as legionaries and a horrid cameo from Kirk Douglas). There is an appearance by The Beatles and mention of the Rolling Menhirs. There is advertising ('It's the right one, it's not the light one … it's a menhir?'), and a young Jacques Chirac (then Mayor of Paris).
>
> (Coren, 2003)

This flair for parody was inspired in the 1950s when Goscinny studied the cartoon trade in New York with the group that went on to found *Mad Magazine* (Beard, 2002). While embraced as a nationalist defence against American cultural imperialism, the comic series is equally critical of French politics; see, for instance, the strip's parody of Chirac:

> Chirac appears as Caius Saugrenus, graduate of a Roman school sounding a lot like the elite École Nationale d'Administration where Chirac himself was educated. Chirac, er, Saugrenus appears as the Roman emperor's jargon-spouting envoy charged with conquering the tiny Gaul village through … capitalism. He succeeds in temporarily inflating the price of rocks, while sowing division and envy among villagers. In the end, they kick him out. Any lessons here for the rest of Europe?
>
> ('Jacques Chirac', 2003)

Similar to the recent slate of Hollywood films based on comic series (*Batman* [Tim Burton, 1989], *Dick Tracy* [Warren Beatty, 1990], *X-Men* [Bryan Singer, 2000] and *Spider-Man*), *Astérix* creates generic verisimilitude through reproducing the *mise en scène* of the comic strip with elaborate sets and costuming, and of course through basing the story on the main characters in the strip. *Astérix* is also reminiscent of the peplum film, a popular genre set in the Greco-Roman era involving a peasant strongman standing up for the people against corrupt politicians. The peplum emerged in Italy in the silent era, but in the post-war years became popular throughout Europe. As production costs and international audiences grew, most peplum films were co-produced with other European countries (Lagny, 1992).

If *Astérix* shares generic Hollywood traits in its fast-pace linear narrative, goal-oriented characters, stars (Christian Clavier, Gérard Depardieu and Roberto Benigni), spectacular special effects and action, it also shares with Hollywood a populist address. Just as Hollywood adaptations of cartoon strips contain heroes who are typically underdogs or outcasts blessed with special powers to fight various institutional forces of oppression, *Astérix* and the peplum invest their everyday heroes with the strength to resist larger forces – a narrative that one reviewer of *Astérix* described as a 'cheeky underdog getting the better of a mightier foe' (Elley, 1999). These are not uncommon themes in Hollywood, and indeed they proliferate in other leading film-export industries such as Hindi and Hong Kong cinema. Popular films that register these power relations suggest that universality resides in lived social injustice rather than Hollywood narrative transparency. Commentators argue that *Astérix*'s popularity across Europe stems in part from a common legacy of Roman imperialism that serves as a ready metaphor for contemporary struggles against global powers. But we must note that when asked about the comic strip's popularity, Goscinny simply replied, 'because he does funny things, and that's all' (quoted in Beard, 2002). Sometimes a Gaul is just a Gaul.

What can these generic measures of textual production and circulation tell us about the relationship between budgetary scale and cultural diversity in co-production through pan-European audiovisual policy? The unprecedented box-office success of *Astérix* throughout Europe is in part the result of tapping into pan-European popular genres (the cartoon strip, the peplum and Hollywood) that do more than simply mimic Hollywood. After all, the film only obtained an extremely limited release in the US, proof that big-budget European films can succeed without catering to US popular-cultural sensibilities. This is also evidence that while the rise and fall of US art-house theatre circuits correlates closely with the volume of highbrow European imports, populist European films have been locked out of Hollywood-controlled US distribution.

Astérix stands as a sharp corrective to claims that the competitive and polyglot US market is the sole breeding ground for textual universalism. Quickly paced narratives, stars and action sequences are no less culturally specific and diverse than art-house, auteurist personal visions. Small budgets and high status should not be bureaucratic litmus tests for European cultural diversity, just as generic pleasures, star affiliation and populist themes should not be left to Hollywood. It is doubtful that the slapstick of *Astérix* is what the framers of EU cultural policy see as bringing Europe's 'common cultural heritage to the fore' – yet it is hard to find a more exacting example. It is also hard to find a more fitting instance of how the deregulation and horizontal integration of European media have birthed synergistic commodity forms across the media (comic books, film and video games) and beyond (theme parks). This process seeks to colonise the widest possible audience in crowded media environments through attempts to be everywhere all the time. It follows the twin logics of a commercial industry: textual standardisation (genres, sequels, series, serials, remakes, reruns and synergy) and differentiation (spectacle, stars, post-production and high-concept marketability) – not the desired prescription for diversifying European cinema.

Under the stated goal of promoting a pan-European audiovisual market-place, the COE and EU media policies set into play two opposing regimes of value, best represented by MEDIA's desire to 'embrace liberalization without uniformity' and Eurimages' distinguishing appropriations for works with 'circulation potential' from those with 'artistic value'. This value hierarchy splits cultural decision-making between *dirigistes*, who judge artistic worth and cultural heritage, and financiers and distributors, who calculate risk, efficiency and marketability. In this twin regime, there is little space outside market mechanisms for policy to engage generic pleasures with roots in collective history, memory and popular culture – the visceral pleasures of spectacle and the populist sentiments that provide spaces for imagining the empowerment of the everyday.

Recent sentiments among France's intelligentsia embrace the new Euro-populism against Hollywood. *Nouvel Observateur* found the second *Astérix* 'wonderful', just the thing to challenge 'the Anglo-Saxon hordes of the *Lord of the Rings* and *Harry Potter* [that] have been taking our multiplexes by storm, knocking our *Amélie* off her throne'. One commentator remarked, 'French intellectuals and politicians have used the new *Astérix* film ... to renew their attacks on what is seen as the evil of American-led globalisation' (Bremner, 2002). An Australian critic shared a similar sentiment:

> *Astérix* is not so much French as non-American. .... As the American empire
> tightens its grip, *Astérix* is our last hope. Only he can unite Europe in
> resistance against these Roman legionaries in casual polyester leisurewear. Parc
> *Astérix* offers disgruntled Europeans the opportunity to boycott the Disney
> empire yet still keep the children happy – a vital but frequently overlooked
> factor in the blueprint of many a revolution. Across Europe, people may have
> qualms about the idea of a European federal state. But rename it 'the Gaulish
> village', and they'll be flocking to its wooden fence.
>
> (Laville, 2001)

Enlisting children in this anti-Hollywood Gallic revolution became more complicated, however, when McDonald's replaced Ronald with Astérix in advertising campaigns in France to coincide with the release of *Astérix et Obélix: Mission Cléopatre*. As 'ancient Gallic hamburgers' joined the menu, many were outraged that this emblematic sign of Yanqui cultural imperialism had appropriated the popular freedom fighter. A French commentator lamented that 'by capturing our very heritage, McDonald's has achieved a striking revenge over Bové', referring to the peasant farmers' leader José Bové, who gained prominence in 1999 when he attacked a McDonald's restaurant (Sage, 2001). While McDonald's in France attempted to localise its image, Claude Berri planned to make the third *Astérix* instalment less French, because the second film's overseas receipts were disappointing. He remarked that 'the Chabat film was too Canal Plus – it was less visual than the first, too dependent on typically French dialogue. The next one won't be like that; it will have jokes and special effects but it will really tell a story' (quoted in James, 2002).

Equity Co-production

> Hollywood movies move; European ones linger; Asian ones sit and contemplate.
>
> ('Not the Last', 1995)

Even as pan-European film has shown signs of valuing popular culture, liberalisation has fostered transnational European media conglomerates that bet on Hollywood's hold on pan-European cultural expression through investing in Hollywood itself, via equity co-productions.

In 1998, Paramount released *Hard Rain* (Mikael Salomon) in 2,100 US theatres. The film was a high-concept generic hybrid that mixed a stagecoach heist with the disaster film and was inspired by the 1993 floods across the US Midwest. Armoured-car security guard Christian Slater faced off with outlaw Morgan Freeman and his henchman over bank spoils against the backdrop of a major flood, while English actress Minnie Driver sported a Midwestern accent and Danish director Salomon provided water-picture credentials courtesy of his camerawork on *The Abyss* (James Cameron, 1989). *Hard Rain* was firmly a product of the Los Angeles talent pool. Orchestrated by the independent Mutual Film Company, five hundred cast, crew and other key personnel were assembled through informal networks that characterise post-studio Hollywood NICL production (Bates, 1998; London Economics, 1992).

Mutual finances its projects through an international consortium of six distribution giants from Europe and Japan. Financing for *Hard Rain* came from Union Générale Cinématographique (UGC), France's largest cinema chain, Britain's public broadcaster, the BBC, the formerly Dutch-owned French film distributor Polygram Film Entertainment, the German television rights distributor Telemunchen (TMG) and the Danish studio Nordisk Film. Financing from Japan came from the Marubeni Corporation, a video and television rights distributor, and the film distributor Toho-Towa Company ('Paramount', 1996; Hindes, 1998a; Herskovitz, 1998). Although US independents have sought financing from abroad for decades, including De Laurentiis in the 1970s, Cannon in the 1980s and Carolco in the 1990s, Mutual's projects give an equity stake to its partners, rather than just territory rights. In other words, Mutual's partners have a say in the projects that are developed, and offer creative input on what will attract audiences in their respective regions. For example, Toho-Towa opted not to invest in *Blues Bros. 2000*, but backed Mike Nichols' *Primary Colors* (1998). As a Toho executive said, 'If you just see [*Primary Colours*] as a political satire, that's a problem. But we see it as a well-crafted human drama, directed by a great, famous director' (quoted in Hindes, 1998a). Mutual's consortium has produced big-budget films, including *12 Monkeys* (Terry Gilliam, 1995), *The Jackal* (Michael Caton-Jones, 1997), *The Relic* (Peter Hyams, 1997) and *Virus* (John Bruno, 1999), as well as the medium-budget pictures *A Simple Plan* (Sam Raimi, 1998), *Man on the Moon* (Milos Forman, 1999) and *Wonder Boys* (Curtis Hanson, 2000). But certain Mutual projects have been less risky, and perhaps too Yanqui, to obtain international money predicated on difference. Mutual developed *Saving Private Ryan* (1998) before Spielberg became interested. It subsequently lost all equity in the picture, and co-produced for a fee with Dream-Works and Paramount (Eller, 1998). The same thing happened with *The Patriot* (Roland Emmerich, 2000), which Mutual co-produced with Sony. Mutual, TMG, Toho-Towa and the BBC responded by creating a three-year, US$200 million revolving credit to finance films outside the studios (Guider, 2000b).

The Mutual consortium is just one example of how highly capitalised theatrical and television distributors in Hollywood's largest export markets have become integral players in facilitating rather than challenging the Hollywood NICL. Twenty integrated media conglomerates in Japan and Europe have pushed foreign financing for big-budget Hollywood films to 70 per cent (Groves and D'Alessandro, 2001). As noted in Chapter 1, the most recent influx of funding has come from Germany's Neuer Markt, the Frankfurt-based new media and technology stock exchange. In 1999 and 2000, thirteen German film licensing companies raised €1.9 billion on the Neuer Markt, 1.3 billion of which flowed to Hollywood (Harding, 2000). With the collapse of the market in 2001, many of these rights-holders (Senator, Kinowelt, Helkon) are considered ripe for takeover by European and Hollywood conglomerates (Dawtrey and Foreman, 2001).

This emerging source of funding from new media (cable, satellite and the Internet) has shifted the foreign financial base for Hollywood from bankers to rights-seeking electronic distributors. Revenue streams for Hollywood feature films have increasingly moved away from theatre and video to free and pay-TV, particularly in Europe. European television buyers created such a steady source of income for Hollywood in the late 1990s that they became central partners in equity co-productions with Hollywood majors and independents to the extent that these revenues dwarfed funding levels for treaty-based co-productions. A survey of this growth is warranted to challenge the efficacy of European media policy's embrace of liberalisation as a means of fortifying European cultural expression.

European Conglomerates and Hollywood

> Trade is much more than goods and services. It's an exchange of ideas. Ideas go where armies cannot venture. The result of idea exchange as well as trade is always the collapse of barriers between nations.
>
> (Jack Valenti, 2000a)

For over a decade now, viewers in Europe have spent more on film via video than in the theatre. In 1998, they paid US$4.8 billion at the box office and US$7.2 billion either buying or renting videos (*Screen Digest*, November 1999: 296). But the key new site is pay-TV, which increased at a rate of 23 per cent in the last five years of the 1990s (*Screen Digest*, August 1999: 2). In the EU, pay-TV spending grew from 14 per cent of total film expenditure in 1988 to 34 per cent in 1996, while video spending dropped from 45 per cent to 35 per cent, and box-office receipts from 41 per cent to 31 per cent. Of the five largest European film markets, pay-TV as a percentage of movie spending is considerably larger in France and Britain than Spain, Italy and Germany. In France, pay-TV accounted for 48 per cent of movie spending in 1996, the box office 27 per cent and video 25 per cent, while in Britain, pay-TV accounted for 42 per cent, video 39 per cent and box office 19 per cent (*Screen Digest*, January 1997: 11, 13). Of the estimated US$9 billion Western European pay-TV market in 1999, 68 per cent came from these two countries (*Screen Digest*, November 1999: 301).

This shift in motion-picture revenue from theatre and video to pay-TV has implications for Hollywood distribution and finance. For while Hollywood has maintained cartel-like control over the world theatrical distribution of motion pictures, as we shall see in Chapter 5, it lacks dominance in television distribution. The regulatory structures of television in Europe, and indeed in the US, have their origins in national broadcasting as a means of protecting and augmenting the public interest, a policy logic that has restricted foreign ownership and fostered the regulation of state and private national broadcasting monopolies (Negrine and Papathanassopoulos, 1990: 15–24).

Deregulation, commercialisation and the rise of cable and satellite across Europe have transformed state-regulated national public television and facilitated the growth of such national and pan-European audiovisual conglomerates as Mediaset and Telipiu in Italy, Canal Plus in France and Murdoch's BSkyB in Britain. These media giants, with ownership positions in free and pay-TV, are increasingly important sources of financing for Hollywood, and have signed valuable multi-year contracts for European television rights to Hollywood films. For example, in 1996 Germany's Leo Kirsch signed contracts with US majors worth over a billion dollars for movie rights extending up to ten years, and paid a reported US$30 million for German-language rights to *Jurassic Park* (Steven Spielberg, 1993) and *Schindler's List* (Steven Spielberg, 1993) (*Screen Digest*, July 1997).

Europe's largest media companies consolidated pay-TV in the new century. Vivendi Universal, of particular interest below, and News Corporation comprise the most expansive systems. In 2003, Spain's two pay-TV providers, Sogecable (part owned by Canal Plus) and Via Digital merged, while in Italy, News Corporation's Stream acquired Vivendi Universal's Telipui. The News Corporation's BSkyB became Britain's lone satellite TV provider when ITV Digital collapsed in 2002 (Godar, 2003; Meller, 2003). Pay-TV proved disastrous for Kirsch Media, whose Premiere World swamped the media company with debt, leading to bankruptcy proceedings in 2002 (Landler, 2003). Premier World failed to attract subscribers in a market that offered an inexpensive basic pay-cable service via thirty channels screening several thousand feature films per year (Frater, 2003), and was unable to capitalise on its purchase of rights to the 2002 men's football World Cup. But the financially struggling pay-TV systems continue to purchase proven Hollywood box-office successes over independent European films (Brown, 1995). To consider the place of these emerging pan-European broadcasters, and their relationship to Hollywood co-production and financing, we turn now to Canal Plus, Europe's largest pay-TV service.

Canal Plus

> The whole idea that France is being destroyed by global popular culture misunderstands the modern media, which increasingly create separate products for each national market rather than peddling a single imperial product.
>
> (Sebastian Mallaby, 2002)

Universal had been owned by the Japanese electronics company Matsushita and then the Canadian spirits company Seagram. In 2000, Vivendi, Canal Plus' owner, became the third foreign conglomerate to own the studio, at a price tag of US$33 billion, only to sell it to NBC in 2003. While this was not the first time the French had invested in Hollywood, the sales return was perhaps not surprising, given the battles that have characterised Franco-American cinema relations. As we have seen, these struggles began in the silent era, continued with *étatiste* French film policy based on quotas and production subsidies, and peaked in the Uruguay Round of the GATT (Jeancolas, 1998; Miller, 1996). *Variety*'s long-time editor Peter Bart ironically, yet bitterly, complained that the Vivendi offer to purchase Universal represented reverse 'cultural imperialism'. His charge reflected the Los Angeles-based trade weekly's commitment to Hollywood boosterism and echoed the widespread xenophobic response to Japanese investments in Hollywood in the 1980s. At the same time, French filmmakers protested the merger, for fear that the station was 'being dissolved into a global, Americanized behemoth'. Canal Plus President Pierre Lescure declared that this would in fact be a successful move into Hollywood, unlike foreign ownership of MGM, which he described as 'run by an exotic and sulphurous Italian' (quoted in Tartaglione, 2000). Corporate idiocy and bigotry are indeed transnational.

Since its launch as a government-backed French terrestrial pay-TV channel in 1984, Canal Plus has grown to become Europe's largest pay-TV service, with 14 million subscribers throughout Belgium (since 1989), Germany (1989),

Spain (1990), French-speaking North Africa (1991), Poland (1995), Italy (1997), the Netherlands (1997) and Scandinavia (1997). The French subscription channel remains the corporate cash crop. It attracts half the total European-wide subscribers and garners 63 per cent of corporate revenues. Movies and sports make up most of the programming schedule, with 400 films aired per year, 300 of which are first-run (Canal Plus *Annual Report*, 1999).

In the late 1980s, Canal Plus began creating cable/satellite thematic channels, including Planète, Canal Jimmy, Ciné Cinémas, Ciné Classics and Canal Saisons, a nature and outdoor sporting channel. Canal Plus used these channels to launch an analogue satellite service in 1992, a digital package in 1996 and twenty-five themed channels in fourteen European countries, owned by Canal Plus, Vivendi and Liberty Media. Canal Satellite organises its thirty-nine basic services into nine themes (Sport, Discovery, Entertainment, Music, Youth, News, General Interest, Services and Games) and offers up to 200 pay-per-view and interactive services, including home banking, home betting, local news, job search, classified advertising and email. Much of Canal Plus' success across Europe stems from its control over interactive decoding and encryption technologies. It licenses a digital-access system and interactive software technology to major media service providers in the US (MediaOne), India (Zee TV) and Japan (Pioneer) (Canal Plus *Annual Report*, 1999).

Canal Plus' pre-eminence in pan-European television and Internet delivery is not simply the outcome of liberalising and privatising public broadcasting across Europe. It is beholden to the French system of broadcast regulation that some have referred to as 'land-owning capitalism'. Here, the government awards licences on the basis of the political affiliations and discretion of government bureaucrats, rather than through a venture-capitalist approach based on competitive bidding. For example, state control of broadcasting in France ended when Mitterand's government awarded the first commercial licence to Canal Plus in 1984. Mitterand then appointed his Chief of Staff, André Rousselet, as Chairman and Managing Director, and Canal Plus was granted a ten-year licence extension in 1994 without competitive bidding (Regourd, 1999: 35–36). Yet both the venture-capitalist and land-owning capitalist routes to deregulation and privatisation in Europe have created proprietary concentration through conglomeration. In the late 1990s, Canal Plus lost its *de facto* monopoly in pay-TV in France when a competing bouquet of satellite channels (TPS) was launched through an alliance of French public and private television channels (France Television TF1), a public utility company, France Telecom and the German media giant Bertelsmann (Palmer, 1999: 153–54).

But this integral relationship between the state and capital in France has benefited European film production as well as Canal Plus' pan-European expansion. Under a special agreement with the Conseil Supérieur de l'Audiovisuel, Canal Plus was granted the right to show recent films one year after their theatrical release, and one to two years before other channels. In exchange,

Canal Plus was required to allocate 20 per cent of its budget to film production, 60 per cent of which must be spent on European works, and 45 per cent on French-language films. This contrasted with requirements that other public and commercial broadcasters such as TF1, France 2, France 3 and M6 contribute 3 per cent to film. Although Canal Plus agreed not to use advertising in exchange for special access to recent films, in 1985 it was allotted a portion of the prime-time schedule for unscrambled advertising-sponsored programming, a combination that provided a valuable opportunity for Canal Plus to promote its scrambled pay service (Jäckel, 1999: 181; Mazdon, 1999; Palmer, 1999: 149; Buchsbaum, 2004).

Canal Plus is involved in financing 80 per cent of all current French films, and has manoeuvred to establish a major European movie studio and theatrical distribution network. Le Studio Canal Plus produces medium-budget French-language films with co-production partners or independent producers, and Canal Plus funds internationally known filmmakers such as Italy's Nanni Moretti, Spain's Alejandro Amenábar and Germany's Tom Tykwer. Le Studio Canal Plus also co-produces and funds US independent films, such as *Ghost Dog: The Way of the Samurai* (Jim Jarmusch, 1999) and *The Straight Story* (David Lynch, 1999), and holds the European rights to films from Francis Ford Coppola's Zoetrope studio until 2011 (Williams, 1999).

Canal Plus' state-facilitated ascent to the position of largest pan-European pay-TV network, a majority financier of French-language cinema and a production and distribution infrastructure has provided a foundation of support for European film. But Canal Plus has also been Hollywood's most substantial source of European funding, including two phases of equity co-production in the 1990s. The first, in the early 1990s, consisted of three co-production and co-financing agreements with Hollywood independents and majors, and a later phase involved arrangements with newborn independents. In 1990, Canal Plus paid US$30 million for a 5 per cent stake in Carolco Pictures, producer of the successful Rambo franchise and one of a number of independent Hollywood film companies in the late 1980s and early 1990s that packaged high-budget, star-driven, special-effects films financed by pre-sales of foreign distribution rights to Europe and Japan. Carolco was widely credited with this shift to ultra-high-budget films and the escalation of star fees, such as the reported US$12 million paid to Michael Douglas for his role in *Basic Instinct* (Paul Verhoeven, 1992). Despite the success of *Basic Instinct* and *Terminator II: Judgment Day* (James Cameron, 1991), Carolco lost US$353 million in 1991 and 1992. In 1993, Canal Plus raised its share in Carolco to 17 per cent and invested in individual films in need of further funds. With bank creditors pressing for forced bankruptcy in 1994, Carolco hastily pushed forward its final picture, the pirate film *Cutthroat Island* (Renny Harlin, 1995), which lost over US$100 million. While the Carolco executives received multi-million-dollar minimum fees to bring the film to market, and thus had nothing to lose, given that everyone understood this was Carolco's final film, foreign backers like Canal Plus lost a great deal of money banking on big-budget Hollywood movies, despite the fact that Carolco's twenty-three films averaged US$115 million at the box office. Carolco was sold in 1995 to 20th Century-Fox for US$50 million, and Canal Plus purchased the Carolco library in 1996 (Eller, 2000b; Balio, 1998a; Willman and Citron, 1992; Sterngold, 1996; Parkes, 1995; 'Canal Plus', 1999).

Canal Plus entered an equity partnership in 1991 with Warner Bros. and Germany's pay-TV group Scriba & Deyhle to produce twenty films through independent producer Arnon Milchan's Regency International Pictures. Warner Bros. offered US$400 million to cover marketing costs in exchange for domestic rights, and US$600 million came from Canal Plus and Scriba, which received theatrical and pay-TV rights in their territories and access to Warners' European theatrical distribution network. As all rights return to the joint venture after initial distribution, the partners have equity in the library of films produced by Milchan, an important asset for the European television distributors. Coming on the eve of 'Television Without Frontiers', for its part, Warner Bros. benefited from contracts with leading European pay-TV companies (quoted in Nussbaum, 1991).

The Carolco–Canal Plus co-production deal represented an aspect of Hollywood globalisation that meant a turn to star-driven, high-budget, action-centred, special-effects spectacles. The affiliation with Milchan presents a different trajectory, a global Hollywood that finds new European media giants investing less in global-event projects than in producers who have demonstrated skills in attracting creative talent and packaging deals. Milchan came to Hollywood from Israel, where he amassed a fortune in chemical and plastics, and gained notoriety as the country's largest arms dealer. By the early 1990s, he had built a reputation for producing the films of such prestigious directors as Martin Scorsese (*King of Comedy*, 1983) and Sergio Leone (*Once upon a Time in America*, 1984), as well as *War of the Roses* (Danny DeVito, 1989) and *Pretty Woman* (Garry Marshall, 1990). Canal Plus' involvement in the consortium was short-lived, for although in two years the group had box-office successes such as *JFK* and *Under Siege* (Andrew Davis, 1992), a string of flops such as *Memoirs of an Invisible Man* (John Carpenter, 1992), *The Power of One* (John G. Avildsen, 1992) and *Mambo Kings* (Arne Glimcher, 1992) led to heavy losses (Bardach, 2000; Bates, 1993). Canal Plus' third co-production arrangement was with Universal. Each side could choose which projects to participate in. The first was Robert De Niro's *A Bronx Tale* (1993), but the arrangement was again short-lived, perhaps because of the heavy commitments Canal Plus had made with Carolco and Regency ('Principal Photography', 1992; West, 1991).

Meanwhile, a new generation of Hollywood independents emerged that had risk-sharing ties to the studios and thus more stable and leveraged projects than

Carolco, plus additional sources of capital through the emerging European and Japanese media conglomerates. In 1998, Canal Plus signed equity agreements with three such independents: Bel Air Entertainment (Warner Bros.), Mandalay (Paramount) and Spyglass (Disney). Each was run by prominent producers or ex-studio heads: Steven Reuther (New Regency), Peter Guber (Sony) and Gary Barber and Robert Birnbaum (20th Century-Fox). The deals range from a fifty-fifty partnership between Canal Plus and Warner Bros. for Bel Air pictures, including *Message in a Bottle* (Luis Mandoki, 1999) and *The Replacements* (Howard Deutch, 2000), a twelve-picture deal with Mandalay that included *Sleepy Hollow* (Tim Burton, 1999) and Jean-Jacques Annaud's *Enemy at the Gates* (2001), to a fifteen-picture deal with Spyglass that has produced *The Sixth Sense* (M. Night Shyamalan, 1999) and Jackie Chan's *Shanghai Noon* (Tom Dey, 2000). In 2000, Canal Plus signed a US$900 million deal with Michael Ovitz' new production company for fifteen films over three years, continuing a trend of foreign money financing known producers through newly emerging independent companies (Carver, 1999b; Hindes, 1998b; Eller, 2000a; James, 2000).

The emergence of these and other Hollywood independents like Mutual (see above), Franchise, Hyde Park, LakeShore and Beacon Pictures is in part due to cost-cutting measures by the studios at the behest of conglomerate heads. For example, Sumner Redstone of Viacom reduced Paramount's motion-picture budget from US$600 million to US$300 million in two years, and Disney's Eisner cut US$200 million from feature-film budgets. The studios also began co-producing big-budget films such as Paramount and BuenaVista's *Runaway Bride* (Garry Marshall, 1999) and Warner Bros. and Paramount's *Payback* (Brian Helgeland, 1999) and *Southpark: Bigger, Longer and Uncut* (Trey Parker, 1999) (Eller, 2000b; Carver, 1999b; 'Canal Plus', 1999; Williams, 1999; Brodesser and Lyons, 2000).

In purchasing Universal Pictures and the US Networks (which include the cable channels Sci Fi Channel, USA Network and the Trio Channel) for US$44 billion in 2001, Vivendi turned to acquisition rather than rights to secure access to Hollywood films and cable television (Sabbagh, 2002). But this debt, in conjunction with other investments in wireless telephony and the Internet, led to losses of €13.6 billion in 2001 (Crumley, 2002), with a consequent impact on Canal Plus' support for French and European filmmaking. In 2002, trade magazines reported that Canal Plus was making fewer pre-buys of independent US and French and European films, and had ceased purchasing from Asia (Frater and Blaney, 2002). A French distributors' association voiced concern that the historic accords between Canal Plus and the French film industry regarding quotas and investments were less secure (Tartaglione, 2000). In 2003, Canal Plus announced a restructuring plan that involved hundreds of job cuts, even as French pay-TV competitor TPS signed movie-rights deals with Disney and Canal Plus' former partner, Warner Bros. (James, 2003a).

Vivendi Universal's financial woes also hurt filmmaking across Europe. In Italy, the merger between Vivendi pay-TV partner Telipiu and News Corporation's Stream destabilised local film funding. Telipiu had invested US$42 million annually in the Italian industry, but froze that investment in 2002 (Rodier, 2002). Other mergers changed the geography of co-production and film distribution. Spain's newly merged satellite provider was believed to favour the Hollywood contracts of Sogecable over Via Digital's commitments to independent film, and the merger of the two pay-TV operations in Italy gave the new monopoly provider greater bargaining power for Hollywood films. Movie-rights deals soon came under scrutiny, with Italian regulators placing a one-year limit on exclusive movie deals (Godar, 2003). The EC opened an anti-trust inquiry in 2002 into studio use of 'most favoured nation clauses', which require European buyers to pay the same price for films across all studios (Burt and Guerrera, 2003). These anti-trust cases have surged following the EC's continued deregulation of the European media industry.

Canal Plus has also served as a hub for English-language films intended for the international market. In 1998, Canal Plus entered a fifty-fifty partnership with Universal Pictures to co-finance Working Title, the London-based producer of *Four Weddings and a Funeral* (Mike Newell, 1994), *Bean* (Mel Smith, 1997), *Elizabeth* and *Notting Hill*. The five-year contract gave Canal Plus continental television rights to all Working Title films for an investment of between US$100 and 150 million annually. The first film under the deal was the Coen brothers' *O Brother, Where Art Thou?* (2000), a story of escaped convicts in rural Mississippi that indicated the French–British film pact had its sights on the US market (Carver, 1998; Cox, 1998; Rawsthorn, 1999; Dawtrey, 1999; Fry, 1998; Williams, 1999).

More controversial has been Canal Plus' involvement with publicly funded projects. In 1997, the Arts Council of Britain changed its policy of funding film on a per-project basis to allocating lottery money to three production consortia, in an effort to build more stable production and distribution groups, *à la* mini-Hollywood studios. The Council awarded three franchises access to US$153 million in lottery funds to produce British films over six years, with the idea that these groups would be self-sustaining studios after that time. Canal Plus financed the Pathé Pictures franchise, which was awarded access to US$55 million for thirty-five films over the six years. Pathé and Canal Plus have had an ongoing relationship through the studio's 20 per cent ownership of Canal Satellite and a joint venture signed in 1997 that established a pan-European film distribution network throughout France, Britain, Germany and Spain (Dawtrey, 1998; Williams, 1997a). The British press widely criticised the Arts Council for subsidising a US$1.4 billion media conglomerate run by a 'family of French multimillionaires' and a company that had a 17 per cent stake in Murdoch's profitable BSkyB (Purnell, 1999; Walker, 1999; Norman, 2000). By 2001, only one

of the fourteen films financed by the three lottery franchises had made money –
Pathé's star-driven *An Ideal Husband* (Oliver Parker I, 1999) (Stringer, 2001).

The Canal Plus experience embodies the cultural contradictions and possibilities of co-production and cultural policy more generally, as per the chart in
our Introduction (see p. 4). That leads us to address the wider field of commerce and concentration.

European Media Convergence: Liberalisation vs. Democratisation

> Competition . . . does not come easily in communications. . . . Clearly,
> something about the communications business breeds concentration.
>
> (Frances Cairncross, quoted in Gates, 2000:85)

Neoliberal deregulatory policies, which have contributed to Canal Plus' dominance, threaten to usurp the more democratically accountable recommendations
of the European Parliament (EP), the Council of Europe and nationally based
initiatives that favour local rules to ensure a diverse audiovisual culture. The latest
assault on state participation has come from EC 'convergence' policies that bring
more heavily regulated broadcast television industries into line with less regulated telephone industries. This is particularly relevant to the future of European
filmmaking, as most film financing across Europe has come from public-service
broadcasters or funding mandates for private television systems (Hill, 1996). Pay-
TV is situated between broadcast and telephony in the struggle to carry future
telecommunications services to viewers/users. The debate over how it is regulated
is increasingly central to financing film across Europe.

The EC's marketplace approach seeks to 'create conditions for economies of
scale to allow European industries to produce in greater quantities, at the lowest possible price, and to recoup their investment costs' (Morley and Robins,
1995:34). Members of the EU have challenged the EC's neoliberalism in policy
debates over the past decade. During negotiations for TWF in the mid-1980s,
the more democratic EP made three formal requests to limit media concentration as a safeguard of pluralistic media culture. The EC decided against
ownership limits, arguing that the free market would ensure diversity. In the
four years following TWF's ratification, the EP produced two working papers
and three resolutions that called for strict restrictions on media concentration.
The EC filed two Green Papers in response, framing the issues as a problem of
inconsistencies across national markets rather than media concentration. In
drafting a directive, Commissioner Mario Monti invoked the coming 'information revolution' to justify prioritising

> a level playing field so that media undertakings who seek to develop
> themselves and to invest across frontiers, notably with a view to the

development of new information society services, can benefit from the opportunities offered by an area without frontiers to promote the growth and the competitiveness of the European media industry.

(Quoted in van Loon, 2001: 18)

But the 1996 draft directive coincided with renewal of the TWF. During this process, the EP submitted forty-four amendments, which addressed diversity issues through local-content provisions and advertising restrictions. They were rejected by the EC's Council of Ministers. EP members grew understandably sceptical of the Commission's support for diversity issues, and the draft directive on lifting ownership restrictions was withdrawn (Harcourt, 1998). However, at the behest of satellite broadcasters, the Commission harmonised pan-European licensing practices and spectrum management to facilitate the expansion of satellite services (van Loon, 2001).

The Directorate General (DG) XIII of the EC is empowered to regulate telecommunications, and in the mid-1990s issued policy papers regarding the convergence of the telecom and audiovisual industries. They argued that in order to maximise the economic and cultural promise of the information society, media policies across sectors must be harmonised and cross-ownership restrictions lifted. The papers warned that if Europe was to compete with US-based media, which were allowed to converge by the 1996 Telecommunications Act, European media industries must not be restricted from converging as well. Pressure from other international bodies such as the WTO and the OECD also pressed for convergence and deregulation. One report even called for an end to public-service broadcasting, which elicited a backlash in the press and the EP, and motivated the European Broadcast Union to add a statement in the 1997 Amsterdam Treaty to guarantee public broadcasting's survival. Later that year, DG XIII published a Green Paper on telecommunications convergence that warned how national regulatory barriers could prevent media conglomerates from formulating 'unified strategies addressing pan-European markets' and 'hold back the delivery of innovative services' (quoted in Harcourt, 1998: 443–44). The EC has decision-making power over competition policy, and does not require official approval from either the Council of Ministers or the EP. The EC also created a 'Merger Regulation' for quick approval of pan-European mergers.

While the EC has used the promise of the information revolution and convergence to initiate neoliberal policies, despite opposition from democratic bodies such as the EP, the COE submitted a memorandum in 1999, following ten years of deliberation, that made recommendations to member-states regarding media pluralism. Composed of forty-one states, the COE represents a much wider constituency across Europe, but has little legal authority within the EU. The memorandum expressed scepticism that neoliberal policies would maintain media pluralism. While the EC encouraged mergers to fortify an audiovisual sector that could compete with non-European conglomerates, the COE recommended that members strive for a 'diversity of media supply' through a 'plurality of independent and autonomous media' (quoted in van Loon, 2001: 12). The memorandum proposed that member-states establish authorities to set ownership restrictions through audience shares and revenue caps. The COE warned against vertical integration in the media industries, advocating that members continue financial support for public-service broadcasting and require cable and satellite platforms to carry broadcast channels. The memorandum also called for non-discriminatory rules regarding on-screen TV navigation systems. Media scholar Ad van Loon has recognised the potential legal conflicts that may arise between these national policy recommendations and EU laws. If national rules are found to restrict competition or trade among EU states, such as policies which require language-based programming quotas, the EC might have the authority to overturn them (van Loon, 2001: 25–26).

Although the EC has incorporated very few of the diversity initiatives advocated by the EP and COE, it has recognised the strategic importance of fortifying economic plans for unification with cultural initiatives, or as Cris Shore puts it, transforming a ' "Europe of institutional structures" into a popular "People's Europe" '. Throughout its history, but especially since the 1992 Maastricht Treaty, EU policy-makers

> have sought to harness culture as a vehicle for promoting solidarity and social
> cohesion among Europeans, but the Eurocentrism and class bias inherent in
> their conceptions of culture also promote exclusion and intolerance,
> particularly towards those who fall outside the boundaries of official European
> culture, including Africans, Asians and other categories of 'non-European'.
> (Shore, 2001: 109)

EC-supported school textbooks, restoration projects and performing arts have constructed narrow, elitist versions of a common culture anchored in 'ancient Greece, Rome and Christendom', while 'ideas of popular culture, multiculturalism, cultural pluralism and hybridity appear to be alien or anathema to official conceptions of European culture'. Shore argues that such bounded conceptions of Europe's common cultural heritage misrepresent the diversities that comprise European life, and, as such, are likely to be perceived as 'too overtly political and instrumental' in realising market integration at the expense of 'cultural diversity in its own right' (Shore, 2001: 108, 115–16, 119).

How might media pluralism based on diversity and difference rather than a spurious notion of heritage inform audiovisual policy? It should not be surprising that the more widely inclusive COE and more democratic EP express concern for maintaining principles of pluralism on a more local and national level, given that lawmakers within the EC have assigned little weight to such issues. While the EC has invoked a revolutionary rhetoric of the information society to push for media convergence liberalisation, voices within the EP and COE have questioned deterritorialised decision-making powers within the EC and the corporate boards of pan-European media corporations. Messier's fall from these corporate echelons put on public display the distance between popular support for a pay-TV system committed to supporting local cultural production and the neoliberal vision espoused by the EC. Vivendi's Hollywood acquisitions and new-media investments destabilised French film financing to create an environment in 2003 where French film producers claimed they could only cover 5–7 per cent of film budgets from French sources, down from 10–12 per cent previously (James, 2003b). France has been the most successful film industry in Europe, in large part because the French government has required Canal Plus to funnel revenues back into it. In turn, the strong capital base that enabled Canal Plus to expand across Europe was facilitated by the state's decision to grant it a monopoly with special access provisions.

France is one of the few countries in Europe with dual pay-TV services, but Canal Plus' rival, TPS, is not required to support local film. As described above, the dual pay-TV systems in Italy, Spain and Britain have merged or ended in the past two years. This has given pay-TV providers more leverage in negotiating Hollywood film rights, but it concerns local producers, who worry that monopoly providers will consolidate and reduce funding opportunities. With their capital-intensive infrastructures, dual pay-TV systems seem unable to compete within a single market – this was even the conclusion of Commissioner Monti (Meller, 2003). In this respect, pay-TV providers resemble public utilities, defined as natural monopoly providers of essential services, rather than free-market competitors. As such, Vivendi's water/waste utility and pay-TV service might have much in common economically, even though culturally the glamour-less and glamour-laden businesses may seem strange together. As the EC champions the convergence of telecommunications, the public-utility values of universal access to telephone service and public broadcasting should not be lost. These access provisions have been important in keeping the Web a network of networks, rather than a system of competing proprietary systems. As pay-TV and telephony converge to become essential providers of these services, the neoliberal policies of the EC offer little guidance for preserving public-service goals. Considered as public utilities for the information age, rather than simply market participants under the EC's neoliberal policies, pay-TV systems could follow the French cultural exception by requiring information distributors to channel revenues back into local cultural production as an essential public service. As monopoly public utilities, pay-TV systems could negotiate for reasonable prices for Hollywood imports, but also ensure that a vibrant national filmmaking industry is not sacrificed to neoliberal expansionist projects, exemplified by Vivendi.

But national film provision must also consider the diversity issues that

Shore raises about the EU. Nation-building has mobilised conceptions of cultural citizenship that have been committed to preserving heritages rooted in racial exclusion, class hierarchy and colonialism. For example, critics of film provision in France complain of the narrow elite that makes funding decisions. One critic described Canal Plus as 'both a bastion of the French cultural exception and one of the strongholds of the gauche caviar', described as the 'snobbish, Parisian left that rules on the accepted canons of what is politically correct'. But this same critic also complained that Canal Plus should not be considered a symbol of the cultural exception: 'the success of its pay-TV channel rests mainly on its output of soccer, political satire (largely copied from Britain's *Spitting Image*), films (including a heavy reliance on Hollywood), and even a monthly hardcore porn movie' (Parmentier, 2002). But beyond these middlebrow sensibilities that attack Canal Plus for being snobbishly highbrow in its capture by leftist intellectuals, and vulgarly lowbrow in pandering to viewers' appetites for football, Hollywood and porn, a more disturbing trend in France and Western Europe demands attention within national and regional cultural policy-making bodies – namely, the heightened expressions of ethnic and racial intolerance that have fuelled right-wing cultural politics in Austria, Italy, Germany and France.

Concurrent with the Canal Plus debacle that began this chapter, the xenophobic French presidential candidate Jean-Marie Le Pen voiced anti-Americanisation, anti-Europeanisation and anti-globalisation through racist anti-immigration sentiments that garnered 28 per cent of the popular vote in 2003. And Chirac's plan to ban religious symbols in public classrooms was less a defence of secularism than a racial policing of French culture. As one commentator observed:

> The impetus for the law stems largely from the increase in the number of Muslim girls turning up at public schools in head scarves, or even in long, black veils. . . . Most Jewish students who wear skullcaps attend private Jewish schools; there has never been a problem with Catholic students wearing crosses that Mr. Chirac described in his speech as 'obviously of an excessive dimension'.
>
> (Sciolino, 2004)

These right-wing movements remind us that fears of a US cultural invasion can be tied to exclusionist conceptions of national identity. Cultural policy should instead consider Hollywood as in some way internal to, and constitutive of, European popular culture, rather than as a 'foreign' threat to bordered European identity. But more US imports will not minimise the xenophobia, given Hollywood's continued traditions of representing peoples of Arab descent as irrational terrorists in *True Lies* (James Cameron, 1994) or *Aladdin* (Ron Clements and John Musker, 1992), where the protagonists are light-skinned and heroic, the antagonists dark-skinned and villainous (Wingfield and Karaman, 1995). As one critic put it, 'in more than 100 nations every day, viewers see American movie stars – Arnold Schwarzenegger (*True Lies*), Samuel L. Jackson (*Rules of Engagement*) [William Friedkin, 2000], Kurt Russell (*Executive Decision*) [Stuart Baird, 1996] and others – blowing Arabs to smithereens' (Shaheen, 2003). Film policies that require pay-TV distributors to invest in French film might also consider diversity initiatives that build on popular cultural forms, such as the *beur* cinema, which represents immigrant experiences through popular genres (de la Bosséno, 1992). Also, French and EC policy might address anti-immigrant sentiment through projects that more fully represent the lived cultures of the very European residents who have become the target of hate campaigns.

Conclusion

> The countries of Europe, encumbered as they are with all sorts of historic,
> linguistic and sociological barriers, were more or less impervious to each
> other, while the European market – unified – existed only for the Americans.
> (Jack Lang, quoted in Collins, 1999: 200–01)

Co-production marks an important axis of socio-spatial transformation in the audiovisual industries, a space where border-erasing free-trade economics meets border-defining cultural initiatives under the unstable sign of the nation. Co-production works through the NICL to facilitate a transatlantic investment highway. It is traversed westbound by European pay-TV giants enchanted by established popular culture, and eastbound by Hollywood producers enticed by tax incentives and cheap labour. That highway overdetermines European treaty, subsidy and quota provisions designed as alternatives to Hollywood's domination. Those interventions favoured economic liberalisation to create a unified pan-European audiovisual space, fortified culturally by the embrace of a common European heritage, weak quota provisions and subsidies for the artistic expression of a few above-the-line European residents. We think this formula is an inadequate challenge to the NICL, for the following reasons.

First, the tax incentives, currency imbalances and labour bargains that lure Hollywood to European soil provide financial incentives that far exceed treaty, subsidy and quota provisions in support of European audiovisual expression. Our survey of ties between pan-European television distributors and Hollywood reveals that European audiovisual liberalisation largely fuels the NICL, rather than challenging it. While the expansion of cable/satellite technologies has shifted leverage away from Hollywood-controlled theatrical distribution to European-owned pay-TV conglomerates, these rights-buyers have stepped up their equity positions in Hollywood, embracing a NICL that places product development in the hands of a few Los Angeles-based former studio heads and star producers.

Why should we not entrust these exceptional gatekeepers to look after the diversity of our needs? One marketing executive for 20th Century-Fox International admitted that Europe is indeed not a homogeneous market, because Germans favour comedy and Latin countries romance (Field, 2000: 100). While studios operate according to these vulgar pronouncements of cultural difference, below-the-line labourers struggle with wage, currency and tax fluctuations. A first step to any supra-national cultural policy would open up cultural-policy fora to bodies that represent culture-industry workers. This would not only elevate the crucial issues of equitable working conditions, job stability and fair compensation, but bring a diversity of cultural affiliations to the exclusionary and taste-rigid bureaucratic boards that have dominated audiovisual decision-making. Empowering a wider area of cultural workers to make policy decisions would tap into popular genres, stars and narratives.

Second, screen policy should not automatically associate culture with nations or regional trading blocs. The global patterns and histories of empire, trade and migration detailed in Chapter 1 speak to the implausibility and undesirability of confining co-production relations and quotas to the territorial boundaries of EU members. In his assessment of European co-production, Murdock comments that 'the simple dichotomy between market solutions and subsidies' does not account for the many linguistic and historical alliances with territories outside Europe. He calls for policies that 'consider more fluid relationships' (1996: 114). 'Television Without Frontiers' kept TNT and the Cartoon Channel off cable – along with channels in Arabic and Turkish (Sergeant, 1999: 109). To avoid such discrimination, multicultural citizenship groups, rather than residency-based point systems, should be considered in determining screen subsidy. By replacing 'cultural exception' with 'cultural diversity' (Rogement, 2002; Sotinel, 2001), pan-European co-production policy could augment rather than forbid arrangements between France and North Africa, or between Spain/Portugal and Latin America. More initiatives like the ones by BFC and Scottish Screen that supported *Pyar Ishq aur Mohabbat* (Rajiv Rai, 2000), the first Hindi film entirely shot in Britain, point in this direction ('Full', 2001). *Astérix et Obélix: Mission Cléopatre* challenged elitist conceptions of European cultural worth, and tapped into populist pan-European cultural traditions. But countering anti-Muslim and anti-Arab sentiments revealed in France's restricting religious symbols in public classrooms, and in the anti-migrant Le Pen movement, requires more from film culture than a cartoon figure's defence of a caricatured ancient Egypt. Rather than debate commercial viability versus auteur vision, film policy might address cultural disempowerment, devising funding schemes for large- and small-budget films to address pressing social-justice issues. In this sense, if no other, we can find common cause

with neoclassical economists in their *tristesse* at the dominance of rent-seeking producers utilising systems of subvention designed with other aims
(Messerlin, 2000: 289).

The case study of Canal Plus demonstrates the relevance of the state as a critical sponsor of local cinema and a facilitator of transnational pay-TV
expansions. This integral role must not be lost to liberalisation. As cable and
satellite replace analogue broadcasting infrastructures, there is an imperative to
project the public airwaves into the digital future. Pay-TV delivery conduits are
critical hubs that will channel our future collective screen experience, and
decisions regarding access to these public passageways must be open to diverse
participants. As pan-European cable systems fall under the control of conglomerates like Canal Plus and News Corporation, each with vertical ties to
content owners, the state will be an important arbiter in ensuring access for
local and national content (Fabrikant, 2001). The MEDIA programmes succeeded in distributing national films outside their country of origin, but to a
limited extent. Television distributors – whether through cable, satellite, broadcast or the Internet –must continue as custodians of the public air(cable)waves,
and thus key sources for ensuring that cultural productions receive distribution
and finance across the local, national and regional. When the EC ignores
requests by national film councils, the EP and the COE, it becomes clear to us
all that neoliberal policies are predicated on anti-democratic actions, and must
be revealed as such.

A final example vividly illustrates these points. The conflict between a neoliberal EC committed to European unification through a common cultural
heritage, and a more democratic EP that challenges this in defence of national
cultural difference, is playfully invoked in the French-Spanish co-production
L'Auberge espagnole (Cédric Klapisch, 2002). In hopes of securing a job with the
European government, a French student signs up for Erasmus (the EU programme designed to encourage students to enrol in neighbouring member-
states) to study economics in Barcelona. Within the close quarters of a cramped
apartment that he shares with students from Spain, Italy, Denmark, Germany,
England and Belgium, cultural differences of language and demeanour are
negotiated, as each person both conforms to, and defies, the national prejudices
that divide the household. Relationships play out as microcosms of the EU: the
Englishwoman feels the least at home and has a fling with a dopey Yanqui, while
the expressive Spanish woman is frustrated by the subdued emotions of her
Danish boyfriend. In the end, there is unity in the diversity of the household,
which contrasts starkly with the cold, bureaucratic corridors of the EU government offices where the French student takes a job – only to resign on the
first day. The multicultural exchange leaves the protagonist feeling like a
stranger on return to his native Paris. But this destabilised, more hybrid identity is liberating, as his Afro-Catalonian friend had found in Barcelona.

The law is a complex player in the co-production side to the NICL, via binding treaties, quotas, subventions and patterns and systems of ownership. In Chapter 4, we interrogate perhaps the most important legal foundation to the NICL – copyright. Hollywood's harmonisation of diverse national regimes of rights via diplomatic and economic muscle is best understood within the history of intellectual property protection and the production and distribution technologies it engenders. Along the way, we find that statutory issues of piracy and other forms of 'inappropriate' appropriation have a lot to tell us about the labours of creators and users, and the narrowing divide between the two in an age of digital reproduction.

Chapter Four

Hollywood's Global Rights

They run computer manufacturing plants and noodle shops, sell 'designer clothes' and 'bargain basement' CDs. They invest, pay taxes, give to charity, and fly like trapeze artists between one international venue and another. The end game, however, is not to buy a bigger house or send the kids to an Ivy League school – it's to blow up a building, to hijack a jet, to release a plague, and to kill thousands of innocent civilians.

(US Department of Transportation, 2003)

Our Department of Transportation epigraph reads like an updated voiceover from a 1950s 'red-scare' science-fiction film: media pirates and terrorists walk freely among us, cloaked by superficial resemblances; but they are actually pod people, manufactured in a churning vat of commodity fetishism and religious fundamentalism (with a dash of philanthropy thrown in for good measure) that hides their contempt for country and conduct. But this is no remake of *Invasion of the Body Snatchers* (Don Siegel, 1956).

The group that stalks the pod people – and this chapter – is the MPAA's foreign-office distribution equivalent, the MPA. It is made up of Buena Vista International (Disney), Columbia TriStar Film Distributors, 20th Century-Fox International, MGM, Paramount Pictures, Universal International Films and Warner Bros. International Theatrical Distribution. The Association was formed to combat the growing tide of restrictions and barriers to audiovisual entertainment that targeted Hollywood motion-picture export after the Second World War (see Guback, 1984 and 1985). That was its central mission during the 1950s, while Kevin McCarthy was keeping the US safe from aliens who sought to take over US bodies.

But its name has changed from those McCarthyite days. Unlike 1956, its mission today is to prevent aliens from cloning not Yanquis, but movies, as it lobbies for global Hollywood's proprietary rights under the NICL. What had been the Motion Picture Export Association of America became the Motion Picture Association (MPA) in 1994, signifying 'the global nature of audiovisual entertainment in today's global media marketplace' (quoted at www.mpaa.org/about/content.html). However, excising the territorial moniker 'America' points more to the priority of the international market for Hollywood. While

'America' may have been removed from the acronym, territoriality and national specificity still guarantee the MPA's litigation infrastructure.

The equivalence between copyright piracy and terrorism is part of the US enforcement technocracy's hardening anti-piracy rhetoric. As we noted in Chapter 1, after 9/11, Hollywood delayed the release of big-budget disaster spectaculars and re-edited scenes of urban catastrophe in *Spider-Man* and *The Time Machine* (Simon Wells, 2002), and went to war. Like the linkage of Saddam Hussein and al-Qaeda in the years to come, the justification for Hollywood's twenty-first-century crusade rested on a mixture of evidentiary sleight-of-hand, bellicose rhetoric and the sheer urgency of a venerable but unbending militarism searching for new targets to acquire. Borrowing Bush Minor's precedent of retrofitting connections to substantiate unilateral intervention, Hollywood translated contemporary intellectual property threats into millenarian hyperbole.

Fear lies at the heart of such discourses; and a Chinese wholesale market at the turn of the twenty-first century is certainly a terrifying place for the US. At the US$3 billion-per-year Yiwu market, which attracts 200,000 visitors a day, 33,000 stalls and shops offer shrink-wrapped tributes to brand fetishism: Rolex watches, Gillette razor blades, Sony TVs, American Standard toilets, Beanie Babies, Viagra pills (even Viagra soup), Suzuki motorcycles, Evian bottled water, Duracell batteries, Timberland boots, Levi jeans, Marlboro cigarettes and Microsoft Windows. As regular shoppers know – indeed, this is the reason why many come in the first place – an estimated 80 per cent of goods sold at Yiwu are fakes. Testifying to the international desire for forgeries, Yiwu distributors have opened branches in Brazil and South Africa and plan to expand in Nigeria, Pakistan and Thailand. The flag of Hollywood flies prominently aboard this pirate ship, where 90 per cent of video discs are illegal copies that play on PCs, 75 million earlier-generation VCD players and 20 million DVD players (cheaply bought in greyware hardware markets like Yiwu). The MPA estimates that members lose close to US$170 million to Chinese DVD piracy every year. Closer religiously to the alleged heart of terrorism, Bangladeshis can look up movie titles online, then find them at Dakar's Rifles Square market as pirate DVDs (Mohaiemen, 2004).

Mission: Impossible 2, released in the US on 24 May 2000, was in Chinese shops three days later. *Titanic*, pirated a few days after its US release and nine months before its projected video release in China, sold 300,000 legal units and between 20 and 25 million pirate copies, mostly on the streets, for the equivalent of US$2–4. Prices have dropped quickly since then, and pirate DVDs of *Gladiator*, *Shanghai Noon* and the *Harry Potter* films are available for a dollar on the street (theatrical admissions in urban centres are anywhere from four to ten times as expensive, and rentals twice to three times as much). Demonstrating a humour lacking in Hollywood's sternly worded copyright manifestos, the pirate version of *The Matrix Reloaded* is called *Hacker Empire*, and was available in Guangzhou shortly after its US release in 2003. In Beijing, pirate Hollywood is just around the corner from the US embassy in Xiushui Street (better known to foreign tourists as Silk Alley), a huge counterfeit apparel and electronics market. Chinese college students can make up to US$30 per film by entering subtitles on the pirate copies from Hollywood scripts distributed over the Internet, or hard copies that travel the ancient heroin-smuggling routes (Behar, 2000; Long, 1998; Smith, 2000b: 13; Leow, 2003; Buckley, 2003).

This chapter tells the story of piracy's grand pursuer: Hollywood's intellectual property (IP) regime. We track its history, from a fledgling domestic industry flaunting loopholes in late-nineteenth-century US copyright law to pirate French film, through to today's global corporate powerhouse, desperate to control digital reproduction and direct other national copyright systems. From the Film Theft Committee of the late 1910s and the Copyright Protection Bureau of the 1920s, to contemporary alignments between the MPA and national governments, the US film lobby has struggled to keep up with new distribution technologies (including piracy) and legislation across local and global contexts. To trace copyright's role in the NICL, we look at:

- copyright history and theory
- its intrication with state security
- borrowing versus piracy
- the international record; and
- dilemmas and opportunities posed by the Internet.

The question Hollywood has not asked, which we pose here, is whether it should acknowledge piracy as a viable form of film distribution. As we will see, the ever-proprietary MPA's strategies to combat Hollywood's estimated annual US$3 billion losses to piracy include the surveillance and prosecution of IP malefactors, local consumer-education campaigns indoctrinating children into copyright's civic virtues, and the international coordination of customs and excise departments in piracy hotspots such as Indonesia, Singapore, Hong Kong, Macao, the Middle East and Eastern Europe.

Despite the detail and flavour of the anecdotes above and to come, it is difficult to measure the overall extra-legal trade in audiovisual products. The passage of audio, video and digital signals is rarely prevented or counted at borders and customs checkpoints. But there are ways to estimate revenues lost to piracy, and some even have the status of orthodoxy in the screen trade (like the assumption that one counterfeit DVD, CD or VHS cassette seized by enforcement authorities corresponds to the loss of another legally purchased product). The neatness of statistical reflexivity forms a framework of objectivity for trade disputes and the groundwork for their articulation, what Foucault calls a 'condition of validity for judgments and a condition of reality for statements' (1972: 127). Official statistics bolster the power of the state to secure enforcement budgets to manage culture, since it often has control over the agencies assigned to enumerate cultural trade. The implied objectivity of governmental data obscures the fact that they have been gathered to suit particular interests (Acheson and Maule, 1999: 39–50). For example, lack of coordination among national and international survey groups on the revenue generated by audiovisual industries can bloat trade deficits and inflate figures on cross-border transactions. However, we are not calling for the rationalisation of measurement schemes in search of a perfect picture of international screen trade. Rather, we suggest that the statistical imperative central to IP is a legacy of modern governmentality. The enumerative gestures of contemporary IP, their implied transparency and objectivity, are part of a history that includes seventeenth-century political arithmetic, the management of populations and the emergence of systems of 'rational' bookkeeping in early mercantilism (Poovey, 1998). The moral retribution of anti-piracy rhetoric can be seen as a deep suspicion of activity that resists assimilation into enumeration.

Locating new legal imperatives within the history and philosophy of copyright law, and outlining tensions between audience and corporate ownership rights, this chapter shows how Hollywood uses IP law to lubricate international exhibition and open up new areas of information management. The advent of new delivery and screen-duplication technologies (also examined in Chapter 5) presents IP challenges and risks at the same time that Hollywood strives to extend its market into new digital distributional arenas. With Washington's attention shifting in the post-9/11 political economy from free trade to imperialist warmongering, Hollywood and other corporate intellectual property owners began to propagate the idea that IP was not just the economic sign noted in the Introduction and Chapter 1, but a strategic weapon. If left unguarded by the state, it could fall into the hands of rogues, criminals, terrorists and unwitting consumers.

A Brief History of Screen Copyright

> Who can be blind today to the threat of a world gradually invaded by an identical culture, Anglo-Saxon culture, under the cover of economic liberalism?
>
> (François Mitterand, quoted in Brooks, 1994: 35)

Even before the statutory 'invention' of copyright in the eighteenth century gave birth to the author as a legal category, owners of texts devised ways to control the dissemination of the printed word. Monasteries, for example, where most transcription and copying of scripture took place, used their geographical remoteness to institute complex lending procedures for tracking a book's whereabouts. Later, European university libraries would take a page from the protection strategies of their ancient predecessors, securing books to one another and then finally to chest-high lecterns by means of a chain. Removing them required the complex and cumbersome detachment of rings and rods. Indeed, 'reading within the length of the chain' remains an apt metaphor for copyright's central imperatives to this day (Petroski, 1999: 60).

Copyright is, literally, the right to make copies of a given work while preventing others from making copies without permission. The historical origins of copyright as a legal determination are intimately linked to the industrial development of duplication technologies, beginning with the printing press, but it protects seemingly intangible products of the human mind – 'fugitive' property that resists easy legal circumscription. Spatial metaphors are apt, because copyright law is based on where infringements occur. In film, copyright gives distributors the ability to control exhibition (Huettig, 1944: 113). Therefore, a Hollywood studio that charges a New Zealander/Aotearoan with copyright infringement for pirating videocassettes will have to plead the case under New Zealand/Aotearoan rather than US law. Such territorial differences have increased copyright-owners' desires for international harmonisation. In addition to the articulation of space under regimes such as copyright protection, complex changes are under way with the advent and proliferation of digital technology, because the Internet fractures the traditional spatial infrastructure of TIS. While simultaneity is the general condition of any service – where the production of the service and its consumption are coterminous – innovation in information technology produces trans-border data flows that reconfigure the spatial parameters of trade between consumer and producer that were perhaps more 'concrete' in traditional forms of TIS, such as tourism, migration, sport and the mail (Nayyar, 1988).

Copyright is one of three traditional forms of IP. The other areas are covered by patent law, which deals with technological invention and protects the intellectual labour involved in creating new products, and trademark law, which polices marketing and advertising and protects symbols that identify a single product or product source. Put simply, copyright covers laws of duplication, patents are laws of invention and trademarks are laws of recognition and discrimination (Goldstein, 1994). Only patents protect ideas – trademarks and copyrights locate protection in their *material expression*. The distinctions between content and carriage are, however, often provisional markers rather than firm boundaries.

In calling copyright officials 'guardians at the gates', who 'build barricades tight and strong to defend the sanctity of copyright',[1] Valenti seems to engage characteristically contradictory forms of institutional address (quoted in 'With a Wild', 1996). The author as a legal/economic hybrid, what David Saunders and Ian Hunter call a 'monstrous contingency', has its roots in the very formation of copyright law (1991: 485; see also Foucault, 1977). In another instance of his mytho-poetic rhetoric, Valenti (1998b) notes that 'IP which leaps full blown and imagined from the brain pan of creative talent is antagonistic to artificial barriers, defies regulation, and resists official definition'. This articulation of authorship – a rhetorical swipe at the division of cultural labour – has been invoked for the past two hundred years or so whenever geographic fragmentation has offered a conduit to accumulation.

Driven by the exigencies of establishing an international market for literary works and redefining the dimensions of book publishing, the nineteenth-century internationalisation of copyright was part of the drive to create a world market by overcoming spatial and temporal barriers that might impede the turnover of publishing capital (Feltes, 1994). In addition to the regulation of international publishing, by the late nineteenth century, the 'creation of indigenous national producers seemed to have acquired importance as an exportable product and the source of cultural legitimacy', the economic incentive of a national literary patrimony (a 'national literature') that could be legitimated through its export to other states (Saunders, 1992: 171). Nations differed in their respective domestic articulations of authorial domicile. Some used territoriality as the threshold definition of authorial rights, others adopted a citizenship criterion. But the primary motivations behind internationalisation were curtailing literary piracy and codifying a universal notion of authorship. The Swiss government's boosterist invitation to 'all civilised nations' to join a new international copyright convention in 1883 and Valenti's rhetoric today exhibit inevitable contradictions:

> It is, in fact, in the nature of things that the work of man's genius, once it has seen the light, can no longer be restricted to one country and to one nationality. If it possesses any value, it is not long in spreading itself in all countries, under forms which may vary more or less, but which, however, leave in its essence and its principal manifestations the creative idea.
>
> (Ricketson, 1987: 54)[2]

The internationalisation of film copyright has a turbulent history. In some countries, screenplay writers were most closely associated with copyright protection, with films considered to be adaptations of screenplays. The 1908 Berlin revision to the Berne Convention for the Protection of Literary and Artistic Works folded cinema under the rubric of adaptation. The Convention did not recognise film as an independent category until its 1948 revision in Brussels. In the 1967 Stockholm revision, a new article attempted to resolve the issue of film authorship by shifting protection away from the author towards the work, thus blunting individual 'moral rights' in favour of corporate ownership. After noting that 'ownership of copyright in a cinematographic work shall be a matter for legislation in the country where protection is claimed', Section 2b of the Berne Convention's Article 14bis states that in the countries of the Union, which, by legislation include among the owners of copyright in a cinematographic work authors who have brought contributions to the making of the work, such authors, if they have undertaken to bring such contributions, may not, in the absence of any contrary or special stipulation, object to the reproduction, distribution, public performance, communication to the public by wire, broadcasting or any other communication to the public, or to the subtitling or dubbing of texts, of the work.

The Stockholm revision also considered whether to extend copyright protection to film in its *unfixed* transmission, for example over live television, but decided to leave the matter to national discretion, although coverage was available under the revision. The crucial policy change was expressed in a subtle language shift: the 1948 revision protected 'reproduction or production *obtained* by any other process analogous to cinematography; the 1967 revision protected works *expressed* by a process analogous to cinematography' (Salokannel, 1997: 66–67). Such distinctions are part of the semantic gymnastics of international trade policy, with linguistic contortions struggling to steady the (ever-narrowing) bar between legal protection and its denial.

Hollywood has always articulated its copyright initiatives with a forked tongue. US-based IP owners have characterised infringements of their rights as trade barriers for well over half a century. We often hear that these barriers restrict the free flow of US motion picture and television entertainment around the world. In fact, as Ronald Bettig notes, 'new communications technologies have caused this programming to flow *too freely*' (1990: 65): digital reproduction and the distributive capabilities of the Internet break through geographic and legal restrictions. While Hollywood's early international history consists of attempts to remove barriers that impeded the free flow of its media forms, new media and reprographic technologies present challenges because of their *excessive* distributional freedom. Clearly, the discourse of the '*free* flow of information and entertainment never meant "without charge!"' It exists to legitimise 'US government and multinational corporate efforts to pry foreign markets open' for US copyright-related export (Bettig, 1990: 65). The rhetorical lifting of restrictions takes a backseat when ownership and trade are confronted by the relatively borderless data flows in piracy's shadow politics of distribution.

Copyright concerns more than ownership, however. Beyond the statutory sphere, copyright permeates everyday assumptions about the uses of culture, conditioning ideas of authenticity and originality and drawing boundary lines that divide winners from losers in cultural production. It systematises the 'semiotic affluence' of reception practices through the enumeration, governance and disciplining of audiences (Hartley, 1996: 66). Since its inception, copyright has fragmented media consumption into public and private terrain, often with convoluted results. For example, while eighteenth-century English law withheld copyright protection (which allows for dissemination to a paying public) from printed works deemed pornographic, that lack of protection ensured a work's place in the public domain. Hence, the public that is served by copyright's commercial imperatives (rewarding legitimate creators with an economic incentive) and ostensibly protected from the immorality of 'obscene' literature can pirate pornography for private and public free use (see Saunders, 1990). Copyright's characteristic equations of the commercial with the public have often resulted in proactive protections of privacy. In the US, cases on the legality of private copying, whether by photocopying or videotaping, affirm most local copyright decisions of the last two centuries, which generally understand copyright to be a law of 'public places and commercial interests'. This means that only public performances can constitute infringement. Non-commercial use is more likely to be protected under fair-use clauses than commercial use, where economic detriment can be demonstrated (Goldstein, 1994: 131). By bringing the issue of cultural ownership into play, copyright legitimises certain forms of media consumption and prohibits others. While art historian Otto Kurz notes that forgeries 'translate the work into present-day language' and 'serve the same purpose as translations and modernizations in literature' (1967: 320), copyright traditionally refuses to grant legitimacy to pirated products.

If this history shows that that 'genius' is free to roam in the supra-national, it also benefits from spatial restriction. Copyright's historical roots in the reconceptualisation of land as 'the paradigm of alienable, marketable property' in the eighteenth century make the relationship between land and author clear. The first English copyright statutes take advantage of the 'transformation of land into the model against which other types of interests were analogized or compared to assess market value' (Aoki, 1996: 1327). Referring to what he calls 'the invasion of the copyright snatchers', Valenti admits that digital piracy takes advantage of a redefined 'IP landscape where there are no protective signs that warn intruders: "THIS IS PRIVATE COPYRIGHTED PROPERTY" ' (quoted in 'Protecting America's', 1998).

And in its evocation of ethical self-management, moral invigilation and spatial ubiquity, Hollywood is tapping into a much older connection between piracy and terrorism. This equation is clearly indicated in the history of 'universal jurisdiction'. In recent applications of international law, this category has been used by national courts to prosecute human-rights abuses in foreign nations. In these cases, the moral heinousness of crimes against humanity circumvents the normal territorial sovereignty of national jurisdiction. However, for centuries prior to the post-Second World War application of universal jurisdiction against genocide, apartheid and war crimes, *maritime piracy* was the only crime deemed heinous enough to warrant universal jurisdiction under international law (Bassiouni, 2001). While rarely invoked in actual application, linking piracy and crimes against humanity was established in late-eighteenth-

and nineteenth-century theoretical treatises that argued for extra-territorial jurisdiction. Although state-sanctioned piracy or 'privateering' was widely condoned – maritime piracy has always been legitimate business of the state – stealing on the high seas without a licence was long the most serious transgression of international law (Kontorovich, 2004). The moral righteousness of contemporary anti-piracy initiatives draws on precedent for the universally accepted immorality of piracy, still understood by the community of nations as exceeding even the sovereign power of national jurisdiction.

Hollywood's global rights intersect with the NICL in complicated ways. The US and the EU recently derailed a World IP Conference by disagreeing over movie royalties in audiovisual trade. The thorny issue was the transfer of performers' rights (which state that a performer has the right to 'object to any distortion, mutilation or other modification of his performances that would be prejudicial to his reputation') from the protection-rich and creative labour-friendly terrain of European copyright law to the litigation-heavy and producer-friendly landscape of the US (McClintock, 2000b). Clearly, the US negotiation team was frustrated in its desire to bring the NICL to the lowest common denominator of legal protection by extending domestic copyright provisions to other places. Differences in the territorial protection of performers' rights can result in such intricate stories of international litigation as the *Asphalt Jungle* colourisation controversy described in Chapter 2.

As the patent wars that enveloped the early US film industry indicate, securing monopoly rights over new technologies paves the way for distributional hegemony. Modern media piracy circumvents national citizenship protection, labour rights and state subvention – precisely those national arenas where differences are exploited by the NICL. Piracy's negligible production costs run on the model of small-scale manufacture. Of course, counterfeiting has different economies of scale. The worldwide trade in counterfeit apparel uses low-paid workers in huge underground Chinese factories. Entry into the pirate video-disc market simply requires a certain degree of entrepreneurial and computer savvy, a few duplication machines, a small air-conditioned space in which to do business and a table to fill out mail orders. Media piracy takes full advantage of its commodity's infinite reproducibility more fully and flexibly than any other form of manufacture. There is a reason why most copyright enforcement materialises at the retail level: it is much harder to capture pirates at the moment of production, because manufacture is so dispersed, operations so small and distribution pipelines so informal. Much pirate media distribution operates along an organisational structure detailed by cyberpunk guru William Gibson's account of trademark and logo advertising fifteen minutes into the future: 'relatively tiny in terms of permanent staff, globally distributed, more post-geographic than multinational ... a high-speed low-drag life-form in an [ecology] of lumbering herbivores' (2003: 6). At the same time, piracy is as embedded in localities as are traditional forms of cultural labour. For example, in the 1980s, government reports suggested that the Indian trade in porno-graphic videos relied on unemployed teenagers hired by a network of video entrepreneurs to travel to Nepal (via Katmandu), Bangkok, Hong Kong and Singapore to purchase pornographic videotapes, after which they were smug-gled over the Indo-Nepali border; another frequent route included travel by land over Burma and Bangladesh or by sea to Thailand (Holloway, 1989). In the 1990s, Hollywood film piracy might involve recording the film in a US theatre, sending the tapes to China for dubbing and photo enhancement, stamping the discs in Taiwan and retailing them in Latin America. National dif-ferences in the protection of IP law most often dictate where pirate production occurs, and pirate distribution is concentrated in sectors that are last in line for hard-top theatrical exhibition (which is why Hollywood's major anti-piracy tactic is worldwide simultaneous film release). The contemporary moment's technological and economic innovations mark a shift in the centre of copyright enforcement from the global North to the global South. Must its theory change as well?

Copyright as a Theory of Distribution

> In our country we don't have copyrights, we feel free to read and do whatever we like.
>
> (Iranian director Dariush Mehruji after his film was pulled from a 1998 New York
> Film Festival for its alleged resemblance to J. D. Salinger's *Franny and Zooey*,
> quoted in 'IP Watch', 1999)

As our above accounts suggest, several types of distribution exceed 'legal' intel-lectual property consumption. The first references tactical and informal transactions at the everyday level of street exchange through mobile, small-scale pirate networks that cater to local populations rooted in the practices of 'transformative appropriation'. They engage in what Michel de Certeau and Luce Giard call the 'daily murmur of secret creativity' (1997: 96). The second form of extra-legal IP distribution references large-scale pirate industries of reproduction, rooted in the classical political economy of uneven development and comparative advantage. Of course, local networks have always been embedded with global ones. Contemporary international media distribution maps onto the extra-legal movements of capital, people, goods and services: piracy does not simply invert the conventional circuits of the 'authentic' com-modity through social space. Extra-legal movements may be symmetrical, asymmetrical or interdependent with the circuits of 'authorised' cultural trade, part of continually shifting alignments between legal and pirate economies. The demarcation lines were once drawn by state apparatuses; new technologies of distribution have 'fuzzied' the traditional forms and logics of distinction between legality and its assumed other (Sundaram, 2000; Liang, 2003). In addition to explaining the exploitation of uneven development in the terrain of international labour that spools Hollywood around the world, the NICL explains the tensions between pirate production and distribution. For example, relatively lax national copyright enforcement can accelerate the domestic production of pirate media, outstripping traditional import chains. So, Russia's twenty-six optical disc factories, with a capacity of 300 million units, have curtailed pirate imports into the country; at the same time, large-scale domestic production has facilitated Russia's emergence as a new centre for international piracy (Wolf, 2003). Copyright addresses an issue at the heart of the NICL: what do culture and ownership have to do with one another?

Cultural ownership motivates a number of non-Western nations to undermine international legislative homogeneity (especially the notion of equal national treatment). They correctly diagnose Western initiatives on copyright internationalisation as a thinly veiled recapitulation of traditional dependency, and seek to prevent foreign monopolisation of cultural ownership or the flight of foreign exchange. Some economists claim that stronger IP protection in less-developed countries rises as foreign direct investment from developed nations increases (Lai, 1998; Seyoum, 1996). Others suggest that this correlation polarises domestic copyright regimes into extremes of high and low protection, and that Hollywood services foreign markets with moderate levels of national IP protection in a variety of ways, from local studio affiliates to licensing agreements (McCalman, 2004).

The mass media produce public goods – their value does not necessarily diminish as the number of users rises. Media commodities are also intangible goods; while they are embodied in material products such as videotape, satellite and the Internet engage with media as *immaterial* forms of service, as signal (Duarte and Cavusgil, 1996). As the complex distinctions between content and carriage suggest, media owners have trouble anticipating usages of immaterial goods except retroactively, i.e. their use by people (Frow, 1997: 188). This is precisely why control of delivery is of utmost importance to the MPA, which brokers media product through IP protection and permits access to cultural knowledges by *renting* consumers access. As Frow notes, media ownership continually struggles with the dual 'problems of defining and enforcing exclusive property rights in something intangible' and 'attaching exchange value to an entity which has almost limitless use-value'. There are, of course, infrastructures that provide for the uncertainty of media via copyright, the control of distribution channels, obsolescence, state subsidy and the 'institution of authorship, which remains the single most important channel for the creation of textual desire and the minimization of market scarcity' (Frow, 1997: 188–90). Yet this circumscription of use enervates what is unique about information. Unlike Igor Kopytoff's (1986) 'terminal commodities', whose social biographies involve only one journey from production to consumption, information leads multiple lives. They embody *transversality*, a 'dimension that overcomes the impasses of pure verticality and mere horizontality [that] tends to be achieved when there is maximum communication among the different levels and, above all, in the different directions' (Félix Guattari quoted in Bosteels, 1998: 157). Information moves from production to reception and back at a velocity that outstrips the declarative injunction of 'proper' use mandated by legal consumption. Such transverse commodities cut across the common intersections and agglomerations of production and use, creating new affiliations. In the legal arena, the commodity imperative overrides the public good. Ownership of copyrighted materials is conferred as an economic incentive to be creative. The problematic position of the public good – which reveals the tensions between public and private property – is generative of copyright's crucial distinction between idea and expression (Boyle, 1996: 57–58): ideas are not subject to copyright protection, but their material instantiation is. IP laws endeavour to draw boundary lines between private property and the public domain. They deal with the essential contradictions between free expression and a free market. Indeed, in recent years, alongside the privatisation of the public domain – which 'turns the information superhighway into a toll road' (Venturelli, 1997: 69) – copyright infringement claims are invoked because information has become 'too free'. This encourages us to suggest that questions of legal propriety must turn not only on *where* and *how* to draw boundary lines, but *why* to draw them at all?

To merit copyright, an expression must be 'fixed' as a work, leading to the exclusion of production within oral traditions. At the same time, the intensity of protection extended to productions that qualify as works of authorship tends to bar their use for new creative purposes, making outlaws of those who draw on such works for their raw material. Since it is derived from Western, especially Continental, principles of authors' rights, the international copyright regime that governs relations between developed and developing nations has huge problems. It is a structural feature of the NICL that while the traditional, folkloric and collaborative productions of these countries circulate internationally and are subject to appropriation by the culture industries of the developed world, for the most part they go unprotected by both national laws and international copyright (see Jaszi and Woodmansee, 1996, and Hayden, 2003, for pharmacological and bioprospecting IP issues). James Boyle astutely summarises the 'author concept' as a

> gate that tends disproportionately to favor the developed countries' contribution to world science and culture. Curare, batik, myths, and the dance 'lambada' flow out of developing countries, unprotected by IP rights, while Prozac, Levis, Grisham and the movie *Lambada!* [we note that three different films with this title came out in 1990 and 1991, directed respectively by Joel Silberg, Giandomenico Curi and Fábio Barreto] flow in – protected by a suite of IP laws, which in turn are backed by the threat of trade sanctions.
>
> (Boyle, 1996: 124–28)

The primary marker of protection in textual dissemination constitutes the author as a privileged frame or node. The temporal and spatial considerations of authorship and policy are crucial in the production of juridical knowledges. While reproduction has different valencies and taxonomies of repetition and replication, copyright law engages reproduction as a social *practice*. As Celia Lury notes, reproduction is regulated 'through specific regimes of rights of copying'. Although *juridically* determined, they are the 'outcome of economic, political and cultural struggles between participants in cycles of cultural reproduction'. Imbricated in the constitution of particular types of cultural work as IP, such regimes 'define the terms under which such property may be copied and distributed for reception' (1993: 4). Using the definitional rubrics of 'originality', 'innovation' and 'novelty', copyright law

> adjudicates between the need to secure the free circulation of ideas, a process which is commonly accepted to be integral to the functioning of the democratic public sphere, and the commercial demand for monopoly rights in copying and the associated creation of markets in cultural commodities. ....
> Regimes of copying rights can thus be considered in terms of both the possibilities and constraints they offer cultural producers in the organization of the processes of internalization, and the actual constraints that they offer for reactivation.
>
> (Lury, 1993: 8)

Legal possibilities and constraints and particular constructions of the audience constitute the field of cultural consumption: copyright law adjudicates the realm of acceptable behaviour in cultural consumption, in best DEM-GEM fashion. The central assumption of copyright systems is that creators of intellectual works need economic incentives. Economic reward is implied in the exclusive right to exploit copyrighted work, which is meant to motivate intellectual and artistic activity and ensure creators a source of income. The argument goes that if copyright functions in this way, it is a social good, because it stimulates creativity. That is not to say that duplication is an issue restricted to the courtroom. Cultural quotation and recycling, such as genre, are also ways of dealing with difference and repetition. Entangled with duplication technologies such as the printing press, genre makes clear the cultural delimitations of textuality and obligation alongside the more juridical parameters of ownership and use. In addition, genre is indebted to a legal conception of the public domain that understands creativity as a collective process. As early as 1845, US courts recognised that 'every book in literature, science and art, borrows, and must necessarily borrow, and use much which was well known and used before' (quoted in Cohen, 1996: 1006). Many copyright decisions of the early twentieth century understood that the textual stuff of genre – 'plots, titles, characters, ideas, situations and style' – were part of the public domain, as were textual similarities among works that could be counted as elements of the social lingua franca: as trite, common, idiomatic or cliché (Litman, 1990: 986–93).

Emergent media technologies remind us of fundamental contradictions at the heart of copyright law itself. Copyright law is predicated on securing and individuating the fruits of artistic labour to encourage and diversify creative innovation. However, copyright's historical implementation only highlights the tendency towards monopoly control and privatisation of IP by a shrinking number of multinational media conglomerates. In addition, IP's transformation of knowledge into property traditionally prioritises ownership over use, creators over audiences and production over reception.

For Frow, 'the tension between free public provision and the pressures to treat information as a commodity with a price is ... an aspect of the aporia that organizes liberal and neoliberal theories of the market' (1997: 209). Through the construction of consumption and prohibition in the public sphere, copyright law plays an important role in the formation of audiences and practices of reception. This is primarily due to the fact that 'the law is never a simple reflection or instrument of socioeconomic processes [and therefore] can register with ... detailed exactitude the slow historical transformation of social categories' (Frow, 1997: 132). The most significant outcome of the continuing pressures put upon extant copyright law is to question privacy, public interest, access and economic gain.

Political-economy theories of copyright protection have been instrumental in recognising the historical conditions that led to the protection of cultural products as forms of intellectual and private property. But economic imperatives and an analysis of state intervention alone cannot explain Hollywood's engagement with copyright. On the one hand, Hollywood uses the proprietary logic of ownership to buttress distribution. On the other, it strategically espouses a freedom-of-dissemination doctrine that should value piracy's role in creating audiences and demand for media products. Indeed, that role sets the stage for Hollywood marketing strategies in many parts of the world. It also points beyond the legal regime imposed upon IP by the jurisdictional authority of the territorial state. In some cases, piracy even inverts the conventional expectations that media will somehow follow patterns of uneven development. In his reincarnation as Tony Blair's 'Third Way' guru, New-Labour lapdog 'Lord' Anthony Giddens makes this point for us:

> A friend of mine studies village life in central Africa. A few years ago, she paid her first visit to a remote area where she was to carry out her fieldwork. The day she arrived, she was invited to a local home for an evening's entertainment. She expected to find out about the traditional pastimes of this isolated community. Instead, the occasion turned out to be a viewing of 'Basic Instinct' on video. The film at that point hadn't even reached the cinemas in London, where we lived.
>
> (Giddens, 2002: 6)

How quaint. For such cosmopolitans, 'London' and 'Africa' are located at the alpha and omega of copyright's temporal and imperial regime – the world out of spatial joint. This story illustrates how media piracy disrupts the conventional time-lag between centre and the periphery, between modernity and its native other. The frenetic, confounding spatiality of piracy is a source of the copyright industry's exasperation and its desperate attempt to link the disjointed spatiality of piracy to stateless terrorism. The national plays a key role here: as the war on terror focuses on the global circuits of the information commodity, the national tames the affective anxieties brought on by the frenetic movements of contemporary intellectual property, the uncanny ubiquity of piracy. In fact, the moral commensurability of piracy and terrorism – as equal partners in the heresy of spatial dislocation – is ensured by their simultaneous threats to the nation.

Yet, the national is affiliated with social practices of identity and domicile. The territoriality of the national is not simply mapped on a pre-existing space: social practices under the sign of nations *perform* the territorial as a provisional and improvisational spatial marker (Ford, 1999). We can see this exemplified in competing domains of the national that are invoked in large-scale media exchange. For example, in Malaysia, media pirates have been, as in many other places, prosecuted under Trade Descriptions Acts for proffering fraudulent 'Made in USA' labels. 'True Name and Address' statutes, which form the backbone of the MPAA's Yanqui anti-video piracy litigation, impose 'criminal penalties for the rental and sale of videocassettes that do not bear the true name and address of the manufacturer'. Similarly, new Russian copyright laws mandate that every CD, DVD and cassette must display the name and location of its manufacturer along with a unique licensing number (Nurton, 2002). Yet US and Russian copyright law's insistence on registering location to designate authenticity falls under the ambit of international maritime law, where registered goods can end up in cargo vessels bearing an imprimatur of national origin that can be openly traded in the international market. These marks of national origin are called 'flags of convenience' and can be obtained from numerous governments willing to sell their national attribution to third-party shipping distributors in exchange for a portion of the profits on a percentage basis or a one-time fee. Such forked evocations of national authenticity and locational primacy are part-and-parcel of territorially governed IP regimes that respond to contemporary spaces of circulation.

Fundamentally, then, copyright establishes relations between textuality, ownership and use. It provides a mechanism for differentiating among texts and articulating relations between the labour of textual production as a form of property and restrictions placed upon textual reception. Securing reception nodes becomes important precisely because of the indeterminacy of the information commodity's *use*. Establishing scarcity through exclusivity is one of the enduring aims of copyright protection. The information commodity relies on its circulation as a protected form of legal property that can serve as a subsidy for the enormous costs of its production. Distribution and predictability become key in the corporate control of IP, deflecting the law (at least in its Yanqui incarnation) away from authorship and towards ownership.

By engaging media copyright in its institutional and symbolic form, we recognise the transitory, palimpsestic and permeable nature of producers and consumers, and the ways in which legal, public and cultural policy has manifested the audience as a fictive, yet constitutive marker of social difference, action and mobilisation, veering between the DEM and the GEM. While we are clearly interested in the disciplinary shifts towards institutional and policy analysis in cultural studies, we do not wish to reinscribe Tony Bennett's provocation that the 'network of relations that fall under the *properly* theoretical understanding of policy have a substantive priority over the semiotic properties of such practices' (1992: 28). This prescription results from his interests in '*severing* the connection between philosophical aesthetics and Marxist socioeconomic analyses' (Bennett, 1990: 117–90), but distinctions between textuality and policy are untenable when one works on copyright and IP. The semiotics of image and content analysis are *absolutely* critical in policy determinations of duplication, where legal determination of what constitutes fair use and juridical notions of substantial similarity turn on *textual* resemblance. In addition, by arguing for a productive relation between post-structuralist literary theory and law, some have suggested that copyright's evocation of the singular work might be shifted to a conception of a de-propertised, dynamic textuality that recognises the fundamentally incomplete nature of all forms of cultural production and reimagines the audience as co-creators of textual forms (see Rotstein, 1992, and Aoki, 1993b). We favour a hybrid methodology that approaches policy and institutions as they are imbricated in both the political economy of cultural enumeration and the signifying power of ownership in everyday life. That is clearly what the MPAA and the US government utilise when they tie IP to national security.

IP and the National Security State

The prospect of piracy is terrorizing.

(Jack Valenti, quoted in Machan, 1997)

In many ways, the digital signals an apocalypse to Hollywood. File-sharing on peer-to-peer (P2P) networks at the end of 2003 made close to 60,000 unauthorised copies of *Terminator 3: Rise of the Machines* (Jonathan Mostow, 2003) and *Finding Nemo* available for free at more than 200,000 websites, many run on network servers beyond the jurisdictional authority of the US. BayTSP, a California-based Internet policing company contracted to a number of Hollywood studios, claims that there are between 1 and 3 million copyright infringements per day (Kipnis, 2004). Assimilating file-sharing within existing risks – video piracy, theatrical print theft, signal and broadcast piracy, and parallel imports – the MPA upped its rhetorical strategies to address the mounting threat as 'a national issue that should concern the citizens of this free and loving land'. Two years after 9/11, and armed with self-comparisons to Winston Churchill and John F. Kennedy, Valenti (2003b) decried the 'kidnapping' and 'illegal abduction' of film as it travelled from theatrical to home VHS and DVD exhibition windows. By defining piracy as an abrogation of film's right to proceed on its 'natural' journey from production to profit, Hollywood has cleverly hijacked something of its own: an equivalence between copyright infringement and terrorism.

As usual, Hollywood was not inventing something new here. The equivalence between piracy and terrorism gained legitimacy in 1995, when New York's Joint Terrorism Taskforce claimed that profits from counterfeit T-shirt sales – sold in the very shadow of the twin towers – helped fund the 1993 bombing of the World Trade Center. Post-9/11, policy proposals from the EC have naturalised the relationship between IP piracy and terrorism, suggesting that financing networks have gone global. A widely circulated 2002 US customs report notes that

> anti-terrorist organizations in the US and abroad are homing in on the close connections between transnational crime and terrorism. Before 9/11, law enforcement defined both as strategic threats, but tended to approach each problem separately. ... Today, in a post 9/11 environment, agencies like Customs and Interpol understand that the international underworld is a breeding ground for terrorism, providing groups like Al Qaeda, Hamas, Hezbollah and the IRA with funds generated by illegal scams.
>
> (Millar, 2002:1)

Valenti used the same report as the centrepiece of his testimony before the US House of Representatives in 2003 on 'International Copyright Piracy: Links to Organized Crime and Terrorism'. Valenti urged the US security establishment to crack down on international syndicates thought to funnel money to terrorists. After noting that new forms of digital reproduction and distribution (primarily over the Internet) were supplanting older forms of analogue video piracy, Valenti borrowed Bush Minor's favourite clause from his stockpile of millenarian hubris: 'And then the world changed'.

Before the world changed, international-relations orthodoxy had directed its criticism of the global trade in counterfeit goods at the relative porosity of state borders. To counter this, theorists called for states to criminalise piracy and share information and resources to enforce IP (see Friman and Andreas, 1999). Some pushed for international cooperation because counterfeit and other 'grey-area phenomena' were threats to the stability of sovereign-states (see Chalk, 1997); others claimed that border controls offered more than a simple deterrent to the clandestine trade, that they 'projected an image of moral resolve and [a] propping up of the state's territorial legitimacy ... in times of high societal insecurity' (Andreas, 2003: 107). Valenti appeared to crib from these sources (without footnotes) when he told the House Piracy Committee that 'to deal with this kind of organized crime', the MPA

> and our fellow copyright associations need the help of governments – both here and abroad. It is simply not possible for a private sector organization to penetrate this kind of organized, criminal endeavor without the help of governments. Governments need to dedicate the same kinds of legal tools to fighting piracy that they bring to other kinds of organized crime: money laundering statutes, surveillance techniques, and organized crime laws. . . . Large, violent and highly organized criminal groups are getting rich from the theft of Hollywood's copyrighted products. Only when governments around the world effectively bring to bear the full powers of the state against these criminals can we expect to make progress.
>
> (Valenti, 2003b)

At a 2003 hearing, the US House International Relations Committee noted the 'human costs' of copyright piracy. In a display of nationalist bravado, the Chair of the Committee, former Clinton inquisitor Henry Hyde, professed extreme 'concern that our most valuable export, American ingenuity and the blood, sweat and tears behind it, is being taken from us as a nation' (quoted in 'Intellectual Property', 2003). Despite Hyde's clichéd advocacy for the libidinal economy of authorship, the language of Yanqui homeland security dominated proceedings. The Secretary-General of the International Police Organization (Interpol), Ronald Noble, was also among the witnesses present, the first time the head of Interpol had testified in a Congressional hearing (Johnston, 2003). He set up Interpol's first IP working group in 2002, after years of intensive lobbying by the International Federation of the Phonographic Industry and EC reports that pirated CDs accounted for almost half of a US$2 billion counterfeiting trade in the EU in 2001 (Masson, 2002). Interpol had adopted resolutions to police audiovisual trade since the mid-1970s, but raised the bar at its annual meeting in 2003 when Noble addressed the links between organised crime and large-scale counterfeiting, adding Chechen separatists and Northern Ireland paramilitaries (who traffic in Disney's *The Lion King* [Roger Allers and Rob Minkoff, 1994] and Sony PlayStation video games) to the growing list of organisations suspected of using profits from pirated software, film and music to fund their networks. The two nationalist groups joined a growing list of others linked to both terrorism and IP piracy, from usual suspects like al-Qaeda, Hezbollah and Hamas, to Albanian and Basque separatists, anti-Arroyo agitators in the Philippines, the FARC in Colombia and the Sicilian Cosa Nostra and its international affiliates. A report issued by Interpol at the end of

2003 notes that one kilogram of pirated CDs or DVDs is more profitable than a kilo of cannabis resin (Oliver, 2003). Heady material.

But Hollywood, the US government and Interpol are not the only copyright monopolists drunk on state-sanctioned anti-terrorism. British police have claimed that Pakistani DVDs account for 40 per cent of their anti-piracy confiscations, and that profits from pirated versions of *Love Actually* (Richard Curtis, 2003) and *Master and Commander* go to Pakistan-based al-Qaeda operatives ('Terrorists Run', 2003). In India, anti-piracy evangelist Julio Riberio, Punjab's former Director-General of police and current IP tsar for the music industry, has alleged that pirate CD factories in Pakistan fund Inter-Services Intelligence, Pakistan's premier spy agency. Meanwhile, Hindu nationalists consider the Bombay film industry a front for Islamic terrorism. Washwood gained some bilateral traction in the region when the Indian Deputy Prime Minister declared that crime magnate 'Dawood Ibrahim has the same resonance in India as Osama bin Laden has in the US', and the corporate media asserted that Ibrahim's music and video pirate trade in Karachi funds al-Qaeda and Kashmiri separatists like Lashkar-e-Toiba (Kartik, 2003; Chengappa *et al.*, 2003).

Hollywood's command over this unruly sector of the NICL is clearly uneven, even as it maps onto conventional targets. In 2003, responding to a cease-and-desist email from the MPA, the Palestinian P2P file-sharing site Earthstation 5 (www.earthstation5.com) declared war on the MPA and the Recording Industry Association of America (RIAA). Claiming physical location in the Jenin refugee camp on the West Bank and Gaza City, Earthstation 5 says it has over 550 employees and field agents throughout the region as well as in India, Mexico and Russia. Managed by a mix of Palestinians, Israelis, Jordanians and Russians, Earthstation 5 is backed by close to US$2 million a month in financing. While other locally based file-sharing companies doubt Earthstation 5's estimate of 19 million active online users, the president of Earthstation 5 (who goes by the pseudonym 'Ras Kabir' – Arabic for 'big head') addressed the copyright majority in language familiar to active *Star Trek* audiences: 'The next revolution in P2P file sharing is upon you. Resistance is futile and we are now in control' (Abbey, 2003; 'Sex, Lies', 2003; 'Earth Station 5', 2003).

Earthstation 5's clever geopolitical manoeuvre offers an example of ways to stymie Hollywood's latest anti-piracy campaign, while the sheer volume and speed of Internet distribution confound conventional surveillance and enforcement. In response, the MPAA has sought to manage domestic consumption via a pedagogy that internalises anti-piracy as a moral source of national subjectivity. In 2003, it invested in a middle-school programme for US pupils called 'What's the Diff: A Guide to Digital Citizenship'. The programme has been promoted with public-service announcements released in 5,000 US movie theatres, with above- and below-the-line labourers arguing that piracy threatens their livelihoods. One such advertisement articulates moviegoers' cynicism about the *real* copyright beneficiaries, the major distributors, with testimony from a

Hollywood set painter who proudly references his contributions to *Dick Tracy*, *Beverly Hills Cop* (Martin Brest, 1984) and *The Natural* (Barry Levinson, 1984):

> the piracy issue ... I don't think it will affect the producers. I mean, it does affect them, but it's minuscule to the way it affects me, the guy working on construction, the lighting guy, the sound guy, because we're not million-dollar employees.
>
> (Quoted in Scott, 2003)

Volunteer teachers from the business sector were deployed to 36,000 classrooms to convince 900,000 students in grades 5–9 that P2P file-sharing was improper. Designed in collaboration with Junior Achievement, the initiative urges teachers to:

> bring home the message that P2P downloading is illegal, immoral and wrong ... as students recognize that there is essentially 'no diff' (i.e. no difference) between the illegal and unethical nature of these practices, it is our hope that they will begin to adopt more appropriate attitudes and beliefs about digital media, which will help guide their future behavior.

Well aware that altruism is no match for bribery in lessons of citizenship, the MPAA offers DVDs, CDs, players, movie tickets and expenses-paid trips to Hollywood for students who write prize-winning essays denouncing piracy. The contest rules for the 'Xcellent Xtreme Challenge' note that 'best of all, when you and your friends help stop the downloading of files from the Internet, EVERYBODY WINS!' (Motion Picture Association of America, 2003; Regardie, 2003). While the National Education Association is sanguine about corporate involvement in cash-strapped classrooms, the non-profit cybertarian watchdog group, the Electronic Frontier Foundation, complains about 'Soviet-style education'. Meanwhile, in the classroom itself, teenagers are rolling their eyes at lectures from guest speakers like a PriceWaterhouse tax accountant. 'It's not illegal if you decide to give it away', says one thirteen-year-old who enjoys burning music CDs for friends: 'it's a gift, you're not selling it' (quoted in Harris, 2003).

Corporate IP owners delight in their born-again identity as warriors against transnational terrorism, because the claim that pirate commodity chains enrich terrorist economies serves to normalise Hollywood's tightening control over cultural consumption. The mundane business of empirically proving piracy's harms is forgotten, as the narrative of homeland security turns IP into a strategic asset against terrorism. For IP advocates, the parallel trajectories of the pirate and the terrorist, from Davao City to Ciudad del Este, threatens the international body politic. Nowadays, IP monopolists claim that the viral threat of piracy overlaps with terrorism's wild, ubiquitous spatiality: 'piracy can be found everywhere', declares Microsoft's Web portal (at www.microsoft.com/piracy/).[3]

But the actual evidence of a link between terrorist funding and counterfeit com-modities is sparse and culled from a variety of disparate events, like a raid on a New York souvenir shop that turned up counterfeit watches and Boeing 767 manuals with notes written in Arabic, or the seizure of eight tons of counterfeit Vaseline petroleum jelly, Head and Shoulders shampoo, Oil of Olay cream, Vicks Vaporub and Chanel No. 5 perfume shipped by a suspected al-Qaeda operative from Britain to Dubai in 2002 (Hering, 2002; 'Al-Qa'idah Trading', 2002). And while pirate media culture disrupts and infiltrates flows of commodity exchange, as Brian Larkin (2004) notes, the polarisation of legal and pirate media obscures 'the fact that for many people outside the West, legal and illegal media are inter-dependent and part of a common infrastructure of reproducing media'.

Hollywood has followed this logic of transposing today's spectral ubiquity of terror with the frenetic movements of the pirate commodity (especially in dig-ital form); or as Valenti (2003a) puts it, 'the mysterious magic of being able, with a simple click of a mouse, to send a full-length movie hurtling with the speed of light to any part of the planet'. At the same time that Hollywood and other commercial film industries have collectively embraced the equivalence between IP piracy and terrorism to justify enforcement assistance to stem file-sharing, along with video, VCD and DVD bootlegging, the 'What's the Diff' campaign to educate youth on proper forms of reception demonstrates that the labour of consumption is within hailing distance of the state. This pedagogy of 'infantile citizenship' – to borrow Lauren Berlant's (1997) formulation – depends on an ethical self-management that combines social obligation with sovereign consumption (see Chapter 5). It turns out that, in addition to all the complex international harmonisation initiatives and technological locks that we describe in this chapter, Hollywood and the copyright establishment still bid for hearts and minds.

Texts for Rent?

> The Internet marauders argue that copyright is old-fashioned, a decaying relic of a non-Internet world. But suppose some genius invented a magic key that could open the front door of every home in America and wanted to make the keys available to everyone under a canopy sign that read, 'It's a new world – take what you want'.
>
> (Jack Valenti, 2000b)

In a 2000 speech outlining corporate strategy in the new digital environment, Disney CEO and head Mouseketeer Eisner gave a visual presentation that dem-onstrated the indebtedness of *Dinosaur* (Eric Leighton and Ralph Zondag, 2000) to *The Lost World* (Harry O. Hoyt, 1925), *King Kong* (Merian C. Cooper and Ernest B. Schoedsack, 1933), *Godzilla* (Roland Emmerich, 1998) and *Juras-sic Park*. Noting that Disney had obtained copyright clearance to show clips from most of these films (but not *Jurassic Park*), Eisner explained that IP law provided economic and moral incentives to create art. He neglected to mention the loopholes in patent law that allow film studios to reverse-engineer the software code in patented high-tech special effects technologies and save valuable research-and-development time and money, and that genre takes advantage of viewers' cultural competencies. While all art is in a sense derivative, terms like originality, skill and labour have complex valencies when legal ownership is to be decided (see Van Camp, 1994). And the big corporate owners are often on the other side of the litigation fence: Disney has itself been sued for copyright violation (albeit mostly unsuccessfully) for stealing: the idea for a sports complex; the 'tinkerbell' trademark from a perfume company; screen treatments; children's magazine formats; and the concepts behind *The Lion King* and *Finding Nemo* (Henley, 2004). Of course, Disney's zealousness about its own IP is not a new issue; in 1989, the House of Mouse sniffed out three South Florida pre-schools that had painted some Disney characters on their outside walls and pursued retribution in the courts (Verrier, 2000).

Eisner offers this five-point plan for copyright protection:

1 avoid extending compulsory licensing (which requires, for example, broadcasters to make their signal available to cable companies)
2 coordinate global legal efforts
3 foster civic education
4 erect technological firewalls; and
5 lobby for fair pricing.

His list brings demarcations between commerce and art in IP law into sharp relief. The central and (to stay within Disney's purview) animating question is who will set prices and establish the logic of distribution – workers, who invest their intellectual labour and creativity in the manufacture of an art object; corporations, which finance and invest in the material production of these objects; or the consuming public?

The success of most copyright-infringement suits turns on the relationship between economics and use. Section 107 of the US Copyright Act of 1976 excludes certain forms of use from the category of infringement. These forms of 'fair use' allow copying for a limited range of activities (teaching and scholarship, social criticism and commentary and news reporting) so long as these activities do not cause economic detriment to the copyright holder. The section on statutory fair use in the Copyright Act outlines four factors in considering whether usage constitutes infringement:

1 the purpose and character of the use (whether it is of a commercial nature or for not-for-profit educational purposes)
2 the nature of the copyrighted work

3   the amount/substantiality of the portion used relative to the copyrighted
    work as a whole; and
4   the effect of use on the potential value of the copyrighted work.

In the historical evocation of Section 107, the key element separating fair use from
infringement has often been the last issue – commercial worth. Since the statute
makes clear that some forms of use are public and others private, the major problem for corporate copyright owners like the Hollywood studios is how to
substantiate the key category of 'detrimental effect': can the owners of copyrighted
material like songs and films specify the money they have lost because of unsanc-
tioned proliferation, for instance through new duplication technology? Once the
potential effect on the market is substantiated by the copyright owner, however, it
has been very difficult to overturn the commercial limitations on fair use.

   In *Universal City Studios, Inc.* v. *Sony Corp of America* (1979), the corporate
owners of copyrighted images claimed 'contributory infringement' and sought
to impose liability on manufacturers of VCRs. The court decided that most uses
of VCRs, such as time shifting or accumulating private libraries, were protected
under fair use. Upon appeal in 1981, the decision was reversed in favour of Universal (joined by Disney). As the case reached final arbitration in the Supreme
Court two years later, the MPAA suggested a fixed royalty on VCRs and blank
videotapes to compensate for purported losses. The key issue, again, was private copying and time shifting. The court decided that these were
non-infringing uses and granted Sony's appeal. In other words, although VCR
hardware could be used for infringing purposes, fair use of the technology out-
weighed any infringement. The Sony case lives on in current debates about the
encryption of digital television transmissions to prevent the possible taping of
'superpremium' pay-TV programming and other digital content. Recent cases
regarding digital multimedia have sought the legal protection of 'transformative use' – i.e. the use significantly changes the dimensions of the original, and
multimedia developers are authors too (see Goldberg, 1995). Consumer electronics is again locked in a struggle with the corporate owners of copyrighted
materials, and fair use will determine the outcome (Goldstein, 1994).

Piracy and the MPA's International Imperatives

   There's no free Hollywood.
                                           (Jack Valenti, quoted in Streif, 2000)

   Look at *Titanic* – it's a Hindi film. *Gladiator* is a Hindi film. Woody Allen's
   Everybody Says I Love You is beautiful, just like a Hindi film. James Bond
   always does well in India – that's a Hindi film. Man, I want to be James Bond.
   Please make me the first Indian James Bond.
                                           (Shah Rukh Khan, quoted in Dalton, 2002)

In order to secure its interests in making Hollywood a global form, however, the MPA knows that it has to be more fluid than copyright's evocations of spatial metaphor suggest, and focus on the geographic and politico-territorial referents that abound in US statutory language on intellectual property (Aoki, 1996: 1300). In addition to its espousal of authenticity and ownership in a specified time and space, the MPA engages spatial flexibility.

Hollywood's unitary conception of IP protection is *based* on territorial boundaries in order to 'produce not only the conceptual, but also the actual physical spaces of the information age' (Aoki 1996: 1297). As Kevin Cox puts it, spatial *organisation* – not its traditional annihilation theorised by many discourses of media globalisation – 'becomes a productive force rather than a discrete set of exchange opportunities and offers capital with competitive advantages. Accordingly, capital can become impeded in particular localities and dependent upon their reproduction' (1997: 131). We shall look here at the MPA's recent history to uncover the strategies that Hollywood adopts to police textuality in the NICL.

But this does not signify a preparedness yet to slacken copyright vigilance. In 1990, the Singapore High Court ruled that the country's Board of Film Censors must disclose information about pirated tapes submitted for review. Valenti said of the court decision that 'it became a favorite ploy of the pirates to submit their illegally copied tapes to the Film Board for review in order to win its approval, making them appear legitimate to unaware buyers'. After Singapore's Copyright Act came into effect in 1987, the then MPEAA reported that in just two years, the island's piracy rate had dropped from 90 per cent to 15–20 per cent, albeit that parallel imports (where a video cassette was licensed in another market) were being brought into the country for sale or rental ('MPEAA Victory', 1990). The Association reported that over a million pirated video cassettes were seized in 1991, 20 per cent more than in 1990. In the same year, the organisation initiated over 21,000 piracy investigations, collecting over US$1.13 million dollars in international piracy court cases, in addition to US$4.19 million received by its member companies in US cases. Forecasting an annual loss of US$1.2 billion, the MPEAA singled out Indonesia, Thailand, Taiwan and Eastern European countries for their lack of copyright protection, and Greece and Italy as judicially lenient. Its worldwide director for anti-piracy noted that 'piracy represents a moving target ... once a serious problem is brought under control in one country – for example Korea in 1991 – we can divert our attention to another area, such as Thailand'. In addition, the MPEAA committed what it called 'significant funds' against black-market audiovisual trade in Eastern Europe, taking advantage of Czechoslovakia's recent accession to the Berne Convention ('MPEAA: Piracy', 1992; Franklin, 1991). In 1993, the Association consolidated anti-piracy operations in Europe, Africa and the Middle East into a single office based in Brussels – adding to their Far East operations centred in Singapore and their Latin American operations based in Los

Angeles. The same year, with a suspected US$2 billion lost in revenue, it conducted over 20,000 investigations and 11,500 anti-piracy raids, seizing close to 2 million cassettes and initiating almost 5,000 legal actions ('MPEAA Merges', 1993; 'In Short', 1994).

With the opening of US–Russian trade relations under perestroika, and Time Warner poised to build multiplexes there, the US–USSR trade agreement signed at the turn of the 1990s obliged the Soviets to enact copyright law consistent with the Berne Convention. Though the MPEAA only sent a handful of films there via the Moscow Film Festival, the vast network of small exhibition sites at trade union and club venues – in the range of 150,000 projection units – provided both sources of pirate screenings and a possible infrastructure for the MPEAA to exploit later on. Seeking retroactive coverage for older releases under the new copyright law, it looked forward to exploiting the lack of constitutional copyright provisions in Russian law – provisions that made it impossible for the MPAA to enact *ex post facto* terms of copyright protection under the US Constitution (Marich, 1999). In 1995, the Russian Society for Intellectual Property (RISP), an anti-piracy monitoring service for a number of major domestic distributors, called on the MPA to provide technical and financial support against piracy after a number of successful court actions against local TV stations: RISP estimated that only 5 per cent of programming broadcast on the 250 local TV stations was legal ('Russia Calls', 1995). When Russian authorities committed to greater anti-piracy action after meeting with US representatives in 1997, Valenti claimed that the Russian government lost US$300 to US$400 million dollars a year in tax revenue (with the distribution and production industry losing US$500 million). Valenti also pledged that US companies would train Russian film professionals in new technology. But Russia topped the MPA's 1999 list of problem countries (Birchenough, 1997; Marich, 1999). That year, Russian police were featured on world television driving tanks over a half-million pirate software disks outside Moscow to demonstrate the government's commitment to combating IP infringement.

In 1998, the MPA estimated that its revenue losses due to piracy amounted to US$320 million in Russia, US$200 million in Italy, US$149 million in Japan, US$125 million in Brazil and US$120 million in China – where illicit duplication operations were moving to Hong Kong and Macao. The same year, piracy was estimated at close to 100 per cent in eleven countries, with the MPA incurring losses estimated at US$2 million in Bolivia and US$5 million in Vietnam. In Nigeria, the MPA had no representation. It continued to wait for compensation for assets seized during the nationalisation of the film industry in 1981 (Marich, 1999). In 1997, the Association joined forces with the World Customs Organization, which represented customs divisions in 144 countries. While the MPA participated in an estimated 40,000 piracy investigations and seized 5 million cassettes in 1996 alone, the Association wanted to increase surveillance of digital piracy. As a spokesperson noted, 'we're looking to boost the interception of pirated product as it crosses frontiers ... to increase investigative programs and foster effective criminal prosecutions' (Williams, 1997). In 1999, the MPA signed an agreement with the International Federation of the Phonographic Industry (IFPI) (which represented over 1,400 record producers in 76 countries) to share resources in the fight against optical disc and Internet piracy. The IFPI calculated that piracy cost its industries US$4.5 billion a year, while the MPA estimated piracy losses in 1999 at US$2.5 billion ('In Brief', 2000).

The MPA estimates that video piracy cost the US studios over US$550 million in lost revenues in Asia in 2000, and that 90 per cent of the video industry was illegally controlled in China and Indonesia, 85 per cent in Malaysia, 52 per cent in Thailand and 25 per cent in Singapore (Groves, 2000b). In 1999, MPA liaisons with government agencies resulted in large cable crackdowns in Pakistan, where copyright laws were relatively lax, and the MPA played a prominent role in a New Delhi ruling prosecuting the two largest Indian cable providers for illegal transmission of films. In China, tightening copyright regulation is understood as a necessary corollary to its fourteen-year ascent to the WTO, as it was for Taiwan. In mid-1996, the US Trade Representative threatened China with US$2 billion in trade sanctions, citing its poor record on IP enforcement and the wide-scale piracy of US-owned copyrighted material to the tune of US$2.3 billion (L. Atkinson, 1997). The threat was withdrawn after the Chinese Propaganda Department and Press and Publications Administration cracked down on new pirate CD factories, and the Public Security Bureau promised to strengthen IP monitoring in such centres of piracy as Guangdong (Crock et al., 1997).

India has between 40,000 and 70,000 cable operators, with over 2,000 in Delhi alone, largely unregulated and without firm licensing procedures for film exhibition (Lall, 1999). Malaysia's Johor Baru is home to a number of pirate VCD firms, and Hollywood is deeply worried about a 2000 Malay court decision that copyright owners must be present to execute affidavits of ownership in infringement suits, rather than submit them via local company representatives. The International IP Alliance, which represents the key US copyright industries, reports that Malaysia is a major supplier of pirated product throughout Asia and even as far as Latin America, and the MPA lists Malaysia second only to China in projected piracy losses (at about US$40 million in 1998) (Oh, 2000). And while the MPA insists that free trade depends on loosening protective national barriers and securing IP provisions, a significant feature of the 1996 Asia-Pacific Economic Cooperation Forum was the extension of free-trade agreements to the region, using NAFTA's language to block *Hollywood* imports.

In India, the numerous regional-language cinemas borrow liberally from each other's scripts and character typologies, and Hollywood has been used as a wellspring of themes and plot ideas since the early history of Indian cinema.

As we noted above, generic forms emerge from the works that precede them. In 'the genre world, every day is *Jurassic Park* day' (Altman, 1998: 24). Especially with the anarchic state of film financing in India, with most producers interested in short-term investments and quick profits, and the underdeveloped state of ancillary industries like video cassette and international sales which amortise Hollywood production, relying on the proven success of a Hollywood genre to provide script ideas helps to diminish the Indian film producer's risk. This form of pre-selling existed long before Hollywood's international copyright initiatives and India's domestic provisions. The remaking of Hollywood film has long been a mainstay of Indian film production. A US writer had this to say in the mid-1950s:

> Hollywood supplies a great deal of the Indian movie industry's raw material in plots and ideas, without having anything to say about it. Local producers watch imported features with an eagle eye and frankly plagiarize the more popular productions scene by scene. One producer explained that he saw nothing ethically wrong with this, as otherwise the Indian masses who do not understand English, and have few chances to see foreign films anyway, would be denied these masterpieces.
>
> (Trumbull, 1953)

These Indian remakes have long been a sore spot for Hollywood, particularly as the Indian industry became the most prolific in the world and domestic protective measures were enacted to ensure its national dominance. In the 1980s alone, it was estimated that US majors lost over US$1 billion in royalties and remake fees in India alone, based on a figure for remake rights of about US$100,000 per film.

Coming to America (John Landis, 1988) had little box-office impact when it arrived in India in 1989, but its Tamil-language remake was very successful, as was *Appu Raja* (Kamal Hassan, 1990), based on *Twins* (Ivan Reitman, 1988). In the early 1990s, at least three versions of *Pretty Woman* and four versions of *Ghost* (Jerry Zucker, 1990) were being remade in a number of Indian languages, and film songwriters often rewrote song lyrics and soundtracks from Hollywood films as well, integrated into the richly textured polyphonic space of Indian 'cassette culture' (Manuel, 1993). Ram Gopal Varma's *Raat* (1992), for example, evokes the familiar background score from *Halloween* (John Carpenter, 1978). Up to 1990, the only time a Hollywood company successfully sued an illegal remake was when Warner Bros. took the producers of *Khoon Khoon* (Mohammed Husain, 1973) to court for remaking *Dirty Harry* (Don Siegel, 1971) scene by scene. Warners received US$50,000 in punitive damages against the producers of the film, Eagle Films. Eagle acted differently when it decided to remake Billy Wilder's *Irma la Douce* (1963) and obtained remake rights from Universal (Pais, 1990).

With the wide availability of Hollywood on multiplex screens and cable tele-vision, Bollywood's remake culture has blossomed in more recent years: *Qayamat* (Harry Baweja, 2003) revisits *The Rock* (Michael Bay, 1996); *Dewaangee* (Aneez Bazmee, 2002) mirrors *Primal Fear* (Gregory Hoblit, 1996); *Jism* (Amit Saxena, 2003) does a double-take on *Double Indemnity* (Billy Wilder, 1944); *Meri Yaar Ki Shaadi Hai* (Sanjay Gadhavi, 2002) is a literal trans-lation of *My Best Friend's Wedding* (P. J. Hogan, 1997); *Humraaz* (Abbas Mastan, 2002) recommits *A Perfect Murder* (Andrew Davis, 2002); *Kucch to Hai* (Anil Kumar, 2003) recalls *I Know What You Did Last Summer* (Jim Gillespie, 1997). The list (and our bad puns) are practically endless. Sometimes, Bolly-wood operationalises the Hollywood remake beyond the usual confines of generic intertextuality: the producers of *Kaante* (Sanjay Gupta, 2002) remade *Reservoir Dogs* (Quentin Tarantino, 1992) in Los Angeles with a crew partially drawn from Tarantino's 'original' (itself a remake of *Long Hu Feng Yun* [*City on Fire*, Ringo Lam, 1987]). One Hollywood lawyer notes that 'until now it has not been worth our time tangling with film-makers in a Bombay court. But if this *Reservoir Dogs* rehash starts making serious money . . . we will have to start investigating how closely such movies are copying the originals' (Harlow, 2002).

Such legal entanglements may well be on the rise. A high-profile civil lawsuit brought by the best-selling Yanqui author Barbara Taylor Bradford against Sahara Television's production of the soap opera *Karishma* resulted in mud-slinging on both sides. Bradford contended that

> they are stealing, pinching intellectual properties every hour, on the hour.
> Bollywood people grab a film or a novel and make a Hindi version . . .
> unfortunately, the world is becoming a global village – thanks to the Internet –
> and it's easy to find out now.
>
> (Quoted in Abdi, 2003)

The editor of the Bombay-based *Trade Guide* claims that Indian remake-happy screenwriters are 'mere translators' (Badam, 2003). Hollywood's support of the globalisation and greater exposure of mainstream Indian cinema – 20th Century-Fox recently became the first Hollywood studio to pick up an India-made film *The Rising* (Ketan Mehta, 2004) for wide international release – is seen as the greatest deterrent against copyright infringement in remakes. When the producers of the Bombay film *Aankhen* (Vipul Shah, 2002), learned that a US producer wanted to remake their film for Hollywood, they insisted on one clause in their contract, 'in the credits of the Hollywood version, we just want one line saying the film is based on *Aankhen*' (quoted in 'Hollywood Eyes', 2002).

The MPA's anti-piracy push now has outposts in over seventy countries. Large-scale operations have been conducted in Malaysia, Mexico, Poland, Italy,

Israel, Germany, Peru, Panama, Brazil and Greece, with new initiatives targeting Russia, China and Ireland. In 1999, the MPA and the Mexican film industry
created a joint committee to tackle bi-national issues of piracy (which saw the
local government upgrade piracy convictions from misdemeanours to felonies,
expedite search-warrant request criteria, and severely restrict bail and pre-trial
release for piracy arrests), co-productions and government incentives to keep
the Mexican industry afloat (Watling, 1999).

US government support for Hollywood's anti-piracy campaign has been
linked to the larger role of the state in helping US capital exploit foreign
markets, as per the story told in Chapter 1. As IP rights are really 'privileges
granted by the State through a form of statutory subsidy' (Raghavan, 1990:
116), government intervention via IP law has been crucial to Hollywood. Prior
to the Uruguay Round of the GATT and the formation of the WTO, international copyright agreements such as the Berne Convention and the Universal
Copyright Convention contained no real enforcement procedures. IP rights
have only become subject to international trade negotiation and harmonisation at the regional (e.g. the EU) as well as the global level in the last decade.
For a long time, refusal to recognise or enforce IP rights was a deliberate policy on the part of many non-US or non-Western European countries, who were
concerned to prevent foreign monopoly ownership of culture and the outflow
of foreign exchange (Chartrand, 1996).

Given capital's voracious appetite for new markets, it is perhaps inevitable
that existing and emerging forms of human artistic and intellectual creativity
were integrated into global marketing. So, the pressure on national governments for greater copyright protection comes from both locally based
oligopolistic media industries and multinational media companies. Sometimes
the US has paid a price for internationalism. For example, as part of the
implementation infrastructure of both NAFTA and the GATT, the US gave
retroactive copyright protection to foreign works that had gone into the US
public domain due to foreign ignorance of certain bureaucratic formalities or
the lack of a bilateral agreement between the US and the foreign country. Of
course, the US fully expects such restorative copyright protection for its own
works in foreign countries (Sobel, 1995). Washington has pursued three strategies to eradicate piracy in foreign markets:

1   bilateral trade-leveraging against countries where piracy was rampant
2   free-trade agreements with selected partners that incorporate IP protection
    into their frameworks; and
3   multilateral efforts such as the GATT.

The US Copyright Office asks US embassies to collect data about local copyright, patent and trademark activity and infrastructures for the publication,
distribution and performance of protected works. US advisers train foreign

lawyers, police and customs officials to enforce copyright. Under Section 301 of the 1988 Trade Act, the Office of the US Trade Representative has the authority to put foreign nations on a watchdog list for up to two years, after which the President is required to take retaliatory action, ranging from termination of trade agreements to suspension of any trade benefits that had been granted to the importing nation. Often, the rationales behind IP protection and the threat of US sanctions are more than merely symbolic Marshall planning: they are central to Washington's international diplomacy. For example, as India, along with China, was targeted for Section 301 investigation in the late 1980s, the piracy of US products was related to Cold War concerns over imported supercomputers and the proliferation of atomic technologies. So, pursuing the US$66 million that the MPA lost to Indian piracy in 1997 is part of a diplomatic heritage that includes nuclear non-proliferation and new entry for US banking and insurance sectors alongside lifting restrictions and quotas on Hollywood in the Indian market (Thomas, 1999: 281, 284).

International piracy, counterfeiting and other unauthorised expropriations of US IP came to the forefront of US trade policy in the early 1980s once it became conventional wisdom that the future success of US global entertainment was predicated upon the production, ownership and marketing of IP-based goods and services. Accordingly, state efforts to advance Hollywood's copyright interests were part of a much larger effort to institute the international legal infrastructure to support IP-based industries. As US IP-based industries sought to secure their rights in foreign markets, they forged alliances with foreign capitalists with the same goal. Added to the GATT under the primary support of the US, Europe and Japan, Trade Related IP (TRIPs) agreements extend hitherto ambiguous coverage of ownership to natural *and* legal persons; that is, both single authors and corporate owners. It does not specifically address the moral rights component of the Berne Convention. And when the US finally signed the Convention in the late 1980s, the moral rights distinction that had held up its signature for a century was effectively nullified, since Berne gave the author of a work a moral right, while in the US, ownership was synonymous with authorship. Accordingly, the Berne Convention Implementation Act allowed for the continuation of federal and state-mandated rights that were in contradistinction to its own, relatively strong, language of moral rights. Yet, continued US compliance with Berne may well be contingent on its extension of moral rights to authors (Chinni, 1997). How might this take place in the environment of digital reproduction? The extension of moral rights will not suffice as a panacea for copyright's problems, and the distributional apparatus of film makes it difficult for an authorial maverick to hold out under the protective umbrella of moral rights. As director Marcel Ophuls once put it, 'if we were to cling to the notion of moral rights we wouldn't work at all' (quoted in Puttnam with Watson, 1998: 242).

Coming into effect at the beginning of 1995, TRIPs established minimum standards for: protection (defining the object to be protected, the rights that accompany its ownership, exceptions and minimum duration of protection); enforcement (civil and administrative procedures, prosecutions and penalties); and dispute settlement. Failure to uphold IP provisions now subjects the offending nation to retaliatory sanctions under unfair trade provisions. The 'Copyright and Related Rights' section of TRIPs (the others deal with 'Trademarks', 'Geographical Destinations' and 'Patents') incorporates the 1971 Berne Convention, whose Article 10 provided for protection of computer programs (in source or object code) as literary works – the culmination of a decade-long effort by Western software manufacturers. In addition, TRIPs affords protection to such neighbouring or related rights as sound recordings and broadcast signals.

Commenting on agricultural law in eighteenth-century Britain, E. P. Thompson (1975) notes that the law is so imbricated in production relations that it is indistinguishable from the mode of production. IP enforcement attempts to regulate the relations of cultural production, the operation of power in the workplace and a redefinition of that workplace to include 'pirates'. IP law also guarantees the consolidation of textual control on behalf of corporate owners of the screen image. Hollywood's fervent interaction with new international governing bodies (like the WTO) convened to organise disparate national copyright regimes is partly an extension of this domestic strategy. But is it that simple? After all, 'doing nothing' is one of the many legitimate strategies that corporate owners have when it comes to IP protection. When dealing with counterfeit cultural products to a Third World region where it has few legal exports, Hollywood might be better off (even in terms of a simple cost-benefit analysis) to avoid bad publicity and take the opportunity of free promotion. Maybe copyright infringement is simply an unofficial tax for doing business in, say, China or India. Backing off on copyright protection might help imbue aspirations that contribute to the cultures of anticipation that buttress Hollywood's ancillary merchandising markets, so that affinities for pirated brand images 'can be converted to authentic products when the market becomes more developed' (Schultz and Saporito, 1996: 22). New directions for Hollywood as it endeavours to come to terms with markets where IP protection is scant (notably China) may include forfeiting an iron-clad grip over media property in favour of stabilising distribution via 'bureaucratic coordination of flows of programs and profits with an eye to maintaining the system overall' (Streeter, 1996: 273). Hardware piracy is not significantly addressed in the Sino-American trade agreement passed by the US Senate in 2000, although copyright is. Hollywood knows that, to play its copyrighted software, you need the hardware – counterfeit or not. Similarly, in late 1995, Sony Pictures Entertainment consolidated its movement into India by teaming with a Singapore-based entertainment company, Argos Communications, to launch a satellite-TV service with some Hindi-language programming. Sony provided 2,000 dish antennae free of charge to cable operators to ensure smooth and quick access to the new channel (da Cunha, 1995b).

The vexed question of publicity is tied to shifting relations between copyright law and trademark law. Films, especially blockbusters, have come to be judged in terms of their capacity to act as logos or have a distinct product image. In these cases, the film sells records, clothes, toys, video games, books, magazines, drinks and food (see Chapter 5). A partial shift in legislative practice since the 1940s, from a conception of textual ownership as copyrightable to a codification of its value as a trademark, is designed to engage texts as icons, systematising regulation through the recognition of symbols rather than readerly semiosis. While trademark law's earlier claims to civic management showed 'deference to context, convention and genre', attempts to prevent consumer confusion between commercial products, giving property-like rights to individual signs (accreted over time by statutory decisions) has 'frequently trumped free-speech concerns in several US state law anti-dilution cases which have ruled against "recodings", or subsequent unauthorized uses of marks, even in the absence of consumer confusion' (Aoki, 1993b: 832; see also Denicola, 1999). The recent enactment of TRIPs agreements at the international level attests to the reach of trademark provision:

> Any sign, or combination of signs, capable of distinguishing the goods or services of one undertaking from those of other undertakings, shall be capable of constituting a trademark. Such signs, in particular words including personal names, letters, numerals, figurative elements and combinations of colours as well as any combination of such signs, shall be eligible for registration as trademarks. Where signs are not inherently capable of distinguishing the relevant good or services, Members may make registrability depend on distinctiveness acquired through use. Members may require, as a condition of registration, that signs be visually perceptible.
>
> (Article 15 of TRIPs)

The shift from copyright to trademark as the legal infrastructure for dealing with digital reproduction has a history in the older notion of trademark as a form of goodwill branding that guarantees a quality product at the same time as it sets the terms for evaluating quality. Indeed, product education is also part of Hollywood's new international anti-piracy initiatives, as per the domestic curriculum described earlier. Even in the Internet bootleg film market, 'trademarked' copies of *The Phantom Menace* (George Lucas, 1999) serve as signs of quality. In India, where Hollywood has long nurtured alliances with the major regional film industries, the director of Asia/Pacific anti-piracy operations at the MPA noted in 1996 that 'our aim is not to pursue every violator, because we don't have that kind of clout or resources in a country as vast as India', but to 'educate viewers and cable operators to insist on the visual quality of the genuine product' (da Cunha, 1996).

Valenti's effort to educate audiences around the world on the inferior quality of pirated Hollywood product redeploys trademark law's nineteenth-century rationale that, as Keith Aoki puts it, 'prevented consumer confusion over competing marketing goods', in the service of a more modern focus that protected the corporate owners of IP from 'dilution and appropriation of a set of positive meanings which have been created by the trademark owner's investment' (1993a: 4). The assimilation of authorial legitimacy and consumer protection within the discourse of civil restraint is part of trademark law's history of signalling quality assurance and consistency in the field of commodity purchase. As the film industry continues to deal with digital transactions, the reputations of sellers will become ever more important as distributors (both legal and otherwise) proliferate – the key will be maximising product differentiation, making sure that people realise that YOU put out a superior, quality product (within narrowly defined criteria of superiority).

The founder of Digimarc, a digital watermarking firm, is a former physicist who developed a process to clean up digital images of outer space. Worried that his doctored images might be considered public property, he added an almost imperceptible ownership mark to the photographs. This led to the development of both watermarking techniques (which are now themselves patented) and sophisticated search engines that scour the Internet for copyrighted material (Golden, 1998). This is not unprecedented in film history: the French cinema company Pathé once stamped its red rooster trademark on silent-film inter-title cards – not specifically to deter copyright (Pathé never sought copyright protection for its films in the US, and the Copyright Act of 1790 automatically relegated foreign works into the public domain) but to circulate them 'as a recurring symbol of goodwill that, in guaranteeing the quality of its product's performance on stage or screen, incited increased consumer demand' (Abel, 1999: 18–19). Confronted with the lack of industry standards and the remarkably simple ways of circumventing contemporary copy protection – like using a felt-tip marker to cover a digital disc's outer data ring – media industries are clearly returning to older forms of product differentiation based on consumer reputation.

The Work of Hollywood in the Age of Digital Reproduction

copy protection n.
A class of methods for preventing incompetent pirates from stealing software and legitimate customers from using it. Considered silly.
(*The New Hacker's Dictionary*, www.tuxedo.org/~esr/jargon/jargon.html)

I love film, but it's a 19th Century invention. The century of film has passed.
(George Lucas, quoted in Sabin, 2000)

A recent spate of Internet piracy has made over sixty films available for public download, including *Armageddon* (Michael Bay, 1998), *Godzilla*, *The Matrix*, *Entrapment* (Jon Amiel, 1999), *Saving Private Ryan* and *The Phantom Menace*. The MPAA estimated in 2001 that, on an average day, 275,000 pirated movies were downloaded (Graham, 2001a); the figures for 2004 put the number in the millions. Three factors contribute to the proliferate status of the digital form: fidelity, compression and malleability (Goldstein, 1994: 197). In a contemporary international application of the *Sony* VCR case, the Dutch music rights organisation Buma Stemra lost a suit against the P2P service KaZaa when an appeals court overturned a lower court's decision, citing *Sony* as providing protection for P2P software providers and their 'substantial non-infringing' uses (Radcliffe and Sazama, 2002). And in 2003, a federal judge in Los Angeles also cited *Sony* in dismissing a joint record- and movie-industry suit against file-sharing services Streamcast Networks and Grokster, noting that 'policy, as well as history, supports our consistent deference to Congress when major technological innovations alter the market for copyrighted materials' ('Music Industry', 2003).

Although film directors protest when 'their' work is altered for video, television and airline exhibition, most infringement suits are brought by corporate owners of film copyright, since directors are considered 'workers for hire' under US law and hence are not authors. The notion of corporate citizenship, where corporations enjoy similar legal status to individuals, has been crucial in ongoing copyright battles, especially the recording industry. The recording companies initiated infringement actions against Napster.com, an Internet clearing house for sharing digital music files, despite the pro-copyright involvement of musical acts like Metallica (one of the few groups that own its songs). Internet services such as Scour, iMesh, Gnutella and the cleverly named Metallicster and Wrapster allow users to locate and download digital material from others' hard drives. These companies also learned from Napster that cooperation with the corporate owners of copyright materials is the best way to navigate the legal terrain. Even as Scour fights a copyright-infringement suit brought against it by the Hollywood majors and a number of record companies, it is negotiating licences with Miramax (a plaintiff). Miramax is also allowing Sightsound.com to distribute a number of its titles over the Internet. But Valenti (2000b) argues that, 'a number of new movies, the ones now in theaters, have already been put on the Internet by pilfering zealots eager to unfold films in the same embrace now choking the music world'. He reserves Hollywood's greatest ire for P2P networks like KaZaa, which allow users to exchange downloaded movie files:

> We know that the infestation of P2P not only threatens the well-being of the copyright industries but consumers and their families as well. ... It can bring into your home and expose your children to pornography of the most vile and

depraved character imaginable. Most insidious of all, the pornography finds its way to your children disguised as wholesome material: your son or daughter may 'search' for 'Harry Potter' or 'Britney Spears,' and be confronted with files that contain bestiality or child pornography. The pornography distributed through P2P networks is so horrific that the District Attorney from Suffolk County, New York, recently called it the worst his office had ever seen on the Internet. And the most disturbing fact of all is that any 10-year old can easily and swiftly bring down this unwelcome perversion. Therefore, the business model that current P2P networks celebrate as 'the digital democracy' is built on the fetid foundation of pornography and pilfered copyrighted works.

(Valenti, 2003b)

Unlike Napster, the new file-sharing services like Morpheus and KaZaa do not link users through a centralised server; instead they enable file-swappers to connect directly to each other's machines, creating a decentralised and tactical distribution network whose shape and infrastructure shift according to usage patterns. KaZaa is incorporated in the South Pacific Island of Vanuatu, which doubles as a tax haven.

The RIAA shut down Napster in 2001 and handed out subpoenas, cease-and-desist orders and some 261 lawsuits in September 2003, seeking an average of US$150,000 per violation, but settling most for around US$3,000 (including a case involving a twelve-year-old downloader). The RIAA bundled cases against 532 computer users in four lawsuits filed in 2004, insisting that music sales are suffering because of 2.6 billion files are being exchanged every month; the MPAA supports the RIAA tactics, claiming that some 600,000 digital and analogue copies of films exchange hands daily. Nielsen Soundscan data show that 687 million CDs were sold in 2003 compared with 693 million in 2002 – a decline of less than 1 per cent – yet those facing lawsuits have inverted the RIAA insistence that file-sharing is a theft of creative labour: after being sued and fined in 2003, one litigant insisted that

we are hardly in the position to pay the recording industry as their sacrificial lamb . . . we feel victimized and angry, but mostly we feel hurt. We are good, honest, hardworking people. My husband works two jobs and I work one. We have never stolen anything.

(Maier, 2004)

The RIAA and the MPAA have suffered some setbacks in their copyright drive. US courts have overturned suits against file-sharing sites like Grokster, noting that the 1998 DMCA (Digital Millennium Copyright Act) mandate for ISPs to surrender customer names and profiles does not extend to file-sharing networks. And Hollywood's bid to curtail Internet piracy suffered a public-relations embarrassment when a study by AT&T Labs suggested that the primary source of new movies on P2P networks was movie-industry insiders, not consumers (Holson, 2003). Sharman Networks, the company behind KaZaa, filed a federal lawsuit in 2003 against the RIAA and other entertainment companies for violating its copyrights by downloading an unauthorised version of its software to troll the Internet for alleged downloaders (Gross, 2003). Accounts of innovative file-sharing abound in the popular press. For example, fans of *Harry Potter* have used file-sharing software to distribute the tasks of translating the books in areas where 'official' translations are unavailable, resorting to email when the copyright industries try to shut down their P2P networks (Harmon, 2003). And independent and alternative media companies claim that P2P represents a business model that supports innovation, insisting that 'in artist development, file-sharing – it's not really hurting you' (Nelson, 2003).

The divergent forms of address manifest the difficulty in 'signifying' the Internet, which has so many possible uses for Hollywood. The Internet is a spatial force that is both *centripetal*, in that it preserves gates and barriers, and *centrifugal*, in that it hurls us into new relations between producers and consumers. It is all at once: a delivery conduit; an exhibition site; a distribution philosophy; a content gathering and talent-differentiating device; an advertising platform; and a globally linked network of copying machines. Even the act of downloading visual media can mean a number of different, simultaneous money-making schemes for Hollywood, from being a sale (the Internet as a point-of-purchase) to a broadcast (the Internet as transmitter technology) to a mechanical copy (the Internet as a copy-clearance centre) (see Mann, 2000).

These qualities explain Hollywood's cosmic ambivalence about the Internet. One film industry executive referred to the computer as 'our nemesis' (Alexander, 2000). The Academy of Motion Picture Arts and Sciences has ruled that films shown on the Internet prior to theatrical release are ineligible for Oscar consideration. Blockbuster Video plans to stream video, bypassing the Internet in favour of a private network provided by phone companies. In the face of the *de facto* strike by Hollywood talent over contract negotiations in 2001, members of the DGA, WGA, Cartoonist Union Local 839 and SAG signed agreements with Internet content producers that were not yet fully amalgamated into the Alliance of Motion Picture and Television Producers (Swanson, 2000). And when the MPA recently shut down companies offering movies over the Internet for US$1, like Movie88.com (based in Taiwan) and Film88.com (based in Iran), it was protecting its own future Internet distribution plans (see Chapter 5). The MPA's digital duplicity stresses the economic eradication of geographic space alongside its reterritorialisation. Valenti notes that

> the fury of the future is already upon us. The explosion of channel capacity,
> the hurling to homes by direct satellite, the multiplicity of optic fiber, among

other magic, are the new centurions of the digital age, marching over
continents and across geographic borders, breaking down artificial
government barriers, the most powerful audiovisual armies ever known.

(Quoted in 'Quo Vadis?', 1996)

The industry's attacks on Internet piracy began in 1999 via a collaboration
between Lucasfilm Ltd, the FBI, the MPAA and the Department of Justice, when
Lucasfilm shut down more than 300 Internet sites offering pirated copies of its
latest *Star Wars* instalment. Counterfeit versions of the film were available in
Malaysia two days after its domestic release, and a few days later in Hong Kong,
with Chinese-language jackets (for the equivalent of less than US$3) courtesy
of one of four CD printing machines in Hong Kong, each capable of producing
20,000 discs per day (Michael, 1999). Filmed with a camcorder in a US theatre,
this version was quickly supplanted by copies made from a stolen print. Digital
piracy's shadow politics of distribution honoured *The Phantom Menace* as the
first feature to be downloaded illegally in the UK from servers in Eastern Europe.

While the Internet has been notoriously difficult to police, the MPAA has
recently created its own Internet investigative unit. Recalling the imagery of
medieval chastity belts, Valenti calls this unit 'a technological armor plate that
guards our movies from being hauled out in a profligate manner by everybody
with a computer'. The appointment of a former digital scanning and imaging
company executive as its Chief Technology Officer reflects the MPA's mandate
for 'creating technical standards for the digital transmission and distribution
of films' and safeguarding against digital piracy ('MPA Appoints', 1999).

Following strong lobbying by the MPA and the Consumer Electronics Manufacturers Association for a digital anti-copying bill to protect the 'sanctity of
copyright', Congress began to take a number of measures. After the No Electronic Theft Act in 1997, it passed the DMCA in 1998, in accord with the World
IP Organization Treaties signed in Geneva in late 1996. The DMCA is separate
to the Federal Copyright Act. It is designed to provide legal coverage for new
digital technologies and contains an 'anti-circumvention provision' that prohibits the distribution of devices that crack copyright encryption; exonerates
online service providers for copyright infractions committed on their system
by subscribers; and codifies penalties and prison terms for convicted infringers.
The statute was designed to ban 'black boxes' that might promote the piracy of
copyright works. But as Pamela Samuelson suggests, 'the ban is far broader than
this and threatens to bring about a flood of litigation challenging a broad range
of technologies, even where there is no proof that the technologies have or real-
istically would be widely used to enable piracy' (1999: 563–64). At the most
basic level, the DMCA admits corporate tracking technologies to PCs to ascer-
tain whether an infringement is taking place.

US courts have circumscribed the protective materiality of digital data.
Through a number of cases dating back to 1993, they have affirmed that the

right of reproduction contained in copyright law is subject to infringement when a digital copy is stored in a computer's memory (Sullivan, 1996). Anticipating digital distribution of films over the Internet or on digital television set-top boxes, Hollywood teamed up with computer manufacturers like IBM to develop rights-protection technology that uses unique serial numbers on recordable media to create single encryption keys, ensuring that downloaded material can only be saved to a single source. The MPAA maintains that this technology will extend to hard drives, so that 'copy-once protection technology goes beyond just a pay-per-view business model to a pay-per-copy business model' (Chmielewski, 2000). Thus, Hollywood is revisiting the sealed-set hardware innovation of commercial radio that made the medium a technology of reception rather than relay.

However, the legal terrain in software protection is harrowing indeed. Do computer games, for example, meet the criteria for 'aesthetic representation' maintained by a number of countries? Does interactivity render obsolete the traditional notion of an authorial right? In France, a bastion of support for authorial rights, new software provisions in national copyright law resemble the 'work for hire' doctrine of US copyright law, where the employer gains 'all the rights' of an 'author' working under their contract (McColley, 1997). Some countries have drawn up 'composite work' criteria, with different aspects of the same media object protected under a number of IP provisions (which means that the musical score and still images in a video game are protected under separate criteria). The accreting logic of legal protection is designed, of course, to limit access to the design playing-field. Furthermore, the countries that Hollywood pursues for IP harmonisation are also high on the software piracy list: for example, China is accused by the Software Publishers Association of selling US$1.5 billion in pirated business software in 1997 via 'compilation CD-ROMS' (which contain tens of thousands of dollars of retail business software) that cost under US$10. In the Philippines, an estimated 80 per cent of business software is pirated, with government offices the major culprits (Tanzer, 1998).

Studying the contexts of legal and cultural history can help us understand these forms of image duplication and the audiences that are constituted by them. For example, a late-1960s case in the US (*Williams and Wilkins Co.* v. *The United States*) was brought on by new Xerox copying technology, which allowed libraries to keep photocopies of journals in their collection without compensating the publisher. The subsequent establishment of copyright clearance houses and licensing fees for photocopies may become a precedent for digital-film downloading and transformations after the model of fair use, since such copying technologies allow for the creation of derivative works. Copying and creativity would converge as forms of digital use. Barring this radical redefinition of reception – which begins with a foundational acceptance of fair use rather than its invocation as a pothole in the road to full commercial exploitation of the work – Hollywood might borrow from the American Society of

Composers, Authors and Publishers and track royalty revenue for each download. Integrated digital systems designed for online transactions and the generation of customer databases for profiling purposes are also a means of implementing technological and price restrictions on uses of copyrighted works (Cohen, 1996: 984).

'Trusted system' technology, designed to track a work via digital property-rights language, is in development at places like IBM and Xerox. Forms of trusted system hardware might look and feel like a normal duplication platform (e.g. a printer, a VCR, a stereo) but would have the capability to implement a copyright holder's restrictions over usage in a number of arenas:

- rendering (to play, print or export media via the translation of digital code to a usable form)
- transportation (to copy, transfer or lend digital works among other trusted systems); and
- derivation (to extract, edit or embed a copyrighted work in a derivative usage).

Along with the implementation of digital watermarking technologies, trusted system technology allows a tremendous level of control over the use of digital works (Gimbel, 1998: 1677–80). While it was once commonly understood that information commodities 'can never be endowed with real scarcity, since its most important quality is its inexhaustible reproducibility' (Frow, 1997: 188), the techno-bureaucratic management of film threatens to impose new regimes of scarcity.

When the fifteen-year-old Norwegian teenager Jon Johansen and two friends wrote a program that descrambled the anti-piracy Contents Scrambling System (CSS), which Hollywood encrypts on DVDs, and posted it on the Internet in the autumn of 1999, they incurred the MPAA's wrath. And after the Web magazine *2600: The Hacker Quarterly* posted the descrambling software (called DeCSS) on its website, Hollywood sued under new DMCA guidelines. Interestingly, those same issues of creativity and originality came to bear when a computer scientist claimed on the witness stand that 'if the court upholds this injunction, what would happen is that certain uses of computer language – my preferred means of expression – would be illegal' (Harmon, 2000). Copyright and the US Constitution's First Amendment guarantees of free speech come together when computer code is deemed a form of personal expression. In the DeCSS case, a US District Court judge distinguished code from speech, noting that 'computer code is not purely expressive any more than the assassination of a political leader is purely a political statement'. How are such forms of expression to be weighed against more traditional forms of IP, such as copyright, which secure the expressive content of the owner? Cognisant of shifts in determinations of expressivity, the MPA's Director of Legal Affairs notes that 'this case is not about infringement of copyright, but about the illegal tracking in the device (code) that makes illegal copies' (Alexander, 2000). Nevertheless, copies of DeCSS are available from Internet sites based in the Czech Republic, Finland, Russia, Slovenia, Israel, Greece and Mexico (VerSteeg, 2000: 12A).When an Oslo court eventually cleared Johansen of copyright violation, he said he would 'celebrate by watching a few DVDs on unauthorized equipment'. In the years since inventing DeCSS, Johansen has also cracked Apple's online music distribution service's encryption code, cementing his position as a maverick whose aim, in the words of his lawyer, was to 'defend the principle of consumer rights' (quoted in 'Setback', 2003).

In an effort to address the commercial possibilities of digital distribution with the attendant forms of high-fidelity piracy, the MPA, along with the US government, is attempting to extend TRIPs-related protections. At the 1996 World IP Conference in Geneva, US negotiators outlined a possible future for copyright in the global information society. Although its most strongly worded policy suggestions were derailed (the WIPO has always been aligned with relatively Third World-friendly organisations like UNESCO and UNCTAD), the negotiators worked towards draft language that would find powerful proponents in both the US copyright industries and within the government (and possibly for future WTO/GATS accords, which, as we have seen, are aligned with the IMF and the World Bank). In calling for protection for temporary reproductions of copyrighted works in a private PC's random-access memory (therefore treating digital *transmissions* as distribution *copies*), the US team upheld President Clinton's Information Infrastructure Task Force's 1995 White Paper, which 'deprived the public of the "first sale rights" it had long enjoyed in the print world' and conceived of 'electronic forwarding as a violation of both the reproduction and distribution rights of copyright law' (Samuelson, 1996: 136). The 'first-sale' statute, guaranteed by Section 109(a) of the US Copyright Act of 1976, reaffirmed that the purchaser of a particular work is entitled, without the permission of the copyright owner, 'to sell or otherwise dispose of the possession of that copy'. While copyright owners had struggled against the statute for years, it nevertheless prevented movie studios from claiming a royalty on video rentals, or book/record owners from claiming a royalty on copies loaned from a public library. In conceptualising the distribution of digital works as inherently a form of copying, the US WIPO team subtly sidestepped the first-sale restrictions. The drafters of copyright's digital initiatives could therefore argue for an elimination of fair-use rights wherever a licensed use was possible, as well as buttress their demands for encrypted tracking software designed to police the use of digital media (Samuelson, 1996: 136).

The US characterises digital transmission as the distribution of copies, because it is necessary to copy a digital work in order to reproduce it. This makes such transfers amenable to copyright protection, part of a larger agenda at the WIPO to limit user rights and curtail 'fair use and kindred privileges under which private or personal copying of protected works has often found shelter' (Samuelson, 1997: 398). This stance has effectively rolled back fair-use precepts upheld by US courts that allowed private videotaping of audiovisual programming in the early 1980s. Here we find the savvy corporate owners of copyright using the distinctive technology of the digital against itself, since one must copy a text in order to read it (i.e. materialise in some new way, even as signals). Conveniently, 'copyright's legal threshold of originality is a simple requirement of creation *without* any copying' (Litman, 1990: 1000). Infringement is assimilable to every act of reception – the 'transient reproduction in use' addressed by the US at the WIPO. Every act of digital reading is, therefore, an act of copying. As the President of the US Consumer Electronics Association recently put it, 'if the content industry has its way, the "play" button will become the "pay" button' (Snider, 2001). For example, say you watch a movie (accessed *legally* from a studio website) on your computer. While it plays, parts of it are stored within your PC's random-access memory, and because a copy (of sorts) is being created, the studio has the right to make sure that you are not circumventing its encrypted rights management software, something that it can only do by entering the domain of your PC. Privacy evaporates in a puff of logic. Surveillance takes its place (for which see Chapter 5).

The RIAA and MPAA used file-sharing networks to send anti-piracy pop-up messages to users logged on the network, which begs the question, couldn't they do the same for advertising and promotion? While the partial assimilation of P2P within corporate IP regimes is likely – much like the corporate support of open-source software development – Hollywood's copyright idolatry will, of course, be renewed. Meanwhile, the new architectures of digital surveillance continue to expand copyright criminality to include previously legal forms of circumvention. Clearly, trusted systems and digital-rights management are the latest allies in the coalition of anti-terror metaphors, part of an overarching logic of pre-emption that justifies unilateralism in anti-piracy and anti-terrorism alike. While the global and the digital complicate territoriality in cultural exchange, this crisis has spurred new forms of reverence. The para-territories of the national, and the mnemonic traces of digital-rights management, are motivated by IP's newly invigorated mission. For those tallying gains and losses in the global war on terror, piracy has become a matter of great urgency. From the pre-emptive strikes of digital-rights management and the moral invigilation of consumption, to alternate national jurisdiction and its erasure with the invocation of genocide and maritime piracy, modern IP initiatives have orchestrated an action-adventure melodrama. The pirate, the consumer, the terrorist and the hysterical manager are locked together in a fatal attraction that any moviegoer can learn to love. The current GATS negotiations are designed to outmanoeuvre European cultural exemptions through liberalisation of online services. The MPA is fully poised to enter new communications services markets in Europe, challenging 'the EC's freedom to maneuver and regulate emerging services due to their massive economic potential' (Wheeler, 2000: 258). In a globalised digital environment, where the WTO guarantees that customs duties will not be levied on electronic transmissions, and the US leads the way in 'the creation of a market-driven policy architecture for this new digital economy' (US Government Working Group on Electronic Commerce, 1998: 30), the danger looms that the neoclassical tenets of copyright (fundamental to IP's economic imperative) will overwhelm the public domain and free use.

Conclusion

> 'The law, my boy, puts us in everything.'
>
> (Al Pacino in *The Devil's Advocate*, Taylor Hackford, 1997)

With over 8,500 video-rental stores in 29 countries, and worldwide sales topping US$5 billion a year, Blockbuster became the world's largest video/DVD rental chain in the 1990s. As part of its parent company Viacom's expansion strategy, Blockbuster entered Hong Kong in 1999, buying up stores from a local video-rental chain facing receivership to tap into the local film industry and catapult rental business revenue on the mainland. Blockbuster's corporate parent, Viacom, then focused attention on the Chinese mainland. MTV, another of Viacom's subsidiaries, was broadcast in programme blocks by local cable networks, and given broadcasting rights to air in Chinese in Guangdong in 2003, capping the southern province's meteoric rise as the foreign media portal to the rest of the mainland. In early 2004, however, Blockbuster announced that it was not renewing the lease on its twenty-four Hong Kong stores and was putting off its push into China for 'the forseeable future', even as the chain's US success was dwindling. Beginning in 1997, Blockbuster had steadily edged out independent video-rental shops in the US by using its Hollywood connections (Viacom also owns Paramount) to negotiate revenue-sharing agreements with the major studios. While one independent video retailer claimed that Blockbuster was 'killing the market with copy depth' (Coolidge, 2002), 'copy theft' killed Blockbuster in Hong Kong. The MPA reported that close to 45 million pirated DVDs were seized in its Asia-Pacific jurisdiction in 2003 – a 12 per cent upswing in piracy that 'cost' the film industry well over US$700 million, part of a US$1.85 billion overall loss for the US IP industries in China alone (Craven, 2004; Luk, 2004).

Viacom's experience in China demonstrates the complex spatial invocation of contemporary IP: DVD rental revenue based on the rental of physical space may fail, but television syndication provides a way forward. Hollywood's growth in China is conditioned by material and immaterial forms of property acquisition, rendered legible through the familiar territorial grammar of intellectual property, where multiplex construction through local partnerships takes place alongside tailored programming that fits 'local' tastes (see Chapter 5).

As the Internet and digital duplication continue to disarticulate the geographic sensitivities of the MPA, regulation and enforcement policies struggle to recapitulate this spatial imperative of corporate capital. Clifford Schultz and Bill Saporito (1996) suggest a number of strategies for IP protection:

- 'grin and bear it', trusting in the mythic levelling 'even hand' of capitalism
- co-opt offenders and offer them legitimate business opportunities
- educate the public
- eradicate demand for piracy through advertising
- erect investigative and surveillance procedures
- engineer labels and embed anti-piracy technologies
- create a constantly evolving product
- lobby for IP legislation
- build coalitions with international organisations, foreign governments and local enforcement agencies; and
- cede certain sectors of the industry.

The priority of IP control is manifested in the proliferation of alliances and mergers in the media trade: for example, DreamWorks and Microsoft, AOL and Time Warner, and a hostile takeover bid for Disney from Comcast, the US' largest cable company, which has a growing Internet presence. These mergers of content and distribution promise Hollywood access to digital pipelines without compromising their IP, although some suggest that content will have to take a backseat to Internet telephony (see Norris, 2004). How these developments play out alongside Hollywood's attempt to enter hitherto hostile digital IP terrain is unclear. NICL-influenced convergence strategies consolidate creative workforces through the 'vertical integration of new production with inventory management of owned information' (Benkler, 1999: 401), moving towards further privatisation and enclosure of information. When problems arise in Hollywood mergers – as in the debacle of AOL–Time Warner, or the more prosaic separation of Pixar and Walt Disney – management volatility and a clash of corporate cultures are most often blamed. Distribution, labour and IP ownership still drive the engine of corporate media synergy – even in reverse.

At the beginning of this chapter, we raised the thorny question of whether Hollywood should acknowledge piracy as a viable form of film distribution. We maintain that cultural policy should reformulate traditional forms of IP ownership in recognition of the proliferate status of media *readerships*. This means that, along with fracturing the singularity of authors, policy should recognise the multiplicity of readers. As John Hartley notes, reading is not a 'solitary, individualist, consumptive, supplementary act of silent subjection to a series of imperial graphic impressions', but 'a social, communal, productive, act of writing, a dialogic process which is so fundamental to (and may even *be*) popular culture' (Hartley, 1996: 51). There is little doubt that the sheer proliferation of digital reproduction ensures that the MPA make use of piracy's powerfully signifying vernacular. At the same time, as it tries to extend markets into places where it has traditionally been a minority culture – markets that encompass almost half the globe – Hollywood will have to be more innovative about disentangling media from proprietary ownership. Borrowing from observations made during the aforementioned Sony case, Hollywood might recognise that piracy has forms of fair use in areas where traditional forms of distribution/exhibition result in market failure. In India and China, where structural and socio-economic factors impede the 'legitimate' distribution of Hollywood, provisional fair use might be extended to piracy for three reasons: (a) market flaws exist; (b) transfer of use is socially and economically desirable (it creates the cultures of anticipation that buttress Hollywood's merchandising markets); and (c) substantial economic injury is not really a factor (Gordon, 1982: 1614).

Of course, Hollywood and its representatives in the USTR would be the first to 'Yank' such provisional fair-use privileges once the market became profitable. With the advent of new digital technologies, international IP law and attendant public policy might structure textual ownership across variegated terrain rather than yoking it to antiquated and dubious notions of singular authorial genius. For example, taxation and licensing schemes, horizontal private law and centralised purchasing relationships 'might be preferable to a strong interference from the state in the shape of the vertical relationships' established by traditional copyright (Van der Merwe, 1999: 313). Ultimately though, something much stronger and more fundamental must take place. With the explosive interrelation of convergence and diversification engendered by new forms of distribution and duplication technology, ordinary consumers' rights must be taken more seriously – with their reception practices recognised as forms of creative labour: 'moves in a conversation rather than as endpoints for the delivery of product' (Benkler, 2000: 564). In 2004, Morris County, New Jersey, resident Michele Scimeca was making her own cultural policy. After being accused of sharing 1,400 copyrighted songs through the Internet (part of her child's research project), Ms Scimeca and 531 others across the country charged record-company executives with racketeering in their attempts to extort funds by terrorising citsumers (Coughlin, 2004).

Sociological orthodoxy in the early twentieth century linked consumer culture with a loss of social control exacerbated by the insecurities of a changing world (Lears, 1989). The early twenty-first century's linkage of piracy (an over-conspicuous form of consumption) with terrorism proves that nothing much has changed in a hundred years: one mouse-click keeps us from becoming potential accessories to 9/11 after the fact. Why has not cultural policy simply asked consumers what *they* want out of the audiovisual media? Of course, Hollywood has been doing that for a while. The next chapter shows how.

Notes

1   The software giant also has to face the rather delicate fact that the 9/11 hijackers' use of counterfeit Microsoft 'Flight Simulator' programs helped to popularise pirated versions of the program, which is now sold in many parts of the world with bin Laden's face on the cover. In another uncanny doubling with the hijackers' mission, Microsoft deleted the World Trade Center from new versions of the Flight Simulator software beginning in 2001. As one company spokesman put it, 'we did decide, after some careful consideration, that we wanted to do the appropriate thing, the right thing, so we decided to remove the Towers' (Gaudiosi, 2001; for background and critique of this post-traumatic drama of deletion, see Govil, 2002).

2   Carey Heckman, co-director of the Stanford Law and Technology Policy Center, compares the new Internet copyright issues to the barbed wiring that attended new property rights on open territory in the Wild West at the turn of the nineteenth century. See Jonathan Rabinovitz, 'Internet Becomes New Frontier in Copyright Battles', *San Jose Mercury News* (7 November, 1999). Indeed, Westerns provide the gun-slinging with a lingua franca, since the MPA offers a whistle-blowing reward programme called 'The Bounty for Pirates Program', which allows those concerned with combating the civic evils of copyright violation – a 'cancer that cheats the consumer', as Valenti puts it – to pursue temporary deputation under the legal aegis of the MPAA (quoted in MPAA press release, 'Almost 18,000 Pirate Videos Seized Nationwide', 8 February 1995). Piracy is a form of contagion in the rhetoric of the MPAA, illegal video disc plants in China are 'the cancerous core of piracy problems', producing 'poisoned product'; piracy is the 'cancer in the belly of global business', a 'toxin for which there is no known cure' except stronger legislation, penalties and national resolve (MPAA press releases: 'Valenti Announces Enhanced MPAA/VSDA Anti-Piracy Hotline', 21 May 1995; 'Valenti Testimony before the Senate Subcommittee on East Asian and Pacific Affairs', 29 November 1995; 'Quo Vadis?', 23 May 1996).

3   International copyright law originated in the years immediately following the French Revolution, when French national law made no distinctions between French and foreign authors and freely granted French copyright to foreign works. Such reciprocity, it was hoped, might engender similar protection of French works in other nations. But underlying this reciprocity was the idealism of a burgeoning modernism, deployed in the push towards unilaterality. A universal law of copyright would *transcend* nationality and territoriality, and would, as Sam Ricketson notes: 'accord directly with the

conception of the author's natural right of property in his work, existing independently of, and prior to, the formal rules and sanctions of positive law and admitting no artificial restrictions such as a limited term or protection or national boundaries' (1987: 40).

Chapter Five

Getting the Audience

In most societies in which supernatural elements are important in attaining success, some form of divination is practiced, because foreknowledge is one way of control. In parts of East Africa, the entrails of chickens are used for divining the future, while among the Karen of Burma it is the gall bladder of a pig; in Hollywood polls are used to determine the mysterious tastes of the audience.

(Hortense Powdermaker, 1950: 285)

Entertainment is one of the purest marketplaces in the world. If people don't like a movie or record they won't see it or buy it. The fact that the American entertainment industry has been so successful on a worldwide basis speaks to the quality and attractiveness of what we're creating.

(Robert Shaye, Chair of New Line Pictures, quoted in Weinraub, 1993)

The DVD phenom is part of the more customized, individualized approach to leisure that is turning the phrase 'mass audience' into an oh-so-20th-century concept.

(Elisabeth Guider *et al.*, 2004)

We have travelled from globalisation, cultural imperialism and Hollywood's historical structure, through the labour that gives films meaning and value and the policies and laws that police them. In this chapter, we look at the target of these processes – viewers – through three lenses: marketing; surveillance; and distribution and exhibition.

The Conditions of Film Marketing

Viacom boss Sumner Redstone recently told Bill Kartozian, president of the National Association of Theatre Owners, that he had a special formula for reducing film production spending. 'We're not going to make any more bad movies,' he said.

('Hollywood's Incredible', 1999)

Commodities elicit desire by smelling, sounding, tasting, feeling or looking nice in ways that are borrowed from romantic love but then reverse that relationship: people learn about correct forms of romantic love from commodities themselves. The term 'commodity aesthetics' covers the division between what commodities promise (pleasure) and what animates them (profit) (Haug, 1986: 14, 17, 19, 35). At the 1913 meeting of the US National Association of Advertisers, an electric sign emblazoned 'TRUTH' in letters ten-feet high – quite a provocation for an industry built on lies in labelling. The meeting produced the 'Baltimore Truth Declaration', a code of conduct that specified and denounced misleading advertising. This commitment to truth as a productive force and a banner for the industries of persuasion was two-sided. It combined an internal uncertainty – what was 'true' in a rapidly changing world characterised by competing definitions of need and agency – with an external anxiety: the state might intervene in the Association's business via unwelcome regulation (Lears, 1983: 20). That shift, between self-governance and public governance, is the key to Hollywood marketing as it has emerged from this most Yanqui of industries. Three years after the sign of truth blazed away, Baldwin Pictures hired advertisers to conduct a survey of exhibitors about audiences. The agency decided to lie about itself and its real reasons for undertaking the study, posing as a disinterested research agency (Lewis, 1930: 437). Thus shall we know them.

Marketing research and promotion are central to Hollywood's quest for the missing link between the drive towards standardisation to minimise costs and innovation to maximise difference. Except for a brief period in the 1960s when the majors flirted with experimentation and director-driven films, an ethos of aversion to risk turned them towards such strategies as repeated use of formulae, sequels, the event film and 'bankable' stars, directors and writers (Litman, 1998: 26; Wyatt, 1994: 69–94). In common with most managerial warlockcraft, these logics are scrupulously observed rhetorically, but rarely investigated empirically or with any conceptual rigour. Risk-reduction strategies did not eliminate risk; they were merely symptoms of the growing frenzy that 'demand uncertainty' had created in Hollywood's business culture (Litman and Ahn, 1998: 173). Structural uncertainty began to draw increased investment in marketing and audience research in the 1970s. Marketing took firm hold of global Hollywood in the Reaganite 1980s. By then, marketers had spread throughout the industry in 'bureaucratic layers' of the distribution sector (Litman, 1998: 24). Hollywood became

> an industry town dominated by media conglomerates more comfortable with MBAs than with movie moguls. The new breed of studio executive already spoke the language of market research. Several marketing firms moved to Hollywood to take advantage of what promised to be a booming business opportunity.
>
> (Lerner, 1999: 18)

As noted in Chapter 1, marketing has become one of the most expensive of Hollywood's protectionist barriers to outsiders. In keeping with the irresponsibly profligate and violent Reagan era, the cost of marketing spiralled into a 'drain on profits' (Litman, 1998: 59). Today, Hollywood invests nearly twice as much money in marketing activities as do other comparable industries. According to *Advertising Age*, if major film studios, including DreamWorks and MGM/UA, were lumped together as a single brand category, their 1999 advertising expenditure of US$2.55 billion would have placed them third in cost after the automotive and retail industries (Endicott, 2000). Average costs of film promotion increased from US$19.8 million in 1996 to US$22.2 million in 1997 as a means of differentiation from competing cultural industries and national cinemas (European Audiovisual Observatory, 1998), and the process has continued.

US FILM MARKETING COSTS, 2000, US$MILLIONS

Sony	3,593.0
Disney	3,039.0
Time Warner	1,685.5
News Corp	1,264.2

SOURCE: Euromonitor, 2002

Marketing expenditures on film promotion can grow because price is not a factor in gaining market share in the first-run US theatrical film market. Under these circumstances, rival firms compete through campaigns that differentiate their films. Such costs escalate when an oligopoly of five or six companies controls the film distribution market using expensive marketing campaigns to beat their rivals and hold back new competitors, as they collectively build and maintain what neoclassical economists call a 'product differentiation barrier to entry' (Litman, 1998: 277, 59) via the accumulation over time of consumer preferences (Hoskins *et al.*, 1997: 61). The so-called 'accumulative preference' of consumers builds on such advertising clichés as 'from the creative genius of Walt Disney', or 'from the producers of *Titanic*'. This gives the majors a hypothetical monopoly on filmgoers' knowledge. But 'accumulative preference' alone does not sustain Hollywood's hegemony or justify the cost of marketing.

First, the risk-reduction strategy of the slate finds the studios making vast numbers of pictures, predicated on the correct assumption that they know nothing about audience tastes and that approximately 95 per cent of films will fail abysmally. No other filmmaking economy has sufficient capital formation to embark on such a high-risk strategy. This creates a barrier to competition in distribution, which makes it possible to force foreign exhibitors to engage in block-booking – you only get the Spielberg film if you take the Jean-Claude Van Damme movie. Second, scale necessitates a large multifaceted marketing structure to ensure that product differentiation is ongoing and systematic. This involves a massive sales effort for particular films, using the conventional tools of marketing: advertising, promotions, retailing, innovation and product design. But it also entails expanded tasks of advocacy (corporate advertising, public relations and political lobbying – see below) and, because they know nothing about audiences, extensive surveillance (consumer 'behaviour' and audience and market research). Finally, it helps to remember that 'market failure' is not a dirty little secret; it is fundamental to Hollywood. The anxiety involved in the filmmaking business provokes an extraordinary need for the ritualised use of marketing in all phases of a film's life. Barry Litman and Hoekyuhn Ahn (1998: 173) have suggested that the fear of making a movie without market knowledge is akin to the fear of building a skyscraper only to find out on the day it opened that nobody liked it. With the stakes so high, it is no surprise that, as one former marketing executive put it, a 'marketing campaign is tackled with the same zeal and methodical planning as a general preparing an invasion' (Lukk, 1997: ix).

Vast sums of money thus channel into film marketing for reasons (and superstitions) that go beyond the conventional promotional work of building 'accumulative preference'. Marketing:

- consoles movie executives who live with the risk of box-office failure
- makes product differentiation a barrier to entry
- regulates populations of moviegoers through consumer surveillance; and
- promotes positive associations with Hollywood's distribution cartel.

Fundamentally, the persistent and growing investment in marketing reinforces barriers to competitors in film distribution worldwide (Hoskins *et al.*, 1997: 61–62). Evidence of the way US films are themselves marketed abroad indicates that advertising expenditure has its major impact on exhibitors, not audiences. Extended overseas runs for Hollywood films frequently correlate with marketers efficiently targeting theatrical chains (Elberse and Eliashberg, 2003).

The audience is therefore not a *locus* of demand, but of calculation. Three basic systems of fantasising about consumers have dominated marketing over the two decades that the industry has viewed an emergent global homogeneity of taste. These concepts are individual, regional and global. The first is animated by ideas of race, class, gender and psyche; the second by geopolitical clusters; and the third by a growing cosmopolitanism (Hassan *et al.*, 2003: 446-47).

Marketing supposedly helps to make an industry competitively open. In theory, smaller specialty and B-movie distributors can use it to challenge the majors. In practice, competitive marketing now requires investments on a scale beyond the reach of smaller distributors everywhere. In fact, chipping away at the majors' 75–85 per cent market share in the US alone can mean spending more on *marketing* than *making* a movie. That is why Gramercy Pictures paid twice the production costs of *Four Weddings and a Funeral* to market it in the

US (Lukk, 1997). Gramercy was a joint venture of Polygram Film Entertainment and Universal Pictures, which kept the reassuring jingle of deep and full pockets within earshot of this speciality distributor. Finally, with the accelerated capitalisation and organisational reach of film marketing, marketers have scaled up the authorship ladder to occupy a strategic position inside global Hollywood's screen machine.

Of course, you hardly need a film scholar to tell you that marketing has made a big impact on the movies – it is abundantly clear when you see Meg Ryan and Tom Hanks drinking coffee at Starbucks or using AOL email to fall in love. It was funny to watch Mike Myers' Dr Evil plot Austin Powers' destruction over a cup of Starbucks coffee, and hard to ignore it when John Travolta bellied up to the Krispy Kreme counter in *Primary Colors* mumbling that he 'shouldn't eat so many of the glazed treats', only to hear Danny, a Krispy Kremer, tell him: 'Well, you know, you gotta eat something' (Herman, 2000). This list goes on: the cast of *The Faculty* (Robert Rodriguez, 1998) costumed by Tommy Hilfiger; Columbia's *Big Daddy* (Dennis Dugan, 1999) furnished with enough Sony audiovisual equipment to start a small retail electronics store; Matt Damon and Ben Affleck sharing Dunkin' Donuts in *Good Will Hunting* (Gus Van Sant, 1997); Tom Cruise 'racing' a packet of Sweet 'n' Low along Nicole Kidman's thigh in *Days of Thunder* (Tony Scott, 1990); ET washing Reese's Pieces down with Coors beer (sales of the sweetmeat rose by 66 per cent afterwards); FedEx featuring in *Cast Away* (Robert Zemeckis, 2000) in return for funding 80 per cent of its costs (Wenner, 2004); and Gene Hackman offering Tom Cruise a Red Stripe in *The Firm* (Sydney Pollack, 1993), leading to a 50 per cent increase in US sales and the eventual purchase of the brewery by a global firm (Buss, 1998). And you certainly don't need anyone to point out that movie characters and stories populate toy stores, big-box discount stores, speciality retail shops, bookstores, music stores and theme parks. Beyond the obvious, what can screen studies say about marketing's effect on its primary object of interest, the film text?

One author who has taken up this question is Justin Wyatt (1994). He endeavoured to reconcile the history of marketing's incursion into filmmaking with a humanist narrative that preserves both an authorial presence for individual filmmakers and an aesthetic experience for filmgoers. This econo-aesthetic comprehension of film marketing offers a helpful starting point from which to record marketing's textual effects as well as its historical significance. Wyatt represents 'high concept' as a distinct film aesthetic engendered during the 'post-classical' period of motion-picture history. This was the moment when a new product differentiation orthodoxy gave filmmakers more opportunities to make individual films with varying quality and different looks, even as the oligopoly of major distributors encouraged the homogenisation of product lines (Wyatt, 1994: 104). Wyatt reinscribes concentration and conglomeration as conditions, rather than obstructions, of aesthetic possibility.

From this historical perspective, he perceives the ascendancy of 'industrial expressivity': that is, the self-conscious use of marketing conventions over the 'authorial expressivity' that characterises art-cinema conventions (1994: 60–64). The mutual infiltration of these expressive modes became a general condition of filmmaking after the 1960s.

Of all the formulae to emerge from this aesthetic alchemy, 'high concept' was the one marked with the most 'coherent and repeated structuring of … its elements around the marketing possibilities in the project' (Wyatt, 1994: 64). Marketing's 'industrial expressivity' made its mark on a film as formal 'excess' motivated by sheer commercial interest. This mark of 'excess' stands out whenever there is a 'gap in the [artistic] motivation of the work': that is, whenever sizeable parts of a film are unnecessary to advance the story or establish a visual style. Wyatt separates commercially motivated excess from melodrama's narrative excesses. When 'excess' is used for commercial ends, it aestheticises elements to improve marketability – for example, exaggerated decoration, high-tech settings or any special effects that disturb an otherwise consistent and coherent set of formal and narrative elements. Stars are another commonly used component of commercial excess, in particular when their presence in a film is determined by their 'bankability'. The makers of 'high-concept' films allow the logic of the marketplace to dictate these stylistic choices. 'Excess' becomes a signature of corporate authorship (Wyatt, 1994: 28, 34, 24, 36).

This 'industrial expressivity' would be useless if the marketable elements in a film, its 'excesses', were intractable for film advertising and associated merchandising. Wyatt details the numerous ways in which marketable film content flows from film texts to marketing texts. For example, music and image can be extracted from a film and repackaged in modules 'separate from the narrative', then moved to television as a music video promoting the film (1994: 40–44). Modular 'excesses' reappear in other media and promotional forms as well, including radio, trailers, poster art, the Internet, print advertisements, cross-promotions and tie-ins. As these marketing modules become widely disseminated through domestic and global distribution, they form what Gary Hoppenstand calls a 'film environment' (1998: 232). The externalisation of these modules of 'excess' is an integral part of 'high concept' and film marketing generally. However, the modules serve more than an economic function, for when they penetrate public space, they also affect the aesthetic experience of filmgoing. By maximising 'points of contact with the film', they multiply 'the possible meanings' one might derive 'from the film narrative' (Wyatt, 1994: 46; see also Hoppenstand, 1998: 232). Wyatt suggests that this process not only pluralises textual possibilities, but has the potential to enhance people's enjoyment of movies. He argues that marketing, in particular the promotional music video, creates a number of intertextual influences that, as Barbara Klinger says, 'cannot be settled within the textual system', but spill over into a zone of competing interpretations outside the film narrative (quoted in Wyatt, 1994: 44–45).

The econo-aesthetic method fosters appreciation for the textual complexity of 'high-concept' films, and argues for their worthiness as objects of study. In this account, marketing enlarges the experience of filmgoing as well as related experiences of popular music, eating out, child care, education, branded clothing and so on. Wyatt's account of the industrial and corporate imperatives that drive marketing 'excesses' into the movies and into other areas of cultural consumption also invites us to see the movies, and related intertextual encounters, as sites of intertextual wrangling over meanings.

By focusing on the aesthetic dimensions of film marketing, this approach restrains criticism of marketing's textual predilections (is it really a matter of taste or pleasurably ambiguous meanings?) and diverts attention from marketing's role in defending the distribution cartel. Further, the econo-aesthetic method foregrounds textual production within narrowly defined film-industrial conditions, overlooking the coordinated efforts of large entertainment-information conglomerates to annex cultural consumption and elevate market criteria over other ways of interpreting culture's value (Schiller, 1974 and 1989; Miller, 1987; Maxwell, 2001). Finally, in elaborating his econo-aesthetic method, Wyatt criticises the industry's audience research on technical grounds. But he does not question the fundamental problem of surveillance in marketing research's attention to feelings, desires, memory, tastes, dislikes and other behavioural features associated with the moviegoing experience (Litman and Ahn, 1998: 180; De Silva, 1998: 145). Litman and Ahn have criticised this linkage of economic concepts and aesthetic and marketing approaches, which, they argue, installs highly questionable presumptions about the filmgoer into an otherwise useful economic model. Style might be identifiable in film content, but its allure cannot be measured. If the impact and significance of the textual elements 'seem to lie in the viewer's mind', as Litman and Ahn put it, then such factors do not belong with the objective criteria that will predict a film's success at the box office. After all, a film's success is about how many tickets are sold, not the quality of film perceived as a statistical projection of audience taste or thought. For years, there was no empirical test for this gamble on quality, only unreliable predictors such as stars, directors and critics, though contemporary marketing scholars claim to have established correlations (Austin, 1989; Basuroy et al., 2003). Most people writing on the industry accept William Goldman's famous saying: 'NOBODY KNOWS ANYTHING' (Goldman, 1985: 39).

The distribution oligopoly has carved out an occupational growth area for marketers in global Hollywood. Marketers labour for huge sums of money to tell their clients what a probable audience wants in a film, desires in association with it and thinks about its stars, director, special effects, studio, genre and so on. Part of the growing investment in marketing seeks to find out whether marketers did their job – getting people to their clients' movies. It has even become a common feature of infotainment journalism to analyse a distributor's marketing strategy, going so far as to treat successes and failures as 'news'. Of course, the entertainment media have a hard time representing the immanent failure of their own industry without deepening a romantic myth perpetuated by the film industry itself: taking risks makes them come across as glamorous and daring. Confusion in screen studies helps the myth persist: Wyatt (1994) thinks marketing works, and marvels at its wizards' derring-do; Litman does not, endorsing only a popular adage about advertising: it works half the time, but nobody knows which half (see Litman and Ahn, 1998: 180; also see De Silva, 1998: 145). This myth is further perpetuated by the secretive way that the industry's own research on marketing's efficacy is guarded as proprietary information, which is publicly disseminated via journalistic reports of widespread, constant monitoring of marketing activities and their routinely urgent modification, indicating a universal lack of confidence in the power of any particular marketing idea. This is echoed in the executive mantra, 'marketing is just a tool'.

The tool showed that Scorsese's *Cape Fear* (1991) tested badly in previews, but it ended up being his most profitable movie; and research was negative on *Stuart Little* (Rob Hinkoff, 1999), which 'did huge business', in the argot of the linguistically challenged who create clichés for and about warlockcraft (Willens, 2000: 20). The most notorious blunder, according to industry lore, was the prediction that Spielberg's *E.T. the Extra-Terrestrial* (1982) would not interest anyone over the age of four. Market researchers at Columbia proposed that production be scrapped (Andrews, 1998: 1). And, of course, there is the celebrated failure of New Coke, which still generates enough inward embarrassment and outward *Schadenfreude* to keep marketers from making final decisions in any industry.

When marketers are wrong, the shaky foundation underlying market knowledge becomes clear. Marketers have tried 'everything short of hooking up an audience to a machine' (Klady, 1998: 9). They know that 'respondents' are not candid; that they are silent about viewing pleasures that embarrass them; and that the non-response rate – that is, outright resistance to audience surveys – is too high to make authoritative statistical findings. As one researcher put it, predicting a film's success is like 'sending a rocket to a distant planet. If you're off by half a degree, you wind up in another galaxy' (Klady, 1998: 9). In response, marketing executives keep a favourite scapegoat at hand in the sovereign consumer – who by 'word of mouth' rebelliously makes or breaks a film. This returns us to Nazi, Marxist, functionalist and cultural-studies true believers in the active audience. What a party!

Of course, there is a problem with this vision of the audience as a powerbroker. Movie executives decide what gets made and what is exhibited, not audiences, and there is not a single executive in Hollywood who, under pressure from the parent firm and financiers, would make a movie that lacks elements to market, advertise, promote and so on. In sum, the faith in marketing – even if its research is persistently wrong, and advertising only works half the proverbial time – has real effects: on the screen, on the manner in which Hollywood production advances, on the dispositions guiding the work within the distribution sector of the NICL and on the bureaucratic rationalisation of what Gitlin (1983) has called the science of the second-guess. More than that – the paper that won the oleaginously named 'Best New Thinking Award' at the 2003 Market Research Society Conference let the hypocrisy sing when it acknowledged that effective marketing does not adopt a 'view of the consumer as an individual' but rather 'part of the herd' (Earls, 2003:311). So there you have it. Welcome to mad-audience disease, as diagnosed by the marketing department. The DEM/GEM is under surveillance in intensive care.

Writers who still envision a formal wall between film art and commerce are rendered unintelligible, and those who treat production and distribution as autonomous realms of labour (one side 'creative' the other 'business') are baffled by the infiltration of distribution's economic pressures and marketers' selective perception in the production phase. Marketing assails these assumptions by installing a high regard for what Oliver Stone calls the 'product oriented business' up front in the 'creative' pre-production and production parts of filmmaking (quoted in Wyatt, 1994: 157). To be sure, there has always been tension between the 'creatives' and the marketing people, but this hardly matters more than the ritual disputes between advertising 'creatives' and market researchers. Commercialisation is only rhetorically questioned, while the real fight is over whose ideas work best for getting bankers' approval and creating marketability and commercial success. The perceived or hoped for independence of culture from the political economy is further smashed by marketing's growing presence in contemporary storytelling.

Textual Gatekeepers: Positioning, Playability, Marketability

> British filmmakers need to learn that great quality doesn't guarantee box-office success. [T]hey should add a dash of focus group and polling, and be prepared to change their product if necessary – just as the major Hollywood studios do. Either that, or keep their integrity and stay poor.
>
> (Darius Sanai, 1999: 12)

> *Jurassic Park* is a very different film. People came for the curiosity: you know, what is a dinosaur? And how has a Hollywood film been dubbed first time in Hindi? There was a curiosity value attached to it – that's no longer the case.
>
> (Rajat Barjatya, marketing director of Rajshri Productions, quoted in Ganti, 2002: 285)

In a sense, marketing information appears to reduce everyday risks associated with spending money. After all, you cannot try out a film before paying to see it, as you would a pullover in a department store. So one might think that film marketing is an informational gift that helps customers make a rational ticket purchase under circumstances that actually force them to do something very irrational – namely, to buy a product sight unseen. Yet it should be obvious by now that marketing is not in the business of consumer protection. Marketers do not work for you, and their clients certainly do not wish you to make an independent decision about how to spend your money. Marketers and marketing executives play a strategic gatekeeping role for Hollywood, blessing only those film projects with commercial potential and marketability and making sure such films appear in advertisements and theatres near you. Marketing safeguards the major distributors' market power and Hollywood's hegemony, despite its claim to be simply providing audiences with information on which to base their choices of entertainment.

Marketers read stories and watch movies differently from most people, scanning pages and screens for elements called positioning and playability, which give them a way to make sense of a project's commercial potential. Positioning is not about a film's setting or exhibition, but what marketers want to 'do to the mind of the prospect' (marketing warlocks' word for a person). That is, they 'position the product in the mind of the prospect'. The inventors of the positioning concept tell us that its 'basic approach … is not to create something new and different, but to manipulate what's already up there in the mind, to retie the connections that already exist' (Ries and Trout, 1981: 2, 5). The mind of the audience, or 'prospect', is conceived as an organ seeking guidance through the clutter of information and entertainment. 'The only defense a person has in our overcommunicated society', say Al Ries and Jack Trout, 'is an oversimplified mind' (1981: 6). Positioning a film to the oversimplified mind of the audience means finding elements of a film's story that can be communicated as simply as possible. These are its selling points, and they make positioning possible.

The marketing executives at Gramercy Pictures, for example, positioned *Four Weddings and a Funeral* in a variety of ways. For one 'prospect', it was presented as a story of 'two people who belong together but may never be'; to another, it was about friends going to humorous weddings and the funny things that happen to them. Positioning gets further simplified with the narrowing of these probable audiences into what marketers call segments, which are demographic pools for different positionings of the same film. *Four Weddings* was positioned for the 18- to 24-year-old segment as 'a comical look at the perils of being single', while the 25- to 34-year-old segment would see the film as 'an English-humor romantic comedy, a high concept expressed as Monty Python meets *Sleepless in Seattle*', and the 35-plus segment would go to 'a non-Shakespearian *Much Ado About Nothing*' (Lukk, 1997: 5).

In similar fashion, each US film is allotted a hundred generic descriptions for use in specific markets. *Dances with Wolves* (Kevin Costner, 1990) was sold in France as a documentary-style dramatisation of Native American life, while

Malcolm X (Spike Lee, 1991) was promoted there with posters of the Stars and Stripes aflame (Danan, 1995: 131–32, 137). *Sliver* (Phillip Noyce, 1993) was shown in the US with four minutes cut by Paramount censors. It was then promoted overseas as 'The film America didn't see' and returned double its domestic revenue in foreign sales (Augros, 2000: 159). The overseas release of *The Sweetest Thing* (Roger Kumble, 2002) included a segment considered too touchy for US audiences. A performance number called 'The Penis Song' featured the female leads singing 'You're too big to fit in' at their restaurant (Groves, 2002b). *Pearl Harbor* was promoted in Japan as a love story rather than the blend of righteous revenge and forgiving passion that provided a focus elsewhere. Its trailer showed a Japanese airman warning children to take cover. All this added considerably to the reported total promotional cost of US$125 million (Eller and Muñoz, 2002; Smith, 2002).

After *Minority Report* (2002) had failed domestically, Spielberg and Cruise travelled everywhere they could to recoup their seemingly unwise investment via personal appearances in the auteur reaches of Europe, and new commercials that made the film 'not like schoolwork'. *Master and Commander: The Far Side of the World* was sold by Fox to transnational audiences by linking it to the 2003 men's Rugby World Cup. Star Russell Crowe appeared on Fox Sports World, interspersed with footage of rugby games and his performance in the film, talking about how rugby was both a metaphor and a technique for male bonding on the set. This also allowed the network to cross-promote the movie with its coverage of a sports spectacle. Whereas US trailers for *Moulin Rouge!* featured a syrupy moment of terpsichory between lovers, Japanese audiences were provided a deathbed scene both of and as consumption, in view of their alleged interest in tragedy as honour – but the film failed there (Eller and Muñoz, 2002; latimes.com/moulintrailers). *XXX* was of concern to the studios because Vin Diesel had failed to attract non-Yanquis in the past, but he spent eight weeks in twelve nations to promote it and had his first international success (King, 2002). Promotion of a particular brand of cigarette in Japan was timed to coincide with the release of *Licence to Kill*, in which the hero used the brand to detonate a bomb (Mekemson and Glantz, 2002: i85). In Nigeria, British American Tobacco handed out cigarettes to spectators as part of its 2002 'Rothmans Experience It Cinema Tour', which also offered viewers theatrical facilities far beyond the norm and new Hollywood action adventure (James Bates, 2003b).

Overseas-audience targeting explains why several big-budget, small-dialogue films of the 1990s were made, such as war epics and disaster movies (Cook, 2000: 21). Gérard Depardieu appeared in *102 Dalmatians* (Kevin Dima, 2000), Michelle Yeoh in *Tomorrow Never Dies* and Tcheky Karyo in *The Patriot* to boost the films' appeal outside the US (Martin, 2000). International co-productions also cross-breed cultural preferences in order to position films on multiple national screens.

Strong positioning of US movies is not always politically acceptable in Hollywood. In the post-9/11 period, as events led up to the US invasion of Afghanistan, Hollywood sensed a rise in effective positioning for *The Quiet American* (Phillip Noyce, 2002), but not the kind that suited it politically. Instead of marketing the movie to position it in the minds of billions of anti-imperialists worldwide, the distributor Miramax chose to censor it for a year after 9/11 because Yanqui test audiences 'didn't appreciate moviemakers taking a swipe at America', as Noyce put it (quoted in Biskind, 2004: 463–64; Lyman, 2002b: 1). Several films were also censored, some for reasons of kindness to the families of 9/11 – like *Collateral Damage*, which depicts a firefighter's family being killed by narco-terrorists – and others because they were positioned in the anti-militarist mind, such as another Miramax picture, *Buffalo Soldiers* (Gregor Jordan, 2001), which was finally released to video stores in 2004.

In general, the arbitrary interpretations of positioning simplify the meanings of a film in order to appeal to the imaginary impulses of distinct national audiences. If a film lacks selling points, positioning is still imperiously applied. Preview audiences either loved or walked out of *Pulp Fiction* (Quentin Tarantino, 1994). Those who said they liked it belonged to no clear marketing segment, which meant one thing to the marketing geniuses at Miramax: 'it was different' and 'had something for everyone' (Lerner, 1999: 18; Lukk, 1997: 22). For those executives, numerous positionings of *Pulp Fiction* (those who hated it were not counted) would be randomly assigned to the audience in upmarket, blue-collar and ethnic categories, then further subdivided by geography and age. In an attempt to position films for forty-something audiences, distributors have begun to advertise in such media as 'easy-listening' FM radio and television guides, associating films like *The Italian Job* (F. Gary Gray, 2003) with nostalgia for the 1960s (Grimshaw, 2003: 7).

Obviously, such random guesswork can make a lot of blunders. *Faux* southern accents in *The Legend of Bagger Vance* (Robert Redford, 2000) and *Cold Mountain* grate on southerners' ears. The stereotype of 'some barefooted Jethro Clampett with chicken poop between [his] toes' strikes many as clumsy at best, and biased at worst ('Hollywood's Southern', 2003). Also confounding the regional expectations of marketing executives in California, Disney's Spanish-language version of *The Emperor's New Groove* (Mark Dindal, 2000) failed with Spanish-speaking audiences in the US, who went to see the English version instead. This unsuccessful attempt to cultivate a Latino audience (75 per cent of Latinos in the US do not go to the movies) via an apparently fail-safe positioning strategy was especially embarrassing for marketers in Los Angeles, where nearly half of all potential moviegoers are Latino/a. As a reporter for the Spanish news agency EFE noted, 'Hollywood just doesn't know how to address itself to this bilingual audience' ('Fracasa el Estreno Ultimo', 2001). In the US, as Sony Pictures Classics President Michael Barker put it, 'once the French were the big thing, now it's the Latin American', with 400 screens allotted to

Spanish-language films (quoted in 'España Promocionará', 2000). But this address of domestic difference is always and everywhere contingent. We also see reactions like the following after a major broadcast network invested in a Spanish-language channel: 'people come up to you and say, "So, you're serious about this Spanish thing?"' (NBC President and Chief Operating Officer Andrew Lack quoted in 'Hispanic-American', 2002).

Waiting to Exhale (Forest Whitaker, 1995) was first broadly positioned as a 'chick flick' (*sic*). When that audience failed to show up, it was repositioned for the segment that did, as 'an African-American chick-flick' (Lukk, 1997: 39). This 'discovery' had more to do with defending marketing's weak techniques than it did with identifying the mind of the middle-class US black filmgoer. Still, Hollywood began positioning one or two 'black' films per year. This effort at cultivating the black segment has extended to Africa with the help of the US State Department, which has sponsored a film festival in Yaoundé, Cameroon, to highlight African-American themed movies, along with a few films from Nigeria and Cameroon. According to the US embassy there, the Yaoundé festival aims to develop African markets as well as filmmaking labour in the region ('African, American', 2003). Domestically, however, films about black themes are given a mere six weeks of opportunity each year, in the period between Martin Luther King, Jr's birthday and the end of Black History Month.

Whereas positioning is about finding the right place to put a film in an audience's (imagined) collective mind, playability is about predicting how satisfied that audience will be with the positioning. In determining playability, marketers stop looking at the movie and start conducting surveys, choosing to question people whose outward characteristics match those of an audience they suspect will be predisposed to like the film or its animating logic. This is where pre-tests, test screenings and tracking are important. Test screenings and tracking are often used to gauge what warlocks call, in their more oleaginous incantations, 'the overcome' and 'the want-to-see'. The overcome is a noun describing an obstacle in the way of clear positioning (Lukk, 1997: 85), as in 'we had a very difficult overcome with the audience for *Meshes in the Afternoon*' (Maya Deren and Alexander Hammid, 1943). Often pronounced 'the wannasee', this second noun refers to the level of awareness and desire surrounding a particular movie, as in '*Titanic* had great wannasee' (Lukk, 1997: 8–9).

The test of *Pulp Fiction*'s playability, which 'scored' well among US 'urban' and 'ethnic' audience segments, helped marketers build the movie's want-to-see. As one executive commented, the 'audience just went wild' when the trailer came on with the volume 'really pumped up' for the song 'Jungle Boogie' (quoted in Lukk, 1997: 26). He was referring to a trailer carrying an R-rating, itself a sign that is thought to position a film in the minds of audiences as akin to action-adventure and thriller movies. The trailer also sought a position in the minds of baby-boomers' children by combining clips of action sequences, always highly marketable elements, with a retro 1970s music track. Other ways of creating the want-to-see have surfaced in e-promotions that publicise new film releases via the Internet, which is thought to offer its own strong positioning capabilities. For example, *Lord of the Rings: The Fellowship of the Ring* had the biggest one-day download of an Internet film promotion (1.6 million), beating *Phantom Menace*'s previous record of 1 million ('New Line', 2000). The numbers keep growing each year.

Academic warlocks identify four film marketing possibilities via the Internet: promotional and informational material on screenings; selling merchandise; paratextual trivia such as outtakes; and creating fan groups (adapted from Finn *et al.*, 2000: 368–69). We would add a fifth: surveillance.

Marketability differs from a film's commercial potential (positioning and playability), because it is based on a calculation of elements that can be used to promote and advertise a film through trailers, posters, television, radio, magazines and the Internet. It is also based on a film's pre-sold fit with special cross-promotions involving retailers, fast-food restaurants and other entertainment media, especially recorded music. The larger the number of advertising-friendly elements – including a film's imagery, storyline, music, genre and stylisation – the greater the marketability (Wyatt, 1994; Lukk, 1997). From a warlock's perspective, a film might have high playability and great commercial potential, but still lack marketability, a problem that confronted the documentary *Hoop Dreams* (Steve James, 1994) (Lukk, 1997: 97).

Thus far, we have seen how the appraisal of commercial potential (positioning and playability) and marketability is based on restrictive market criteria, and also how this process fosters a technical jargon and methodology that lend social-scientific credibility, or at least a professional aura, to marketers' judgments of a movie's value. Marketing's influence is not confined to post-production and release phases, however. Commercial potential and marketability are assessed *and* manipulated in a film's textual elements during pre-production and production, effectively merging distribution into production and blurring the old scalar and spatial divisions of this labour process. 'The minute you start the process of deciding to make a film and you're communicating that vision to anyone,' says producer Peter Guber, 'you're in the process of selling. If you don't understand that, you're not in show business. You're just not' (quoted in 'The Monster', 2001).

Pre-production calculation and manipulation of marketability are done with an eye to both the level of interest in a film while it is still in production and future tie-ins and cross-promotions of recorded music, fast food, video games, toys and other merchandising features that form part of a film's aural and visual design. At this stage, the movie is often little more than a title. For example, Disney's *Armageddon* was the name of a marketing concept for a film that had yet to be written (McChesney, 1999: 39). Even marketers have an ironic awareness of this trend in Hollywood. A recent television commercial for a soft drink famously mocked this process by portraying marketing executives designing advertising and merchandising details for a movie about a giant man-eating slug. The only thing left to do was make the actual film (Lowe & Partners, Sprite brand).

One well-known result of pre-planned marketability involves product placement, which began seventy years ago with autos, diamonds, alcohol and tobacco, *inter alia* (Wasko, 1994; Wenner, 2004), and now has its own peak body, the Entertainment Resources and Marketing Association (ERMA), and the capacity to tailor placements to specific audiences via digital insertion. Major distributors employ placement specialists and independent placement companies or brokers to ensure that 'Virtually everything you see [in a film], other than background stuff, is a negotiated deal' (Herman, 2000: 48) through logos, background advertisements or actual use of the product, of which the latter is the most costly, since the object is animated within the diegesis through the labour of acting (DeLorme and Reid, 1999). An example is Tom Hanks' reference to the 'computing machine' with 'the fruit' in *Forrest Gump* (Robert Zemeckis, 1994). Some directors and stars try to put their favourite brands into movies. Many of these preferences are induced through payments and other incentives from marketers to the directors and stars (once again, see smokefreemovies.ucsf.edu).

There are about thirty-five product placement companies in the US. ERMA links manufacturers to its members' placement operations and offers visitors to erma.org a primer on the wonders of making consumer goods integral to a film's scenery. Retailers and consumer-goods producers pay placement companies annual retainer fees of US$50,000 or more to scan hundreds of film scripts a year for scenes in which to place their brand names and products. One placement company boasts that product placement is 'legitimately the only way to pay one time for an "ad" that appears forever' (Herman, 2000: 48). When merchandisers miss the opportunity to place their goods in the film, they are given another chance during planning for video, DVD and television releases. Jennifer Lopez never touched Proctor & Gamble's Swiffer duster in *Maid in Manhattan* (Wayne Wang, 2002), though she now appears on the DVD cover with one, thanks to computer-generated mischief (Ebenkamp, 2003). As part of making *Swordfish*, Halle Berry, John Travolta and Hugh Jackman lent their characters' likenesses to Heineken for a US$10 million international marketing campaign (Scevak, 2001).

The most enduring franchise for global product placement is the 007 series, where gratuitous commercial inserts have become both controversial and wildly successful. When BMW was selected as Bond's car for the first three Pierce Brosnan movies, it obtained staggering results: the Z3 model sold out prior to reaching showrooms. That launch, plus the boost to its 750iLs and R1200c motorcycle, were valued at more than US$100 million. Most recently, Aston Martin – of course, now owned by Ford – bought its way back as Bond's motor for *Die Another Day* with approximately US$40 million, as part of a strategy to increase annual worldwide sales from 1,500 to 5,000. The company was seeking an association with 'solving global crises'. Ford was one of twenty-five promotional 'partners' that paid US$70 million towards the production, while eleven other companies spent over US$100 million in cross-marketing campaigns to associate themselves and promote the text, which was quickly renamed *Buy Another Day* within the advertising industry (Norm Marshall & Associates, n. d.; 'New Bond', 2002; Stewart-Allen, n. d.; Trebay, 2002; '007', 2002; 'A View', 2002). For another espionage fantasy, *Spy Kids* (Robert Rodriguez, 2001), marketable film elements were tied to high-tech spy toys from Compaq, RCA, Sprint and others, and promoted in advertisements for the electronics retailer Radio Shack.

Televisa's Mexican *telenovelas* have product placements that change with each foreign sale (Wenner, 2004), and Coca-Cola and Pepsi now invest in Bollywood product placement (Kahn, 2002). New Line has formed a marketing department specifically devoted to generating tie-in and placement deals throughout the life of a single film or franchise (Stanley, 2003: 8). As the Chief Executive Officer of Associated Film Promotions remarked in the 1980s: 'Life in the 20th century is a life of commercialism. Films are becoming more real. Face it, doesn't life look like a commercial?' (quoted in Prince, 2000: 139). Even satires like *Josie and the Pussycats* (Harry Elfont and Deborah Kaplan, 2001) become exemplars rather than critiques of product placement, and it remains for David Mamet in *State and Main* (2001) to ironise from beyond, via his character who finds the million dollars he needs for his film by placing a dot-com logo in a nineteenth-century locale (Scevak, 2001).

Cross-promotions and merchandising tie-ins, whether planned during production or distribution phases, draw on a film's marketable elements to raise awareness of it across media and non-media publicity channels. For example, Gramercy cross-promoted *Four Weddings and a Funeral* with a 'Just Say I Do' vacation sweepstakes via a partnership with a French airline and a travel agency that offered winners a honeymoon in Tahiti. The promotion was also sold through Starbucks coffee shops, a national dating service, bridal shops and florists. Gramercy arranged promotional screenings with the same US dating service and mail-order florist, and found television stations willing to promote the film by holding contests for the best wedding video (Lukk, 1997: 15). DreamWorks' Shrek cartoon character sells Barilla pasta in Italy and around the world ('Barilla si allea con Spielberg'), while Universal's *The Cat in the Hat* (Bo Welch, 2003) can be seen hawking products from fast food to US postage stamps (Ebenkamp and Hein, 2003: 4). The Mount Earnslaw region of New Zealand has been plucked from *The Lord of the Rings* trilogy to promote consumer goods ('Ringing Up', 2002). Cars lead cross-promotions, with T-3 Toyotas in *Terminator 3*, Fords in projects under way at Revolution Studios and Miramax's come-hither request of US$35 million from any automaker who wants their car to be the centrepiece of *The Green Hornet* (forthcoming) (Grover, 2003a: 88; Greenberg, 2003: 4; Linnett and Friedman, 2003: 1).

The pushers of boozing and cruising have begun a new trend of producing films whose title characters are products themselves. BMW started this as an Internet advertising campaign called *The Hire*, based on a David Fincher treatment, and made up of eight short films by auteurs John Woo, Joe Carnahan, Ang Lee, Wong Kar-Wai, Tony Scott, Guy Ritchie, John Frankenheimer and González-Iñárritu. Bombay Gin maker Bacardi followed suit with a series of branded short films, in which hip young directors talk about themselves on the Independent Film Channel (Hein, 2003: 13). The ultimate product placement/tie-in/merchandising/cross-promotion film is *Foodfight!* (Lawrence Kasanoff, forthcoming), scheduled for release sometime in 2005. It will be a two-hour computer cartoon in which leading consumer brands battle 'Brand X' for control of a supermarket after closing time. A Santa Monica firm called Threshold Digital Research Labs (TDRL) is producing the film using digital-animation technology that allows icons to be replaced and customised as familiar brands from wherever in the world the film is screened. *Foodfight!* is also a prototype for a new decentralised computer processing system developed by IBM. IBM invested 'multiple millions' in TDRL to make the film, using its proprietary 'on-demand' processing network, which it plans to market to other industries using *Foodfight!* as a selling point. IBM wants to price and sell computer processing like a utility – when there is an increase in demand, it supplies more computing power to any user on the grid, eliminating the need for the client to buy more computers, but also making the user dependent on IBM's supply. TDRL gets access to large-scale digital processing owned by the major studios and shortens the turnaround time for digital products (Maney, 2003).

The Internet presence of merchandising, promotion and tie-in deals is spreading. Websites devoted to single film promotions are common now. Marketing at these sites dramatically increases immediately prior to the initial theatrical release. After that, activity usually declines until the site is eventually abandoned. The Internet is littered with dead pages for films that are no longer in circulation, except on video-store shelves. The content of the typical site has grown quickly, and now can include not only downloadable trailers and promotional photographs, but discussion boards, online games and links to fan clubs and vendors of related products, including books, clothing, toys and electronic and board games (Maas, 2003: 16–18). Many fans start their own sites, but the major distributors and the licensees of their brand icons carry the heavy commercial work. Film advertising via the Internet has yet to make a dent in a market dominated by television and print, but for certain films, marketers draw on Internet positioning (the putative geeky minds of young men on computers) to create a want-to-see. For example, marketing executives at Fox Searchlight are convinced that the US$1 million they spent on saturating nerdy websites with banner ads for *28 Days Later* (Danny Boyle, 2003) was the reason their US$9 million movie made US$21 million in its first two weeks in the US (Smith, 2003: 57; Grover, 2003b). And Microsoft and Universal cite the MSN

Internet service portal as integral to launching *How the Grinch Stole Christmas* (Ron Howard, 2000).

Merchandise

> There's one group there to discuss the marketing tie-ins. How much will McDonald's or Burger King put up? There's somebody else there to discuss merchandising toy companies and so forth. Someone else is there to discuss what the foreign co-financiers might be willing to put up. So everyone is discussing the business aspects of this film. And it's sometimes unusual for someone actually to circle back and talk about the script, the cast, the package – whether the whole damn thing makes any sense to begin with.
>
> (Peter Bart quoted in 'The Monster', 2001)

Of course, the goal of cross-promotions and merchandising tie-ins, in whatever form, is to sell both the movie and the products associated with it. The practice began in 1929 when Mickey Mouse appeared on a pencil box. The difference is that the money for these items is now central to budgeting for film production itself, all the way from movie vouchers to see *Scooby-Doo* that accompanied purchases of its endorsed flea medication, through to *Spider-Man's* bewildering array of cereal, pop and clothing. And television is a key node for sales, given the number of dedicated children's channels. The stakes are high, with a 2002 global toy market worth US$27 billion, and children's TV shows earning US$2 billion ('The Spider's', 2002). Sony Signatures, the consumer-products division of Sony Pictures Entertainment, arranged for the director and stars of *Stuart Little* to appear at a major trade fair for toys, because the 'character of Stuart lends itself to a world of licensing and merchandising possibilities'. Cross-promotion partners included Hasbro (general toys), HarperCollins (publishing) and Learning Curve (speciality toys) ('Columbia Pictures' *Stuart Little*', 1999). The Canadian Toy Testing Council (2001) notes that international toy fairs have become 'an advertising campaign . . . launched for the toys together with a two-hour commercial', such as *Space Jam* (Joe Pytka, 1996). Sony orchestrated similar tie-ins for the 'brands' *Godzilla, Men in Black, The Mask of Zorro*, 'Godzilla: The Series', 'Men in Black: The Series', *Dawson's Creek* and 'Extreme Ghostbusters'. Similarly, the Burger King Corporation spent an estimated US$40 million in advertising and themed meals, toys and packaging based on the story and characters in *Chicken Run* (Peter Lord and Nick Park, 2000). Children could hear Mel Gibson's voice on television asking them to save the chickens by eating Burger King's 'Whoppers'. According to a Burger King press release, young consumers at the company's fast-food restaurants were encouraged to 'reenact escape scenes from the movie by making airplane shaped Chicken Tenders part of their meal'. British Airways invested in *Chicken Run*, with a 'Fly the coop to London' campaign. In total, Dream-

Works attained US$100 million worth of promotional partnerships, which also included Chevron petroleum, Clorox Co., Gold Circle Farms and a California supermarket chain (Friedman, 2000a). As we noted earlier, in the case of *The Hunchback of Notre Dame*, films that fare poorly in theatrical receipts can make money thanks to toys. It is widely believed that *Teenage Mutant Ninja Turtles* (Steve Barron, 1990) failed to find an audience in Japan precisely *because* it lacked merchandise (Prince, 2000: 139).

In many countries, Disney merchandise was made locally via site licences, until a 1990s expansion saw the company set up a number of subsidiaries. So rather than its former policy of receiving a fee and a sales percentage from independent companies that made and sold its cartoon characters, in 1997 the firm set up Disney Enterprises Southern Africa, which is also its entrepôt to the rest of the continent. Disney collaborated with the South African Broadcasting Corporation to sponsor afternoon cartoons encouraging young black viewers to associate their viewing with merchandise (Burton, 2001: 258–59). In Korea, with a new openness to foreign film after the 1980s, Disney has pursued a number of strategies to ensure merchandise-based profits. For example, it sets up goodwill for itself by hosting pseudo-humanitarian events. Children with cancer are given a special screening of *Sleeping Beauty* (Joan Sugarman, 1992), while poor children go to a preview of *The Hunchback of Notre Dame*. The state's new policy of teaching students English is enabled via videos featuring Disney animation, while cross-promotion is undertaken with Kellogg's and McDonald's 'food'. These occasions are tied in with release promotions for films and toys. Supermarkets feature large screens with Disney characters, there is aggressive telemarketing and local vendors are offered unprecedentedly low rates of retail return (Kim and Lee, 2001: 192–94).

As part of its struggle with Disney, Universal Studios launched a US$1.7 billion theme park in Osaka in 2000. Universal itself only has a US$90 million investment in the facility, but owns 24 per cent of the park. Universal's Japanese partners include the Osaka local government, the Sumitomo Group, Hitachi and over forty other shareholders, while Universal's corporate marketing strategy is buttressed by twenty-three separate deals with marketing partners (O'Brien, 2001; Emmons, 2001). Taking lessons from problems at Fox's theme park in Sydney and Universal Studios Beijing (a joint development between a Hong Kong developer and Universal that has been under-performing), Universal extended its usual strategy of avoiding spending its own dollars on theme parks, and took advantage of 'strategic partners ready to step up with money to leverage' (Hirsch, 2001). The *Jaws* attraction is co-sponsored by All-Nippon Airways, Fuji Film supports '*Jurassic Park*: The Ride' and Toyota sponsors the '*Back to the Future*' exhibit (though Marty McFly probably still drives a stainless-steel DeLorean rather than a Camry). Conveniently located with access to Kyoto, Nara and Kobe, and part of a larger Osaka bid to attract the Olympics in 2008, Universal Studios Japan is only the second major movie-themed park to open in Asia, with very few amusements tailored to 'Japanese tastes'. Hollywood's adaptation strategies are not necessarily invoked at the level of textual attraction, but hinge on the insurance of local investment through what amounts to leasing a Hollywood brand.

Lucas is the undisputed leader in merchandising tie-ins and cross-promotions. Weeks before *The Phantom Menace* was released, licensed merchandise 'flooded toy stores, Web sites, fast-food restaurants, computer stores, music stores, supermarkets, bookstores and newsstands'. Hasbro Toys, which guaranteed Lucas US$500 million in royalties from *Phantom Menace* dolls, 'light sabres' and toy 'podracers', has even created a special office for 'an executive vice president for Star Wars' (Elliot, 1999: 1). The Pepsi-Cola Company spent US$2 billion to sponsor *The Phantom Menace* and sequels. Not surprisingly, *The Phantom Menace*'s relatively small advertising budget of US$20 million (it ended up spending only US$14 million) benefited from the marketing campaigns of its licensees, merchandisers and retailers as well as the 'Mexicans with mobiles' from Chapter 2 who actually made it happen. To save on royalty payments, Hasbro has since halved its movie-licensing deals, as these products were taking up almost 25 per cent of its inventory by the end of the 1990s (Fasig, 2003). The only worry seems to be what the warlocks call 'over-merchandising', which resulted in piles of unsold light sabres, Neo dolls and Godzilla toys languishing on toy-store shelves. The British publisher of 'books' derived from *Star Wars: Episode 1* was left with £14 million of unsold inventory. For this reason, Warner Bros. appears to have had little trouble abiding by J. K. Rowling's demand to limit merchandising of her Harry Potter characters to 'a mere 75 or so product licenses' ('Harry Potter', 2003; Austin, 2002: 40 n. 84).

So, whether or not people finally buy a ticket to the movies, marketing executives have already decided that an audience exists for a film with the right combination of playability, positioning and marketability. If marketers fail to sense the presence of this trinity, they may not bless a film project, though they are more likely to propose changes that normalise the project's commercial content and value. An important effect of marketing's textual gatekeeping is the multiplication of corporate partnerships that result from cross-promotions and merchandising. Potential links to retail marketers can be indexed to the level of marketability found in a film project. Greater marketability not only means more film elements congenial to advertising but also entails more partnerships with consumer goods and services corporations. And when corporate interests proliferate, the slightest sign of box-office failure sends 'shudders down Wall Street' (McChesney, 1999: 39), threatening marketing's credibility among its most important patrons. Projects that lack marketers' endorsements may still get made, if they can find studio executives or large investors to shepherd them through the system. Also, exhibitionary outlets for Hollywood are very numerous, and the majors can always depend on block booking and blind bidding, the safety nets of oligopoly, to ensure that even 'unsuccessful' films may eventually produce a profit – with the precise details obscured by one kind of creative accounting for taxation officials and another for investors.

In addition to the selective filter that the marketing bureaucracy uses to determine which movies get made and what content will endow the screen with marketability, marketing executives also decide when and where a movie will be exhibited. They come up with a rough sixty-day estimate for a film's release date, which they calculate after learning when they will receive a final print, the earliest date they can screen it for the media and how long it will take for the media to start publicising the film. Once this is done, they look at the competition coming out at the same time and make whatever scheduling adjustments are needed before deciding on a domestic release date (Lukk, 1997: 3). Distributors habitually release expected hits and executive favourites on holiday weekends, though this ingrained practice appears to be based more on institutional superstitions about 'seasonality' than empirical evidence that higher demand coincides with those dates (Einav, 2002: 28–29).

Prior to a film's release, marketers flood public space with trailers, posters and television and print advertisements – all of which cut up a film's main visual selling points and condense them into simple images to lure people to the theatre and subsequent exhibition windows (Wyatt, 1994: 131). The Friday and Sunday editions of the *New York Times* are showcases for theatrical releases in the US, largely because marketers believe that as a national paper, it 'can position a film for regional audiences as well as critics' (Lukk, 1997: 27). Print advertisements in general-circulation and specialty magazines also draw on the visual attributes of a film. In 2001, major distributors planned to reduce investment in print advertising, which took up about US$900 million in annual newspaper advertising alone (Friedman, 2001: 1), while expanding television advertising and promotion, already the dominant channel for most film marketing. This was largely due to growth in national cable channels and the overlap of national network advertising in local markets, where newspaper advertising was seen as redundant. Cable has enhanced marketers' ability to pick and choose their target audiences, especially music television, which offers tremendous flexibility for positioning films among their key segment, 14 to 24-year-old males (Wyatt, 1994: 44–52). It has also become axiomatic for film marketers to buy network television time on Thursday evenings. According to marketers, this is the week night when the largest potential film audience congregates in front of the television and decides on a first-choice film for the weekend (Lukk, 1997; Litman, 1998: 41).

Advocacy Marketing and its Others

> Mr. Valenti himself rarely sees the inside of a theatre. As the major studios' chief lobbyist, he spends much of his time hounding his own and foreign governments for more action to staunch the drain on Hollywood revenues

from film pirates. He is off again later this month with a bunch of business
dignitaries trailing U.S. Commerce Secretary William Daley to Asia, a hotbed
of counterfeiting and copyright thievery.

('Hollywood's Incredible', 1999)

To some extent, movie executives, trade magazines, film critics, film scholars
and the news media are advocates for the film industry. But the constant din of
advocacy marketing surrounds the power and profit centres of distribution,
marketing and exhibition. Advocacy marketing is closely related to the sales
effort, so it amplifies during cyclical saturation releases, and is also devoted to
polishing corporate images, especially in response to the occasional headline
about Hollywood cartel abuses of children and women, the latest mega-merger
or the threat of a labour strike. Apart from Valenti's singular role as the con-
queror of cultures, advocacy is left largely to professional marketers, lobbyists
and public-relations firms to promote political support, public knowledge and
general acclaim of the industry. The brand or trademark is a form of symbolic
equity that can be accumulated through regular advocacy, giving major distributors a 'trademark advantage' over newcomers. A studio's brand equity is
also bolstered by each film's publicity and advertising campaign, by stars
appearing on television, trailers, billboards, posters and theatre displays, and
product tie-ins (Litman, 1998: 32–33). Stars are both brands and brand boost-
ers. Their presence is said to be worth 20 per cent of a film's revenues. As bearers
of such brand equity, stars are protected by the major distributors and the stars'
publicists, who closely monitor how journalists pose questions and represent a
star's brand assets. Any perceived diminishment of a star's brand equity can
lead to the excommunication of journalists from all-expenses-paid travel and
press conferences ('Back Scratching', 2001). The kind of advocacy best known
for generating popular acclaim occurs in publicity, promotion and media coverage of trade shows (that is, film festivals) and awards ceremonies. The most
celebrated awards ceremony, the Oscars, is sponsored yearly by the Academy of
Motion Picture Arts and Sciences. Important annual trade shows include Santa
Monica, Cannes, Monte Carlo, Berlin, San Sebastian, Sundance, Toronto, Tel-
luride and the Hamptons. Throughout the year, these marketing festivals
spotlight new releases and offer a venue for producers and distributors to min-
gle and close any unfinished deals. Similar advocacy activities include the Film
Information Council's awards for 'Best Marketed Movie of the Month'.

Advocacy takes a more disciplinary turn when powerful trade organisations
like the AFMA and the MPAA engage in political lobbying, contribute millions
of dollars to influence major political parties and conduct international
relations through cooperative as well as imperious trade efforts, most notably
in the transnational corporate fight for copyright protectionism (see Chapters
1 and 4). The AFMA works for independent motion-picture and television
companies that make and distribute English-language films around the world.

Headed by former New Zealand Film Commissioner Ruth Harley, it represents 150 companies that generate about US$4 billion a year, including New Line, Miramax, Polygram, King World, Saban Pictures International, HBO Enterprises, NBC Enterprises, Endemol, Capitol Films, Intermedia and Kushner-Locke ('Acronym Alert', 2003). As we have seen, the most important trade organisation is the studios' own MPAA. Most people in the US know the MPAA only for its rating system, which is also a form of advocacy marketing. As a marketing feature of film packaging, a rating conveys something about a film's content, but its core advocacy function is to reinforce the idea that the industry is capable of self-regulation. The MPAA rating system invites people to think that the industry has ethical codes and follows noble ideals, such as protecting children from harmful influences. It is part of the DEM.

By turning *The Phantom Menace* into an event of film marketing, LucasFilm attracted unprecedented advocacy publicity via cover articles in *Entertainment Weekly, GQ, Newsweek, Premiere, Time, Vanity Fair, Wired, Popular Mechanics* ('The Machines of "Star Wars" '), *Vogue* (' "Star Wars" Couture') and *TV Guide*. As one trade magazine described the *Star Wars* phenomenon: 'the marketing of an entertainment property is becoming the story instead of the property itself' (Elliot, 1999: 1). This success at capturing media space has since been copied by *Lord of the Rings: The Fellowship of the Ring*, the promotion of which took over the cover and pages of 'news' copy in an issue of its corporate cousin, *Time* magazine. Event film marketing of blockbusters is now de rigueur, as the likes of the *Lord of the Rings* trilogy, the *Matrix* trilogy and the *Harry Potter* franchise demonstrate. This is not only aimed at children. For the British release of *Bram Stoker's Dracula* (Francis Ford Coppola, 1992), Columbia TriStar arranged a fashion show for journalists to encourage talk about a new Goth look, leading to a spot on the BBC's *Clothes Show* and stories in *Harpers and Queen* (Austin, 2002: 127). For someone thinking about going to the movies, this kind of advocacy marketing may appear to be a service. Advertisements, film reviews and publicity events provide information upon which to make a decision about what to see. The three categories were blended in 2001 when Sony Pictures Entertainment promoted endorsements of *A Knight's Tale* (Brian Helgeland, 2003) and *The Animal* (Luke Greenfield, 2001) by the critic David Manning. But the corporation's creativity went further – it invented the reviewer and his writings (Basuroy *et al.*, 2003: 103). You can read all about it at museumofhoaxes.com or in publicity surrounding the payment by Sony to the Connecticut government and its promise neither to repeat this fabrication nor continue to pay Sony employees posing as 'people on the street' who endorse the company's releases ('Connecticut', 2002). Sony's website does not, however, provide links to Manning's oeuvre. In Greece, Disney provides film reviewers with gifts such as travel and tickets to Disneyland Paris and various festivals (Kaitatzi-Whitlock and Terzis, 2001: 144). Clearly, this valuable service enables the critics to be fiercely independent in their evaluation of the firm's output. Needless to say, it is a short step from these cynical forms of advocacy to surveillance.

Surveillance

Mr. Louden, who is directing an effort with the behavioral science unit of the FBI to create empirical records on serial killers, rapists and other criminal types, said that the McDermott film list could be useful as part of a psychological reconstruction. 'You have to look at the totality,' he said. 'And someone's movie preferences, when laid out at such length, would be helpful.' [Louden is referring to the Amazon.com video-DVD 'wish-list' of a man arrested for shooting seven people to death in a suburban Boston office.]

(Pamela L. O'Connor, 2001)

We work with a very efficient combination of calling and electronic capture. We do what's best, the most efficient and accurate way at any given time. From our clients' perspective it doesn't matter how we obtained the data, as long as they receive what they want and when they need to.

(Tonya Bates, President of Nielsen EDI, quoted in Fuchs, 2003a: 60)

The industry's interest in audiences has seen another, seemingly conflictual paradigm emerging, under the sign of Foucault. It considers the contemporary moment as an electronic transformation of a long history of surveillance under modernity that stretches from the panoptic prison designs of Jeremy Bentham to the all-seeing gaze and internalisation of today's mall security, virtual home cinemas and global positioning satellite (GPS) stalkers (Denzin, 1995; Lyon, 2001).

The guiding ethos of immanent/imminent business failure has a curious side-effect on Hollywood's vision of audiences. Bad or good, films are judged at the box office. Yet, as we have seen, marketing researchers are anxious about filmgoers' power as the ultimate arbiter of a movie's success – they are a threat to be controlled rather than respected. Audiences are, after all, the causes of uncertainty; they are responsible for the Hollywood frenzy. In this sense, marketing scapegoats filmgoers for the industry's failure while providing apparent solutions for controlling them. Today, the presumption that audiences are an untamed labour force that must be domesticated for consumption justifies film marketing's ever-deepening surveillance of people's feelings, opinions, loves and hates in a much more intense, even righteous, quest for knowledge of the filmgoing experience.

This perception of audiences motivated early filmmakers and opinion pollsters to develop rudimentary audience research: silent-movie comedians tested films for laughs (comedies still undergo more tests than most genres), studios collected audience opinions on 'idiot cards' and George Gallup monitored audience opinions while a movie played (Lerner, 1999). Noted social scientist Paul Lazarsfeld and CBS executive Frank Stanton invented the Lazarsfeld–Stanton Program Analyzer, a device originally designed to survey radio listeners as they made their way through a show that was later transferred to the screen. Other systems included the wonderfully named Cirlin Reactograph and the Hopkins Electronic Televoting Machine. By the 1950s, the foreign departments of the major studios had also begun audience research into preferences for dubbing versus subtitles as correlated with social class, notably in Latin America (Handel, 1950: 46–50, 218–21).

While there are useful studies of audience research, very little has been written on how these activities form part of a wider system of surveillance. That is perhaps a result of focusing too narrowly on the form and results of pre- and post-production surveys, focus groups, consumer panels, pre-release test screenings and audience or box-office tracking. Wyatt's (1994) econo-aesthetic interpretation of high concept, for instance, relies on the same unexamined presumptions about filmgoing as marketers themselves. For marketing to work, Wyatt's audience must perceive a film's difference in order for it to stand out as a 'differentiated product'; yet this same audience must also perceive a film's similarity to other films in order to minimise box-office uncertainty.

Surveillance nests in the unstable foundation of this paradoxical presumption. The probability of an audience perceiving difference and/or sameness can only be guessed at after enquiring into people's tastes, preferences and abilities to articulate opinions about variety and quality. Litman and Ahn confirm that most research used by the film industry is based on 'uncertainty about audience preferences', which 'necessitates the development of an often vague "audience image" that governs much of the decision-making in the economic stages of the movie business' (1998: 193). Thus, in addition to surveillance, assessing audiences relies on pre-scripted accounts of their psychology as actors in a story of economic rationality. So marketers conduct surveillance not to discover something new and wonderful about people's boundless diversity, identification and creativity, but to sort people into predetermined marketplace identities with propensities to like certain kinds of movies or movie components and buy certain goods and services. The best that marketers can do under these conditions is match film elements to those probable consumption habits. Banks and assorted investors who want their brands inscribed in film narratives via product placement pay for an integrated marketing concept that can sell both the film and associated merchandise. No wonder Alec Baldwin called film marketing a 'suppository into the society' on the Charlie Rose show (9 January 2004).

Marketers profess a better way to judge and sell a film than intuition or strong feelings about a project, or outright saturation of theatres. This confidence derives from the use of survey research to endow their decisions and recommendations with an aura of science. Most studio executives who use marketing research today find utility in such hubris, since it gives marketing the immediate disciplinary function of bending the ears of uncooperative directors and producers to make them 'hear something' from the test audiences that 'they don't want to hear from us'. If a major distributor wants to change a movie, it manipulates marketing research to support its point of view. As director Andrew Bergman puts it, 'if the test is bad, the studio panics', and the Hollywood frenzy crashes down on the director. But, adds Bergman, 'If it goes well they say, "It doesn't mean anything" and the studio heatedly demands changes anyway.' With the hammer of marketing research behind them, said the late John Frankenheimer, 'they have the power' to put 'terrible pressure' on the director 'to make the movie they want' (quoted in Willens, 2000: 20, 11).

There are signs pointing to common ground between filmgoers and filmmakers opposed to marketing, a place we revisit in the Conclusion. For now, we note that there is deep discord among many directors, producers and actors. They see any 'research' designed to fine-tune their film as 'part of the dumbing down of the business'. For a few dissenters, like Oliver Stone or Francis Ford Coppola, who do not mind the basic principle of giving a film a final test in front of audiences, the problem is, as Stone puts it, when testing reduces filmmaking to 'a product-oriented business' that ruins a film's integrity and makes the director a mere 'cog in the machine' (quoted in Willens, 2000: 20). Nevertheless, there are as many, if not more, cogs in the machine who, in exchange for aggressive and well-financed sales and promotion by distributors, happily surrender their movie to the scrutiny of audience research and distributor demands.

Many small firms subcontract surveillance from distributors. For instance, marketing executives at Gramercy hired thirty separate advertising agencies to promote *Four Weddings and a Funeral*. Each agency drew on files from databases of consumer information collected for previous jobs. Their goal was to identify other advertisers whose customers matched Gramercy's idea of *Four Weddings*' probable audience (Lukk, 1997). By cross-matching information from earlier consumer surveillance, these agencies found retailers with whom Gramercy formed alliances to promote each other's products (florists, travel agents, airlines, specialty coffee shops, bridal stores).

The sales effort may involve dozens of firms, but one company dominates surveillance of audiences. The National Research Group (NRG), renamed NielsenNRG in 2002, controls about 80 per cent of this US$90 million industry, holding exclusive contracts with all major distributors and most prominent second-tier companies (Milmo, 2003: 20). As Mark Horowitz (1997), producer of *Kindergarten Cop* (Ivan Reitman, 1990) and *The Nutty Professor* (Tom Shadyac, 1996), said of NRG's research, 'everybody in the industry, the ones who are really in the game, looks at this stuff'.

NielsenNRG's offices are located in Hollywood. They are 'purposefully anonymous quarters with claustrophobic corridors, lots of opaque glass and all the personality of a CIA front' (Lerner, 1999: 18). NielsenNRG has amassed a proprietary consumer database for 'every major motion picture released since 1982, cross-referenced by actor, director, box office, genre, studio, country and just about any other index imaginable' (Lerner, 1999: 18). It tracks awareness of upcoming releases, conducts preview screenings and post-viewing focus groups, and undertakes overseas market analysis. It tests in terms that also apply to video/DVD sales and other exhibition windows, and evaluates film titles and how television spots and print advertising for films are working (Klady, 1998: 9). Prices for these services range from US$15,000 per test screening up to US$500,000 charged to big-budget movies for full-service market research. NielsenNRG was founded during the late-1970s boom in marketing research. After making a big impression on its first client, Coppola, for testing *Apocalypse Now* (1979), NielsenNRG became best known for the tests of *Fatal Attraction* (Adrian Lyne, 1987) that caused Warner Bros. to change the ending to satisfy audiences who wanted to see a character murdered, rather commit suicide, as the director had planned. More recently, NielsenNRG research caused producers to change the ending of *Big Daddy* to include an 'uplifting' party at a 'Hooters' restaurant (Dutka, 2003).

About 2,000 people work full time for NielsenNRG in the US, but the bulk of the surveillance legwork is carried out by unskilled, part-time interviewers. Writer Preston Lerner (1999) followed these 'recruiters' around to detail their labour. He found them roaming 'suburban malls and multiplexes with ever-present clipboards' looking for prospective interview subjects. The recruiters were instructed to gather a group that matched the test film's broadest probable audience. This statistically correct test audience was supposed to be 'plucked', as Lerner aptly put it, 'from the heartland of the bell curve'. But because these young workers' wages depended on the number of people they delivered, they were 'notoriously and understandably reluctant to reject test-screening candidates'. This seriously compromised the statistical protocols they were expected to follow. To help ensure that the 550 people waiting to be interviewed shared attributes with the presumed audience for the film, the recruiters were told to make sure that the recruits were between 17 and 49 years of age, did not work in the entertainment-information industry and had seen at least two of the following movies: *Scream* (Wes Craven, 1996), *Scream II* (Wes Craven, 1997), *Wild Things* (John McNaughton, 1998), *Mimic, An American Werewolf in Paris* (John Landis, 1997), *I Know What You Did Last Summer* and *Alien Resurrection* (Jean-Pierre Jeunet, 1997). Apparently, these films were analogous in some way with the test film so NielsenNRG could assess its positioning. A flyer handed to recruits revealed that the film was called *The Whole Nine Yards* (Jonathan Lynn, 2000), and described it as 'an outrageous dark comedy' starring Bruce Willis in 'a life-and-death struggle with disastrous but hilarious consequences'. At the end of the movie, the work of the recruits began. Interviewers distributed two-page questionnaires to the people they had corralled into the theatre, which asked: 'How would you rate the performances? Which scenes did you like? What do you think of the ending? Where were you confused?' Later, a smaller focus group was formed from this sample audience to work on clarifying the survey answers (Lerner, 1999: 18). In addition to these special test screenings, NielsenNRG conducts phone interviews with about 400 people across the US three times a week to assess film awareness and choices (Klady, 1996: 3).

NielsenNRG research affects almost all major Hollywood releases in the US and Europe. Challenges to its dominance have come from Lieberman Research, which tried and failed to win business away from NielsenNRG in the mid-1990s. Even the venerable Gallup organisation could not compete, despite relaunching its Motion Picture Research Division in 1994 after forty years (Klady, 1994). Current rivals include MarketCast, OTX (Online Testing Exchange), specialising in online tracking of audience preferences for promotional material, and CA Walker (Dutka, 2003). In 2003, MarketCast's owner, Reed Elsevier (publisher of *Variety*) filed a lawsuit against NielsenNRG, claiming that it was using its monopoly purchasing power to discourage other research companies from providing data to MarketCast (Milmo, 2003: 20).

Another challenger is Moviefone, a consumer spy operation owned by Time Warner that is disguised as a phone service offering movie times, locations and bookings. In pursuit of its goal to sell box-office revenue predictions, Moviefone has amassed a huge database on filmgoers' preferences and spending habits from the over 2 million weekly calls it gets in twenty-eight US metropolitan areas. One Moviefone executive could not sugarcoat his spying disposition: 'We know who our callers are,' he said, 'and have set up tests to monitor their preferences' (quoted in Klady, 1996). The number of enquiry calls received on this service mirrors later ticket sales, and so it has become a surveillance device for predicting audience moves (Sreenivasan, 1997; for a benign interpretation, see Orwall, 2001). Moviefone and smaller competitors MovieTickets.com and Fandango hold exclusive contracts with different theatre chains, frustrating online and phone purchases for erstwhile customers who were unable to book tickets because, unbeknown to them, they were using a rival's service (Pristin, 2003).

The latest challengers to NielsenNRG's dominance are in the Internet consumer-surveillance industry, which received a boost from a Simmons Research Consumer Study in 2002 that found '84% of all moviegoers who've seen at least one film in the last three months are now online users' (quoted in Dutka, 2003). While NielsenNRG works this angle to develop research with sister companies Nielsen Media Research, Reel Research and NetRatings, newer firms like OTX, a subsidiary of Ifilm.com, have expanded surveillance of Internet-using filmgoers. 'We can access everyone from Asian laxative users to African American women who saw a film last weekend,' boasts OTX President Kevin Goetz, a former tester for NRG (quoted in Dutka, 2003). DreamWorks is banking on cyberteens taking so much pleasure in their own surveillance/uptake of their free labour that they will tell their friends it is fashionable. This happened when DreamWorks sent emails to sixteen-year-old girls asking them to pick a logo for *Win a Date with Tad Hamilton!* (Robert Luketic, 2004). One cyberteen was so delighted that her choice had appeared in the film's trailer that she told 'a bunch of friends at school [and] well over 10 or 20 people'. 'Oh my God,' she said, 'they do listen. It does matter' (abcnews.go.com/sections/Business/Living/marketing_teens_forbes_040122-1.html). Inroads into children's lives via the Internet provide one of the biggest attractions of online surveillance. By 2003, according to Nielsen NetRatings, 27 million (or one out of five) Internet users in the US were between 2 and 17 years of age (www.netratings.com/pr/pr_031021.pdf). In Europe, the number of children using the Internet in 2003 was about 13 million ('More Children', 2003).

Young people link to OTX surveillance on-site by interacting with a skateboard-wielding teen. Then at one point they read this:

> Now we'd like to put your 6–12 year old child on to answer some questions. During the interview we will be asking some questions about children's advertising and showing some commercials you may or may not have seen before. Please do not push the 'next' button until your child is in front of the computer monitor. Remember, we want your child's opinion. Please do not assist your child unless necessary.
>
> (www.otx.ifilm.com)

Another online research company is the Hollywood Stock Exchange (HSX), owned by a unit of Cantor Fitzgerald, a Wall Street firm. As of 2004, HSX had about a million registered users, mostly affluent young men, who trade stocks of movies and bonds of stars. Every movie or star traded on the site has a value in *faux* H-dollars, though Cantor hopes one day to be trading real money. Music groups are also traded. HSX makes up starting prices based on past performances and sales, then lets trading determine price fluctuations, which it tracks as if it were a Wall Street exchange. Ersatz trading on HSX found Piper Perabo's 'StarBond' 'trending upwards' of H$1,100 in 2000, while *Coyote Ugly* (David McNally, 2000), a film in which Perabo appears, was trading stock in the H$30 range, far below *Space Cowboys'* (Clint Eastwood, 2000) stock, in the high US$50s. Winona Ryder's StarBond hovers above Eastwood's, while neither star has reached Kevin Bacon's H$2,218 high; and so it goes (Friedman, 2000b). *The Cat in the Hat* traded at H$130 a share on its opening day, 'meaning that the market expected four-week box office receipts of $130 million' (it actually made US$94 million). *Spider-Man 2* (Sam Raimi, 2004) outranked that at H$235 a share (Alster, 2003).

'HSX was conceived as a game to take advantage of the public's obsession with box-office numbers', said one of the founders, but the real plan is to sell forecasts based on 'information it has collected on the folks who frequent the site' (founder quoted in Bates, 2000). HSX's success in predicting such otherwise unforeseen successes as *The Blair Witch Project* (Daniel Myrick and Eduardo Sánchez, 1999) did not convince major distributors to rely on its services at first. Part of the problem was the statistical profile of its users, who are mostly twenty-something male movie fans, with average household incomes of more than US$53,000. But interest has grown steadily since Cantor took over in 2001. As one *Los Angeles Times* reporter wondered, 'maybe it's true: rich young guys do rule pop culture' (Bates, 2000). By 2004, Cantor was offering its HSX research to the majors, promoted as 'a real-time update of consumer opinion … using the predictive market versus going out on the street with a clipboard and asking people questions' (Alster, 2003). Thus surveillance becomes 'the interactivity that matters', by 'cracking human personality in real time' (Burke, 2003).

Digital interactive television is another key innovation for spying on the public via a set-top box that can provide masses of information about viewers to marketers and advertisers, from use of mute buttons to psychographics. For those untroubled by corporate knowledge of their intimate practices and pleasures as a quid pro quo for technology, it is worth noting that this 'research' can also be done at the behest of the state, which has already ordered such firms to share their data with other commercial interests across the audiovisual sector whose texts are being recorded, viewed and eluded (Chmielewski, 2002).

The irony that flows from the screen industries' apparently insoluble problem of how to 'know' audiences might help attenuate worries about the surveillance activities taking place in global Hollywood. But it is important to recall that the main users of marketing information and labour are large entertainment conglomerates. The gamble of predicting the whereabouts and desires of audiences, while generating many amusing stories of blunders and missteps, is no joke to them. They demand from all who work for them the defence of their marketing assets, whether these are built upon a product-differentiation barrier to entry, a lucrative marketing unit or some other highly capitalised venture involving marketing and marketing research. This creates constant pressure on marketing executives and researchers to refine their techniques, to build better methods of data collection and bigger databases. In short, marketers encounter two structural challenges at once. They must strive to overcome their fragile reputation and satisfy unyielding corporate demand for more, and more accurate, information on people's lives. These structural pressures drive marketing research inexorably into ever more extensive and invasive areas of surveillance. The outcome may not really be successful predictions of filmgoing, but rather intimate knowledge of citizens and consumers.

Marketing research firms have opted for a few different strategies to advance information gathering and analysis. In 2002, Nielsen Media Research, for example, began tests in South Africa of a tracking device that will be carried by 'volunteers', whose exposure to billboards and other outdoor advertisements can be measured via a GPS that relays the information to Nielsen's databases in Oldsmar, Florida, where data are protected within a 'small-missile impact resistant' building (Cane, 2002: 2; Harrington, 2003: E1). By 2003, the project was being tested in Chicago with lighter-weight tracking mechanisms that encode sex, age and other demographic information into the system (Bickerton, 2003). Nielsen is also planning an 'active-passive' meter that can detect single television programmes watched within a multichannel digital signal (Harrington, 2003: E1). Yanqui research firms Alaris Media Network and MobilTrak are developing a device attached to electronic billboards that eavesdrops on passing cars to 'deduce demographic information from the radio stations drivers are listening to and then [instantly change the billboard] advertising aimed at them based on income, sex, race, and buying habit data'. Said one company official: 'We can tell you the percentage of people who drove past that were married, shop at Petsmart, that make over $100,000' (Richtel, 2002: C1, C5). Perhaps the most invasive technology applied to consumer surveillance has been Magnetic Resonance Imaging (MRI) used by a band of warlocks known as 'neuromarketers', who measure brain activity in response to commercial imagery. Bypassing rational filters that might urge self-restraint in the face of a stimulating image, neuromarketers claim to know if we truly, madly, secretly fall for a sales pitch, a seductive gaze or a product design. 'To an M.R.I., you cannot misrepresent your responses. Your medial prefrontal cortex will start firing when you see something you adore, even if you claim not to like it' (Thompson, 2003: 57).

As we have seen, the computer industry offers new Internet tracking devices that surpass traditional research strategies' invasiveness and mendacity. Silicon Valley hardware makers also offer new spy machines concealed within Digital Video Recorders (DVR). DVRs have been advertised as a means to record television shows and bypass commercial advertisements. Initially, the major versions of these devices only worked when subscribers hooked them up to the Internet to allow service providers, TiVo and ReplayTV, to collect information on every choice, channel change and skipped commercial. In addition to amassing a huge database of consumer information, they pinpointed the identities and actions of individual television viewers (Lewis, 2000: 40; Rose, 2001b). After protests from consumer groups in 2001, TiVo allowed subscribers to opt out of surveillance. Then it established a partnership with Nielsen to improve the tracking of those customers who did not opt out. Meanwhile, ReplayTV claimed it simply stopped collecting data. Television network owners, anxious about ratings, initially hated DVRs, but have learned to love them as one more source of consumer information with which to seduce advertisers (Rose, 2001b). Distributors complained when ReplayTV began selling its DVR series 4000, which allowed subscribers to email recorded films to one another. In 2002, they sued ReplayTV's owner, Sonicblue, to stop selling the machines, subsequently winning an order from a federal magistrate in Los Angeles to have

Sonicblue turn over subscriber information to the studios so they could identify those people who were exchanging copies of movies. Eventually, a higher court prohibited the studios from gathering this data, Sonicblue declared bankruptcy, ReplayTV's new owners, a Japanese holding company, discontinued the sale of the series 4000 DVR and the studios dropped their lawsuit (Evangelista, 2002; 'ReplayTV', 2004).

Like HSX and Moviefone, these surveillance operations concealed their spying activities by offering what looked like a free or low-cost gift – a game, a directory service or a way to enhance television viewing. Each exchange appears to favour consumer needs, but in actuality is a lure to get users to generate personal information, which the company then transforms into proprietary market research. In effect, they create an involuntary informational labour market from which they can surreptitiously exploit the effort that gives value to their enterprise. Whenever the Internet and digital technology are involved, the entertainment media always get more from you than you get from them (Raphael, 2001).

None of these schemes measure up to the scale and scope of concentration and conglomeration strategies in the consumer-surveillance industry. As large marketing companies reach limits to innovation and growth, they have begun purchasing competitors and merging databases, software and licensing deals into even larger corporations to get better surveillance results. Concentration in consumer research creates global surveillance services on a sufficiently large scale and with enough variety to meet the demands of MNCs, whose businesses encompass interlocking interests in the media, entertainment and retail. The globalisation of consumer surveillance has resulted in unprecedented capitalisation in proprietary marketing research, with one multinational conglomerate rising to dominate this area in the 1990s.

We have seen that NielsenNRG exemplifies the NICL's surveillance sector, and not merely for its singular role in testing and tracking film audience preferences. More importantly, NielsenNRG forms part of a much larger surveillance network owned by the Dutch firm Verenigde Nederlandse Uitgeversbedrijven (VNU), or United Dutch Publishers. NielsenNRG is one of twenty-two market-research subsidiaries operated by VNU Marketing Information Group (MIG) and Media Measurement & Information Group (MMIG), which operate in over a hundred countries. VNU has become a leading business-information provider through newsletters, magazines, trade shows and directories in Europe, Asia, South Africa and Puerto Rico. Since 2001, VNU has sold off most of its consumer media holdings to focus on directory as well as business and trade publishing, involving prominent magazines such as *Editor & Publisher, Hollywood Reporter, Adweek, Brandweek* and *Billboard*, among others. It owns several financial data services and a film company that specialises in expositions and trade fairs, and holds 96 per cent of ORG-MARG, the leading market-research company in India, which it recently merged with ACNielsen India. The company is also expanding operations in China and Hong Kong, where it is building huge databases in partnership with the data-storage firm, EMC. VNU was the first company allowed to track Internet use in China (Perez, 2002). VNU's Business Media Group also manages the Clio Awards, which celebrate and promote goodwill towards the advertising industry ('VNU', 2000; 'VNU NV', 2000; VNU, 2002).

By 2000, VNU had become one of the leading business information and service providers in the world, largely through its control over the principal US commercial and consumer-surveillance companies. VNU's 1997 acquisition of NRG from Saatchi & Saatchi was followed in 1999 by its US$2.5 billion purchase from Dun & Bradstreet of both Nielsen Media Research (television and Internet audience measurement) and a majority share (65 per cent) in Nielsen NetRatings (Internet-user measurement), giving it leading audience and consumer-tracking companies for film, television and the Internet. In 2000, as part of an anti-trust settlement following the Nielsen purchases, VNU sold Competitive Media Reporting – the biggest advertising tracking service in the US and, until then, the leader in Internet-usage surveillance – to the world's fourth-largest market-research company, Taylor Nelson Sofres, which already dominates media tracking in Europe through its UK Tellex and French TNS Secodip operations (Tomkins, 2000). Soon after, VNU completed its absorption of the old Nielsen empire when it paid US$2.3 billion for ACNielsen Corporation, the dominant global company in consumer-behaviour surveillance and analysis (Elliot, 2000). In addition to its Nielsen holdings, VNU consumer-surveillance operations include Claritas USA (it sold Claritas Europe in 2003), Scarborough, Spectra (49 per cent), Trade Dimensions and others. Finally, as a symbol of its growing wealth, VNU signed the largest lease for New York City property in 1999 to house its headquarters in a former department store in the East Village, a deal that 'came with about US$9 million in tax incentives from the city and state' (Kanter, 1999; VNU, 2002).

VNU Marketing Information Group (MIG)

ACNielsen – *surveillance and analysis of consumer behaviour, consumer profiling, test marketing.*

Spectra Marketing Systems, Trade Dimensions, Claritas USA, Solucient (36 per cent) – *consumer surveillance and analysis using lifestyle research, geo-demographics, segmentation, targeting, database marketing and analysis.*

VNU Media Measurement & Information Group (MMIG)

Media Measurement Division: Nielsen Media Research (sixteen countries) – *in the US, television ratings and competitive advertising intelligence; outside the US, TV and radio audience surveillance, print, advertising and customised data collection.*

Internet Measurement Division: Nielsen NetRatings – *Internet-usage tracking and analysis.*

Entertainment Information Division: Aircheck, Music Control, Nielsen EDI (fourteen countries and 50,000 film screens), NielsenNRG, Nielsen ReelResearch, Nielsen BDS, Nielsen Retail Entertainment Information, Nielsen Entertainment Marketing Solutions (EMS) – *box-office results, audience testing of film, TV and advertising content, music-programming tracking, point-of-sale tracking of music, video/DVD, and book retail sales and bibliographic data – EDI pioneered overnight overseas box-office reports via the delicious acronym BOFFO (Box Office Flash Figures Online).*

Media Solutions Division: IMS, Interactive Market Systems (UK), IMS/Mediaplan (US), Interactive Market Systems (Canada), MRP (Marketing Resources Plus), Scarborough Research (49 per cent), SRDS, PERQ/HCI – *media spending and circulation tracking and analysis; healthcare data, geo-demographic consumer surveillance.*

In a trend that is sure to continue, VNU established a strategic alliance with Equifax in 2000, a move that extended its surveillance network into new areas. Equifax is a credit reporting agency that gathers personal information related to individual debt, income and purchasing across the Americas and Europe. The company determines hundreds of millions of people's creditworthiness for credit-card transactions, loans, cheques and insurance. The relationship with Equifax began when VNU purchased National Decision Systems (merged with Claritas) from it in 1996. This partnership in marketing and cross-licensing consumer-surveillance products not only gave VNU 'one of the most robust databases in the industry', in the words of the then President of VNU MIG, but also made VNU one of the few firms to offer a single source for predicting the 'demographic, lifestyle and financial behaviour of consumers' ('Equifax', 2000).

Prior to purchasing ACNielsen Corp., VNU had already contracted to help the company globalise and strengthen entertainment-audience research. The purchase gave VNU undisputed dominance in tracking box-office sales, through ACNielsen's subsidiary Entertainment Data Inc. (Nielsen EDI), and in global consumer research, where ACNielsen has operations in over one hundred countries. The acquisition further expanded VNU's surveillance network by offering a 'single source of complete consumer insights' for home-video distributors and related trade and consumer media ('VNU and ACNielsen', 1999). The initial alliance with ACNielsen was formed to market VNU's VideoScan, which provides home-video distributors with video and DVD point-of-sale tracking, and is often credited with boosting distributors' acceptance of the DVD format. ACNielsen's surveillance of sales through discount mass merchandisers, drug stores and grocers, including information and analysis from its trademarked consumer panel, was thus merged with VideoScan's records of purchases from specialty retailers, direct mail and Internet. VideoScan is also the dominant source of video-industry information for *Billboard, Hollywood Reporter, Video Business, Video Week*, the *New York Times*, the *Los Angeles Times*, the *Wall Street Journal* and other trade and consumer publications ('VNU and ACNielsen', 1999). VNU had previously integrated consumer surveillance with its trade magazines to sell information on sport fans and amateur athletes through one of its subsidiary holdings, Sports Trend Info, a marketing research firm that tracks retail sporting-goods sales and sells consumer data to sub-scribers and advertisers of *Sporting Goods Dealer* magazine (which merged with *Sporting Goods Business* in 2002) (VNU, 2002).

The NielsenNRG story reveals that research into film marketing is located in a much wider political economy of consumer surveillance. The horizon stretches in line with the growing concentration and conglomeration of enter-tainment industries in Europe and the US, laying down corporate roots around the world. Even if VNU's 'bigger-is-better' idea does not eliminate the inherent problem of knowing the film audience, it helps to make Hollywood global by meeting the demand of entertainment conglomerates that must now imagine filmmaking within an integrated marketing concept, one that includes all the major exhibition windows plus recorded music and publishing, as well as tie-ins to merchandising and cross-promotions with retailers, restaurants and other entertainment or leisure promotions. In Malaysia, for example, US-style surveillance permits the continuation of US texts on prime-time television. They rate lower than domestic programmes, but the consumption pattern of their ruling-class fans is more powerful than the taste of ordinary viewers in attracting national advertisers (Karthigesu, 1998: 50).

Finally, it is important to note that, at present, globalisation of audience research is still largely financed through massive surveillance of the US popu-lation. That is, while the large MNCs are globalising the consumer-surveillance business, most investment in audience research remains focused on US filmgo-ers. More than 50 per cent of VNU profits come from US operations. This is, in part, an effect of the non-existent/shamefully pro-business privacy laws in the US, which pale when measured against the EU's protections from surveillance and for consumer rights (Maxwell, 1999). The surveillance bias towards the US filmgoer also reflects the lack of business opportunities for film-audience research firms outside the US. Audience research requires heavy investment that is hard to justify in small national film markets. It is virtually non-existent in all but a few urban enclaves of the poor regions of Asia, Eastern and Central Europe, Latin America and Africa – though VNU is working to change that, especially in China and South Asia. Consider that for most British films it is cost-effective simply to wait until a film opens in order to judge its commercial potential, given the comparatively small national audience (Andrews, 1998). In contrast, the sheer size of the US filmgoing population guarantees a better return on investments in motion-picture audience research and consumer research generally. In this way, the US population functions as a valuable asset for the majors and market-research MNCs like VNU, to the near exclusion of other groups, including Dutch VNU's Anglo-Dutch rival Reed Elsevier. This is another instance where major distributors are able to exploit economies of scale to purchase and accumulate consumer information that most independent and non-US competitors cannot afford. Understanding these political-economic conditions helps explain why global consumer surveillance in general, and audience research in particular, concentrates its spying on the US population.

Distribution and Exhibition

The studios don't want to be in production any more. They want to be in distribution.

(J. P. Morgan Chase, quoted in Parkes, 2002)

Marketing . . . is like air to all of us. It is a crucial resource that you must be breathing from the beginning.

(Peter Guber, quoted in 'The Monster', 2001)

FBI + CIA = TWA + Pan Am
(Graffito written by Eve Democracy in Jean-Luc Godard's *One + One*, 1969)

As we have seen, many reasons are advanced for the supremacy of Hollywood cinema worldwide: production values, cartel conduct, cultural imperialism manufacturing the transfer of taste rather than technology or investment, and US sign-value as the epicentre of transcendental modernity – fixing social and individual problems via love, sex and commodities. *Pace* Godard's quotation that begins this section, we have avoided simple equations that explain Hollywood's success, endeavouring instead to rethink it as contingent on Hollywood's contestable control of the NICL, which is sustained via the exploitation of national cultural labour markets, replication through international co-production of a particular business culture and the application and enforcement of IP rights as a coercive strategy in screen trade. Capitalism is constitutively contingent – after all, neither Pan Am nor TWA exist any more! And in keeping with the merchant-bank quotation above, there appear to be major shifts within the industry as well. So we need some history both to enliven and comprehend the fourth and most prosaic set of processes and practices that have enabled Hollywood to exert control over the conditions and possibilities of cultural labour – wholesale and retail.

Asu Aksoy and Kevin Robins argue that 'the Hollywood studios owe their long-standing position in the film industry to their strategy of controlling the critical hubs in the film business, that is distribution and finance', and history has revealed that the key to securing the latter is control over the former (1992: 15). Thus, the key to the high volume of audiovisual trade is not cheap reproduction, but the vast infrastructure of distribution that secures financing for production. And as marketing expenditures increase as a percentage of production costs, they are unaffected by the cost of reproduction altogether. So, despite the fact that Greek copyright legislation allows for movies to be exhibited theatrically for five years after their release, Disney insists that films be removed from cinemas after a year, thereby expediting revenue from other sources, such as DVDs (Kaitatzi-Whitlock and Terzis, 2001: 140). Time Warner puts it like this:

> No competitor can match our lineup of quality products. But just as impressive is how we distribute them. We are the only company of its kind that owns and controls 100 per cent of its worldwide distribution networks. We can control the flow of our products to market and aren't required to share our distribution profits.
>
> (Quoted in Prince, 2000: 140)

Distribution is wholesale, exhibition is retail. Distributors lease movies to exhibitiors, and organise scheduling, delivery and collection (Huettig, 1944: 7). Exhibitors show the texts. Hollywood has experienced four phases of distribution and exhibition. In the period to 1948, there was intense integration with production, and US theatres were mostly located in lucrative urban markets, with some overseas holdings in New Zealand, South Africa, France, Britain and Australia (Acland, 2003: 135). They showed whatever their own studios had made, so there was less need for the organised and aggressive promotion of films we see today. This was followed by a decade of divestiture as per a consent decree with anti-trust federal forces. Distribution became the locus of industry power, and film marketing began its inexorable move to the centre of industry activities. In fact, the cinema became one of the first US industries to place faith in social-science methods and intellectuals, because Hollywood was exercised by the prospect of products that potentially lasted only a few days (Bakker, 2003) but were not cheap to make, unlike the similarly perishable fruit or vegetables. Television arrived to compete for film audiences, stimulating technical innovations like widescreen, 3-D and other marketing ploys. Increasing consolidation occurred from that point until the 1980s, since which time deregulation has led to reintegration (Steinbock, 1995: 109–10). Most overseas audience research was retrospective rather than testing out new products. It generally relied on analysing box-office trends, unlike Hollywood's domestic-surveillance techniques, which included toilet ethnography (taping discussions in cinema restrooms) (Bakker, 2003: 107–08). As the 1960s began, the studios sought additional control over their audience by integrating international distribution and exhibition. They gained pre-sales in Europe to finance production at one end of the labour process, and purchased theatre chains in Africa and Europe at the other (Storper, 1994: 207–08).

Distribution forms a dense occupational sediment of the NICL via its network of 'accountants, sales personnel, warehouse managers and others'. As Albert Moran (1996: 2) observes, distribution workers are 'low on glamour' and invisible to the public, even though they labour everywhere in global Hollywood, from national to global distribution in theatrical and subsidiary markets for pay-cable, pay-per-view, commercial television and home video. In the Los Angeles area, over 22,000 people are employed in this sector of the industry (Scott, 2002: 969). And no wonder, for with annual returns on production for studios running at between 1 and 2 per cent, the appeal of controlling distribution is clear (Parkes, 2002). Overseas revenue from distribution varied in 2002 between US$2 billion to Miramax and US$16 billion to Warner Bros. (European Audiovisual Observatory, 2003: 12).

Distributors charge exhibitors a percentage of box-office profits – often as much as 40 per cent – in 'film rental' (Goldberg, 1991: 5). They take 25 per cent in fees for film sales to TV networks and 30–40 per cent to cable (Daniels *et al.*, 1998: 104), using what is euphemistically called 'creative accounting' to conceal these profits from foreign organisations that are due a share of revenue. In the US, distribution is basically an oligopoly, with 96 per cent of the market controlled by thirteen companies, and nine of the top ten run by studios (Scott, 2002: 969). The movie studios operate vertically integrated networks to control access to audiences, and utilise a massive domestic TV market to ensure returns on investment, even from their multiple failures in theatrical exhibition. Each major studio and most big so-called independents have output arrangements with associated distributors. That means one-third of production costs will be returned to them regardless of a film's popularity.

Hollywood realised early on that its dominance of the world market depended on owning the means of distribution. World distribution is dominated by the US (World Trade Organization, 1998) via arrangements that would be illegal domestically because of their threat to competition. UIP, Fox, Warner Bros., Buena Vista (Disney) and Columbia (Sony) all operate in this manner. UIP emerged from Cinema International Corporation, which Universal and Paramount had created in 1970 to distribute in Latin America, South Africa and Europe. MGM joined them in 1973. When it merged with United Artists in 1981, the agency was renamed UIP (Cook, 2000: 21). Warner Bros., Fox and Columbia TriStar have their own international distribution networks. Other studios operate joint ventures that vary with the territory, sometimes with one another and sometimes with local firms or front-organisation subsidiaries. UIP released for MGM, Paramount and Universal until MGM left for Fox International. In Canada, distributors collude to assist multinational multiplex owners, while in Spain every 'national' distributor is a subsidiary of a Hollywood major. UIP is buying rights to more and more Asian films for distribution in the region (Durie *et al.*, 2000: 87; Short, 1997; Augros, 2000: 160; Moerk, 2000; 'Canada Probes', 2000; Shackleton, 2003). UIP lobbied the competition directorate of the EU for five years to extend its anti-trust exemption status, finally winning an extension through 2004 (*Variety*, 20–26 September 1999: 30). When the EU ordered UIP's pay-TV division to disband in 1997, this had little effect on its member studios, because most of their contracts with broadcasters in Europe and around the world had been conducted individually (*Daily Variety*, 14 March 1997: 50).

This 2001 breakdown of how prices are calculated by small US producers (i.e. not the studios) for sales overseas indicates how films are licensed to match up with their cost and the wealth of the country where they are to be distributed:

SITE DISTRIBUTION COST US$	BUDGET US$750,000–1 MILLION	BUDGET US$1–3 MILLION	BUDGET US$3–6 MILLION	BUDGET US$6–12 MILLION
FRANCE	25–60,000	60–150,000	150–350,000	350,000–1M
GERMANY/AUSTRIA	40–100,000	100–300,000	300–600,000	600,000–1M
GREECE	5–10,000	10–15,000	15–25,000	25–50,000
ITALY	50–70,000	70–2000,000	200–400,000	400–800,000
NETHERLANDS	25–50,000	50–90,000	90–150,000	150–400,000
PORTUGAL	5–15,000	15–30,000	30–60,000	60–90,000
SCANDINAVIA	40–70,000	70–100,000	100–300,000	300–450,000
SPAIN	50–100,000	100–175,000	175–300,000	300–600,000
BRITAIN	40–80,000	80–200,000	200–350,000	350–750,000
AUSTRALIA/NEW ZEALAND	25–50,000	50–100,000	100–200,000	200–350,000
HONG KONG	10–20,000	20–30,000	30–40,000	40–100,000
INDONESIA	5–10,000	10–20,000	20–25,000	25–40,000
JAPAN	35–90,000	90–250,000	250–500,000	500,000–1.3M
MALAYSIA	5–15,000	15–25,000	25–40,000	40–60,000
PHILIPPINES	5–20,000	20–35,000	35–60,000	60–90,000
SINGAPORE	10–20,000	20–30,000	30–50,000	50–90,000
SOUTH KOREA	30–90,000	90–175,000	175–400,000	400–800,000
TAIWAN	15–40,000	40–90,000	90–175,000	175–350,000
ARGENTINA/PARAGUAY/URUGUAY	15–35,000	35–75,000	75–125,000	125–175,000

SITE DISTRIBUTION COST US$	BUDGET US$750,000 –1 MILLION	BUDGET US$1– 3 MILLION	BUDGET US$3– 6 MILLION	BUDGET US$6– 12 MILLION
BOLIVIA/PERU/ECUADOR	5–10,000	10–20,000	20–50,000	50–75,000
BRAZIL	20–50,000	50–100,000	100–175,000	175–300,000
CHILE	15–30,000	30–50,000	50–90,000	90–125,000
COLOMBIA	5–10,000	10–20,000	20–50,000	50–90,000
MEXICO	25–50,000	50–100,000	100–200,000	200–350,000
VENEZUELA	5–10,000	10–20,000	20–40,000	40–80,000
CZECH REPUBLIC/SLOVAKIA	5–15,000	15–30,000	30–75,000	75–125,000
FORMER YUGOSLAVIA	5–10,000	10–15,000	15–25,000	25–50,000
HUNGARY	5–15,000	15–30,000	30–75,000	75–125,000
RUSSIA	10–25,000	25–50,000	50–100,000	100–200,000
CHINA	10–20,000	20–40,000	40–60,000	60–150,000
INDIA	5–15,000	15–30,000	30–60,000	60–175,000
ISRAEL	5–10,000	10–20,000	20–40,000	40–75,000
ARAB STATES	5–15,000	15–35,000	35–65,000	65–100,000
PAKISTAN	4–10,000	10–15,000	15–30,000	30–40,000
SOUTH AFRICA	10–20,000	20–30,000	30–60,000	60–120,000
TURKEY	5–15,000	15–40,000	40–80,000	80–175,000

SOURCE: Adapted from DeWayne, 2002: 220

The majors have two systems for distributing their own and other US films overseas. The first consists of spreading the risk – an amazing euphemism, as the system sees producers receiving nothing unless their films succeed universally overseas – or the risk being borne by the local distributor (Augros, 2000: 161). In television, the system works through a series of trade fares where executives and their apparatchiks convene to purchase series: the National Association of Television Program Executives (NATPE) in the US; MIPCOM and MIP-TV in France; and Los Angeles screenings. The 2000 NATPE event drew 17,500 people, more than a third of them overseas buyers (Bielby and Harrington, 2002: 215).

The consequence of this capacity to suit pricing to locale, along with distributional oligopolies, is the exercise of power over a nation's cultural curriculum. In Greece, Disney times its releases seasonally. When holiday seasons are starting, a rerun or small film is distributed as a means of promoting the brand. At Christmas, when workers receive a special bonus and children are out of school, major releases come out, with all the usual merchandise on sale in cinema kiosks (Kaitatzi-Whitlock and Terzis, 2001: 144). These schedules can run counter to audience interest. Consider the British film *Riff-Raff* (Ken Loach, 1990). It was doing a roaring trade in Britain until the exhibitor was required by a distributor to displace it with *Backdraft* (Ron Howard, 1991), which was already a spectacular failure in the US and continued that way else-where. Angus Finney (1996: 70, 140–41, 145) reports that *Damage* (Louis Malle, 1993) was removed from a theatre in Britain after a week, having broken all box-office records, in favour of pre-booked US material. Of course, *The Full Monty* posted phenomenal sales figures and was nominated for an Academy Award for Best Picture. Is its success attributable to the fact that the British sud-denly, magically, made a commercial film? No, all this depended on Fox's decision to release the picture. The holy grail of worldwide release by a US dis-tributor guaranteed an audience and fair play for the appeal of the text. In the UK, *The Full Monty* was the kind of film – an account of bleak post-industrial Northern disemployment – that people would generally have to travel fifty miles to see. But the multiplex exposure brought by Fox amounted to hundreds of screens across the country. The film's producer, Uberto Pasolini, puts it like this:

> Distribution, distribution, distribution – that's the issue ... the whole business
> of people saying to European producers that you just need to make films
> audiences want to see is complete crap. There are American movies that
> should not be in 100 theatres, ghastly movies with terrible reviews that no one
> cares about, but because a major has the muscle they get them onto those
> screens.
>
> (Pasolini, quoted in Dawtrey, 1997: 9)

Quite the opposite occurred with *The Quiet American*, a film depicting mur-derous CIA operations in Vietnam during the 1950s, which Miramax censored for a year before briefly releasing it with a lukewarm marketing campaign that ensured audiences would not see it. The assumption that it would not succeed in the post-9/11 political climate was certainly self-fulfilling (Biskind, 2004: 463).

Distribution is similarly important in the video market, which has under-gone tremendous consolidation since the end of the 1990s. Here, majors sell tapes to retailers, mostly rental stores. Many titles that did not have theatrical releases are available. Whereas films are distributed purely as wholesale activi-ties, video and DVD rentals link wholesale and retail functions, and studios do not always use the same overseas affiliates for the two functions (McCalman, 2004: 113). Universal is the wholesale distributor in the US video market for

DreamWorks, Lion's Gate and Playboy. Artisan distributes Hallmark Entertainment, Trimark, Family Home Video and others. Warner Bros. distributes
New Line. MGM distributes its own video products, but uses Warners' shipping facilities (Wasko, 1994: 138, 140). Smaller producers benefit from selling
percentages of their films to major video distributors via overall savings on distribution costs and the boost their products receive from the majors' economies
of scale in manufacturing, shipping, marketing, sales force, trademark advantage and, in the case of selling to major retailers, being bundled with 'A' titles
in order to capture shelf space.[1] But even that distinction between the creative
producer and the middle-person distributor is misleading. For very early on in
the life of a film, it may obtain financing through a pre-sale, whereby distributors are sufficiently taken with a proposal that they guarantee to pass it on via
exhibition deals already struck or likely to be so.

Major cable operators typically wait forty-five to fifty-two days after film
shipments arrive at video stores before they air pay-per-view (PPV) and video-
on-demand (VOD) movies. In 2003, they began to look for deals with the major
studios to cut that waiting period by a third, banking on the fact that studios
receive a larger revenue share from VOD (60 per cent) than video rental. Their
aim is to gain equal placement as a release window with video, but this will ultimately depend on cable operators buying more movies and people using VOD.
In 2003, VOD was available in about 10 million US households, though only
about 10 per cent of those actually used it, while 95 per cent of those households had a VCR or DVD player. Nevertheless, the studios are interested
in matching certain titles to earlier VOD releases to boost sales – for instance,
Shallow Hal (Bobby and Peter Farrelly, 2001) was the most successful VOD
release in 2002 (Whitney, 2003). Projections suggested that VOD in general
would increase from US$991 million in 2003 to more than US$4.5 billion in
2007 (Hu and Olsen, 2004). Hollywood is also waiting for the emergence of
high-definition DVDs, which carry much more data than the current format
(Rojas, 2004) and hold out the prospect of yet more sales of the same text.

The notion that distribution is a hard-headed enterprise is correct. But the
assertion that this leads to real competition is ludicrous – it ensures market
domination by US producers. For all the blathering to the effect that US audiences have no interest in foreign film, in addition to university screenings across
the thousands of US colleges, there is a vast array of small companies striving
to meet the needs of this supposedly non-existent demand.

SELECT US DISTRIBUTORS OF FOREIGN-LANGUAGE AND INDEPENDENT US FILM 2000–02

COMPANY	CITY	STATE	WEBSITE
Arenas Entertainment	Los Angeles	CA	www.arenasgroup.com
Arrow Films International	LA	CA	
Artisan Entertainment	LA	CA	www.artisanentertainment.com
Artistic License Films	New York	NY	www.artflic.com
AtomFilms	Seattle	WA	www.atomfilms.com
Attitude Films	NYC	NY	www.attitudefilms.com
Bullfrogs Films	Oley	PA	www.bullfrogsfilms.com
Capitol Entertainment Corp.	Bethesda	MA	www.capitolent.com
Code Red Films	NYC	NY	
Cowboy Booking International	NYC	NY	www.cowboybi.com
Crystal Pictures	Asheville	NC	
Entertech Releasing Corp.	LA	CA	www.entertechmedia.com
Esparza/Katz Productions/Maya Cinemas	LA	CA	www.mayacinemas.com
Facets Multimedia	Chicago	IL	www.facets.org
Film Forum	NYC	NY	www.filmforum.com
Filmakers Library	NY	NY	www.filmakers.com
Filmopolis Pictures	LA	CA	www.filmopolis.com
Films for the Humanities & Sciences	Princeton	NJ	www.films.com

COMPANY	CITY	STATE	WEBSITE
Fine Line Features	LA	CA	www.flf.com
Fireworks Pictures	LA	CA	www.watchfireworks.com/wfw _pictures.html
First Look Pictures	LA	CA	www.flp.com
First Run Features	NYC	NY	www.firstrunfeatures.com
Fox Searchlight	LA	CA	www.foxsearchlight.com
Frameline	San Francisco	CA	www.frameline.org
Good Machine Intl.			
GPN	Lincoln	NE	mall.unl.edu
Greycat Releasing	Las Vegas	NV	
Highland Crest Pictures	LA	CA	www.highlandcrestpix.com
IFC	LA	CA	www.ifctv.com
Independent Artists	LA	CA	www.independentartists.net
Jour de Fete Films	LA	CA	
Kino International	NYC	NY	www.kino.com
Kit Parker Films	Sand City	CA	www.kitparker.com
Latin Star	LA	CA	
Latin Universe	Sherman Oaks	CA	www.universolatino.net
Leisure Time Features	NYC	NY	www.leisurefeat.com
Leo Films	Van Nuys	CA	www.leofilms.com
Lions Gate Films	LA	CA	www.lionsgatefilms.com
Lot 47, Inc.	NYC	NY	www.lot47.com
Manga Entertainment	Chicago	IL	www.manga.com

COMPANY	CITY	STATE	WEBSITE
Merrimack Films	Belmont	MA	
Milestone Film & Video	NYC	NY	www.milestonefilms.com
Miramax Films	NYC	NY	www.miramax.com
Miravista	LA	CA	
Myriad Pictures	LA	CA	www.myriadpictures.com
New Latin Pictures	Sand City	CA	www.newlatin.com
New Video Group	NYC	NY	www.newvideo.com
New Yorker Films	NYC	NY	www.newyorkerfilms.com
Palm Pictures	NYC	NY	www.palmpictures.com
Panorama Entertainment	Port Chester	NY	
Paramount Classics	LA	CA	www.paramountclassics.com
Phaedra Cinema International	LA	CA	www.phaedracinema.com
Picture This!	LA	CA	www.picturethisent.com
Red Diaper Productions	NYC	NY	www.reddiaper.com
Roxie Releasing	San Francisco	CA	www.roxie.com
Samuel Goldwyn Films	NYC	NY	
Seventh Art Releasing	LA	CA	www.7thart.com
Shadow Distribution	Waterville	ME	www.mint/net/movies/shadow
Sony Pictures Classics	NYC	NY	www.sonyclassics.com
Starz Encore Group	Engle-wood	CO	www.encoremedia.com
Strand Releasing	LA	CA	www.strandrel.com

COMPANY	CITY	STATE	WEBSITE
Stratosphere Entertainment	NYC	NY	www.prime.ground0.com
Sundance Channel	NYC	NY	www.sundancechannel.com
Tapestry International	NYC	NY	
The Cinema Guild	NYC	NY	www.cinemaguild.com
The Shooting Gallery	LA	CA	www.shootinggallery.com
The Video Project	Benlomond	CA	www.videoproject.org
Third World Newsreel	NYC	NY	www.twn.org
Trimark Pictures	LA	CA	www.trimarkpictures.com
Turbulent Arts	San Francisco	CA	www.turbulentarts.com
Universal Pictures	LA	CA	www.universalpictures.com
USA Films	NYC	NY	www.octoberfilms.com
Vanguard Films	Huntington Beach	CA	www.moviesource.com/ vanguard
Venevision Intl	Miami	FL	
Video Data Bank	Chicago	IL	
W. P. Donnelly & Associates	LA	CA	
Water Bearer Films	NYC	NY	www.waterbearer.com
Wellspring Media	NYC	NY	www.wellspring.com
Women Make Movies	NYC	NY	www.wmm.com
York Home Video	LA	CA	
Zeitgeist Films Limited	NYC	NY	www.zeitgeistfilm.com

Decisions about the number of prints are also important during the final promotional effort for exhibition. Combined with the advertising budget, prints often raise marketing costs to 50 per cent of a feature film's total value. From a marketing perspective, the investment is justified, because more prints mean more opportunities for poster displays and for the film's title to occupy available marquee space, much like a billboard announcing a new product. Release strategies, therefore, usually include consideration of an optimal volume of prints as part of a single marketing event with advertising and other promotions. Major distributors usually opt for wide US release, with 1,000 to 2,000 prints distributed and advertised on a nationwide basis, including '100 theatres in Los Angeles and eighty theatres in New York'. Wide releases have come to 'represent about three-quarters of total box office revenue' (Lukk, 1997: 6–7). In contrast, speciality distributors use a method called platforming, in which they release prints in three to five key theatres in Los Angeles and New York to build awareness through the local press and then 'platform' their films to other cities (Lukk, 1997: 6; Wyatt, 1994: 110; Brunella, 2001). Limited releases are those that do not appear beyond two or three major cities.

A Hollywood movie typically makes 40 per cent of its total domestic revenues in the first week of release, 70 per cent from the weekend sales (Einav, 2002: 5). Though most movies perceived to lack mass marketability are relegated to limited or platform releases, one of the main strategies in bringing an expensive but clearly unmarketable movie to cinemas is film-print saturation to ensure it can 'make as much money as possible before [the proverbial] word-of-mouth kills the film at the box office' (Lukk, 1997: 7).

In 2001, the studios demoted their overseas-desk mavens, on the basis that global revenues were now *so* crucial that they no longer needed their own management systems or promotional budgets, but could be incorporated in US domestic planning (Dunkley and Harris, 2001). Some have interpreted these changes as signs of hubris by 'domestic distribution czars', a failure to acknowledge difference that will undermine Hollywood dominance (Williams-Jones, 2001; see also Lewis, 2001). Whether or not this 'streamlining' turns out to be a brief fad of managerial warlockcraft, global simultaneity of distribution seems assured. Whereas there used to be delays of six months and more between the release of films in the US and overseas, it is now standard to open them everywhere within a month of domestic exhibition, regardless of issues such as climate or local holidays (DiOrio, 2001: 16). UIP is applying a new marketing database to track ticket sales in 'real time' around the world to gauge the effectiveness of advertising campaigns and change them instantly. Networked database marketing increases the velocity with which UIP marketers can manage the advertising campaign of films released simultaneously worldwide. This became quite a feat with the much-discussed schedule for the third *Matrix* film, which had a synchronised release in sixty countries, including:

- 6 a.m. Los Angeles
- 9 a.m. New York
- 2 p.m. London
- 5 p.m. Moscow
- 7.30 p.m. New Delhi
- 11 p.m. Tokyo.

(Gupta, 2003)

After the date of first domestic release, US feature-fiction films have at least nine opportunities to bring in revenue:

- US theatres, for 4 months from US release
- foreign theatres (4–18 months)
- US video (6–30 months)
- foreign video (9–24 months)
- US cable television (12–36 months)
- US broadcast television (36–60 months)
- foreign broadcasters (48–60 months)
- second US cable television (66–72 months); and
- US syndication (72 months).

(Adapted from Gershon, 1997: 40)

This efflorescence of formats and sites has been a bonanza for Hollywood. As recently as a quarter of a century ago, direct consumer purchase in the EU and the US was only an option through theatrical attendance. In the late 1990s, that accounted for just 31.3 per cent of spending, with pay-TV at 34 per cent, video purchase 20.4 per cent and video rental 14.2 per cent. As measured across all these outlets, for example, British expenditure on films increased 750 per cent between 1981 and 1997 (Durie *et al.*, 2000: 15–17; Hettrick, 2001).

When distributors have done their work, exhibition becomes the next marketing tool, as theatrical releases themselves promote texts for resale in more lucrative venues. The exhibition system has been modernised during the 1990s with the globalisation of the multiplex, itself a subset of developments in fast-food franchises and merchandise agglomeration via the growth of the shopping mall, where local shops often subsidise theatres. This convergence of space with other retail sectors also applies at the level of managerial systems, with chain ownership displacing independence, and the return of Hollywood producer-distributors to theatrical interests (Litman, 1998: 18, 33; Blackstone and Bowman, 1999). By 2002, global theatrical sales of food and drink had reached US$4.5 billion, and the trend was for exhibitors to make more from concessions than tickets ('New Research', 2002).

Up to the 1990s, Western Europe had seen a decline in the number of screens and admissions. Theatre numbers fell by 60 per cent between 1960 and 1990, while total Western European admissions diminished from 2.9 billion to 564 million as alternative leisure-time activities and ways of watching 'films' multiplied. The trend was not reversed until 1997, when EU admissions rose to 758.5 million (Durie *et al.*, 2000: 10–11). This reversal was fuelled in part by the US$1.65 billion construction of new venues in Britain alone, most of which was bankrolled by United Cinemas International (a joint venture of MCA and Paramount), Warner Bros. and AMC. Warners claimed that its British building programme was 'not so much to generate profits as to encourage cinemagoing *per se*' (quoted in Acland, 2003: 156). Rather than offering sufficient screens to permit diverse selections from around the world (or even the country of domicile), multiplexes have encouraged distributors to seek multiple slots for each film within the one complex. Minor exceptions can be found: the thirty screens in Birmingham's Star City included six dedicated to Bollywood (Durie *et al.*, 2000: 10–11, 153; Younge, 2000). International audiences typically used to wait six months for US films to be screened, but that dropped to four weeks during the 1990s – creating further pressure on space for local material (Short, 1997). Often derided in Europe as 'fronts for the American blockbusters' that have undermined independent outlets (European Audiovisual Observatory, 1998), multiplexes have been described by Valenti as 'comfortable, clean' (1993: 148). Designers claim to customise them to local needs, as per the proud boast of catering to the 'number of fixtures required in the gentlemen's toilets' in Indian multiplexes, which is deemed 'unusually high' by Yanqui standards (Mesbur, 2003). At the same time, the ambitious building and renovation programmes went too far, at least domestically, and from 1999, domestic exhibitors were mostly bankrupt. The result, of course, was additional consolidation (Los Angeles County Economic Development Corporation, 2001: 1).

The technologies of distribution and exhibition are today subject to even more radical change. Worldwide consumer spending on DVD software reached US$22.7 billion in 2002, overtaking consumer spending on VHS (US$19.6 billion) for the first time. The DVD market sees US$17.2 billion in sales compared with US$5.6 billion in rentals, whereas for video, rentals are more than 50 per cent greater than purchases (US$11.9 billion compared with US$7.7 billion),

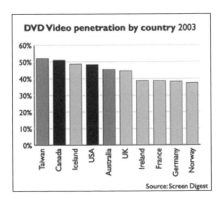

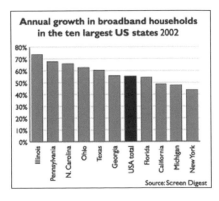

while the uptake of broadband in key coastal markets of the US ensured the transfer of this method of transmission to cinema (*Screen Digest*, 8 January 2004).

During the annual ShoWest trade fair convened by the National Association of Theatre Owners in 2000, executives from big theatrical operations such as UCI and Warner Bros. International Theatres (WBIT) expressed concern about cinema overbuilding in mature markets such as the US and Western Europe, and announced plans to shift investment to Latin America, Eastern Europe and especially Asia. While forecasting the decline of traditional film projection is something of a cottage industry, recent demonstrations of direct-to-theatre satellite delivery have convinced a number of Hollywood distributional arms to create executive departments to pursue this new technology and thereby cut jobs in distribution and exhibition. The average 35mm film costs $3,000 for each copy, which would be reduced many times over with manufacture and delivery through hard disk, CD-ROM, broadband or satellite. This would also save perhaps US$200 million a year in duplication and shipping by diminishing the number of prints required for an opening, and offer up to four times the resolution of the existing system. Digital distribution would shave over US$10 million in domestic post-production print manufacturing costs from a film like *Godzilla* (Natale, 2000). If the 39,000 screens in North America were to switch to digital projection today, film studios would save the US$800 million they spend annually on making, insuring and shipping film prints (Sabin, 2000). At the same time, revenue from DVD/VHS rentals and sales accounted for 62 per cent of Hollywood's 2002 domestic revenue and 49 per cent in Europe, so Hollywood is also compressing the time-lag between hard-top and home exhibition (Burgess, 2004).

Although distributors hope to save millions of dollars in print reproduction from digitalisation, the enormous cost of even partial conversion of traditional theatres, as well as the much greater problem of hackers breaking the encryption keys that are supposed to keep satellite delivery piracy-free, has set Hollywood on a firm course to seek ever more complex methods of copyright control and surveillance. Art cinemas have already diminished in number as part of the chains' recovery strategies, sacrificed so that their owners could stay in business and prepare for the coming costs of digitisation (estimated at US$175,000 per screen) (Holden, 2002; Parthasarathy, 2003; Tubridy, 2001).

Star Wars: Episode II (George Lucas, 2002) was the first feature film downloaded from a Boeing aerospace satellite for exhibition (to the 116 screens out of 130,000 worldwide that had the technology). It is claimed that there will be 10,000 digital screens by 2005 and that the system will be ubiquitous within two decades. This has major implications for imported films, as distributors will be unwilling to pay for making additional copies of non-digital movies, but subtitles will be easily added to suit exhibitionary sites (Culkin and Randle, 2002; Chellam, 2003; Forde, 2002; Carus, 2003). In response, the UK Film Council invested £19 million for a network of digital-projection cinemas in Britain that it hopes will ensure independent films can reach regional audiences who may be affected by cuts in print duplication that could result from digitisation (Burrell, 2003).

For now, most films are still shot on film, then scanned by post-production firms that add special effects and do off-line editing before saving the master that is scanned back to film. In the US, the number of digital screens in 2002 was still just 124 out of over 35,000 (Carus, 2003; Motion Picture Association of America Worldwide Market Research, 2003: 23–24), and in the UK, only five theatres had digital screens (Burrell, 2003). Only China was embarked on a serious digital building policy, with thirty-four screens by early 2003 (Brown, 2003). But 5,000 theatres across the world already had digital pre-show systems for advertising by the end of 2003, and most people in the industry believed that 2004–05 would see major US expansion once standardised systems for compression, encryption, resolution and contrast had been attained ('Digital Directions', 2003; Fuchs, 2003b: 28). Meanwhile, China provided the first major data on the appeal of Hollywood films in digital versus film theatres.

PERCENTAGE DIFFERENCE OF DIGITAL VERSUS CONVENTIONAL RELEASES

TITLE	*STAR WARS 2*	*HARRY POTTER–CHAMBER*	*FINDING NEMO*
Screen #	1.7	4	8.4
Box Office	11.6	14.25	22
Admissions	248.8	290	151.02
Ticket Price	171.8	138	155.84
Revenue per Screening	426.3	247	234.7

SOURCE: Adapted from Zhou, 2004

As for the Internet, in 1987, the Motion Picture Experts Group (MPEG) of the Geneva-based International Organization for Standardization began looking into ways to compress digital video, resulting in the 1992 MPEG format, whose Layer-3 version gives it the well-known MP3 moniker. So, even though patents on software systems designed to broadcast movies on the Internet were issued in the US in the early 1990s (like Scott Sander and Arthur Hair's 'Method for Transmitting a Desired Digital Video or Audio Signal' that became the basis for their sightsound.com website), as we saw in Chapter 4, Hollywood only took serious note when a recent spate of Internet piracy put over sixty films online.

Today, the studios seek to duplicate their success in the international multi-channel television market, and have launched PPV Internet channels. Satellite, digital television, broadband, VOD and other technologies of digital distribution (like the table-top hybrid of television and the PC, forecast by techno-futurists and studio heads alike) allow them to cut out the middle people who facilitate Hollywood distribution in foreign countries. Sony Pictures, successful in the multichannel television market, with thirty-three networks around the world (which earn about US$150 million in advertising revenue, 80 per cent from Asia) and a huge programme-syndication business, formed Sony Pictures Digital Entertainment to leverage Sony's programming in the digital environment (Galetto and Dallas, 2000). Sony also has an online VOD service called Moviefly, which is designed to replace the PPV cable and satellite business that did not meet the expectation that it would be a platform for the premiere of films (Graham, 2001b). Driven by the need to maximise the value of their content, Hollywood studios look to the Internet and companies like iBeam and CinemaNow – major players in Internet distribution of film (Winslow, 2001; 'iBeam and CinemaNow', 2000). And with hundreds of millions of consumers online and 95 per cent of major media companies broadcasting on the Internet, e-commerce is a game with a lot at stake and few rules (Pham, 2000). By 2001, as we saw in Chapter 4, experiments were under way at hardware firms and at Miramax and several US Internet companies, using encryption technology that made pay-per-download films uncopyable and, after twenty-four hours, unplayable. These efforts did not advance as planned (Arthur, 2001), and several early ventures, including a Disney-Fox project called Movies.com, failed.

In 2002, a collaboration between Warner Bros., MGM, Universal, Sony and Paramount called Movielink was established, offering major studio films for downloading after release on video and before TV (Graser, 2002; Bedell, 2003). It is designed to avoid illegal copying by using encryption technology – and latterly, to try to save AOL from failure (Hu and Olsen, 2004). Bollywood innovated digital downloads in 2003 with *Supari* (Padam Kumar, 2003) via KaZaa for US$2.99, with other texts following from Australia and Singapore. By 2004, the only major studio Internet distributors were Movielink and CinemaNow (financed by Viacom's Blockbuster, Microsoft and Lion's Gate Entertainment) (Bedell, 2003). Internet distribution will depend on steady growth in broadband use and software improvements. By early 2004, nearly 40 per cent of US Internet households had broadband capability, a 27 per cent increase over the previous six months (www.nielsen-netratings.com/pr/pr_040108_us.pdf). Proposed innovations to move Internet distribution to television viewing – a niche that Microsoft is hoping to capture with a proprietary appliance attached to new TV sets – suggest that Internet distribution will supersede pay-TV and video rental, as happened in pornography, though theatrical distribution should survive this technology shift, just as it weathered the impact of television and video recorders (Moore, 2000: 202–05). Seven of the major studios announced a Digital Cinema Initiative late in 2003 (Chellam, 2003).

The goal of Internet video distribution is to inhibit piracy, reduce costs while achieving a direct link to audiences for surveillance purposes, and defend the majors' position as principal distributors in home entertainment against competing pay-TV and video-rental services (Peers, 2001; Mathews, 2001). For US independents, the Internet film distributor Intertainer announced a new service plan in 2002. The initiative, known as Film Marketplace, permits producers to pay Intertainer a fee for encoding, storage and streaming, then charge their own viewing price ('Intertainer', 2002). Atomfilms.com and SightSound.com offer similar arrangements.

At least until the shift to digital systems is complete, international theatrical distribution will remain very expensive, due to the cost of prints, advertisements and labour – the multiple media and sites necessitate a huge bureaucracy. Yet as production costs continue to rise for Hollywood films, the relative cost of the physical distribution cycle (both legal and illegal) is declining. This is especially the case for the highly capitalised and integrated entertainment conglomerates that own Hollywood studios, because they are structured to cross-subsidise failures and risks from various media businesses and ensure cash flow, and can coordinate marketing across territories to cut the cost of market research and promotional activities (Durie *et al.*, 2000: 89–90; Litman, 1998: 24). Driven by the possibilities of syndicating its considerable television library, Sony's Columbia TriStar is involved in producing a Putonghua version of *Charlie's Angels* for China and historical costume epics for India, two places that are traditionally hostile to Hollywood's business. And while most Hollywood exports are still only dubbed into German, Italian, Spanish and French, with the rest of the world reading subtitles, there is a trend towards hiring 'local' actors across the thirty largest language groups to dub high-budget films (Orwall, 2000).

This brings us to two sites, somewhere still beyond Hollywood's control but not its reach, where projects are under way that engage each sector of this chapter. In all these debates about global expansion, the hidden desire of Hollywood is to gain easy and profitable access to Indian and Chinese audiences. As these markets are so often heralded as the future – the *People's Daily* estimates potential revenue in the PRC to be US$1–1.5 billion annually ('Hollywood Movies', 2003) – we devote considerable space to them here.

India

Hollywood's tried and true formulas, the poor boy and the rich girl and vice versa; the love triangle, and the action spectacle like Samson and Delilah also go over big. Some of these reveal, perhaps, India's national yearnings – to be richer, to be braver, to win the beautiful girl – in which the average Indian is no different from the average American. Some are wondering how far the 'love' movie will help break down India's rigid caste barriers and the universal customs of marriage wherein bride and bridegroom are chosen by the respective parents, and rarely see each other until the wedding ceremony.

(Trumbull, 1953)

Hollywood regards India as one of its keys to prosperity in Asia (Rosenberg, 2003). In 2001, seventy features were released there, and Columbia TriStar claims 5 per cent of the national market. Imports are increasingly dubbed into regional languages as well as Hindi, which has expanded business (Kumar, 2002). *Die Another Day* broke records for Hollywood revenues there and was released nationally (Kapoor, 2002). But after a century of screen trade, these are rather paltry achievements. What happened?

The US share of the import market in India doubled between 1900 and 1913, from 1.7 per cent to 3.8 per cent. With the onset of war, Hollywood took advantage of the absence of European companies – whose film industries were also affected by shortages and rationing – to establish a strong foothold in the Indian market. With wartime building restrictions lifted in 1919, theatre construction resumed. The US Department of Commerce estimated that US films made up almost 95 per cent of all imports (Thompson, 1985: 48, 144). By the mid-1920s, Universal's distribution company was selling over 150 films, split evenly between features, comedies and newsreels. Madan Theatres Ltd was a major importer of US product, accounting for 90 per cent of its screen time, and by 1927, 15 per cent of films exhibited in India were domestic productions, while 85 per cent were foreign, the vast majority from Hollywood (Barnouw and Krishnaswamy, 1980: 41–42). Even though India produced 100 films in 1926–27 (compared to 47 in Britain the same year), US films comprised 80 per cent of screenings (Singh, *c.* mid-1930s). As an indication of the government's recognition of industrial capital's investment in cinema, and the growth in the urban working classes that formed the backbone of the viewing public, an entertainment tax on film exhibition was levied in Calcutta in 1922 and Bombay the following year.

A few years later, writing derisively about the state of much popular Indian film (for example, commenting that 'Indian films are slow in movement, necessarily so because of the people who go to see them') F. M. de Mello noted that, while Indian films 'have not yet attracted the cultured classes to the extent that American and British films have', it would nevertheless

be a mistake to agitate, as some people are tempted to do, for restrictions on imported films; for these films are to a large extent noncompetitive with Indian films and in any case cannot carry nationalism to the point of cutting off ourselves from foreign culture. What Indian producers might do – and the

best of them are doing – is to go abroad and study every aspect of the
industry. It might then be easier to improve the quality of their pictures in
order to win the attention of the cultured classes both at home and abroad.

(de Mello, 1937)

In an article that valorised the formation of the Motion Picture Society in
Bombay, the US equivalent was described as 'an example to the Indian Film
Industry' ('An Example', 1933). And in 1939, the newly formed Cine Finance
and Banking Corporation of India proposed to send a British representative to
the US in order to study Hollywood and contact producers of motion-picture
equipment ('India Company', 1939).

One source maintains that the maximum market for English-language films
(based on educational level and an approximation of nationality derived from
census evidence) in 1930s Bombay was 11.6 per cent (or about 135,000) ('Bombay Theatremen', 1937). In the late 1930s and early 1940s, India was the most
lucrative market for Hollywood in South and East Asia, and the only market
besides the Philippines that offered four-digit returns. For example, *Algiers*
(John Cromwell, 1938) grossed US$7,613 in India and *Arabian Nights* (John
Rawlins, 1942) yielded US$30,000 in gross earnings (against over US$650,000
in Britain) (Glancy, 1999: 34, 36). Some reports put the larger US grosses in the
early 1940s at between US$50,000 and US$75,000 each in Indian exhibition
('No Title', 1941).

On a stopover in the US, producer/director Mehboob Khan maintained that
'our movie makers are artistic and competent and if they can obtain entry to
world markets, and particularly to US theatres, I believe we can make a favor-
able showing before non-Indian audiences'. Travelling with Khan, the
distributor J. P. Jhalani noted that Hollywood musicals were particularly popular with Indian audiences, and that 'if a reciprocal agreement could be made
with some large American company to help us build up our studios and equip
them with the best American facilities, it would be of material benefit to both
our countries' (quoted in Fox, 1947). These sentiments were echoed by a major
West India exhibitor, Keki Modi, who noted that action films were the most
popular among foreign movies, adding that Hollywood might take advantage
of the fact that there were no government-imposed restrictions on profit repa-
triation on money earned by films released in India by US distributors
('Report', 1948).

Just after Independence, Indian producers pressed for protectionist quotas
and bans on the dubbing of imported films; especially strong protests were lobbied against the 700 per cent increase in censorship fees ordered by the Central
Board of Film Censors (Doraiswamy, 1951). However, MGM's general manager
in India, Pakistan, Burma and Ceylon insisted in 1950 that Hollywood films did
not represent a serious threat to the Indian industry, noting that in Bombay,
only five houses screened first-run English-language films, while fifty-five

showed Indian films. Remarking upon the prodigious runs for locally produced film (a 28-week engagement was not unusual), the executive cited the 102-week run of *Kismet* (William Dieterle, 1944), while MGM's own *The Three Muske-teers* (George Sidney, 1948) ran for six weeks at its theatre in Bombay ('US Films', 1950).

In 1952, almost a hundred theatres in India showed only foreign films. Over 400 US features entered the country, in addition to the usual flow of newsreels, cartoons and shorts (Eswar, 1953). Nevertheless, the degradation of political relations between India and the US was felt in Hollywood's tightening export business as the 1950s wore on, and not only on the balance sheet.

The rhetoric of the Cold War began to infuse US depictions of the Indian film industry: in a 1959 article in *Time*, the annual audience was estimated at some 730 million ('Movies Abroad', 1959). The grandson of Gandhi, who worked for Moral Rearmament, called on the US to supplement its financial aid to India with 'an ideal for which we can fight against the forces that seek to overthrow our government'. This ideal, which, according to Rajmohan Gandhi, might 'help save India from Communism', could take shape in Hollywood – though in a modified way: 'Sex and sensationalism will never destroy communism ... What is needed is the kind of movie which will spread the word of democracy with entertainment, not preaching' ('Gandhi Pleads', 1959).

In the late 1960s, raw stock shortages and scarce resources for film financing fuelled regional Indian dubbing industries, allowing independent producers to give a film a specific regional appeal (or the Hindi 'all-India' demographic) at about 25 per cent of the outlay cost for an original production. Dubbing had proved unsuccessful for *Bambi* (David Hand, 1942) and *Samson and Delilah* (Cecil B. DeMille, 1949), and US films were almost exclusively screened in English. Nevertheless, driven by the 'universal' genres of the costume drama and the historical spectacle, as of 1964, the greatest Hollywood success in India was *The Ten Commandments* (Cecil B. DeMille, 1956), followed by *Ben-Hur* and *The Guns of Navarone* (J. Lee Thompson, 1961) ('Cine Exec', 1970; Scheuer, *c.* 1964). In early 1965, Paramount's *Hatari!* (Howard Hawks, 1962) was in the middle of a sixteen-week run in Bombay, after success in Calcutta. Distributors expected a gross of about US$560,000 using between five and seven prints. *Ben-Hur* ran for thirty-six weeks in Bombay and *My Fair Lady* (George Cukor, 1964) for over twenty-seven weeks ('India's Prolific', 1965; Scott, 1965). Occasionally, securing the success of certain Hollywood films mediated the battle between distributors and the print media over advertising rates. For example, B. K. Karanjia, critic for *The Times of India*, was banned from MGM press screenings following her review of *Dumbo* (Ben Sharpsteen, 1941) as 'mediocre'. *The Times* had been at odds with distributors in the mid-1960s over advertising rates, and had stopped film reviews for a time because of lack of distributor interest in buying up ad space (Brady, 1963). Hollywood's screen trade in India in the mid-1960s involved a mix of company allegiances – MGM released Universal film, the Rank organisation dealt with Disney and Allied Artists and Fox handled United Artists. Theatres joined in the mix: Keki Modi's chain once played Fox releases, but began to realise exhibition deals with distributors Rank, Paramount and MGM and occasionally screened Warner Bros. product ('India's Prolific', 1965).

The restarting of Universal Pictures in India and reports of the Rank organisation reinitiating business in the subcontinent were reasons for optimism among institutions involved in the distribution of Hollywood film. At the end of the decade, *Where Eagles Dare* (Brian G. Hutton, 1968) grossed US$8,000 at Bombay's Metro theatre after playing for nine weeks at the nearby Strand, an indication of the action film's staying power. At the same time, the government was being asked to consider screen quotas on foreign film and rescind preferential treatment accorded to British and US productions. Hollywood had been enjoying years of monopoly as independent importers had severely cut back on their patronage of Continental European fare. British imports were fairly negligible during the same time (Eswar, 1970). Scheduling mistakes were still being made, however. The success of *The Sound of Music* (Robert Wise, 1965) did not, for example, translate into brisk business for *West Side Story* (Jerome Robbins and Robert Wise, 1961), and optimistic predictions for *Easy Rider* were woefully off (Reed, 1970). Some, like *Variety*'s N. V. Eswar, bemoaned that fact that critically acclaimed Indian films, like the Venice prize-winning *Bhuvan Shome* (Mrinal Sen, 1969), were made to compete with foreign films during their matinee screenings in Indian urban theatres (Eswar, 1971).

US feature-film exports to India climbed from 103 in 1968 to 132 in 1969. Total Indian domestic box office increased from US$146 million in 1968 to US$155 million in 1969. The US Department of Commerce figured that foreign film accounted for some 10 per cent of this, and since US product obtained some 80 per cent of foreign grosses, revenue in India in 1969 could be estimated at close to US$12.5 million ('80%', 1970; 'Cine Exec', 1970).

In 1971, there was a crisis in Indo-US film relations, with MPEAA companies stuck with US$6.5 million in non-repatriable money and the Indian government still skittish about the flight of foreign exchange. No wonder that negotiations between the Indian government and the MPEAA were seen as critical to the future of Hollywood in the subcontinent. The number of US features had dropped from 132 in 1969 to 106 in 1970 (out of a total 168 foreign features released in India in 1970, down from 211 in 1969 and 182 in 1968). The Indian government's claim that the MPEAA had failed to promote Indian film in the US was one of the reasons for the eventual expiration of the contract, which led effectively to a ban on the import of new US films. The MPEAA responded to these criticisms with the well-practised free-trade rhetoric that assimilated the overseas cartel within the logic of US trade law: namely, that it could not force US theatres to screen Indian films, because 'that would be a violation of our anti-trust laws' ('India Reports', 1971; 'Breach',

1971). With the MPEAA complaining about the relatively slight profit available in the Indian market and deeming the domestic distribution a cartel, the Hollywood cartel decided to stand firm and stop sending new films into India until 1975.

In 1974, Valenti and the MPEAA coordinated diplomatic initiatives to renew Hollywood's presence in India with the help of both Secretary of State Henry Kissinger and Ambassador Pat Moynihan. Valenti held a party for the 1975 International Film Festival in India. Ingeniously utilising 'blocked funds' for the party at the US embassy, he used the event to re-establish cordial relations with the Indian government (Pendakur, 1985: 63). In early 1975, a three-year ban on US film imports was lifted. Under the terms of the new agreement between the Indian government and the MPEAA, US companies could repatriate 15 per cent of their earnings in foreign exchange, up to a limit of US$310,000. US companies also agreed to funnel 20 per cent of earnings into US–Indian co-productions and give 20 per cent towards interest-free loans to national corporations. The remaining money would presumably cover local expenses. However, relations continued to be tense, with suggestions in late 1976 that the Indian Film Finance Corporation would be made the sole agent for the import and distribution of foreign film once the agreement with the MPEAA expired in 1979 ('Lift', 1975; 'Hint', 1976).

In the mid-1970s, the MPAA's Delhi representative, Captain Dennis Pereira, forecast that the majors might distribute 150 features in India, up from the current total of 120. Remittances ran to about US$350,000 a year, plus money from blocked funds during the early 1970s when no US pictures entered India. The average run for a US feature was about a month, with some notable exceptions like *The Towering Inferno* (Irwin Allen and John Guillermin, 1974) lasting forty-four weeks. A number of spectacular action films like *The Poseidon Adventure* (Ronald Neame and Irwin Allen, 1972), *Enter the Dragon* (Robert Clouse, 1973) and *Diamonds are Forever* (Guy Hamilton, 1971) also succeeded in the mid-1970s, and a repeat showing of *The Ten Commandments* ran for fifteen weeks in a local theatre. In 1978, the Kinematograph Renter's Society, which represented US firms, offered the Indian Film Finance Corporation an interest-free loan of 10 million rupees (culled from the vast store of Hollywood funds blocked in India) on condition that the money be used for the construction of new theatres. The Indian government accepted, and while repayment would be delayed for five years – at which point the funds would be converted and remitted – Hollywood was convinced that investment in the Indian theatrical sector would allow greater exhibition venues for US feature product ('US Majors', 1977; 'US Film', 1977; Segrave, 1997: 218). Following the release of *Gandhi*, there was talk about dubbing *E.T.* into Hindi and a general upswing of interest in foreign film in the country (Wilkerson, 1983). According to 1982 certification data from the Censor Board, ninety-one Hollywood films were imported into the country ('Censor', 1983).

As part of its commitment to the New Economic Policy, in 1992 the Indian government lifted its ban on the importation and distribution of US film, ending, as Valenti put it, 'a long and unhappy period of strained relations between India and the U.S. motion picture industry ... I applaud the government of India for removing artificial restraints that have denied the people of India the choice to view American films.' In addition, the government was considering allowing foreign companies to enter the video-rental business in India and remedy music and video piracy (Valenti quoted in 'India Promises', 1992).

In keeping with continuing liberalisation, following the removal of film tariffs in 1992, the government abolished selection committees and registration fees for imported raw stock and films. While the MPEAA was happy about not having to pay the US$10,000 canalisation fee, the Indian National Film Development Corporation was concerned about funding its small and medium-budget productions, and government subsidy seemed unlikely as ever. As *The Silence of the Lambs* (Jonathan Demme, 1991) played to full houses in Bombay, local producers worried about competition from foreign films, although the President of the Importers Association of Bombay, Jiten Hemdev, noted that 'there's always room for good cinema. Our producers will have to learn to cope with competition' (quoted in Gahlot, 1992). The MPEAA's repatriation limits were upped to US$6 million in box-office revenue per year. Mid-1990s optimism on the part of the Hollywood majors was mainly centred around increased efficiency in censorship clearance and other forms of regulation. Renewed calls for 'quality product' were voiced by proponents of liberalisation, who insisted that ending canalisation fees would encourage independent import of foreign films by diasporic Indian importers competing with debased Hollywood forms (Pendakur, 1996).

Attempting to duplicate *Gandhi*'s bilingual release strategy, UIP (which handled distribution for Universal, Paramount and MGM-UA) geared up for the release of *Jurassic Park*, with 102 Hindi prints and 30 English copies. *Jurassic Park* was not the first Hollywood film dubbed into Hindi; that was probably *The Thief of Bagdad* (Raoul Walsh, 1924), starring Douglas Fairbanks, Sr. (da Cunha, 1994; Dahlburg, 1994). It *was*, however, the first Hollywood film in a decade to be dubbed into Hindi. Distributor N. N. Sippy argued at a meeting of the Film Federation of India that 'we should not allow dubbed versions of Hollywood films to be screened since [their] excessive sex and violence will have a deep impact on the Indian psyche' (quoted in Groves and da Cunha, 1994). While most popular Hollywood films were released on thirty screens, *Jurassic Park* was released on 117. UIP spent more than 10 million rupees (US$320,000) promoting the film on television, print and billboard advertising, and promotional tie-ins with consumer product. After a three-week run across some 260 theatres, the film was estimated to have generated more than 4 million admissions (*Sholay* [Ramesh Sippy] was estimated to have sold 500 million tickets since its 1975 debut) (Lall, 1994; Dahlburg,

1994). By mid-August, *Jurassic Park* had grossed US$5.8 million, compared to the average US$30,000 performance of a Hollywood film and US$140,000 for a hit.

Soon after these figures were released, WBIT announced an agreement with the Maharashtra state government to build a dozen ten-screen multiplexes in key Indian cities, at a total cost of US$60 million (Lall and Ludemann, 1994). In a more comfortable regulatory and investment environment, and as a way to avoid the entertainment taxes that ate up box-office revenue, a number of Hollywood companies invested in the Indian film-exhibition sector. United Artists Theatres joined with a major Indian entertainment conglomerate in planning almost two dozen multiplexes, and a stock exchange to secure foreign investment. Many companies focused on regions within the country with the lowest entertainment taxes, which are set locally – Delhi was a favourite site for development, because its tax rate was set as almost 40 per cent, whereas some other areas had entertainment taxes that might exceed 125 per cent. Western exhibitors lobbied the Indian government in election run-ups to reduce the tax and aid cinema construction (Groves, 1995; Ludemann, 1996).

Jurassic Park influenced other Hollywood majors in India. Disney began distributing again in 1994 after a two-year hiatus, pursuing a joint venture and licensing agreement with a major Indian media conglomerate, as did its independent wing, Miramax. Another of Disney's many subsidiaries, Buena Vista Television International, supplied programming to the government network Doordarshan and managed Disney's dubbing operations, some of which were done in LA for 'quality control reasons' (da Cunha, 1995a).

Since India had finally allowed the dubbing of foreign films, other Hollywood majors jumped on the Indian distribution bandwagon, with an accompanying rise of amateur dubbings of pirated Hollywood films on videotape. Fox's *Speed* (Jan de Bont, 1994) followed *Jurassic Park*'s distribution strategy, with Murdoch's Star Movies satellite movie channel co-sponsoring marketing initiatives for the film alongside local companies. The next year, joint ventures between Indian industrialists and video distributors and foreign interests (such as Buena Vista, Sony, Time Warner, Reuters and Disney Consumer Products) proliferated.

Indian conglomerate Modi Films International signed an exclusive distribution deal with Buena Vista International to release *Aladdin* that was publicised (as is common with co-production's localisation strategies) as a way to funnel profits towards in-house production of both Indian TV and feature films. Independent US film distribution in India was spearheaded in 1995 by Miramax, but while MPAA product accounted for only US$8 million of a total domestic box office of US$500 million in India, any measurement of market penetration in dollars seems deflated because of pirated video distribution and rampant cable piracy. US distributors began to look towards other strategies that could avoid heavy taxes on entertainment tickets by investing in new theatres and dubbing English-language features into Hindi, Telegu and Tamil.

Release strategies for *Independence Day* and *Eraser* (Chuck Russell, 1996) were based on regional linguistic preferences – focusing on the south, for example, where English-language features had been successful. The Indian nationals who ran Hollywood's local divisions made sure that innovative marketing strategies and audience targeting spurred on *Anaconda* (Luis Llosa, 1997) (it took US$2 million in one month). The following year, Columbia Tri-Star Film Distributors International and Buena Vista International duplicated their convergence strategies in Singapore, Malaysia and Thailand, and signed a theatrical distribution pact in India, with Columbia TriStar handling all Buena Vista International product beginning with *Armageddon*. The same year's economic recession did not overly affect Hollywood films, and, following the wake left by *Titanic*, *The Mask of Zorro*, *Godzilla* and *Dr Dolittle* (Betty Thomas, 1998) exceeded expectations, mostly in dubbed versions.

Though syndication rights for US programming rose as deals were struck in dollars instead of local currency, Yanqui media companies involved in cable television discovered by the mid-1990s that *regional programming* was cheaper and invited friendlier relations with market-control institutions. For example, in 1994, Murdoch acquired Zee Television and then announced plans to launch a 24-hour Hindi channel. Sony planned to set up Indian film and television production facilities to feed a new joint-venture satellite channel that would screen films from the Columbia TriStar film libraries, and tentatively planned to produce Hindi films for theatrical exhibition. Sony's corporate vision, as its Executive President put it, was a combination of 'Japanese regional precision, American know-how and Indian flair'. Sony soon moved into international theatrical distribution of Hindi films, and Fox planned for international distribution via STAR-TV (da Cunha, 1995b; Lall, 2000). Columbia TriStar announced it would invest in domestic film production and acquire distribution rights to Hindi music from films.

The PRC

> We're just waiting for those theatres to be built in China. Everything will change – Lucy Fisher, former vice-chairman of Columbia-Tristar.
>
> (Quoted in 'The Monster', 2001)

In China during the 1930s and 1940s, Hollywood maintained distribution offices in Guangzhou, Beijing, Tianjin and Shanghai (Hu, 2003: 20), but major changes came in 1949. Ideological issues aside, Hollywood distribution in China was long hampered by the state's insistence on buying films for a fee rather than sharing revenue. The MPAA reacted by refusing to deal with the country from the 1950s to the late 1980s, so the nation could only see independents' films – one more tiresome example of the US tendency to walk away from any environment that it does not control, and engage in censorship by monopoly capital. But in 1986, a new formula was established that blended a flat fee with revenue-sharing (Wan and Kraus, 2002: 423). Further stimulus was close by.

In 1982, the domestic box office was US$21 billion. It dropped to US$4.5 billion in 1991 (Nickerson and Lappin, 1993; see also Zhu, 2002). The environment was very similar to the profit squeeze experienced during the 1920s. Each moment generated a new openness to Hollywood films (Hu, 2003: 61), marked in the 1990s by Premier Jiang Zemin's review of *Titanic* (Rosen, 2002 and 2003). The local film industry had borrowed Hollywood's techniques of organisation to reinvigorate efficient storytelling, and the local government was interested in borrowing its techniques of political propaganda to rejuvenate nation-binding (Wan and Kraus, 2002). In an attempt to get the populace back to theatres, the Chinese government decided in 1994 to bring in ten foreign films annually on a revenue-sharing basis. Prior to that, only a small number of Hollywood films had been allowed into the Chinese market each year, at a flat fee of US$30,000–50,000 each (Groves, 1994b). Under the new quota system, in which Valenti had played an instrumental role, the importation of *The Fugitive* from Warner Bros. marked China's first step in opening up its film industry. It brought the major Hollywood studios closer to their ambition of open access to the vast, largely untapped and potentially lucrative Chinese market. At the same time, pressure from the US government was mounting for the Chinese government to loosen its rigorous approval procedure for imported films and increase its annual import quota on a revenue-sharing basis prior to its accession to the WTO in 2001. In 1995, another six revenue-sharing Hollywood movies were imported. The films led to a big surge in box office, which increased 50 per cent in the first half of 1995 over the same period the previous year. Attendance at theatres in Beijing that summer increased by 70 per cent, which also drew audiences to domestic releases, though much less significantly. *True Lies* opened in 1995 and grossed 102 million yuan (Kuhn, 1995). While some in the Chinese industry hoped that these Hollywood imports might revive national cinema, the films' success spurred a heated debate on how to protect the indigenous film industry. That debate continues. Jinhua Dai has expressed her deep concern about the fate of the enfeebled Chinese national cinema, given the aggressive entry of the 'wolf' under essentially 'unequal' and 'unfair' competitions around the world, including the cinematically strong and culturally resistant France ('Tiaozhan Dayu Jiyu', 2002). She also laments the profit-driven behaviour of state-controlled distributors and theatres, which promote Hollywood films while neglecting domestic ones (over seventy local films were shelved without reaching theatres that year). This tendency 'further intensifies the squeezing power of transnational capital over domestic films' (Dai, 1999). The ten Hollywood imports each outperform domestic films at the box office, accounting for over half of annual receipts (Rosen, 2002: 56–57). To alleviate this massive imbalance and theatres' overdependence on Hollywood films, in 1996, the government ruled that at least two-thirds of screen time be reserved for domestic films, but foreign imports benefited most from the surge in box office. In 1998, *Titanic* set a box-office record of 359.5 million yuan (about US$44 million), taking a quarter of that year's total ticket sales (Rosen, 2002: 61). There is a nice commentary on this in Zhang Yimou's *Wodi Fuqin Muqin* (1999), in which a teacher's house in a remote village is adorned with posters advertising *Titanic*.

Meanwhile, domestic film production in 1998 fell to 37 from the standard output since 1980 of 100, and Xi'an Film Studio, cradle of some of the most renowned fifth-generation filmmakers, had to lay off more than 10 per cent of its employees (Liu, 1999). The dire picture of the Chinese film industry in 1998 led Dai to voice even gloomier pessimism. She warned that 'like *Titanic*, the Chinese film industry is sinking amidst tender feelings and happiness, almost without any measures of resistance' (1999).

Nevertheless, Hollywood found the gap between achievement and expectation discouraging. In addition to the annual quota of ten revenue-sharing films, refusal of direct distribution rights in China put marketing, cinema booking and scheduling firmly in the hands of China Film, which had a monopoly over importing and distributing foreign films. And although under the revenue-sharing terms, Hollywood distributors and China Film are to divide box-office revenues in half, after the exhibitors' cut, taxes and other fees, the final return for Hollywood companies is only around 13 per cent, as opposed to its portion of the box office elsewhere – typically between 40 and 50 per cent (Groves, 2000c). Even for a substantial success such as *The Lion King*, which met projections of 20 million yuan (US$2.4 million) in box-office receipts in its first ten days, the ultimate return was comparable to a small Central European country ('Disney's', 1995). And in 1998, the year of *Titanic*, Hollywood revenues in the PRC were a mere US$18 million, equivalent to its earnings in Peru (Bates and Farley, 1999). Referring to the arduous sixteen months negotiating release of *The Lion King*, the short notice to prepare its marketing kit and the poor cinema infrastructure that generally denies a good scale of exhibition, Senior Vice-President of Buena Vista International (BVI) Larry Kaplan declared, 'there's a future, but there's not much of a present' (quoted in Stanley, 1996: 37). But sales of the film's soundtrack (over 700,000 copies in China) and the potential size of the market made BVI 'see huge opportunity for Disney'. It was prepared to 'seed the garden and harvest returns later' ('Disney's', 1995).

China's strict censorship has kept Hollywood studios from introducing overly violent and sexually explicit films. From time to time, studio executives are also puzzled by the fact that successes in the US and other territories fail in the PRC (e.g. *The Mummy Returns* [Stephen Sommers, 2001] grossed less than US$1 million), while obscure, far less commercially successful films in the US, such as *Meet the Parents* (Jay Roach, 2000), can succeed (Markham-Smith,

2001). Special-effects-laden films that are quintessentially Hollywood are usually popular, but other genres and styles can be surprise hits. *The Bridges of Madison County* (Clint Eastwood, 1995) set a Beijing box-office record of 1.9 million yuan (US$228,900) during its first three days of screening in 1996 (Major, 1997). Sony Pictures TriStar probably obtained 30–35 per cent in the PRC (Lee and Cox, 1999). This contrasts to the standard foreigner's share from distributing an imported film there (around 13 per cent, though the gross can be very different). Such figures are potentially good financial returns from global markets for a relatively low investment, and, more importantly, represent a foothold in the market for future distribution deals and other business opportunities. Ironically, while *Crouching Tiger, Hidden Dragon* was the highest-grossing foreign-language film ever in the US, it drew a rather lacklustre response in China, grossing only 10 million yuan (US$1.2 million) for the opening month of October 2000. It was perceived across Asia as a cultural 'chop suey' catering to Western audiences (Elley, 2001).

As one US major's Asian representative pointed out in the summer of 2001, no Hollywood import had grossed over 3 billion yuan (US$3.6 million) in the previous two years (Groves, 2001c). In 2002, only three films from Hollywood made it to the top-ten list in China. The domestic release *Hero* topped the box-office record with 245 million yuan, winning by a wide margin over the second-ranking *Lord of the Rings: The Two Towers* at 60 million yuan (Brent, 2003). *Mulan* (Barry Cook, 1998) was based on a local story, developed following three weeks of ethnography by Disney executives in China (Michael Wayne, 2003: 96). However, it failed to resonate there, because the narrative had been customised for the US. This cultural barrier may remain a long-term, tougher challenge to Hollywood than quotas. But for Sumner Redstone of Viacom, the 'village-idiot intervenes' style of US executives is central to all myths of business success: 'If there's a problem in China you don't wait three months to fix it, you get on a plane tomorrow with a go-for-it, seize-the-day attitude' (quoted in Eisenmann and Bower, 2000: 352).

China has long determined to keep film distribution out of Hollywood's control by putting a strict ban on any foreign involvement in China's film distribution, regarding it as critical to autonomy, while allowing the domestic sector to become a stronger competitor (Brent, 2000). Yet, how long that last barrier could be sustained amid the latest cascade of concessions to Hollywood is hard to project. Some predict that restrictions on foreign investment in Chinese film distribution will be lifted within the next five years (Brent, 2003). Hollywood has spared no efforts to increase the import quota and end the local distribution monopoly. In Disney's 1999 negotiations with the Chinese government, the studio argued that increasing the number of distributors of US films would benefit the Chinese film industry through enhanced expertise in marketing. In 2003, the Huaxia Film Distribution Co. was established as China's second distributor of imported films, ending China Film's fifty-year monopoly with distribution of *Terminator 3* ('New Company', 2003). A joint venture of nineteen enterprises, the new company may distribute imported films, but not import them directly ('No More', 2003). According to a senior executive of the second distributing company, with the introduction of competition, the new company and China Film will both put more emphasis on attracting audiences and maximising revenues, thereby supposedly enhancing Chinese theatres and the domestic film industry.

This fits Hollywood's desires for an improved distribution structure and handing over more power to warlocks (Markham-Smith, 2001). Valenti has welcomed the reforms, though he also expressed reservations, because the future remains unclear (Lyman, 2002a). Yet, the world seems to be approximating the promising picture he depicted for the Senate: 'Although China is now a small market for the MPAA member companies ... We believe over time it will become a most alluring and expanded marketplace' (quoted in 'Valenti Urged', 2000).

China's theatrical infrastructure has been largely underdeveloped, with a very low screen:population ratio of one screen per 122,000 people, as compared to one screen per 8,600 people in the US. Most of its cinemas are unwelcoming to potential moviegoers. Hollywood has long eyed the Chinese exhibition market agnuopically ('Valenti Supports', 1999). At the annual CineAsia Film Exhibitors Convention in 1997, Valenti publicised Hollywood's wish to join with partners 'throughout Asia, especially in China' in building 'modern cinema auditoriums' to accommodate the growing number of Asian moviegoers with an 'epic viewing' experience unavailable at home (Valenti, 1997). Yet, the Chinese government did not lift the ban on foreign investment in Chinese cinemas until the 1999 WTO agreement. Peter Dobson from WBIT remarked that China 'is just sitting there waiting for the taking' (quoted in 'D'Allesandro and Goldsmith', 2000). In 1999, after sensing a shift in the policy climate, WBIT undertook warlock investigations of the film audience's composition, taste and consumption level and feasible sites in high-traffic commercial areas of Shanghai (Lyman, 2002a). Talks followed with local cinemas about potential partnerships (Chen, 2003). WBIT worked with Shanghai Paradise, an active and successful participant in distribution and exhibition in Shanghai and neighbouring provinces. It owned one of China's largest theatre chain of 57 cinemas and developed a nine-screen, 1,398-seat multiplex in Shanghai, which opened in 2002. After much anxious waiting, the partnership was finally approved by the Chinese government, and the theatre, originally named Shanghai Paradise Film City, was renamed Shanghai Paradise Warner Cinema City in 2003, with its ownership split 51–49 per cent between Shanghai Paradise and WBIT (Rong and Xu, 2003). The two partners plan to offer renovation, engineering technologies and management-training programmes to Chinese multiplex cinemas. WBIT management will be involved in the operation of the new theatre and maintain or upgrade it on a yearly basis in accordance with its own standards. More importantly, it will promote and manage its own films, as demonstrated in the release of *Matrix II*. The new joint-venture theatre obtained exclusive screening rights for the film's China 2003 premiere to coincide with the site's official renaming and opening ceremony, one week earlier than the film's nationwide release (Chen, 2003). Chinese industry insiders believe that WBIT wishes to cultivate the growing movie audience, exert increasing pressure to import more Hollywood films to fill the screens and eventually dominate distribution (Rong and Xu, 2003). Warner Bros. sees this as a major strategic step towards long-term goals in China, rather than an immediate source of financial return (Lyman, 2002a). For now, the idea is to establish a cinema chain in Shanghai, the single largest film market in China, which has grown at a steady annual rate of 15 per cent in recent years. The company is selecting potential sites for a second multiplex in Shanghai as well as other cities (Chen, 2003). In 2004, WBIT announced it would construct thirty multiplexes across the country in shopping malls (Jones, 2004). Plans suggest a thousand new multiplexes by 2006 (Rosenberg, 2003: 44).

The latest change in governmental policy, announced in 2003 with effect from 2004, raised the cap on foreign investment share in Chinese cinema to 75 per cent in seven major Chinese cities on an 'experimental' basis. It forbids any foreign company to set up cinema chains or be the sole investor in a Chinese cinema (Wang, 2003; Brown, 2003). The first implementation of the new ruling granted WBIT a 51 per cent stake in a joint venture with Shanghai United Circuit for an eight-screen multiplex scheduled to open in 2004 in Nanjing. WBIT's majority share with the same partnership for a ten-screen multiplex in Wuhan awaits government approval (Groves, 2004). The first Western investor allowed majority ownership in a Chinese cinema, WBIT has embarked on a more ambitious scheme for the territory, engaging with different partners. In early 2004, WBIT reached a deal in principle with Guangzhou Performance Co. to invest an estimated US$30 million to build between eight and ten state-of-the-art multiplexes in southern China in the next several years (Ludemann, 2004). More significantly, WBIT signed a management and licensing deal with the Chinese real-estate company Dalian Wanda Group to build thirty multiplexes in shopping malls across China by 2006 (Sun, 2004). According to the deal, Wanda Group will invest in the construction, while WBIT will provide technical support as well as operate and manage the cinemas; and WBIT has the option to take 51 per cent equity in any of those venues at a time of its choosing (Sun, 2004; Groves, 2004). So far, fifteen sites have been chosen. Provisionally named Warner Wanda Cinemas, the chain reportedly will feature the Warner Bros. shield and use the studio's Looney Tunes characters (Jones, 2004). WBIT's new breakthrough will probably usher in other major Hollywood exhibitors, and Loews has been evaluating the feasibility of entering the alluring Chinese market (Groves, 2004).

This new relaxation in exhibition policy appears to be a bigger concession than Hollywood had expected. Even prior to China's formal accession to the WTO, studio executives reasoned that the rationale behind a more accommodating policy was officials' realisation that a steady flow of US films and greater foreign control of theatres would encourage investment and rejuvenate Chinese cinema. Jim Burk, UCI's Executive Vice-President, remarked that market access for US films would be a major incentive for his company to explore business opportunities in China, because 'ultimately there will be a market in China; it's a matter of timing' (quoted in Groves, 2000a: 7). Official figures state that the industry takes US$120 million a year in receipts, which Hollywood projections suggest can increase fifteen times by 2015 (Rosenberg, 2003: 28).

The US has also sought entry to TV. Both Disney and Fox have altered programming to satisfy the government. Murdoch removed the BBC from Star TV in 1994, because it angered officials by reporting human-rights violations. He was rewarded with a cable station in Guangdong. In 2001, his son James, who happened to be in charge of Star TV through one of those meritocratic processes that characterise his father's business, attacked the state's bitter foe, the Falun Gong, and criticised Western media assaults on human rights in China (Mike Wayne, 2003: 85). And Eisner met with officials to apologise for the raft of anti-PRC films from his company (Sakr, 2001: 83). When business leeches support state socialism, more unearned income must be nearby. The proximity of capital to surveillance is illuminated once more, however accidentally. So what alternatives actually exist?

Alternatives

> It is no longer Bollywood Vs Hollywood. It is now an era of co-existence, it is Bollywood and Hollywood.
>
> (Vikramjit Roy, Columbia TriStar, quoted in Gupta, 2003)

While advocacy activities strengthen both popular praise and formal political support for Hollywood's domestic and international hegemony, rival national and pan-regional campaigns support the promotion and distribution systems that control the NICL. For example, the National Screen Institute of Canada joined with Toronto-based Cultural Enterprises International to launch a 'Going To Market' programme aimed at 'increasing the marketing and deal-making savvy of Canadian producers [and] to set Canadian writers, directors and producers above the crowd at international markets ... through specific, festival-related intelligence' (Binning, 1999a). Canadian marketers have also sought out 'Hispanic Canadians' through the Toronto-based Hispano-American Film Festival, an advocacy venue for Latino-Canadian, Latin American and Spanish films (Dinoff, 2003).

As the 1990s saw decreased export figures (Finney, 1996: 145, 140), national cinemas in Europe sought policies to bolster distribution and marketing. We saw in Chapters 1 and 3 that France, the US' perennial foe in the GATT and the WTO over cultural protection and a (flawed) symbol of hope against US cultural and, latterly, military imperialism, offers distributors financial and tax incentives to purchase local films and facilitate their release, provided that full liability is taken and the funds actually go to ensure circulation within a specified time. But the top-ten distributors in France are all US-owned. Germany, another critic of US hegemony, offers interest-free loans to aid financing, distributing, copying and advertising, and there are also municipal mechanisms in place. Italy provides 'soft loans' to assist local distribution and overseas penetration. Britain has not given as much assistance as other European countries. Half of the sixty-nine films produced there in 1994 had still never been screened two years later. The Spanish government has begun a number of initiatives with an eye towards the elimination of the EU exhibition quota system, including a programme of subsidies to Spanish filmmakers and another to promote Spanish and Latin American co-productions. The plan for the Audiovisual Development and Promotion of Cinematography rewards partnerships with commercially oriented projects like Ibermedia, a fund created by Iberomericana de Chile to support co-productions across the Spanish-speaking world (KPMG, 1996: 68–69, 87, 138; Finney, 1996: 146; 'España Promocionará', 2000). In 2003, British cinema's share of the local market was 9.5 per cent, but Hollywood majors distributed all but 0.4 per cent of these, including *Love Actually* and *Johnny English* (Peter Howitt, 2003), released by Universal/United International Pictures (UIP), *Calendar Girls* (Nigel Cole, 2003) by Buena Vista, *S Club Seeing Double* (Nigel Dick, 2003) by Columbia TriStar, and *Nicholas Nickelby* (Douglas McGrath, 2002) by UA/Fox (Dawtrey, 2003). In Spain, Disney's local producer and distributor BVI Spain released *Football Days* (David Serrano, 2003), *Carmen* (Vicente Aranda, 2003), *La Fiesta* (Carlos Villaverde, 2003) and *Fourth Floor* (Antonio Mercero, 2003), which collectively grossed US$27 million in 2003.

Titanic drew attention to a phenomenon that had been quietly developing over a decade – a coalition of studios, in this case Paramount and Fox, that split national and global distribution (European Audiovisual Observatory, 1998). Regional alliances have offered advocacy marketing and funding for pan-European distribution. This was recognised as necessary across the then European Economic Community thirty years ago (Hunnings, 1972), but it took the rise of a culturalist mission, along with the new significance of TIS, for it to be realised programmatically via the blend of internal liberalism and external protection offered by the 1989 Directive on Broadcasting, the 1992 Maastricht Treaty and the 1997 Amsterdam Treaty (Ó Siochrú et al., 2002: 61–62). European Film Promotion (EFP), for example, was founded in 1997 to help sell European cinema in the international audiovisual market. It comprises twenty promotion and export organisations from eighteen European countries,[2] with headquarters in Hamburg provided by the German Federal Government Commissioner for Cultural Affairs and the Media. Its major activity so far has been a road show called 'Shooting Stars', in which new directors and actors from member countries travel to international film festivals, from Berlin to Pusan, to show the diversity of film production across Europe and promote their own work and careers through exposure to the international press and buyers.

Backing the EFP alliance is the MEDIA programme, as we saw in Chapter 3, which was launched during the early 1990s with the aim of making European film production regionally cohesive in the interests of profitability, while also being responsive to local cultures – an attempt to blend commerce and culture through the exchange of media within the EU across new forms of distribution, rather than via international co-production. The first five years saw annual funding below the production costs of a Hollywood blockbuster. The more substantial MEDIA II (US$405 million) ran from 1995 to 2000, adding a particular focus on distribution, development and training plus the global circulation of European texts. As in the case of the first MEDIA, highbrow production was privileged and successful films tended only to travel within their linguistic community of origin, unlike their Hollywood rivals. MEDIA III (MEDIA Plus) aimed at similar interventions. Its US$355 million budget is to stimulate 300,000 new jobs in the EU audiovisual sector between 2001 and 2005 through a link between market success and public subvention, alongside e-Europe, an Internet initiative (Theiler, 1999: 570–71, 576; 'European Commissioner', 1999; Stern, 1999 and 1999–2000). In 2004, the EU limits to members' capacity to link film subsidies to national production were set to increase, adding to a market incentive (Johnson and Dombey, 2004).

In Asia, a regional alliance with a different structure but similar goals has formed through the work of the Network for the Promotion of Asia-Pacific Cinema (NETPAC)[3] (www.pacific.net.sg/siff and www.asianfilms.org). NETPAC began in 1994 as a series of conferences supported in part by UNESCO, which helped build its network of participants and establish Asian Film Centres around the world. It includes critics, filmmakers, festival organisers and curators, distributors, exhibitors and film educators, and helps new directors promote their work in the international audiovisual market. NETPAC participates in festivals and conferences in India, Japan, Hawaii, Rotterdam, Singapore, the Philippines and Korea. While it designs educational materials and coordinates non-commercial international exchange to raise awareness of pan-Asian work (in effect, a counter-curriculum to global Hollywood's), NETPAC also conducts promotional and advocacy marketing through such programmes as 'The Asian Film Discovery Selection', which markets packages of Asian films using a single topic or theme (e.g. Asian women directors, Asian documentaries and Asian youth cinema).

Thai industry representatives have also formed GMT Entertainment to market Thai films at the major festivals in the US, France and Italy (Ywin, 2003). When Thai cinephiles celebrated the fact that *Beautiful Boxer* (Ekachai Uekrongtham, 2003) bested US rivals for high revenue in December 2003, they weighed the fact that, unlike previous local successes, it had been distributed by a subsidiary of 20th Century-Fox (Shackleton, 2003). And India's National Film Development Corporation, which promotes entertainment exports, initiated its 'Film Bazaar' programme to market Indian movies in Australia, Mauritius, Malaysia, China, Japan, South America and countries from the former USSR (Dey, 2003). The diasporic South Asian audience encouraged Sony Entertainment Television to begin targeting Bollywood fans based in the US from 1999, and Fox started distributing Bollywood in India (Pendakur, 2003: 44; Kripalani and Grover, 2002). And Singapore is seeking to transform its traditional brokerage services into a tightly targeted niche in digital cinema distribution, acting as a teleporting entrepôt between Hollywood and Asia, with films sent to a central digital hub where dubbing, subtitling and other forms of customisation can be undertaken prior to 'release' (Chellam, 2003).

All the above efforts to sustain state-sponsored, public service or commercial programmes have funded distribution outside and across Hollywood's oligopoly, primarily targeting financial and technical aid to small domestic producers. However, as neoliberal policy menaces public funding, the traditional political safeguards for production and distribution of undercapitalised film projects are disappearing, marking a shift to dependence on private funds from investment capitalists.

When financial capital takes over the bookkeeping, as in Hollywood, this augments the power of large commercial distributors, because banks see distributors who offer a slate of films as better bets than the small film producer who comes with a one-off project (the reverse of traditional public-funding criteria). When the money that used to come from public programmes evaporates, textual power shifts to distributors. As we have seen, they translate the banks' pressure to meet the numbers into market criteria for funding films. As one Canadian investor put it: 'distributors are the cash cows, they pay the loans' (Binning, 1999a). Independent projects, already undercapitalised and lacking equity, lose out.

The abiding logic of the EU's audiovisual policy is now commercial and profit-oriented, clearly favouring existing large concerns. Viviane Reding, the key European Commissioner, proclaimed that MEDIA Plus would ensure 'European audiovisual production which no longer relies on its inventiveness and originality, reflecting our cultural diversity, but sets out resolutely to win over European audiences and the rest of the world'. The tactic was clearly a concentration on film distribution and marketing rather than production (Theiler, 1999: 570–71, 576; 'European Commissioner', 1999; Reding quoted in 'Circulation', 1999; Stern, 1999 and 1999–2000).

This push to displace, or at least synchronise, public-sector investment and distribution with large-scale commercial projects encouraged several EU members, such as Spain (where domestic films in 2000 made up about 9 per cent of theatrical exhibition) to seek a greater share of private investment for domestic cinema and international co-production. The trade group Federación de Asociaciones de Productores Audiovisuales de España (FAPAE) and the multinational telecommunication and entertainment conglomerate Telefónica have formed alliances with over one hundred media businesses across Latin America and Spain to carry out trade talks on Iberoamerican audiovisual co-production, where a major goal is finding strategies to reach Spanish speakers living in the US. The orientation of this group was reflected in a Brazilian marketer's comment: 'we must not end up as we always do, by attacking the major Hollywood distributors. It's better to learn from them, not attack them' (quoted in 'Distribuidores Apuntan', 2000).

Conclusion

'High risk is only in the minds of people. Everybody covers investment by selling. And when you hit the bull's eye, profits can be as high as 500 per cent,' says Sanjay Bhattacharya, vice-president, UTV Motion Pictures [Bollywood]. ... If Bollywood can manage that, multi-billion dollar Hollywood may yet find true and tough competition.

(Shankar Aiyer, 2000)

For U.S. audiences, the mean, green title character in Universal Pictures' new film 'Dr Seuss' How the Grinch Stole Christmas' needs no introduction. But outside the U.S., mention of the Grinch often elicits a 'Who?' – and they're not talking about the residents of Whoville.

(Bruce Orwall, 2000)

We have raised a number of questions that need to be historicised, interpreted and criticised by screen studies as a core part of its labours. This chapter has shown how solidarity around commercial interests is cultivated and reproduced through the continuing and extensive business relations of consumer goods and service companies, the distribution oligopoly and a myriad of marketing operations. That relation is so robust that it creates a value system of its own, in which the quality of a film, apart from technical questions, is determined by commercial potential and marketability, what Wyatt (1994) calls the 'look, hook, and book'. This value system is carried through the nexus of pre-production, production, distribution and exhibition from our Introduction's diagrams. The distribution oligopoly necessitates the enrichment and legitimacy of marketing and extends the marketing bureaucracy throughout the NICL. It ensures a preponderance of commercialised texts in the cultural curriculum and exposure to commercial signs in social space. In dim contrast, people's preferences in global Hollywood, whether popular or intellectual interpretations of a film's value, barely influence what gets screened (less what gets made) via the figure of the audience, a construct built from, and known through, the institutional discourses of the state, the academy and the film industry.

If VNU is an indication of things to come, consumer surveillance will follow the trend towards greater concentration of corporate control over the infrastructure of consumption. Moviefone, MovieTickets and Fandango are talking about merging, VNU is buying up smaller research firms and distributors are destabilising movie-sharing technologies like the ReplayTV 4000 with egregious lawsuits. With its rapacious appetite for 'knowing' filmgoers, the industry's construction of audiences will continue to be ascendant, absorbing much of the depoliticised discourse of active audiences as well as a deracinated vision of the globe-trotting, deal-making citizen. These are fictive marketplace citizens, whose labours of interpretation, judgment and enjoyment are exploited without much contest (so far) in the informational labour market created and regulated by consumer research in the service of global Hollywood. With this in mind, we draw attention again to integrated marketing that depends on research that tracks filmgoing, consumer tastes, television viewing, Internet use, financial information, whereabouts, conduct and faith. These surveillance capabilities are poised to converge with recent technological innovations in digital telecommunication film and television delivery. They embody the DEM, but as a tool of control rather than critique. Whereas the state and critics see the audience as a dope in need of protection, marketers view it as a dope in need of exploitation. The result is a regime of surveillance that produces the GEM as a negative political reaction and the DEM as a negative psychic one. In each case, the audience is a drastically overextended signifier, onto which are projected fantasies of consumption. TiVo, OTX and HSX (the dead labour of active audiences?) are just beginning to experiment with new modes of real-time tracking of audiences over the Internet (the living labour of audiences made even more productive for capital).

When digital film delivery arrives, filmgoers should expect the industry to alter images surreptitiously for product and commercial placement, which sport fans exposed to digital inserts on televised events already see, and as drivers passing Alaris billboards in California may have noticed. In this scenario, filmgoers will view scenes with digitally placed brands, retail signage and other 'brandable' features in the background that can be assigned to fit viewing locations, targeting specific places with commercials for local retailers. The active-audience member will walk out of the cinema and encounter a shop or brand that had just appeared in a film, and, in marketers' dreams, be disposed to buy something (of course, this will be touted in public as the voluntary action of an independent mind, but understood privately as 'herd behaviour').

As long as filmgoers' cultural citizenship is represented through the marketers' vision of audiences – and the franchise of one dollar, one vote – this is bound to happen. For those who question the influence of marketing on the movies, not to mention the commercialisation of everything, this forecast is appalling. The *next* question is whether marketing and audience-bearing discourses will continue to influence the way movies are made. The answer has a lot to do with how we imagine the society we want to live in.

This should be an abiding lesson for screen studies: the medium's promiscuity points every day and in every way towards social inequalities. The screen is three things, all at once: a *recorder* of reality (the unstaged pro-filmic event); a *manufacturer* of reality (the staged and edited event); and *part of* reality (watching film as a social event on a Saturday night, a protest event over sexual, racial or religious stereotyping, or a site in which one's patterns of desire are analysed). The DEM and the GEM apply to both citizen and consumer – audience categories that are as real and purposive, unfortunately, as the people whose lives they purport to describe, even as they draw them into Hollywood's division of labour. DEM and GEM are probably invincible, so fixed are they at the centre of public, academic, media and governmental discourse. But they can at least be read for what they are – signs of activity in search of control, not sources of empirical truth.

Notes

1   Thanks to Colleen Petruzzi, Senior Account Executive at Universal Music and Video Distribution, for these insights.

2   EFP member organisations are the Austrian Film Commission, British Council, Danish Film Institute, Export-Union des Deutschen Films, Film Fund Luxembourg, Finnish Film Foundation, Flanders Image, Greek Film Centre, Holland Film, Icelandic Film Fund, Instituto de Cine (ICAA) Spain, Instituto do Cinema, Audiovisual E Multimédia (ICAM) Portugal, Irish Film Board, Italia Cinema – Italian Cinema Promotion Agency, Norwegian Film Institute, Swedish Film Institute, Swiss Film Center, Unifrance Film International and Wallonie-Bruxelles Images.

3   NETPAC includes the following participants: Alpha Film (Turkey), Asia Pacific Media Center-Annenberg Center at the University of Southern California, Asian Film Centre (Sri Lanka), China Film Import & Export Corporation, Choijiv Nergui (Mongolia), *Cinemaya: The Asian Film Quarterly*, New Delhi, *Daily News* newspaper (Thailand), Export & Film Promotion (Pakistan), Films from the South Film Festival (Norway), Fribourg International Film Festival (Switzerland), Hong Kong Arts Center, International Film Festival Rotterdam, International Forum for New Cinema (Germany), Japan Film Library Council, Kelab Seni Filem Malaysia, Korean Motion Picture Corporation, Melbourne International Film Festival, Mowelfund Film Institute (Manila), Protishabda Alternative Communication

Center (Bangladesh), Pusan International Film Festival (South Korea), Singapore International Film Festival, Sub-Commission on the Arts (Philippines), Taiwan Film Center, The Japan Foundation ASEAN Cultural Center, Vietnam Cinema Association and the Vietnam Cinema Department.

Conclusion

At the end of 50 years journeying the American Motion Picture Industry stood on a mountaintop from which the beacon of its silver screen was sending rays of light and color and joy into every corner of the earth.

(Will Hays, 1938, quoted in Grantham, 2000: 1)

What's the point of saying no to America's nuclear ships when we've said yes, a thousand times yes, to the Trojan Horse of American Culture, dragging it through our city gates into our very lounge-rooms. MGM is mightier than the CIA. . . . We are, all of us, little by little, becoming ventriloquial dolls for another society. We are losing our authenticity, our originality, and becoming echoes.

(*Australian Weekend Magazine*, quoted in Pendakur, 1990: 16–17)

The Washington Family, the large painting which Edward Savage completed in Philadelphia in 1796, aptly captured Washington's vision for the seat of empire. In it the family sits around a map of the federal city with the wide majestic Potomac River behind them. Washington rests his arm on the shoulder of young George Washington Parke Custis. The boy, symbolic of the next generation, rests his hand on the globe.

(Kenneth Bowling, 1991: 208)

While *How the Grinch Stole Christmas* dominated US theatres in late 2000, PRC *flâneurs* could already buy pirated dubbed or subtitled DVD versions of *Gui-jingling* for US$1.20 apiece – and pirated copies of the government's anti-corruption video, *Life and Death Choice*. Both discs were playable on technology made in state-owned factories. Illegal use of the format became popular after pirated copies of *Titanic* outsold the more expensive legal ones – sales of 25 million versus 300,000 (Smith, 2000a). The same week as the *Grinch*'s theft, SAG announced that actors' earnings for 1999 had gone up by just 1.3 per cent on the previous year, despite the booming US economy and the extraordinary amounts paid to big stars (Kiefer, 2000). Across town, two other monetary deals were revealed. The MPAA released a study showing that copyright contributed more to the US economy in 1999 than any other industrial sector, with

US$79.65 billion in overseas sales (McClintock, 2000a). And with copyright on its Mouse about to expire, Disney gave Trent Lott money for his re-election on the very day that the then Republican Congressional leader sponsored a bill extending its copyright of the rodent by another twenty years (Bromley, 1999). Meanwhile, Time Warner was busy issuing cease-and-desist orders against young fans of the *Harry Potter* books around the world who had the gall to create Web pages without obtaining permission from the rights holders, who were looking forward to a profitable film about the young hero's gripping adventures (Ingram, 2001). We shall have more on *Harry Potter* later.

The following northern spring, just days after attending an advance press screening of *Pearl Harbor* in Manhattan, one of us entered Shenzen and found DVDs of the film on sale there. Returning to New York, he was pulled aside by an alert customs official and hailed as someone in 'a group'. Our colleague assumed this meant a tourist group, but the officer meant a rock band. That assumption made our author a suspect person in copyright terms, and he had to be spoken to about piracy violations at some length in a back room, then shown DVDs of live performances that he was told had been donated to US customs by 'groups' in return for the lightest of inspections for drugs.

The US Customs Service was organising people into obedience in one frame of this story, and encouraging/condoning illegality in another. Each tendency was a corollary of entering world capitalism's groping embrace, and duelling with the role of government in the process. These are essentially political and economic stresses deriving from globalisation, a tendency that was dramatised by the blend of risk and consumerism that emerged from 9/11 and the US government's subsequent drive 'to help unleash the productive potential of individuals in all nations' as an antidote to poverty-driven radicalism (The White House, 2002). This little series of anecdotes encapsulates the complex intersection of law, the state and labour in global Hollywood.

Globalisation's significance for the screen varies between concerns over US-dominated cultural flow, as per cultural imperialism, the international spread of capitalistic production and conglomerates via the NICL, and attempts to govern the chaotic, splintered circulation of signs across cultures. Ownership is concentrated in a diminishing number of increasingly large corporations. What used to be nationally dominated markets for terrestrial television have undergone vast changes. Companies like Disney are in a position to produce films, promote them across a variety of subsidiaries, screen them on an owned network, and generate television replicas – not to mention CDs, reading material, toys and branded apparel – and all with an eye to external profits (but they may cower in the face of Marguerite Duras' condemnation of EuroDisney as a 'cultural Chernobyl') (McChesney, 1999: 4; Duras quoted in Van Maanen, 1992: 26). All of this is purposive, much of it is facilitated by (formally) democratically accountable politicians, and none of it is 'necessary'. It can be reversed or changed.

As we have noted, some theorists are sanguine about such developments, stressing the skill of audiences in negotiating texts, or offering multicultural business strategies, themselves a segment of US transnationalism extending its domain. Others focus on the direction of multinational finance, that Hollywood studios have recently been foreign-owned and are increasingly beholden to cross-cultural audiences for their success. But at the same time as this apparent diversity appears, the means of communication, association and political representation are converging (Jacka, 1992: 5, 2; Jameson, 1991: xiv–xv; Reeves, 1993: 36, 62; Sreberny-Mohammadi, 1996: 3–8). Yanqui late-night talk-show host Jay Leno's mid-1990s promotional spot for NBC's pan-European Super Channel promised 'to ruin your culture just like we ruined our own' – this from the man who slavishly supported the candidacy of Mr Shriver (aka Arnold Schwarzenegger) for the Governorship of California in 2003. Cultural-imperialism discourse is now so commonsensical and so connected to the US as a political entity that it has become material for stand-up, which in turn has become a site of politics.

Thankfully, counter-power to the Washington Consensus is always at work. Textiles, shipping and agriculture remain massively subsidised across the world. The US, supposedly a poster-child for free trade and true competition, has hundreds of anti-dumping measures aimed at blocking imports where prices have been 'unfairly' set, and maintains a semi-secret deal with Japan to restrict steel sales, while the EU remains firm in its refusal to import genetically modified beef. Environmentalists, trade unions and consumer groups have problematised globalisation as defined by neoliberal *nostrums*. The Seattle 1999, Washington 2000, Genoa 2001 and Miami 2003 actions illustrated as much. All of this leads the *Economist*, a key business advocacy voice, to admit that 'Globalization is not irreversible' ('Storm over Globalization', 1999: 15–16).

Bourdieu postulates a model of world culture that continues the bipolarity of the Cold War, if without its political ramifications, military corollaries and economic isolations. His vision of the struggle for world culture pits the US against France – *laissez-faire* dogma juxtaposed against cultural nationalism. This Enlightenment conflict between anomic monads and collective identities sets bourgeois individualism against collaboration, with reincarnations of the Depression and Sovietism hanging over each model. Bourdieu calls for a pre-Marxist, Hegelian way through the debate, a democratic mode that favours the state neither as an aid to capital accumulation nor as totalitarian, but as the expression of a popular will that contemplates itself collectively rather than atomistically, and acts under the sign of a general interest rather than singular egotism (Bourdieu, 1999: 20). That struggle – of structure and agency, of capital and state intricated in the production and symbolism of culture – requires analysis via political economy mixed with cultural studies.

In this conclusion, we enact these conflicts in key areas:

- cultural-policy reform in the name of citizens, not consumers
- labour reform in the name of workers, not corporations
- regional production in the name of citizens, not corporations
- copyright reform in the name of audiences, not producers
- marketing reform in the name of audiences, not producers; and
- a finale, in keeping with the remit of any sequel.

Cultural-Policy Reform

Equipped with the theoretical modifications and political and historical reminders from Chapter 1, we can begin to articulate cultural policy within cultural-imperialism critique. First, there is a need to preserve a local infrastructure that encourages public debate about national culture, whether in the name of a regressive, liberatory or invented heritage – as a space for locally conducted and stimulated talk and disagreement (Baker, 2000). In addition, attention must shift from an exclusive focus on textuality and national identity to the NICL, as we explore cultural work, mediation and customisation. It is clear that the contradictory nature of ideas-in-trade may not make for a docile cultural workforce, and that any policy we articulate will have to stand up against pressure from cultural MNCs for national cultural labour markets that conform to the NICL.

Cultural leftists face a critical dilemma. In an era of globalised film and television, the idea that audiovisual spaces should be accountable to local viewers as well as far-distant shareholders is a powerful one. But how much can be expected from citizenship and consumer ideals when for the first time:

- trade between corporations exceeds that between states
- deregulation sees monopoly capital converging and collaborating
- screen texts are designed to transcend linguistic and other cultural boundaries
- textual diversity is a myth
- cultural production is not independent of the state; and
- many of us live in societies that deny or limit our citizenship and consumption claims?

Does this mean that citizenship and consumption have become irrelevant in discussing accountability, sovereignty and democracy, because of the culture industries? No, for recent developments are not so much turns away from cultural policy in favour of industry policy, but continuities with what has always been a blend of culture with commerce (Goldsmith and O'Regan, 2002: 5).

In rethinking the links between citizen, consumer and labour, cultural policy must remove the conditions that lead marketers to deepen, and hide, their complicity with major distributors and their corporate parents. This necessitates enfranchising the desires and needs of filmmakers, filmgoers and others, and reducing the representational authority of major distributors, large marketing firms, banks and studio executives. We can imagine, for example, cultural workers allying with marketing to amplify the presence of labour in public discourse, to bring attention to working conditions and the process of alienation, and to revitalise the relation between filmmaking and filmgoing. Such a policy converts the currently one-way surveillance of filmgoers into a mode of sociality that raises awareness of the differences between values invested by film workers in making movies and values that people derive from watching them. A greater ethical regard for each constituency's needs, values and desires could flow from this re-functioning of film marketing and its surveillance operations. It has the potential to end differences between the institutional identities of producer and consumer, offering instead a vision of culture work as interdependent efforts of production, distribution and consumption that bring value and meaning into the world. Such a policy would have to ensure some level of subsidy and legal freedom to organise new institutions, both domestically and through international networks.

When the US government (2000) offered the WTO a strategy for liberalising the screen, it actually proposed some limits to untrammelled commerce. This sop to critics was based on measures in the GATT and the GATS 'necessary to protect public morals'. Hollywood showed a similar taste for dispensing fat-free human kindness milk when the studios won a case in the Mexican Supreme Court in 2000 against a Federal Film Law provision that required subtitles rather than dubbing for feature imports, on the basis that this discriminated against the 20 million Mexicans who do not read because of age, sight or literacy issues (Tegel, 2000). This concern for the audience takes us back to where we began in the Introduction and the moral panics and panaceas conjured up by silent-cinema critics, Depression-era Payne Fund sociologists and post-war ethnographers that grew into the positivistic reign of psychologists and communications scholars, via the DEM, and cultural mavens, via the GEM.

But as we saw in Chapter 3, culture has a moral authority that provides terrain for struggle against neoliberalism. It is ambivalent space for the left to occupy, given connections between 'public morals' and religion/superstition, oppression of women, racism, homophobia and limits to free expression. But it is also space to be grabbed, as in the case of ethical debates that have ensued recently over limits to patents and the affordability and availability of HIV/AIDS drugs. Ethical issues such as fair use, the surveillance of screen audiences and fair-trade comparability of wages for screen workers are all questions that should be raised under the rubric of morality.

They alert us to the more sinister aspects of the 'Third Way', that polite amalgam of social conscience and pro-capitalist sentiment that moderates its redistributive conservatism with cultural liberalism and a commitment to the investment in human capital beloved of 'progressive' neoliberals (Burbach, 2001: 148). Whereas culture has frequently permitted the South a certain political and social differentiation, the Third World has not been allocated a substantive role under the new arrangements that are tranforming the international political economy, beyond providing a kind of avant-garde anthropological laboratory for music, medication and minerals. For example, compliance with TRIPs diverts money away from basic needs and towards expensive computer equipment and costly bureaucrats with the skills and resources to evaluate and police copyright, trademarks and patents. This is in keeping with the deskilling of Hollywood and its reorchestration around managerialism rather than labour's creativity. In the mid-1980s, around 30 per cent of the industry's workforce was employed in administration. Today, the figure is close to 45 per cent (Parkes, 2002). This is not a creative revolution. It is a moment in the transformation of capital that sees financial and managerial intermediaries at the centre of control and employment. That suggests the need for labour reform in addition to the initiatives we have already outlined.

Since the WTO's 1997 decision denying Canada the right to protect local print media through limiting the importation of split-run magazines (McKercher, 2001), Canadian policy-makers have led efforts to create an international consensus on rules that would allow states to design policies to foster cultural diversity. In 1999, a coalition of Canadian civic organisations prepared the report *New Strategies for Culture and Trade: Canadian Culture in a Global World*, which recommended creating a New International Instrument on Cultural Diversity that would recognise trade exceptions for domestic policies that seek to ensure cultural diversity. In subsequent trade talks, the Canadian government refused to make commitments that would restrict its ability to achieve cultural diversity goals until this international instrument was secured. The Canadians and other culture ministries formed an International Network on Cultural Policy that met in Mexico (1999), Greece (2000) and Switzerland (2001) to exchange information regarding diversity initiatives (Goldsmith, 2002). These and other efforts led UNESCO to create a working group on cultural diversity, which culminated in the adaptation of a Declaration on Cultural Diversity in November 2001 (see below).

The Declaration links cultural rights to universal human rights through 'the possibility for all cultures to have access to the means of expression and dissemination'. To realise this, cultural goods must not be treated as 'mere commodities or consumer goods', because 'market forces alone cannot guarantee the preservation and promotion of cultural diversity'. International regulations must allow each state, through public and private partnerships, 'to define its cultural policy and to implement it through the means it considers fit, whether by operational support or appropriate regulations'. As such, the Declaration challenges neoliberalism, which has dominated free-trade initiatives. But it invokes aspects of citizenship that have tended to subordinate cultural difference and exclude non-citizens, under the guise of fostering cultural unity. For example, in stating that 'heritage in all its forms must be preserved, enhanced and handed on to future generations as a record of human experience and aspirations', the Declaration privileges heritage preservation over renewed historical understandings of how heritage has been used to subordinate minority groups and exclude non-citizens. As we saw in Chapter 3, the EU's cultural policies that promote a pan-European common culture based on a white colonial Christian heritage are examples of heritage in need of redefinition, not preservation. Also, in stating that 'policies for the inclusion and participation of all citizens are guarantees of social cohesion, the vitality of civil society and peace', the UNESCO Declaration links diversity to cohesion, which has also been a form of citizenship used to police rather than proliferate difference.

In a report commissioned and endorsed by the forty-four members of the COE, Tony Bennett presents a methodological approach to cultural citizenship that reconfigures previous conceptions based on homogenisation and cultural unity to one based on heterogeneity and cultural diversity. Rather than positioning cultural diversity as a subset of social-inclusion policies, Bennett argues that cultural policy should address the needs and demands of those who have experienced historical dispossession and support the cultural right to be different:

> what distinguishes the cultural perspectives of diasporic communities and indigenous peoples, for example, is less their demand for equal and inclusive cultural entitlements with all other members of society – although, this is of course, a legitimate aspect of both indigenous and diasporic aspiration – than the demand for the right to maintain and develop specific cultural practices that will function as the organising foci for cultural lives that are not centered on the notional mainstream of a nationally defined society.
>
> (Bennett, 2001: 17, 25)

While the UNESCO Declaration reflects a growing movement to incorporate cultural rights into international policy arenas, its function as a deliberative body intent on 'deepening the debate', 'exchanging information', 'involving civil society' and creating 'forums for dialogue between the public sector and the private sector', without legal force within international trade agreements, limits its effectiveness to combat neoliberal policies that continue to transform the legal arenas for cultural trade (www.unesco.org/culture/pluralism/diversity/html_eng/decl_en.shtml).

One way to incorporate these principles of cultural diversity within world trade fora is to link fundamental cultural rights to the international labour movement's efforts to include minimum labour standards in international trade agreements. Just as UNESCO connects cultural rights to human rights, as per the International Covenant on Economic, Social and Cultural Rights, international trade agreements could frame cultural diversity in terms of the human rights of cultural workers. Rather than focus cultural diversity principally on preserving cultural heritage or sovereignty, modern notions that do not account for the accelerating international circulation of peoples and cultures, diversity principles might take the form of rights to participate fully and fairly in the production of culture, with particular attention to cultural labourers who have been left outside the dominant category of the citsumer. Within the EU, this would focus cultural policy on creating opportunities for workers with affinities to the Arab, East Asian, Turkish, South Asian and African diasporas, to ethnic communities from new EU member countries from Eastern and South-Eastern Europe, and to religious minorities throughout Europe. Instantiated as cultural labour rights within international trade agreements, UNESCO's declared cultural diversity rights would begin an enforceable challenge to the NICL:

UNESCO UNIVERSAL DECLARATION ON CULTURAL DIVERSITY
IDENTITY, DIVERSITY AND PLURALISM
Article 1 – Cultural diversity: the common heritage of humanity
Culture takes diverse forms across time and space. This diversity is embodied in the uniqueness and plurality of the identities of the groups and societies making up humankind. As a source of exchange, innovation and creativity, cultural diversity is as necessary for humankind as biodiversity is for nature. In this sense, it is the common heritage of humanity and should be recognized and affirmed for the benefit of present and future generations.

Article 2 – From cultural diversity to cultural pluralism
In our increasingly diverse societies, it is essential to ensure harmonious interaction among people and groups with plural, varied and dynamic cultural identities as well as their willingness to live together. Policies for the inclusion and participation of all citizens are guarantees of social cohesion, the vitality of civil society and peace. Thus defined, cultural pluralism gives policy expression to the reality of cultural diversity. Indissociable from a democratic framework, cultural pluralism is conducive to cultural exchange and to the flourishing of creative capacities that sustain public life.

Article 3 – Cultural diversity as a factor in development
Cultural diversity widens the range of options open to everyone; it is one of the roots of development, understood not simply in terms of economic growth, but also as a means to achieve a more satisfactory intellectual, emotional, moral and spiritual existence.

CULTURAL DIVERSITY AND HUMAN RIGHTS
Article 4 – Human rights as guarantees of cultural diversity
The defense of cultural diversity is an ethical imperative, inseparable from respect for human dignity. It implies a commitment to human rights and fundamental freedoms, in particular the rights of persons belonging to minorities and those of indigenous peoples. No one may invoke cultural diversity to infringe upon human rights guaranteed by international law, nor to limit their scope.

Article 5 – Cultural rights as an enabling environment for cultural diversity
Cultural rights are an integral part of human rights, which are universal, indivisible and interdependent. The flourishing of creative diversity requires the full implementation of cultural rights as defined in Article 27 of the Universal Declaration of Human Rights and in Articles 13 and 15 of the International Covenant on Economic, Social and Cultural Rights. All persons should therefore be able to express themselves and to create and disseminate their work in the language of their choice, and particularly in their mother tongue; all persons should be entitled to quality education and training that fully respect their cultural identity; and all persons should be able to participate in the cultural life of their choice and conduct their own cultural practices, subject to respect for human rights and fundamental freedoms.

Article 6 – Towards access for all to cultural diversity
While ensuring the free flow of ideas by word and image, care should be exercised that all cultures can express themselves and make themselves known. Freedom of expression, media pluralism, multilingualism, equal access to art and to scientific and technological knowledge, including in digital form, and the possibility for all cultures to have access to the means of expression and dissemination are the guarantees of cultural diversity.

Article 7 – Cultural heritage as the wellspring of creativity
Creation draws on the roots of cultural tradition, but flourishes in contact with other cultures. For this reason, heritage in all its forms must be preserved, enhanced and handed on to future generations as a record of human experience and aspirations, so as to foster creativity in all its diversity and to inspire genuine dialogue among cultures.

Article 8 – Cultural goods and services: commodities of a unique kind
In the face of present-day economic and technological change, opening up vast prospects for creation and innovation, particular attention must be paid to the diversity of the supply of creative work, to due recognition of the rights of authors and artists and to the specificity of cultural goods and services which, as vectors of identity, values and meaning, must not be treated as mere commodities or consumer goods.

Article 9 – Cultural policies as catalysts of creativity

While ensuring the free circulation of ideas and works, cultural policies must create conditions conducive to the production and dissemination of diversified cultural goods and services through cultural industries that have the means to assert themselves at the local and global level. It is for each State, with due regard to its international obligations, to define its cultural policy and to implement it through the means it considers fit, whether by operational support or appropriate regulations.

CULTURAL DIVERSITY AND INTERNATIONAL SOLIDARITY

Article 10 – Strengthening capacities for creation and dissemination worldwide

In the face of current imbalances in flows and exchanges of cultural goods and services at the global level, it is necessary to reinforce international cooperation and solidarity aimed at enabling all countries, especially developing countries and countries in transition, to establish cultural industries that are viable and competitive at national and international level.

Article 11 – Building partnerships between the public sector, the private sector and civil society

Market forces alone cannot guarantee the preservation and promotion of cultural diversity, which is the key to sustainable human development. From this perspective, the pre-eminence of public policy, in partnership with the private sector and civil society, must be reaffirmed.

Article 12 – The role of UNESCO

UNESCO, by virtue of its mandate and functions, has the responsibility to:

(a) Promote the incorporation of the principles set out in the present Declaration into the development strategies drawn up within the various intergovernmental bodies;

(b) Serve as a reference point and a forum where States, international governmental and non-governmental organizations, civil society and the private sector may join together in elaborating concepts, objectives and policies in favour of cultural diversity;

(c) Pursue its activities in standard-setting, awareness-raising and capacity-building in the areas related to the present Declaration within its fields of competence;

(d) Facilitate the implementation of the Action Plan, the main lines of which are appended to the present Declaration.

SOURCE: www.unesco.org/culture/pluralism/diversity/html_eng/decl_en.shtml

Great care must be taken ensure industry compradores do not overdetermine cultural policy. George Yúdice (2000, 2002 and 2003) and García-Canclini

(2001) have elaborated alternative models of citizenship and consumption that improve on standard left-wing critiques of cultural imperialism (watching US drama will turn rural people around the world into Idaho potato farmers) and invectives about socially responsible shopping (purchasing environmentally sound toilet paper and free-range chicken will transform the world, one roll/wing at a time). Yúdice argues that it may no longer be possible to speak of citizenship and democracy without also considering consumption, by combining First World practices, such as juridical prosecution of discrimination in the private workplace, and Latin American ones – for example, the need to go beyond individual consumer choices in cultural politics to consider the collaboration of local groups, transnational businesses, financial institutions, media and non-governmental organisations.

Labour Reform

As we noted earlier, labour is relegated to the status of 'X-category inefficiency' in bourgeois economics, always already a problem because it costs money (and makes value, but that understanding is rejected). Labour is even more of a problem when it becomes self-consciously an 'it' – when workers have a political self-consciousness and organise themselves. But the stability, knowledge base and welfare offered by unions has been severely underestimated as a positive contributor to economic transformations in the cultural sector.

In the US, organised labour has supposedly been an endangered species since the 1980s – ready for fossilisation (White, 2001). Business leeches and their emissaries argue that high technology has rendered unions anachronistic. In 2000, with Internet workers happy to change employers regularly and the new technology empowering them to see a future in 'meritocracy' rather than 'seniority', this new flexibility was allegedly a great boon to all – so, down with collective bargaining and job security. Harris Miller, President of the Information Technology Association of America, proudly suggested that 'The philosophy is, Till death us do part – until I get a better offer' (quoted in Dreazen, 2000a). But many people in the high-technology industries saw cracks widen beneath their feet, reading the signs in Federal Reserve Chair Alan Greenspan's blunt remark that European and Japanese domestic investments in the 'New Economy' had not been as profitable as the US, where it is easy to hire and fire and there is minimal health insurance (Petras, 2000). Of course, in the wake of 9/11, the underlying cracks in revenue also began to appear with consequent effects on the 'no-collar' utopia (Ross, 2003). Nevertheless, the decline of collective bargaining and industry wage-setting, together with the rise in long-term employment, have militated powerfully against unions across industries. The screen sector's fetishised labour and project-based hiring present a post-Fordist model for the economy more generally (Saundry, 2001).

Union membership in the US has reached its highest level of the past two decades (265,000 new subscriptions in 1999), in part due to mergers that mimic the functions of capital. There are now 16.5 million unionists in the US (Dreazen, 2000b). Managerial high-technology people are organised (but not as unions) into the Association of Internet Professionals (AIP), a quasi-guild that includes executives as well as 'creatives' and freelancers. The Communication Workers of America (CWA) triumphed in 2000 over Verizon, the new Esperantish drag-name of Bell Atlantic, chosen to mark the company's emergence as part of the 'New Economy'. The very week that the drag-name was announced, CWA members compromised the magic by striking – and won their struggle in a fortnight. The CWA is looking to assist workers with Microsoft and Amazon.com as they deal with an employer sleight-of-hand that categorises them as temporary employees or independent contractors as a means of denying retirement and health benefits (Dreazen, 2000a; Amman, 2002). These brutal practices have seen Microsoft face a class-action lawsuit from its 6,000 temps (Greenhouse, 1999a). The Washington Alliance of Technological Workers and the CWA have fought for the right of Amazon.com workers to unionise. The company has retaliated by moving part of its customer services to Delhi and areas of the US with poorer conditions than its original Pacific Northwest home, where working life is satirised nightly by veteran ex-employee Mike Daisey, whose one-man comedy show always keeps a seat vacant for Amazon emperor Jeff Bezos (McNary, 2001; Gumbel, 2001; Preston, 2001; Amman, 2002). Meanwhile, the AFL-CIO has a Silicon Valley not-for-profit temp agency that offers healthcare coverage to workers, and has successfully pressed for the highest minimum-wage legislation in the country (double what had been paid) (Greenhouse, 1999b). And studies proliferate that the fantasy of cultural jobs substituting effectively for primary and secondary industry is often just that – a fiction (van den Besselaar, 1997). But for now, the workplace is frequently deterritorialised even when the work itself stays still, as the risk of dislocation stifles employees' ability to negotiate by threatened as much as actual departure (Collins, 2002).

The screen unions' numerical growth and willingness to strike during the dominance of Republican union-busting was a beacon through the 1980s. They stand today against virulent anti-union legislation in so-called 'right-to-work' states of the US, the appeal to capital of the NICL and pressure for workers to de-unionise in order to retain employment. (Industry analysts use the terms 'non-union or flexible-union territories outside of Hollywood' to refer to scab labour, noting cost reductions of up to 40 per cent for productions that evade unions.) SAG has 135,000 members across twenty-six national production sites, and the WGA represents 11,000 members. SAG, AFTRA and DGA obtained Internet jurisdiction in 2000. All these groups have important internal divisions between so-called 'talent' and 'craft', and between the heavily unionised (film and broadcast workers) and the non-union workforce (such as less well-paid, but increasingly more numerous, cable employees). Women and minorities remain proportionally under-represented and stuck in secondary labour markets. But these unions have a collective consciousness. T-shirts with crossed-out maple leaves and 'how 'bout some work, eh?' proliferate among disemployed workers in the Los Angeles screen sector (Ryan, 1999). FTAC Chair Jack Degovia said of the Canadian government and industry: 'They came after us. They got us. The effects companies in Silicon Valley are next' (quoted in Stroud, 1999). This may be the start of a major backlash against the NICL (Madigan, 1999b; Screen Actors Guild, 2000).

There are also indications of a growing internationalist sentiment among unions, as they start to mirror the globalism of capital: Los Angeles cooks visit Tokyo in a pan-Pacific labour action against a hotel conglomerate; French and German metalworkers organise collaboratively; Mexican farm labourers work with the US Farm Labour Organizing Committee against the importation of cut rates at a Mexican tomato-paste factory; and a Council of Ford Workers represents Mexican, Canadian and US labour interests. Such transnational labour networks are essential to ensure acceptable levels of worker control and affluence. And in 2000, there were major strikes in India, Argentina, Uruguay and South Africa against globalisation, the WTO and the IMF (Smithsimon, 1999; O'Brien, 2000a and b; Munck, 2000; Howard, 1995; Brecher et al., 2000: 105; Buckley, 2003; Frundt, 2000; Burbach, 2001: 145; Stevis and Boswell, 1997).

US unions joined the AFMA and MPAA in opposing cultural exemptions to the GATT, letting down their brothers and sisters in the European group of the International Federation of Actors, and adopted a neutral stance on NAFTA, other than IATSE worrying about a new Mexican studio (Wasko, 1998: 183–87). But certain film unions in Canada have shown international solidarity ('Solidarity', 2000; 'Defend', 1999), and the International Federation of Actors seeks parity of pay-scales (Grumiau, 1998). The venue for discussion of labour issues at a peak level remains vexed. Other parties to NAFTA would rather work through the ILO, which has stringent contract-labour standards. But embracing internationally agreed and democratic labour standards is, predictably, more than the Office of US Trade Representative (2001b) can stomach. The same struggles apply to dealings with the WTO and its links to labour (Hughes and Wilkinson, 1998). The North American Agreement on Labour Cooperation was supposed to police infringements of workers' rights under the parent agreement, but has been largely ineffectual. Rued by Hollywood union activists, this ultimately led to anti-NAFTA demonstrations, the first cross-union political actions in fifty years. But many activists despair of effective union radicalism and point to racial segregation as a problem in closed shops (Bacon, 1999; Everett, 1999; Wuliger, 2000; Malcolm, 2000). In 2000, a Union Network International was formed to bind together world screen workers across as many divisions as possible in order to deal with capital's mobility and government's impotence (International Labour Office, 2000a).

Even as producer Peter Sussman fetishised Canada's workers – 'like any labour pool it keeps cloning and breeding itself' (quoted in Kirkland and Buckley, 2001) – on the last day of the Clinton administration, the US Department of Commerce released a report on offshore filming. Secretary Norman Mineta gravely intoned that 'Runaway film production has affected thousands of workers in industries ranging from computer graphics to construction workers and caterers' (quoted in Gentile, 2001). The Democrats had presided over the most radical tranformation of the NICL imaginable, but even within that administration, labour's flame continued to smoulder.

To humanise the NICL, we need institutionalised labour standards that will maintain and develop the situation of workers across the global North and South. These core values and practices can ensure that skills and methods are easily transferable across sites, thereby promoting efficiency at the same time as they commit governments, unions and corporations to economic development at all points of both the commodity cycle and the world atlas. The ILO provides a good guide. Following Thomas I. Palley (2004: 23), we have adapted its fundamental Conventions, further adapting them ourselves to apply to screen culture:

- Freedom of association, guaranteeing the right to unionise without hindrance by the state, with direct links to major Northern unions that can aid with plans, finances and negotiations with Hollywood on the points below.
- Collective bargaining, prohibiting corporations setting up pseudo-unions that do their bidding, with the state offering mechanisms to encourage negotiations that also consider cultural specificity and localism in public incentives to offshore production.
- Elimination of forced and child labour, minimising environmental and health issues to do with the screen industries.
- Elimination of discrimination, ensuring equal pay for work of equal value and undermining the gendered exploitation of the NICL.

Regional Production

We saw in Chapter 3 how the 'Television Without Frontiers' directive deregulated national industries and fostered pan-European pay-TV conglomerates, filling Hollywood coffers at rates that far outpaced co-production treaty provisions. We also noted that while co-productions facilitated pan-European collaboration and distribution, they did so through exclusionary, art-house-centred boards that privileged artistic above-the-line talent without care for below-the-line labour standards or the openness of decision-making. Moreover, the existence of the NICL collapses the equation of the US with entertainment and Europe with education. The globalisation of cultural labour makes art cinema a 'Euro-American' genre in terms of sweat, finance, marketing and management (Lev, 1993). A seeming discontinuity with earlier concerns, when the EU had a primarily economic personality, is misleading: cultural sovereignty underpins concerns vis-à-vis the US, but so too does support for European monopoly capital and the larger states inside its own walls (Burgelman and Pauwels, 1992).

If we turn to other First World regions that have sought to parlay cultural policy into industry policy, we once more encounter the contingency of their success. Consider one of the least-polite incomplete sentences of 2002, uttered at a UCLA event by Mark Ordesky, President of First Line Pictures, about *The Lord of the Rings*: 'If a bunch of Kiwis can do it . . .' (quoted in Parkes, 2002). New Zealanders were immensely proud of the films, which they felt had put their country in the forefront of filmmaking, with the Labour government appointing a Minister in Charge of Lord of the Rings, funding studies of how it was 'Enhancing Brand New Zealand' (NZ Institute of Economic Research, 2002: vii) and spending nearly US$5 million refitting the theatre where the world premiere of the third instalment was shown (Huffstutter, 2003). Public expenditure for the premiere also included US$600,000 to fly in foreign journalists and the same amount for a celebration, including photographs taken by Viggo Mortensen, plus new subvention policies that would only apply to high-budget NICL ventures. But progressives were forced to recognise that the 'most profitable film ever made in New Zealand' was '*not* a New Zealand film' in the national-cinema sense, noting that the government's subsidy to the series could have been spent on buying every New Zealander tickets to the trilogy (Zanker and Lealand, 2003: 67; Calder, 2003; Hufstutter, 2003). Meanwhile, even as the country's exposure from the films was being trumpeted, local actors noted a lack of interest from Hollywood and wondered where their next job might come from ('Wrung', 2004). There are, then, many good reasons to be sceptical about the model of industrial policy creating audiovisual space. So, what can an alternative strategy learn from it?

As the case of co-production attests, state provision is key to maintaining a diverse audiovisual culture through local, national and regional work. Perhaps the most productive state-capital alliance has been Canal Plus, which has spent 60 per cent on European works in exchange for its prominent position in pay-TV. This support has given France the strongest national film industry in Europe, which suggests that policy must amplify Europe's long history of broadcasting in the public interest, and extend this citizen-based philosophy from (what remain) public airwaves to the new media conduits of cable, satellite and the Internet. With the digital convergence of telephony and television, these conduits could become new gateways of public expression. Rather than freeways for Hollywood to take off in search of the NICL, they could draw on the example of the public library. This is of particular importance now, as European policy on convergence faces pressures to liberalise policy from the US, the WTO and the OECD via Washington's various front organisations such as the Coalition of Service Industries. As one OECD representative suggests, 'there will be no need to have separate broadcasting and telecommunications regulators' under technological convergence. Because telecommunications policies on competition and foreign ownership are historically less restrictive than in broadcasting, it is important that legal reform quickly brings public-interest and universal-access rules to convergence policy initiatives (Harcourt, 1998: 442).

Recent events heighten urgency in these matters – 1999 mergers and acquisitions in Europe totalled US$1.3 trillion, a threefold increase since 1997. Much of this activity consisted of telecommunications mergers, such as the British firm Vodafone's hostile US$179 billion takeover of rival Mannesmann in 2000. Emerging global telecom conglomerates Vodafone, Vivendi and the Spanish Telefónica have been acquiring content producers to position themselves for televisual and telephonic convergence through the Internet (Hopewell, 2000). Behind the market forces unleashed through privatisation and deregulation is the promise of a technological revolution and universal access to participatory expression. Yet as Shalini Venturelli has argued, liberalisation has facilitated 'proprietary concentration' rather than democratising expression (1998: 56–58). Vivendi (the former owner of Universal) holds stakes in the pan-European cable/satellite systems of Canal Plus (49 per cent) and BSkyB (25 per cent), and has an alliance with the world's largest wireless phone service, Vodafone AirTouch. This extends Vivendi's multi-access Internet portal Vizzavi to a potential 80 million subscribers. Unless the EU stalls this trend of convergence and concentration, there will be no place for public-service policies such as the one that called on Canal Plus to support the national film industry (Goldsmith, 2000; James and Dawtrey, 2000). In addition, the global trend for TV stations to proliferate splinters the audience and drives up competition for programming, leading to increases in the cost of US material, but not to the point where it threatens to be as costly as locally produced drama (Friends of Canadian Broadcasting, 2003: 11–12). For all the flaws with cultural policy that we have identified in this book, its regionalism remains a key potential bulwark against such consolidation.

Learning from the cultural blancmange problems of the EU, Latin America – a more homogeneous linguistic region – could make audiovisual sectors key components of its economic integration, albeit with great care, given the leadership sought by the US in both integration and screen texts, by concentrating on subregional activity as well as larger groupings (Yúdice, 2002). The same goal should be set by the African Union, the Arab League and the Association of South-East Asian Nations. But it will not come to pass easily or quickly.

Latin America has very limited regional arrangements by comparison with the EU, though the Organisation of American States/Organización des Estados Americanos has set up a cultural ministers' forum. The 1989 NAFTA between Canada and the US specifically exempted the culture industries, but permitted commercial retaliation against any exclusion of materials. Mexico did not seek an equivalent exemption in 1994. Indeed, according to Mexican negotiators, thirty centuries of cultural tradition dating back to pre-Aztec times would maintain Mexico's autonomy (Miller and Yúdice, 2002: 176). And the Mercado Común del Sur of the southern cone and Brazil has introduced few cultural initiatives other than a trade preference for intra-Mercado TV (Ó Siochrú *et al.*, 2002: 61–63).

For its part, ASEAN held an Information Ministers event in 1989 to deal with globalisation, principally the representation of the Third World in Northern media. Although media policies were agreed on, no binding principles or mechanisms were set up, and the variant attitudes within the Association have not been overcome. Malaysia, Singapore and Indonesia require centralised state control for fear of social dislocation from foreign media, but Thailand and the Philippines welcome TIS and see openness to Western cultural exchange as part of economic development (Atkins, 2002: 32–33, 73).

When centralised bodies such as the EC draw upon neoliberalism to disregard democratic voices within the COE and the EP that call on members to create cultural policies that nurture local and national diversity, we must gather support around a growing international movement to safeguard cultural rights within international trade agreements. Although García-Canclini acknowledges that the private takeover of state cultural functions has 'compounded the already existing problems of the inadequate development and instability of our democracies' (2001: 2) and threatens Latin American civil society, he also believes it is necessary to expand notions of citizenship to include consumption of health, housing and education.

Yúdice and García-Canclini propose a regional federalism to promote a specifically Latin American media space, with:

- quotas for Latin American productions in movie theatres, radio broadcasts and television programming
- a Foundation for the Production and Distribution of Latin American media; and
- policies to strengthen Latin American economies and regulate foreign capital in order to foster a citizenship that promotes multiculturalism and democratises the relationship between populations and states.

(Yúdice, 1995)

García-Canclini (1996) criticises the widespread neoliberal dismissal of government as an inappropriate arbiter of regulation and control. He argues that the market and civil society are not the same thing, thus challenging those tenets of neoclassical economics that assert that *laissez-faire* serves society at large. This does not mean a return to the critiques of left-wing cultural commentators that transnational culture perverts pure indigenous traditions. Indeed, his theory of hybridity (1990) precludes such analysis. Nor does it elicit more aristocratic complaints that mass dissemination corrupts high art. Rather, it challenges neoliberal policy-makers and authors such as Vargas Llosa who assert that the free market finally allows peripherally produced cultural products such as *Like Water for Chocolate* (Alfonso Arau, 1992) to be disseminated around the world. García-Canclini asserts instead that without reviving nationalism, there must be state intervention that recognises 'culture is too important to be relinquished exclusively to the competition among international markets' (1996: 155). Yúdice (2000) states that the creation of regional/continental trading blocs, organised with the intent of moderating US audiovisual dominance and providing space for local cultural expression outside national frameworks, must involve non-governmental organisations, the state and industry.

This strategy to create an alternative media space diverges from the European model of pan-regional audiovisual culture in one fundamental way. It rejects the abiding logic of the EU's audiovisual cultural policy of privatisation and expansion of existing large industrial concerns. García-Canclini (2001) asserts that the proposal of an audiovisual space is appropriate for Latin America, because its particular way of being multicultural and modern is very different from both Europe and the US: Latin America prioritises solidarity over sectarianism. In this way, multiculturalism avoids separatism, which he states is the case in the US and Europe. The Zapatistas in Chiapas, for example, link their regional and ethnic demands to the nation and to globalisation, mounting an inclusive critique of modernity that goes beyond isolated local interests. García-Canclini attributes this to the hybrid ethnic and national identities in Latin America, which comprise a particularly uneven form of modernity that includes complicated mixtures of tradition, modernity and post-modernity, and link the continent in a way that does not apply to Europe, because the former is almost entirely dominated by the Spanish language (with the notable but changing exception of Brazil). The organic unity of this language has been crucial, for example, in the international success of the *telenovela*, which sees production sites, labour and intertextual references drawn from the entire continent, providing a precedent for a broader Latin American linkage in terms of both personnel and cultural signification (Mato, 1999: 248–49; Mazziotti, 1996).

As a resistive cultural policy depends on organic linkages, it is drawn into conflict with the chauvinism of national cultures and their border wars. The theory of cultural imperialism needs to be modified to account for its lost intellectual cachet, as we urged in Chapter 1. We have pulled our theory of cultural imperialism away from its historical attraction to the sovereign-state, which was resistive in its own moment through the 1950s and 1960s. This dialectic took us back, in a sense, to a more fundamental source of culture: work. Our proposal is to return to the person as labourer, but not as an idealistic category of identity. We have installed a political and ethical regard for labour and its alienation into a model of citizens and consumers that allows us to question the role of states and markets in extending or stemming global Hollywood. Such a model of citizenship, we suggest, must deal with de-domiciled workers, with all the dispossession entailed in that status. Citizenship assumes governmental policing of rights and responsibilities. Does this apply when a NICL is in operation, and either the deregulation or the protection of media bourgeoisies seem to be the only alternatives? To whom do you appeal if you are unhappy with the silencing of your local dramatic tradition through television imports, but demoralised by the representation of ethnic and sexual minorities or women within so-called national screen drama or network news? We have seen first the slow and now the quick dissolution of cultural protectionism on screen.

Copyright Reform

Policies that disarticulate IP from corporate interests remove the cornerstone of Hollywood's global control over the resources for making and watching movies, beginning instead with the practical problems that already weaken the corporate enclosure: first, the prioritisation of copyright law alone fails to ensure monopoly rights, because it neglects the shift towards trademark law embraced by licence-based industries (like television); second, copyright is difficult to enforce in so-called emerging markets; and third, it has trouble working in new distributional arenas without compromising user privacy. Further weaknesses can be found in the liberal foundation to policy reform – whether to shore up progressive moral-rights provisions against corporate control, or give corporations a human face. First, artistic livelihoods are sustained only *accidentally* by copyright. More often than not, copyright involves signing away moral rights under work-for-hire doctrine. Second, copyright is tied to forms of legislation that grant legal personhood to corporations, who become 'authors' in the act of contractual transfer. Finally, there is no equality in IP trade, because the slippery realpolitik transfer of moral-rights provisions privileges ownership-oriented regimes (which finally saw the US sign the Berne Convention). In sum, moral-rights arguments work well within the narrow purview of tributary rights attached to creative work (i.e. that it cannot be 'distorted' without approval from its author and that the authorship must always be attributed); however, by design, moral rights are incapable of negotiating the everyday ways that IP relations are subject to the *commercial transfer* inherent 'in the work'.

Perhaps we need a more nuanced approach to ownership. Rather than attending exclusively to ownership at the level of production, why not consider the act of *consumption*? Acts of consumption generate ownership in a myriad of ways. Taking advantage of limited rights attached to screen a copyrighted programme, you may screen Blockbuster videos within the confines of your own home, or in non-profit educational arenas. However, the rolling-back of first-sale rights (discussed in Chapter 4) creates digital property in the very act of consumption; this transitory act of ownership is used by the copyright industries as a warrant to install tracking technologies in personal computers. Clearly, copyright cuts across the spatio-temporal parameters of ownership in specific ways.

Instead of endlessly recycling ownership ideals rooted in property, we suggest that cultural policy shift the debate to consumer rights. Rather than protect sites of creation (rights to own) through the phantasmatic evocation of authorship under copyright law, policy might protect *rights to consume* (which are under fire in recent DMCA legislation). This would involve a thorough consideration of the public domain and fair use – not merely as byproducts designed to compensate for the possible excesses of IP, but at a more fundamental level that ensures people have rights to do things beyond signing them away in the act of creation as per common law. Moral rights for the act of consumption rather than an originary act of creation might go a long way towards extending fair use. This retooling takes us away from fair use's traditional evocation as a form of subsidy given by copyright owners (see Ginsberg, 1997b), towards a subsidy to users. Presently, their labour as audiences is exploited by market research, then protected in survey form as IP.

Since market research understands audiences as an untamed labour force that requires domestication, users might demand compensation in the form of an extension of fair use. In addition, a user's rights would redeploy the public domain away from its conceptualisation as the maligned progeny of IP (Cain to the commercial imperative's Abel), which fences off discrete areas of knowledge from public use or serves as the public's toll for conferring private property rights in authorship. Instead, we might recognise the public domain as 'a device that permits the rest of the system to work by leaving the raw materials of authorship available for others to use' (Litman, 1990: 968–69). In other words, the public domain must be the constitutive ground upon which creativity rests, rather than its remainder. This idea is at the heart of the open-source movement.

In search of this reorientation in US legal discourse, the EFF funds ongoing legal challenges to the DMCA. By providing financial and strategic support to plaintiffs who deploy legal arguments based on the open-source movement, the EFF hopes to counter attempts to lock up intellectual property in corporate hands. One industry analyst worries that by 'forcing the government to defend the law over and over', the EFF poses a 'far more serious challenge in their battle to assert their intellectual property rights in cyberspace than a bunch of college kids swapping music via the Internet' (Sweeting, 2001).

Consider two further approaches to establishing greater audience control over copyright: use as a speech act and as an act of labour. While 'US First Amendment jurisprudence has defined readers' rights only incidentally' (Cohen, 1996: 1003), there are reasons to limit copyright's power to diminish democracy – the constitutional guarantee of freedom of speech. Melvin Nimmer, for example, argued in 1970 that there existed a 'speech interest with respect to copyright'. Copyright should be violated if the act of copying sustained a 'unique contribution to an enlightened public dialogue' (1193, 1197). While he had in mind a scenario in which copyrighted photographs of the My Lai massacre might be withheld from a critical public, Paul Goldstein (1970) used Howard Hughes' attempt to stop Random House from publishing his biography by creating a corporate façade that bought the rights to articles written about him, to claim that copyright infringement should be excused when it supports the public interest.

Media and legal theorists on the left often equate the copy-related rights of information creators with forms of speech (see, for example, Braman, 1998: 81) or maintain that copyright itself regulates speech (Benkler, 1999: 446). Some suggest copyright law pertains to speech rather than texts (Rotstein, 1992: 739–42). Still others argue that the conflation of speech rights with property rights – even in its progressive modality – simply recapitulates the public/private and commons/commodity orthodoxies inscribed in IP law (Coombe, 1996: 239, 241, 247).

We are suggesting a reorientation of property rights (which underpin the NICL) towards labour rights. Such a fundamental move away from a politics of ownership to a politics of work recognises that, for fair use and the public domain to have any meaning, audience labour is a form of speech act. Julie Cohen (1996: 1038–39) notes that 'reading is intimately connected with speech', and is therefore amenable to constitutional protections. Hartley adds that reading as a form of media response is 'a universal technology of communication, while not an already-existing attribute of persons' (1996: 119, 66). We suggest that, like speech, reading deserves protection.

The equation of basic human rights with reading is more than just rhetoric. Under the strict schedules of harmonisation posed by the WTO, 'communications rights and human rights as expressed in communication policy and social policy can be contested on the grounds that they act to constrain trade through a set of non-commercial public interest requirements whether in infrastructure or content' (Venturelli, 1997: 63).

Following free-speech precepts, communications policy must think itself out of traditional IP rights to protect forms of creativity that stimulate the 'production of media content at the fringes of the range of preferences, thus promoting equal access to diverging preferences and opinions in society' (Van Cuilenburg, 1999: 204). But the DMCA curtails free-speech protection with anti-circumvention provisions that state consumers may not use devices or services designed to bypass copyright-management systems (such as watermarking). The only way corporate owners of copyrighted products can prevent such infringements is to monitor the entire terrain of media consumption; as such, anti-circumvention policies pose a significant invasion of privacy as well as fair use. Cultural policy must deflate the widespread corporate acceptance of rights-management software that threatens significant sectors of use, and 'contemplate built-in technological limits on copyright owners' monitoring capabilities' (Cohen, 1996: 988). In arguing for the anonymity of media users technologically, Cohen notes:

> Reading is an intellectual association, pure and simple. As such, it is profoundly constitutive of identity as direct interpersonal association. There are reasons for according even stronger protection to reading, moreover. Interpersonal association and group affiliation are, by definition, voluntary expressions of a common purpose or interest.
>
> (Cohen, 1996: 1014)

To modify the mostly individualist language of these rights, cultural policy might draw from the 1996 report by UNESCO and the UN's World Commission on Culture and Development. *Our Creative Diversity* notes that one of the challenges in the wake of the GATT is maintaining a 'balance between those countries that export copyright and those that import it' (Pérez de Cuéllar, 1996: 244). Defining an intermediary sphere of IP rights between individual authorial rights and the national/international public domain, *Our Creative Diversity* suggests that certain cultures deserve IP rights as *groups* (Pérez de Cuéllar, 1996). Not surprisingly, the protection of collective authorship (specifically with regard to folklore) was not raised at the 1997 WTO meeting in Geneva, and when Third World countries supported such protection at a joint UNESCO/WIPO meeting later that year, the move was opposed by US and British delegates:

> when the US delegate said that since most of the folklore that was commercially exploited was US folklore, Third World countries would have to pay a lot of money to the US if an international convention should come about. The Indian lawyer, Mr. Purim, answered that that was already the case with existing conventions and by the way all US folklore except the Amerindian one was imported to the US from Europe and Africa. . . . Thus the money should go to the original owners of that folklore.
>
> (Kirster Malm, quoted in Smiers, 2000: 397)

A current case involving modern folklore illustrates the powerful correlation of consumption and speech act – the *Harry Potter* controversy, touched on earlier.

After Time Warner's inelegant bullying of fans and website owners, the latter engaged in a war of position. The formation of such sites as www.potterwar.org.uk and the cleverly named www.harrypotter-warnercan suemyarse.co.uk was followed by the 'Defense Against the Dark Arts' (DADA) Project (www.dprophet.com/dada/), which urged a boycott of *Harry Potter* merchandise and the first film (though, interestingly, *not* the books). DADA suggested that reparations be made to *Potter* fans by Warner Bros., 'whether this is in a substantial donation to UNICEF, or tickets to the premiere to the actual fans who were threatened themselves; we'd like to see Warner Brothers come up with a plan that shows how sorry they feel'. In rallying support for an upcoming constitutional battle, DADA described the corporate policing actions in this way:

> There are dark forces afoot, darker even than He-Who-Must-Not-Be-Named, because these dark forces are daring to take away something so basic, so human, that it's close to murder. They are taking away our freedom of speech, our freedom to express our thoughts, feelings and ideas, and they are taking away the fun of a magical book.

Although Time Warner stopped sending the cease-and-desist letters – no doubt swayed by the tremendous negative publicity their trademark protection generated – it is applying and registering 2,000 trademarks connected to *Harry Potter* (Demarco, 2001: 4). This is part of a long line of corporate policing efforts that stretch from *Star Wars* websites to *The Simpsons*, *Star Trek* and the *X-Files* (see Tushnet, 1997).

In addition to conceptualising consumption as a form of speech, which is protected under most forms of democratic constitutional provision, cultural policy must recognise that every act of consumption is an act of authorship that hybridises the traditional parameters of singular gatekeeping authority, that authorship 'in any medium is more akin to translation and recombination' than a spurious originary act (Litman, 1990: 966).

We have already shown how IP law fails to recognise collectively authored work like folklore, which become secured through use. Ironically, corporate-friendly initiatives substantiate our claim for the labour of consumption. In Chapter 4, we discussed the US negotiating team's position at the 1996 WIPO conference, which said that reproduction was inherent in every digital transmission. In effect, this makes *all* users of digital media *writers* – as Pool puts it, 'to read a text stored in electronic memory, one displays it on the screen: one writes to read it' (quoted in Van der Merwe, 1999: 311).

Labour as consumption redeploys Lockean labour theory (which traditionally underpins the romantic idea of authorship) towards a socialist vision of property rights gained by adding one's labour (Boyle, 1996: 57). Although such conceptualisations of labour have supported worker exploitation, since wages transfer the property right of labour to the employer, they have also prioritised the *creative* labour that makes the author's work his or her own. Conceiving of a more open public use as a *symbolic* wage for users works through the dilemma of monopoly rights, even though it acknowledges that property is the heart of media transactions.

Borrowing from studies of subcultural practices, Aoki refers to 'audience recoding rights'. He notes that focusing on the dynamic and fluid nature of textuality (with audiences equal partners in the creative act) might 'dilute the property-ness of interests protected by copyright'. Such an approach, focused on 'texts-as-speech-events, would begin allowing space for a judicial consideration of "recoded" cultural productions and enhanced respect for free speech values' (Aoki, 1993b: 826–27). While Aoki recognises that this might introduce commercial imperatives into the regulation of speech, understanding media consumption as a collaborative network of productive labour takes us part of the way towards a wider definition of 'fair use'.

Jane Ginsberg (1997a) has suggested that traditional forms of fair use privilege certain types of users and redistribute copyright value to them. Audiences are otherwise 'paedocratised' as dopes by both academic and governmental cultures for supposedly being incapable of either 'critical distance, scepticism or reason, or with being able to integrate, compare or triangulate media discourses with others elaborated in different institutional sites' (Hartley, 1996: 59). Redirecting fair use towards ordinary people would recognise the transient nature of reading rather than the fixed site of authorship. Fair use, as Wendy Gordon notes, has not often been extended to 'ordinary users', since 'the public interest served by second authors [creators of derivative works or specialised users using the stuff of public domain] are likely to be stronger than the interests served by ordinary consumers' (1982: 1653). This prejudice recapitulates copyright's espousal of the author as a principle that impedes the free circulation and recomposition of cultural production. Authorship provides the common terrain for laws that claim that lists of telephone numbers are not copyrightable by directory publishers – because there is no proof of 'sweat of the brow' labour (see *Feist Publications Inc.* v. *Rural Telephone Service Co.*, 499 US [1991]) – unlike statutory protections of market-research firms' computer databases as copyrightable 'literary works', with all the ownership benefits of authorship.

Technology such as the 'trusted systems' and 'rights management tracking software' discussed in Chapter 4 is beginning to supplant copyright's traditional function (which includes a significant, if underdeveloped, evocation of fair use). Legal manoeuvrability within the statutory sphere is becoming even more difficult: 'every single copy of a digital work would become its own tollbooth' (Benkler, 1999: 422). Of course, there will always be hackers, the last guardians of an old system that recognises some forms of the public domain and private use.

'The tendency to undervalue the public domain', writes Boyle, 'is a worldwide phenomenon' (1996: 130). Public policy designed to control knowledge capital by monopoly rents instead of a public archive-based consensual access to knowledge represents, as Frow notes, a 'major erosion of the public domain' (2000: 182). While the public domain has traditionally signified as the abject detritus of non-copyrightable materials, its roots in European feudalism (as the true public commons, scarce land reserved for public use) mask the fact that 'knowledge actually increases when it is shared' (Frow, 2000: 182). Yochai Benkler calls for two policy proposals alongside free and open source-software strategies that might meaningfully sustain the public domain and resist its enclosure: 'identifying and sustaining a series of commons in the resources necessary for the production and exchange of information', and a 'shift in distributive policies from low cost or free reception to ubiquitous access to the facilities necessary for production and dissemination of information' (2000: 576).

The market model theorised by Napster suggests a group of peer users exchanging information. Internet-based rights might be conceived along a service-based approach via the shared-resource market network. Bundling users into groups that share resources, rather than individuals who consume in private singular acts, clearly threatens both the existence of copyright as well as the corporate distributional brokers who mediate between traditional artists and consumers.

Cultural policy that privileges reception as an *act of creative labour* can similarly fracture the authorial underpinnings of copyright and encourage the proliferation of responses to new aesthetic forms. To use John Perry Barlow's (n. d.) words, a politics of labour (which prioritises *doing*) rather than of objects (which favours *owning*) reconceptualises media interaction as conduct 'in a world made more of verbs than nouns'.

Marketing Reform

Our call for a labour theory of consumption that inverts the negative liberties granted by the NICL is based, in part, on the acts of surveillance performed on media users. We have shown, in Chapter 5, how spectators are alienated from their labour as subjects of market research. Like the broadcast media it supports, market research structures the diversity of user activity into suspected or probable sorts of 'audience', wherein consumers *themselves* become the product. When audience labour is owned by market research and protected by corporate IP laws, research subjects are denied access to the very speech acts that constitute reception.

Hollywood's marketers confront vexing and arbitrary connections between what they think people are, as members of a suspected audience, and the personal stories people elaborate for themselves as filmgoers. In working through this contradiction, marketing identifies some ways to build attendance, but guesswork plays a big part. Constant monitoring of filmgoers works to improve the guesswork. An important ethical dilemma flows from this. Even though they regularly get it wrong, marketers must make up audiences into images that suit their clients' needs. To do so they probe, analyse and interpret filmgoing habits. There is no respect for experiences that do not fit into pre-scripted versions of probable audience behaviour. Even when they shift responsibility to the sovereign consumer, marketers still rely on pre-scripted notions of who and what people 'are'. Tracking this ethical problematic a bit further can help locate additional points of departure for innovative cultural policy.

Imagine an encounter in which marketers come face to face with the people they presume to know, rather than the usual pre-scripted and automated encounter of surveillance. Here the proxies of the corporate view of film and its audiences might have to acknowledge the unknowable; namely, an unruly, unpredictable filmgoer or an ineffable filmgoing experience. Such an encounter would expose the deficiency inside marketing's will to predict audience behaviour. All marketers do is cast a statistical shadow of a made-up audience, nothing substantial. People might laugh at these corporate soothsayers and wonder how they cannot but laugh at themselves. This encounter might also disclose how marketers make up audiences and call them to account for the elaborate deception covering their surveillance. Such an encounter would be full of sources for an ethical and political awakening. Yet, it might also give marketers an opportunity to appeal to the moral authority that comes from two institutional sources: legitimate (for now) business operations and legitimate (for now) research. Perhaps a textual example can help us imagine such an encounter.

At the beginning of *Magic Town* (William Wellman, 1947), news spreads that the 'Institute of Public Opinion', run by Lawrence 'Rip' Smith (Jimmy Stewart), is going out of business. A clerk scoffs: 'Gettin' opinions from the public; that's a screwy way to make a livin'.' 'Hold on,' says a customer, 'lotsa guys clean up on it. Look at Gallup. You know, big corporations pay a lot of money to find out what you and I think.' 'They do?' exclaims the befuddled clerk. We know they do, for in that moment, Rip's luck changes as he reads a letter from an old army pal telling him about Grandview, a town where opinions mirror the nation as a whole across sex, income, political party and other demographic markers. 'I'm gonna make a million bucks on this,' Rip exclaims.

The next morning, he steps off the train at Grandview, posing as an insurance salesman from Hartford, because 'people in that town can't know what we're doing there, so we gotta have a cover. Sooner or later they're gonna get self-conscious, and that's fatal.' As Rip gazes across the town square, he rhapsodises: 'the moment Columbus first sighted land must have been just like this'. Rip motions towards one of the natives and comments: 'I know all about him.' 'He's married, he has 1.7 children, out of his income he spends 11.2 for rent, 23.5 for food, 17.2 for clothing.' Rip's partner Ike interrupts. 'Poor guy,' he grumbles. 'He's just a series of fractions. He oughtta stop acting like a human being.' Rip wins the people's trust with his 'devotion to the basketball team' and his antic flirtations with Mary Peterman (Jane Wyman), the acting editor of the local newspaper. All the while, though, Rip has secretly collected everyone's opinions and thoughts; only his partners and his old army pal know what he is doing.

Rip's personal involvement begins to threaten the research. Ike wonders if

Rip is getting too close to Mary: 'Howdya like to kick this whole deal over?' Ike asks. Rip says he has not worked his whole life to 'kick it over' now – 'What kind of lame-brain do you think I am?' At the town dance, his army pal suggests that Rip 'must be having an awful tussle' with his conscience. 'Don't worry about my conscience,' Rip snaps. Life is a rat race, he says, but at least he's out in front of it. Rip leaves the dance to phone Ike, who tells him that the survey results are perfect; they will make them very rich. Just then, a concerned Mary enters the front office looking for Rip, who had left the dance upset. Looking around for him, she sees a sheet of tabulations that alerts her to Rip's con game. Then she picks up the phone and hears Rip say: 'I'll handle the Peterman girl'.

Rip emerges from the back room and stands face to face with Mary, unwilling to let her begin an ethical critique of his actions: 'We had to work secretly,' he told her, adding coldly, 'Nobody's been hurt by it, have they?' He cannot hear her heart break. Rip becomes increasingly self-righteous as he tries to stop Mary from writing an article that would expose his deception to the people of Grandview. This is the limit point for him. 'You can't go around telling people they're special,' he says, 'not even these people. It's deadly.' Rip cannot see his mendacity as a form of violence. Instead, he passes the burden of killing the town to the messenger. What she will kill, he implies, is the town's innocence – a pious judgment based on the moral authority of his social science. Mary stands for a competing ethical orientation, one that is open and solicitous without being pious and exploitative: her act of writing will only kill Rip's ability to exploit innocence. By removing the researcher's mask of friendship and solidarity, she creates the conditions for the town's ethical and political awakening.

At this point, the story of *Magic Town* closes around the representational authority inscribed in Rip's institutional identity – the social scientist would be proven right. Mary's article changes the town. Opinions 'are our chief export', Grandview's mayor declares. 'We're through giving them away.' So they build opinion-collecting booths, each containing a reference library to ensure people say smart things. Journalists, tourists and house-hunters from the big city overrun magic town. Property values and speculation soar. Rip spends his remaining days in Grandview drunk and disorderly, never missing an opportunity to tell Mary that she is to blame for turning Grandview into a circus. Eventually, Rip leaves, Grandview's self-made poll flops and the town becomes a national joke. At the end, Rip returns, professes his love for Mary, and saves the town from itself. 'We murdered a town', Mary confesses after realising that Grandview could have lived as before had it not been alerted to Rip's scheme.

Magic Town introduces constituencies that help us to imagine a cultural policy that can reconfigure consumption and consumer surveillance for the new politics of citizenship suggested by Yúdice. There are those who, by remaining innocent, become susceptible to marketing research. Their identities are interpreted and judged within a moral framework determined by business and statistical research. They 'live', to borrow from *Magic Town*'s lament, for as long as they work for the research. Once they awaken to their conditions as subjects of surveillance, they are dead to the researchers.

In our view, this is a salutary death, for it creates new conditions of possibility for cultural policy. We can imagine, for instance, a policy that bans the exploitation of innocence through consumer surveillance. Full disclosure of audience and consumer research would immediately offer more freedom. The citizen is in the house of consumption. People could opt in to the research, but in so doing they would already make it a much weaker form of surveillance. Given what we know about the expanding surveillance network that interlocks multiple sites of cultural consumption, this policy would have to have a wider remit. Imagine, then, that all point-of-sale tracking required the buyer's permission, that no information about a CD, video or DVD purchase could be gathered or sold without consent. The burden of the added cost of disclosure would be carried by the retailer and marketer, as would the tax that paid for policing the legal use of personal information and the punishment of commercial offenders, which together would probably be great enough to reduce the commercial incentive for, and limit the growth of, the exposed surveillance system. In this context, current EU policy on personal data protection in global data trade is instructive: in particular, how it succeeds, and where it fails, in creating a mode of comprehending supra-national commitments to citizenship while accommodating the commercial logic of audiovisual policy, especially in defence of a right to know the surveyors, correct one's own data and be informed when personal information is being extracted for surveillance purposes (Maxwell, 1999). Banning the exploitation of innocence is only a first step in this policy scenario. If people become aware of the extent of consumer surveillance, they may participate more fully in the resulting economy of display, forging an entrepreneurial bridge between citizens, consumers and workers via personal-information businesses, polling one another and selling the information themselves.

Major studios have recently banded together with NRG and other marketers to demonise one such opinion entrepreneur, Harry Knowles, who formed a network of people to infiltrate test screenings and leak home-made reviews on ain't-it-cool-news.com (Lerner, 1999). Marketers complain that this corrupts the research process. But they may be angry because Harry is telling us to listen to his friends, not to the industry's version of audiences (his own version of *Magic Town* statisticide). For this constituency of small-time marketers and survey researchers, a policy that assures them adequate resources to compete with large marketers and the state could become a feature of our policy. Of course, their ability to survey their neighbours would come under the same scrutiny and ethical commitments that are applied to larger firms: no secrets or deceptions, opt-in only rules and proportional tax levies.

Because such a small-business policy encourages the socialisation of the economy of surveillance and display, it demands sharper inspection (see Maxwell, 1999). It would at a minimum necessitate a radical critique of the liberal principles underlying the rights conferred upon owners of proprietary information gathered through surveillance, as well as the extremely limited privacy protection based in the same property standards. In theory, the heartbreak suffered by betrayal of a confidence or friendship would be minimised, because the human-scale marketers hear and see the violence of their mendacity.

But how does this theory of a little liberation from surveillance avoid recapitulation of governmentality and discipline in another, apparently more humane form (Maxwell, 1996a)? In practice, these marketers might still feel drawn to the moral authority embedded in their research technique, or the fees and instructions they receive from clients. Our policy has to build in a principle of cooperation and solidarity that forces the individual marketer to cultivate ethical regard for personal information, minimising the draw of methodological purity or money. One such principle might derive from García-Canclini's proposal to socialise consumption, thereby promoting collaboration of constituencies across a number of social and cultural fields (health, housing and education were already mentioned; we would add communication). The US offers audiences minimal protection of privacy by comparison with the EU, and Microsoft and others are lobbying fiercely to prevent democratic accountability of business practices via the usual strategy – let us take care of you by writing software and bundling it into your system. Their partners in US corporate self-regulation are mostly in accord, and the Republican Party never misses an opportunity to deride European safeguards (Simpson, 2001a and b; Sykes and Simpson, 2001; Bridis, 2001). This is evidence enough that such reform would wrest power away from reactionaries!

We think there is a strong constituency to support such reforms – US college students. In the 1980s and early 1990s, they would nervously shift in their seats in response to the cultural-studies professor's query, 'Who here likes soap operas?' A subsequent (mutual) confession to fandom humanised professors in their eyes. Or so we hoped. Today, the cutting question is 'Who downloads?', and the answer does not serve as a Membership Categorisation Device for resistive readers – it can imply a jail sentence or significant fine. And Movielink is not only seeking custom for VOD; it is also funding surveillance of students downloading 'illegally' (Hu and Olsen, 2004). 'Cool stuff' is something more than unruly decoding today, and young people know it.

Finale

Global Hollywood 2 has wrestled throughout with a variety of complex trends that inhibit making policy progressive. We have endeavoured to write for readers whose identities rival the ones generated for and about them by global Hollywood. In so doing, we envisage a reader with capacious interests that take into account these ethical and political problems of the contemporary political economy of culture:

- 'Americanisation' of production, distribution and exhibition, with its persistent vision of separate spheres of work and consumption
- bureaucratisation of national policy and privatisation of global policy
- impact of deregulated markets
- dominance of the 'Washington Consensus'
- spread of the NICL
- cooptation of resistive national cultural policy by bourgeoisies and Hollywood itself
- harmonisation of copyright under neoliberal evangelism
- power of the US domestic audience; and the
- force of DEM/GEM logics of citizenship and consumption.

Our critique of screen trade has also come up against the pre-eminence of exchange value defended by IP, a relation that disguises or displaces labour behind the fetishisms of text, interiority and authorship, even as, in the US alone, countless films are 'pirated' each day (Valenti, 2001c).

In the Introduction, we posed these questions:

- is Hollywood global – and in what sense?
- what are the implications of that dominance?; and
- where is Hollywood?

Here are our answers. Yes, Hollywood *is* global. It sells to virtually every nation, through a system of copyright, promotion and distribution that uses the NICL to minimise cost and maximise revenue. The implications are that we need to focus on the NICL and the global infrastructure of textual exchange in order to make world film and television more representative, inclusive and multiple in their sources, texts and effects. Understanding how Hollywood 'works' might not exactly make us free, but it could provoke us to confront the NICL and imagine alternative, more salutary conditions and possibilities for our own cultural labour and for our brothers and sisters in the culture works everywhere.

Until that moment, we can only agree with Powdermaker in the 1950s abjuring Hollywood's '"darling" and "sweetheart" terms of address and demonstrations of affection and love in situations of hostility, hatred, and lack of respect' (1967: 223) and the propensity to treat 'people as property and as objects to be manipulated' (1950: 332). Fifty years later, the *New Yorker* observed that

> Hollywood seems to exemplify the most joyless aspects of capitalism. The 'industry,' as it insists upon calling itself, packages artistic ideas and images as commodities and then values those commodities according to how they 'penetrate' markets, support 'platforms' of ancillary commodities (tie-in

Burger King action figures), and 'brand' a company as a reliable purveyor of similar commodities.

(Friend, 2003: 41)

The magazine also ran a cartoon of a man, woman and child in Central Park. The child is playing with a ball, the woman looking at the man as he prepares to film them. He offers second thoughts: 'Look, I love the city, too, but would-n't it be cheaper to shoot this in Canada?' (Gregory, in the *New Yorker*, 14–21 July 2003: 90). The culture is becoming alive to the cold winds of capital flight.

Returning to the binaries with which we began the book, here is our rewriting of that original table to give a better idea of what is actually happening:

HOLLYWOOD FILM INDUSTRY	NATIONAL FILM INDUSTRY
Massive state investment in training via film schools and production commissions, major diplomatic negotiations over distribution and exhibition arrangements	Major state subvention of training and production, minimal or no support for distribution and exhibition
Governmental censorship	Governmental censorship
Copyright protection as a key service to capital along with anti-piracy deals	Copyright protection
Monopoly restrictions minimised to permit cross-ownership and unprecedented domestic concentration and international oligopoly	Monopoly restrictions
Export orientation aided by plenipotentiaries, equal reliance on local audience	Import substitution, some export to cognate language groups
Market model, mixed-economy practice	Mixed-economy model
Ideology of pleasure, nation and export of *Américanité*	Ideology of nation, pleasure and job creation
Governmental anxiety over the impact of film sex and violence on the population, as alibi for no cultural-policy discourse	Governmental anxiety over the impact of imported film on the population, as alibi for bourgeois subvention

We might also consider how to evaluate the impact on local/host industries of
domestic versus runaway production:

INDUSTRY IMPACT	DOMESTIC	RUNAWAY
Labour	Developing local talent across the labour process	Contingent labour with risk of migration by talent and/or most technical work done elsewhere
Text	Art cinema	Commercial industry
Marketing	Local or auteur	High concept
Distribution and Exhibition	Limited and contingent	Multinational
Locale	Showcasing the nation, investing in training and plant	Disguising the nation, sporadic business
Budget	Small with full local multiplier effect, may be public	Large with inconsistent multiplier, may be co-financed
Copyright	Locally held	Internationally held
Overall	Follows ISI, cultural-nationalist model	Follows EOI, neoliberal model

None of this is to privilege the local over the international, given the concerns
expressed in our tables comparing the two industry models. It is more a typol-
ogy of value that can be applied to particular cases, following McHoul and
O'Regan's (1992) model of contingent evaluation that we mentioned in the
Introduction, whereby specific interests must be identified and interrogated.

Returning to John Ford's provocation that began this sequel, where *is* Hollywood? For those who must deal with the direct nexus of Hollywood and
militarism ideologically, it is located in Washwood, a transversal between LA
and DC. For those who must deal with that link technologically, it is located in
Siliwood, a transversal between LA and Silicon Valley that occasionally stops off
at the University of Southern California for refreshments. And for those engaged
in an intra-bourgeois struggle between productive and mercantile capital, Hollywood is located between theatres and televisions versus games and computers.

Then there is the Hollywood of an old man walking through Greenwich Village, Santa Monica, Vancouver, a North American Chinatown or Toronto, and
being ordered by a young man to move because his use of a public wayfare is

trespassing on the crew's 'right' to shoot their film, at any hour on any day with any amount of arrogant arrogation of public space, whatever the impact on local people (Brodsky, 2002; Heinzl, 2002; Elmer, 2002). Or the Hollywood that is invited back by St Vincent's ministry of tourism and culture to shoot a sequel to *Pirates of the Caribbean: The Curse of the Black Pearl* (Gore Verbinski, 2003), even as they complain about the fact that people from 'First Mate Productions' (a Disney front organisation) disrupted their lives and exploited their goodwill (Taylor, 2004). This is the Hollywood that takes over the streets we thought were a commons. We are ordered about, for all the world subject to Hollywood martial law. For the technocrats, of course, this experience is relegated to a cliché. They call it 'location burn-out' when residents object to their communities being privatised in this way (Los Angeles County Economic Development Corporation, 2004: 59).

Recall Sydney Smith's 1820 rant about the lack of US culture. He knew even then what potential the nation had, given its avoidance of 'the insanity of garrisoning rocks and islands across the world'. Smith asked whether it would amount to 'a powerful enemy or a profitable friend', querying the US because 'every sixth man is a slave, whom his fellow-creatures may buy and sell and torture' (1844: 139, 137). Today the US garrisons over 130 overseas places, and its friendly and enemy status are blurred, as much by culture as warfare. And in as labour-intensive an industry as the screen, we know that Leno's promised 'ruination' will involve over a million working people in the US alone, most of whom have low weekly earnings. At the same time, we have seen the advent of a cybertarian discourse that blends residues of hippy ideology with bourgeois individualism. Some call this 'Californian Ideology' (Barbrook and Cameron, 1996). Cybertarians ignore the institutional, governmental, scholarly and military foundation to the 'New Economy', celebrating instead putative independence from welfare and business. This cosmic fantasy is ignorant of the state's history and currency of racism, poverty and despoliation, and relies on a dubious appropriation of anti-Establishment rhetoric by capital in the service of labour aristocrats blinded by *laissez-faire* mendacity and a selective fetishisation of the Jeffersonian tradition. Technology is visible, slavery is not.

In 2001, coup beneficiary Bush Minor announced his trade policy. It favoured liberalisation on the basis of three putative benefits that would accrue to 'the American people' (good of him to include Latin America and Canada in this):

1 increased job opportunities and income from exports
2 'freedom', because '[e]conomic freedom creates habits of liberty and habits of liberty create expectations of democracy'; and
3 'our nation's security', which had been threatened over the previous half-century by 'hostile protectionism and national socialism'.

('USTR 2001', 2001)

We agree with Bush Minor. Exports should see income equitably distributed among the workers, who make goods and services that are in demand. Liberty and democracy should exist in workplace politics, both in the US and its partners. And anti-worker corporate welfare and fascism must indeed be resisted. So the basics in terms of philosophical principles are there! The task now is to orient world trade away from its current distributional politics and towards an equitable share of wealth. Perhaps that will not come from the return of state welfare as we knew it; but there will be a continuing role for government in protecting and umpiring, along with tasks that the not-for-profit sector will undertake as part of global governance (Scott, 1998c: 5).

In the planned expansion of NAFTA into the Free Trade Area of the Americas, the US persuaded other nations to permit Time Warner, Microsoft, IBM and others to sit at the table (Anderson, 2001). In keeping with Bush Minor's commitment to 'Americans', the corollary of encouraging business participation must be labour representation. Of course, the fears enunciated in Chapter 1 about the disappearance of US national culture from Hollywood are celebrated by some, who foresee that such dependence on the Asian market will make the future more diverse:

> Ten years from now, *Spider-Man* will make Dollars 1bn in its first week. But when *Spider-Man* takes off his mask, he'll probably be Chinese. And the city in which he operates will not be New York, it will be Shanghai. And yet it will be an international film, it will still be *Spider-Man*.
>
> (Kapur, 2002)

Who knows what part changes in the international political economy will play? The 2001 recession hit the culture industries hard, not least because Republican financiers transferred money away from Silicon Valley/Alley and Hollywood and towards manufacturing and defence as punishments and rewards for these industries' respective attitudes during the election and subsequent coup. Energy, tobacco and military contractors, 80 per cent of whose campaign contributions had gone to Bush Minor, suddenly received unparalleled transfers of confidence. Money fled the cultural sector because 66 per cent of its campaign contributions had gone to Gore Minor. There was a dramatic shift towards aligning finance capital with the new administration – a financial victory for oil, cigarettes and guns over film, music and wires. The former saw their market value rise by an average of 80 per cent in a year, while the latter's declined by between 12 and 80 per cent (Schwartz and Hozic, 2001). The rewards were not compromised despite the scandals surrounding Enron and others. And the post-9/11 remilitarisation of everyday life, as the old Cold War saying 'Duck and Cover' became 'Duct and Cover', saw Hollywood and the Silicon sites turn their attention to imperialist technology and ideology to show their loyalty – to Wall Street and the Presidency alike.

But to return to the Pollyannaish pronouncements we derided so in our Introduction, just as the continuity system is available to all, even if Hollywood's governmental and fiscal power are not, so the wider impact of globalisation is felt everywhere. The US creature grows and grows beyond its control, as global finance and 'freedom to invest' stimulate global labour migration (egads, those people at the door!) and generate forms of resistance that can be transnational and even suicidal (Nairn, 2003). This is no simple world of neoliberal competition, but a struggle of military might, post-national cultural subjectivity and anti-imperial feeling.

In the current conjuncture, the US breaks the rules of financial restraint that it imposes on the rest of the world: gigantic deficits, huge governmental expenditure, massive protectionism, global militarism, unprecedented consumption and a teenager's savings rate. The capacity to do all these things simultaneously rather than deciding between untrammelled militarism and untrammelled consumption relies on selling debt securities in a universal lingua franca (the dollar) that is not tied to anything but one's own wishes for its value; and securing other forms of exchange, such as minerals, by force (Wade, 2003).

What if the era of nationalism contained by the state really were at an end, and defending the nation through arms and projecting it through culture were apotheosised by the US in the blazing end of an epoch? What happens if foreign investors decline to buy US stocks and bonds to sustain the gigantic US current-account deficit and the nation's bizarre consumption rituals, or the euro displaces the dollar as the world's unit of exchange (World Trade Organization, 2003: 2)?

More specific to *Global Hollywood* 2, will the weakening dollar undermine the NICL's current operation and attract additional inflows of capital for US-based production? The answers to these quandaries must await more history. But some responses to queries we have posed can be given now. The craven lies that Washington and Hollywood purvey about their relationship in the pages of the press, the corridors of trade and the ideology of everyday rhetoric can stand no longer. Against all we are told, Hollywood is a citadel of cultural policy, and a model for urban planning.

In this lonely hour of the last instance, we return to those ambiguous figures, Hollywood workers. Their stories represent the labour utilised and then discarded, replaced by others elsewhere or by new technology. In the dehumanising, rent-seeking rhetoric of digital entrepreneur Jeff Bacon, promoting his use of synthespians in games as models for the screen: 'Synthespians don't go on strike, they can speak any language, they don't get old – unless you want them to. If you want to have a character with the voice of Aretha Franklin and the body of Jennifer Lopez, you can get it' (quoted in Kotkin, 2001). The drive towards masculinist domination and racial control is as abhorrent as the fetishising away of workers' humanity. Is it any wonder high-tech disemployed participants in the Boston Labour Day rally of 2003 carried signs reading 'War on Nerds' in opposition to runaway culture industries (Gaither, 2003)? They have clearly learned that with 'freedom of labour' can come 'alienation of life' (Bowring, 2002: 163).

Controversy erupted when the archetypically US tale of *Cold Mountain* was shot overseas, leading to a campaign to prevent the film from winning Oscars. So many jobs were lost, and the issue summed up the sense of loss felt both economically and culturally by below-the-liners. The cinematographers refused a special screening and the FTAC and the United States of America Coalition of Film and Television Workers published articles with titles like 'What Americans Need to Know about "Cold Mountain"', asking for consumer boycotts. These pieces became email chain essays (Horn, 2004; Haffner, 2004).

For our informant Michael, an Irish-American gaffer in the film industry located in Southern California, Hollywood is definitely in LA. Folks from all over the country who work below the line (what we can now recognise as Hollywood's handy term to describe its proletariat, on the margins of the 'creative class') seem to be moving either to LA or New York because of recession. But when they arrive, they find what Michael points to as a set of company unions that work with the studio heads against worker interests, permitting the NICL. He and other reformers want state aid to fight job loss, but only as retaliation against subsidies elsewhere.

On the other hand, for our informant Joe, a Chinese-Jamaican-Canadian set builder in Toronto who walks around with a 550-page government report on cultural policy in his backpack, Hollywood is in the US, despite all the carpentry he has done in Ontario for mini-series that are shot 'there' but set 'here'. It is part of an exploitative culture that pervades his world, against which his country must enact cultural policies designed to maintain a local textuality, but where workers compete for Yanqui dollars to sustain themselves.

Haskell Wexler, the notable cinematographer and director, is also a union activist within IATSE. This is what he had to say in 2002:

> We are hurting from coast to coast. The career counseling, networking techniques, feature screenings and golf tournaments, although all of use, only prove to be diversionary to the problem at hand. The members want priorities put on jobs and health care coverage.
>
> ('Telephone Interview', 2002)

And here are similar snapshots:

Below-the-line workers speak out

I have been a member of the IATSE. Local 705 for the past 20 years. For 14 of those years I have also been a small business owner in the entertainment industry. I am supposed to be living the American Dream. Instead, after 20 years of hard work I am on the verge of living the American Nightmare. I hear about potential jobs all the time. Unfortunately, they are in Canada or Australia.
Jean Rosone, IATSE Local 705

My husband and I have worked in the film industry for over 20 years. We are now seriously considering closing our doors, losing our modest home and facing bankruptcy. It is infuriating for production after production to request bids from our company only to take the work out of the country.
Jennifer E. Manus, Sticks and Stones Studio

The film business is a driving economic force [in] California. The monies spent on filming filter down through our community creating jobs in related industries and providing sales and income tax revenues.
Gary Jackson, President, Jackson Shrub Supply

While we are small employers in the entertainment industry, we have already been forced to reduce our staff by 10 per cent and anticipate that further cuts of up to 25 per cent will be necessary in the near future if this problem is not addressed.
Raymond Claridge, President, CP Enterprises

In its first season back in California, *X-Files* spent $328,494.74 in rentals and expendables, and another $168,000.00 in manufacturing and graphics from our companies. Our company employs 95–125 people with salaries greatly varying. We can't afford to lose even one SHOW.
Gregg H. Bilson, Jr., Executive VP/CFO, Independent Studio Services, Inc.

During the past 12 months, Omega experienced a significant drop in revenue. Moreover, first quarter 1999 figures are down 10 per cent from 1998. Normally studios have several feature films in production in the Spring. Currently we are working only on one feature in US production, and Omega is working closely with the set decorator to control costs.
Barry Pilchard, VP/General Manager, Omega Cinema Props

My business in the past year has seen a decrease of $500,000.00 in revenue resulting in layoffs and consideration of a permanent down sizing.
Frank Uchalik, President, ALPHA Medical Resources, Inc.

> I lost three movies in four months with producers I have worked with for years. I only made $1,800 in the first four months of 1999.
> *David Lewis, Director of Photography, age 53*
>
> For 24 years I have worked as a costume designer making between $80,000 and $120,000 in a good year. I have lost two jobs to Canada in the last year. I did a commercial for three days in January and that's the only work I've had since last March. We're scared of losing our home.
> *Betty Pecha Madden*
>
> I'm trying to stay afloat, but it's tough because of all the money I owe. What I'm finding is a lot of business going toward Canada and out of state. When I do sell something, I have to cut the price by 50–60 per cent.
> *Jesse Hurtado, Owner, Prima Equipment (lighting business)*

SOURCE: Department of Commerce, 2001: 13; also see 'Runaway', 2000

Blaise Gauba's 'Hollywouldn't' cartoon (2003) depicts the four Mounties of an apocalypse riding away with a gigantic Academy Award tethered to their rides, while the Hollywood sign falls to the ground. As two SAG officials put it, troping Don McLean's 'American Pie' but without his sense of meter:

> Bye, Bye Miss American pic,
>   drove my Daimler to the movies to see a foreign-made flic;
>   And good old actors were drinking whiskey and beer,
>   singing this is the day we're unemployed here,
>   this will be the day we're unemployed here.

(Quoted in Ulich and Simmons, 2001: 357)

For those who become itinerant workers, packing up to provide skills to runaways, many negative domestic impacts are associated with long absences, such as sadness, alcoholism, drug use, affairs and difficulties with children (James Bates, 2003a). On days off, some are found playing *State of Emergency*, an electronic game set in the urban dross caused by the 'American Trade Organization', which has in turn declared a state of emergency following a rebellion.

Global Hollywood 2
THE END

But the Global Hollywooders may well be back. For in addition to his unfortunate remark about New Zealanders, Mark Ordesky offered something more to his UCLA listeners while waiting for the *Lord of the Rings* cycle to accumulate. It was to do with the jobs that ran away: 'They're not lost, they've just been relocated' (quoted in Parkes, 2002). Someone has to keep looking for where they've gone.

Bibliography

Articles by title

'No title'. (1941) *Hollywood Reporter*, 6 March.

'007 Stirs the Marketing Mix'. (2002) *Guardian*, 22 November.

'60 Studios in India; Few New; Labs Not Bad'. (1975) *Variety*, 14 May.

'80% of India's Film Imports are American'. (1970) *Variety*, 5 April.

'1999: Une Année de Cinéma dans le Monde'. (2000) *Eurodata TV*, www.euro datatv.com/news/2000/23.06.html.

'Acronym Alert: NZFC CEO Joins AFMA'. (2003) *Onfilm*, October: 4.

'Administration Settles Television Piracy Case'. (2001) Associated Press,23 March.

'Africa's Hollywood'. (1997) *Economist*, 1 November.

'African, American Film Festival in Yaoundé'. (2003) *Panafrican News Agency Daily Newswire*, 27 August.

'After GATT Pique, Pix Pax Promoted'. (1994) *Daily Variety*, 8 June: 1, 16.

'Al-Qa'idah Trading in Fake Branded Goods'. (2002) *BBC Monitoring International Reports*, 11 September.

'American Fiction and Feature Films Continue to Dominate Western European Television Channel Programme Imports'. (2003) European Audiovisual Observatory, 28 January.

'Americans Go On-line with Anti-Canuck Views'. (2001) *Toronto Star*,14 February.

'Andersen Report on Indian Cinema'. (2000) Reuters.

'Animation: The Challenge for Investors'. (2001) *Screen Digest*, www.screendi gest.com/rep_animation.htm.

'Asia's Toonsville'. (1997) *Economist*, 22 February.

'Australia as a Film Location. Wallaby-wood'. (1998) *Economist*, 30 May.

'B3M Fund Will Fight Piracy; Film Industry Unites to Spur Enforcement'. (2000) *Bangkok Post*, 27 December.

'Back Scratching in La-La Land'. (2001) *Sydney Morning Herald*, 15 October.

'Bangkok: A Guide to Shooting Films in Thailand'. (2002) *CB Entertainment & Media World*, 4: 13–15.

'Ban Those Obnoxious Films: Bombay Appeal to Premiers'. (n. d.) Archived at Academy of Motion Picture Arts and Sciences, Margaret Herrick Library, Los Angeles.

'Barilla Si Allea con Spielberg'. (2003) *Il Sole 24 Ore*, January: 16.

' "Baywatch" Goes Out with the Tide'. (1999) *Economist*, 6 March: 39.

'Big Harry Deal! It's an Image Thing'. (2001) *Chicago Tribune*, 27 February.

'Bombay Theatremen Aid Civic Activities: Exhibitors and Managers Participate in Social and Public Life'. (1937) *Motion Picture Herald*, 8 July.

'Bond and Tomb Raider Fuel UK Film Optimism'. (2003) *Guardian*,14 January.

'Boycott the Anti-Indian Producers'. (c. 1938) Archived at Academy of Motion Picture Arts and Sciences, Margaret Herrick Library, Los Angeles.

'Breach of Contract on U.S. Film Import Charged in India'. (1971) *New York Times*, 16 July: 16.

'Brief *Amici Curiae* of Thirty-Three Media Scholars in Interactive Digital Software Association, *et al.* v. St. Louis County, *et al.*'. (2003) *Particip@tions: International Journal of Audience Research*, 1, no. 1.

'Canada Probes 2 Leading Exhibs'. (2000) *Hollywood Reporter*, 20 December.

'Canal Plus at 15: In the Big Leagues'. (1999) *Variety*, 28 June–11 July: 44.

'Censor Data Hints India Used Fewer Foreign Pix in '82'. (1983) *Variety*,4 May.

'Censors in India Frown on Murder, Drinking Scenes'. (1947) *Variety*,31 December.

'China: Opportunities for Co-production of Films in China'. (2002) *CB Entertainment & Media World*, 4: 10–13.

'Chinese Film Industry to Go Global'. (2001) *China Daily*, 29 March.

'Chinese Film Producers Leery Of Open Trade'. (2001) *Rotten Tomatoes*, 22 January, www.rottentomatoes.com/news-1921.

'Cine Exec Paints Feature Industry Bright in India'. (1970) *Hollywood Reporter*, 25 September.

'Circulation of Audiovisual Works and Training of Professionals: Commission Adopts its Proposals for the MEDIA PLUS Programme (2001–2005)'. (1999) Commission of the European Communities RAPID, 14 December.

'Clarity, Bouillabaisse, Story telling and a Tail-Wagging Dachshund. All Part of the Felicities of 1998'. (1999) MPA Press Release, 9 March.

'Columbia Pictures' *Stuart Little* Debuts with Major Event at Toy Fair '99'. (1999) *Business Wire*, 8 February.

'Commerce Secretary Mineta Releases Report on the Impact of the Migration of U.S. Film and Television Production'. (2001) US Department of Commerce Press Release, 18 January.

'Commission Report on the Results Obtained under the Media II Programme (1996–2000) from 1.1.96–30.6.98'. (1999) European Commission.

'Congress to Address Runaway Production'. (2001) International Cinematographers Guild, www.cameraguild.com/news/global/congress_runaway. htm.

'Connecticut Settles with Sony Pictures'. (2002) *Consumer Protection Report*, March: 6.

'Coverage of ShoWest'. (2000) Box Office Online, www.boxoff.com/shows/showest00.

'Culture Wars'. (1998) *Economist*, 12 September.

'Customer Comments: On Financing Flops'. (2003) *Euromoney Institutional Investor*, June.

'The Day the Dream Factory Woke Up'. (1970) *Life*, 27 February: 38–46.

'Defend Culture, Says ACTRA in Seattle for WTO Talks'. (1999) www.actra.com/news/.

'Déjà Vu'. (1994) *Film Journal*, 97, no. 6: 3.

'Digital Directions'. (2003) *Film Journal International*, December: 30–34.

'Disney Games in Spanish'. (2001) *Video Business*, 8 January: 6.

'Disney Labor Abuses in China'. (1999) www.summersault.com/~agi/clr/alerts/disneysweatshopsinchina.html.

'Disney's "Lion King" Comes Out Roaring in Theaters in China'. (1995) *Wall Street Journal*, 30 October.

'A Disquieting New Agenda for Trade'. (1994) *Economist*, 332, no. 7872: 55–56.

'Distribuidores Apuntan Oportunidad Negocio Cine en Español en USA'. (2000) *Efe News Services*, 22 June.

'Docklands Film Studios in the Can'. (2004) *Arts News*, 28 February.

'Earth Station 5 Declares War against the Motion Picture Association of America'. (2003) *PR Newswire*, 19 August.

'Egypt's Censorship Overlooks Egyptian Version of Bay Watch'. (2003) *Al-Bawaba*, 24 May.

'Egyptian Censors Ban US Comic Hit "Bruce Almighty" '. (2003) Agence France Presse, 6 November.

'Egyptians Ban Screening of American Films in Solidarity with Iraq'. (2003) *Al-Bawaba*, 13 April.

'Equifax Forms Alliance with VNU MIS Precision Marketing Group – Long Term Strategic Cross-Licensing Agreement Signed'. (2000) *Business Wire*, 15 May.

'España Promocionará Estreno de Coproducciones con Latinoamerica'. (2000) *Efe News Services*, 20 June.

'Eurimages Grants EUR 650,000 in Support for Filming of Kertesz's *Fateless*'. (2003) *MTI Econews*, 4 December.

'European Commissioner Wants More Film Exchange within EU'. (1999) Agence France Presse, 16 December.

'An Example to the Indian Film Industry: What Self-Help Can Do To Improve Indian Picture Production'. (1933) *Sound and Shadow*, February.

'Fiery End for Australian Jackass'. (2003) *Deutsche Presse-Agentur*, 27 October.

'Film Production and Distribution Trends: Shift in Balance between US and the Rest of the World – Part 1'. (2000) *Screen Digest,* June.

'Film Production Soars in U.K'. (2001) *Rotten Tomatoes*, 23 January, www.rottentomatoes.com/news-1926/.

'Foreign Bums on Seats'. (1998) *Economist*, 15 August.

'Fracasa el Estreno Ultimo del Filme Disney en Español para Hispanos'. (2001) *Efe News Services*, 9 January.

'Full of Eastern Promise'. (2001) *Sunday Times*, 21 January.

'Gandhi Pleads: Movies Asked to Help India'. (1959) *Hollywood Reporter*, 22 January.

'Global Animation Industry Pegged at $70bn by 2005'. (2001) *Indian Express*, 11 March.

'Global Cinema Admissions Overtake World Population'. (2002) *ScreenDaily.com*, 4 July.

'Global Finance: Time for a Redesign?' (1999) *Economist*, 30 January: 4–8 Survey Global Finance.

'Global Investing: Why Hollywood is Losing the Limelight'. (2001) *Financial Times*, 8 March: 24.

'Global Media Breakdown'. (2001) *Variety*, 19–25 February: 14.

'Global Programming Price Guide'. (2002) *Variety*, 7–13 October: A25.

'A Grand Confluence: The Intersection of Storytellers from East and West: A Reciting of the Fruitful Results of an Asian/American Cinema Collaboration', by Jack Valenti, Chairman and CEO, MPAA, presented at CineAsia in Singapore. (1997) MPAA Press Release, 3 December.

'Guide to International Film Production'. (2000) Ernst and Young report available at www.ey.com/global/gcr.nsf/International/2001_Guide_to_International_Film_Production.

'The G-Word'. (1997) *Financial Times*, 30 July: 15.

'Harry Potter and the Publishing Goldmine'. (2003) *Economist.com/Global Agenda*, 23 June: 1.

'Hint FFC May Be India's Sole Film Importer when MPEA Deal Runs Out'. (1976) *Variety*, 6 October.

'Hispanic-American TV Booms'. (2002) *Broadcasting & Cable*, 20 May: 29.

'Hollywood Cashes Runaway Checks in Czech Republic'. (n. d.) International Cinematographers Guild, www.cameraguild.com/ news/global/czech.htm.

'Hollywood Defends Itself against Cultural Imperialism Charges'. (1998) Agence France Presse, 1 July.

'Hollywood Downunder 2: Crucial Time for Attracting US TV Production to Australia'. (2004) *Screen Hub*, 1 March.

'Hollywood Eyes *Aanken*'. (2002) *Times of India*, 10 December.

'Hollywood Heads South of Border to Mexico'. (2000) *Jefferson City News Tribune*, 12 June.

'Hollywood May Be Local Software Co's Next Stop'. (2003) *Economic Times*, 14 March.

'Hollywood Movies Enjoy Great Popularity in China'. (2003) *People's Daily*, 5 December.

'Hollywood on the Vltava'. (2001) *Economist*, 3 February: 65.

'Hollywood Reaches Out to NASA at L.A. Power Lunch'. (2002) Reuters, 24 September.

'Hollywood's Incredible Turkey Machine is as Prolific as Ever'. (1999) *National Post*, 17 March: C09.

'Hollywood's Southern Belles Rarely Ring True'. (2004) *News and Record*, 8 January: 4.

'Home Alone in Europe'. (1997) *Economist*, 22 March.

'Hong Kong: Film Industry Incentives'. (2002) *CB Entertainment & Media World*, 4: 9–10.

'H'wood Buries Overseas Pix'. (1999) *Variety*, 25–31 January: 1, 90–91.

'IATSE Global Rule None'. (2002) *Viewfinder*, 1, no. 4: 10.

'iBeam and CinemaNow Partner to Stream Pay-Per-View Feature Films'. (2000) *Business Wire*, 9 November.

'Ignored: 370 Million! Hindu Says Hollywood is Doing Just That'. (1941) *Hollywood Citizen News*, 23 April: 3.

'The Imbalance of Trade in Films and Television Programmes between North America and Europe Continues to Deteriorate'. (2002) European Audiovisual Observatory, 9 April.

'In Brief'. (2000) *Screen International*, 9 June.

'In Short'. (1994) *Screen International*, 15 April.

'India Bans All Drinking in Films'. (1948) *Hollywood Reporter*, 9 September.

'India Bans Films of Glamorous Vice'. (1955) *Los Angeles Mirror News*, 11 March.

'India Censors on Eampage: Cutting, Banning H'wood Films at Alarming Rate; Even Musicals Scissored'. (1954) *Hollywood Reporter*, 15 November.

'India Company to Study Our Industry'. (1939) *Motion Picture Herald*, 13 May.

p. 26

'India Makes Bid for Attention'. (1946) *New York Times*, 3 November.

'India Reports Opening 82 New Theaters in 1970; Total 6987'. (1971) *Hollywood Reporter*, 21 June.

'India to Permit Only Neutral Pix; Bans Cease Fire'. (n. d., *c.* 1954) *Variety*.

'India's Ban on African Pictures'. (1956) *Hollywood Reporter*, 28 May.

'India's Prolific Film Production'. (1965) *Variety*, 10 February.

'India Promises to Lift its Ban on American Pix'. (1992) *Variety*, 2 March.

'Indian Showbiz Industry Appoints Sleuths at Asian Stores in U.S.'. (2001) *Times of India*, 11 June.

'Indonesian Moslem Youths Call for Ban on American Films'. (2003) *Deutsche Presse-Agentur*, 25 March.

'Intellectual Property Crimes: Are Proceeds from Counterfeited Goods Funding Terrorism?' (2003) Hearing of the House International Relations Committee. *Federal News Service*, 16 July.

'International Film'. (2002) *Screen Finance*, 5 July.

'Intertainer Creates New Platform for Independent Filmakers' [*sic*]. (2002) *TV Meets the Web*, 25 April.

'IP Watch'. (1998) *IP Worldwide*, November/December.

'IP Watch'. (1999) *IP Worldwide*, January/February.

'Jacques Chirac'. (2003) *Financial Times*, 25 February: 12.

'Lift Three-Year Film Ban on US Imports to India'. (1975) *Boxoffice*, 10 March.

'Lumiere'. (2003) European Audiovisual Observatory, 21 March.

'Masters Command'. (2002) *Viewfinder*, 1, no. 4: 7.

'The Monster That Ate Hollywood' (2001). Vince DiPersio and Adam Bardach for PBS Frontline and Riot Pictures, pbs.org/wgbh/pages/frontline/shows/hollywood.

'More Children Surfing the Web'. (2003) *New Zealand Herald*, 2 October.

'Movie Shoot Gives Shot in the Arm to Cambodia'. (2000) *Movie/TV News*, 1 December, us.imdb.com/SB?20001201.

'Movies Abroad: The New Maharajahs'. (1959) *Time*, 5 January.

'MPA Appoints New Technology Officer'. (1999) MPA Press Release, 21 June.

'MPAA Continues Pirate Video Lab Assault'. (1995) MPAA Press Release, 29 November.

'MPAA Identifies Malaysia, Brazil as Problem Areas for Intellectual Property'. (2000) MPAA Press Release, 18 February.

'MPEAA Merges Piracy Ops'. (1993) *Variety*, 16 March.

'MPEAA: Piracy War Seizes Record Spoils'. (1992) *Screen International*, 27 March.

'MPEAA Victory over Singapore Pirates.' (1990) *Screen International*, 17 February.

'Music Industry Reels At Hearing'. (2003) *Sunday Business Post*, 4 May.

'New Bond Film "a Giant Advert" '. (2002) *BBC News*, 18 November.

'New Company Set Up to Deal with Imported Movies'. (2003) *Xinhua*, 8 August.

'New Film Council Analysis Shows Inward Investment Up, Domestic Spending Down, Fewer Films Shooting in UK but Co-productions Flourishing'. (2003) British Film Council, January.

'New Line Cinema Verifies Approximately 1.7 Million Downloads of Exclusive "The Lord of the Rings" Preview During 1st Day of Operation'. (2000) *PR Newswire*, 10 April.

'New Research Reveals the Real Value of Cinema Food Sales'. (2002) *ScreenDaily.com*, 6 August.

'No More Monopoly Distribution of Imported Blockbusters'. (2003) *China Radio International*, 16 August, www.crienglish.com/636/2003-9-1/20@39699.htm.

'Not the Last Picture Show'. (1995) *Economist*, 2 December.

'Paramount Gets New Financing'. (1996) *New York Times*, 14 May: D11.

'Polish Leader Wants EU-wide Worker Movement'. (2000) *United Press International*, 19 December.

'The PolyGram Test'. (1998) *Economist*, 15 August.

'Presidents of SAG, DGA, TV Academy to Join Edward James Almos, Other Actors, Politicians, Union Leaders and Thousands of Filmworkers at March and Rally in

Hollywood on Sunday, Aug. 15'. (1999). *Business Wire*, 8 December.

'Principal Photography Under Way on New Regency's "Made in America" for Distribution by Warner Bros'. (1992) *PR Newswire*, 18 May.

'Producers Warn SAG to Back Off'. (2002) SAG Press Release, 17 May.

'Protecting America's Grandest Trade Prize'. (1998) MPAA Press Release, 10 September.

'Protecting America's Most Prized Export in the Digital World'. (1998) MPAA Press Release, 16 July.

'Protecting Australian Voices under the FTA'. (2004) Minister for Communications Information Technology and the Arts Press Release, 10 February.

'Quo Vadis?'. (1996) MPAA Press Release, 23 May.

'Rank May Use Frozen Funds to Shoot Films in India; Eyes Co-prods'. (1976) *Variety*, 15 December.

'Relocating the Back Office'. (2003) *Economist*, 13 December: 67–69.

'A Renewed Understanding of American Blockbuster Films'. (2003) *Chinese Education and Society*, 36, no. 1: 48–54.

'ReplayTV Users' Lawsuit is Dismissed'. (2004) *Los Angeles Times*, 13 January: C2.

'Report Made by Top Picture Man There'. (1948) *Hollywood Reporter*, 12 December.

'Ringing Up the Cash Register?' (2002) *Onfilm*, April: 13.

'Runaway Production: An Opinion'. (2000).

'Russia Calls on MPA to Enter into Pirate Battle'. (1995) *Screen International*, 17 November.

'SA Premier Challenges FTA'. (2004) *Screen Hub*, 25 February.

'San Miguelwood'. (2004) *Economist*, 10 January: 31.

'Saving Hollywood'. (2001) *Los Angeles Daily News*, 9 January.

'Screens without Frontiers'. (2000) webworld.unesco.org/screens/html/about.html.

'Setback for Hollywood Movie Empire as DVD Jon Acquitted'. (2003) Agence France Presse, 22 December.

'Sex, Lies and Earth Station 5'. (2003) *Economist*, 20 December.

'Shall We, Yawn, Go to a Film?' (1997) *Economist*, 1 February: 85–86.

'Soft Money – The United Kingdom'. (2002) *ScreenDaily.com*, 17 December.

'Solidarity with Striking SAG and AFTRA Members'. (2000) AFTRA Press Release, www.actra.com/news/101900n.htm.

'Sony-Led Consortium Wins Major $314 Million Contract to Build Egyptian "Media Production City"'. (1997) *African Film WebMeeting*, 29 January.

'The Spider's Bite'. (2002) *Economist*, 11 May: 57.

'Statement by Jack Valenti on the 9th Circuit Court of Appeals Ruling on Napster'. (2001) MPAA Press Release, 12 February.

'Statement of Jack Valenti, Chairman and CEO, MPA, before the Committee on Ways and Means Subcommittee on Trade, Regarding US–China Trade Relations and the Possible Accession of China to the WTO'. (1999) MPAA Press Release, 8 June.

'Statement of Jack Valenti, Chairman and CEO, MPA, before the Special 301 Committee'. (1999) MPAA Press Release, 6 June.

'Storm over Globalisation'. (1999) *Economist*, 27 November: 15–16.

'Technology-Labor: New Opportunities for Developing Countries'. (1999) *Inter Press Service English News Wire*, 8 December.

'Telenovela de Caracol Vendida a Walt Disney Company'. (2001) *El Tiempo*, 25 January.

'Telephone Interview with Haskell Wexler'. (2002) *Viewfinder*, 1, no. 4: 1.

'Terrorists Run Pirate DVD Rackets'. (2003) *The Express*, 1 December.

'Thailand Sees Insult to Monarchy as it Bans "Anna"'. (1999) *Wall Street Journal*, 29 December: B11.

'Thailand Wants Joint Ventures with Foreign Film Producers'. (2004) *New Straits Times*, 24 January: 15.

'Tiaozhan Dayu Jiyu: Dai, Jinhau Jiaoshou Tan Shiji Zhijiao de Zhongguo Dianying'. (2002) National Museum of Modern Chinese Literature, Beijing, 6 January, www.wxg.org.cn/jiangzuo.

'TiVo Partners with Nielsen, ASI'. (2000) *Advertising Age*, 24 July: 2.

'Top 100 All-Time Domestic Grossers'. (1994) *Variety*, 17–23 October: M60.

'Tough Girl Lara Needs Armed Bodyguards'.
   (2000) Movie/TV News, 20 October,
   us.imdb.com/WN?20001020.
'Towards an East African Film and TV Industry'.
   (2001) The Nation (Kenya), 14 July.
'Trade Barriers, Erected in Fear, Hurt U.S.
   Workers'. (1997) USA Today, 16 October: 10A.
'TV Fiction Programming: Prime Time is
   Domestic, Off-Prime Time is American'.
   (2001) European Audiovisual Observatory,
   9 October.
'UIP in Digital Overhaul to Enhance Tailored
   Offering'. Precision Marketing,
   19 December: 3.
'U.S. and Australia Complete Free Trade
   Agreement'. (2004) Office of the United
   States Trade Representative Press Release,
   8 February.
'U.S. Elevates Korea to Priority Watch List'.
   (2004) Office of the United States Trade
   Representative, 8 January.
'U.S. Film Receipts Climb in India Despite
   Censors'. (1977) Hollywood Reporter,
   22 April.
'U.S. Films Not Competition in India'. (1950)
   Motion Picture Herald, 27 May.
'U.S. Majors Curbed in India, but Market Has
   Big Potential'. (1977) Variety, 2 February.
'USTR 2001 Trade Policy Agenda and 2000
   Annual Report'. (2001) Office of the
   United States Trade Representative,
   6 March.
'Valenti Announces Formation of Committee
   in Support of China Trade'. (2000) MPAA
   Press Release, 9 February.
'Valenti Calls on Congress to Protect
   Copyright, Says Some Studios to be Online
   within Six Months'. (2001) MPAA Press
   Release, 22 January.
'Valenti Supports Normal Trade Relations for
   China and WTO Accession Conditional on
   Market Access'. (1999) MPAA Press
   Release, 8 June.
'Valenti Urged Senate to Grant PNTR to China'.
   (2000) MPAA Press Release, 11 April.
'A View to Make a Killing'. (2002) Age,
   12 December.
'VNU and ACNielsen to Provide Complete
   Measurement of Pre-recorded Video and
   DVD Sales'. (1999) Business Wire,
   15 September.

'VNU'. (2000) Hoover's Company Profile
   Database – World Companies.
'VNU NV'. (2000) The Major Companies
   Database. Graham & Whiteside Ltd.
'Warner Bros. Exits Australian Exhibition Joint
   Venture'. (2003) ScreenDaily.com, 11
   March.
'Welcome Note from the President'. (2002).
   ASIFA Newsletter, 6.
'Why Hollywood is Losing the Limelight'.
   (2001) Financial Times, 8 March: 24.
' "With a Wild Surmise, Silent, upon a Peak in
   Darien": The Audiovisual Revolution in
   the Americas'. (1996) MPAA Press Release,
   15 July.
'World Cinema: Poor Product Fails
   Multiplexes'. (2000) Screen Digest,
   September.
'A World View'. (1997) Economist,
   29 November.
'Written Testimony of Bonnie J. K. Richardson,
   V. P. Trade and Federal Affairs, MPAA,
   Before the U.S. China Commission Public
   Hearings on WTO Compliance and
   Sectoral Issues'. (2002) Department of
   State, 18 January.
'Wrung Out to Dry'. (2004) Sydney Morning
   Herald, 25 February.
'A Yank in Thirty Days'. (1927) Film Fun,
   February: 56.
'You're Not in Kansas Any More: Hollywood'.
   (1995) Economist, 4 February.

Articles and Books by Author

Abbas, K. Ahmad. (1940) 'The "Filum" in
   India'. Life and Letters 5, no. 40: 192.
Abbey, Alan. (2003) 'Gaza Based Internet
   Company Dares US Industries to Sue'.
   Jerusalem Post, 1 September: 3.
Abdi, S. N. M. (2003) 'Copycat Bollywood Put
   in the Dock'. South China Morning Post, 27
   June: 12.
Abel, Richard. (1999) The Red Rooster Scare:
   Making Cinema American, 1900–1910.
   Berkeley: University of California Press.
Acheson, Keith and Christopher Maule. (1989)
   'Trade Policy Responses to New
   Technology in the Film and Television
   Industry'. Journal of World Trade 23, no. 2:
   35–48.

Acheson, Keith and Christopher Maule. (1991) 'Shadows behind the Scenes: Political Exchange and the Film Industry'. *Millennium Journal of International Studies* 20, no. 2: 287–307.

Acheson, Keith and Christopher Maule. (1994) 'International Regimes for Trade, Investment and Labour Mobility in the Cultural Industries'. *Canadian Journal of Communication* 19: 149–63.

Acheson, Keith and Christopher Maule. (1999) *Much Ado about Culture: North American Trade Disputes.* Ann Arbor: University of Michigan Press.

Acland, Charles R. (2003) *Screen Traffic: Movies, Multiplexes, and Global Culture.* Durham: Duke University Press.

Adler, M. (1985) 'Stardom and Talent'. *American Economic Review* 75, no. 1: 208–12.

Adler, Tim. (2002) 'Audiovisual Eureka Turns to the South East'. *Screen Finance*, 2 August.

Adler, Tim. (2003a) 'Toubon Outlines Eurimages Reform Package'. *Screen Finance*, 15 January.

Adler, Tim. (2003b) 'EU Spending E1.23 Bn a Year on Subsidy'. *Screen Finance*, 26 March.

Adler, Tim. (2003c) 'Financiers Call for Distinct Unit to Police Future International Co-productions'. *Screen Finance*, 19 November.

Adler, Tim. (2003d) 'Media Plus Faces Budget Cutbacks Post 2007'. *Screen Finance*, 19 November.

Ahmed, Ashfaq. (2003) 'Dollywood Studios Opens Floor to Movie Makers'. *Gulf News*, 7 October.

Aiyer, V. Shankar. (2000) 'Film Marketing: Happy Endings'. *India Today*, 6 November: 78.

Aksoy, Asu and Kevin Robins. (1992) 'Hollywood for the Twenty-First Century: Global Competition for Critical Mass in Image Markets'. *Cambridge Journal of Economics* 16, no. 1: 1–22.

Alberge, Dalya and Dominic Kennedy. (1999) 'Lottery-Funded Films Fail to Show a Profit'. *The Times*, 20 May: 36–37.

Albert, Steven. (1998) 'Movie Stars and the Distribution of Financially Successful Films in the Motion Picture Industry'. *Journal of Cultural Economics* 22, no. 4: 249–70.

Alexander, Garth. (2000) 'Cyber-Raiders Attack'. *Sunday Times*, 1 August.

Alford, James and Jon Herskovitz. (2001) 'Japan, Korea Find Common Ground'. *Variety*, 26 February: 28.

Allan, Blaine. (1988) 'The State of the State of the Art on TV'. *Queen's Quarterly* 95, no. 2: 318–29.

Allen, Donna, Ramona R. Rush and Susan J. Kaufman, eds. (1996) *Women Transforming Communications: Global Intersections.* Thousand Oaks, CA: Sage.

Allen, Jeanne Thomas. (1983) 'Copyright and Early Theater, Vaudeville, and Film Competition'. *Film before Griffith.* Ed. John Fell. Berkeley: University of California Press. 176–87.

Alster, Norm. (2003) 'It's Just a Game, but Hollywood is Paying Attention'. *New York Times*, 23 November: C4.

Altman, Rick. (1998) 'Reusable Packaging: Generic Products and the Recycling Process'. *Refiguring American Film Genres: History and Theory.* Ed. Nick Browne. Berkeley: University of California Press. 1–41.

American Academy of Pediatrics. (2001) *Media Matters*, www.aap.org/advo cacy/mediamatters.htm.

Amin, Samir. (1997) *Capitalism in the Age of Globalization.* London: Zed.

Amir, Hussein Y. (1999) 'American Programs on Egyptian Television'. *Images of the U.S. Around the World: A Multilateral Perspective.* Ed. Yahya R. Kamalipour. Albany: State University of New York Press. 319–34.

Amman, John. (2002) 'Union and the New Economy: Motion Picture and Television Unions Offer a Model for New Professionals'. *Working USA* 6, no. 2.

Amsden, Alice H. and Takashi Hikino. (1999) 'The Left and Globalization'. *Dissent* 46, no. 2: 7–9.

Anderson, Benedict. (1983) *Imagined Communities: Reflections on the Origin and Spread of Nationalism.* London: Verso.

Anderson, Kurt. (1993) 'No Tariff on Tom Cruise'. *Time*, 19 July: 67.

Anderson, Sarah. (2001) 'Peddling the E-Ticket to the Development Train'. *Corporate Watch*, 8 March, www.corpwatch.org/trac/issues/net/sanderson. html.

Andreas, Peter. (2003) 'Redrawing the Line: Borders and Security in the Twenty-First Century'. *International Security* Fall: 78–107.

Andrews, N. (1998) 'Roll Up! It's a Launch: Filming a Blockbuster is One Thing; Striking Gold is Another'. *Financial Times*, 3 January: 1.

Aoki, Keith. (1993a) 'Authors, Inventors, and Trademark Owners: Private Intellectual Property and the Public Domain. Part 1'. *Columbia-VLA Journal of Law and the Arts* 18: 1–73.

Aoki, Keith. (1993b) 'Adrift in the Intertext: Authorship and Audience "Recoding" Rights: Comment on Robert H. Rotstein, "Beyond Metaphor: Copyright Infringement and the Fiction of the Work" '. *Chicago-Kent Law Review* 68: 805–39.

Aoki, Keith. (1996) 'Surveying Law and Borders: (Intellectual) Property and Sovereignty. Notes Towards a Cultural Geography of Authorship'. *Stanford Law Review* 48: 1293–355.

Armes, Roy. (1987) *Third World Film Making and the West*. Berkeley: University of California Press.

Arnheim, Rudolf. (1983) 'On Duplication'. *The Forger's Art: Forgery and the Philosophy of Art*. Ed. Denis Dutton. Berkeley: University of California Press. 232–45.

Arthur, Charles. (2001) 'First Film Released for Rental over the Internet'. Independent Digital Ltd.

Association of Internet Professionals. (2000) 'Helping Our Members Succeed in Business', www.association.org/about.cfm.

Atkins, William. (2002) *The Politics of Southeast Asia's New Media*. London: Curzon.

Atkinson, G. (1997) 'Capital and Labour in the Emerging Global Economy'. *Journal of Economic Issues* 31, no. 2: 385–91.

Atkinson, Lisa. (1997) 'What's Entertainment? China's Entertainment Industry'. *China Business Review* 24, no. 2: 38–40.

Audirac, Ivonne. (2003) 'Information-Age Landscape Outside the Developed World: Bangalore, India, and Guadalajara, Mexico'. *Journal of the American Planning Association* 69, no. 1.

Aufderheide, Patricia. (1998) 'Made in Hong Kong: Translation and Transmutation'. *Play it Again, Sam: Retakes on Remakes*. Ed. Andrew Horton and Stuart Y. McDougal. Berkeley: University of California Press. 191–99.

Augros, Joël. (2000) *El Dinero de Hollywood: Financiación, Producción, Distribución y Nuevos Mercados*. Trans. Josep Torrell. Barcelona: Paidós.

Austin, Bruce A. (1989) *Immediate Seating: A Look at Movie Audiences*. Belmont, CA: Wadsworth.

Austin, Thomas. (2002) *Hollywood, Hype and Audiences: Selling and Watching Popular Film in the 1990s*. Manchester: Manchester University Press.

Australian Film Commission. (2002a) *Submission to the Department of Foreign Affairs and Trade*.

Australian Film Commission. (2002b) *Foreign Film and Television Drama Production in Australia: A Research Report*.

Axtmann, Roland. (1993) 'Society, Globalization and the Comparative Method'. *History of the Human Sciences* 6, no. 2: 53–74.

Bacon, David. (1999) 'Is Free Trade Making Hollywood a Rustbelt?' *Labournet*, 19 November, www.labournet.org/x/copy-of-site/news/112399/01.html.

Bacon, David. (2000a) 'Globalization: Two Faces, Both Ugly'. *Dollars and Sense*, 1 March: 18–20, 40.

Bacon, David. (2000b) 'Can Workers Beat Globalisation?' www.focusweb.org/publications/2000/Can%20workers%20beat%20glob alisation.htm.

Badam, Ramola T. (2003) 'Bollywood May Have Lost the Plot'. *Advertiser*, 16 June: 28.

Bagai, Ram. (*c.* 1938) 'The Film Goes Forward in India'. Unsourced article archived at Academy of Motion Picture Arts and Sciences, Margaret Herrick Library, Los Angeles.

Bain, Peter and Phil Taylor. (2002) 'Ringing the Changes? Union Recognition and Organisation in Call Centres in the UK Finance Sector'. *Industrial Relations Journal* 33, no. 3: 246–61.

Baker, C. Edwin. (2000) 'An Economic Critique of Free Trade in Media Products'. *North Carolina Law Review* 78: 1357–435.

Baker, Wayne E. and Robert R. Faulkner. (1991) 'Role as Resource in the Hollywood Film Industry'. *American Journal of Sociology* 97: 279–309.

Bakker, Gerben. (2003) 'Building Knowledge about the Consumer: The Emergence of Market Research in the Motion Picture Industry'. *Business History* 45, no. 3: 101–27.

Baldoz, R., C. Koeber and P. Kraft, eds. (2001) *The Critical Study of Work: Labor, Technology, and Global Production*. Philadelphia: Temple University Press.

Balio, Tino. (1993). *History of the American Cinema, Volume Five: Grand Design: Hollywood as a Modern Business Enterprise, 1930–1939*. New York: Charles Scribner's Sons.

Balio, Tino. (1998a) ' "A Major Presence in all the World's Important Markets": The Globalization of Hollywood in the 1990s'. *Contemporary Hollywood Cinema*. Ed. Steve Neale and Murray Smith. London: Routledge. 58–73.

Balio, Tino. (1998b) 'The Art Film Market in the New Hollywood'. *Hollywood and Europe: Economics, Culture, National Identity 1945–95*. Ed. Geoffrey Nowell-Smith and Steven Ricci. London: British Film Institute. 63–73.

Barbrook, Richard and Andy Cameron. (1996) 'The Californian Ideology'. *Science as Culture* 6, no. 1: 44–72.

Bardach, Ann Louise. (2000) 'The Last Tycoon'. *Los Angeles Magazine* 4, no. 45: 74.

Barker, Ernest. (1927) *National Character and the Factors in its Formation*. London: Methuen.

Barker, Martin. (1993) 'Sex, Violence, and Videotape'. *Sight and Sound* 3, no. 5: 10–12.

Barlow, John Perry. (n. d.) 'The Economy of Mind on the Global Net', www.eff.org/pub/Publications/John_Perry _Barlow/idea_economy.article.

Barnatt, Christopher and Ken Starkey. (1994) 'The Emergence of Flexible Networks in the UK Television Industry'. *British Journal of Management* 5: 251–60.

Barnouw, Erik and S. Krishnaswamy. (1980) *Indian Film*. New York: Oxford University Press.

Baron, James N., Michael T. Hannan and M. Diane Burton. (2001) 'Labor Pains: Change in Organizational Models and Employee Turnover in Young, High-Tech Firms'. *American Journal of Sociology* 106, no. 4: 960–1012.

Barrett, Amy. (2000) 'The Unkindest "Cut!" ' *New York Times Magazine*, 10 September: 22.

Barshefsky, Charlene. (1998) Testimony of the United States Trade Representative before the House Appropriations Committee Subcommittee on Commerce, Justice, State, the Judiciary and Related Agencies, 31 March.

Barson, Steve. (2000) 'Cross-Border Trade with Mexico and the Prospect for Worker Solidarity: The Case of Mexico'. *Critical Sociology* 26, nos. 1–2: 13–35.

Bart, Peter. (2000) 'Will France's Hollywood Souffle Rise?' *Variety*, 19–25 June: 1, 4, 84.

Basel Action Network and Silicon Valley Toxics Coalition. (2002) *Exporting Harm: The High-Tech Trashing of Asia*.

Bassiouni, M. Cherif. (2001) 'Universal Jurisdiction for International Crimes: Historical Perspectives and Contemporary Practice'. *Virginia Journal of International Law* 42: 81–162.

Basuroy, Suman, Subimal Chatterjee and S. Abraham Ravid. (2003) 'How Critical are Critical Reviews? The Box Office Effects of Film Critics, Star Power, and Budgets'. *Journal of Marketing* 67, no. 4: 103–17.

Bates, James. (1993) 'Canal Plus Pulls Back'. *Los Angeles Times*, 21 February: D1.

Bates, James. (1998) 'Making Movies and Moving On'. *Los Angeles Times*, 19 January: 1.

Bates, James. (2000) 'Site Hopes to Put Profitable Spin on Hollywood Fame Game'. *Los Angeles Times*, 19 May: C1.

Bates, James. (2003a) 'On the Road, on Location'. *Los Angeles Times*, 7 January: A1.

Bates, James. (2003b) 'Warner Douses Smoking Promo'. *Los Angeles Times*, 5 March.

Bates, James and Maggie Farley. (1999) 'Hollywood, China in a Chilly Embrace'. *Los Angeles Times*, 13 June: A1, A30.

Bates, Jim. (2003) 'Reassessing Hollywood Job Data'. *Los Angeles Times*, 3 March.

Bauman, Zygmunt. (1998) *Globalization: The Human Consequences*. New York: Columbia University Press.

Beals, Gregory. (2001) 'The Birth of Asiawood'. *Newsweek*, 21 May: 56.

Beals, Ralph L. (1951) 'On Bierstedt's Review of Powdermaker's *Hollywood – The Dream Factory*'. *American Sociological Review* 16, no. 4: 549–50.

Beams, Nick. (2004) 'Another Step in the "Balkanisation" of the World Market'. *World Socialist Web Site*, 12 February.

Beard, Mary. (2002) 'Asterix and the Soul of France'. *Independent*, 4 April, Thursday Review: 1.

Becker, Gary S. (1983) *Human Capital: A Theoretical and Empirical Analysis, with Special Reference to Education*, 2nd edn. Chicago: University of Chicago Press.

Bedell, Doug. (2003) 'Movie Downloads Don't Live Up to Predictions in Titles'. *Dallas Morning News*, 25 December.

Behar, Richard. (2000) 'Beijing's Phony War on Fakes'. *Fortune*, 30 October.

Bellah, Robert N., Richard Madsen, William M. Sullivan, Ann Swidler and Steven M. Tipton. (1992) *The Good Society*. New York: Alfred A. Knopf.

Benhabib, Seyla. (1999) 'Citizens, Residents, and Aliens in a Changing World: Political Membership in the Global Era'. *Social Research* 66, no. 3: 709–44.

Benjamin, Walter. (1968) *Illuminations*. New York: Harcourt, Brace and World.

Benkler, Yochai. (1999) 'Free as the Air to Common Use: First Amendment Constraints on Enclosure of the Public Domain'. *New York University Law Review* 74: 354–446.

Benkler, Yochai. (2000) 'VIACOM-CBS Merger: From Consumers to Users: Shifting the Deeper Structures of Regulation towards Sustainable Commons and User Access'. *Federal Communications Law Journal* 52: 561–79.

Bennett, Dan. (2001) 'Video en Espanol'. *Video Store*, 14–20 October: 22–23.

Bennett, Tony. (1990) *Outside Literature*. New York: Routledge.

Bennett, Tony. (1992) 'Putting Policy into Cultural Studies'. *Cultural Studies*. Ed. Lawrence Grossberg, Cary Nelson and Paula Treichler. New York: Routledge. 23–37.

Bennett, Tony. (2001) *Differing Diversities: Transversal Study on the Theme of Cultural Policy and Cultural Diversity*. Strasbourg Cedex: Council of Europe Publishing.

Bensinger, Ken. (2002) 'Stealing the Show?' *Wall Street Journal*, 27 August: B1, B4.

Berg, Charles Ramírez. (1992) *Cinema of Solitude: A Critical Study of Mexican Film, 1967–1983*. Austin: University of Texas Press.

Berkman, Meredith. (1992) 'Coming to America'. *Entertainment Weekly*, 14 October.

Berlant, Lauren. (1997) *The Queen of America Goes to Washington DC: Essays on Sex and Citizenship*. Durham: Duke University Press.

Berlingame, Jon. (2000) 'The Sound of Work Leaving LA'. *Los Angeles Times*, 23 July.

Berman, Nathaniel. (1992) 'Nationalism Legal and Linguistic: The Teachings of European Jurisprudence'. *New York University Journal of International Law and Politics* 24, no. 1: 1515–578.

Bettig, Ronald V. (1990) 'Extending the Law of Intellectual Property: Hollywood's International Anti-Videotape Piracy Campaign'. *Journal of Communication Inquiry* 14, no. 2: 159–84.

Bettig, Ronald V. (1996) *Copyrighting Culture: The Political Economy of Intellectual Property*. Boulder, CO: Westview Press.

Bettig, Ronald V. (1997) 'The Enclosure of Cyberspace'. *Critical Studies in Mass Communication* 14: 138–57.

Bhagwati, Jagdish. (2002) 'Coping with Antiglobalization: A Trilogy of Discontents'. *Foreign Affairs* 81, no. 1: 2–7.

Bickerton, Ian. (2003) 'VNU to Boost Billboard Technology'. *Financial Times*, 18 August: 23.

Bielby, Denise D. and C. Lee Harrington. (2002) 'Markets and Meanings: The Global Syndication of Television Programming'. *Global Culture: Media, Arts, Policy, and Globalization*. Ed. Diana Crane, Nobuko Kawashima and Ken'ichi Kawasaki. New York: Routledge. 215–32.

Bing, Jonathan. (2002) 'H'W'D Says Good Morning, Vietnam'. *Variety*, 2–8 December: 9, 15.

Binning, Cheryl. (1999a) 'Demand Outstrips Healthy Cash Injections'. *Playback*, 5 April: 23.

Binning, Cheryl. (1999b) 'NSI Launches Marketing Initiative'. *Playback*, 14 June: 2.

Birchenough, Tom. (1997) 'MPA Bows Moscow Antipiracy Putsch.' *Variety*, 23 July.

Biskind, Peter. (2004) *Down and Dirty Pictures: Miramax, Sundance, and the Rise of Independent Film*. New York: Simon & Schuster.

Bjork, Ulf Jonas. (2000) 'The U.S. Commerce Department Aids Hollywood Exports, 1921–1933'. *Historian* 62, no. 3: 575–87.

Blackstone, Erwin A. and Gary W. Bowman. (1999) 'Vertical Integration in Motion Pictures'. *Journal of Communication* 49, no. 1: 123–39.

Blair, Helen. (2003) 'Winning and Losing in Flexible Labour Markets: The Formation and Operation of Networks of Interdependence in the UK Film Industry'. *Sociology* 37, no. 4: 677–94.

Blair, Helen and Al Rainnie. (1998) 'Flexible Films?' Paper presented to the 16th Annual International Labour Process Conference, 7–9 April.

Blair, Helen, Susan Grey and Keith Randle. (2001) 'Working in Film – Employment in a Project Based Industry'. *Personnel Review* 30, no. 2.

Blankstein, Andrew. (2001) 'Company Town: Lawmaker Urges Stop to Runaway Production'. *Los Angeles Times*, 31 January.

Bloom, David. (2002) 'Inside Moves: Yo, "Mama"'. *Variety.com*, 19 May.

Blumer, Herbert. (1933) *Movies and Conduct*. New York: Macmillan.

Blumer, Herbert and Philip M. Hauser. (1933) *Movies, Delinquency and Crime*. New York: Macmillan.

Bobo, Jacqueline. (1995) *Black Women as Cultural Readers*. New York: Columbia University Press.

Bodey, Michael. (2003) 'Battle Swords Drawn in Fight for Hollywood'. *Daily Telegraph*, 26 April: 31.

Bodo, Carla. (2000) *The Film Industry in Italy: The Market and the State in the Nineties*. Report for the European Audiovisual Laboratory.

Boliek, Brooks. (2000) 'Bush's Haul from Hollywood Growing'. *Milwaukee Journal Sentinel*, 1 August: 6B.

Boliek, Brooks. (2003) 'New Coalition Boosts Free Trade'. *Hollywood Reporter*, 17 March.

Bono, Francesco. (1995) 'Cinecittà'. *UNESCO Courier*, 8 July: 68.

Bordwell, David, Kristin Thompson and Janet Staiger. (1988) *The Classical Hollywood Cinema: Film Style and Mode of Production to 1960*. New York: Routledge.

Boryskavich, Krista and Aaron Bowler. (2002) 'Hollywood North: Tax Incentives and the Film Industry in Canada'. *Asper Review of International Business and Trade Law* 2: 25–42.

Bosch, Aurora and M. Fernanda del Rincón. (2000) 'Dreams in a Dictatorship: Hollywood and Franco's Spain, 1939–1956'. *'Here, There and Everywhere': The Foreign Politics of American Popular Culture*. Ed. Reinhold Wagnleitner and Elaine Tyler May. Hanover: University Press of New England. 100–15.

Bosteels, Bruno. (1998) 'From Text to Territory: Félix Guattari's Cartographies of the Unconscious'. *Deleuze and Guattari: New Mappings in Politics, Philosophy and Culture*. Ed. Eleanor Kaufman and Kevin Jon Heller. Minneapolis: University of Minnesota Press. 145–74.

Bourdieu, Pierre. (1998) *On Television*. Trans. Priscilla Parkhurst Ferguson. New York: New Press.

Bourdieu, Pierre. (1999) 'The State, Economics and Sport'. Trans. Hugh Dauncey and Geoff Hare. *France and the 1998 World Cup: The National Impact of a World Sporting Event*. Ed. Hugh Dauncey and Geoff Hare. London: Frank Cass. 15–21.

Bowling, Kenneth. (1991) *The Creation of Washington, DC: The Idea and Location of the American Capital*. Fairfax, VA: George Mason University Press.

Bowring, Finn. (2002) 'Post-Fordism and the End of Work'. *Futures* 34: 159–72.

Bowser, Eileen. (1990) *History of the American Cinema, Volume Two: The Transformation of Cinema, 1907–1915*. New York: Charles Scribner's Sons.

Boyle, James. (1996) *Shamans, Software, and Spleens: Law and the Construction of the Information Society*. Cambridge, MA: Harvard University Press.

Brady, Thomas. (1963) 'On Indian Film: Native Producers Calm as Government Tussles with Western Distributors'. *New York Times*, 1 December.

Braman, Sandra. (1998) 'The Right to Create; Cultural Policy in the Fourth Stage of the Information Society'. *Gazette* 60, no. 1.

Braman, Sandra and Annabelle Sreberny-Mohammadi, eds. (1996) *Globalization, Communication and Transnational Civil Society*. Cresskill, NJ: Hampton Press.

Braudy, Leo and Marshall Cohen. (1999) 'Preface'. *Film Theory and Criticism: Introductory Readings*, 5th edn. Ed. Leo Braudy and Marshall Cohen. New York: Oxford University Press. xv–xviii.

Brecher, Jeremy, Tim Costello and Brendan Smith. (2000) *Globalization from Below: The Power of Solidarity*. Cambridge, MA: South End Press.

Bremner, Charles. (2002) '*Asterix* Prepares to Repel Legions of Hollywood'. *Times*, 2 February.

Brent, William. (2003) 'Chinese Film Industry Steps Out of the Shadows'. *The China Business Review* 30, no. 6: 42.

Brent, Willie. (2000) 'Chinese Wary of WTO Entry'. *Variety*, 3–9 April: 76.

Bridis, Ted. (2001) 'Industry Studies Attack Web-Privacy Laws'. *Wall Street Journal*, 13 March: B6.

Briffa, Peter. (2003) 'It Takes a Moron to Recognise a Good Movie'. *Times*, 9 September.

Briller, B. R. (1990) 'The Globalization of American TV'. *Television Quarterly* 24, no. 3: 71–79.

Brinsley, John. (1999) 'Hollywood's Obsession over Runaway Production: Eyes Wide Shut'. *Los Angeles Business Journal* 21, no. 31: 1.

Broad, Dave. (1995a) 'Globalization and the Casual Labor Problem: History and Prospects'. *Social Justice* 22, no. 3: 67–91.

Broad, Dave. (1995b) 'Globalization Versus Labor'. *Monthly Review* 47: 20–32.

Broadberry, Stephen and Sayantan Ghosal. (2002) 'From the Counting House to the Modern Office: Explaining Anglo-American Productivity Differences in Services, 1870–1990'. *Journal of Economic History* 62, no. 4: 967–98.

Brodesser, Claude. (2003) *Daily Variety*, 17 October: 7.

Brodesser, Claude and Charles Lyons. (2000) 'Pic Partners Do the Splits'. *Variety*, 21–27 February: 1, 57.

Brodsky, Sascha. (2002) 'Chinatown Business Groups Say Movies Hurt Commerce'. *Villager*, 7 August: 3.

Brogan, Kerry. (2002) 'Hollywood Meets Beijing in Tarantino Flick'. *China Daily*, 23 September: 9.

Bromley, Carl. (1999) 'What Hollywood Wants from Uncle Sam'. *Nation*, 5 April: 28.

Bronfenbrenner, Kate. (2000) 'Raw Power: Plant Closing Threats and the Threat to Union Organizing'. *Multinational Monitor*, December: 24–29.

Brooks, David. (1994) 'Never for GATT'. *American Spectator* 27, no. 1: 34–37.

Browett, John and Richard Leaver. (1989) 'Shifts in the Global Capitalist Economy and the National Economic Domain'. *Australian Geographical Studies* 27, no. 1: 31–46.

Brown, Charles, ed. (1995) *Co-production International*. London: 21st Century Business Publications.

Brown, Colin. (2002) 'TV Woes Hamper AFM Trade'. *Screen International*, 1–7 May: 1, 4.

Brown, Colin. (2003) 'China 'Ready' for Foreign-Owned Multiplexes'. *ScreenDaily.com*, 4 March.

Brown, DeNeen L. (2000) 'Canada's New Role: Movie-War Villain'. *Washington Post*, 5 November: A33.

Bruce, David. (1996) *Scotland the Movie*. Edinburgh: Polygon.

Brunella, Elisabetta. (2001) 'Old-World Moviegoing: Theatrical Distribution of European Films in the United States'. *Film Journal International*, March: 28–32.

Brush, Stephen B. and Doreen Stabinsky. (1996) *Valuing Local Knowledge: Indigenous People and Intellectual Property Rights*. Washington: Island Press.

Buchsbaum, Jonathan. (2004) 'L'Engagement Vivendi et le Paysage Audiovisuel Français'. Unpublished paper.

Buck, Elizabeth B. (1992) 'Asia and the Global Film Industry'. *East-West Film Journal* 6, no. 2: 116–33.

Buckingham, David. (1997) 'News Media, Political Socialization and Popular Citizenship: Towards a New Agenda'. *Critical Studies in Mass Communication* 14, no. 4: 344–66.

Buckley, Chris. (2003) 'Helped by Technology, Piracy of DVD's Runs Rampant in China'. *New York Times*, 18 August: C9.

Burawoy, Michael, Joseph A. Blum, Sheba George, Zsuzsa Gille, Teresa Gowan, Lynne Haney, Maren Klawiter, Steven H. Lopez, Seán Ó Riain and Millie Thayer. (2000) *Global Ethnography: Forces, Connections, and Imaginations in a Postmodern World.* Berkeley: University of California Press.

Burbach, Roger. (2001) *Globalization and Postmodern Politics: From Zapatistas to High-Tech Robber Barons.* London: Pluto Press.

Bureau of Labor Statistics. (2000a) *Career Guide to Industries 2000–01.*

Bureau of Labor Statistics. (2000b) *Occupational Outlook Handbook 2000.*

Burgelman, Jean-Claude and Caroline Pauwels. (1992) 'Audiovisual Policy and Cultural Identity in Small European States: The Challenge of a Unified Market'. *Media, Culture & Society* 14, no. 2: 169–83.

Burgess, Kate. (2004) 'DVD Sets Rules for Hollywood'. *Financial Times*, 23 January: 12.

Burke, David. (2003) 'Your TV is Watching You'. *openDemocracy.net*, 6 March.

Burrell, Ian. (2003) 'British Film Chiefs Challenge Hollywood's Dominance'. *Independent*, 6 June.

Burt, Tim and Francesco Guerrera. (2003) 'Brussels Confirms Hollywood Probes'. *Financial Times*, 16 January: 7.

Burton, Simon. (2001) 'South Africa: Disney in South Africa: Towards a Common Culture in a Fragmented Society?' *Dazzled by Disney? The Global Disney Audiences Project.* Ed. Janet Wasko, Mark Phillips and Eileen R. Meehan. London: Leicester University Press. 257–68.

Bush, George W. (2001) 'Address to a Joint Session of Congress and the American People'. *Harvard Journal of Law and Public Policy* 25, no. 2: xiii–xx.

Buss, Dale. (1998) 'A Product-Placement Hall of Fame'. *Business Week*, 22 June.

Butsch, Richard. (2000) *The Making of American Audiences: From Stage to Television, 1750–1990.* Cambridge: Cambridge University Press.

Byrne, Richard. (2002) 'Hollywood vs. Bollywood'. *theGlobalist*, 13 July.

Cairncross, Frances. (1997) *The Death of Distance.* Cambridge: Harvard Business School Press. 155–56.

Calder, Peter. (2003) 'The Hoard of the Rings'. *New Zealand Herald*, 29 November.

California Film Commission. (2000) www.filmcafirst.ca.gov.

Calkins, P. and M. Vézina. (1996) 'Transitional Paradigms to a New World Economic Order'. *International Journal of Social Economics* 23, nos. 10–11: 311–28.

Callahan, Sen. (2004) 'Media Companies Push into Asia'. *BtoB*, 9 February.

Calvo, Dana and Robert W. Welkos. (2002). 'Hollywood Shakes Off Fear of Terror Images'. *Los Angeles Times*, 20 May: 1.

Campbell, Duncan. (2003) 'Hollywood Dips a Toe in Mandarin'. *Guardian*, 10 January.

Campbell, Matthew and Dominic Rush. (2002) 'France Rises Up against the Ego'. *Sunday Times*, 21 April.

Canadian Film and Television Production Association/Association des Producteurs de Films et de Télévision du Québec. (2003) *Profile 2003: An Economic Report on the Canadian Film and Television Production Industry: Risky Business: Canadian Producers in the Global Economy.*

Canadian Toy Testing Council. (2001) '*I Want That': The Impact of Current Trends and Practices Shaping the Advertising of Toys to Children in the Global Marketplace.*

Cane, Alan. (2002) 'Measuring the Audience for Outdoor Advertising'. *Financial Times*, 5 November: 2.

Carson, Diane and Lester D. Friedman, eds. (1995) *Shared Differences: Multicultural Media and Practical Pedagogy.* Urbana: University of Illinois Press.

Carson, Diane, Linda Dittmar and Janice R. Welsch, eds. (1994) *Multiple Voices in Feminist Film Criticism.* Minneapolis: University of Minnesota Press.

Carson, Tom. (1983) 'Homage to Catatonia'. *Village Voice*, 19 April: 58.

Carus, Felicity. (2003) 'Reel Change'. *Guardian*, 20 March.

Carver, Benedict. (1995) 'MPA to Fund Euro Training'. *Screen International*, 27 October.

Carver, Benedict. (1998) 'Bridge Makes Novel Buys to Jumpstart Pic Production'. *Variety*, 9–15 February: 24.

Carver, Benedict. (1999a) 'Hollywood Tack: Grin and Share it'. *Variety*, 13–19 September: 1, 95.

Carver, Benedict. (1999b) 'Bel Air Nails US$225 Mil Bank Line'. *Variety*, 30 August–5 September: 12.

Caves, Richard. (2000) *Creative Industries: Contracts between Art and Commerce*. Cambridge, MA: Harvard University Press.

Center for Entertainment Industry Data and Research. (2002) *The Migration of Feature Film Production from the U.S. to Canada and Beyond: Year 2001 Production Report*.

Chadha, Kalyani and Anandam Kavoori. (2000) 'Media Imperialism Revisited: Some Findings from the Asian Case'. *Media, Culture & Society* 22, no. 4: 415–32.

Chakravartty, Paula. (2001) 'Flexible Citizens and the Internet: The Global Politics of Local High-Tech Development in India'. *Emergences* 11, no. 1: 69–88.

Chakravarty, Sumita. (1993) *National Identity in Indian Popular Cinema, 1947–1987*. Austin: University of Texas Press.

Chalaby, Jean K. (2003) 'Television for a New Global Order: Transnational Television Networks and the Formation of Global Systems'. *Gazette* 65, no. 6: 457–72.

Chalk, Peter. (1997) *Grey Area Phenomena in Southeast Asia: Piracy, Drug Trafficking and Political Terrorism*. Canberra: Strategic and Defense Studies Centre.

Chambers, David. (2002). 'Will Hollywood Go to War?'. *Transnational Broadcasting Studies* 8.

Chang, Leslie. (2002a) 'Made in China: Sneakers, Toys, Now Film'. *Wall Street Journal*, 27 August: B1, B4.

Chang, Leslie. (2002b) 'Film-Making: Tapping a Reservoir'. *Far Eastern Economic Review*, 29 August: 52.

Chartrand, Harry Hillman. (1992) 'International Cultural Affairs: A Fourteen Country Survey'. *Journal of Arts Management, Law and Society* 22, no. 2: 134–54.

Chartrand, Harry Hillman. (1996) 'Intellectual Property Rights in the Postmodern World'. *Journal of Arts Management, Law and Society* 25, no. 4: 306–19.

Chase-Dunn, Christopher. (2002) 'Globalization from Below: Toward a Collectively Rational and Democratic Global Commonwealth'. *Annals of the American Academy of Political and Social Science* 581: 48–61.

Chellam, Raju. (2003) 'The Enigma of Digital Cinema'. *Business Times Singapore*, 24 November.

Chen, Xiaoli. (2003) 'Huana Cangu Yongle Dianyingcheng, Hezi Yingyuan Zaicheng Touzi Redian'. *Oriental Network – Wenhui Daily*, 11 July.

Chengappa, Raj, Sheela Raval and Anil Padmanabhan. (2003) 'War on Terror: Getting Dawood'. *India Today*, 3 November: 16.

Cherbo, Joni Maya. (2001) 'Issue Identification and Policy Implementation: Union Involvement in the Immigration of Temporary Cultural Workers'. *Journal of Arts Management, Law and Society* 31, no. 2: 149–67.

Cherneff, Jill B. R. (1991) 'Dreams are Made Like This: Hortense Powdermaker and the Hollywood Film Industry'. *Journal of Anthropological Research* 47, no. 4: 429–40.

Chidley, Joe. (2000) 'Hollywood's Welfare Bums'. *Canadian Business*, 3 April: 11–12.

Chinni, Christine L. (1997) 'Droit d'Auteur Versus the Economics of Copyright: Implications for the American Law of Accession to the Berne Convention'. *Copyright Law Symposium* 40: 65–92.

Chmielewski, Dawn C. (2000) 'Movie Studios, Tech Firms Team Up to Bolster Copyright-Proof Technology'. *San Jose Mercury News*, 29 December.

Chmielewski, Dawn C. (2002) 'SonicBlue Ordered to Track Digital Video Recorder Users'. *Mercury News*, 2 May.

Christopherson, Susan. (1996) 'Flexibility and Adaptation in Industrial Relations: The Exceptional Case of the U.S. Media Entertainment Industries'. *Under the Stars: Essays on Labor Relations in Arts and Entertainment*. Ed. L. S. Gray and R. L. Seeber. Ithaca: Cornell University Press. 86–112.

Christopherson, Susan and Michael Storper. (1986) 'The City as Studio; the World as Back Lot: The Impact of Vertical Disintegration on the Location of the Motion Picture Industry'. *Environment and Planning D: Society and Space* 4, no. 3: 305–20.

Christopherson, Susan and Michael Storper. (1989) 'The Effects of Flexible Specialization and Industrial Politics and the Labor Markets: The Motion Picture Industry'. *Industrial and Labor Relations Review* 42, no. 3: 331–47.

Chung, Kee H. and Raymond A. K. Cox. (1994) 'A Stochastic Model of Superstardom: An Application of the Yule Distribution'. *Review of Economics and Statistics* 76, no. 4: 771–75.

Clark, Danae. (1995) *Negotiating Hollywood: The Cultural Politics of Actors' Labor.* Minneapolis: University of Minnesota Press.

Clark, Jon. (1997) 'Copyright Law and Work for Hire'. *Copyright Law Symposium* 40: 129–64.

Cochrane, Robert H. (1927) 'Advertising Motion Pictures'. *The Story of the Films as Told by Leaders of the Industry to the Students of the Graduate School of Business Administration George F. Baker Foundation Harvard University.* Ed. Joseph P. Kennedy. Chicago: A. W. Shaw Company. 233–62.

Coe, Neil M. (2000) 'On Location: American Capital and the Local Labour Market in the Vancouver Film Industry'. *International Journal of Urban and Regional Research* 24, no. 1.

Cohen, Julie E. (1996) 'A Right to Read Anonymously: A Closer Look at "Copyright Management" in Cyberspace'. *Connecticut Law Review* 28: 981–1039.

Cohen, Karl. (2003) 'The Cartoon That Came in from the Cold'. *Guardian*, 7 March.

Cohen, Robin. (1991) *Contested Domains: Debates in International Labor Studies.* London: Zed Books.

Cohen, Roger. (1994) 'Aux Armes! France Rallies to Battle Sly and T. Rex'. *New York Times*, 2 January: H1, 22–23.

Coleman, Herbert. (1975) 'Why Shoot in India?' *Variety*, 28 October.

Coletti, Elisabetta Anna. (2000) ' "Made in Italy" Label Gains Celluloid Cachet'. *Christian Science Monitor*, 4 November.

Collins, Jane L. (2002) 'Deterritorialization and Workplace Culture'. *American Ethnologist* 29, no. 1: 151–71.

Collins, Jim. (1992) 'Television and Postmodernism'. *Channels of Discourse, Reassembled: Television and Contemporary Criticism*, 2nd edn. Ed. Robert C. Allen. Chapel Hill: University of North Carolina Press. 327–53.

Collins, Richard. (1999) 'The European Union Audiovisual Policies of the U.K. and France'. *Television Broadcasting in Contemporary France and Britain*. Ed. Michael Scriven and Monia Lecomte. Oxford: Berghahn Books. 198–221.

Connell, David. (2000) 'Customs Clearance: Runaway Production Update'. *Cinematographer.com*, 21 July.

Connell, R. W. and Julian Wood. (2002) 'Globalization and Scientific Labour: Patterns in a Life-History Study of Intellectual Workers in the Periphery'. *Journal of Sociology* 38, no. 2: 167–90.

Connelly, M. Patricia. (1996) 'Gender Matters: Global Restructuring and Adjustment'. *Social Politics* 3, no. 1: 12–13.

Connolly, Kate. (2002) 'Bridge for Hire: $7000 a Morning'. *Guardian*, 12 April: 8.

Cook, David A. (2000) *History of the American Cinema, Volume 9: Lost Illusions: American Cinema in the Shadow of Watergate and Vietnam, 1970–1979.* New York: Charles Scribner's Sons.

Coolidge, Alex. (2002). 'Blockbuster Defends its Arrangement with Studios'. *Sarasota Herald-Tribune*, 18 June: D1.

Coombe, Rosemary. (1996) 'Innovation and the Information Environment: Left Out on the Information Highway'. *Oregon Law Review* 75: 237–47.

Coombe, Rosemary J. (1998) *The Cultural Life of Intellectual Properties: Authorship, Appropriation, and the Law.* Durham: Duke University Press.

Cooper, Marc. (2000a) 'Runaway Shops'. *Nation*, 3 April: 28.

Cooper, Marc. (2000b) 'Acting for Justice'. *Nation*, 9 October: 7, 38.

Cooper, Mark Garrett. (2003) *Love Rules: Silent Hollywood and the Rise of the Managerial Class*. Minneapolis: University of Minnesota Press.

Coren, Giles. (2003) 'Asterix: My Addiction'. *Times*, 15 November: Weekend Review: 2.

Cornford, James and Kevin Robins. (1998) 'Beyond the Last Bastion: Industrial Restructuring and the Labor Force in the British Television Industry'. *Global Productions: Labor in the Making of the 'Information Society'*. Ed. Gerald Sussman and John A. Lent. Cresskill, NJ: Hampton Press. 191–212.

Coslovich, Gabriella and Lawrie Zion. (2002) 'US Protectionism Bushwhacks Australian Films'. *Age*, 2 May: 6.

Costa-Gavras, Michael Eisner, Jack Lang and Benjamin Barber. (1995) 'From Magic Kingdom to Media Empire'. *New Perspectives Quarterly* 12, no. 4: 4–17.

Coughlin, Kevin. (2004) 'Morris Mom Turns Tables in Music Industry Lawsuit'. *Star-Ledger*, 18 February.

Council of Europe. (1992) 'European Convention on Cinematographic Co-production'. The European Treaty Series no. 147. culture.coe.fr/infocentre/txt/eng/econ147.html.

Council of Europe. (2000a) 'Report on the Activities of Eurimages in 1999'. Eurimages, 31 March.

Council of Europe. (2000b) 'Guide: Support for the Co-production of Full Length Feature Films, Animation and Documentaries'. Eurimages.

Cox, Dan. (1998) 'Canal+, Col Jump Bridge'. *Daily Variety*, 13 November: 4.

Cox, Kay. (2000) 'Gaul Systems Go; Asterix Theme Park is Stunning Success Story'. *Sunday Mail*, 25 June: 34–35.

Cox, Kevin R. (1997) 'Globalization and the Politics of Distribution: A Critical Assessment'. *Spaces of Globalization: Reasserting the Power of the Local*. Ed. Kevin R. Cox. New York: Guilford Press. 115–36.

Craven, Neil. (2004). 'Blockbuster Set to Spin After Sale Collapses'. *Retail Week*, 6 February: 6.

Crayford, Peter. (2002) 'The Revolt on Planet Hollywood'. *Australian Financial Review*, 13 July: 45.

Crock, Stan, Dexter Roberts, Joyce Bernathan, Paul Magnusson and Emily Thornton. (1997) 'America and China'. *Business Week*, 3 November.

Crofts, Stephen. (1998) 'Authorship and Hollywood'. *Oxford Guide to Film Studies*. Ed. John Hill and Pamela Church Gibson. Oxford: Oxford University Press. 310–24.

Crumley, Bruce. (2002) 'Battle Lines Drawn'. *Time International*, 29 April: 36.

Culkin, Nigel and Keith Randle. (2002) 'Digital Star Wars Heralds New Dawn'. *Guardian*, 20 May: 23.

Cummins, Kath. (2003) 'The Great Raid'. *City Weekend*, 22 January.

Cunningham, Stuart. (1992) *Framing Culture: Criticism and Policy in Australia*. Sydney: Allen and Unwin.

Cunningham, Stuart and Elizabeth Jacka. (1996) *Australian Television and International Mediascapes*. Melbourne: Cambridge University Press.

D'Alessandro, Anthony. (2000) 'The Top 125 Worldwide'. *Variety* 24–30 January: 22.

D'Allessandro, Anthony and Jill Goldsmith. (2000) 'Exhibs: Help us o'seas', *Variety.com*, 7 March.

da Cunha, Uma. (1994) 'UIP Has Big Plans for "Jurassic Park" '. *Variety*, 10 January: 55.

da Cunha, Uma. (1995a) 'BV Connection'. *Variety*, 12 June: 39.

da Cunha, Uma. (1995b) 'India's "Sunrise" Shines on Sony'. *Variety*, 18 August.

da Cunha, Uma. (1996) 'MPA Reps Lobby Locals to Stem Piracy in India'. *Variety*, 29 July: 10.

Da, Yong. (2003) 'Media Giants Win Lawsuit'. *China Daily*, 8 August: 3.

Dahlburg, Jon-Thor. (1994) 'India Finds "Jurassic Park" a Real Scream'. *Los Angeles Times*, 21 May: F1, F10.

Dai, Jinhua. (1999) 'Zhongguo Dianying: Zai Kuaile Zhong Chenmo …'. *Xiandai Chuanbo* 1: 22.

Dalton, Stephen. (2002) 'Meet the Khan-do Guy'. *The Scotsman*, 14 August: 5.

Danan, Martine. (1995) 'Marketing the Hollywood Blockbuster in France'. *Journal of Popular Film and Television* 23, no. 3: 131–40.

Daniels, Bill, David Leedy and Steven D. Sills. (1998) *Movie Money: Understanding*

Hollywood's (Creative) Accounting Practices. Los Angeles: Silman-James Press.

Davenport, Coral M. (2002) 'Greek Women Trade Aphrodite for Gaunt Model Look'. *Christian Science Monitor*, 14 February.

Davies, Hugh. (1997) 'Kissinger to Advise Disney on Row over Tibet Film'. *Daily Telegraph*, 14 October.

Dawtrey, Adam. (1994) 'Playing Hollywood's Game: Eurobucks Back Megabiz'. *Variety*, 7–13 March: 1, 75.

Dawtrey, Adam. (1997) 'Hollywood Muscle Pushes Brit Pix Blitz'. *Variety*, 11–17 August: 7, 9.

Dawtrey, Adam. (1998) 'Lottery Franchises Mark First Year'. *Variety*, 14–20 December: 74.

Dawtrey, Adam. (1999) 'U, Canal+ Working Jointly'. *Variety*, 17–21 May: 26.

Dawtrey, Adam and Liza Foreman. (2001) 'Biz Takes Pulse of Teuton Quake'. *Variety*, 5–11 March: 8, 12.

Dawtrey, Adam and Rex Weiner. (1995) 'Indie Pic Pioneers Feel Global Warming'. *Variety*, 20 November: 1.

Dawtrey, Adam, Alison James, Liza Foreman, Ed Meza, David Rooney and John Hopewell. (2000) 'Yanks Rank but Locals Tank'. *Variety*, 18–31 December: 1, 77–78.

Day, Mark. (2003) 'US Targets Our Local Content Rules'. *Australian*, 3 April.

De Bens, Els de Smaele and Hedwig de Smaele. (2001) 'The Inflow of American Television Fiction on European Broadcasting Channels Revisited'. *European Journal of Communication* 16, no. 1: 51–76.

de Certeau, Michel and Luce Giard. (1997) 'A Necessary Music'. *The Capture of Speech and Other Political Writings*. Trans. Tom Conley. Minneapolis: University of Minnesota Press. 91–99.

De Grazia, Victoria. (1989) 'Mass Culture and Sovereignty: The American Challenge to European Cinemas 1920–1960'. *Journal of Modern History* 61, no. 1: 53–87.

de la Bosséno, François. (1992) 'Immigrant Cinema: National Cinema – The Case of Beur Film'. *Popular European Cinema*. Ed. Richard Dyer and Ginette Vincendeau. London: Routledge. 47–57.

de la Fuente, Anna Marie and Mike Goodridge. (2003) 'Valenti's Mexican Stand-Off'. *ScreenDaily.com*, 10 February.

De Los Reyes, Aurelio. (1996) 'El Gobierno Mexicano y las Películas Denigrantes. 1920–1931'. *México Estados Unidos: Encuentros y Desencuentros en el Cine*. Ed. Ignacio Durán, Iván Trujillo and Mónica Verea. Mexico: Universidad Nacional Autónoma de México. 23–35.

de Mello, F. M. (1937) 'India-Made Movies'. *Asia Magazine*, September.

De Silva, I. (1998) 'Consumer Selection of Motion Pictures'. *The Motion Picture Mega-Industry*. Ed. Barry R. Litman. Boston: Allyn and Bacon. 144–71.

De Vany, Arthur. (2004) *Hollywood Economics: How Extreme Uncertainty Shapes the Film Industry*. London: Routledge.

De Vany, Arthur S. and W. David Walls. (1996) 'Bose-Einstein Dynamics and Adaptive Contracting in the Motion Picture Industry'. *Economic Journal* 106, no. 439: 1493–514.

De Vany, Arthur S. and W. David Walls. (1997) 'The Market for Motion Pictures: Rank, Revenue, and Survival'. *Economic Inquiry* 35, no. 4: 783–97.

De Vany, Arthur S. and W. David Walls. (1999) 'Uncertainty and the Movie Industry: Does Star Power Reduce the Terror of the Box Office?' *Journal of Cultural Economics* 23, no. 4: 285–318.

De, R. (2002). 'What's afflicting the animation training industry'. *IT People*, 4 February.

De, R. and S. Glancy. (2001) 'Can India Become a Global Animation Leader?' *Express Computer*, 11 December.

DeFillippi, Robert J. and Michael B. Arthur. (1998) 'Paradox in Project-Based Enterprise: The Case of Film Making'. *California Management Review* 40, no. 2: 125–39.

DeLillo, Don. (2001) 'In the Ruins of the Future'. *Harper's Magazine*, December.

DeLorme, Denise E. and Leonard N. Reid. (1999) 'Moviegoers' Experiences and Interpretations of Brands in Films Revisited'. *Journal of Advertising* 28, no. 2.

Demarco, Peter. (2001) 'Legal Wizards Crack Whip at Harry Potter Fan Sites'. *Daily News*, 22 February: 4.

Demers, David. (1999) *Global Media: Menace or Messiah?* Cresskill, NJ: Hampton Press.

Denicola, Robert. (1999) 'Freedom to Copy'. *Yale Law Journal* 108: 1661–86.

Denzin, Norman. (1995) 'The Birth of the Cinematic, Surveillance Society'. *Current Perspectives in Social Theory* no. 15: 99–127.

Department of Commerce. (1997) *Commercial Opportunities in the Western Cape Film Industry*. Washington, D.C.

Department of Commerce. (2001) *The Migration of U.S. Film and Television Production*. Washington, D.C.

Department of Commerce. (2003) *U.S. International Trade in Goods and Services*. Washington, D.C.

Devine, Jeremy M. (1999) *Vietnam at 24 Frames a Second*. Austin: University of Texas Press.

DeWayne, Mark. (2002) *Making Your Film for Less Outside the U.S.* New York: Allworth Press.

Dey, Sudipto. (2003) 'Entertainment Industry Targets New Shores'. *Economic Times of India*, 10 October.

Diawara, Manthia. (1992) *African Cinema*. Bloomington: Indiana University Press.

Diawara, Manthia, ed. (1993) *Black American Cinema*. New York: Routledge.

Dicken, Peter. (1998) *Global Shift: Transforming the World Economy*, 3rd edn. New York: Guilford Press.

DiMaggio, Paul. (1994) 'Culture and Economy'. *The Handbook of Economic Sociology*. Ed. Neil J. Smelser and Richard Swedberg. Princeton: Princeton University Press. 27–57.

Dinoff, Dustin. (2003) 'HAFF Attendance Climbs'. *Playback*, 9 June: 18.

DiOrio, Carl. (2001) 'Exhibs: Glass Half Full'. *Variety*, 12–18 March: 9, 16.

Directors Guild of America. (2000) 'DGA Commends Action by Governor Gray Davis to Fight Runaway Production'. Press Release, 18 May.

Dobson, John. (1993) 'TNCs and the Corruption of GATT: Free Trade Versus Fair Trade'. *Journal of Business Ethics* 12, no. 7: 573–78.

Donahue, Ann. (2000) 'Confab's Focus Turns to Piracy'. *Variety*, 7–13 August.

Donnelly, Peter. (1996) 'The Local and the Global: Globalization in the Sociology of Sport'. *Journal of Sport & Social Issues* 20, no. 3: 239–57.

Doraiswamy, V. (1951) 'Produced 241 in India in '50'. *Motion Picture Herald*, 28 April.

Downing, John H. (1996) *Internationalizing Media Theory: Transition, Power, Culture*. London: Sage.

Dragomir, Marius. (2003) 'Quiet on the Set'. *Prague Business Journal*, 26 January.

Drake, William J. and Kalypso Nicolaïdis. (1992) 'Ideas, Interests, and Institutionalization: Trade in Services and the Uruguay Round'. *International Organization* 46, no. 1: 37–100.

Dreazen, Yochi J. (2000a) 'Old Labor Tries to Establish Role in New Economy'. *Wall Street Journal*, 15 August: B1, B10.

Dreazen, Yochi J. (2000b) 'Labor Unions Turn to Mergers in Pursuit of Growth'. *Wall Street Journal*, 9 September: A2, A6.

Duarte, Luiz Guilherme and S. Tamer Cavusgil. (1996) 'Internationalization of the Video Industry: Unresolved Policy and Regulatory Issues'. *Columbia Journal of World Business* 31, no. 3.

Duke, Paul F. (2000) 'House Vote Cracks China's Great Wall'. *Variety*, 29 May–4 June.

Dunkley, Cathy and Dana Harris. (2001) 'Foreign Sales Mavens See Their Empires Fade'. *Variety*, 15–21 January: 1, 103.

Dupagne, Michel and David Waterman. (1998) 'Determinants of U.S. Television Fiction Imports in Western Europe'. *Journal of Broadcasting & Electronic Media* 42, no. 2: 208–20.

Durie, John, Annika Pham and Neil Watson. (2000) *Marketing and Selling Your Film Around the World: A Guide for Independent Filmmakers*. Los Angeles: Silman-James Press.

Durkheim, Émile. (1984) *The Division of Labor in Society*. Trans. W. D. Halls. New York: Free Press.

Dutka, Elaine. (2003) 'As Technology Evolves and Competition Heats Up, This is a Time of Great Change in Hollywood Market Research'. *Los Angeles Times*, 31 August: E8.

Dyer, Richard. (1992) *Only Entertainment*. London: Routledge.

Earle, John S. and Scott Gehlbach. (2003) 'A
    Spoonful of Sugar: Privatization and Popular
    Support for Reform in the Czech Republic'.
    Economics and Politics 15, no. 1: 1–32.

Earls, Mark. (2003) 'Advertising to the Herd: How
    Understanding Our True Nature Challenges
    the Ways We Think about Advertising and
    Market Research'. International Journal of
    Market Research 45, no. 3: 311–37.

East, James. (2000) 'Raiders of the Lost
    Temple'. Guardian, 8 December: 12.

Ebenkamp, Becky. (2003) '2 Cool 2 Stay Flat,
    Films Soar'. Brandweek 44, no. 25:
    S38–S40.

Ebenkamp, Becky and Kenneth Hein. (2003)
    'Universal Feeds the Kitty'. Brandweek 44,
    no. 22: 4.

Eberts, Derek and Glen Norcliffe. (1998) 'New
    Forms of Artisanal Production in
    Toronto's Computer Animation Industry'.
    Geographische Zeitschrift 86, no. 2: 120–33.

Eco, Umberto. (1972) 'Towards a Semiotic
    Inquiry into the Television Message'. Trans.
    Paola Splendore. Working Papers in
    Cultural Studies 3: 103–21.

Eco, Umberto. (1987) Travels in Hyperreality:
    Essays. Trans. William Weaver. London:
    Picador.

Edelman, Bernard. (1979) Ownership of the
    Image: Elements for a Marxist Theory of
    Law. Trans. Elizabeth Kingdom. London:
    Routledge and Kegan Paul.

Edmunds, Marlene. (2000a) 'Netherlands'.
    Variety, 15–21 May: 54.

Edmunds, Marlene. (2000b) 'Dutch Seek
    Subsidy Cut'. Daily Variety, 25 July: 18.

Edwards, Tony and Anthony Ferner. (2002)
    'The Renewed "American Challenge": A
    Review of Employment Practices in US
    Multinationals'. Industrial Relations Journal
    33, no. 2: 94–111.

Einav, Liran. (2002) 'Seasonality and
    Competition in Time: An Empirical
    Analysis of Release Date Decisions in the
    U.S. Motion Picture Industry'.
    Unpublished manuscript, Stanford
    University, 12 August.

Eisenmann, Thomas R. and Joseph L. Bower.
    (2000) 'The Entrepreneurial M-Form:
    Strategic Integration in Global Media Firms'.
    Organization Science 11, no. 3: 348–55.

Eisner, Michael. (2000) 'Fostering Creativity'.
    Vital Speeches 66, no. 16.

Elberse, Anita and Jehoshua Eliashberg. (2003)
    'Demand and Supply Dynamics for
    Sequentially Released Products in
    International Markets: The Case of Motion
    Pictures'. Marketing Science 22, no. 3:
    329–54.

Eliashberg, J. and S. M. Shugan. (1997) 'Film
    Critics: Influencers or Predictors?' Journal
    of Marketing 61: 68–78.

Eller, Claudia. (1998) 'Producing Partners Step
    Aside for Spielberg with "Saving" Grace'.
    Los Angeles Times, 24 July: D1.

Eller, Claudia. (2000a) 'Spyglass Hopes for
    More Good "Sense" in Future Projects for
    the Record'. Los Angeles Times, 23 May:
    B1.

Eller, Claudia. (2000b) 'After Years of Trying,
    Canal Plus Set to be a Player'. Los Angeles
    Times, 20 June: C1.

Eller, Claudia and Lorenza Muñoz. (2002) 'The
    Plots Thicken in Foreign Markets'. Los
    Angeles Times, 6 October: A1.

Elley, Derek. (1999) 'Review: Asterix and
    Obelix vs. Caesar'. Variety, 1–7 February:
    54.

Elley, Derek. (2001) 'Asia to "Tiger": Kung-
    Fooey'. Variety, 5–11 February: 1.

Elliot, Stuart. (1999) 'The Hype is with Us'.
    New York Times, 14 May: C1.

Elliot, Stuart. (2000) 'Intelligex, a New Web
    Site, Moves into the New World of Online
    Market-Research Exchanges'. New York
    Times, 19 December: C7.

Elmer, Greg. (2002) 'The Trouble with the
    Canadian "Body Double": Runaway
    Productions and Foreign Location
    Shooting'. Screen 43, no. 4: 423–31.

Elsaesser, Thomas. (1989) New German
    Cinema: A History. New Brunswick:
    Rutgers University Press.

Elsaesser, Thomas. (2001) 'The Blockbuster:
    Everything Connects, but not Everything
    Goes'. The End of Cinema as We Know it:
    American Film in the Nineties. Ed. Jon
    Lewis. New York: New York University
    Press. 11–22.

Emmons, Natasha. (2001) 'Setting a New
    Standard with Marketing Partnership'.
    Amusement Business, 5 March: 16.

Endicott, R. C. (2000) 'Studios Soar to New Box-Office Nirvana'. *Advertising Age*, 17 July: S12.

Entertainment Industry Development Corporation. (2001) 'Movies of the Week and Production Flight'. www.eidc.com/MOWwebLR.pdf.

Eswar, N. V. (1953) 'India's Domestic Output Off to 250 Pix in 1952 and Financiers Tie Up Coin'. *Variety*, 7 January.

Eswar, N. V. (1970) 'India's Film Output'. *Variety*, 7 January.

Eswar, N. V. (1971) 'People without Enough Theaters: India's Masses Just Too Poor'. *Variety*, 12 May.

Euromonitor. (2002) Marketing Data. www.euromonitor.com.

European Audiovisual Observatory. (1998) *Statistical Yearbook 1998. Film, Television, Video and New Media in Europe*.

European Audiovisual Observatory. (2002) *Focus 2002: World Film Market Trends/Tendances du marché mondial du film*.

European Audiovisual Observatory. (2003) *Focus 2003: World Film Market Trends/Tendances du marché mondial du film*.

Evangelista, Benny. (2002) 'Sonicblue Ruling Reversed; Judge Says Order for Data Invalid'. *San Francisco Chronicle*, 4 June: B7.

Evans, Peter. (1979) *Dependent Development: The Alliance of Local Capital in Brazil*. Princeton: Princeton University Press.

Everett, Michael. (1999) 'Unionists Chasing Daley and Gore on Trade Issue'. *Labornet*. www.labornet.org/news/123199/06.html.

Fabrikant, Geraldine. (2001) 'A U.S. Cable Baron Bets His Money Overseas'. *New York Times*, 26 March: 1, 14.

Falk, Richard. (1997) 'State of Siege: Will Globalization Win Out?' *International Affairs* 73, no. 1: 123–36.

Farnam, Arie. (2002) 'Filmmakers Flock to Prague for a Cheap Hollywood'. *Christian Science Monitor*, 17 January.

Fasig, Lisa Biank. (2003) 'At Hasbro, Costly Licensing Agreements are out, Classics are Back in'. *Providence Journal*, 23 February.

Faulkner. R. R. and A. B. Anderson. (1987) 'Short-Term Projects and Emergent Careers: Evidence from Hollywood'. *American Journal of Sociology* 92: 879–909.

Featherstone, Mike, ed. (1990) *Global Culture: Nationalism, Globalization and Modernity*. London: Sage.

Featherstone, Mike and Scott Lash. (1995) 'Globalization, Modernity, and the Spatialization of Social Theory: An Introduction'. *Global Modernities*. Ed. Mike Featherstone, Scott Lash and Roland Robertson. London: Sage. 1–24.

Federal Trade Commission. (2000) *Marketing Violent Entertainment to Children: A Review of Self-Regulation and Industry Practices in the Motion Picture, Music Recording & Electronic Game Industries*.

Federation of Indian Chambers of Commerce and Industry. (2000) *The Indian Entertainment Industry: Strategy and Vision*. New Delhi.

Feigenbaum, Harvey B. (2002) 'Ceding Public Power to Private Actors: Public Policy and the Private Sector in Audiovisual Industries'. *UCLA Law Review* 49: 1767–81.

Feltes, N. N. (1994) 'International Copyright: Structuring "the Condition of Modernity" in British Publishing'. *The Construction of Authorship: Textual Appropriation in Law and Literature*. Ed. Martha Woodmansee and Peter Jaszi. Durham: Duke University Press. 271–80.

Ferguson, Iain and Caspar Henderson. (2003) 'Corporate Timeline'. *open Democracy.net*, 12 March.

Ferguson, Marjorie. (1992) 'The Mythology about Globalization'. *European Journal of Communication* 7, no. 1: 69–93.

Field, Heather. (2000) 'European Media Regulation: The Increasing Importance of the Supranational'. *Media International Australia* 95: 91–105.

Film and Television Action Committee. (1999) 'A Statement of Principles'. www.ftac.net/mission.html.

Film and Television Action Committee. (2002) 'Ottawa Hikes Film Tax Breaks Despite U.S. Anger'.

Finn, Adam, Nicola Simpson, Stuart McFadyen and Colin Hoskins. (2000) 'Marketing Movies on the Internet: How does Canada compare to the US?' *Canadian Journal of Communication* 25, no. 3: 367–76.

Finney, Angus. (1996) *The State of European Cinema: A New Dose of Reality*. London: Cassell.

Fitzgerald, Michael. (2000) 'Inside Sydney: Harboring Hollywood'. *Time International*, 31 July: 48.

Fitzpatrick, Liam. (1993) 'Docs Asia Want My MTV? An Interview with Richard Li'. *Hemispheres*, July: 21–23.

Flanigan, Peter. (2002) 'The Environmental Cost of Filmmaking'. *UCLA Entertainment Law Review* 10: 69–95.

Flew, Terry. (2003) *New Media: An Introduction*. Oxford: Oxford University Press.

Footer, Mary E. and Christoph Beat Graber. (2000) 'Trade Liberalization and Cultural Policy'. *Journal of International Economic Law* 3, no. 1: 115–44.

Ford, Peter. (2003) 'Global Pushback against "Titanic" Culture'. *Christian Science Monitor*, 20 October.

Ford, Richard T. (1999) 'Law's Territory: A History of Jurisdiction.' *Michigan Law Review* 97: 843–930.

Forde, Leon. (2002) 'Cinema Expo Seminar Poses the $10bn Digital Question'. *ScreenDaily.com*, 27 June.

Forrester, Chris. (2001) 'High Hopes for Egyptian Media Production City'. *Transnational Broadcasting Studies* 7.

Foucault, Michel. (1972) *The Archeology of Knowledge*. Trans. A. M. Sheridan Smith. New York: Pantheon.

Foucault, Michel. (1977) 'What is an Author?'. *Language, Counter-Memory, Practice*. Ed. Donald F. Bouchard. Trans. Donald F. Bouchard and Sherry Simon. Ithaca: Cornell University Press. 113–38.

Foucault, Michel. (1989) *Foucault Live (Interviews, 1966–84)*. Ed. Sylvère Lotringer. Trans. John Johnston. New York: Semiotext(e) Foreign Agents Series.

Foucault, Michel. (1991) *Remarks on Marx: Conversations with Duccio Trombadori*. Trans. J. R. Goldstein and J. Cascaito. New York: Semiotext(e).

Fox, Fred W. (1947) 'Khan Ends Visit: India's DeMille Lauds Hollywood'. *Hollywood Citizen News*, 24 May.

Fox, William. (1927) 'Reminiscences and Observations'. *The Story of the Films as Told by Leaders of the Industry to the Students of the Graduate School of Business Administration George F. Baker Foundation Harvard University*. Ed. Joseph P. Kennedy. Chicago: A. W. Shaw Company. 301–18.

Franco, Robert J. (2002) 'Beyond the Blockbuster'. *Pharmaceutical Executive* 22, no. 11: 74–80.

Franklin, Anna. (1991) 'MPEAA Leads Pirate Hunt across Eastern Europe'. *Screen International*, 27 September.

Fraser, Graham. (2003) 'Copps Wins Cultural Victory'. *Toronto Star*, 15 October: A06.

Frater, Patrick. (2000) 'Eurowood'. *Screen International*, 4 June: 8–9.

Frater, Patrick. (2002). 'Bollywood Goes Global'. *ScreenDaily.com*, 22 May.

Frater, Patrick. (2003) 'US Turns Up the Heat on Asian Remakes'. *ScreenDaily.com*, 24 February.

Frater, Patrick and Martin Blaney. (2002) 'Euro Media Giants in Turmoil'. *Screen International*, 19–25 April: 1, 2.

Freedman, Des. (2003a) 'Who Wants to be a Millionaire? The Politics of Television Exports'. *Information, Communication & Society* 6, no. 1: 24–41.

Freedman, Des. (2003b) 'Cultural Policy-Making in the Free Trade Era: An Evaluation of the Impact of Current World Trade Organisation Negotiations on Audio-Visual Industries'. *International Journal of Cultural Policy* 9, no. 3: 285–98.

Freeman, Carla. (2000) *High Tech and High Heels in the Global Economy: Women, Work, and Pink-Collar Identities in the Caribbean*. Durham: Duke University Press.

Frew, Wendy. (2004) 'Village Showing a Troubling Story'. *Age*, 27 February.

Friedman, Wayne. (2000a) 'Chicken Plucks US$100 Mil for Media, Marketing Run'. *Advertising Age*, 19 June: 3.

Friedman, Wayne. (2000b) 'Hollywood Swings for Box Office Fences'. *Advertising Age*, 10 July: 24.

Friedman, Wayne. (2001) 'Studios Mull Ad Cuts for Local Papers'. *Advertising Age*, 8 January: 1.

Friend, Tad. (2003) 'Remake Man'. *New Yorker*, 2 June: 40–47.

Friends of Canadian Broadcasting. (2003) *Re: Broadcasting PN CRTC 2003–54: Support for Canadian Television Drama.*

Friman, H. Richard and Peter Andreas, eds. (1999) *The Illicit Global Economy and State Power.* Lanham, MD: Rowman & Littlefield.

Fröbel, Folke, Jürgen Heinrichs and Otto Kreye. (1980) *The New International Division of Labour: Structural Unemployment in Industrialised Countries and Industrialisation in Developing Countries.* Trans. P. Burgess. Cambridge: Cambridge University Press; Paris: Éditions de la Maison des Sciences de l'Homme.

Frow, John. (1992) 'Cultural Markets and the Shape of Culture'. *Continental Shift: Globalisation and Culture.* Ed. Elizabeth Jacka. Sydney: Local Consumption, 1992. 7–24.

Frow, John. (1995) *Cultural Studies and Cultural Value.* Oxford: Clarendon Press.

Frow, John. (1997) *Time and Commodity Culture: Essays in Cultural Theory and Postmodernity.* Oxford: Clarendon Press.

Frow, John. (2000) 'Public Domain and the New World Order in Knowledge'. *Social Semiotics* 10, no. 2: 173–85.

Frundt, Henry. (2000) 'Models of Cross-Border Organizing in Maquila Industries'. *Critical Sociology* 26, nos. 1–2: 36–55.

Fry, Andy. (1998) 'Major Players Backing New Euro Finance Shops'. *Daily Variety*, 27: Special Section 1.

Fry, Andy. (2001) 'Taking TV Deals across Borders'. *Media Monitor*, 8 March: 41.

Fuchs, Andreas. (2003a) 'Nielsen Entertainment Expands its Reach'. *Film Journal International*, July: 60, 70.

Fuchs, Andreas. (2003b) 'The Santa Scenario: Awaiting the Arrival of Digital Cinema'. *Film Journal International*, December: 28–29.

Fung, Richard. (1991) 'Looking for My Penis: The Eroticized Asian in Gay Video Porn'. *How do I Look? Queer Film and Video.* Ed. Bad Object-Choices. Seattle: Bay Press. 14–68.

Fuson, Brian. (1998) 'Valenti Hails $6.4 Bil B.O. but Fears "Fiscal Godzilla" '. *Hollywood Reporter*, 11 March.

Gabler, Neal. (2003) 'The World Still Watches America'. *New York Times*, 9 January: A27.

Gahlot, Deepa. (1992) 'State Scraps Pic Registration Fee'. *Hollywood Reporter*, 12 May.

Gailey, Lynn. (2001) 'The Impact of Globalisation on Audio Visual Industries'. Paper presented to the Union Network International Apro Media Entertainment Conference, Sydney, 6–7 April.

Gaines, Jane. (1991) *Contested Culture: The Image, the Voice, and the Law.* Chapel Hill: University of North Carolina Press.

Gaither, Chris. (2003) 'US Workers See Hard Times'. *Boston Globe*, 3 November.

Galbraith, James K. (1999) 'The Crisis of Globalization'. *Dissent* 46, no. 3: 13–16.

Galetto, Mike and Jo Dallas. (2000) 'Sony's New Gameplan'. *Multichannel News International*, 1 November: 16.

Gandy, Oscar H., Jr. (1992a) 'The Political Economy Approach: A Critical Challenge'. *Journal of Media Economics* 5, no. 2: 23–42.

Gandy, Oscar H., Jr. (1992b) *The Political Economy of Personal Information.* Boulder, CO: Westview Press.

Gandy, Oscar H., Jr. (1998) *Communication and Race: A Structural Perspective.* London: Arnold; New York: Oxford University Press.

Gandy, Oscar H., Jr. and Paula Matabane. (1989) 'Television and Social Perception among African Americans and Hispanics'. *Handbook of International and Intercultural Information.* Ed. M. Asante and W. Gudykunst. Newbury Park: Sage. 318–48.

Ganti, Tejaswini. (2000) *Casting Culture: The Social Life of Hindi Film Production in Contemporary India.* Ph.D. dissertation, New York University.

Ganti, Tejaswini. (2002) ' "And Yet My Heart is Still Indian": The Bombay Film Industry and the (H)Indianization of Hollywood'. *Media Worlds: Anthropology on New Terrain.* Ed. Faye D. Ginsburg, Lila Abu-Lughod and Brian Larkin. Berkeley: University of California Press. 281–300.

García, Beatrice E. (1998) 'Entertainment Industry Survey is Off the Mark'. *Miami Herald*, 5 December: 1C.

García-Canclini, Néstor. (1990) *Culturas Híbridas: Estrategias para Entrar y Salir de la Modernidad*. Mexico: Editorial Grijalbo.

García-Canclini, Néstor. (1996) 'North Americans or Latin Americans? The Redefinition of Mexican Identity and the Free Trade Agreements'. *Mass Media and Free Trade: NAFTA and the Culture Industries*. Ed. Emile D. McAnany and Kenton T. Wilkinson. Austin: University of Texas Press. 142–56.

García-Canclini, Néstor. (2001) *Consumers and Citizens: Multicultural Conflicts in the Process of Globalization*. Trans. George Yúdice. Minneapolis: University of Minnesota Press.

Gardels, Nathan. (1998) 'From Containment to Entertainment: The Rise of the Media-Industrial Complex'. *New Perspectives Quarterly* 15, no. 5: 2–3.

Garfinkel, Harold. (1992) *Studies in Ethnomethodology*. Cambridge: Polity Press.

Gasher, Mike. (1995) 'The Audiovisual Locations Industry in Canada: Considering British Columbia as Hollywood North'. *Canadian Journal of Communication* 20, no. 2.

Gasher, Mike. (2002) *Hollywood North: The Feature Film Industry in British Columbia*. Vancouver: UBC Press.

Gates, Arlan. (2000) 'Convergence and Competition: Technological Change, Industry Concentration and Competition Policy in the Telecommunications Sector'. *University of Toronto Faculty Law Review* 58, no. 83.

Gauba, Blaise. (2003) 'Hollywouldn't'. *The Viewfinder* 2, no. 3: 2.

Gaudiosi, John. (2001) 'Game Makers Blot Out Signs of WTC Tragedy'. *Hollywood Reporter*, 19 September.

Gaudreault, André. (1990) 'The Infringement of Copyright Laws and Its Effects (1900–1906)'. *Early Cinema: Space, Frame, Narrative*. Ed. Thomas Elsaesser. London: British Film Institute. 114–22.

Gentile, Gary. (2001) 'Report Released on Runaway Films'. Associated Press, 19 January.

Gerbner, George. (1994) 'Unesco in the U.S. Press'. *The Global Media Debate: Its Rise, Fall, and Renewal*. Ed. George Gerbner, Hamid Mowlana and Kaarle Nordenstreng. Norwood, NJ: Ablex. 111–21.

Gerbner, George, Hamid Mowlana and Kaarle Nordenstreng. (1994) 'Preface'. *The Global Media Debate: Its Rise, Fall, and Renewal*. Ed. George Gerbner, Hamid Mowlana and Kaarle Nordenstreng. Norwood, NJ: Ablex. ix–xii.

Gershon, Richard A. (1997) *The Transnational Media Corporation: Global Messages and Free Market Competition*. Mahwah, NJ: Lawrence Erlbaum.

Gever, Martha, John Greyson and Pratibha Parmar, eds. (1993) *Queer Looks: Perspectives on Lesbian and Gay Film and Video*. New York: Routledge.

Ghosh, Nirmal. (2003) 'Thailand May Find Movie-Making Pie Hard to Bite into'. *Straits Times*, 9 August.

Gibbons, Fiachra. (2000) 'Tax Could Make Film Industry a Sleepy Hollow'. *Guardian*, 7 February.

Gibson, William. (2003) *Pattern Recognition*. New York: Putnam.

Gibson-Graham, J. K. (1996–97) 'Querying Globalization'. *Rethinking Marxism* 9, no. 1: 1–27.

Giddens, Anthony. (2002) *Runaway World: How Globalization is Reshaping Our Lives*. London: Routledge.

Gille, Zsuzsa and Séan Ó Riain. (2002) 'Global Ethnography'. *Annual Review of Sociology* 28: 271–95.

Gills, Dong-Sook S. (2002) 'Globalization of Production and Women in Asia'. *Annals of the American Academy of Political and Social Science* 581: 106–20.

Gimbel, Mark. (1998) 'Some Thoughts on the Implications of Trusted Systems for Intellectual Property Law'. *Stanford Law Review* 50.

Gindin, Sam and Leo Panitch. (2002) 'Rethinking Crisis'. *Monthly Review* 54, no. 6: 34–46.

Gingrich, Newt and Peter Schweizer. (2003) 'We Can Thank Hollywood for Our Ugly-American Image'. *Los Angeles Times*, 21 January.

Ginsberg, Jane C. (1997a) 'Authors and Users in Copyright'. *Journal of the Copyright Society USA* 45: 1–45.

Ginsberg, Jane C. (1997b) 'Copyright, Common Law, and *Sui Generis* Protection of Databases in the United States and Abroad'. *University of Cincinnati Law Review* 66: 151–76.

Ginsberg, Jane and Pierre Sirinelli. (1991) 'Authors and Exploitations in International Private Law: The French Supreme Court and the Huston Film Colorization Controversy'. *Columbia-VLA Journal of Law and the Arts* 15, no. 2: 135–96.

Ginsburg, Faye D., Lila Abu-Lughod and Brian Larkin, eds. (2002) *Media Worlds: Anthropology on New Terrain*. Berkeley: University of California Press.

Gitlin, Todd. (1983) *Inside Prime Time*. New York: Pantheon Books.

Gitlin, Todd. (1997) 'The Anti-Political Populism of Cultural Studies'. *Cultural Studies in Question*. Ed. Marjorie Ferguson and Peter Golding. London: Sage. 25–38.

Gitter, Robert J. and Markus Scheuer. (1998) 'Low Unemployment in the Czech Republic: "Miracle" or "Mirage"?' *Monthly Labor Review* 121, no. 8: 31–37.

Given, Jock. (2003) *America's Pie: Trade and Culture after 9/11*. Sydney: University of New South Wales Press.

Glancy, H. Mark. (1999) *When Hollywood Loved Britain: The Hollywood 'British' Film, 1939–45*. New York: Manchester University Press.

Godar, François. (2003) 'Pay TV Monopolies Have Majors Reeling'. *Variety*, 24–30 March: A4, A6.

Goldberg, Fred. (1991) *Motion Picture Marketing and Distribution: Getting Movies to a Theatre Near You*. Boston: Focal Press.

Goldberg, Jonathan Evan. (1995) 'Now That the Future Has Arrived, Maybe the Law Should Take a Look: Multimedia Technology and its Interaction with the Fair Use Doctrine'. *American University Law Review* 44: 919–61.

Golden, Peter. (1998) 'Trolling the Net; Digimarc's Watermarking Technology'. *Electronic Business* 24, no. 9.

Golding, Peter and Phil Harris. (1997) 'Introduction'. *Beyond Cultural Imperialism: Globalization, Communication and the New International Order*. Ed. Peter Golding and Phil Harris. London: Sage. 1–9.

Goldman Edry, Sharon. (2002) 'ALA Uses Press to Put Heat on MPAA'. *PRWeek*, 10 June: 19.

Goldman, Michael. (2000) 'The Politics of Post: Lobbying Congress for HD Relief'. *Millimeter*, 1 May.

Goldman, William. (1985) *Adventures in the Screen Trade: A Personal View of Hollywood and Screenwriting*. London: Futura.

Goldsmith, Ben. (2002) 'Cultural Diversity, Cultural Networks and Trade: International Cultural Policy Debate'. *Media International Australia* 102: 35–53.

Goldsmith, Ben and Tom O'Regan. (2002) 'The Policy Environment of the Contemporary Film Studio'. Oct 2–3, Old Parliament House, Canberra, Australia. Communications Research Forum.

Goldsmith, Ben and Tom O'Regan. (2003) *Cinema Cities, Media Cities: The Contemporary International Studio Complex*. Sydney: Australian Film Commission.

Goldsmith, Jill. (2000) 'U Gets New Modus: Vivendi: Gauls Invade Fraternity of Media Behemoths'. *Variety*, 19–25 June: 1, 84.

Goldstein, Adam O., Rachel A. Sobel and Glen R. Newman. (1999) 'Tobacco and Alcohol Use in G-Rated Children's Animated Films'. *Journal of the American Medical Association* 28, no. 12: 1131–36.

Goldstein, Paul. (1970) 'Copyright and the First Amendment'. *Columbia Law Review* 70.

Goldstein, Paul. (1994) *Copyright's Highway: The Law and Lore of Copyright from Gutenberg to the Celestial Jukebox*. New York: Hill and Wang.

Golodner, Jack. (1994) 'The Downside of Protectionism'. *New York Times*, 27 February: H6.

Goodman, Bill and Reid Steadman. (2002) 'Services: Business Demand Rivals Consumer Demand in Driving Job Growth'. *Monthly Labor Review* 125, no. 4: 3–16.

Goodman, William C. (2001) 'Employment in Services Industries Affected by Recessions and Expansions'. *Monthly Labor Review* 124, no. 10: 3–11.

Gordon, Wendy. (1982) 'Fair Use as Market Failure: A Structural and Economic Analysis of the Betamax Case and its Predecessors'. *Columbia Law Review* 82.

Gorman, Steve. (2002). 'ABC to Launch Controversial Wartime "Reality" Show'. Reuters, 20 February.

Gould, Ellen. (2001) 'The 2001 GATS Negotiations: The Political Challenge Ahead'. www.thealliancefordemocracy.org.

Govil, Nitin. (2002) 'The Metropolis and Mental Strife'. *Sarai Reader 02: The Cities of Everyday Life*. Ed. Ravi S. Vasudevan, Jeebesh Bagchi, Ravi Sundaram, Monica Narula, Geert Lovink and Shuddhabrata Sengupta. New Delhi: Sarai/Center for the Study of Developing Societies/Society for New and Old Media. 78–84.

Graham, Jefferson. (2001a) 'Next Napsters Wait in the Wings: As Music-Swap Site Goes Legit, Users Threaten to Quit'. *USA Today*, 8 February.

Graham, Jefferson. (2001b) 'Video on Demand Has Come into View'. *USA Today*, 22 March: 3D.

Grainge, Paul. (1999) 'Reclaiming Heritage: Colourization, Culture Wars and the Politics of Nostalgia'. *Cultural Studies* 13, no. 4: 621–38.

Gramsci, Antonio. (1978) *Selections from the Prison Notebooks*. Ed. and trans. Quintin Hoare and Geoffrey Nowell-Smith. New York: International Publishers.

Grantham, Bill. (1998) 'America the Menace: France's Feud with Hollywood'. *World Policy Journal* 15, no. 2: 58–66.

Grantham, Bill. (2000) '*Some Big Bourgeois Brothel*': Contexts for France's Culture Wars with France. Luton: University of Luton Press.

Graser, Marc. (2002) 'H'wood Plots to Parry Pic Pirates'. *Variety*, 3–9 June: 7.

Gray, L. and R. Seeber. (1996a) 'The Industry and the Unions: An Overview'. *Under the Stars: Essays on Labor Relations in Arts and Entertainment*. Ed. L. S. Gray and R. L. Seeber. Ithaca: Cornell University Press. 15–49.

Gray, L. and R. Seeber. (1996b) 'Introduction'. *Under the Stars: Essays on Labor Relations in Arts and Entertainment*. Ed. L. S. Gray and R. L. Seeber. Ithaca: Cornell University Press. 1–13.

Greenberg , Karl. (2003) 'Ford Navigates into Film with Revolution'. *Brandweek* 44, no. 40: 4.

Greenhouse, Steven. (1999a) 'Unions Need Not Apply'. *New York Times*, 26 July: C1, C14.

Greenhouse, Steven. (1999b) 'The Most Innovative Figure in Silicon Valley? Maybe This Labor Organiser'. *New York Times*, 14 November: 32.

Greenwald, William I. (1952) 'The Control of Foreign Trade: A Half-Century of Film Trade with Great Britain'. *Journal of Business of the University of Chicago* 25, no. 1: 39–49.

Greider, William. (2000) 'It's Time to Go on the Offensive. Here's How'. *Globalize This! The Battle against the World Trade Organization and Corporate Rule*. Ed. Kevin Danaher and Roger Burbach. Monroe, ME: Common Courage Press. 143–57.

Grey, Rodney de C. (1990) *Concepts of Trade Diplomacy and Trade in Services*. Hemel Hempstead: Harvester Wheatsheaf.

Grimshaw, Colin. (2003) 'Mellow Tempts 40-somethings with Films'. *Marketing*, 17 July: 7.

Gritten, David. (2001) 'Hey, World! Hollywood's Coming!' *Daily Telegraph*, 31 March: 8.

Gross, Grant. (2003) 'KaZaa Files Copyright Complaint against RIAA, Others'. *Infoworld Daily News*, 26 September.

Grossberg, Lawrence. (1997) *Bringing it All Back Home: Essays on Cultural Studies*. Durham: Duke University Press.

Grover, Ronald. (2001). 'Power Lunch'. *Business Week*, September 21.

Grover, Ronald. (2003a) 'Lights! Camera! Investors! T-3 Has Yet to Open, but its Producers are Already in the Black'. *Business Week*, 26 May: 88.

Grover, Ronald. (2003b) 'Things that Go Bump at the Box Office'. *Business Week On-line*, 14 July.

Groves, Don. (1992) ' "1492" Sinks in Italy, Cruises in Germany'. *Daily Variety*, 9 October: 14.

Groves, Don. (1994a) 'O'seas B. O. Power Saluted at Confab'. *Variety* 356, no. 4: 18.

Groves, Don. (1994b) 'Bamboo Curtain Rises for H'wood'. *Daily Variety*, 21 March: 1.

Groves, Don. (1995) 'Cashing in on Nat'l Pastime'. *Variety*, 12 June: 42.

Groves, Don. (1999) 'A Major Force O'seas'. *Variety*, 12–18 April: 9.

Groves, Don. (2000a) 'Trade Push May Crack Great Wall for US Pix'. *Variety*, 15–21 May: 7, 75.

Groves, Don. (2000b) 'CineAsia Basks in Rebound'. *Variety*, 20–26 November: 45.

Groves, Don. (2000c) 'Boffo B.O. Bucks Foreign Coin Ills'. *Variety*, 18–31 December: 9, 74.

Groves, Don. (2001a) 'China Sez it Can't Handle 20 U.S. Pix'. *Variety*, 12–18 March: 20.

Groves, Don. (2001b) 'Foreign Exchange Flattens H'wood'. *Variety*, 2–8 April: 7, 45.

Groves, Don. (2001c) 'U.S.–China Tiff Almost Shanghais U Pic Exex'. *Variety*, 23–29 April: 40.

Groves, Don. (2001d) 'H'w'd Pix Driving Key Film Reforms'. *Variety*, 30 July–5 August: 10, 11.

Groves, Don. (2002a) 'Australia'. *Variety*, 28 October–3 November: 5.

Groves, Don. (2002b) 'Rejigged Marketing Helps U.S. Pics Soar'. *Variety*, 28 October–3 November: 14.

Groves, Don. (2004) 'Warners Flexes Chinese Plexes'. *Daily Variety*, 30 January: 1.

Groves, Don and Anthony D'Alessandro. (2001) 'H'W'D Frets over Foreign Aid'. *Variety*, 12–18 February: 1, 77.

Groves, Don and Mark Woods. (1999a) 'Co-production Battle Lines Set'. *Variety*, 8 August: 28.

Groves, Don and Mark Woods. (1999b) 'Oz Tinkers with Co-production Rules'. *Variety*, 5 September: 159.

Groves, Don and Uma da Cunha. (1994) 'India's Dino-Size Legacy'. *Variety*, 15 August: 41–42.

Grumiau, Samuel. (1998) 'Behind the Scenes with the Show-Business Trade Unions'. *Trade Union World*, 9 January.

Grumiau, Samuel. (2000) 'The Hollywood Union'. *Trade Union World*, 2 November.

Guback, Thomas H. (1969) *The International Film Industry: Western Europe and America Since 1945*. Bloomington: Indiana University Press.

Guback, Thomas H. (1974) 'Cultural Identity and Film in the European Economic Community'. *Cinema Journal* 14, no. 1: 2–17.

Guback, Thomas H. (1984) 'International Circulation of U.S. Theatrical Films and Television Programming'. *World Communications: A Handbook*. Ed. George Gerbner and Marsha Siefert. New York: Longman. 153–63.

Guback, Thomas H. (1985) 'Hollywood's International Markets'. *The American Film Industry*. Ed. Tino Balio. Madison: University of Wisconsin Press. 463–86.

Guback, Thomas H. (1987) 'Government Support to the Film Industry in the United States'. *Current Research in Film: Audiences, Economics and Law Vol. 3*. Ed. Bruce A. Austin. Norwood, NJ: Ablex. 88–104.

Gubernick, Lisa and Joel Millman. (1994) 'El Sur is the Promised Land'. *Forbes* 153, no. 7: 94–95.

Guha, K. (1999) 'Expansion through the Acquisition Trail'. *Financial Times*, 2 June: 4.

Guider, Elizabeth. (1999) 'Sony Ups its Local Payoff'. *Variety*, 26 July–1 August: 23.

Guider, Elizabeth. (2000a) 'Report Sees US$10 Bil B.O. Decade Rise'. *Variety*, 14–20 February: 20.

Guider, Elizabeth. (2000b) 'Mutual Pacts O'seas on Pix'. *Daily Variety*, 9 May: 4.

Guider, Elizabeth. (2001) 'Majors' Local TV Push'. *Variety*, 22–28 January: 53, 60.

Guider, Elizabeth and Don Groves. (1995) 'Asian Markct Paradox'. *Variety*, 1 December: 35.

Guider, Elizabeth, Adam Dawtrey, Ed Meza, Lukas Schwarzacher, Alison James, Nick Vivarelli, John Hopewell, Marlene Edmunds, Don Groves, Tom Birchenough, Barbara Hollender, Cathy Meils and Ken Bensinger. (2004) 'The Incredible Shrinking Aud'. *Variety*, 5–11 January: 1.

Gumbel, Andrew. (2001) 'Short Shrift for Unions in Amazon's Silicon Jungle'. *Independent*, 3 February.

Gupta, Shubhra. (2003) 'It's a Revolution, Ahoy!' *Business Line*, 10 November.

Guttridge, Peter. (1996) 'Our Green and Profitable Land'. *Independent*, 11 July: 8–9.

Haffner, Craig. (2004) 'It's Up to Us to Bring Movies Home'. *Los Angeles Times*, 9 February: E6.

Hainsworth, Paul. (1994) 'Politics, Culture and Cinema in the New Europe'. *Border Crossing: Film in Ireland, Britain and Europe*. Ed. John Hill, Martin McLoone and Paul Hainsworth. Belfast: Institute of Irish Studies in Association with the University of Ulster and the British Film Institute. 8–33.

Hall, Stuart. (1980) 'Encoding/Decoding'. *Culture, Media, Language*. Ed. Stuart Hall, Dorothy Hobson, Andrew Lowe and Paul Willis. London: Hutchinson. 128–39.

Hall, Stuart and Paddy Whannell. (1965) *The Popular Arts*. New York: Pantheon.

Hamelink, Cees. (1990) 'Information Imbalance: Core and Periphery'. *Questioning the Media: A Critical Introduction*. Ed. John H. Downing, Ali Mohammadi and Annabelle Sreberny-Mohammadi. Newbury Park, CA: Sage.

Hamelink, Cees. (2001) 'Remember Herbert Schiller: Our Common Efforts'. *Television & New Media* 2, no. 1: 11–16.

Hames, Peter. (2000) 'Czech Cinema: From State Industry to Competition'. *Canadian Slavonic Papers* 42, no. 1: 63–85.

Hamilton, Annette. (1992) 'The Mediascape of Modern Southeast Asia'. *Screen* 33, no. 1: 81–92.

Hancock, David. (1998) 'Global Film Production'. Paper prepared for EURO-MEI Venice Conference, 29–30 August.

Hancock, David. (1999) *Film Production in Europe: A Comparative Study of Film Production Costs in Five European Territories France-Germany-Italy-Spain-UK*. European Audiovisual Laboratory.

Handel, Leo A. (1950) *Hollywood Looks at its Audience*. Urbana: University of Illinois Press.

Hanrahan, John. (2000) 'Studios Busy with All Aspects of Production'. *Variety*, 4–10 December: 58.

Hansen, Miriam. (1994) *Babel and Babylon: Spectatorship in American Silent Film*. Cambridge, MA: Harvard University Press.

Harcourt, Alison. (1998) 'The European Commission and the Regulation of the Media Industry'. *Cardozo Arts and Entertainment Law Journal* 16: 425–49.

Harding, James. (2000) 'Angst for the Blue Angels of German Film Neuer Markt Backers Who Poured Money into Hollywood are Now Rushing for the Exits'. *Financial Times*, 30 November: 25.

Harford, Sonia. (2003) 'La Dolce Vita One More Time'. *Age*, 24 March.

Harley, John Eugene. (1940). *World-Wide Influences of the Cinema: A Study of Official Censorship and the International Cultural Aspects of Motion Pictures*. Los Angeles: University of Southern California Press.

Harlow, John. (2002) 'When Producers in India Say "That's a take", They Mean it'. *Australian*, 16 September: 15.

Harmon, Amy. (2000) 'Free Speech Rights for Computer Code'. *New York Times*, 31 July: C1.

Harmon, Amy. (2003) 'Harry Potter and the Internet Pirates'. *New York Times*, 14 July: C1, C5.

Harrington, C. Lee and Denise D. Bielby. (1995) *Soap Fans: Pursuing Pleasure and Making Meaning in Everyday Life*. Philadelphia: Temple University Press.

Harrington, Jeff. (2003) 'Measuring up?' *St. Petersburg Times*, 4 August: E1.

Harris, Ron. (2003) 'Hollywood's Cold War on Swapping'. www.wired.com/news/digiwood.

Hartley, John. (1987) 'Invisible Fictions: Television Audiences, Paedocracy, Pleasure'. *Textual Practice* 1, no. 2: 121–38.

Hartley, John. (1996) *Popular Reality: Journalism, Modernity, Popular Culture*. London: Arnold.

Harvey, David. (1999) *The Limits to Capital*, 2nd edn. London: Verso.

Hassan, Salah S., Stephen Craft and Wael Kortam. (2003) 'Understanding the New Bases for Global Market Segmentation'. *Journal of Consumer Marketing* 20, no. 5: 446–62.

Hassen, Fakir. (2001) 'S. Africa Battles to Stop Illegal Indian Video, Music Piracy'. *Times of India*, 12 January.

Haug, W. F. (1986) *Critique of Commodity Aesthetics: Appearance, Sexuality and Advertising in Capitalist Society*. Trans. Robert Bock. Cambridge: Polity Press.

Havens, Timothy. (2002) ' "It's Still a White World out There": The Interplay of Culture and Economics in International Television Trade'. *Critical Studies in Media Communication* 19, no. 4: 377–97.

Hay, James. (1987) *Popular Film Culture in Fascist Italy: The Passing of the Rex*. Bloomington: Indiana University Press.

Hayden, Cori. (2003) *When Nature Goes Public: The Making and Unmaking of Bioprospecting in Mexico*. Princeton: Princeton University Press.

Hayes, Dade. (2000) 'Global Release Sked Tightens'. *Variety*, 19–25 June.

Hayes, Dade. (2001) 'Late Rally Lifts Wilted Wickets'. *Variety*, 8–14 January: 9, 16.

Hays, Will. (1927) 'Supervision from Within'. *The Story of the Films as Told by Leaders of the Industry to the Students of the Graduate School of Business Administration George F. Baker Foundation Harvard University*. Ed. Joseph P. Kennedy. Chicago: A. W. Shaw Company. 29–54.

Hays, Will. (1931) Speech, 12 May, J. Walter Thompson Collection, Duke University, Creative Staff Meeting File, Monday Evening Meetings.

Hayward, Susan. (1993) 'State, Culture and the Cinema: Jack Lang's Strategies for the French Film Industry'. *Screen* 34, no. 4: 382–91.

Hearon, Fanning. (1938) 'The Motion-Picture Program and Policy of the United States Government'. *Journal of Educational Sociology* 12, no. 3: 147–62.

Heilemann, John. (1994) 'Feeling for the Future: A Survey of Television'. *Economist* 330, no. 7850: Survey 1–18.

Hein, Kenneth. (2003) 'Bombay Sapphire, Sky Undertake Spirited Searches for Indie Filmmakers'. *Brandweek* 44, no. 19: 13.

Heinzl, Mark. (2002) 'Toronto Residents Rally against Hollywood Onset'. *Wall Street Journal*, 27 August: B4.

Hejma, Ondrej. (2000) 'Quality Filmmakers Turn to Prague When They Can't Afford Hollywood'. *Columbian*, 22 September: Weekend.

Held, David, Anthony McGrew, David Goldblatt and Jonathan Perraton. (1999) *Global Transformations: Politics, Economics and Culture*. Stanford: Stanford University Press.

Hellen, Nicholas. (1999) 'Labour Cuts Film Funding for Flops'. *Sunday Times*, 7 November.

Helmi, Ashraf. (2003) 'The Italian Stallion in Cairo?' *Egypt Today*, September.

Henley, Jon. (2004) 'Nemo Finds Way to French court'. *Guardian*, 24 February.

Henné, Peter. (2001) 'Worldly Distributors'. *Film Journal International*, November: 142, 154.

Hering, Ingrid. (2002) 'How to Beat the Pirates'. *Managing Intellectual Property*, 1 September: 41.

Herman, K. (2000) 'Screen Test'. *Chain Leader* 5, no. 2: 48.

Herod, Andrew. (1997) 'Labor as an Agent of Globalization and as a Global Agent'. *Globalization: Reasserting the Power of the Local*. Ed. K. R. Cox. New York: Guilford Press. 167–200.

Herod, Andrew. (2001) *Labor Geographies: Workers and the Landscapes of Capitalism*. New York: Guilford Press.

Herold, Anna. (2003) 'European Public Film Support within the WTO Framework'. *IRIS plus* 6.

Herskovitz, Jon. (1998) 'Bridging Culture Gap'. *Variety*, 18–24 May: 47.

Hettrick, Scott (2001) 'Tarzan Puts Grinch in Cidlock'. *Variety*, 8–14 January: 1, 79.

Higgott, Richard. (1999) 'Economics, Politics, and (International) Political Economy: The Need for a Balanced Diet in an Era of Globalisation'. *New Political Economy* 4, no. 1: 23–36.

High, Peter B. (2003) *The Imperial Screen: Japanese Film Culture in the Fifteen Years' War, 1931–1945*. Madison: University of Wisconsin Press.

Higson, Andrew and Richard Maltby. (1999) ' "Film Europe" and "Film America": An Introduction'. *'Film Europe' and 'Film America': Cinema, Commerce and Cultural Exchange*. Ed. Andrew Higson and Richard Maltby. Exeter: University of Exeter Press. 1–31.

Hill, John. (1994a) 'The Future of European Cinema: The Economics and Culture of Pan-European Strategies'. *Border Crossing: Film in Ireland, Britain and Europe*. Ed. John Hill, Martin McLoone and Paul Hainsworth. Belfast: Institute of Irish Studies in association with the University of Ulster and the British Film Institute. 53–80.

Hill, John. (1994b) 'Introduction'. *Border Crossing: Film in Ireland, Britain and Europe*. Ed. John Hill, Martin McLoone and Paul Hainsworth. Belfast: Institute of Irish Studies in association with the University of Ulster and the British Film Institute. 1–7.

Hill, John. (1996) 'British Television and Film: The Making of a Relationship'. *Big Picture Small Screen: The Relations between Film and Television*. Luton: University of Luton Press. 151–76.

Hill, John. (1999) *British Cinema in the 1980s: Issues and Themes*. Oxford: Clarendon Press.

Hill, John and Martin McLoone, eds. (n. d.) *Big Picture Small Screen: The Relations Between Film and Television*. Luton: University of Luton Press/John Libbey Media.

Hill, John, Martin McLoone and Paul Hainsworth, eds. (1994) *Border Crossing: Film in Ireland, Britain and Europe*. Belfast: Institute of Irish Studies in association with the University of Ulster and the British Film Institute.

Hills, Jill. (1994) 'Dependency Theory and its Relevance Today: International Institutions in Telecommunications and Structural Power'. *Review of International Studies* 20, no. 2: 169–86.

Himpele, Jeffrey D. (1996) 'Film Distribution as Media: Mapping Difference in the Bolivian Cinemascape'. *Visual Anthropology Review* 12, no. 1: 47–66.

Hindes, Andrew. (1998a) 'US Co-pros Play Well in Japan'. *Variety*, 18–24 May: 52.

Hindes, Andrew. (1998b) 'Mandalay Pacts with C I P'. *Variety*, 21–27 September: 26.

Hindley, B. (1999) 'A Bogey and its Myths'. *Times Literary Supplement*, 22 January: 28.

Hirsch, Jerry. (2001) 'Universal Puts Growth of New Parks on Hold'. *Los Angeles Times*, 7 May: 31.

Hirsch, Paul M. (2000) 'Cultural Industries Revisited'. *Organization Science* 11, no. 3: 356–61.

Hirst, Paul. (1997) 'The Global Economy – Myths and Realities'. *International Affairs* 73, no. 3: 409–25.

Hirst, Paul and G. Thompson. (1996) *Globalization in Question: The International Economy and the Possibilities of Governance*. Cambridge: Polity Press.

Hiscock, John. (1998) 'Hollywood Backs British Film Drive'. *Daily Telegraph*, 24 July: 19.

Hobsbawm, Eric. (1998) 'The Nation and Globalization'. *Constellations* 5, no. 1: 1–9.

Hoekman, Bernard M. and Michel M. Kostecki. (1995) *The Political Economy of the World Trading System: From GATT to WTO*. Oxford: Oxford University Press.

Holden, Wade. (2002) 'Movie Exhibition: The Road to Recovery'. *Boxoffice.com*, 1 April.

Holley, David. (2000) 'Prague: AKA "Hollywood East" '. *Bergen Record*, 27 August.

Holloway, Ron. (1989) 'Porno Trafficking on rise in India.' *Hollywood Reporter*, 21 February.

Hollows, J. and M. Jancovich. (1995) 'Popular Film and Cultural Distinctions'. *Approaches to Popular Film*. Ed. J. Hollows and M. Jancovich. Manchester: Manchester University Press. 1–14.

Holmlund, C. and C. Fuchs, eds. (1997) *Between the Sheets, in the Streets: Queer, Lesbian, Gay Documentary*. Minneapolis: University of Minnesota Press.

Holson, Laura M. (2003a) 'As Animation Goes Digital, Disney Fights for its Crown'. *New York Times*, 10 February.

Holson, Laura M. (2003b) 'Film Industry Joins War on Internet File Sharing'. *International Herald Tribune*, 26 September: 14.

Hong Kong Christian Industrial Committee. (2001) *Beware of Mickey: Disney's Sweatshop in South China.*

Hong Kong Trade Development Council. (2003) News release, 25 September.

Hook, Janet. (2000) 'Film Industry Lobbies for China Trade Bill'. *Los Angeles Times*, 23 May.

Hopewell, John. (2000) 'Deregulation Causes Euro Takeovers to Triple'. *Variety*, 15–21 May: 58.

Hopewell, John. (2001) 'Das Werk Takes Street into Spain'. *Variety*, 12–18 February: 22.

Hopewell, John. (2003) 'Spain'. *Variety*, 5–11 January.

Hoppenstand, Gary. (1998) 'Hollywood and the Business of Making Movies: The Relationship between Film Content and Economic Factors'. *The Motion Picture Mega-Industry*. Ed. Barry R. Litman. Boston: Allyn and Bacon. 222–42.

Horn, John. (2004) 'A "Cold" War over Foreign Filming'. *Los Angeles Times*, 4 February: E1.

Horowitz, M. (1997) 'How to Make a Blockbuster'. *New York Times Magazine*, 16 November: 140.

Horst, Carole. (2002) 'Back Lot Legend Casts Wider Net'. *Variety*, 2–8 December: A4.

Hoskins, Colin, Stuart McFadyen and Adam Finn. (1997) *Global Television and Film: An Introduction to the Economics of the Business*. Oxford: Clarendon Press.

Hostetter, Martha. (2004) 'Arts Groups Look to Congress to Ease Cultural Exchanges'. *Gotham Gazette*, 2 February.

Howard, Andrew. (1995) 'Global Capital and Labor Internationalism in Comparative Historical Perspective: A Marxist Analysis'. *Sociological Inquiry* 65, nos. 3–4: 365–94.

Hozic, Aida A. (1999) 'Uncle Sam Goes to Siliwood: Of Landscapes, Spielberg and Hegemony'. *Review of International Political Economy* 6, no. 3: 289–312.

Hozic, Aida A. (2001) *Hollyworld: Space, Power, and Fantasy in the American Economy*. Ithaca: Cornell University Press.

Hu, Jim and Stefanie Olsen. (2004) 'AOL to Offer Movie Downloads'. *News.com*, 20 January.

Hu, Jubin. (2003) *Projecting a Nation: Chinese National Cinema before 1949*. Hong Kong: Hong Kong University Press.

Huck, Peter and Victoria Gurvich. (2003) 'The Lure of the Big, Wide World'. *Age*, 9 September: 4.

Huettig, Mae D. (1944) *Economic Control of the Motion Picture Industry: A Study in Industrial Organization*. Philadelphia: University of Pennsylvania Press.

Huffstutter, P. J. (2003) 'Aiming to Keep Cameras Rolling'. *Los Angeles Times*, 21 December.

Hughes, Steve and Rorden Wilkinson. (1998) 'International Labour Standards and World Trade: No Role for the World Trade Organization?' *New Political Economy* 3, no. 3: 375–89.

Hunnings, Neville. (1972) 'The Film Industry and the EEC'. *Sight and Sound* 41, no. 2: 82–85.

Husband, Warren. (1994) 'Resurrecting Hollywood's Golden Age: Balancing the Rights of Film Owners, Artistic Authors and Consumers'. *Columbia-VLA Journal of Law and the Arts* 17, no. 3.

Hutchinson, John. (1999) 'Re-interpreting Cultural Nationalism'. *Australian Journal of Politics and History* 45, no. 3: 392–407.

Hutton, Will. (2002) 'The Wheel of Fortune'. *Guardian*, 6 July.

I'Anson-Sparks, Justin. (2000) 'Hollywood Goes Even Further East'. *Independent*, 3 August.

Idato, Michael. (1999) 'Mission Not Impossible: We Could be Tinseltown'. *Daily Telegraph*, 5 May.

Ingram, Mike. (2001) 'AOL-Time Warner Threatens Children Running Harry Potter Fan Sites'. *World Socialist Web Site*, 28 February.

International Labour Office. (1999) *Key Indicators of the Labour Market, 1999*. Geneva.

International Labour Office. (2000a) *Sectoral Activities Programme: Media; Culture; Graphical*. Geneva.

International Labour Office. (2000b) *Symposium on Information Technologies in the Media and Entertainment Industries: Their Impact on Employment, Working Conditions and Labour-Management Relations*. 28 February–3 March. Geneva.

International Monetary Fund. (2000) *Globalization: Threat or Opportunity.*

Iordanova, Dina. (2002) 'Feature Filmmaking within the New Europe: Moving Funds and Images across the East–West Divide'. *Media, Culture & Society* 24, no. 4.

Izod, John. (1988) *Hollywood and the Box Office 1895–1986.* New York: Columbia University Press.

Jacka, Elizabeth. (1992) 'Introduction'. *Continental Shift: Globalisation and Culture.* Ed. Elizabeth Jacka. Sydney: Local Consumption. 1–22.

Jäckel, Anne. (1996) 'European Co-production Strategies: The Case of France and Britain'. *Film Policy.* Ed. Albert Moran. London: Routledge. 85–97.

Jäckel, Anne. (1999) 'Broadcasters' Involvement in Cinematographic Co-productions'. *Television Broadcasting in Contemporary France and Britain.* Ed. Michael Scriven and Monia Lecompte. Oxford: Berghahn Books. 175–97.

Jacob, Preminda. (1998) 'Media Spectacles: The Production and Reception of Tamil Cinema Advertisements'. *Visual Anthropology* 11, no. 4: 287–322.

Jagannathan, Venkatachari. (2002) 'Animated Growth'. *Domain-b.com*, 12 June.

Jaikumar, Priya. (1999) *British Cinema and the End of Empire: National Identity in Transition, 1927–1947.* Ph.D. dissertation, Northwestern University, Evanston, IL.

James, Alison. (2000) 'Canal Plus Shares its Bonbons with Ovitz'. *Variety*, 10–16 July: 7.

James, Alison. (2002) 'Featured Player'. *Variety*, 18 November: 15.

James, Alison. (2003a) 'Canal Plus Programming on the Chopping Block'. *Variety*, 24–30 March: A4.

James, Alison. (2003b) 'Gallic Distribs Soldier on Despite Beating'. *Variety*, 12–18 May: 38.

James, Alison and Adam Dawtrey. (2000) 'Oui are the World'. *Variety*, 19–25 June: 1, 85.

James, Nick. (2001) 'In Bed with the Film Council'. *Sight and Sound* 11, no. 1: 14–17.

Jameson, Fredric. (1991) *Postmodernism, or, the Cultural Logic of Late Capitalism.* London: Verso.

Jameson, Fredric. (1996) 'Five Theses on Actually Existing Marxism'. *Monthly Review* 47, no. 11: 1–10.

Jameson, Fredric. (2000) 'Globalization and Political Strategy'. *New Left Review* 4: 49–68.

Jarvie, Ian. (1998) 'Free Trade as Cultural Threat: American Film and TV Exports in the Post-War Period'. *Hollywood and Europe: Economics, Culture, National Identity: 1945–95.* Ed. Geoffrey Nowell-Smith and Steven Ricci. London: British Film Institute. 34–46.

Jaszi, Peter and Martha Woodmansee. (1996) 'The Ethical Reaches of Authorship'. *South Atlantic Quarterly* 95, no. 4: 947–77.

Jauss, Hans Robert. (1982) *Toward an Aesthetic of Reception.* Trans. T. Bahti. Minneapolis: University of Minnesota Press.

Jeancolas, Jean-Pierre. (1998) 'From the Blum-Byrnes Agreement to the GATT Affair'. *Hollywood and Europe: Economics, Culture, National Identity: 1945–95.* Ed. Geoffrey Nowell-Smith and Steven Ricci. London: British Film Institute. 47–60.

Jihong, Wan and Richard Kraus. (2002) 'Hollywood and China as Adversaries and Allies'. *Pacific Affairs* 75, no. 3: 419–34.

Johnson, Greg. (2000) 'Can Settlement Lure Runaway Production Home?' *Los Angeles Times*, 24 October.

Johnson, Jo and Daniel Dombey. (2004) 'French Filmmakers Fear the "Exception Culturelle"'. *Financial Times*, 8 January.

Johnston, David. (2003) 'Fake Goods Support Terrorism, Interpol Official is to Testify'. *New York Times*, 16 July: A10.

Johnston, Eric. (1947) 'The Motion Picture as a Stimulus to Culture'. *Annals of the American Academy of Political and Social Science* 254: 98–102.

Johnston, Eric. (1950) 'Messengers from a Free Country'. *Saturday Review of Literature*, 4 March: 9–12.

Jones, Arthur. (2002) 'Shanghai Backlots Subs for Philippines in "Raid"'. *Variety*, 25 November–1 December: 13.

Jones, Arthur. (2004) 'Warner Bros. Int'l Pacts for More Chinese Theaters'. *Variety*, 18 January.

Jones, Candace. (1996) 'Careers in Project Networks: The Case of the Film Industry'. *The Boundaryless Career: A New Employment Principle for a New Organizational Era.* Ed. Michael B. Arthur and Denise M. Rousseau. New York: Oxford University Press. 58–75.

Jones, Candace. (2001) 'Co-evolution of Entrepreneurial Careers, Institutional Rules and Competitive Dynamics in American Film'. *Organization Studies* 22, no. 6: 911–44.

Jones, Candace and Robert J. DeFillippi. (1996) 'Back to the Future in Film: Combining Industry and Self-Knowledge to Meet the Career Challenges of the 21st Century'. *Academy of Management Review* 10, no. 4: 89.

Jones, Martha. (2002) *Motion Picture Production in Canada: Requested by Assembly Member Dario Frommer, Chair of the Select Committee on the Future of California's Film Industry.* California Research Bureau, California State Library.

Joseph, May. (1995) 'Diaspora, New Hybrid Identities, and the Performance of Citizenship'. *Women and Performance* 7, nos. 2–8, no. 1: 3–13.

Jury, Louise. (1996) 'Mission Possible: Red Tape Cut to Boost Film Industry'. *Independent*, 4 July: 3.

Jury, Louise. (2004) 'UK Film Industry Exceeded Expectations with over Pounds 1bn Spent on Movies in 2003'. *Independent*, 12 January: 10.

Justice for Maya Bay International Alliance. (2000) 'No to Hollywood's "The Beach"! Boycott the Bulldozer Movie'.

Kahn, E. J., Jr. (1981) *Jock. The Life and Times of John Hay Whitney.* Garden City, NY: Doubleday.

Kahn, Gabriel. (2002) 'India's Bollywood Has a New Focus: Product Placement'. *Wall Street Journal*, 4 September: B5C.

Kaitatzi-Whitlock, Sophia and George Terzis. (2001) 'Greece: Disney's Descent on Greece: The Company is the Message'. *Dazzled by Disney? The Global Disney Audiences Project.* Ed. Janet Wasko, Mark Phillips and Eileen R. Meehan. London: Leicester University Press. 135–59.

Kakabadse, Mario. (1995) 'The WTO and the Commodification of Cultural Products: Implications for Asia'. *Media Asia* 22, no. 2: 71–77.

Kamel, Yomna. (2000) 'Media Free Zone Opens Egypt to the World'. *Middle East Times*, 4.

Kandil, Heba. (2000) 'The Media Free Zone: An Egyptian Media Production City Finesse'. *Transnational Broadcasting Studies* 5.

Kantebet, S. R. (1932) Letter to the President of the Academy of Motion Picture Arts and Sciences, 15 September. Special Collections, Margaret Herrick Library. Academy of Motion Picture Arts and Sciences, Los Angeles.

Kanter, L. (1999) 'Dutch Publishing Firm Colonizes U.S.: Nielsen Deal Caps VNU's Buying Spree'. *Crain's New York Business*, 23 August: 1.

Kapoor, Pankaj. (2002) 'Why Another Day? Xmas Suits Bond!' *Times of India*, 26 December.

Kapur, Shekhar. (2002) 'The Asians are Coming'. *Guardian*, 23 August: 9.

Karthigesu, R. (1998) 'Transborder Television in Malaysia'. *TV without Borders: Asia Speaks Out.* Ed. Anura Goonasekera and Paul S. N. Lee. Singapore: Asian Media Information and Communication Centre. 38–77.

Kartik, G. (2003) 'Pirated CDs Fuel Terror Outfits'. *Times of India*, 17 October.

Kasilag, Giselle. (2003) 'Mission Accomplished'. *Business World*, 13 June: 32.

Katz, Alfred. (1954) 'The Indian Movie Scene: Busy Producers Keep Native Customers Happy but Offer Little for Export'. *New York Times*, 20 June.

Katz, Elihu. (1990) 'A Propos des médias et de leurs effets'. *Technologies et Symboliques de la Communication.* Ed. L. Sfez and G. Coutlée. Grenoble: Presses Universitaires de Grenoble.

Kay, Jeremy. (2002) 'Columbia Marches into Korea with Remake of Mamet Film'. *ScreenDaily.com*, 19 November.

Kay, Jeremy. (2003) 'Village Roadshow Ups Funding Capacity in Warner Co-financing Deal'. *ScreenDaily.com*, 12 February.

Kehr, Dave. (1999) 'Planet Hollywood Indeed'. *New York Times*, 2 May: 23, 33.

Keil, Charlie. (2001) ' "American" Cinema in the 1990s and Beyond: Whose Country's Filmmaking is it Anyway?' *The End of Cinema as We Know it: American Film in the Nineties*. Ed. Jon Lewis. New York: New York University Press. 53–60.

Kellner, Douglas. (1990) *Television and the Crisis of Democracy*. Boulder, CO: Westview Press.

Kempster, Norman. (2001) 'Federal Study Backs Claims of Lost Movie Jobs'. *Los Angeles Times*, 20 January.

Kendall, David E., Joel M. Litvin, Kevin T. Baine and Dennis M. Black. (2000) *Amicus Curiae* for MPAA *et al*. Napster v. A&M Records *et al*. Appeal nos. 00–16401 and 00–16403 US Court of Appeals for the Ninth Circuit.

Kennedy, Joseph P. (1927) 'General Introduction to the Course'. *The Story of the Films as Told by Leaders of the Industry to the Students of the Graduate School of Business Administration George F. Baker Foundation Harvard University*. Ed. Joseph P. Kennedy. Chicago: A. W. Shaw Company. 3–28.

Kenny, Jim and Elena Pernia. (1998) 'The Filipino's Window on the World: Viewing Foreign Television in the Philippines'. *TV without Borders: Asia Speaks Out*. Ed. Anura Goonasekera and Paul S. N. Lee. Singapore: Asian Media Information and Communication Centre. 78–140.

Kent, Sidney R. (1927) 'Distributing the Product'. *The Story of the Films as Told by Leaders of the Industry to the Students of the Graduate School of Business Administration George F. Baker Foundation Harvard University*. Ed. Joseph P. Kennedy. Chicago: A. W. Shaw Company. 203–32.

Kerr, Aphra and Roddy Flynn. (2003) 'Revisiting Globalisation through the Movie and Digital Games Industries'. *Convergence* 9, no. 1: 91–113.

Kessler, Kirsten L. (1995) 'Protecting Free Trade in Audiovisual Entertainment: A Proposal for Counteracting the European Union's Trade Barriers to the U.S. Entertainment Industry's Exports'. *Law and Policy in International Business* 26, no. 2: 563–611.

Keynes, John Maynard. (1957) *The General Theory of Employment Interest and Money*. London: Macmillan; New York: St Martin's Press.

Kiefer, Peter. (2000) 'Screen Actors Guild Members See Slight Rise in Income – Except Those in TV Who Take Home Less'. *Inside.Com*, 11 December.

Kim, Carolyn Hyun-Kyung. (2000) 'Building the Korean Film Industry's Competitiveness'. *Pacific Rim Law and Policy Journal* 9: 353–77.

Kim, Seung Hyun and Kyung Sook Lee. (2001) 'Korea: Disney in Korean Mass Culture'. *Dazzled by Disney? The Global Disney Audiences Project*. Ed. Janet Wasko, Mark Phillips and Eileen R. Meehan. London: Leicester University Press. 182–201.

King, John. (1990) *Magical Reels: A History of Cinema in Latin America*. London: Verso.

King, Tom. (2002) 'How Hollywood Makes the World Take Notice'. *Wall Street Journal*, 15 November: W7.

Kipnis, Jill. (2004) 'Piracy's Next Victim'. *Billboard*, 10 January: 1.

Kirby, Carrie. (2000) 'Hollywood Attacks Digital Movie Piracy'. *San Francisco Chronicle*, 21 July: F1.

Kirkland, Bruce and Claire Buckley. (2001) 'Hollywood vs. Hollywood North'. *Ottawa Sun*, 18 February: S6.

Kirschbaum, Erik. (2001) 'German Thriving Centre for European Film'. *Reuters*, 16 February.

Kissinger, Henry. (1999) Globalization and World Order. Independent Newspapers Annual Lecture, Trinity College Dublin, 12 October.

Klady, L. (1994) 'Gallup Rolls Pic Poll: Film Research Unit to Challenge Dominant NRG'. *Daily Variety*, 21 March: 1.

Klady, L. (1996) 'Moviegoers Stump Science: Despite Reams of Data, Trackers Still Can't Predict Pic's Fate'. *Daily Variety*, 23 August: 3.

Klady, L. (1997) 'Why Can't Johnny Track?' *Variety*, 19–25 May: 7.

Klady, L. (1998) 'More B.O. Oracles Take up Trackin''. *Variety*, 19–25 October: 9.

Klein, Christina. (2003) 'The Asian Factor in Global Hollywood: Breaking Down the Notion of a Distinctly American Cinema'. *YaleGlobal Online*, 25 March.

Kline, Stephen. (2003) 'Media Effects: Redux or Reductive?' *Particip@tions: International Journal of Audience Research* 1, no. 1.

Koerner, Brendan I. (2003). 'Hollywood and Whine'. *Washington Monthly*, January–February.

Kontorovich, Eugene. (2004) 'The Piracy Analogy: Modern Universal Jurisdiction's Hollow Foundation'. *Harvard International Law Journal* 45, no. 1.

Kopytoff, Igor. (1986) 'The Cultural Biography of Things: Commoditization as Process'. *The Social Life of Things: Commodities in Cultural Perspective*. Ed. Arjun Appadurai. Cambridge: Cambridge University Press. 64–91.

Kotkin, Joel. (2001) 'The Digital Divider'. *Los Angeles Times*, 6 May: M1.

Kozul-Wright, R. and R. Rowthorn. (1998) 'Spoilt for Choice? Transnational Corporations and the Geography of International Production'. *Oxford Review of Economic Policy* 14, no. 2: 74–92.

KPMG. (1996) *Film Financing and Television Programming: A Taxation Guide*. Amsterdam: KPMG.

Kracauer, Siegfried. (1949) 'National Types as Hollywood Presents Them'. *Public Opinion Quarterly* 13, no. 1: 53–72.

Kripalani, Manjeet and Ron Grover. (2002) 'Bollywood: Can New Money Create a World-class Film Industry in India?' *Business Week*, 2 December: 48.

Krosnar, Katka, Adam Piore and Stefan Theil. (2001) 'Take One: Prague'. *Newsweek International*, 19 March: 40.

Krugman, Paul. (2000) 'Where in the World is the "New Economic Geography"?' *The Oxford Handbook of Economic Geography*. Ed. Gordon L. Clark, Maryann P. Feldman and Meric S. Gertler with Kate Williams. Oxford: Oxford University Press. 49–60.

Kuhn, Anthony. (1995) 'Raising the Red Curtain'. *Los Angles Times*, 17 October: D1, 7.

Kuhn, Michael. (1998) 'How Can Europe Benefit from the Digital Revolution?' Paper presented to the European Audiovisual Conference, Birmingham, 6–8 April.

Kuhn, Raymond and James Stanyer. (1999) 'Television and the State'. *Television Broadcasting in Contemporary France and Britain*. Ed. Michael Scriven and Monia Lecomte. Oxford: Berghahn Books. 2–15.

Kumar, Sangeeta A. (2002) 'Hollywood Calling: American movies Make Whoopee in India'. *Filmfare*, March.

Kurz, Otto. (1967) *Fakes*. New York: Dover.

LaFranchi, Howard. (1999) 'Mexifilms vs. Mickey Mouse'. *Christian Science Monitor*, 5 January.

Lagny, Michèle. (1992) 'Popular Taste: The Peplum'. *Popular European Cinema*. Ed. Richard Dyer and Ginette Vincendeau. London: Routledge. 163–80.

Lai, Edwin L. C. (1998) 'International Intellectual Property Protection and the Rate of Product Innovation'. *Journal of Development Economics* 55: 133–53.

Lakha, Salim. (1999) 'The New International Division of Labour and the Indian Computer Software Industry'. *The Economic Geography Reader: Producing and Consuming Global Capitalism*. Ed. John Bryson, Nick Henry, David Keeble and Ron Martin. Chichester: John Wiley & Sons. 148–55.

Lall, Bhuvan. (1994) 'Jurassic Park Breaks Indian Resistance'. *Screen International*, 22 April.

Lall, Bhuvan. (2000) 'Sony to Distribute Hindi Movies Worldwide.' *Screen International*, 17 October.

Lall, Bhuvan and Ralf Ludemann. (1994) 'Warner Bros Embarks upon Passage to India'. *Screen International*, 26 August.

Lall, Chander. (1999) 'New Rulings Bolster Copyrights in India'. *IP Worldwide*, May–June.

Landers, Jim. (2000) 'A Tempest Abroad: Other Countries Can be Overwhelmed by American Cultural Exports Such as Music, Movies and Food'. *Dallas Morning News*, 12 November: 1J.

Landler, Mark. (2001) 'A Glut of Cable TV in India'. *New York Times*, 23 March: C1, C12.

Landler, Mark. (2003) 'Hollywood Investor Buys KirchMedia TV unit'. *New York Times*, 18 March: W1.

Lang, Tim and Colin Hines. (1993) *The New Protectionism: Protecting the Future against Free Trade*. New York: New Press.

Lange, André. (1998) 'Andrew Says Local Financing is Reducing the Number of European Co-productions'. *Screen International*, 5 June: 11.

Lange, André. (2003) 'The Financial Situation of the Various Branches of the European Union Audiovisual Industry'. Meeting of Experts on the Reform of the Instruments to Encourage the European Audiovisual Industry, 15–16 November.

Langman, Larry. (2000) *Destination Hollywood: The Influence of Europeans on American Filmmaking*. Jefferson, NC: McFarland & Company.

Larkin, Brian. (2004) 'Degrading Images, Distorted Sounds: Nigerian Video and the Infrastructure of Piracy'. *Public Culture* 16, no. 2.

Larner, Wendy. (2002) 'Calling Capital: Call Centre Strategies in New Brunswick and New Zealand'. *Global Networks* 2, no. 2: 133–52.

Latimer, Joanne. (2003) 'The Guy in That Canadian Film Sounds Like a Noo Yawka, Eh?' *New York Times*, 3 February.

Latour, Bruno. (1993) *We Have Never Been Modern*. Trans. C. Porter. Cambridge, MA: Harvard University Press.

Laurance, Jeremy. (2001) 'The Habit Hollywood Just Can't Stub Out'. *Independent*, 5 January.

Lauzen, Martha M. and David M. Dozier. (1999) 'The Role of Women on Screen and behind the Scenes in the Television and Film Industries: Review of a Program of Research'. *Journal of Communication Inquiry* 23, no. 4: 355–73.

Laville, Helen. (2001) 'The Gaul of These Guys'. *Australian Financial Review*, 14 July: The Fin 6.

Lazarsfeld, Paul F. (1950) 'Foreword'. *Hollywood Looks at its Audience*. Leo A. Handel. Urbana: University of Illinois Press. ix–xiv.

Le Heron, Richard, Ian Cooper, Martine Perry and David Hayward. (1997) 'Commodity System Governance: A New Zealand Discourse'. *Uneven Development: Global and Local Processes*. Ed. M. Taylor and S. Conti. Aldershot, Hants.: Avebury. 81–100.

Lears, Jackson. (1989) 'Beyond Veblen: Rethinking Consumer Culture in America'. *Consuming Visions: Accumulation and Display of Goods in America, 1880–1920*. Ed. Simon J. Bronner. New York: Norton. 73–95.

Lears, T. J. Jackson. (1983) 'From Salvation to Self-Realization: Advertising and the Therapeutic Roots of the Consumer Culture, 1880–1930'. *The Culture of Consumption: Critical Essays in American History, 1880–1980*. Ed. Richard Wightman Fox and T. J. Jackson Lears. New York: Pantheon. 1–38.

Lécuyer, Christophe. (2003) 'High-Tech Corporatism: Management–Employee Relations in U.S. Electronics Firms, 1920s–1960s'. *Enterprise & Society* 4, no. 3: 502–20.

Ledbetter, James. (2002) 'The Culture Blockade'. *The Nation*, 4 November: 37.

Lee, Oliver and Dan Cox. (1999) 'China's Sweet and Sour Pitch'. *Variety*, 1–7 March: 1.

Leets, Laura, Gavin de Becker and Howard Giles. (1995) 'Fans: Exploring Expressed Motivations for Contacting Celebrities'. *Journal of Language and Social Psychology* 14, nos. 1–2: 102–23.

Leff, Lisa. (2000) 'The Past is Prologue'. *Los Angeles Times Magazine*, 29 October.

Legislative Research Service, Library of Congress. (1964) *The U.S. Ideological Effort: Government Agencies and Programs: Study Prepared for the Subcommittee on International Organizations and Movements of the Committee on Foreign Affairs*. Washington.

Lent, John A. (1998) 'The Animation Industry and its Offshore Factories'. *Global Productions: Labor in the Making of the 'Information Society'*. Ed. Gerald Sussman and John A. Lent. Cresskill, NJ: Hampton Press. 239–54.

Leow, Jason. (2003) 'China Has it All'. *The Straits Times*, 10 December.

Lerner, Preston. (1999) 'Shadow Force: Hundreds of Movies Have Been Reshaped as a Result of Work by Joseph Farrell's National Research Group'. *Los Angeles Times Magazine*, 7 November: 18.

Lev, Peter. (1993) *The Euro-American Cinema*. Austin: University of Texas Press.

Lev, Peter. (2003) *History of the American Cinema, Volume 7: Transforming the Screen 1950–1959*. New York: Charles Scribner's Sons.

Levin, Adam and Jenny Schneider Li. (2001) 'Between a Rock and a Hard Place: Writers and Actors Navigate Hollywood's Rough Roads to Employment during Labor Strikes'. *Loyola of Los Angeles Entertainment Law Review* 21: 371–99.

Levinson, Mark. (1999) 'Who's in Charge Here?' *Dissent* 46, no. 4: 21–23.

Levy, Emmanuel. (1989) 'The Democratic Elite: America's Movie Stars'. *Qualitative Sociology* 12, no. 1: 29–54.

Lewis, Gerry. (2001) 'Think Local When Going Global'. *Variety*, 26 February–4 March: 7.

Lewis, Howard Thompson. (1930) *Cases on the Motion Picture Industry with Commentaries: Harvard Business Reports Volume 8*. New York: McGraw-Hill.

Lewis, Justin. (1991) *The Ideological Octopus: An Exploration of Television and its Audience*. New York: Routledge.

Lewis, Michael. (2000) 'Boom Box'. *New York Times Magazine* 13 August: 36+.

Lexington. (1999) 'Pokémania v. Globophobia'. *Economist*, 20 November: 36.

Liang, Lawrence. (2003) 'Porous Legalities and Avenues of Participation'. Presented at the Intellectual Property, Markets, and Cultural Flows Workshop. Social Science Research Council, New York, 24 October.

Light, Julie. (1994) 'Cooperation and Compromise: Co-production and Public Service Broadcasting'. *Screen* 35, no. 1: 78–90.

Lindsay, Vachel. (1970) *The Art of the Moving Picture*. New York: Liveright.

Linnett, Richard and Wayne Friedman. (2003) ' "Green Hornet" Shops for a Car'. *Advertising Age*, 26 May: 1, 35.

Litman, Barry R. (1998) *The Motion Picture Mega-industry*. Boston: Allyn and Bacon.

Litman, Barry R. and Hoekyun Ahn. (1998) 'Predicting Financial Success of Motion Pictures: The Early '90s Experience'. *The Motion Picture Mega industry*. Barry R. Litman. Boston: Allyn and Bacon. 172–97.

Litman, Jessica. (1990) 'The Public Domain'. *Emory Law Journal* 39.

Liu, Xitao. (1999) 'Jiaru shimao, Zhongguo Dianying Shou Menglie Chongji'. *Qiaobao*, 24 November: B1.

Loeb, Hamilton. (2000) 'The Management and Resolution of Cross-Border Disputes as Canada/U.S. Enter the 21st Century. Telecommunications and Culture: Transborder Freedom of Information or Cultural Identity?' *Canada-United States Law Journal* 26: 303–12.

London Economics. (1992) *The Competitive Position of the European and US Film Industries*. Report for the Media Business School (an initiative of the MEDIA programme of the European Community, London).

Long, Doris E. (1998) 'China's IP Reforms Show Little Success'. *IP Worldwide* November–December.

López, Ana M. (2000) 'Facing up to Hollywood'. *Reinventing Film Studies*. Ed. Christine Gledhill and Linda Williams. London: Arnold. 419–37.

Los Angeles County Economic Development Corporation. (2001) *Film Industry Profile of Los Angeles County*.

Los Angeles County Economic Development Corporation. (2004) *2004–2005 Economic Forecast and Industry Outlook for California & the Los Angeles Five-County Area Including the National & International Setting*.

Lowry, Brian. (2000) 'Greetings from Vancouver'. *Los Angeles Times*, 1 October.

Ludemann, Ralf. (1996) 'Majors Set Sights on India'. *Screen International*, 2 February.

Ludemann, Ralf. (2004) 'Warner Theaters Plans Chinese Expansion'. *ScreenDaily.com*, 8 January.

Luk, Sidney. (2004) 'Blockbuster Quits HK as High Rents Take Toll'. *South China Morning Post*, 30 January: 1.

Lukk, T. (1997) *Movie Marketing: Opening the Picture and Giving it Legs*. Los Angeles: Silman-James Press.

Lumiere Data Base on Admissions of Films Released in Europe. (n. d.) 'Methodology – Limitations of the *Lumiere* Database'. lumiere.obs.coe.int/web/sources/EN/metho.html.

Lury, Celia. (1993) *Cultural Rights: Technology, Legality and Personality*. New York: Routledge.

Lyman, Eric J. (2000) 'Hollywood Goes to Rome'. *Adageglobal*, December.

Lyman, Rick. (2002a) 'China is Warming to Hollywood's Glow: Before Big Profits, Hurdles Remain'. *New York Times*, 18 September: 1.

Lyman, Rick. (2002b) 'British Star Speaks up for "Quiet American" '. *New York Times*, 18 November: E1.

Lyon, David. (2001) *Surveillance Society: Monitoring Everyday Life*. Maidenhead, Berks.: Open University Press.

Lyons, Charles. (2002) 'Remakes Remodel Foreign Pix'. *Variety*, 21–27 October, 24.

Maas, John-Michael. (2003) 'Brave New Branding'. *Publishers Weekly* 250, no. 51: 14, 16–18.

MacDougall, J. Paige. (2003) 'Transnational Commodities as Local Cultural Icons: Barbie Dolls in Mexico'. *Journal of Popular Culture* 37, no. 2: 257–75.

Machan, Dyan. (1997) 'Mr. Valenti Goes to Washington'. *Forbes*, 1 December.

Mackenzie, Drew. (2000) 'Mel's Making a Monkey of Me'. *Mirror*, 2 December: 3.

Mackey, Robert. (2004) 'A World of Ticket Prices'. *New York Times*, 11 January: 7.

MacMillan, Scott. (2002) 'Prague Slashes Location Shooting Fees'. *ScreenDaily.com*, 3 October.

MacMillan, Scott. (2003a) 'Barrandov Studios to be Re-nationalised?' *ScreenDaily.com*, 22 January.

MacMillan, Scott. (2003b) 'Dreamworks Joins Prague Production Influx'. *ScreenDaily.com*, 7 March.

MacMillan, Scott. (2003c) 'Location Prague Attracts Two New US Productions'. *ScreenDaily.com*, 20 March.

Madigan, Nick. (1999a) 'Prod'n Headed North'. *Variety*, 28 June–11 July: 12.

Madigan, Nick. (1999b) 'Runaways Inspire Taxing Questions'. *Variety*, 23–29 August: 7.

Madigan, Nick. (1999c) 'Flight or Fight? Industry Gears up to Keep Production in Area'. *Variety*, 22–28 November: L3–4.

Madigan, Nick. (2000) 'Surviving the Odds'. *Variety*, 13–19 November: 43–44, 46, 50.

Magder, Ted. (1998) 'Franchising the Candy Store: Split-Run Magazines and a New International Regime for Trade in Culture'. *Canadian-American Public Policy* no. 34: 1–66.

Magder, Ted and Jonathan Burston. (2001) 'Whose Hollywood? Changing Forms and Relations inside the North American Entertainment Economy'. *Continental Order? Integrating North America for Cybercapitalism*. Ed. Vincent Mosco and Dan Schiller. Lanham, MD: Rowman & Littlefield. 207–34.

Maguire, Joseph. (1999) *Global Sport: Identities, Societies, Civilizations*. Cambridge: Polity.

Mahendra, Sunanda. (1996) 'A Note on Television in Sri Lanka'. *Contemporary Television: Eastern Perspectives*. Ed. David French and Michael Richards. New Delhi: Sage. 221–27.

Mahmood, Hameeduddin. (1980) No Title. *Hollywood Reporter*, 29 April.

Maier, Timothy W. (2004) 'Arresting Kids for Downloading Music'. *Insight on the News*, 1 March: 29.

Major, Wade. (1997) 'Hollywood's Asian Strategy: The Asian Millennium Could Catch Hollywood Flat-Footed'. *Transpacific* 68.

Malcolm, Paul. (2000) 'Below the (Color) Line'. *LA Weekly*, 20–26 October.

Mallaby, Sebastian. (2002) 'France's Strange Resentments'. *Washington Post*, 22 April: A19.

Mallet, James. (2001) 'Lights, cameras ... but No Action'. *Observer*, 25 March.

Mallory, Michael. (2003) 'The Cutting Room'. *Los Angeles Times*, 17 February.

Maney, Kevin. (2003) 'IBM Makes Play for "Next-Generation Pixar" '. *USA Today*, 24 July. www.usatoday.com/tech/techinvestor/techc orporatenews/ 2003–07–24–ibm_x.htm.

Mann, Charles C. (2000) 'The Heavenly Jukebox: Efforts to Obtain Control Access to Sound Recordings from the Internet'. *Atlantic Monthly*, 1 September.

Mann, Chik. (1997) 'Korea Slams 5 Majors'. *Variety*, 21 March.

Mann, Michael. (1993) 'Nation-States in
    Europe and other Continents:
    Diversifying, Developing, not Dying'.
    Daedalus 122, no. 3: 115–40.

Mann, Michael. (2003) *Incoherent Empire.*
    London: Verso.

Manuel, Peter. (1993) *Cassette Culture: Popular
    Music and Technology in North India.* New
    Delhi: Oxford University Press.

Marich, Bob. (1999) 'Russia Leads MPA's '98
    Piracy-Loss List'. *Los Angeles Times*, 3
    February.

Markham-Smith, Ian. (2001) 'China Sets to
    Open up to Hollywood Movie Giants'.
    International Market News, 26 July.

Marshall, Don D. (1996) 'Understanding Late-
    Twentieth-Century Capitalism: Reassessing
    the Globalization Theme'. *Government and
    Opposition* 31, no. 2: 193–215.

Martin, Judith N. and Thomas K. Nakayama.
    (2000) *Intercultural Communication in
    Contexts*, 2nd edn. London: Mayfield
    Publishing.

Martín, Lydia. (1998) 'Studio Miami: How
    Does an Entertainment Capital Rise from
    the Ground up? Cash, Connections and
    Cool'. *Miami Herald*, 13 December: 11.

Martin, Reed. (1995) 'The French Film
    Industry: A Crisis of Art and Commerce'.
    Columbia Journal of World Business 30:
    6–17.

Martin, Reed. (2000) 'The Casting Accent is on
    Foreign Appeal'. *USA Today*, 13 December.

Martín-Barbero, Jesus. (1993) *Communication,
    Culture, and Hegemony: From the Media to
    Mediations.* London: Sage.

Marvasti, A. (1994) 'International Trade in
    Cultural Goods: A Cross-Sectional
    Analysis'. *Journal of Cultural Economics* 18,
    no. 2: 135–48.

Marvasti, A. (2000) 'Motion Pictures Industry:
    Economies of Scale and Trade'.
    *International Journal of the Economics of
    Business* 7, no. 1: 99–115.

Marx, Karl. (1906) *Capital: A Critique of
    Political Economy.* Trans. Samuel Moore
    and Edward Aveling. Ed. Frederick Engels.
    New York: Modern Library.

Masson, Gordon. (2002) 'Interpol Forms
    Intellectual Property Rights Group'.
    Billboard, 10 August: 6.

Masur, Richard and Jack Shea. (1999) 'Letter to
    the Editor'. *Los Angeles Business Journal.*

Mathews, Anna Wilde. (2001) 'Studios Have
    Their Own Movies-on-Demand Plans'.
    Wall Street Journal, 29 January: B1.

Mato, Daniel. (1999) 'Telenovelas:
    Transnacionalización de la Industria y
    Transformación del Género'. *Las Industrias
    Culturales en la Integracion
    Latinoamericana.* Ed. Néstor García-
    Canclini and Carlos J. Moneta. Mexico:
    Grijalbo. 245–82.

Mato, Daniel. (2003) 'The Telenovela Industry:
    Markets and Representations of
    Transnational Identities'. *Media
    International Australia* 106: 46–56.

Mattelart, Armand. (1979) *Multinational
    Corporations and the Control of Culture:
    The Ideological Apparatuses of Imperialism.*
    Trans. Michael Chanan. Brighton:
    Harvester Press; Atlantic Highlands:
    Humanities Press.

Mattelart, Armand. (2002) 'An Archaeology of
    the Global Era: Constructing a Belief'.
    Trans. Susan Taponier with Philip
    Schlesinger. *Media Culture & Society* 24,
    no. 5: 591–612.

Mattelart, Armand and Michèle Mattelart.
    (1992) *Rethinking Media Theory: Signposts
    and New Directions.* Trans. James A. Cohen
    and Marina Urquidi. Minneapolis:
    University of Minnesota Press.

Mattelart, Armand and Michèle Mattelart.
    (1998) *Theories of Communication: A Short
    Introduction.* Trans. Susan Gruenheck
    Taponier and James A. Cohen. London:
    Sage.

Mattelart, Armand, Xavier Delcourt and
    Michèle Mattelart. (1988) 'International
    Image Markets'. *Global Television.* Ed.
    Cynthia Schneider and Brian Wallis. New
    York: Wedge Press; Cambridge, MA: MIT
    Press. 13–33.

Mattelart, Michèle. (1986) 'Women and the
    Cultural Industries'. Trans. Keith Reader.
    *Media, Culture & Society: A Critical
    Reader.* Ed. Richard Collins. London: Sage.
    63–81.

Maxwell, Richard, ed. (2001) *Culture Works.*
    Minneapolis. University of Minnesota
    Press.

Maxwell, Richard. (1996a) 'Ethics and Identity in Global Market Research'. *Cultural Studies* 10, no. 2: 218–36.

Maxwell, Richard. (1996b) 'Out of Kindness and into Difference: The Value of Global Market Research'. *Media, Culture & Society* 18, no. 1: 105–26.

Maxwell, Richard. (1999) 'The Marketplace Citizen and the Political Economy of Data Trade in the European Union'. *Journal of International Communication* 6, no. 1.

May, Christopher. (2002) 'The Political Economy of Proximity: Intellectual Property and the Global Division of Information Labour'. *New Political Economy* 7, no. 3: 317–41.

Mayer, Gerald M. (1947) 'American Motion Pictures in World Trade'. *Annals of the American Academy of Political and Social Science* 254: 31–36.

Mayer, J. P. (1946) *Sociology of Film: Studies and Documents*. London: Faber and Faber.

Mayrhofer, Debra. (1994) 'Media Briefs'. *Media Information Australia* 74: 126–42.

Mazdon, Lucy. (1999) 'Cinema and Television: From Enmity to Interdependence'. *Television Broadcasting in Contemporary France and Britain*. Ed. Michael Scriven and Monia Lecompte. Oxford: Berghahn Books. 71–82.

Mazdon, Lucy. (2000) *Encore Hollywood: Remaking French Cinema*. London: British Film Institute.

Mazurkewich, Karen. (2002) 'Sony's "Big Shot's Funeral" Tops Record for Commercial Films in Mainland China'. *Wall Street Journal*, 30 January: B5.

Mazurkewich, Karen. (2003) 'Hollywood Sees Starry Remakes in Asian Movies'. *Wall Street Journal*, 11 July: B1.

Mazziotti, Nora. (1996) *La Industria de la Telenovela: La Producción de Ficción en América Latina*. Buenos Aires: Paidós.

McCalman, Phillip. (2004) 'Foreign Direct Investment and Intellectual Property Rights: Evidence from Hollywood's Global Distribution of Movies and Videos'. *Journal of International Economics* 62, no. 1: 107–23.

McCann, Paul. (1998) 'Hollywood Film-Makers Desert UK'. *Independent*, 14 August: 7.

McChesney, Robert W. (1999) *Rich Media, Poor Democracy: Communication Politics in Dubious Times*. New York: New Press.

McClintock, Pamela. (2000a) 'Valenti Touts Value of Copyright Biz'. *Variety Extra*, 13 December.

McClintock, Pamela. (2000b) 'Treaty Trips, Falls: US–Euro Rift Thwarts Thesp Film Royalty Accord'. *Daily Variety*, 21 December: 7.

McClintock, Pamela. (2002). 'H'Wood Steps up War Effort'. *Variety*, 3–9 June: 3.

McColley, Carolyn. (1997) 'Limitations on Moral Rights in French "Droit d'Auteur"'. *Copyright Law Symposium* 41.

McDonald, Kevin. (1999) 'How Would You Like your Television: With or Without Borders and With or Without Culture – A New Approach to Media Regulation in the European Union'. *Fordham International Law Journal* 22: 1991–2031.

McDowell, Stephen D. (2001) 'The Unsovereign Century: Canada's Media Industries and Cultural Policies'. *Media and Globalization: Why the State Matters*. Ed. Nancy Morris and Silvio Waisbord. Lanham, MD: Rowman & Littlefield. 117–32.

McHoul, Alec and Tom O'Regan. (1992) 'Towards a Paralogics of Textual Technologies: Batman, Glasnost and Relativism in Cultural Studies'. *Southern Review* 25, no. 1: 5–26.

McKercher, Catherine. (2001) 'Commerce Versus Culture: The Print Media in Canada and Mexico'. *Continental Order? Integrating North America for Cybercapitalism*. Eds Vincent Mosco and Dan Schiller. Lanham, MD: Rowman & Littlefield. 189–206.

McMichael, Philip. (1996) *Development and Social Change: A Global Perspective*. Thousand Oaks, CA: Pine Forge.

McMichael, Philip. (2000a) *Development and Social Change: A Global Perspective*, 2nd edn. Thousand Oaks, CA: Pine Forge.

McMichael, Philip. (2000b) 'Globalisation: Trend or Project?' *Global Political Economy: Contemporary Theories*. Ed. R. Palan. London: Routledge.

McNary, Dave. (2001) 'Guild by Association'. *EV*, February: 3.

McQuire, Scott. (1999) 'Digital Dialectics: The Paradox of Cinema in a Studio without Walls'. *Historical Journal of Film, Radio and Television* 19, no. 2: 379–97.

McRobbie, Angela. (2002) 'From Holloway to Hollywood: Happiness at Work in the New Cultural Economy?' *Cultural Economy: Cultural Analysis and Commercial Life.* Ed. Paul du Gay and Michael Pryke. London: Sage. 97–114.

Meils, Cathy. (1998) 'Prague Studio Steels for Future'. *Variety*, 22–28 June: 46.

Meils, Cathy. (2000a) 'More Pix Say "Czech, Please"'. *Variety*, 1–7 May: 88.

Meils, Cathy. (2000b) 'Milk and Honey Cuts in with *Blade 2* Prod'n'. *Daily Variety*, 28 November: 38.

Meils, Cathy. (2000c) 'Czech it out: Studio Biz Good, Sale is on'. *Daily Variety*, 22 December: 8.

Meils, Cathy. (2002–03) 'Brit Prod'n Firm Tosses Hat in Ring with Prague Studios'. *Variety*, 23 December–5 January: 16.

Mekemson, C. and S. Glantz. (2002) 'How the Tobacco Industry Built its Relationship with Hollywood'. *Tobacco Control* 11: i81–i91.

Meller, Paul. (2003) 'Murdoch Cleared to Buy Italian TV Venture'. *New York Times*, 3 April: W1, W7.

Menon, Vinay. (2001) 'Foreign Filming Makes Gains in T.O.'. *Toronto Star*, 7 February.

Merchant, K. (2001). 'Defining the Indian Software Brand in a Competitive World'. *Financial Times*, 21 February: 14.

Mesbur, David. (2003) 'Worldwide Designs'. *Film Journal International*, November: 42.

Messerlin, Patrick. (2000) 'Regulating Culture: Has it "Gone with the Wind"?' *Achieving Better Regulation of Services.* Canberra: Productivity Commission. 287–318.

Meurs, Mieke and Rasika Ranasinghe. (2003) 'De-development in Post-Socialism: Conceptual and Measurement Issues'. *Politics & Society* 31, no. 1: 31–53.

Mezias, John M. and Stephen J. Mezias. (2000) 'Resource Partitioning, the Founding of Specialist Firms, and Innovation: The American Feature Film Industry, 1912 1929'. *Organization Science* 11, no. 3: 306–22.

Michael, Ian. (1999) 'Pirates in Space'. *Times*, 19 June.

Michaels, Eric. (1990) 'A Model of Teleported Texts (with Reference to Aboriginal Television)'. *Continuum* 3, no. 2: 8–31.

Michie, Jonathan and Maura Sheehan. (2003) 'Labour Market Deregulation, "Flexibility" and Innovation'. *Cambridge Journal of Economics* 27: 123–43.

Miège, Bernard. (1989) *The Capitalization of Cultural Production.* Trans. J. Hay, N. Garnham and UNESCO. New York: International General.

Mies, Maria. (1998) *Patriarchy and Accumulation on a World Scale: Women in the International Division of Labour,* 2nd edn. London: Zed.

Mi-hui, Kim. (2003) 'World's Interest in Korean Film Growing'. *Korean Herald*, 20 March.

Milkman, Ruth. (2000) 'Immigrant Organizing and the New Labor Movement in Los Angeles'. *Critical Sociology* 26, nos. 1–2: 59–81.

Millar, Kathleen. (2002) 'Financing Terror: Profits from Counterfeit Goods Pay for Attacks'. *U.S. Customs Today*, 38, no. 11.

Millea, Michael. (1997) 'Czech Privatisation: The Case of Fimove Studio Barrandov'. *Journal of International Affairs* 50, no. 2: 489–505.

Miller, Daniel. (1987) *Material Culture and Mass Consumption.* Oxford: Blackwell.

Miller, Danny and Jamal Shamsie. (1996) 'The Resource-Based View of the Firm in Two Environments: The Hollywood Film Studios from 1936 to 1965'. *Academy of Management Journal* 39, no. 3: 519–43.

Miller, J. D. B. (1981) *The World of States: Connected Essays.* London: Croom Helm.

Miller, J. D. B. (1984) 'The Sovereign State and its Future'. *International Journal* 39, no. 2: 284–301.

Miller, Toby. (1990) 'Mission Impossible and the New International Division of Labour'. *Metro* 82: 21–28.

Miller, Toby. (1996) 'The Crime of Monsieur Lange: GATT, the Screen and the New International Division of Cultural Labour'. *Film Policy: International, National and Regional Perspectives.* Ed. Albert Moran. London: Routledge. 72–84.

Miller, Toby. (1998a) *Technologies of Truth: Cultural Citizenship and the Popular Media*. Minneapolis: University of Minnesota Press.

Miller, Toby. (1998b) 'Hollywood and the World'. *The Oxford Guide to Film Studies*. Ed. John Hill and Pamela Church Gibson. Oxford: Oxford University Press. 371–81.

Miller, Toby and George Yúdice. (2002) *Cultural Policy*. London: Sage.

Miller, Toby, Geoffrey Lawrence, Jim McKay and David Rowe. (2001) *Globalisation and Sport: Playing the World*. London: Sage.

Miller, Toby, David Rowe, Jim McKay and Geoffrey Lawrence. (2003) 'The Over-Production of US Sports and the New International Division of Cultural Labor'. *International Review for the Sociology of Sport* 38, no. 4: 427–40.

Milmo, Dan. (2003) 'Biblical Battle in Tinseltown'. *Guardian*, 15 October: 20.

Mingo, J. (1997) 'Postal Imperialism'. *New York Times Magazine*, 16 February: 36–37.

Minnesota Film Board. (2000) www.mnfilm.org.

Minns, Adam. (2002) 'UK Shooting Costs Come under Fire'. *ScreenDaily.com*, 2 December.

Mishra, Vijay. (2002) *Bollywood Cinema: Temples of Desire*. New York: Routledge.

Mitchell, Peter. (2003) 'Dollar Puts Pressure on Films'. *Herald Sun*, 26 December: 74.

Mittell, Jason. (2000) 'The Cultural Power of an Anti-Television Metaphor: Questioning the "Plug-in Drug" and a TV-Free America'. *Television & New Media* 1, no. 2: 215–38.

Mittelman, James H. (1995) 'Rethinking the International Division of Labour in the Context of Globalisation'. *Third World Quarterly* 16, no. 2: 273–95.

Miyoshi, Masao. (1993) 'A Borderless World? From Colonialism to Transnationalism and the Decline of the Nation-State'. *Critical Inquiry* 19: 726–51.

Moerk, Christian. (2000) 'Studios See Leaner, Greener Times'. *Variety*, 10–16 January: 9, 30.

Mohaiemen, Naeem. (2004) 'The League of Extraordinary Subtitles'. *AlterNet*, 19 February.

Mohammadi, Ali, ed. (1997) *International Communication and Globalization*. London: Sage.

Mokhiber, Russell and Robert Weissman. (1999) 'The Globalization Horror Picture Show'. *Focus on the Corporation*. lists.essential.org/corp-focus/ msg00036.html.

Monaco, Paul. (2001) *History of the American Cinema, Volume 8: The Sixties: 1960–1969*. New York: Charles Scribner's Sons.

Monbiot, George. (2003) 'The Flight to India'. *Guardian*, 21 October.

Monitor. (1999) *U.S. Runaway Film and Television Production Study Report*, Cambridge, MA.

Moore, Schuyler M. (2000) *The Biz: The Basic Business, Legal and Financial Aspects of the Film Industry*. Los Angeles: Silman-James Press.

Moore, Solomon. (2002) 'Cape Town Relishes its Role as a Stand-in'. *Los Angeles Times*, 13 December.

Moran, Albert. (1996) 'Terms for a Reader'. *Film Policy*. Ed. Albert Moran. London: Routledge. 1–20.

Moran, Albert. (1998) *Copycat TV: Globalisation, Program Formats and Cultural Identity*. Luton: University of Luton Press.

Morley, David and Kevin Robins. (1995) *Spaces of Identity: Global Media, Electronic Landscapes and Cultural Boundaries*. London: Routledge.

Morris, Meaghan. (1990) 'Banality in Cultural Studies'. *Logics of Television: Essays in Cultural Criticism*. Ed. Patricia Mellencamp. Bloomington: Indiana University Press; London: British Film Institute. 14–43.

Motion Picture Association of America. (2001) *2000 US Economic Review*. Los Angeles.

Motion Picture Association of America. (2003) 'What's the Diff: A Guide to Digital Citizenship'. http://www.ja.org/programs/programs_su pple ments_citizenship.shtml.

Motion Picture Association of America Worldwide Market Research. (2003) *U.S. Entertainment Industry: 2002 MPA Market Statistics*. Los Angeles.

Mowlana, Hamid. (1993) 'Toward a NWICO for the Twenty-First Century?'. *Journal of International Affairs* 47, no. 1: 59–72.

Mowlana, Hamid. (1996) *Global Communication in Transition: End of Diversity?* Newbury Park: Sage.

Mowlana, Hamid. (2000) 'The Renewal of the Global Media Debate: Implications for the Relationship between the West and the Islamic World'. *Islam and the West in the Mass Media: Fragmented Images in a Globalizing World*. Ed. Kai Hafez. Cresskill, NJ: Hampton Press. 105–18.

Munck, Ronaldo. (2000) 'Labour and Globalisation: Results and Prospects'. *Work, Employment and Society* 14, no. 2: 385–93.

Muñoz, Lorenza. (2003). 'Anti-Piracy Swords Drawn in Theaters'. *Los Angeles Times*, 3 March.

Muñoz, Lorenza. (2004) 'Movie Ticket Sales Finish 2003 Down 5%'. *Los Angeles Times*, 5 January: E10.

Murdoch, Rupert. (1998) Presentation Prepared for the European Audiovisual Conference, Birmingham, 6–8 April.

Murdock, Graham. (1995) 'Across the Great Divide: Cultural Analysis and the Condition of Democracy'. *Critical Studies in Mass Communication* 12, no. 1: 89–95.

Murdock, Graham. (1996) 'Trading Places: The Cultural Economy of Co-productions'. *European Co-productions in Television and Film*. Ed. Sofia Blind and Gerd Hallenberger. Heidelberg: Universitätsverlag C. Winter. 103–14.

Murphy, David G. (1997) 'The Entrepreneurial Role of Organised Labour in the British Columbia Motion Picture Industry'. *Industrial Relations* 52, no. 3: 531–54.

Murray, Alan. (1999) 'The American Century: Is it Going or Coming?' *Wall Street Journal*, 27 December: 1.

Muscio, Giuliana. (2000) 'Invasion and Counterattack: Italian and American Film Relations in the Postwar Period'. *'Here, There and Everywhere': The Foreign Politics of American Popular Culture*. Ed. Reinhold Wagnleitner and Elaine Tyler May. Hanover: University Press of New England. 116–31.

Nader, Ralph. (1999) 'Introduction'. *The WTO: Five Years of Reasons to Resist Corporate Globalization*. Lori Wallach and Michelle Sforza. New York: Seven Stories Press. 6–12.

Naficy, Hamid. (2002) 'Islamizing Film Culture in Iran: A Post-Khatami Update'. *The New Iranian Cinema: Politics, Representation and Identity*. Ed. Richard Tapper. London: I. B. Tauris. 26–65.

Nagaraj, S. (1999) 'Hot Effects from Cool Labs'. *Computers Today*, 15 June: 41.

Nain, Zaharom. (1996) 'The Impact of the International Marketplace on the Organization of Malaysian Television'. *Contemporary Television: Eastern Perspectives*. Ed. David French and Michael Richards. New Delhi: Sage. 157–80.

Nairn, Tom. (1993) 'Internationalism and the Second Coming'. *Daedalus* 122, no. 3: 155–70.

Nairn, Tom. (2003) 'Democracy & Power: American Power & the World'. *open Democracy.net*, 9, 16 and 23 January; 4 and 20 February.

Nakayama, Thomas K. (1994) 'Show/Down Time: "Race", Gender, Sexuality, and Popular Culture'. *Critical Studies in Mass Communication* 11: 162–79.

Nakayama, Thomas K. (1997) 'Dis/orienting Identities'. *Our Voices*, 2nd edn. Ed. A. González, M. Houston and V. Chen. Los Angeles: Roxbury. 14–20.

Nakayama, Thomas K. and R. L. Krizek. (1995) 'Whiteness: A Strategic Rhetoric'. *Quarterly Journal of Speech* 81: 291–309.

Nakayama, Thomas K. and Judith N. Martin, eds. (1999) *Whiteness: The Communication of Social Identity*. Thousand Oaks, CA: Sage.

Natale, Richard. (2000) 'Year in Review: Hollywood – What Really Lies Beneath?' *Los Angeles Times*, 24 December.

Nathan, Ian. (2003) 'Union of Greek Film-Makers Boycott'. *Times*, 31 March: 2, 16.

Navarro, Vicente, John Schmitt and Javier Astudillo. (2004) 'Is Globalisation Undermining the Welfare State?' *Cambridge Journal of Economics* 28, no. 1: 133–52.

Nayyar, Deepak. (1988) 'The Political Economy of International Trade in Services'. *Cambridge Journal of Economics* 12: 279–98.

Neale, Steve. (1995) 'Questions of Genre'. *Film Genre: A Reader II*. Ed. Barry Keith Grant. Austin: University of Texas Press. 159–83.

Negrine, R. and S. Papathanassopoulos. (1990) *Internationalisation of Television*. London: Pinter Publishers.

Nelson, Craig. (2003) 'Upstart Labels See File Sharing as Ally, Not Foe'. *New York Times*, 22 September: C1, C7.

Nelson, Randy A., Michael R. Donihue, Donald M. Waldman and Calbraith Wheaton. (2001) 'What's an Oscar Worth?' *Economic Inquiry* 39, no. 1: 1–16.

Netherby, Jennifer. (2001) 'Latin at Ground Zero'. *Video Business*, 5 November: 23.

Nevin, Tom. (2002) 'Lights, Camera . . . Action'. *African Business*, November: 12–16.

New York City Office of Film, Theatre and Broadcasting. (2000) www.ci.nyc.ny.cs/html/filmcom.

Newcomb, Horace. (1996) 'Other People's Fictions: Cultural Appropriation, Cultural Integrity, and International Media Strategies'. *Mass Media and Free Trade: NAFTA and the Cultural Industries*. Ed. Emile G. McAnany and Kenton T. Wilkinson. Austin: University of Texas Press. 92–109.

Newman, Matthew and Michael M. Phillips. (2000) 'WTO Says U.S. Copyright Law Violates Global Trade Rules on Musical Rights'. *Wall Street Journal*, 8 June: A6.

Ng, Crystal and Bradley Dakake. (2002) *Tobacco at the Movies*. Boston: Massachusetts Public Interest Research Group.

Nickerson, Deidre L. and Todd Lappin. (1993) 'Frustration in Peking: Chinese Directors Win Acclaim Abroad but Not at Home'. *Far Eastern Economic Review*, 12 August: 57.

Nightingale, Virginia. (2001) 'Australia: Disney and the Australian Cultural Imaginary'. *Dazzled by Disney? The Global Disney Audiences Project*. Ed. Janet Wasko, Mark Phillips and Eileen R. Meehan. London: Leicester University Press. 65–87.

Nimmer, Melvin. (1970) 'Does Copyright Abridge the First Amendment Guarantees of Free Speech and the Press?' *UCLA Law Review* 17: 1180–1204.

Noam, Eli M. (1993) 'Media Americanization, National Culture, and Forces of Integration'. *The International Market in Film and Television Programmes*. Ed. Eli M. Noam and Joel C. Millonzi. Norwood, NJ: Ablex. 41–58.

Norcliffe, Glen and Olivero Rendace. (2003) 'New Geographies of Comic Book Production in North America: The New Artisan, Distancing, and the Periodic Social Economy'. *Economic Geography* 79, no. 3: 241–63.

Norm Marshall & Associates, Inc. (n. d.) *Product Placement: A Global Medium*.

Norman, Neil. (2000) 'Controversy as Gilliam's Film Gets 2m Lottery Boost'. *Variety*, 25 April: 7.

Norris, Floyd. (2004) 'A Deal's Outlines Suggest Content is No Longer King'. *New York Times*, 12 February: C7.

Nowell-Smith, Geoffrey. (1998) 'Introduction'. *Hollywood and Europe: Economics, Culture, National Identity: 1945–95*. Ed. Geoffrey Nowell-Smith and Steven Ricci. London: British Film Institute. 1–18.

Nowell-Smith, Geoffrey, James Hay and Gianni Volpi. (1996) *The Companion to Italian Cinema*. London: Cassell/BFI.

Nurton, James. (2002) 'Plusses Outweigh Minuses in Westward Expansion'. *Managing Intellectual Property*, 1 June: S17.

Nussbaum, Bruce. (1991) 'The Worldwide Web Steve Ross is Weaving'. *Business Week*, 13 May: 82.

Nye, Joseph S., Jr. (2002–03). 'Limits of American Power'. *Political Science Quarterly* 117, no. 4: 545–59.

NZ Institute of Economic Research. (2002) *Scoping the Lasting Effects of The Lord of the Rings*.

O'Brien, Robert. (2000a) 'The Difficult Birth of a Global Labour Movement'. *Review of International Political Economy* 7, no. 3: 514–23.

O'Brien, Robert. (2000b) 'Workers and World Order: The Tentative Transformation of the International Union Movement'. *Review of International Studies* 26, no. 4: 533–55.

O'Brien, Tim. (2001) 'Thousands Flock to Universal Studios Japan'. *Amusement Business*, 9 April: 12.

O'Connor, Pamela L. (2001) 'Tracking a Suspect on an Online Trail'. *New York Times*, 8 January: C4.

O'Donnell, Hugh. (1999) *Good Times, Bad Times: Soap Operas and Society in Western Europe*. London: Leicester University Press.

O'Regan, Tom. (1992) 'Too Popular by Far: On Hollywood's International Reputation'. *Continuum* 5, no. 2: 302–51.

O'Regan, Tom. (1993) '(Mis)taking Policy: Notes on the Cultural Policy Debate'. *Australian Cultural Studies: A Reader*. Ed. John Frow and Meaghan Morris. Urbana: University of Illinois Press.

O'Shea, Alan. (1989) 'Television as Culture: Not Just Texts and Readers'. *Media, Culture & Society* 11, no. 3: 373–79.

Ó Siochrú, Seán and Bruce Girard with Amy Mahan. (2002) *Global Media Governance: A Beginner's Guide*. Lanham, MD: Rowman & Littlefield.

Ochoa, Ana María. (2003) *Músicas Locales en Tiempos de Globalización*. Buenos Aires: Grupo Editorial Norma.

Office of the US Trade Representative. (2001a) *The President's 2000 Annual Report on the Trade Agreements Program*. Washington.

Office of the US Trade Representative. (2001b) *The FTAA and Labor Issues*. Washington.

Office of the US Trade Representative. (2001c) *WTO Services – U.S. Negotiating Proposals*. Washington.

Oh, Errol. (2000) 'Change in Tack'. *Malaysian Business*, 16 March.

Oliver, Joe. (2003) 'Ulster Warned Poor-Quality Fake DVDs Could be Xmas Turkeys'. *Belfast Telegraph*, 7 December.

Ollman, Bertell. (2000) 'What is Political Science? What Should it be?' *New Political Science* 22, no. 4: 553–62.

Olson, Scott R. (2000) 'The Globalization of Hollywood'. *International Journal on World Peace* 17, no. 4: 3–17.

Olson, Scott Robert. (1999) *Hollywood Planet: Global Media and the Competitive Advantage of Narrative Transparency*. Mahwah, NJ: Lawrence Erlbaum.

Orwall, Bruce. (1999) 'Studios Try to Hush Box-Offices Guesses'. *Wall Street Journal*, 25 October: 16.

Orwall, Bruce. (2000) 'Can Grinch Steal Christmas Abroad?' *Wall Street Journal*, 16 November: B1, B4.

Orwall, Bruce. (2001) 'Ticket to Nowhere'. *Wall Street Journal*, 26 March: R15.

Owens-Ibie, Nosa. (2000) 'Programmed for Domination: U.S. Television Broadcasting and its Effects on Nigerian Culture'. *'Here, There and Everywhere': The Foreign Politics of American Popular Culture*. Ed. Reinhold Wagnleitner and Elaine Tyler May. Hanover: University Press of New England. 132–46.

Pais, Arthur. (1990) '4 "Ghosts" Meet 3 "Pretty Women" in India's Ripoffs'. *Variety*, 11 December.

Palley, Thomas I. (1999) 'Toward a New International Economic Order'. *Dissent* 46, no. 2: 48–52.

Palley, Thomas I. (2004) 'The Economic Case for International Labour Standards'. *Cambridge Journal of Economics* 28, no. 1: 21–36.

Palmer, Michael. (1999) 'Multimedia Multinationals: Canal Plus and Reuters'. *Television Broadcasting in Contemporary France and Britain*. Ed. Michael Scriven and Monia Lecomte. Oxford: Berghahn Books. 140–67.

Paquet, Darcy. (2002) 'Korean Cinemas Exceeding Local Quota Requirements'. *Screen Daily*, 2 August.

Paquet, Darcy. (2004) 'Asian Film Commissions Join Forces to Attract Shoots'. *Screen Daily*, 23 February.

Park, Robert S. (1943) 'Education and the Cultural Crisis'. *American Journal of Sociology* 48, no. 6: 728–36.

Park, Seah. (2003) 'Coming to a Theater Near You? South Korean Movie Exports Mark Shift Away from Manufacturing'. *Wall Street Journal*, 31 October: A10.

Parker, Alan. (2002) 'Building a Sustainable UK Film Industry'. *ScreenDaily.com*, 5 November.

Parker, Richard A. (1991) 'The Guise of the Propagandist: Governmental Classification of Foreign Political Films'. *Current Research in Film: Audiences, Economics and Law Vol. 5*. Ed. Bruce A. Austin. Norwood, NJ: Ablex. 135–46.

Parkes, Christopher. (1995) 'Carolco Bought by Murdoch for US$50m'. *Financial Times*, 13 November: 23.

Parkes, Christopher. (2002) 'Farewell, My Lovely'. *Financial Times*, 4 April: 25.

Parkin, Frank. (1971) *Class Inequality and Political Order*. London: Magibbon and Kee.

Parmentier, Guillaume. (2002) 'Canal Plus: Slaughtering a Sacred Cow'. *Financial Times*, 2 May: 13.

Parthasarathy, Anand. (2003) 'Indian Film in Internet Distribution Wave'. *The Hindu*, 11 December.

Patel, Baburo. (1951) 'Rape of Our Heritage', reprinted in W. R. Wilkerson (1952) 'Trade Views'. *Hollywood Reporter*, 9 October.

Paul, Alan and Archie Kleingartner. (1994) 'Flexible Production and the Transformation of Industrial Relations in the Motion Picture and Television Industry'. *Industrial & Labor Relations Review* 47, no. 4: 663–77.

Pauwels, Caroline and Jan Loisen. (2003) 'The WTO and the Audiovisual Sector: Economic Free Trade vs Cultural Horse Trading?'. *European Journal of Communication* 18, no. 3: 291–313.

Peers, Martin. (2001) 'Video on Demand Arrives – Sort of'. *Wall Street Journal*, 29 January: B1, B10.

Pelegrine, Louis. (1976) 'India Film Industry Seeking U.S. Deals'. *Hollywood Reporter*, 10 June.

Pendakur, Manjunath. (1985) 'Dynamics of Cultural Policy Making: The U.S. Film Industry in India'. *Journal of Communication* 35, no. 4: 52–72.

Pendakur, Manjunath. (1990) *Canadian Dreams and American Control*. Toronto: Garamond.

Pendakur, Manjunath. (1996) 'India's National Film Policy: Shifting Currents in the 1990s'. *Film Policy*. Ed. Albert Moran. New York: Routledge. 148–71.

Pendakur, Manjunath. (1998) 'Hollywood North: Film and TV Production in Canada'. *Global Productions: Labor in the Making of the 'Information Society'*. Ed. Gerald Sussman and John A. Lent. Cresskill, NJ: Hampton Press. 213–38.

Pendakur, Manjunath. (2003) *Indian Popular Cinema: Industry, Ideology and Consciousness*. Cresskill, NJ: Hampton Press.

Peres, Shimon and Sydney Pollack. (1998) 'Out of Hollywood'. *New Perspectives Quarterly* 15, no. 5: 9–12.

Perez, Bien. (2002) 'EMC to Aid ACNielsen's China Hopes'. *South China Morning Post*, 11 September: 10.

Pérez de Cuéllar, J. (1996) *Our Creative Diversity: Report of the World Commission on Culture and Development*. Paris: UNESCO.

Perlmutter, Shira. (1998) 'Future Directions in International Copyright'. *Cardozo Arts and Entertainment Law Journal* 16, nos. 2–3: 369–82.

Peters, Anne K. (1974) 'Aspiring Hollywood Actresses: A Sociological Perspective'. *Varieties of Work Experience*. Ed. P. L. Stewart and M. G. Cantor. Cambridge, MA: Schenkman.

Peters, Anne K. and Muriel G. Cantor. (1982) 'Screen Acting as Work'. *Individuals in Mass Media Organisations: Creativity and Constraint*. Ed. James S. Ettema and D. Charles Whitney. Beverly Hills: Sage. 53–68.

Peterson, Richard A. (1978) 'The Production of Cultural Change: The Case of Contemporary Country Music'. *Social Research* 45.

Peterson, V. S. (1996) 'The Politics of Identification in the Context of Globalization'. *Women's Studies International Forum* 19, nos. 1–2: 5–15.

Petras, James. (2000) 'Estados Unidos: Una Democracia en Venta'. *El Mundo*, 31 August: 4.

Petroski, Henry (1999). *The Book on the Bookshelf*. New York: Alfred A. Knopf.

Pew Internet & American Life Project. (2003) *Consumption of Information Goods and Services in the United States*.

Pew Research Center for the People & the Press. (2002) *What the World Thinks in 2002: How Global Publics View: Their Lives, Their Countries, The World, America*.

Pew Research Center for the People & the Press. (2003) *Views of a Changing World*.

Pfister, Bonnie. (2000) 'Movie May Help Hurt Mexican Village'. *San Diego Union-Tribune*, 31 May.

Pham, Alex. (2000) 'Technology and Innovation'. *Boston Globe*, 30 November: C1.

Phillips, Richard. (2003) 'Australian Film Industry: The Futility of Calls for "Cultural Protection"'. *World Socialist Web Site*, 9 December.

Pierson, Michele. (2002) *Special Effects: Still in Search of Wonder*. New York: Columbia University Press.

Pietrolungo, Kathryn E. and Brian Tinkham. (2002–03) 'Global Rule One: SAG's Answer to Runaway Production'. *Southwestern Journal of Law and Trade in the Americas* 9: 357–90.

Piore, Michael J. and Charles F. Sabel. (1984) *The Second Industrial Divide: Possibilities for Prosperity*. New York: BasicBooks.

Pius XI. (1936) *Encyclical Letter of Pope Pius XI on the Motion Picture Vigilanti Cura*. www.vatican.va/holy_father/pius_xi/ encyclicals/ documents/hf_p-xi_enc_ 29061936_vigilanti-cura-en.html.

Pius XII. (1957) *Miranda Prorsus: Encyclical Letter on Motion Pictures, Radio and Television*. www.vatican.va/holy_father/ pius_xii/ encyclicals/documents/hf_pxii_ enc_ 08091957_miranda-prorsus_en.html.

Plate, Tom. (2002) 'Hollywood Faces New Competition: World Film Industry is Globalization at its Best'. *Honolulu Advertiser*, 25 August.

Pokorny, Michael and John Sedgwick. (2001) 'Stardom and the Profitability of Filmmaking: Warner Bros. in the 1930s'. *Journal of Cultural Economics* 25, no. 3: 157–84.

Polan, Dana. (1996) 'Globalism's Localisms'. *Global/Local: Cultural Production and the Transnational Imaginary*. Ed. Rob Wilson and Wimal Dissanayake. Durham: Duke University Press. 255–83.

Pool, Ithiel de Sola. (1983) *Technologies of Freedom*. Cambridge, MA: Harvard University Press.

Poovey, Mary. (1998) *A History of the Modern Fact: Problems of Knowledge in the Sciences of Wealth and Society*. Chicago: University of Chicago Press.

Porter, Eduardo. (2000) 'Hispanic Actors Await End of Strike'. *Wall Street Journal*, 22 September: B3.

Porter, Michael E. (1990) *The Competitive Advantage of Nations*. New York: Free Press.

Porter, Michael E. (1998) 'Clusters and the New Economics of Competition'. *Harvard Business Review*, November–December: 77–90.

Porter, Michael E. (2000) 'Locations, Clusters and Company Strategy'. *The Oxford Handbook of Economic Geography*. Ed. Gordon L. Clark, Maryann P. Feldman and Meric S. Gertler with Kate Williams. Oxford: Oxford University Press. 253–74.

Porter, Vincent. (1978) 'Film Copyright: Film Culture'. *Screen* 19, no. 1.

Postrel, Virginia. (1999) 'The Pleasures of Persuasion'. *Wall Street Journal*, 2 August.

Powdermaker, Hortense. (1950) *Hollywood: The Dream Factory: An Anthropologist Looks at the Movie-Makers*. Boston: Little, Brown and Company.

Powdermaker, Hortense. (1967) *Stranger and Friend: The Way of an Anthropologist*. London: Secker & Warburg.

Prasad, Monica. (1998) 'International Capital on "Silicon Plateau": Work and Control in India's Computer Industry'. *Social Forces* 77, no. 2: 429–53.

Prelypchan, Erin. (2003) 'Adultery Still Sells'. *Far Eastern Economic Review*, 6 November: 70–71.

Preston, Morag. (2001) 'My Life as a Dot.com Dog at Amazon'. *Independent*, 5 March.

Primo, Alex Fernando Teixeira. (1999) 'The Paradoxical Brazilian Views Concerning American Media Products'. *Images of the U.S. around the World: A Multilateral Perspective*. Ed. Yahya R. Kamalipour. Albany: State University of New York Press. 179–95.

Prince, Stephen. (2000) *History of the American Cinema, Volume 10: A New Pot of Gold under the Electronic Rainbow, 1980–1989*. New York: Charles Scribner's Sons.

Pristin, Terry. (2003) 'No Waiting in Line, Just Online; Moviegoers Say Buying in Advance can be Confusing, Not Convenient'. *New York Times*, 15 February: B1.

Program on International Policy Attitudes. (2002) *Americans & the World*.

Pryor, Thomas M. (1956) 'Sukarno Praises Role of U.S. Films'. *New York Times*, 2 June: 13.

Publicized government document online. (n. d.). www.sarft.gov.cn/manage/publishfile/20/1251.html.

Puente, Enrique. (2001) 'Latin Universe'. Paper for Fifth Congress of the Americas, Puebla.

Purnell, Sonia. (1999) 'The Pathe to 33m. Pounds'. *Daily Mail*, 11 February: 17.

Puttnam, David, with Neil Watson. (1998) *Movies and Money*. New York: Alfred A. Knopf.

Pye, Lucian W. (1965) 'Introduction: Political Culture and Political Development'. *Political Culture and Political Development*. Ed. Lucian W. Pye and Sidney Verba. Princeton: Princeton University Press. 3–26.

Quester, George H. (1990) *The International Politics of Television*. Lexington, MA: Lexington.

Quinlivan, Beth. (2003) 'Lights, Cameras but No Action'. *Business Review Weekly*, June 26: 14.

Raboy, Marc. (2002) 'Media Policy in the New Communications Environment'. *Global Media Policy in the New Millennium*. Ed. Marc Raboy. Luton: University of Luton Press. 3–16.

Raco, Mike. (1999) 'Competition, Collaboration and the New Industrial Districts: Examining the Institutional Turn in Local Economic Development'. *Urban Studies*, May: 951–70.

Radcliffe, Mark and Jill Sazama. (2002) 'Hollywood Confronts the Napster Challenge'. *Managing Intellectual Property*, 1 October: 73–84.

Radner, Hilary. (2001) 'Hollywood Redux: *All about My Mother* and *Gladiator*'. *The End of Cinema as We Know it: American Film in the Nineties*. Ed. Jon Lewis. New York: New York University Press. 72–80.

Raghavan, Chakravarthi. (1990) *Recolonization, GATT, the Uruguay Round and the Third World*. London and Penang: Zed Books/Third World Network.

Rajagopal, Arvind. (2001) *Politics after Television: Religious Nationalism and the Reshaping of the Indian Public*. Cambridge: Cambridge University Press.

Ramsaye, Terry. (1947) 'The Rise and Place of the Motion Picture'. *Annals of the American Academy of Political and Social Science* 254: 1–11.

Rantanen, Terhi. (2002) *The Global and the National: Media and Communications in Post-Communist Russia*. Lanham, MD: Rowman & Littlefield.

Raphael, Chad. (2001) 'The Web'. *Culture Works: The Political Economy of Culture*. Ed. Richard Maxwell. Minneapolis: University of Minnesota Press.

Ravid, S. Abraham. (1999) 'Information, Blockbusters and Stars: A Study of the Film Industry'. *Journal of Business* 72, no. 4: 463–92.

Rawsthorn, Alice. (1997) 'Return of the Blockbuster Moviemakers'. *Financial Times*, 6 May: 18.

Rawsthorn, Alice. (1999) 'Canal Plus in Film Link with Universal'. *Financial Times*, 14 May: 33.

Raz, Aviad E. (2003) 'The Slanted Smile Factory: Emotion Management in Tokyo Disneyland'. *The Cultural Study of Work*. Ed. Douglas Harper and Helene M. Lawson. Lanham, MD: Rowman & Littlefield. 210–27.

Reed, Rochelle. (1970) 'Film Production in India More Leisurely Than Here'. *Hollywood Reporter*, 10 December.

Reeves, Geoffrey. (1993) *Communications and the 'Third World'*. London: Routledge.

Regardie, Jon. (2003). 'Putting the Fear of Valenti into Your Kids'. *Variety*, 8 December: 68.

Regourd, Serge. (1999) 'Two Conflicting Notions of Audiovisual Liberalisation'. *Television Broadcasting in Contemporary France and Britain*. Ed. Michael Scriven and Monia Lecomte. Oxford: Berghahn Books. 29–45.

Reich, Robert. (1999) 'Brain Trusts'. *New York Times Book Review*, 19 December: 10.

Reis, Raul. (2001) 'Brazil: Love it and Hate it: Brazilians' Ambiguous Relationships with Disney'. *Dazzled by Disney? The Global Disney Audiences Project*. Ed. Janet Wasko, Mark Phillips and Eileen R. Meehan. London: Leicester University Press. 88–101.

Rendon, Jim. (2004) 'Unions Aim to Share in the Success of Reality TV'. *New York Times*, 25 January.

Rettig, Ellen. (1998) 'Lights, Camera, Tax Incentives?'. *Indianapolis Business Journal*, 28 September: 3.

Rhines, Jesse Algeron. (1996) *Black Film/White Money*. New Brunswick, NJ: Rutgers University Press.

Rice-Oxley, Mark. (2004) 'In 2,000 Years, Will the World Remember Disney or Plato?'. *Christian Science Monitor*, 15 January.

Rich, B. Ruby. (2001) 'Mexico at the Multiplex'. *The Nation*, 14 May: 34–36.

Richard, Julie. (2000) 'U.S. Projects Bolster Blighty's Studio, Post Facilities'. *Variety*, 11–17 December: 55–56.

Richtel, Matt. (2002) 'New Billboards Sample Radios as Cars Go by, Then Adjust'. *New York Times*, 27 December: C1, C5.

Ricketson, Sam. (1987) *The Berne Convention for the Protection of Literary and Artistic Works: 1886–1986*. London: Centre for Commercial Law Studies.

Riding, Alan. (1999) 'French Comic Book Heroes Battle Hollywood's Hordes'. *New York Times*, 10 February: E2.

Ries, Al and Jack Trout. (1981) *Positioning: The Battle for Your Mind*. New York: McGraw-Hill.

Riley, Michael. (1999) 'Producers Find Magic in Mexico'. *Houston Chronicle*, 3 December.

Roach, Colleen. (1997) 'Cultural Imperialism and Resistance in Media Theory and Literary Theory'. *Media, Culture & Society* 19, no. 1: 47–66.

Robins, James A. (1993) 'Organization as Strategy: Restructuring Production in the Film Industry'. *Strategic Management Journal* 14: 103–18.

Robins, Kevin and John Cornford. (1992) 'What is "Flexible" about Independent Producers?' *Screen* 33, no. 2: 190–200.

Robinson, Jim. (2000) 'Reel Renaissance'. *Business Mexico* 10, no. 4: 51–55.

Robinson, W. I. (1996) 'Globalization: Nine Theses of our Epoch'. *Race and Class* 38, no. 2: 13–31.

Robles, Alfredo C. (1994) *French Theories of Regulation and Conceptions of the International Division of Labour*. New York: St Martin's Press.

Rockett, Kevin, Kevin Gibbons and John Hill. (1988) *Cinema and Ireland*. Syracuse, NY: Syracuse University Press.

Rockwell, John. (1994) 'The New Colossus: American Culture as Power Export'. *New York Times*, 30 January: H1, H30.

Roddick, Nick. (1994) 'A Hard Sell: The State of Documentary Film Marketing'. *Dox* 2: 30–32.

Rodier, Melanie. (2002) 'The Pan-European Fall Out'. *Screen International*, 26 April–2 May: 1, 2.

Rogement, Marcel. (2002) 'Quel avenir pour le cinéma, en France et en Europe'. *Les Documents d'Information de l'Assemblée Nationale*. Paris: Commission des Affaires Culturelles. 3642: 69.

Rojas, Peter. (2004) 'Waiting for DVDs, the Sequel'. *Wired News*, 1 March.

Rong, Li and Xu Zhengfeng. (2003) 'Time Warner Spearheads China's Potentially Huge Cinema Market'. *Xinhua*, 19 June.

Rooney, David. (2002) 'Italy'. *Variety*, 28 October–3 November: 5.

Rose, Marla Matzer. (2001a) 'Film Industry Profile'. *Business.Com*.

Rose, Marla Matzer. (2001b) 'Television Industry Profile'. *Business.Com*.

Rosen, S. (1981) 'The Economics of Superstars'. *American Economic Review* 71, no. 5: 845–57.

Rosen, Stanley. (2002) 'The Wolf at the Door: Hollywood and the Film Market in China'. *Southern California and the World*. Ed. Eric J. Heikkila and Rafael Pizarro. Westport, CT: Praeger. 49–77.

Rosen, Stanley. (2003) 'China Goes Hollywood'. *Foreign Policy* 134: 94–96.

Rosenberg, Scott. (2001) 'Thailand Puts Arm around H'w'd'. *Variety*, 12–18 February: 22.

Rosenberg, Scott. (2003) 'The Asian Outlook'. *Film Journal International*, November: 28–29, 44.

Rosenthal, A. M. (1955) 'Off the Indian Screen'. *New York Times*, 12 June.

Ross, Andrew. (2003) *No-Collar: The Humane Workplace and its Hidden Costs*. New York: Basic Books.

Ross, Bob and Kevin Walker. (2000) 'Hollywood on the Bay'. *Tampa Tribune*, 10 October: 1.

Ross, Murray. (1947) 'Labor Relations in Hollywood'. *Annals of the American Academy of Political and Social Science* 254: 58–64.

Ross, Robert and Kent Trachte. (1990) *Global Capitalism: The New Leviathan*. Albany: State University of New York Press.

Rosten, Leo C. (1947) 'Movies and Propaganda'. *Annals of the American Academy of Political and Social Science* 254: 116–24.

Roth, Scott. (2002) Letter to Melissa Gilbert, 17 May.

Rothkopf, David. (1997) 'In Praise of Cultural Imperialism'. *Foreign Policy* 107: 38–53.

Rotstein, Robert H. (1992) 'Beyond Metaphor: Copyright Infringement and the Fiction of the Work'. *Chicago-Kent Law Review* 68: 725–804.

Rotter, Andrew J. (2000) *Comrades at Odds: The United States and India, 1947–1964*. Ithaca: Cornell University Press.

RSVP Film Studios. (n. d.) 'Why Shoot in the Philippines'. www.rsvpfilm.com/shoot.htm.

Ryall, Tom. (1998) 'Genre and Hollywood'. *The Oxford Guide to Film Studies*. Ed. John Hill and Pamela Church Gibson. Oxford: Oxford University Press. 327–38.

Ryan, James. (1999) 'Action Heats up in Film Biz War'. *Toronto Sun*, 29 August: 50.

Sabbagh, Dan. (2002) 'Echoes of Napoleon in the Rise and Fall of an Almost Perfect Young Man'. *The Times*, 28 November.

Sabin, Rob. (2000) 'The Movies' Digital Future is in Sight and it Works'. *New York Times*, 26 November: B1.

Sage, Adam. (2001) 'Asterix Succumbs to McDonald's Dollar'. *The Times*, 20 December: Overseas News.

Sakr, Naomi. (2001) *Satellite Realms: Transnational Television, Globalization and the Middle East*. London: I. B. Tauris.

Salokannel, Marjut. (1997) *Ownership of Rights in Audiovisual Productions*. Boston: Kluwer Law International.

Sama, Emmanuel. (1996) 'African Films are Foreigners in Their Own Countries'. *African Experiences of Cinema*. Ed. Imruh Bakari and Mbye B. Cham. London: British Film Institute. 148–56.

Samuelson, Pamela. (1996) 'The Copyright Grab'. *Wired*, January.

Samuelson, Pamela. (1997) 'The Digital Agenda of the World Intellectual Property Organization (Principal Paper): The US Digital Agenda at the WIPO'. *Virginia Journal of International Law* 37: 369–439.

Samuelson, Pamela. (1999) 'Intellectual Property and the Digital Economy: Why the Anti-Circumvention Regulations Need to be Revised'. *Berkeley Technology Law Journal* 14: 519–66.

Sanai, Darius. (1999) 'Taking a Leaf out of Hollywood's Book – British Film-Makers Need to Learn That Great Quality Doesn't Guarantee Box-Office Success'. *Independent*, 30 March: 12.

Sánchez-Ruiz, Enrique. (2001) 'Globalization, Cultural Industries, and Free Trade: The Mexican Audiovisual Sector in the NAFTA Age'. *Continental Order? Integrating North America for Cybercapitalism*. Ed. Vincent Mosco and Dan Schiller. Lanham, MD: Rowman & Littlefield. 86–119.

Sankowski, Edward. (1992) 'Ethics, Art and Museums'. *Journal of Aesthetic Education* 26, no. 3: 1–15.

Sardar, Ziauddin. (1998) 'Hollywood Postmodernism: The New Imperialism'. *New Perspectives Quarterly* 15, no. 5: 23–32.

Sardar, Ziauddin and Merryl Wyn Davies. (2002) *Why do People Hate America?* Cambridge: Icon Books.

Sartre, Jean-Paul. (1990) *What is Literature?* London: Routledge.

Saunders, David. (1990) 'Copyright, Obscenity and Literary History'. *ELH* 57, no. 2: 431–44.

Saunders, David. (1992) *Authorship and Copyright*. London: Routledge.

Saunders, David and Ian Hunter. (1991) 'Lessons from the Literary: How to Historicize Authorship'. *Critical Inquiry* 17.

Saundry, Richard. (1998) 'The Limits of Flexibility: The Case of UK Television'. *British Journal of Management* 9: 151–62.

Saundry, Richard. (2001) 'Employee Relations in British Television – Regulation, Fragmentation and Flexibility'. *Industrial Relations Journal* 32, no. 1: 22–36.

Sauvé, Pierre and Karsten Steinfatt. (2000) 'Towards Multilateral Rules on Trade and Culture: Protective Regulation or Efficient Protection?' *Achieving Better Regulation of Services*. Canberra: Productivity Commission. 323–45.

Scevak, Niki. (2001) 'The Evolution of Product Placement'. *Australia.Inter net.com*, 15 June.

Schaeffer, R. K. (1997) *Understanding Globalization: The Social Consequences of Political, Economic, and Environmental Change*. Lanham, MD: Rowman & Littlefield.

Schatz, Thomas. (1988) *The Genius of the System: Hollywood Filmmaking in the Studio Era*. New York: Pantheon.

Schatz, Thomas. (1997) *History of the American Cinema, Volume 6: Boom and Bust: The American Cinema in the 1940s*. New York: Charles Scribner's Sons.

Scheuer, Philip K. (*c.* 1964) 'Story of Taj Mahal Set for $8 Million'. Unsourced article archived at Academy of Motion Picture Arts and Sciences, Margaret Herrick Library, Los Angeles.

Schiller, Dan. (1996) *Theorizing Communication: A History*. New York: Oxford University Press.

Schiller, Herbert I. (1974) *Mind Managers*. Boston: Beacon Press.

Schiller, Herbert I. (1976) *Communication and Cultural Domination*. New York: International Arts and Sciences Press.

Schiller, Herbert I. (1981) *Who Knows: Information in the Age of the Fortune 500*. Norwood, NJ: Ablex.

Schiller, Herbert I. (1984) *Information and the Crisis Economy*. Norwood, NJ: Ablex.

Schiller, Herbert I. (1989) *Culture Inc.: The Corporate Takeover of Public Expression*. Oxford: Oxford University Press.

Schlesinger, Philip. (1991) *Media, State and Nation: Political Violence and Collective Identities*. London: Sage.

Schou, Soren. (1992) 'Postwar Americanisation and the Revitalisation of European Culture'. *Media Cultures: Reappraising Transnational Media*. Ed. Michael Skovmand and Kim Christian Schroder. London: Routledge, 142–58.

Schulberg, Budd. (1950) 'Hollywood Primitive'. *New York Times*, 15 October: BR4.

Schultz, Clifford J. and Bill Saporito. (1996) 'Protecting Intellectual Property: Strategies and Recommendations to Deter Counterfeiting and Brand Piracy in Global Markets'. *Columbia Journal of World Business* 31, no. 1: 18–28.

Schulze, Jane and Geoff Elliott. (2004) 'Big Three Will Run World's Media, Says Murdoch'. *Australian*, 12 February.

Schwab, S. (1994) 'Television in the 90's: Revolution or Confusion?'. Tenth Joseph I. Lubin Memorial Lecture, New York University, 1 March.

Schwartz, Herman M. and Aida Hozic. (2001) 'Who Needs the New Economy?'. *Salon.com*, 16 March.

Sciolino, Elaine. (2004) 'French Sikhs Defend Their Turbans and Find Their Voice'. *New York Times*, 12 January: A4.

Scott, A. O. (2003) 'These are Your Movies on Piracy'. *New York Times*, 16 November: 15.

Scott, Allen J. (1996) 'The Craft, Fashion, and Cultural-Products Industries of Los Angeles: Competitive Dynamics and Policy Dilemmas in a Multisectoral Image-Producing Complex'. *Annals of the Association of American Geographers* 86, no. 2: 306–23.

Scott, Allen J. (1998a) 'From Silicon Valley to Hollywood: Growth and Development of the Multimedia Industry in California'. *Regional Innovation Systems: The Role of Governances in a Globalized World*. Ed. Hans-Joachim Braczyk, Philip Cooke and Martin Heidenreich. London: UCL Press. 136–62.

Scott, Allen J. (1998b) 'Multimedia and Digital Visual Effects: An Emerging Local Labor Market'. *Monthly Labor Review* 121, no. 3: 30–38.

Scott, Allen J. (1998c) *Regions and the World Economy: The Coming Shape of Global Production, Competition, and Political Order*. Oxford: Oxford University Press.

Scott, Allen J. (2002) 'A New Map of Hollywood: The Production and Distribution of American Motion Pictures'. *Regional Studies* 36, no. 9: 957–75.

Scott, John L. (1965) 'India Film Industry Flourishes'. *Los Angeles Times*, 25 August.

Screen Actors Guild. (2000) 'The Guild's Efforts to Address Runaway Film and Television Production'. www.sag.org/runaway/sagaddresses.html.

Screen Actors Guild. (2001) *Screen Actors Guild Employment Statistics Reveal Increases in Total TV/Theatrical Roles and Increases for All Minorities in 2000*. www.sag.orf/diversity/castingdata.html.

Sedgwick, John. (2002) 'Product Differentiation at the Movies: Hollywood, 1946 to 1965'. *Journal of Economic History* 62, no. 3: 676–705.

Sedgwick, John and Michael Pokorny. (1998) 'The Risk Environment of Film-Making: Warners in the Inter-War Period'. *Explorations in Economic History* 35, no. 2: 196–220.

Segrave, Kerry. (1997) *American Films Abroad: Hollywood's Domination of the World's Movie Screens from the 1890s to the Present*. Jefferson, NC: McFarland.

Segrave, Kerry. (2002) *Piracy in the Motion Picture Industry*. Jefferson, NC: McFarland.

Seguin, Denis. (2003) 'The Battle for Hollywood North'. *Canadian Business*, 15 September: 55.

Seiter, Ellen. (1999) *Television and New Media Audiences*. Oxford: Clarendon Press.

Sen, Krishna. (1994) *Indonesian Cinema: Framing the New Order*. London: Zed.

Seneviratne, K. (2002) 'Film-Asia: Asian Animation Industry Draws on Ancient Heritage'. *Inter Press Service*, 11 December.

Seno, Alexandra A. and R. Mitton. (2001) 'Toy Story too?' *AsiaWeek*, 27 April: 39.

Seno, Alexandra A. and Siem Reap. (2001) 'Lights, Camera – Tourists!'. *Asia Week*, 2 March: 38.

Sergeant, Jean-Claude. (1999) 'Cable Television'. *Television Broadcasting in Contemporary France and Britain*. Ed. Michael Scriven and Monia Lecompte. Oxford: Berghahn Books. 107–19.

Sethi, Sunil. (1984) 'The Cinema in India'. *Screen International*, 7 January: 14–16.

Sewell, James P. (1974) 'UNESCO: Pluralism Rampant'. *The Anatomy of Influence: Decision Making in International Organization*. Ed. Robert W. Cox and Harold K. Jacobson. New Haven. CT: Yale University Press. 139–74.

Seyoum, Belay. (1996) 'The Impact of Intellectual Property Rights on Foreign Direct Investment'. *Columbia Journal of World Business* 31, no. 1.

Shackleton, Liz. (2003) 'Thai Triumph Shines Light on Hollywood's Asian agenda'. *South China Morning Post*, 7 December: 4.

Shaheen, Jack. (2003) 'Will Hollywood Stop Arab-Bashing?'. *Los Angeles Times*, 21 April: Calendar Desk 3.

Shamim, M. (2001) 'Malaysia's Help May be Sought to End Film Piracy'. *The Hindu*, 10 March.

Sharma, A. (2003). 'India Winning Higher-Status Jobs from the US'. *Christian Science Monitor*, 18 June: 1.

Shatilla, Christopher Andrew. (1996) *Reaching a Global Audience: The Economic Geography of Toronto's Film and TV Industry*. MA thesis, Queen's University at Kingston, Canada.

Shaw, Lisa. (2003) 'The Brazilian *Chanchada* and Hollywood Paradigms (1930–1959)'. *Framework* 44, no. 1: 70–83.

Shiva, Vandana. (2002) *Water Wars: Privatization, Pollution, and Profit*. Boston: South End Press.

Shively, JoEllen. (1992) 'Cowboys and Indians: Perceptions of Western Films Among American Indians and Anglos'. *American Sociological Review* 57, no. 6.

Shohat, Ella and Robert Stam. (1994) *Unthinking Eurocentrism: Multiculturalism and the Media*. New York: Routledge.

Shore, Cris. (2001) 'The Cultural Policies of the European Union and Cultural Diversity'. *Differing Diversities: Transversal Study on the Theme of Cultural Policy and Cultural Diversity*. Ed. Tony Bennett. Strasbourg Cedex: Council of Europe Publishing.

Short, David. (1996) 'Pearson Resists Pressure for a Focus on Television'. *European*, 21 March: 24.

Short, David. (1997) 'Batman and Robbing'. *European*, 31 July: 28–29.

Simonet, T. (1980) *Regression Analysis of Prior Experience of Key Production Personnel as Predictors of Revenue from High Grossing Motion Pictures in American Release*. New York: Arno Press.

Simpson, Glenn R. (2001a) 'The Battle over Web Privacy'. *Wall Street Journal*, 21 March: B1, B4.

Simpson, Glenn R. (2001b) 'U.S. Officials Criticise Rules on EU Privacy'. *Wall Street Journal*, 27 March: B7.

Sinclair, John. (1999) *Latin American Television: A Global View*. Oxford: Oxford University Press.

Sinclair, John, Elizabeth Jacka and Stuart Cunningham, eds. (1996) *New Patterns in Global Television: Peripheral Vision*. Oxford: Oxford University Press.

Sinclair, Scott. (2000) *GATS: How the World Trade Organization's New 'Services' Negotiations Threaten Democracy*. Canadian Centre for Policy Alternatives.

Singh, Eripa. (*c.* mid-1930s) *India: A Market for American Products: A Bird's Eye View*. Publisher unknown: 18. Pamphlet archived at Academy of Motion Picture Arts and Sciences, Margaret Herrick Library, Los Angeles.

Sjolander, Claire Turner. (1992–93) 'Unilateralism and Multilateralism: The United States and the Negotiation of the GATS'. *International Journal* 48, no. 1: 52–79.

Sklair, Leslie. (2002) *Globalization: Capitalism & its Alternatives*. Oxford: Oxford University Press.

Slotin, Ian. (2002) 'Free Speech and the *Visage Culturel*: Canadian and American Perspectives on Pop Culture Discrimination'. *Yale Law Journal* 111, no. 8: 2289–319.

Smiers, Joost. (2000) 'The Abolition of Copyright: Better for Artists, Third World Countries and the Public Domain'. *Gazette* 62, no. 5: 379–406.

Smith, Adam. (1970) *The Wealth of Nations Books I–III*. Ed. A. Skinner. Harmondsworth: Penguin.

Smith, Anthony D. (1990) 'The Supersession of Nationalism?' *International Journal of Comparative Sociology* 31, nos. 1–2: 1–31.

Smith, Anthony D. (1996) 'LSE Centennial Lecture: The Resurgence of Nationalism? Myth and Memory in the Renewal of Nations'. *British Journal of Sociology* 47, no. 4: 575–98.

Smith, Craig S. (2000a) 'Copyright Pirates Strike at Beijing'. *International Herald Tribune*, 6 October: 6.

Smith, Craig S. (2000b) 'Tale of Piracy: How the Chinese Stole the Grinch'. *New York Times*, 12 December.

Smith, Craig S. (2000c) 'Turnabout: China's Copyright Pirates Steal the Grinch'. *International Herald Tribune*, 13 December: 20.

Smith, Roger. (2002) 'Why Studio Movies Don't Make (Much) Money'. *Film Comment* 38, no. 2: 60–62.

Smith, Sean. (2003) 'How to Out-Fox the Big Boys'. *Newsweek* 142, no. 10: 57.

Smith, Sydney. (1844) *The Works of the Rev. Sydney Smith*. Philadelphia: Carey and Hart.

Smithsimon, Greg. (1999) 'Transnational Labor Organizing: Opportunities and Obstacles for Unions Challenging Multinational Corporations'. *Socialist Review* 27, nos. 3–4: 65–93.

Smoodin, Eric. (1993) *Animating Culture: Hollywood Cartoons from the Sound Era*. New Brunswick, NJ: Rutgers University Press.

Snider, Mike. (2001) 'No Copying, No Trading? No Kidding: Copyright Fight Might Narrow Our Options'. *USA Today*, 6 March.

Snoddy, Raymond. (2002) 'Bronfmans Plot New Move to Oust Messier'. *The Times*, 29 June: 50.

Sobel, Lionel S. (1995) 'Back from the Public Domain'. *Entertainment Law Reporter* 17, no. 3.

Sochay, S. G. (1994) 'Predicting the Performance of Motion Pictures'. *Journal of Media Economics* 7: 1–20.

Soriano, Cesar G. (2001) 'Top 3 Prove Hard to Cast Out'. *USA Today*, 23 January.

Sorlin, Pierre. (1991) *European Cinemas, European Societies 1939–1990*. London: Routledge.

Soros, George. (1997) 'The Capitalist Threat'. *Atlantic Monthly*, February.

Sorrosa A., Raúl. (2001) 'Praga: ¿El Hollywood del Este?' *Chasqui: Revista Latinoamericana de Comunicación* 76.

Sotinel, Thomas. (2001) 'Jean Marie-Messier signe la fin de l'exception culturelle'. *Le Monde*, 19 December.

Sreberny-Mohammadi, Annabelle. (1996) 'Globalization, Communication and Transnational Civil Society: Introduction'. *Globalization, Communication and Transnational Civil Society*. Ed. Sandra Braman and Annabelle Sreberny-Mohammadi. Cresskill, NJ: Hampton Press. 1–19.

Sreenivasan, Sreenath. (1997) 'What is a Hit Film? Moviefone May Know'. *New York Times*, 2 June: D9.

Srinivas, Alam. (2003) 'Other Side of Midnight'. *OutlookIndia.com*, 17 November.

Staiger, Janet. (1983) 'Combination and Litigation: Structures of US Film Distribution, 1896–1917'. *Cinema Journal* 23, no. 2.

Stalker, Peter. (2000) *Workers without Frontiers: The Impact of Globalization on International Migration*. Boulder, CO: Lynne Reinner.

Stam, Robert. (1989) *Subversive Pleasures: Bakhtin, Cultural Criticism and Film*. Baltimore: The Johns Hopkins University Press.

Stanbery, Jennifer. (2001) 'Hollywood Envy? Europe's Films Struggle to Compete'. Reuters, 9 February.

Standard & Poors. (2002) *Industry Surveys: Movies & Home Entertainment*, 14 November.

Stanley, T. L. (1996) 'Hollywood Heads East'. *Brandweek* 37, no 5: 37–8.

Stanley, T. L. (2003) 'New Line Forms Marketing Group'. *Advertising Age* 74, no. 39: 8.

Steinbock, Dan. (1995) *Triumph and Erosion in the American Media and Entertainment Industries*. Westport, CT: Quorum.

Stern, Andy. (1994a) 'Film/TV Future Tops Confab Agenda'. *Variety*, 27 June– July: 39.

Stern, Andy (1994b) 'Valenti Denis Euro TV Crisis'. *Daily Variety*, 23 June: 1, 17.

Stern, Andy. (1999) 'Reding Plans More Green for Distrib'n'. *Variety*, 1–7 November: 18.

Stern, Andy. (1999–2000) 'EC Funnels $355 Mil to Boost Pix'. *Variety*, 20 December–2 January: 20.

Stern, Christopher. (1997) 'China, Hollywood Hug and Thaw out'. *Variety*, 17–23 November: 4, 6.

Stern, Christopher. (1998) 'US Ideas Top Export Biz'. *Variety*, 11–17 May.

Sterngold, James. (1996) 'Debacle on the High Seas'. *New York Times*, 31 March: 1.

Stevens, Tracy, ed. (2000) *International Motion Picture Almanac*, 71st edn. La Jolla, CA: Quigley.

Stevenson, Richard W. (1994) 'Lights! Camera! Europe!' *New York Times*, 6 February: 1, 6.

Stevis, Dimitris and Terry Boswell. (1997) 'Labour: From National Resistance to International Politics'. *New Political Science* 2, no. 1: 93–104.

Stewart-Allen, Allyson. (n. d.) 'And Now, a Word from Our Sponsor . . . Product Placement in Europe'. *Marketing News Magazine*.

Stiglitz, Joseph. (2002) 'The Roaring Nineties'. *Atlantic Monthly* 290, no. 3: 75–89.

Stokes, Bruce. (1999) 'Lights! Camera! More Inaction'. *National Journal*, July: 2106.

Stonor Saunders, Frances. (1999) *Cultural Cold War: The CIA and the World of Arts and Letters*. New York: New Press.

Storper, Michael. (1989) 'The Transition to Flexible Specialisation in the U.S. Film Industry: External Economies, the Division of Labour, and the Crossing of Industrial Divides'. *Cambridge Journal of Economics* 13: 273–305.

Storper, Michael. (1993) 'Flexible Specialisation in Hollywood: A Response to Aksoy and Robins'. *Cambridge Journal of Economics* 17, no. 4: 479–84.

Storper, Michael. (1994) 'The Transition to Flexible Specialisation in the US Film Industry: External Economies, the Division of Labour and the Crossing of Industrial Divides'. *Post-Fordism: A Reader*. Ed. Ash Amin. Oxford: Blackwell. 195–226.

Storper, Michael and Susan Christopherson. (1987) 'Flexible Specialization and Regional Industry Agglomerations: The Case of the U.S. Motion Industry'. *Annals of the Association of American Geographers* 77, no. 1: 104–17.

Strange, Susan. (1995a) 'The Defective State'. *Daedalus* 124, no. 2: 55–74.

Strange, Susan. (1995b) 'The Limits of Politics'. *Government and Opposition* 30, no. 3: 291–311.

Stratton, David. (2003) 'Vodka Lemon'. Variety, 22–28 September: 28.

Straubhaar, Joseph. (2001) 'Brazil: The Role of the State in World Television'. Media and Globalization: Why the State Matters. Ed. Nancy Morris and Silvio Waisbord. Lanham, MD: Rowman & Littlefield. 133–53.

Strauss, William Victor. (1930) 'Foreign Distribution of American Motion Pictures'. Harvard Business Review 8, no. 3: 307–15.

Streeter, Thomas. (1996) Selling the Air: A Critique of the Policy of Commercial Broadcasting in the United States. Chicago: University of Chicago Press.

Streif, Tilman. (2000) 'Movies are Next Battle Zone in War over Digital Copyrights'. Deutsche-Presse-Agentur, 25 July.

Stringer, Robin. (2001) 'Lottery's £92m for Film Flops'. Evening Standard, 2 January: 1.

Strode, Louise. (2000) 'France and EU Policy-Making on Visual Culture: New Opportunities for National Identity?' France in Focus: Film and National Identity. Ed. Elizabeth Ezra and Sue Harris. Oxford: Berg. 61–75.

Stroud, Michael. (1999) 'Valley to Lose Film Jobs?' Wired News, 26 June.

Subramaniam, A. (2003) 'Next, an Animated Boom'. Business Standard, 12 February.

Sullivan, Jeanne English. (1996) 'Copyright for Visual Art in the Digital Age: A Modern Adventure in Wonderland'. Journal of Arts Management, Law and Society 26, no. 1.

Sullivan, Maureen. (1999) 'H.K. Mulls Harsher Piracy Fines'. Daily Variety, 25 February: 10.

Sum, Ngai-Lin. (2003) 'Information Capitalism and U.S. Economic Hegemony: Resistance and Adaptations in East Asia'. Critical Asian Studies 35, no. 3: 373–98.

Sun, Yubo. (2004) 'Huana Jituan yu Dalian Wanda Jituan Gongjian Hezi Yingyuan'. XinhuaNet, 18 January.

Sundaram, Ravi. (2000) 'Beyond the Nationalist Panopticon: The Experience of Cyberpublics in India'. Electronic Media and Technoculture. Ed. John Caldwell. New Brunswick, NJ: Rutgers University Press. 270–94.

Surowiecki, James. (2004) 'The Pipeline Problem'. New Yorker, 16–23 February: 72.

Sussman, Gerald and John A. Lent, eds. (1998) Global Productions: Labour in the Making of the 'Information Society'. Cresskill, NJ: Hampton Press.

Sutcliffe, Bob. (2003) A More or Less Unequal World? World Income Distribution in the 20th Century. Amherst, MA: Political Economy Research Institute Working Paper Series no. 54.

Sutter, Mary. (1998a) 'Viva Mexico! – Hollywood Heads South of the Border'. Kempos, 21–27 December: 1, 4–5.

Sutter, Mary. (1998b) 'Woman on Top in a Macho Man's Union'. Kempos, 21–27 December: 8.

Svetkey, Benjamin. (1994) 'Why Movie Ratings Don't Work'. Entertainment Weekly 250: 26–33.

Swanson, Tim. (2000) 'Writers Reboot'. Variety, 31 July–6 August.

Sweeting, Paul. (2001) 'The Movie and Music Industries Have Good Reason to Feel Picked on'. Video Business, 12 March: 12.

Swift, Brent. (1999) 'Film and Television Action Committee Past and Present'. www.ftac.net/about.html.

Swyngedouw, Erik. (1997) 'Neither Global Nor Local: "Glocalization" and the Politics of Scale'. Spaces of Globalization: Reasserting the Power of the Local. Ed. Kevin R. Cox. New York: Guilford Press. 137–66.

Sykes, Jason and Glenn R. Simpson. (2001) 'Some Big Sites Back P3P Plan; Others Wait'. Wall Street Journal, 21 March: B1, B4.

Tagliabue, John. (2003) 'Vivendi Posts a Net Profit as it Seeks a New Loan'. New York Times, 3 December: W1.

Talcin, Marsha. (n. d.) 'Many Film Productions Hopping the Northern Border'. Showbiz Industry Digest. www.showbizdigest.com.

Tanzer, Andrew. (1998) 'Tech-Savvy Pirates'. Forbes, 7 July.

Tartaglione, Nancy. (2000) 'The Final Vote: Canal Plus Shareholders Approve Vivendi-Universal Merger'. [Inside] 8 December: 17.

Tashiro, Charles S. (2002) 'The Twilight Zone of Contemporary Hollywood Production'. Cinema Journal 41, no. 3: 27–37.

Taylor, Diane. (2004) 'Hollywood Pirates Ripped Us Off, Claim St Vincent Islanders'. Independent, 28 February.

Taylor, Paul. (1998) *Responding to the Shock of the New: Trade, Technology and the Changing Production Axis in Film, Television and New Media*. Ph.D. dissertation, University of Washington.

Taylor, Paul W. (1995) 'Co-productions – Content and Change: International Television in the Americas'. *Canadian Journal of Communication* 20: 411–16.

Teeple, G. (1995) *Globalization and the Decline of Social Reform*. New Jersey: Humanities Press.

Tegel, Simeon. (2000) 'Hollywood Gets Last Word in Mexican Dubs'. *Variety*, 13 March.

Tegel, Simeon. (2001a) 'Sand and Stardust'. *Business Mexico*, 1 February.

Tegel, Simeon. (2001b) 'Celluloid Chic'. *Latin Trade*, August.

Tegel, Simeon. (2002) 'Cue the Governor's Helicopter'. *Latin Trade*, December.

Tepper, Steven Jay. (2002) 'Creative Assets and the Changing Economy'. *Journal of Arts Management, Law and Society* 32, no. 2: 159–68.

The White House. (2002) *The National Security Strategy of the United States of America.*

Theiler, Tobias. (1999) 'Viewers into Europeans?: How the European Union Tried to Europeanize the Audiovisual Sector, and Why it Failed'. *Canadian Journal of Communication* 24, no. 4: 557–87.

Thomas, Pradip. (1999) 'Trading the Nation: Multilateral Negotiations and the Fate of Communications in India'. *Gazette* 61, nos. 3–4: 275–92.

Thompson, Clive. (2003) 'There's a Sucker Born in Every Medial Prefrontal Cortex'. *New York Times Magazine*, 26 October: 54–58, 85.

Thompson, E. P. (1975) *Whigs and Hunters: The Origins of the Black Act*. New York: Pantheon.

Thompson, Kristin. (1985) *Exporting Entertainment: America in the World Film Market 1907–1934*. London: British Film Institute.

Thompson, Paul and Chris Smith. (1999) 'Beyond the Capitalist Labor Process: Workplace Change, the State and Globalisation'. *Critical Sociology* 24, no. 3: 193–215.

Throsby, David. (2001) 'Defining the Artistic Experience: The Australian Experience'. *Poetics* 28: 255–71.

Ting Yu, Liza Hamm, Fran Brennan, Michelle Caruso, Alison Gee, Jennifer Longley and York Member. (2000) 'Czech, Please!' *People*, 9 October: 26.

Tomkins, R. (2000) 'Taylor Nelson Buys into Internet Trends Group'. *Financial Times*, 13 March: 24.

Tomlinson, John. (1991) *Cultural Imperialism: A Critical Introduction*. Baltimore: The Johns Hopkins University Press.

Toto, Dominic. (2000) 'Job Growth in Television: Cable Versus Broadcast, 1958–99'. *Monthly Labor Review* 123, no. 8: 3–14.

Townson, Don. (1999) 'H'wood Techs Migrate North'. *Variety*, 23–29 August: 9.

Tracy, James F. (1999) 'Whistle While You Work: The Disney Company and the Global Division of Labor'. *Journal of Communication Inquiry* 23, no. 4: 374–89.

Trebay, Guy. (2002) 'Secret Agent's Commission'. *Sydney Morning Herald*, 4 November.

Triana-Toribio, Núria. (2003) *Spanish National Cinema*. London: Routledge.

Tricot, Agnès. (2000) ' "Screens Without Frontiers": Project to Establish a Database for Television Programs for Use of the Public Television Channels of Developing Countries'. UNESCO/URTI.

Truffaut, François with Helen G. Scott. (1967) *Hitchcock*. New York: Touchstone.

Trumbull, Robert. (1953) 'Movies are Booming: In Bombay'. *New York Times Magazine*, 5 July: 17.

Trumpbour, John. (2002) *Selling Hollywood to the World: U.S. and European Struggles for Mastery of the Global Film Industry, 1920–1950*. Cambridge: Cambridge University Press.

Tubridy, Michael. (2001) 'Movie Theater Closings and Shopping Centers'. *International Council of Shopping Centers Research Express* 2, no. 3.

Tunstall, Jeremy. (1981) *The Media are American: Anglo-American Media in the World*. London: Constable.

Tunstall, Jeremy and David Machin. (1999) *The Anglo-American Media Connection.* Oxford: Oxford University Press.

Tuohy, Wendy. (2003) 'US Talks Threaten Film, TV Industry'. *Age*, 1 June: 4.

Turner, Graeme. (1988) *Film as Social Practice.* London: Routledge.

Tushnet, Rebecca. (1997) 'Legal Fictions: Copyright, Fan Fiction and a New Common Law'. *Loyola of Los Angeles Entertainment Law Journal* 17: 651–85.

Tyner, James A. (1998) 'Asian Labor Recruitment and the World Wide Web'. *Professional Geographer* 50, no. 3: 331–44.

Ugalde, Victor. (2004) 'Cine Mexicano, a Diez Años del TLC'. *Infodac – Suplemento Especial* 52.

UK Film Council. (2003) *Post-Production in the U.K.*

Ukadike, Nwachukwu Frank. (1994) *Black African Cinema.* Berkeley: University of California Press.

Ulff-Moller, Jens. (1999) 'Hollywood's "Foreign War": The Effect of National Commercial Policy on the Emergence of the American Film Hegemony in France, 1920–1929'. *'Film Europe' and 'Film America': Cinema, Commerce and Cultural Exchange.* Ed. Andrew Higson and Richard Maltby. Exeter: University of Exeter Press. 181–206.

Ulich, Pamela Conley and Lance Simmons. (2001) 'Motion Picture Production: To Run or Stay Made in the U.S.A'. *Loyola of Los Angeles Entertainment Law Review* 21: 357–70.

UNDP. (1999) *Human Development Report.*

UNESCO. (2000a) 'Cinema: A Survey on National Cinematography'. www.unesco.org/culture/industries/cinema /html_eng/trade.shtm.

UNESCO. (2000b) 'Statistics'. unescostat.unesco.org/statsen/Statistics/ year book/tables/CultAndCom/ Table_IV_12_America.html.

UNESCO. (2002) 'Culture, Trade and Globalisation'. www.unesco.org/cul ture /industries/trade/html_eng/question1.sht.

Ungureit, Heinz. (1991) 'Le Groupement Européen de production: rassembler les forces du service public . . .'. *Dossiers de l'Audiovisuel* 35.

United Nations Development Programme. (1999) *Human Development Report.* Oxford: Oxford University Press.

United States Government. (2000) 'Communication from the United States: Audiovisual and Related Services'. World Trade Organization. Council for Trade in Services Special Session. S/CSS/W/21, 18 December.

Ursell, Gillian. (2000) 'Television Production: Issues of Exploitation, Commodification and Subjectivity in UK Television Labour Markets'. *Media, Culture & Society* 22, no. 6: 805–25.

US Department of Transportation, Office of Safety and Security. (2003) *Transit Security Newsletter* 36: 2.

US Government Working Group on Electronic Commerce. (1998) 'First Annual Report'. www.ecommerce.gov.

USIA. (1997) '1997 National Trade Estimate Report – European Union'. M2 Press Wire.

Valenti, Jack. (1993) 'Expanding Competition in the International Market – An Industry Perspective'. *The International Market in Film and Television Programs.* Ed. Eli M. Noam and Joel C. Millonzi. Norwood, NJ: Ablex. 147–50.

Valenti, Jack. (1997) 'A Grand Confluence: The Intersection of Storytellers from East and West: A Reciting of the Fruitful Results of an Asian/American Cinema Collaboration'. *CineAsia*, Singapore, 3 December.

Valenti, Jack. (1998a) 'Collapse of the Common Wisdom: How Movies Beat the Competition! A Recounting of a Very Good Year'. MPA Press Release, 10 March.

Valenti, Jack. (1998b) 'Cinema Renaissance – "it's Morning in Britain" – by Jack Valenti'. MPA Press Release, 16 June.

Valenti, Jack. (2000a) 'Valenti Announces Formation of Committee in Support of China Trade'. MPA Press Release, 9 February.

Valenti, Jack. (2000b) 'There's No Free Hollywood'. *New York Times*, 21 June: A23.

Valenti, Jack. (2001a) 'Copyright and Creativity – The Jewel in America's Crown'. Address to the International Trademark Association, Santa Monica, 22 January.

Valenti, Jack. (2001b) 'Opinion: Copyright and Creativity'. *Newsweek*, 19 March.

Valenti, Jack. (2001c) 'Traveling That Sweet Road That Leads to Success'. Address to ShoWest, Las Vegas, 6 March.

Valenti, Jack. (2003a) 'Intellectual Copyright Piracy: Links to Organized Crime and Terrorism'. Testimony before Subcommittee on Courts, the Internet, and Intellectual Property Committee on the Judiciary US House of Representatives, 13 March.

Valenti, Jack. (2003b). 'Thoughts on the Digital Future of Movies'. Testimony before Senate Committee on Governmental Affairs Hearing on 'Privacy and Piracy': The Paradox of Illegal File Sharing on Peer-to-Peer Networks and the Impact of Technology on the Entertainment Industry', 30 September.

Valentine, John. (1997) 'Global Sport and Canadian Content: The *Sports Illustrated* Controversy'. *Journal of Sport & Social Issues* 21, no. 3: 239–59.

Van Camp, Julie. (1994) 'Creating Works of Art from Works of Art: The Problem of Derivative Works'. *Journal of Arts Management, Law and Society* 24, no. 3: 209–22.

Van Cuilenburg, Jan. (1999) 'On Competition, Access and Diversity in Media, Old and New: Some Remarks for Communications Policy in the Information Age'. *New Media and Society* 1, no. 2.

Van den Besselaar, Peter. (1997) 'The Future of Employment in the Information Society: A Comparative, Longitudinal and Multi-Level Study'. *Journal of Information Science* 23, no. 5: 373–92.

Van der Merwe, Dana. (1999) 'The Dematerialization of Print and the Fate of Copyright'. *International Review of Law Computers* 13, no. 3.

Van Elteren, Mel. (1996a) 'Conceptualizing the Impact of US Popular Culture Globally'. *Journal of Popular Culture* 30, no. 1: 47–89.

Van Elteren, Mel. (1996b) 'GATT and Beyond: World Trade, the Arts and American Popular Culture in Western Europe'. *Journal of American Culture* 19, no. 3: 59–73.

van Loon, Ad. (2001) 'Freedom Versus Access Rights in a European Context'. *Media Law and Policy*, Fall: 18.

Van Maanen, John. (1992) 'Displacing Disney: Some Notes on the Flow of Culture'. *Qualitative Sociology* 15, no. 1: 5–35.

Vargas Llosa, Mario. (2000) 'The Culture of Liberty'. *Foreign Policy*, February.

Vasey, Ruth. (1992) 'Foreign Parts: Hollywood's Global Distribution and the Representation of Ethnicity'. *American Quarterly* 44, no. 4: 617–42.

Vasey, Ruth. (1997) *The World According to Hollywood, 1918–1939*. Madison: University of Wisconsin Press.

Vasudevan, Ravi. (2000) 'National Pasts and Futures: Indian Cinema'. *Screen* 41, no. 2: 119–25.

Venturelli, Shalini. (1997) 'Prospects for Human Rights in the Political and Regulatory Design of the Information Society'. *Media and Politics in Transition: Cultural Identity in the Age of Globalization*. Ed. Jan Servaes and Rico Lie. Leuven: Acco. 61–74.

Venturelli, Shalini. (1998) 'Cultural Rights and World Trade Agreements in the Information Society'. *Gazette* 60, no. 1: 47–76.

Venturelli, Shalini. (n. d.) *From the Information Economy to the Creative Economy: Moving Culture to the Center of International Public Policy*. Washington: Center for Arts and Culture.

Verini, James. (2004) ' "Mr Ferrer Can't be with Us Tonight" '. *Guardian*, 18 February.

Veronis Suhler Media Merchant Bank. (2000) *Communications Industry Forecast*, 14th edn. New York.

Verrier, Richard. (2000) 'Disney's Big Ideas: Company is a Magnet for Accusations of Intellectual Thefts'. *Orlando Sentinel*, 2 August: H1.

VerSteeg, Jac Wilder. (2000) 'A Wild West – with No Sheriffs'. *Palm Beach Post*, 19 September.

Villa, Joan. (2002) 'Retailers, Studios Increasingly Eye Hispanic Market'. *Video Store*, 7–13 April: 12.

Vivarelli, Nick. (2003) 'Cinecittà Lot Loaded with U.S. Biz'. *Variety*, 27 October: 16.

Vlessing, Etan and Peter Kiefer. (2003) 'Canada Boosts Film Tax Credits'. *Back stage.com*, 21 February.

VNU. (2002) *Annual Report*. Haarlem.

Vogel, Harold L. (1998) *Entertainment Industry Economics: A Guide for Financial Analysis*, 4th edn. Cambridge: Cambridge University Press.

Wade, Robert Hunter. (2003) 'The Invisible Hand of the American Empire'. *openDemocracy.net*, 13 March.

Wagnleitner, Reinhold and Elaine Tyler May. (2000) 'Here, There, and Everywhere: Introduction'. *'Here, There and Everywhere': The Foreign Politics of American Popular Culture*. Ed. Reinhold Wagnleitner and Elaine Tyler May. Hanover: University Press of New England. 1–13.

Walker, Alexander. (1999) 'Adding Insult to Injury'. *Evening Standard*, 9 February: 46.

Walker, Alexander. (2000) 'The Split Screen'. *Evening Standard*, 5 October: 31.

Wallace, W. Timothy, Alan Seigerman and Morris B. Holbrook. (1993) 'The Role of Actors and Actresses in the Success of Films: How Much is a Movie Star Worth?'. *Journal of Cultural Economics* 17, no. 1: 1–27.

Wallerstein, Immanuel. (1989) 'Culture as the Ideological Battleground of the Modern World-System'. *Hitotsubashi Journal of Social Studies* 21, no. 1: 5–22.

Wallerstein, Immanuel. (2000) 'Introduction'. *Review* 23, no. 1: 1–13.

Walsh, Michael. (1997) 'Fighting the American Invasion with Cricket, Roses, and Marmalade for Breakfast'. *Velvet Light Trap* 40: 3–17.

Wan, Jihong and Richard Kraus. (2002) 'Hollywood and China as Adversaries and Allies'. *Pacific Affairs* 75, no. 3: 419–39.

Wang, Jiangen. (2003) 'Waishang Touzi Yingyuan Zhengce Zuo Zhongda Tiaozheng'. *China Culture Net*, 15 December.

Wanger, Walter. (1939) '120,000 American Ambassadors'. *Foreign Affairs* 18, no. 1: 45–59.

Wanger, Walter. (1950) 'Donald Duck and Diplomacy'. *Public Opinion Quarterly* 14, no. 3: 443–52.

Wasko, Janet. (1982) *Movies and Money: Financing the American Film Industry*. Norwood, NJ: Ablex.

Wasko, Janet. (1994) *Hollywood in the Information Age: Beyond the Silver Screen*. Cambridge: Polity Press.

Wasko, Janet. (1998) 'Challenges to Hollywood's Labor Force in the 1990s'. *Global Productions: Labor in the Making of the 'Information Society'*. Ed. Gerald Sussman and John A. Lent. Cresskill, NJ: Hampton Press. 173–89.

Wasko, Janet. (2001) 'Is it a Small World, After All?' *Dazzled by Disney? The Global Disney Audiences Project*. Ed. Janet Wasko, Mark Phillips and Eileen R. Meehan. London: Leicester University Press. 3–28.

Wasko, Janet. (2003) *How Hollywood Works*. London: Sage.

Wasser, Frederick. (1995) 'Is Hollywood America? The Trans-Nationalization of the American Film Industry'. *Critical Studies in Mass Communication* 12, no. 4: 423–37.

Wasser, Frederick. (2001) *Veni, Vidi, Video: The Hollywood Empire and the VCR*. Austin: University of Texas Press.

Waterman, David and Krishna P. Jayakar. (2000) 'The Competitive Balance of the Italian and American Film Industries'. *European Journal of Communication* 15, no. 4: 501–28.

Waters, Dan. (1999) 'Throwing Cash at Movieland'. *Sacramento Bee*, 23 April.

Waters, Mary C. (2003) 'Once Again, Strangers on Our Shores'. *The Fractious Nation? Unity and Division in Contemporary American Life*. Ed. Jonathan Rieder. Assoc. ed. Stephen Steinlight. Berkeley: University of California Press. 117–30.

Watling, John. (1999) 'Co-production: Mexico, MPA Team up on Issues'. *Hollywood Reporter*, 21 July.

Waxman, Sharon. (1999) 'Location, Location: Hollywood Loses Films to Cheaper Climes'. *Washington Post*, 25 June: C1.

Wayne, Michael. (2003) 'Post-Fordism, Monopoly Capitalism, and Hollywood's Media Industrial Complex'. *International Journal of Cultural Studies* 6, no. 1: 82–103.

Wayne, Mike. (2003) *Marxism and Media Studies: Key Concepts and Contemporary Trends*. London: Pluto Press.

Weatherall, Ernest. (1978) 'Blocked Rupee Funds Invite Yanks to Make Film in India, but Gotta Know Local Scene'. *Variety*, 17 May.

Wedell, George. (1994) 'Prospects for Television in Europe'. *Government and Opposition* 29, no. 3: 315–31.

Weil, Lynn (1998) 'Italian Film Biz Slumping'. *NPR Morning Edition*, 5 May.

Weinraub, Bernard. (1993) 'Directors Battle over GATT's Final Cut And Print'. *New York Times*, 12 December: L24.

Weinstein, Mark. (1998) 'Profit-Sharing Contracts in Hollywood: Evolution and Analysis'. *Journal of Legal Studies* 27, no. 1: 67–112.

Welch, L. S. and R. Luostarinen. (1988) 'Internationalization: Evolution of a Concept'. *Journal of General Management* 14, no. 2: 34–55.

Welkos, Robert W. (1999) 'Chinese Head to Hollywood, Ready to Deal'. *Los Angeles Times*, 19 Febuary: F2.

Weller, Jerry. (1999) Congressional Testimony, 5 August.

Weller, Jerry. (2000) Congressional Testimony, 27 October.

Wenders, Wim. (1991) *The Logic of Images: Essays and Conversations*. Trans. Michael Hofmann. London: Faber and Faber.

Wenner, Lawrence A. (2004) 'On the Ethics of Product Placement in Media Entertainment'. *Handbook of Product Placement in the Mass Media: New Strategies in Marketing Theory, Practice, Trends, and Ethics*. Ed. Mary-Lou Galician. Binghamton, NY: Best Business Books/Hayworth Press.

Wesselius, Erik. (2002) *Behind GATS 2000: Corporate Power at Work*. Amsterdam: Transnational Institute.

West, Stephen. (1991) 'Universal to Make Films with European Pay-TV Firm'. *Los Angeles Times*, 15 July: D2.

Wexler, Haskell. (2002) 'Western Region Residency Requirements Relaxed for Eastern Region Members'. *Viewfinder* 1, no. 4: 7.

Wheeler, Mark. (2000) 'Research Note: "The Undeclared War" Part II'. *European Journal of Communication* 15, no. 2: 253–62.

Whitaker, Barbara. (2000). 'Private Sector; Trading on Hollywood's Future'. *New York Times*, 29 October.

White, Jerry. (2001) 'Union Membership in US at Lowest Level in 60 Years'. *World Socialist Web Site*, 26 February. www.wsws.org.

Whitney, Daisy. (2003) 'Cablers Ask Film Studios for Parity'. *Television Week* 22, no. 32: 15.

Whyte, Murray. (2003) 'In the Film Biz, Reality Bites'. *Toronto Star*, 6 September: H4.

Wicker, Heidi Sarah. (2003) 'Making a Run for the Border: Should the United States Stem Runaway Film and Television Production through Tax and Other Financial Incentives?' *George Washington International Law Review* 35: 461–99.

Wildman, Steven S. and Stephen E. Siwek. (1993) 'The Economics of Trade in Recorded Media Products in a Multilingual World: Implications for National Media Policies'. *The International Market in Film and Television Programs*. Ed. Eli M. Noam and Joel C. Millonzi. Norwood, NJ: Ablex. 13–40.

Wilkerson, Cynthia. (1983) 'Foreign Films' Popularity Rises in India with "Gandhi" Release'. *Hollywood Reporter*, 3 February: 3.

Wilkerson, W. R. (1952) 'Trade Views'. *Hollywood Reporter*, 9 October.

Willens, M. (2000) 'Putting Films to the Test, Every Time'. *New York Times*, 25 June: 11, 20.

Williams, Michael. (1994) 'The Future Speaks English'. *Variety*, 12–18 December: 57.

Williams, Michael. (1997a) 'Canal+, Pathe in Pic Pact'. *Variety*, 2–8 June: 9.

Williams, Michael. (1997b) 'MPA Inks Piracy Pact with World Customs Org'. *Variety*, 1 September.

Williams, Michael. (1999) 'US Pix Get French Kiss'. *Variety*, 15–21 November: 1.

Williams, Raymond. (1989) *The Politics of Modernism: Against the New Conformists*. London: Verso.

Williams-Jones, Michael. (2001) 'Global Biz Requires Global Expertise'. *Variety*, 19–25 February: 7.

Willman, David and Alan Citron. (1992) 'Carolco Pictures Pins Hopes for Rescue on its "Universal Soldier"'. *Los Angeles Times*, 10 July: D1.

Willnat, Lars, Zhou He, Toshio Takeshita and Esteban López-Escobar. (2002) 'Perceptions of Foreign Media Influence in Asia and Europe: The Third- Person Effect and Media Imperialism'. *International Journal of Public Opinion Research* 14, no. 2: 175–92.

Wingfield, Marvin and Bushra Karaman. (1995) 'Arab Stereotypes and American Educators'. American Arab Anti-Discrimination Committee. adc.org.

Winslow, George. (2001) 'Hollywood Wired'. *Multichannel News International*, 1 January.

Wolf, Jessica. (2003) 'MPA Testifies in Congress on Piracy'. *Video Store*, 30 March: 12.

Wolf, Michael J. (1999) *The Entertainment Economy: How Mega-media Forces are Transforming Our Lives*. New York: Random House.

Woodmansee, Martha. (1984) 'The Genius and the Copyright: Economic and Legal Conditions of the Emergence of the "Author"'. *Eighteenth Century Studies* 17: 425–48.

Woods, Mark. (1999a) 'That Championship Season'. *Variety*, 11–17 January: 9, 16.

Woods, Mark. (1999b) 'Foreign Pix Bring Life to Biz'. *Variety*, 3–9 May: 37, 44, 46, 59.

Woods, Mark. (2000) 'More Players Split O'seas Pie'. *Variety*, 10–16 January: 9–10.

Woolf, Marie. (1998) 'Why the Next English Patient Will be British'. *Independent on Sunday*, 20 December: 9.

World Trade Organization. (1998) 'Audiovisual Services: Background Note by the Secretariat'. S/C/W/40 of 15 June.

World Trade Organization. (2000) 'Growth Rate of World Merchandise Trade Expected to Double in 2000, According to Latest Report by WTO Secretariat'. www.wto.org/english/news_e/pres00_e/pr200_e.htm.

World Trade Organization. (2001) 'Overview of the State-of-Play of WTO Disputes'.

World Trade Organization. (2003) *World Trade Developments in 2001 and Prospects for 2002*. Geneva.

Worth, Sol. (1981) *Studying Visual Communication*. Ed. Larry Gross. Philadelphia: University of Pennsylvania Press.

Wuliger, Deborah. (2000) Posting on *Citizens' Media Watch Forum*, 6 December. oneworld.net:8080/~mediachannel/read?2619,358.

Wyatt, Justin. (1994) *High Concept: Movies and Marketing in Hollywood*. Austin: University of Texas Press.

Yang, Fang and James Shanahan. (2003) 'Economic Openness and Media Penetration'. *Communication Research* 30, no. 5: 557–73.

Ye, Tan. (2003) 'Hollywood and the Chinese Other'. *Cineaction* 60: 10–20.

Yong-Shik, Choe. (2002) 'Korean Pop Culture Sets Pace in East Asia'. *Korea Herald*, 28 June.

Younge, Gary. (2000) 'The Big Picture'. *Guardian*, 26 July.

Yúdice, George. (1995) 'Civil Society, Consumption, and Governmentality in an Age of Global Restructuring: An Introduction'. *Social Text* 45: 1–27.

Yúdice, George. (2000) 'The Creation of a Latin American Cultural Space'. Paper presented at the Crossroads in Cultural Studies Conference, Birmingham, 21–25 June.

Yúdice, George. (2002) 'Las Industrias Culturales: Más Allá de la Lógica Puramente Económica, el Aporte Social'. *Pensar Iberoamérica: Revista de Cultura* 1.

Yúdice, George. (2003) *The Expediency of Culture: Uses of Culture in the Global Era*. Durham: Duke University Press.

Ywin, Ken. (2003) 'Making Movies: Thai Films Set for Big US Airing'. *Nation* (Bangkok), 18 February.

Zanker, Ruth and Geoff Lealand. (2003) 'New Zealand as Middle Earth: Local and Global Popular Communication in a Small Nation'. *Popular Communication* 1, no. 1: 65–72.

Zecchinelli, Cecilia. (1994) 'Gaps Seen for EU TV Meet'. *Daily Variety*, 26 June: 13.

Zhou, Tiedong. (2004) 'China: The Operation and Development of Digital Cinemas'. *European Cinema Journal* 6, no. 1: 3.

Zhu, Ying. (2002) 'Chinese Cinema's Economic Reform from the Mid-1980s to the Mid-1990s'. *Journal of Communication* 52, no. 4: 905–21.

Zolberg, Vera. (1995) 'Museum Culture and GATT'. *Journal of Arts Management, Law and Society* 25, no. 1: 5–16.

Zollars, C. L. and M. G. Cantor. (1993). 'The Sociology of Culture Producing Occupations: Discussion and Synthesis'. *Current Research on Occupations and Professions* 8: 1–29.

Zuckerman, Ezra W. and Tai-Young Kim. (2003) 'The Critical Trade-Off: Identity Assignment and Box-Office Success in the Feature Film Industry'. *Industrial and Corporate Change* 12, no. 1: 27–67.

Zuckerman, Ezra W., Tai-Young Kim, Kalinda Ukanwa and James von Ritterman. (2003) 'Robust Identities or Nonentities? Typecasting in the Feature-Film Labor Market'. *American Journal of Sociology* 108, 5: 1018–74.

Zwick, Steve. (2000) 'Top Marks for Hollywood: German Film Production Companies are Pouring into Big U.S. Movies – with Mixed Results'. *Time International*, 16 October: 58.

Index